THE WAYS OF RELIGION

THE WAYS OF RELIGION

An Introduction to the Major Traditions

SECOND EDITION

Edited By

ROGER EASTMAN

New York   Oxford

OXFORD UNIVERSITY PRESS

1993

Oxford University Press

Oxford   New York   Toronto
Delhi   Bombay   Calcutta   Madras   Karachi
Kuala Lumpur   Singapore   Hong Kong   Tokyo
Nairobi   Dar es Salaam   Cape Town
Melbourne   Auckland   Madrid

and associated companies in
Berlin   Ibadan

Copyright © 1975, 1993 by Roger Eastman

Published by Oxford University Press, Inc.
200 Madison Avenue, New York, New York 10016

Oxford is a registered trademark of Oxford University Press, Inc.

First edition originally published in 1975 by Harper & Row, Publishers

Library of Congress Cataloging-in-Publication Data
The Ways of religion : an introduction to the major traditions
edited by Roger Eastman. — 2nd ed.
p. cm.   Includes bibliographical references and indexes.
ISBN 0-19-507596-X
1. Religions.   I. Eastman, Roger.
BL74.W3   1992   291—dc20   92-19530

3 5 7 9 8 6 4 2

Printed in the United States of America
on acid-free paper

To
Arturo B. Fallico
Professor of Philosophy, San Jose State

and
John L. Mothershead
Professor of Philosophy, Stanford

Preface

The Ways of Religion is a collection of readings for the course in the world's religions. It is an attempt to combine in a single volume a cross section of materials that introduce the unique claims, hopes, and wisdom of those religions.

Why an Anthology?

For the most part, each religion is represented by selections from its scriptures, prophets, and scholars—each is heard in its own voices, so to speak. Thus Sarvepalli Radhakrishnan introduces Hinduism, and the Dalai Lama writes about Buddhism. There are selections from the Analects and the Tao Te Ching. The Confucianist Tu Wei-ming, the Zen Buddhist D. T. Suzuki, and the Muslim Fazlur Rahman are here. This is religion first-hand, at least as far as print goes.

The few exceptions to the unofficial rule of using sources from within the traditions should require little justification: they include, for example, Huston Smith's reflections on Taoism and Joseph Epes Brown's "The Spiritual Values of Native Americans." The *overriding* rule for choosing materials was to go with what was authoritative, central to the religion, of vital interest, and lucidly written.

A Second Edition

Of the sixty-four reading selections in the pages that follow, forty-four are new to this edition. Among the latter are several recent translations, notably those by Wendy Doniger O'Flaherty (The Rig Veda, 1981), Barbara Stoler Miller (The Bhagavad-Gita, 1986), John Ross Carter and Mahinda Palihawadana (Dhammapada, 1987), and the Jewish Publication Society (The Holy Scriptures, 1985). The New Testament selections are from the New Revised Standard Version, 1989.

The chapter on Shinto and the final chapter, "Religion in America: A Sampler," appear here for the first time.

Acknowledgments

At the risk of belaboring the obvious, I would nevertheless like to say that my primary debt is to the authors whose work is the substance of this volume: *The Ways of Religion* is the product of their sweat, tears, and genius.

I remain indebted to the National Endowment for the Humanities for a generous fellowship, which some years ago was the point of origin for this and other work.

At Oxford University Press, Senior Editor Cynthia Read responded enthusiastically to an early outline and then provided valuable suggestions and criticism. The copyediting of Catherine Clements improved the text throughout and saved me from frightful embarrassments.

Reedley, Calif.   R. E.
August 1992

Contents

THE WAYS OF RELIGION

I

HINDUISM
Himalayas of the Soul

Lead me from the unreal to the real.
Lead me from darkness to light.
Lead me from death to immortality.

Brihadaranyaka Upanishad

Its origins are obscured by the shadows of antiquity; its sacred literature is vast. Its sects and forms of worship are innumerable. One stream of its thought claims that there is ultimately *one* Absolute, an unseen *Brahman,* and yet there are those thousands upon thousands of gods. Such is Hinduism. R. C. Zaehner called it "the proliferating jungle,"[1] a phrase that aptly suggests the luxurious growth of the religion through the ages.

"There has been no such thing as a uniform, stationary, unalterable Hinduism whether in point of belief or practice," Sarvepalli Radhakrishnan has written. "Hinduism is a movement, not a position; a process, not a result; a growing tradition, not a fixed revelation."[2] Radhakrishnan summarizes, nevertheless, in the pages that follow, certain themes that have characterized much of Hindu thought. He notes first of all the overwhelming emphasis upon the "spiritual," an emphasis again evident in his discussion of "The Four Ends of Life." (The end that really matters, of course, is the spiritual end.)

Similarly, in an essay later in this chapter, Rabindranath Tagore discusses the idealized "stages of life": that of the student, that of work, then that of retreat for study and meditation on matters of the spirit. The fourth and culminating stage is that of freedom from all the concerns of this world, as *moksha,* liberation, is achieved. The *sannyasin* (perhaps "saint" is close) at last awaits a final death and release from turmoil, confusion, and the endless cycles of births and deaths and time itself. *Moksha,* however, "is so rare a condition that to attain it much more effort and patience are necessary than, say, for emptying the sea drop by drop with

1. *Hinduism* (New York: Oxford University Press, 1966), p. 3.
2. *The Hindu View of Life* (New York: Macmillan, 1927), p. 91.

3

a blade of grass."[3] Many lifetimes may be required. One will live again and again in this world until life's purposes have been accomplished.

Yoga is one of the means whereby these very difficult spiritual ends are sought: it refers to various methods of self-discipline, training, meditation, devotion, and concentration that are designed to lead one to a realization of or contact with the Divine. There are varieties of yoga: *raja* yoga is the "royal" *(raj)* road of yoga, the classic system that leads to *samadhi*, the experience of oneness with Brahman. *Bhakti* yoga is the way of love, of devotion. (Some Hindus see Christianity as an expression of *bhakti* yoga.) This form of yoga entails belief in and worship of a personal God. *Karma* yoga is for those who express themselves most fully in their work. *Jnana* yoga is the yoga of knowledge, for those who are intellectually inclined. The different types of yoga are a recognition of the simple fact that there are different types of people. Hinduism covers a lot of ground and a lot of history.

The earliest period of Hindu thought is the Vedic—the Age of the Vedas. The date for the beginning of the period is a matter of speculation; some authorities say it was as early as 2500 B.C.E., others say 1500 B.C.E. The period closes somewhere around 600 B.C.E. and is followed by the Age of the Epics, which extends to about 200 C.E.

The literature of the Vedic period—known collectively as the *Vedas*—comprises the most sacred scriptures of Hinduism. It is termed *sruti*, that which was "heard." The Vedas are divided into four groups: *Rig Veda, Sama Veda, Yajur Veda,* and *Atharva Veda.* These, in turn, are each made up of three parts, which are historical strata. There are, first, the early hymns, prayers, and rites of the *Samhitas.* Then there are the *Brahmanas*, which are later commentary and explanatory material attached to the Samhitas, and finally there are the *Aranyakas,* the "Forest Treatises." These books culminate in the *Vedanta* (literally, the "end of the Vedas") which is also called the *Upanishads,* and these date from the last centuries of the Vedic period. Of all the Vedic literature, that deemed most significant are the hymns of the Rig Veda and the very philosophical Upanishads,[4] both of which are represented by selections in this chapter.

The literature of the Age of Epics is *smirti*, that which has been "remembered" and transmitted by tradition, and it includes the vast *Mahabharata*, one small portion of which is the *Bhagavad-Gita.* While this literature is technically considered less authoritative than the Vedic literature, the influence of much of it, particularly the Bhagavad-Gita, upon the life of India has been incalculable. Often called the "Bible" of India, the Bhagavad-Gita contains most of the major strands of Hindu religious thought. Selections from the Gita are in the pages that follow, in a recent translation by Barbara Stoler Miller.

The chapter concludes with excerpts from the writings of Mahatma Gandhi. The well-known words of Robert Payne may help to put the phenomenon of Gandhi in perspective:

3. Mahatma Gandhi, in Ragavan Iyer (ed.), *The Moral and Political Writings of Mahatma Gandhi* (Oxford: Clarendon Press, 1986), Vol. 1, p. 141.

4. The subtitle of this chapter, "The Himalayas of the Soul," used here to honor the spiritual heights achieved by the Hindu religion, was the title, in 1938, of Juan Mascaro's translation of the *Upanishads.*

When Gandhi died, a part of India died with him. The small man with the bright eyes and the enchanting smile towered above his compatriots; he had been more powerful than any maharaja or viceroy. He had never occupied high office, never commanded an army, never claimed any special sanction for his words, but for nearly two generations he had been the conscience of his country.[5]

5. *Saturday Review,* 4 October 1969, p. 26.

The Brahman in the Pit

Roy C. Amore and Larry D. Shinn

The little story that follows is taken from the Mahabharata, that compendium of Indian myth, folklore, and philosophy. But slight as "The Brahman in the Pit" is, it touches on themes central to Hinduism and, indeed, to all our lives.

Just as Dante, in The Inferno, *awoke to find himself alone in gloomy woods, so here a Brahman is lost in a deep dark forest. It is a common problem. Notice that the forest, like life itself, is crawling with every sort of horror and that there is no escape. The Brahman runs frantically (as do we all) but to no avail, and time gnaws its way toward the Brahman's inevitable death. He is trapped. At the same time, remarkably (in view of his circumstances), the Brahman is distracted—by the taste of "honey."*

Roy C. Amore is Professor of Religious Studies at the University of Windsor; Larry D. Shinn is Professor of Religion at Oberlin College. Their book, Lustful Maidens and Ascetic Kings, *from which "The Brahman in the Pit" is taken, is among those recommended at the end of this chapter.*

A certain brahman who lived in this world wandered into a deep dark forest that was filled with ferocious wild animals. The forest was populated with lions, bull elephants, and other animals that roared incessantly. It was so terrifying that even the god of death, Yama, would cringe at entering this malevolent realm. Realizing he was lost, the brahman became very alarmed and began to run in circles hoping to find the way out. Attempting to elude the frightening creatures which were all around, the panicked man ran deeper into the forest. Still, he could not rid himself of his pursuers.

The brahman looked up and saw that the forest was surrounded by a net held by a huge woman with outstretched arms. Serpents with five heads also encompassed the forest and were so tall that their heads reached nearly up to the heavens. In a clearing, there was a deep pit covered with creeping vines and underbrush. As the brahman ran frantically through the forest pursued by a wild elephant, he stumbled into the open pit and became lodged halfway down the hole in the vines that grew over it.

As the brahman hung upside down, tangled in the vines, he saw a huge serpent at the bottom of the hole. Looking up, he saw an elephant at the top of the hole. The dark-skinned elephant had six faces and twelve feet and seemed intent on maintaining its vigil at the mouth of the hole. In the vines that held the brahman, bees had built hives filled with honey. These hives dripped honey near him, and he reached out to catch the sweet nectar in his mouth as he hung there. The more honey the brahman ate, the more he wanted; his thirst could not be quenched. Meanwhile, black and white rats gnawed away at the roots of the vines which held him. With elephant above, serpent below, bees buzzing all around, and rats gnawing at his life-support, the brahman continued to reach out for more honey.

The Hindu View of Life

Sarvepalli Radhakrishnan

Born and educated in India, Sarvepalli Radhakrishnan (1888–1975) was a professor of philosophy at various Indian colleges and Spaulding Professor of Eastern Religion and Ethics at Oxford University. He served as vice chancellor of Andhra University, held the same position at Benares Hindu University, and was chancellor of Delhi University. Apart from his academic posts, he worked for years as head of the Indian delegation to UNESCO and was chairman of the executive board and president of that organization. He was appointed Indian ambassador to the Soviet Union and was vice-president and then president of India. Knighted in 1931, he held honorary degrees from over fifty universities.

Radhakrishnan is the author or translator of Indian Philosophy *(2 vols.),* The Hindu View of Life, Eastern Religions and Western Thought, The Bhagavadgita, The Dhammapada, The Principal Upanishads, An Idealist View of Life, The Philosophy of the Upanishads, East and West in Religion, The Brahma Sutra, *and many other books.*

The Spirit of Indian Philosophy

At the very outset, it should be emphasized that Indian philosophy has had an extremely long and complex development, much more complex than is usually realized, and probably a longer history of continuous development than any other philosophical tradition.

. . .

Accordingly, it is very difficult to cite any specific doctrines or methods as characteristic of Indian philosophy as a whole and applicable to all the multitudinous systems and subsystems developed through nearly four millenniums of Indian philosophical speculation.

Nevertheless, in certain respects there is what might be called a distinct spirit of

"The Spirit of Indian Philosophy" is from Sarvepalli Radhakrishnan and Charles A. Moore (eds.), *A Sourcebook in Indian Philosophy.* Copyright © 1957 by Princeton University Press. Reprinted by permission of Princeton University Press.

"The Four Ends of Life" is from Sarvepalli Radhakrishnan, *Eastern Religions and Western Thought* (2nd ed., 1940). Reprinted by permission of The Clarendon Press, Oxford.

Indian philosophy. This is exemplified by certain attitudes which are fairly characteristic of the Indian philosophical mind or which stand as points of view that have been emphasized characteristically by Indians in their philosophies.

(1) The chief mark of Indian philosophy in general is its concentration upon the spiritual. Both in life and in philosophy the spiritual motive is predominant in India. Except for the relatively minor materialistic school of the Cārvāka and related doctrines, philosophy in India conceives man to be spiritual in nature, is interested primarily in his spiritual destiny, and relates him in one way or another to a universe which is also spiritual in essential character. Neither man nor the universe is looked upon as physical in essence, and material welfare is never recognized as the goal of human life, except by the Cārvāka. . . .

(2) Another characteristic view of Indian philosophy is the belief in the intimate relationship of philosophy and life. This attitude of the practical application of philosophy to life is found in every school of Indian philosophy. While natural abundance and material prosperity paved the way for the rise of philosophical speculation, philosophy has never been considered a mere intellectual exercise. The close relationship between theory and practice, doctrine and life, has always been outstanding in Indian thought. Every Indian system seeks the truth, not as academic "knowledge for its own sake," but to learn the truth which shall make men free. This is not, as it has been called, the modern pragmatic attitude. It is much larger and much deeper than that. It is not the view that truth is measured in terms of the practical, but rather that the truth is the only sound guide for practice, that truth alone has efficacy as a guide for man in his search for salvation. Every major system of Indian philosophy takes its beginning from the practical and tragic problems of life and searches for the truth in order to solve the problem of man's distress in the world in which he finds himself. There has been no teaching which remained a mere word of mouth or dogma of schools. Every doctrine has been turned into a passionate conviction, stirring the heart of man and quickening his breath, and completely transforming his personal nature. In India, philosophy is for life; it is to be lived. It is not enough to *know* the truth; the truth must be *lived.* The goal of the Indian is not to know the ultimate truth but to *realize* it, to become one with it.

Another aspect of the intimate inseparability of theory and practice, philosophy and life, in Indian philosophy is to be found in the universally prevalent demand for moral purification as an imperative preliminary for the would-be student of philosophy or searcher after truth. Śaṁkara's classic statement of this demand calls for a knowledge of the distinction between the eternal and the noneternal, that is, a questioning tendency in the inquirer; the subjugation of all desire for the fruits of action either in this life or in a hereafter, a renunciation of all petty desire, personal motive, and practical interest; tranquillity, self-control, renunciation, patience, peace of mind, and faith; and a desire for release *(mokṣa)* as the supreme goal of life.

(3) Indian philosophy is characterized by the introspective attitude and the introspective approach to reality. Philosophy is thought of as *ātmavidyā,* knowledge of the self. Philosophy can start either with the external world or with the internal world of man's inner nature, the self of man. In its pursuit of the truth, Indian philosophy has always been strongly dominated by concern with the inner life and

self of man rather than the external world of physical nature. Physical science, though developed extensively in the Golden Age of Indian culture, was never considered the road to ultimate truth; truth is to be sought and found within. The subjective, then, rather than the objective, becomes the focus of interest in Indian philosophy, and, therefore, psychology and ethics are considered more important as aspects of branches of philosophy than the sciences which study physical nature. This is not to say that the Indian mind has not studied the physical world; in fact, on the contrary, India's achievements in the realm of positive science were at one time truly outstanding, especially in the mathematical sciences such as algebra, astronomy, and geometry, and in the applications of these basic sciences to numerous phases of human activity. Zoology, botany, medicine, and related sciences have also been extremely prominent in Indian thought. Be this as it may, the Indian, from time immemorial, has felt that the inner spirit of man is the most significant clue to his reality and to that of the universe, more significant by far than the physical or the external.

(4) This introspective interest is highly conducive to idealism, of course, and consequently most Indian philosophy is idealistic in one form or another. The tendency of Indian philosophy, especially Hinduism, has been in the direction of monistic idealism. Almost all Indian philosophy believes that reality is *ultimately* one and *ultimately* spiritual. Some systems have seemed to espouse dualism or pluralism, but even these have been deeply permeated by a strong monistic character. If we concentrate our attention upon the underlying spirit of Indian philosophy rather than its variety of opinions, we shall find that this spirit is embodied in the tendency to interpret life and reality in the way of monistic idealism. This rather unusual attitude is attributable to the nonrigidity of the Indian mind and to the fact that the attitude of monistic idealism is so plastic and dynamic that it takes many forms and expresses itself even in seemingly conflicting doctrines. These are not conflicting doctrines in fact, however, but merely different expressions of an underlying conviction which provides basic unity to Indian philosophy as a whole.

·   ·   ·

(5) Indian philosophy makes unquestioned and extensive use of reason, but intuition is accepted as the only method through which the ultimate can be known. Reason, intellectual knowledge, is not enough. Reason is not useless or fallacious, but it is insufficient. To know reality one must have an actual experience of it. One does not merely *know* the truth in Indian philosophy; one *realizes* it. The word which most aptly describes philosophy in India is *darśana,* which comes from the verbal root *dṛś,* meaning "to see." "To see" is to have a direct intuitive experience of the object, or, rather, to realize it in the sense of becoming one with it. No complete knowledge is possible as long as there is the relationship of the subject on one hand and the object on the other. Later developments in Indian philosophy, from the time of the beginning of the systems, have all depended in large part upon reason for the systematic formulation of doctrines and systems, for rational demonstration or justification, and in polemical conflicts of system against system. Nevertheless, all the systems, except the Cārvāka, agree that there is a higher way of knowing reality, beyond the reach of reason, namely, the direct perception or

experience of the ultimate reality, which cannot be known by reason in any of its forms. Reason can demonstrate the truth, but reason cannot discover or reach the truth. While reason may be the method of philosophy in its more intellectualistic sense, intuition is the only method of comprehending the ultimate. Indian philosophy is thus characterized by an ultimate dependence upon intuition, along with the recognition of the efficacy of reason and intellect when applied in their limited capacity and with their proper function.

(6) Another characteristic of Indian philosophy, one which is closely related to the preceding one, is its so-called acceptance of authority. Although the systems of Indian philosophy vary in the degree to which they are specifically related to the ancient *śruti,* not one of the systems—orthodox or unorthodox, except the Cārvāka—openly stands in violation of the accepted intuitive insights of its ancient seers, whether it be the Hindu seers of the Upaniṣads, the intuitive experience of the Buddha, or the similarly intuitive wisdom of Mahāvīra, the founder of Jainism, as we have it today. Indian philosophers have always been conscious of tradition and, as has been indicated before, the great system-builders of later periods claimed to be merely commentators, explaining the traditional wisdom of the past. While the specific doctrines of the past may be changed by interpretation, the general spirit and frequently the basic concepts are retained from age to age. Reverence for authority does not militate against progress, but it does lend a unity of spirit by providing a continuity of thought which has rendered philosophy especially significant in Indian life and solidly unified against any philosophical attitude contradicting its basic characteristics of spirituality, inwardness, intuition, and the strong belief that the truth is to be lived, not merely known.

·   ·   ·

(7) Finally, there is the over-all synthetic tradition which is essential to the spirit and method of Indian philosophy. This is as old as the *Ṛg Veda,* where the seers realized that true religion comprehends all religions, so that "God is one but men call him by many names." Indian philosophy is clearly characterized by the synthetic approach to the various aspects of experience and reality. Religion and philosophy, knowledge and conduct, intuition and reason, man and nature, God and man, noumenon and phenomena, are all brought into harmony by the synthesizing tendency of the Indian mind.

The Four Ends of Life

1. *Mokṣa.* The chief end of man is the development of the individual. The Upaniṣad tells us that there is nothing higher than the person. But man is not an assemblage of body, life, and mind born of and subject to physical nature. The natural half-animal being with which he confuses himself is not his whole or real being. It is but an instrument for the use of spirit which is the truth of his being. To find the real self, to exceed his apparent, outward self, is the greatness of which man alone of all

beings is capable.[1] "Verily, O Gārgī, he who departs from this world without knowing this Imperishable one is a vile and wretched creature."[2] To inquire into his true self, to live in and from it, to determine by its own energy what it shall be inwardly and what it shall make of its outward circumstances, to found the whole life on the power and truth of spirit, is *mokṣa* or spiritual freedom. To be shut up in one's own ego, to rest in the apparent self and mistake it for the real, is the root of all unrest to which man is exposed by reason of his mentality. To aspire to a universality *(sarvātmabhāva)* through his mind and reason, through his heart and love, through his will and power, is the high sense of his humanity.

2. *Kāma.* Is this perfection consistent with normal living? There is a prevalent idea that the Hindu view concedes no reality to life, that it despises vital aims and satisfactions, that it gives no inspiring motive to human effort. If spirit and life were unrelated, spiritual freedom would become an unattainable ideal, a remote passion of a few visionaries. There is little in Hindu thought to support the view that one has to attain spiritual freedom by means of a violent rupture with ordinary life. On the other hand, it lays down that we must pass through the normal life conscientiously and with knowledge, work out its values, and accept its enjoyments. Spiritual life is an integration of man's being, in its depth and breadth, in its capacity for deep meditation as well as reckless transport. *Kāma* refers to the emotional being of man, his feelings and desires.[3] If man is denied his emotional life, he becomes a prey to repressive introspection and lives under a continual strain of moral torture. When the reaction sets in, he will give way to a wildness of ecstasy which is ruinous to his sanity and health.

3. *Artha.* The third end relates to wealth and material well-being. Though it is not its own end, it helps to sustain and enrich life. There was never in India a national ideal of poverty or squalor. Spiritual life finds full scope only in communities of a certain degree of freedom from sordidness. Lives that are strained and starved cannot be religious except in a rudimentary way. Economic insecurity and individual freedom do not go together.

4. *Dharma.* While the spontaneous activities of interest and desire are to be accepted, their full values cannot be realized if their action is unrestrained. There must be a rule, a guidance, a restraint. *Dharma* gives coherence and direction to the different activities of life. It is not a religious creed or cult imposing an ethical or social rule. It is the complete rule of life, the harmony of the whole man who finds a right and just law of his living. Each man and group, each activity of soul, mind, life, and body, has its *dharma.* While man is justified in satisfying his desires, which is essential for the expression of life, to conform to the dictates of his desires is not the law of his being. He will not get the best out of them if he does not conform to the *dharma,* or the rule of right practice. A famous verse of the Mahābhārata says: "I cry with arm uplifted, yet none heedeth. From righteousness *(dharma)* flow forth pleasure and profit. Why then do ye not follow righteousness?" *Dharma* tells us that

---

1. The Bhāgavata says, "The chief end of life here is not the attainment of heaven popularly known to be the result of pious duties. It is the desire to enquire into truth" (i. 2. 10).

2. Brhadāranyaka Up. iii. 8. 10.

3. Bhāgavata i. 2. 10.

while our life is in the first instance for our own satisfaction, it is more essentially for the community and most of all for that universal self which is in each of us and all beings. Ethical life is the means to spiritual freedom, as well as its expression on earth.

The *dharma* and its observance are neither the beginning nor the end of human life, for beyond the law is spiritual freedom, not merely a noble manhood but universality, the aim which ennobles the whole life of the individual and the whole order of society. Man's whole life is to be passed in the implicit consciousness of this mysterious background.

The four ends of life point to the different sides of human nature, the instinctive and the emotional, the economic, the intellectual and the ethical, and the spiritual. There is implanted in man's fundamental being a spiritual capacity. He becomes completely human only when his sensibility to spirit is awakened. So long as man's life is limited to science and art, technical invention, and social programmes, he is incomplete and not truly human. If we are insolent and base, unfair and unkind to one another, unhappy in personal relationships, and lacking in mutual understanding, it is because we remain too much on the surface of life and have lost contact with the depths. When the fountains of spirit from which the creative life of the individual and society is fed dry up, diseases of every description, intellectual, moral, and social, break out. The everlasting vagrancy of thought, the contemporary muddle of conflicting philosophies, the rival ideologies which cut through national frontiers and geographical divisions, are a sign of spiritual homelessness. The unrest is in a sense sacred, for it is the confession of the failure of a self-sufficient humanism with no outlook beyond the world. We cannot find peace on earth through economic planning or political arrangement. Only the pure in heart by fostering the mystical accord of minds can establish justice and love. Man's true and essential greatness is individual. The scriptures could point out the road but each man must travel it for himself. The law of *karma* affirms the responsibility of each individual for his life. "The sins ye do by two and two, ye shall pay for one by one," as Kipling called Beelzebub to remark. There is no salvation by proxy or in herds. In primitive societies there is collective responsibility, but on the hypothesis of rebirth, the guilt of an action attaches to its author. The punishment must fall on the individual, if not in this life, then in the next or perhaps in a later. The dignity and responsibility of the individual soul are recognized.

Hymns from the Rig Veda

Wendy Doniger O'Flaherty (translator)

The Rig Veda is the earliest of the Vedas; it consists of slightly more than a thousand hymns. Composed by unknown poets over hundreds of years (the dates, as has been mentioned, are uncertain), the hymns accordingly express a wide range of hopes and fears and speculation. They are attempts, in the main, to come to grips with a world as mysterious then as it is now.

Born in New York, Wendy Doniger O'Flaherty (1940–   ) studied Sanskrit at Radcliffe College and holds doctoral degrees in Indian literature from both Harvard and Oxford Universities. She has taught at the University of London and the University of California, Berkeley; she is presently the Mircea Eliade Professor of the History of Religions at the University of Chicago. Among her publications are Siva: The Erotic Ascetic; The Origins of Evil in Hindu Mythology; Women, Androgynes, and Other Mythical Beasts; Dreams, Illusion, and Other Realities; Tales of Sex and Violence: Folklore, Sacrifice, and Danger in the Jaiminiya Brahmana; *and* Other Peoples' Myths: The Cave of Echoes. *She has edited* Karma and Rebirth in Classical Indian Traditions, The Critical Study of Sacred Texts, *and* Textual Sources for the Study of Hinduism. *She is the translator of* Hindu Myths *and* The Laws of Manu.

Creation Hymn

The best known of all the hymns of the Rig Veda, the "Creation Hymn" was meant, suggests O'Flaherty, "to puzzle and challenge, to raise unanswerable questions, to pile up paradoxes."

———

There was neither non-existence nor existence then; there was neither the realm of space nor the sky which is beyond. What stirred? Where? In whose protection? Was there water, bottomlessly deep?

There was neither death nor immortality then. There was no distinguishing sign of night nor of day. That one breathed, windless, by its own impulse. Other than that there was nothing beyond.

Darkness was hidden by darkness in the beginning; with no distinguishing sign, all this was water. The life force that was covered with emptiness, that one arose through the power of heat.

Desire came upon that one in the beginning; that was the first seed of mind. Poets seeking in their heart with wisdom found the bond of existence in non-existence.

Their cord was extended across. Was there below? Was there above? There were seed-placers; there were powers. There was impulse beneath; there was giving-forth above.

Who really knows? Who will here proclaim it? Whence was it produced? Whence is this creation? The gods came afterwards, with the creation of this universe. Who then knows whence it has arisen?

Whence this creation has arisen—perhaps it formed itself, or perhaps it did not—the one who looks down on it, in the highest heaven, only he knows—or perhaps he does not know. (10.129)

The Unknown God, the Golden Embryo

There are many creation hymns in the Rig Veda; "The Unknown God, the Golden Embryo" is another of them. As with the "Creation Hymn," the emphasis is on the questions. *The answer provided in the last verse is thought to have been appended to the hymn at a later date.*

In the beginning the Golden Embryo arose. Once he was born, he was the one lord of creation. He held in place the earth and this sky. Who is the god whom we should worship with the oblation?

He who gives life, who gives strength, whose command all the gods, his own, obey; his shadow is immortality—and death. Who is the god whom we should worship with the oblation?

He who by his greatness became the one king of the world that breathes and blinks, who rules over his two-footed and four-footed creatures—who is the god whom we should worship with the oblation?

He who through his power owns these snowy mountains, and the ocean together with the river Rasā, they say; who has the quarters of the sky as his two arms—who is the god whom we should worship with the oblation?

He by whom the awesome sky and the earth were made firm, by whom the dome of the sky was propped up, and the sun, who measured out the middle realm of space—who is the god whom we should worship with the oblation?

He to whom the two opposed masses looked with trembling in their hearts, supported by his help, on whom the rising sun shines down—who is the god whom we should worship with the oblation?

When the high waters came, pregnant with the embryo that is everything, bringing forth fire, he arose from that as the one life's breath of the gods. Who is the god whom we should worship with the oblation?

He who in his greatness looked over the waters, which were pregnant with Dakṣa, bringing forth the sacrifice, he who was the one god among all the gods—who is the god whom we should worship with the oblation? Let him not harm us, he who fathered the earth and created the sky, whose laws are true, who created the high, shining waters. Who is the god whom we should worship with the oblation?

O Prajāpati, lord of progeny, no one but you embraces all these creatures. Grant us the desires for which we offer you oblation. Let us be lords of riches. (10.121)

Puruṣa-Sūkta, or "The Hymn of Man"

"The function of myth is to make sense of things that are not otherwise understandable," O'Flaherty has said.* In the following poem, the attempt to understand is palpable in the line, "Thus they [the gods] set the worlds in order."

The man has a thousand heads, a thousand eyes, a thousand feet. He pervaded the earth on all sides and extended beyond it as far as ten fingers.

It is the Man who is all this, whatever has been and whatever is to be. He is the ruler of immortality, when he grows beyond everything through food.

Such is his greatness, and the Man is yet more than this. All creatures are a quarter of him; three quarters are what is immortal in heaven.

With three quarters the Man rose upwards, and one quarter of him still remains here. From this he spread out in all directions, into that which eats and that which does not eat.

From him Virāj was born, and from Virāj came the Man. When he was born, he ranged beyond the earth behind and before.

When the gods spread the sacrifice with the Man as the offering, spring was the clarified butter, summer the fuel, autumn the oblation.

They anointed the Man, the sacrifice born at the beginning, upon the sacred grass. With him the gods, Sādhyas, and sages sacrificed.

From that sacrifice in which everything was offered, the melted fat was collected, and he made it into those beasts who live in the air, in the forest, and in villages.

From that sacrifice in which everything was offered, the verses and chants were born, the metres were born from it, and from it the formulas were born.

Horses were born from it, and those other animals that have two rows of teeth; cows were born from it, and from it goats and sheep were born.

*Interview with Alvin P. Sanoff, *U.S. News and World Report,* 15 July 1991, p. 49.

When they divided the Man, into how many parts did they apportion him? What do they call his mouth, his two arms and thighs and feet?

His mouth became the Brahmin; his arms were made into the Warrior, his thighs the People, and from his feet the Servants were born.

The moon was born from his mind; from his eye the sun was born. Indra and Agni came from his mouth, and from his vital breath the Wind was born.

From his navel the middle realm of space arose; from his head the sky evolved. From his two feet came the earth, and the quarters of the sky from his ear. Thus they set the worlds in order.

There were seven enclosing-sticks for him, and thrice seven fuel-sticks, when the gods, spreading the sacrifice, bound the Man as the sacrificial beast.

With the sacrifice the gods sacrificed to the sacrifice. These were the first ritual laws. These very powers reached the dome of the sky where dwell the Sādhyas, the ancient gods. (10.90)

Dawn and the Aśvins

See how the dawns have set up their banner in the eastern half of the sky, adorning and anointing themselves with sunlight for balm. Unleashing themselves like impetuous heroes unsheathing their weapons, the tawny cows, the mothers, return.

The red-gold lights have flown up freely; they have yoked the tawny cows who let themselves be yoked. The dawns have spread their webs in the ancient way; the tawny ones have set forth the glowing light.

They sing like women busy at their tasks, coming from a distant place with a single harnessed team, bringing refreshing food day after day to the man of good actions, the man of generosity, the man who sacrifices and presses the Soma.

Like a dancing girl, she puts on bright ornaments; she uncovers her breast as a cow reveals her swollen udder. Creating light for the whole universe, Dawn has opened up the darkness as cows break out from their enclosed pen.

Her brilliant flame has become visible once more; she spreads herself out, driving back the formless black abyss. As one sets up the stake in the sacrifice, anointing and adorning it with coloured ornaments, so the daughter of the sky sets up her many-coloured light.

We have crossed to the farther bank of this darkness; radiant Dawn spreads her webs. Smiling like a lover who wishes to win his way, she shines forth and with her lovely face awakens us to happiness.

The shining daughter of the sky, bringing rich gifts, is praised by the Gotamas. Measure out offspring and strong men as the victory prizes, Dawn, the rewards that begin with cattle and culminate in horses.

Let me obtain great riches of glory and heroic men, Dawn, riches that begin with slaves and culminate in heroes. Fortunate in your beauty, incited by the victory prize you shine forth with the fame of great achievements.

Gazing out over all creatures, the goddess shines from the distance facing straight towards every eye. Awakening into motion everything that lives, she has found the speech of every inspired poet.

The ancient goddess, born again and again dressed in the same colour, causes the mortal to age and wears away his life-span, as a cunning gambler carries off the stakes.

She has awakened, uncovering the very edges of the sky; she pushes aside her sister. Shrinking human generations, the young woman shines under her lover's gaze.

Spreading out her rays like cattle, like a river in full flood the brightly coloured one shines from the distance. The fortunate goddess does not break the laws of the gods but becomes visible, appearing by the rays of the sun.

Dawn, you who hold the victory prize, bring us that brightly coloured power by which we establish children and grandchildren.

Dawn, rich in cows, rich in horses, resplendent giver of gifts, shine your riches upon us here and now.

Harness your red-gold horses now, O prize-giving Dawn, and bring all good fortunes to us.

O Aśvins who work wonders, turn your chariot that brings cattle, that brings gold, and with one mind come back to us.

You Aśvins who gave a shout from heaven and made light for mankind, bring us strength.

May those who wake at dawn bring here to drink the Soma the two gods who work wonders and give joy, moving on paths of gold. (1.92)

Night

The goddess Night has drawn near, looking about on many sides with her eyes. She has put on all her glories. The immortal goddess has filled the wide space, the depths and the heights. She stems the tide of darkness with her light.

The goddess has drawn near, pushing aside her sister the twilight. Darkness, too, will give way.

As you came near to us today, we turned homeward to rest, as birds go to their home in a tree.

People who live in villages have gone home to rest, and animals with feet, and animals with wings, even the ever-searching hawks.

Ward off the she-wolf and the wolf; ward off the thief. O night full of waves, be easy for us to cross over.

Darkness—palpable, black, and painted—has come upon me. O Dawn, banish it like a debt.

I have driven this hymn to you as the herdsman drives cows. Choose and accept it, O Night, daughter of the sky, like a song of praise to a conqueror. (10.127)

Selections, *The Upanishads*

Swami Prabhavananda and Frederick Manchester (translators)

Swami (a title comparable to the Protestant "Reverend" and the Catholic "Father")
Prabhavananda (1893–1976) was born in India and while still a boy came under
the influence of the teachings of Ramakrishna and his followers. Joining the Ramak-
rishna Order, he was ordained and came to the United States in 1923 to assist at
the Vedanta Society of San Francisco. He went on to found Vedanta societies in
Portland, Oregon, and in Southern California (1929). The latter society, located in
Hollywood, attracted considerable attention through some of its eminent mem-
bers—notably the writers Gerald Heard, Aldous Huxley, and Christopher Isher-
wood (who has written most entertainingly of Prabhavananda and Vedanta in My
Guru and His Disciple [*1980*]*).*

Prabhavananda also translated The Song of God: Bhagavad Gita, Shankara's
Crest-Jewel of Discrimination, *and* How to Know God: The Yoga Aphorisms of
Patanjali *(all with Isherwood). Among his other titles are* Religion in Practice, Vedic
Religion and Practice, Yoga and Mysticism, Eternal Companion, *and* The Sermon
on the Mount According to Vedanta.

Frederick Manchester also worked with Prabhavananda on The Spiritual Heritage of India. *A poet, he was active in the Vedanta Society of Los Angeles; he was*
formerly a professor of English literature at the University of Wisconsin.

Although they often draw their themes from older Vedic literature, the Upani-
shads are usually held to be the earliest philosophical literature of India. In all, there
are over a hundred Upanishads, but thirteen or so receive the most attention. They
do not express an entirely consistent point of view (having been composed by differ-
ent authors in different times and places), but one bold thesis does predominate: that
the Atman, the individual "soul," is one with Brahman, the Absolute. It is the idea
summarized in the classic line from the Chandogya Upanishad, "THAT ART
THOU." *Hence the quest for Truth in the Upanishads turns inward: the Ground of*
Being is to be found within oneself.

There follow excerpts from three Upanishads. The Chandogya *and* Brihadaranyaka *Upanishads are both held in the highest esteem, the latter being also the*
longest and probably the oldest of all the Upanishads. The nature of death is dis-
cussed in the Katha *Upanishad.*

From Swami Prabhavananda and Frederick Manchester (eds. and trans.), *The Upanishads: Breath of the*
Eternal. New York: New American Library. Copyright © 1957 by the Vedanta Society of Southern California. Reprinted by permission of the Vedanta Society of Southern California.

From the Chandogya Upanishad

When Svetaketu was twelve years old, his father Uddalaka said to him, "Svetaketu, you must now go to school and study. None of our family, my child, is ignorant of Brahman."

Thereupon Svetaketu went to a teacher and studied for twelve years. After committing to memory all the Vedas, he returned home full of pride in his learning.

His father, noticing the young man's conceit, said to him: "Svetaketu, have you asked for that knowledge by which we hear the unhearable, by which we perceive the unperceivable, by which we know the unknowable?"

"What is that knowledge, sir?" asked Svetaketu.

"My child, as by knowing one lump of clay, all things made of clay are known, the difference being only in name and arising from speech, and the truth being that all are clay; as by knowing a nugget of gold, all things made of gold are known, the difference being only in name and arising from speech, and the truth being that all are gold—exactly so is that knowledge, knowing which we know all."

"But surely those venerable teachers of mine are ignorant of this knowledge; for if they had possessed it, they would have taught it to me. Do you therefore, sir, give me that knowledge."

"Be it so," said Uddalaka, and continued thus:

.   .   .

"As the bees make honey by gathering juices from many flowering plants and trees, and as these juices reduced to one honey do not know from what flowers they severally come, similarly, my son, all creatures, when they are merged in that one Existence, whether in dreamless sleep or in death, know nothing of their past or present state, because of the ignorance enveloping them—know not that they are merged in him and that from him they came.

"Whatever these creatures are, whether a lion, or a tiger, or a boar, or a worm, or a gnat, or a mosquito, that they remain after they come back from dreamless sleep.

"All these have their self in him alone. He is the truth. He is the subtle essence of all. He is the Self. And that, Svetaketu, THAT ART THOU."

"Please, sir, tell me more about this Self."

"Be it so, my son:

"The rivers in the east flow eastward, the rivers in the west flow westward, and all enter into the sea. From sea to sea they pass, the clouds lifting them to the sky as vapor and sending them down as rain. And as these rivers, when they are united with the sea, do not know whether they are this or that river, likewise all those creatures that I have named, when they have come back from Brahman, know not whence they came.

"All those beings have their self in him alone. He is the truth. He is the subtle essence of all. He is the Self. And that, Svetaketu, THAT ART THOU."

"Please, sir, tell me more about this Self."
"Be it so, my child:

                                    .   .   .

... Bring a fruit of that Nyagrodha tree."
"Here it is, sir."
"Break it."
"It is broken, sir."
"What do you see?"
"Some seeds, extremely small, sir."
"Break one of them."
"It is broken, sir."
"What do you see?"
"Nothing, sir."
"The subtle essence you do not see, and in that is the whole of the Nyagrodha tree. Believe, my son, that that which is the subtle essence—in that have all things their existence. That is the truth. That is the Self. And that, Svetaketu, THAT ART THOU."
"Please, sir, tell me more about this Self."
"Be it so. Put this salt in water, and come to me tomorrow morning."
Svetaketu did as he was bidden. The next morning his father asked him to bring the salt which he had put in the water. But he could not, for it had dissolved. Then said Uddalaka:
"Sip the water, and tell me how it tastes."
"It is salty, sir."
"In the same way," continued Uddalaka, "though you do not see Brahman in this body, he is indeed here. That which is the subtle essence—in that have all things their existence. That is the truth. That is the Self. And that, Svetaketu, THAT ART THOU."

From the Brihadaranyaka Upanishad

YAGNAVALKYA (to his wife) Maitreyi, I am resolved to give up the world and begin the life of renunciation. I wish therefore to divide my property between you and my other wife, Katyayani.

MAITREYI My lord, if this whole earth belonged to me, with all its wealth, should I through its possession attain immortality?

YAGNAVALKYA No. Your life would be like that of the rich. None can possibly hope to attain immortality through wealth.

MAITREYI Then what need have I of wealth? Please, my lord, tell me what you know about the way to immortality.

YAGNAVALKYA Dear to me have you always been, Maitreyi, and now you ask to learn of that truth which is nearest my heart. Come, sit by me. I will explain it to you. Meditate on what I say.

It is not for the sake of the husband, my beloved, that the husband is dear, but for the sake of the Self.

It is not for the sake of the wife, my beloved, that the wife is dear, but for the sake of the Self.

It is not for the sake of the children, my beloved, that the children are dear, but for the sake of the Self.

It is not for the sake of wealth, my beloved, that wealth is dear, but for the sake of the Self.

It is not for the sake of the Brahmins, my beloved, that the Brahmins are held in reverence, but for the sake of the Self.

It is not for the sake of the Kshatriyas, my beloved, that the Kshatriyas are held in honor, but for the sake of the Self.

It is not for the sake of the higher worlds, my beloved, that the higher worlds are desired, but for the sake of the Self.

It is not for the sake of the gods, my beloved, that the gods are worshiped, but for the sake of the Self.

It is not for the sake of the creatures, my beloved, that the creatures are prized, but for the sake of the Self.

It is not for the sake of itself, my beloved, that anything whatever is esteemed, but for the sake of the Self.

The Self, Maitreyi, is to be known. Hear about it, reflect upon it, meditate upon it. By knowing the Self, my beloved, through hearing, reflection, and meditation, one comes to know all things.

Let the Brahmin ignore him who thinks that the Brahmin is different from the Self.

Let the Kshatriya ignore him who thinks that the Kshatriya is different from the Self.

Let the higher worlds ignore him who thinks that the higher worlds are different from the Self.

Let the gods ignore him who thinks that the gods are different from the Self.

Let all creatures ignore him who thinks that the creatures are different from the Self.

Let all ignore him who thinks that anything whatever is different from the Self.

The priest, the warrior, the higher worlds, the gods, the creatures, whatsoever things there be—these are the Self.

As, when the drum is beaten, its various particular notes are not heard apart from the whole, but in the total sound all its notes are heard; as, when the conch-shell is blown, its various particular notes are not heard apart from the whole, but in the total sound all its notes are heard; as, when the vina is played, its various particular notes are not heard apart from the whole, but in the total sound all its notes are heard—so, through the knowledge of the Self, Pure Intelligence, all things and beings are known. There is no existence apart from the Self.

As smoke and sparks arise from a lighted fire kindled with damp fuel, even so, Maitreyi, have been breathed forth from the Eternal all knowledge and all wisdom—what we know as the Rig Veda, the Yajur Veda, and the rest. They are the breath of the Eternal.

As for water the one center is the ocean, as for touch the one center is the skin, as for smell the one center is the nose, as for taste the one center is the tongue, as for form the one center is the eyes, as for sound the one center is the ears, as for thought the one center is the mind, as for divine wisdom the one center is the heart—so for all beings the one center is the Self.

As a lump of salt when thrown into water melts away and the lump cannot be taken out, but wherever we taste the water it is salty, even so, O Maitreyi, the individual self, dissolved, is the Eternal—pure consciousness, infinite and transcendent. Individuality arises by identification of the Self, through ignorance, with the elements; and with the disappearance of consciousness of the many, in divine illumination, it disappears. Where there is consciousness of the Self, individuality is no more.

This it is, O my beloved, that I wanted to tell you.

MAITREYI "Where there is consciousness of the Self, individuality is no more": this that you say, my lord, confuses me.

YAGNAVALKYA My beloved, let nothing I have said confuse you. But meditate well the truth that I have spoken.

As long as there is duality, one sees *the other,* one hears *the other,* one smells *the other,* one speaks to *the other,* one thinks of *the other,* one knows *the other;* but when for the illumined soul the all is dissolved in the Self, who is there to be seen by whom, who is there to be smelt by whom, who is there to be heard by whom, who is there to be spoken to by whom, who is there to be thought of by whom, who is there to be known by whom? Ah, Maitreyi, my beloved, the Intelligence which reveals all—by what shall it be revealed? By whom shall the Knower be known? The Self is described as *not this, not that.* It is incomprehensible, for it cannot be comprehended; undecaying, for it never decays; unattached, for it never attaches itself; unbound, for it is never bound. By whom, O my beloved, shall the Knower be known?

This it is that I teach you, O Maitreyi. This is the truth of immortality.

From the Katha Upanishad

[*Translator's note:* Granted three wishes, or "boons," by Death, the young Nachiketa as his third wish asks of Death the secret of what happens to a man after he dies.]

And then Nachiketa considered within himself, and said:

"When a man dies, there is this doubt: Some say, he is; others say, he is not. Taught by thee, I would know the truth. This is my third wish."

"Nay," replied Death, "even the gods were once puzzled by this mystery. Subtle indeed is the truth regarding it, not easy to understand. Choose thou some other boon, O Nachiketa."

But Nachiketa would not be denied.

"Thou sayest, O Death, that even the gods were once puzzled by this mystery, and that it is not easy to understand. Surely there is no teacher better able to explain it than thou—and there is no other boon equal to this."

To which, trying Nachiketa again, the god replied:

"Ask for sons and grandsons who shall live a hundred years. Ask for cattle, elephants, horses, gold. Choose for thyself a mighty kingdom. Or if thou canst imagine aught better, ask for that—not for sweet pleasures only but for the power, beyond all thought, to taste their sweetness. Yea, verily, the supreme enjoyer will I make thee of every good thing. Celestial maidens, beautiful to behold, such indeed as were not meant for mortals—even these, together with their bright chariots and their musical instruments, will I give unto thee, to serve thee. But for the secret of death, O Nachiketa, do not ask!"

But Nachiketa stood fast, and said: "These things endure only till the morrow, O Destroyer of Life, and the pleasures they give wear out the senses. Keep thou therefore horses and chariots, keep dance and song, for thyself! How shall he desire wealth, O Death, who once has seen thy face? Nay, only the boon that I have chosen—that only do I ask. Having found out the society of the imperishable and the immortal, as in knowing thee I have done, how shall I, subject to decay and death, and knowing well the vanity of the flesh—how shall I wish for long life?

"Tell me, O King, the supreme secret regarding which men doubt. No other boon will I ask."

Whereupon the King of Death, well pleased at heart, began to teach Nachiketa the secret of immortality.

KING OF DEATH The good is one thing; the pleasant is another. These two, differing in their ends, both prompt to action. Blessed are they that choose the good; they that choose the pleasant miss the goal.

Both the good and the pleasant present themselves to men. The wise, having examined both, distinguish the one from the other. The wise prefer the good to the pleasant; the foolish, driven by fleshly desires, prefer the pleasant to the good.

Thou, O Nachiketa, having looked upon fleshly desires, delightful to the senses, hast renounced them all. Thou hast turned from the miry way wherein many a man wallows.

Far from each other, and leading to different ends, are ignorance and knowledge. Thee, O Nachiketa, I regard as one who aspires after knowledge, for a multitude of pleasant objects were unable to tempt thee.

Living in the abyss of ignorance yet wise in their own conceit, deluded fools go round and round, the blind led by the blind.

To the thoughtless youth, deceived by the vanity of earthly possessions, the path that leads to the eternal abode is not revealed. *This world alone is real; there is no hereafter*—thinking thus, he falls again and again, birth after birth, into my jaws.

To many it is not given to hear of the Self. Many, though they hear of it, do not understand it. Wonderful is he who speaks of it. Intelligent is he who learns of it. Blessed is he who, taught by a good teacher, is able to understand it.

The truth of the Self cannot be fully understood when taught by an ignorant man, for opinions regarding it, not founded in knowledge, vary one from another. Subtler than the subtlest is this Self, and beyond all logic. Taught by a teacher who knows the Self and Brahman as one, a man leaves vain theory behind and attains to truth.

The awakening which thou hast known does not come through the intellect but rather, in fullest measure, from the lips of the wise. Beloved Nachiketa, blessed, blessed art thou, because thou seekest the Eternal. Would that I had more pupils like thee!

Well I know that earthly treasure lasts but till the morrow. For did not I myself, wishing to be King of Death, make sacrifice with fire? But the sacrifice was a fleeting thing, performed with fleeting objects, and small is my reward, seeing that only for a moment will my reign endure.

The goal of worldly desire, the glittering objects for which all men long, the celestial pleasures they hope to gain by religious rites, the most sought-after of miraculous powers—all these were within thy grasp. But all these, with firm resolve, thou has renounced.

The ancient, effulgent being, the indwelling Spirit, subtle, deep-hidden in the lotus of the heart, is hard to know. But the wise man, following the path of meditation, knows him, and is freed alike from pleasure and from pain.

The man who has learned that the Self is separate from the body, the senses, and the mind, and has fully known him, the soul of truth, the subtle principle—such a man verily attains to him, and is exceeding glad, because he has found the source and dwelling place of all felicity. Truly do I believe, O Nachiketa, that for thee the gates of joy stand open.

NACHIKETA Teach me, O King, I beseech thee, whatsoever thou knowest to be beyond right and wrong, beyond cause and effect, beyond past, present, and future.

KING OF DEATH Of that goal which all the Vedas declare, which is implicit in all penances, and in pursuit of which men lead lives of continence and service, of that will I briefly speak.

It is—OM.

This syllable is Brahman. This syllable is indeed supreme. He who knows it obtains his desire.

It is the strongest support. It is the highest symbol. He who knows it is reverenced as a knower of Brahman.

The Self, whose symbol is OM, is the omniscient Lord. He is not born. He does not die. He is neither cause nor effect. This Ancient One is unborn, imperishable, eternal: though the body be destroyed, he is not killed.

If the slayer think that he slays, if the slain think that he is slain, neither of them knows the truth. The Self slays not, nor is he slain.

Smaller than the smallest, greater than the greatest, this Self forever dwells within the hearts of all. When a man is free from desire, his mind and senses purified, he beholds the glory of the Self and is without sorrow.

Though seated, he travels far; though at rest, he moves all things. Who but the purest of the pure can realize this Effulgent Being, who is joy and who is beyond joy.

Formless is he, though inhabiting form. In the midst of the fleeting he abides forever. All-pervading and supreme is the Self. The wise man, knowing him in his true nature, transcends all grief.

The Self is not known through study of the scriptures, nor through subtlety of the intellect, nor through much learning; but by him who longs for him is he known.[1] Verily unto him does the Self reveal his true being.

By learning, a man cannot know him, if he desist not from evil, if he control not his senses, if he quiet not his mind, and practice not meditation.

To him Brahmins and Kshatriyas are but food, and death itself a condiment.

Both the individual self and the Universal Self have entered the cave of the heart, the abode of the Most High, but the knowers of Brahman and the householders who perform the fire sacrifices see a difference between them as between sunshine and shadow.

May we perform the Nachiketa Sacrifice, which bridges the world of suffering. May we know the imperishable Brahman, who is fearless, and who is the end and refuge of those who seek liberation.

Know that the Self is the rider, and the body the chariot; that the intellect is the charioteer, and the mind the reins.[2]

The senses, say the wise, are the horses; the roads they travel are the mazes of desire. The wise call the Self the enjoyer when he is united with the body, the senses, and the mind.

When a man lacks discrimination and his mind is uncontrolled, his senses are unmanageable, like the restive horses of a charioteer. But when a man has discrimination and his mind is controlled, his senses, like the well-broken horses of a charioteer, lightly obey the rein.

He who lacks discrimination, whose mind is unsteady and whose heart is impure, never reaches the goal, but is born again and again. But he who has discrimination, whose mind is steady and whose heart is pure, reaches the goal, and having reached it is born no more.

The man who has a sound understanding for charioteer, a controlled mind for reins—he it is that reaches the end of the journey, the supreme abode of Vishnu, the all-pervading.[3]

The senses derive from physical objects, physical objects from mind, mind from intellect, intellect from ego, ego from the unmanifested seed, and the unmanifested seed from Brahman—the Uncaused Cause.

Brahman is the end of the journey. Brahman is the supreme goal.

The Brahman, this Self, deep-hidden in all beings, is not revealed to all; but to the seers, pure in heart, concentrated in mind—to them is he revealed.

The senses of the wise man obey his mind, his mind obeys his intellect, his intellect obeys his ego, and his ego obeys the Self.

Arise! Awake! Approach the feet of the master and know THAT. Like the sharp edge of a razor, the sages say, is the path. Narrow it is, and difficult to tread!

---

1. There is another interpretation of this sentence, involving the mystery of grace: "Whom the Self chooses, by him is he attained."

2. In Hindu psychology the mind is the organ of perception.

3. Vishnu is here equivalent to Brahman.

Soundless, formless, intangible, undying, tasteless, odorless, without beginning, without end, eternal, immutable, beyond nature, is the Self. Knowing him as such, one is freed from death.

THE NARRATOR The wise man, having heard and taught the eternal truth revealed by the King of Death to Nachiketa, is glorified in the heaven of Brahma.

He who sings with devotion this supreme secret in the assembly of the Brahmins, or at the rites in memory of his fathers, is rewarded with rewards immeasurable!

KING OF DEATH The Self-Existent made the senses turn outward. Accordingly, man looks toward what is without, and sees not what is within. Rare is he who, longing for immortality, shuts his eyes to what is without and beholds the Self.

Fools follow the desires of the flesh and fall into the snare of all-encompassing death; but the wise, knowing the Self as eternal, seek not the things that pass away.

He through whom man sees, tastes, smells, hears, feels, and enjoys, is the omniscient Lord.

He, verily, is the immortal Self. Knowing him, one knows all things.

He through whom man experiences the sleeping or waking states is the all-pervading Self. Knowing him, one grieves no more.

He who knows that the individual soul, enjoyer of the fruits of action, is the Self—ever present within, lord of time, past and future—casts out all fear. For this Self is the immortal Self.

He who sees the First-Born—born of the mind of Brahma, born before the creation of waters—and sees him inhabiting the lotus of the heart, living among physical elements, sees Brahman indeed. For this First-Born is the immortal Self.[4]

That being who is the power of all powers, and is born as such, who embodies himself in the elements and in them exists, and who has entered the lotus of the heart, is the immortal Self.

Agni, the all-seeing, who lies hidden in fire sticks, like a child well guarded in the womb, who is worshiped day by day by awakened souls, and by those who offer oblations in sacrificial fire—he is the immortal Self.[5]

That in which the sun rises and in which it sets, that which is the source of all the powers of nature and of the senses, that which nothing can transcend—that is the immortal Self.

What is within us is also without. What is without is also within. He who sees difference between what is within and what is without goes evermore from death to death.

By the purified mind alone is the indivisible Brahman to be attained. Brahman alone is—nothing else is. He who sees the manifold universe, and not the one reality, goes evermore from death to death.

---

4. Brahman, the absolute, impersonal existence, when associated with the power called Maya—the power to evolve as the empirical universe—is known as Hiranyagarbha, the First-Born.

5. The reference is to the Vedic sacrifice. Agni, whose name means fire, is said to be all-seeing, the fire symbolizing Brahman, the Revealer; the two fire sticks, which being rubbed together produce the fire, represent the heart and the mind of man.

That being, of the size of a thumb, dwells deep within the heart.[6] He is the lord of time, past and future. Having attained him, one fears no more. He, verily, is the immortal Self.

That being, of the size of a thumb, is like a flame without smoke. He is the lord of time, past and future, the same today and tomorrow. He, verily, is the immortal Self.

As rain, fallen on a hill, streams down its side, so runs he after many births who sees manifoldness in the Self.

As pure water poured into pure water remains pure, so does the Self remain pure, O Nachiketa, uniting with Brahman.

To the Birthless, the light of whose consciousness forever shines, belongs the city of eleven gates.[7] He who meditates on the ruler of that city knows no more sorrow. He attains liberation, and for him there can no longer be birth or death. For the ruler of that city is the immortal Self.

The immortal Self is the sun shining in the sky, he is the breeze blowing in space, he is the fire burning on the altar, he is the guest dwelling in the house; he is in all men, he is in the gods, he is in the ether, he is wherever there is truth; he is the fish that is born in water, he is the plant that grows in the soil, he is the river that gushes from the mountain—he, the changeless reality, the illimitable!

He, the adorable one, seated in the heart, is the power that gives breath. Unto him all the senses do homage.

What can remain when the dweller in this body leaves the outgrown shell, since he is, verily, the immortal Self?

Man does not live by breath alone, but by him in whom is the power of breath.

And now, O Nachiketa, will I tell thee of the unseen, the eternal Brahman, and of what befalls the Self after death.

Of those ignorant of the Self, some enter into beings possessed of wombs, others enter into plants—according to their deeds and the growth of their intelligence.

That which is awake in us even while we sleep, shaping in dream the objects of our desire—that indeed is pure, that is Brahman, and that verily is called the Immortal. All the worlds have their being in that, and no one can transcend it. That is the Self.

As fire, though one, takes the shape of every object which it consumes, so the Self, though one, takes the shape of every object in which it dwells.

As air, though one, takes the shape of every object which it enters, so the Self, though one, takes the shape of every object in which it dwells.

As the sun, revealer of all objects to the seer, is not harmed by the sinful eye, nor by the impurities of the objects it gazes on, so the one Self, dwelling in all, is not touched by the evils of the world. For he transcends all.

He is one, the lord and innermost Self of all; of one form, he makes of himself many forms. To him who sees the Self revealed in his own heart belongs eternal bliss—to none else, to none else!

6. The sages ascribe a definite, minute size to the Self in order to assist the disciple in meditation.

7. The Birthless is the Self; the city of eleven gates is the body with its apertures—eyes, ears, etc.

NACHIKETA How, O King, shall I find that blissful Self, supreme, ineffable, who is attained by the wise? Does he shine by himself, or does he reflect another's light?

KING OF DEATH Him the sun does not illumine, nor the moon, nor the stars, nor the lightning—nor, verily, fires kindled upon the earth. He is the one light that gives light to all. He shining, everything shines.

This universe is a tree eternally existing, its root aloft, its branches spread below. The pure root of the tree is Brahman, the immortal, in whom the three worlds have their being, whom none can transcend, who is verily the Self.[8]

The whole universe came forth from Brahman and moves in Brahman. Mighty and awful is he, like to a thunderbolt crashing loud through the heavens. For those who attain him death has no terror.

In fear of him fire burns, the sun shines, the rains fall, the winds blow, and death kills.

If a man fail to attain Brahman before he casts off his body, he must again put on a body in the world of created things.

In one's own soul Brahman is realized clearly, as if seen in a mirror. In the heaven of Brahma also is Brahman realized clearly, as one distinguishes light from darkness. In the world of the fathers he is beheld as in a dream.[9] In the world of angels he appears as if reflected in water.

The senses have separate origin in their several objects. They may be active, as in the waking state, or they may be inactive, as in sleep. He who knows them to be distinct from the changeless Self grieves no more.

Above the senses is the mind. Above the mind is the intellect. Above the intellect is the ego. Above the ego is the unmanifested seed, the Primal Cause.

And verily beyond the unmanifested seed is Brahman, the all-pervading spirit, the unconditioned, knowing whom one attains to freedom and achieves immortality.

None beholds him with the eyes, for he is without visible form. Yet in the heart is he revealed, through self-control and meditation. Those who know him become immortal.

When all the senses are stilled, when the mind is at rest, when the intellect wavers not—then, say the wise, is reached the highest state.

This calm of the senses and the mind has been defined as yoga. He who attains it is freed from delusion.

In one not freed from delusion this calm is uncertain, unreal: it comes and goes. Brahman words cannot reveal, mind cannot reach, eyes cannot see. How then, save through those who know him, can he be known?

There are two selves, the apparent self and the real Self. Of these it is the real Self, and he alone, who must be felt as truly existing. To the man who has felt him as truly existing he reveals his innermost nature.

8. The "three worlds" are the sky, the earth, and the nether world.

9. The fathers are the spirits of the meritorious dead, who dwell in another world, reaping the fruits of their good deeds, but subject to rebirth.

The mortal in whose heart desire is dead becomes immortal. The mortal in whose heart the knots of ignorance are untied becomes immortal. These are the highest truths taught in the scriptures.

Radiating from the lotus of the heart there are a hundred and one nerves. One of these ascends toward the thousand-petaled lotus in the brain. If, when a man comes to die, his vital force passes upward and out through this nerve, he attains immortality; but if his vital force passes out through another nerve, he goes to one or another plane of mortal existence and remains subject to birth and death.

The Supreme Person, of the size of a thumb, the innermost Self, dwells forever in the heart of all beings. As one draws the pith from a reed, so must the aspirant after truth, with great perseverance, separate the Self from the body. Know the Self to be pure and immortal—yea, pure and immortal!

THE NARRATOR Nachiketa, having learned from the god this knowledge and the whole process of yoga, was freed from impurities and from death, and was united with Brahman. Thus will it be with another also if he know the innermost Self.

OM . . . Peace—peace—peace.

Selections, *Bhagavad-Gita*
Barbara Stoler Miller (translator)

The Bhagavad-Gita falls outside the Vedic canon, but it is the best-loved of all the texts of Hinduism. Its date is uncertain: Radhakrishnan assigns it to the fifth century B.C.E.; *other scholars, including the present translator, Barbara Stoler Miller, place it as late as the first century* C.E.

The Gita is a small part of the Mahabharata, which revolves around an account of a great war between two closely related families. The Gita itself opens on the eve of that war. Arjuna, the hero of one of the families, is revolted by the prospect of the bloodshed to come. The god Krishna, appearing as Arjuna's charioteer, speaks to Arjuna of his responsibilities, but the dialogue (which is closer to a monologue by Krishna) quickly proceeds to even greater matters—the purpose of life and the nature of reality. (The entire dialogue, it must be added, is a report to the blind King Dhritarashtra by his *charioteer Sanjaya, who appears once in the pages that follow.)*

Barbara Stoler Miller (1940–   ) is a graduate of Barnard College. She received her masters from Columbia University and doctorate from the University of Pennsylvania; she is now a professor of Oriental studies at Columbia. A translator of many works from the Sanskrit, Dr. Miller is also competent in French, Spanish, Hindi, Pali, and Prakrits—and is a novelist, too.

The First Teaching: Arguna's Dejection

Arjuna saw them standing there:
fathers, grandfathers, teachers,
uncles, brothers, sons,
grandsons, and friends. 26

He surveyed his elders
and companions in both armies,
all his kinsmen
assembled together. 27

Dejected, filled with strange pity,
he said this:

"Krishna, I see my kinsmen
gathered here, wanting war.   28

I see omens of chaos,
Krishna; I see no good
in killing my kinsmen
in battle.   31

How can we ignore the wisdom
of turning from this evil
when we see the sin
of family destruction, Krishna?   39

When the family is ruined,
the timeless laws of family duty
perish; and when duty is lost,
chaos overwhelms the family.   40

In overwhelming chaos, Krishna,
women of the family are corrupted;
and when women are corrupted,
disorder is born in society.   41

Saying this in the time of war,
Arjuna slumped into the chariot
and laid down his bow and arrows,
his mind tormented by grief.   47

The Second Teaching: Philosophy and
Spiritual Discipline

Lord Krishna

You grieve for those beyond grief,
and you speak words of insight;
but learned men do not grieve
for the dead or the living.   11

Never have I not existed,
nor you, nor these kings;
and never in the future
shall we cease to exist.   12

Just as the embodied self
enters childhood, youth, and old age,
so does it enter another body;
this does not confound a steadfast man.   13

Our bodies are known to end,
but the embodied self is enduring,
indestructible, and immeasurable;
therefore, Arjuna, fight the battle!   18

He who thinks this self a killer
and he who thinks it killed,
both fail to understand;
it does not kill, nor is it killed.   19

It is not born,
it does not die;
having been,
it will never not be;
unborn, enduring,
constant, and primordial,
it is not killed
when the body is killed.   20

Arjuna, when a man knows the self
to be indestructible, enduring, unborn,
unchanging, how does he kill
or cause anyone to kill?   21

Death is certain for anyone born,
and birth is certain for the dead;
since the cycle is inevitable,
you have no cause to grieve!   27

Be intent on action,
not on the fruits of action;
avoid attraction to the fruits
and attachment to inaction!   47

Perform actions, firm in discipline,
relinquishing attachment;
be impartial to failure and success—
this equanimity is called discipline.   48

Even when a man of wisdom
tries to control them, Arjuna,
the bewildering senses
attack his mind with violence.   60

Controlling them all,
with discipline he should focus on me;
when his senses are under control,
his insight is sure.   61

Brooding about sensuous objects
makes attachment to them grow;
from attachment desire arises,
from desire anger is born.   62

From anger comes confusion;
from confusion memory lapses;
from broken memory understanding is lost;
from loss of understanding, he is ruined.   63

But a man of inner strength
whose senses experience objects
without attraction and hatred,
in self-control, finds serenity.   64

In serenity, all his sorrows
dissolve;
his reason becomes serene,
his understanding sure.   65

Without discipline,
he has no understanding or inner power;
without inner power, he has no peace;
and without peace where is joy?   66

The Third Teaching: Discipline of Action

Lord Krishna

Action imprisons the world
unless it is done as sacrifice;
freed from attachment, Arjuna,
perform action as sacrifice!   9

Arjuna

Krishna, what makes a person
commit evil
against his own will,
as if compelled by force?   36

Lord Krishna

It is desire and anger, arising
from nature's quality of passion;
know it here as the enemy,
voracious and very evil!   37

As fire is obscured by smoke
and a mirror by dirt,
as an embryo is veiled by its caul,
so is knowledge obscured by this.   38

Knowledge is obscured
by the wise man's eternal enemy,
which takes form as desire,
an insatiable fire, Arjuna.   39

The Fourth Teaching: Knowledge

Lord Krishna

I have passed through many births
and so have you;
I know them all,
but you do not, Arjuna.   5

To protect men of virtue
and destroy men who do evil,
to set the standard of sacred duty,
I appear in age after age.   8

He who really knows my divine
birth and my action, escapes rebirth
when he abandons the body—
and he comes to me, Arjuna.   9

As they seek refuge in me,
I devote myself to them;
Arjuna, men retrace
my path in every way.   11

No purifier equals knowledge,
and in time
the man of perfect discipline
discovers this in his own spirit.   38

Faithful, intent, his senses
subdued, he gains knowledge;
gaining knowledge,
he soon finds perfect peace.   39

An ignorant man is lost, faithless,
and filled with self-doubt;
a soul that harbors doubt has no joy,
not in this world or the next.   40

The Fifth Teaching: Renunciation of Action

Arjuna

Krishna, you praise renunciation
of actions and then discipline;
tell me with certainty
which is the better of these two.   1

Lord Krishna

Simpletons separate philosophy
and discipline, but the learned do not;
applying one correctly, a man
finds the fruit of both.   4

Men of discipline reach the same place
that philosophers attain;
he really sees who sees philosophy
and discipline to be one.   5

Renunciation is difficult to attain
without discipline;
a sage armed with discipline
soon reaches the infinite spirit.   6

Relinquishing the fruit of action,
the disciplined man attains perfect peace;
the undisciplined man is in bondage,
attached to the fruit of his desire.   12

The Sixth Teaching: The Man of Discipline

Lord Krishna

"He does not waver, like a lamp sheltered
from the wind" is the simile recalled
for a man of discipline, restrained in thought
and practicing self-discipline.   19

Arming himself with discipline,
seeing everything with an equal eye,
he sees the self in all creatures
and all creatures in the self.   29

Arjuna

Krishna, the mind is faltering,
violent, strong, and stubborn;

I find it as difficult
to hold as the wind.   34

Lord Krishna

Without doubt, the mind
is unsteady and hard to hold,
but practice and dispassion
can restrain it, Arjuna.   35

In my view, discipline eludes
the unrestrained self,
but if he strives to master himself,
a man has the means to reach it.   36

The Seventh Teaching: Knowledge and Judgment

Lord Krishna

Practice discipline in my protection,
with your mind focused on me;
Arjuna, hear how you can know me
completely, without doubt.   1

My nature has eight aspects:
earth, water, fire, wind, space,
mind, understanding,
and individuality.   4

This is my lower nature;
know my higher nature too,
the life-force
that sustains this universe.   5

Learn that this is the womb
of all creatures;
I am the source of all the universe,
just as I am its dissolution.   6

Nothing is higher than I am;
Arjuna, all that exists
is woven on me,
like a web of pearls on thread.   7

I am the taste in water, Arjuna,
the light in the moon and sun,
OM resonant in all sacred lore,
the sound in space, valor in men.   8

I am the pure fragrance
in earth, the brilliance in fire,
the life in all living creatures,
the penance in ascetics.　　　　　　　　　9

Know me, Arjuna,
as every creature's timeless seed,
the understanding of intelligent men,
the brilliance of fiery heroes.　　　　　　10

Of strong men, I am strength,
without the emotion of desire;
in creatures I am the desire
that does not impede sacred duty.　　　　11

Know that nature's qualities
come from me—lucidity,
passion, and dark inertia;
I am not in them, they are in me.　　　　12

All this universe, deluded
by the qualities inherent in nature,
fails to know that I am
beyond them and unchanging.　　　　　13

Composed of nature's qualities,
my divine magic is hard to escape;
but those who seek refuge in me
cross over this magic.　　　　　　　　14

Arjuna, four types of virtuous men
are devoted to me:
the tormented man, the seeker of wisdom,
the suppliant, and the sage.　　　　　　16

Of these, the disciplined man of knowledge
is set apart by his singular devotion;
I am dear to the man of knowledge,
and he is dear to me.　　　　　　　　17

I grant unwavering faith
to any devoted man who wants
to worship any form
with faith.　　　　　　　　　　　　21

The Tenth Teaching: Fragments of Divine Power

Lord Krishna

Great Warrior, again hear
my word in its supreme form;

desiring your good,
I speak to deepen your love.   1

Neither the multitude of gods
nor great sages know my origin,
for I am the source of all
the gods and great sages.   2

A mortal who knows me
as the unborn, beginningless
great lord of the worlds
is freed from delusion and all evils.   3

I am the source of everything,
and everything proceeds from me;
filled with my existence, wise men
realizing this are devoted to me.   8

I am the self abiding
in the heart of all creatures;
I am their beginning,
their middle, and their end.   20

I am Vishnu striding among sun gods,
the radiant sun among lights;
I am lightning among wind gods,
the moon among the stars.   21

I am the song in sacred lore;
I am Indra, king of the gods;
I am the mind of the senses,
the consciousness of creatures.   22

I am gracious Shiva among howling storm gods,
the lord of wealth among demigods and demons,
fire blazing among the bright gods;
I am golden Meru towering over the mountains.   23

Arjuna, know me as the gods' teacher,
chief of the household priests;
I am the god of war among generals;
I am the ocean of lakes.   24

I am the endless cosmic serpent,
the lord of all sea creatures;
I am chief of the ancestral fathers;
of restraints, I am death.   29

I am the beginning, the middle,
and the end of creations, Arjuna;
of sciences, I am the science of the self;
I am the dispute of orators.   32

I am death the destroyer of all,
the source of what will be,
the feminine powers: fame, fortune, speech,
memory, intelligence, resolve, patience.   34

I am the great ritual chant,
the meter of sacred song,
the most sacred month in the year,
the spring blooming with flowers.   35

The Eleventh Teaching: The Vision of Krishna's Totality

Arjuna

If you think I can see it,
reveal to me
your immutable self,
Kirshna, Lord of Discipline.

Lord Krishna

Arjuna, see my forms
in hundreds and thousands;
diverse, divine,
of many colors and shapes.   5

See the sun gods, gods of light,
howling storm gods, twin gods of dawn,
and gods of wind, Arjuna,
wondrous forms not seen before.   6

Arjuna, see all the universe,
animate and inanimate,
and whatever else you wish to see;
all stands here as one in my body.   7

But you cannot see me
with your own eye;
I will give you a divine eye to see
the majesty of my discipline.   8

Sanjaya

O King, saying this, Krishna,
the great lord of discipline,

revealed to Arjuna
the true majesty of his form.   9

It was a multiform, wondrous vision,
with countless mouths and eyes
and celestial ornaments,
brandishing many divine weapons.   10

Everywhere was boundless divinity
containing all astonishing things,
wearing divine garlands and garments,
annointed with divine perfume.   11

If the light of a thousand suns
were to rise in the sky at once,
it would be like the light
of that great spirit.   12

Arjuna saw all the universe
in its many ways and parts,
standing as one in the body
of the god of gods.   13

Arjuna

You aew the gods of wind,
death, fire, and water;
the moon; the lord of life;
and the great ancestor.
Homage to you,
a thousand times homage!
I bow in homage to you
again and yet again.   39

The Fifteenth Teaching: The True Spirit of Man

Lord Krishna

I penetrate the earth
and sustain creatures by my strength;
becoming Soma, the liquid of moonlight,
I nurture all healing herbs.   13

I am the universal fire
within the body of living beings;
I work with the flow of vital breath
to digest the foods that men consume.   14

I dwell deep
in the heart of everyone;
memory, knowledge,
and reasoning come from me;
I am the object to be known
through all sacred lore;
and I am its knower,
the creator of its final truth.   15

The Sixteenth Teaching: The Divine and the Demonic in Man

Lord Krishna

Fearlessness, purity, determination
in the discipline of knowledge,
charity, self-control, sacrifice,
study of sacred lore, penance, honesty;   1

Nonviolence, truth, absence of anger,
disengagement, peace, loyalty,
compassion for creatures, lack of greed,
gentleness, modesty, reliability;   2

Brilliance, patience, resolve,
clarity, absence of envy and of pride;
these characterize a man
born with divine traits.   3

Hypocrisy, arrogance, vanity,
anger, harshness, ignorance;
these characterize a man
born with demonic traits.   4

The divine traits lead to freedom,
the demonic lead to bondage;
do not despair, Arjuna;
you were born with the divine.   5

All creatures in the world
are either divine or demonic;
I described the divine at length;
hear what I say of the demonic.   6

Demonic men cannot comprehend
activity and rest;
there exists no clarity,
no morality, no truth in them.   7

They say that the world
has no truth, no basis, no god,
that no power of mutual dependence
is its cause, but only desire.   8

Mired in this view, lost to themselves
with their meager understanding,
these fiends contrive terrible acts
to destroy the world.   9

Subject to insatiable desire,
drunk with hypocrisy and pride,
holding false notions from delusion,
they act with impure vows.   10

In their certainty that life
consists in sating their desires,
they suffer immeasurable anxiety
that ends only with death.   11

Bound by a hundred fetters of hope,
obsessed by desire and anger,
they hoard wealth in stealthy ways
to satisfy their desires.   12

Confused by endless thoughts,
caught in the net of delusion,
given to satisfying their desires,
they fall into hell's foul abyss.   16

Self-aggrandizing, stubborn,
drunk with wealth and pride,
they sacrifice in name only,
in hypocrisy, violating all norms.   17

Submitting to individuality, power,
arrogance, desire, and anger,
they hate me and revile me
in their own bodies, as in others.   18

These hateful, cruel, vile
men of misfortune, I cast
into demonic wombs
through cycles of rebirth.   19

Life's Stages

Rabindranath Tagore

To say that the work and accomplishments of Rabindranath Tagore (1861–1941) were prodigious is almost to say too little. Born into an eminent and cultured family in Calcutta, India, Tagore considered himself primarily a poet (some sixty volumes), but he was also a prolific playwright, novelist, short story writer, and essayist. There were philosophical treatises and autobiographical works; he was a musician, painter, and actor; and he founded literary journals, businesses, and a school. And there was no shortage of honors: in 1913 he won the Nobel Prize for literature.

Of philosophical interest among his books is the early Sadhana: The Realization of Life *(1913);* The Religion of Man *(1930) is the source for the present reading selection.*

It is noteworthy that in the traditional Hindu scheme of the four stages of life, discussed in these pages by Tagore, the more important tasks—the spiritual tasks— come after *retirement from one's work and the "householder" stage. There is the concept here, as elsewhere in Hinduism, of spiritual progression.*

The tendency of the Indian mind has ever been towards that transcendentalism which does not hold religion to be ultimate but rather to be a means to a further end. This end consists in the perfect liberation of the individual in the universal spirit across the furthest limits of humanity itself.

Such an extreme form of mysticism may be explained to my Western readers by its analogy in science. For science may truly be described as mysticism in the realm of material knowledge. It helps us to go beyond appearances and reach the inner reality of things in principles which are abstractions; it emancipates our mind from the thraldom of the senses to the freedom of reason.

The common-sense view of the world that is apparent to us has its vital importance for ourselves. For all our practical purposes the earth *is* flat, the sun *does* set behind the western horizon; and whatever may be the verdict of the great mathematician about the lack of consistency in time's dealings we should fully trust it in setting our watches right. In questions relating to the arts and our ordinary daily avocations we must treat material objects as they seem to be and not as they are in essence. But the revelations of science, even when they go far beyond man's power of direct perception, give him the purest feeling of disinterested delight and a super-sensual background to his world. Science offers us the mystic knowledge of matter which very often passes the range of our imagination. We humbly accept it, follow-ing those teachers who have trained their reason to free itself from the trammels of appearance or personal preferences. Their mind dwells in an impersonal infinity where there is no distinction between good and bad, high and low, ugly and beau-tiful, useful and useless, where all things have their one common right of recogni-tion, that of their existence.

The final freedom of spirit which India aspires after has a similar character of realization. It is beyond all limits of personality, divested of all moral or aesthetic distinctions; it is the pure consciousness of Being, the ultimate reality, which has an infinite illumination of bliss. Though science brings our thoughts to the utmost limit of mind's territory it cannot transcend its own creation made of a harmony of logical symbols. In it the chick has come out of its shell, but not out of the defi-nition of its own chickenhood. But in India it has been said by the *yogi* that through an intensive process of concentration and quietude our consciousness *does* reach that infinity where knowledge ceases to be knowledge, subject and object become one—a state of existence that cannot be defined.

We have our personal self. It has its desires which struggle to create a world where they could have their unrestricted activity and satisfaction. While it goes on we discover that our self-realization reaches its perfection in the abnegation of self. This fact has made us aware that the individual finds his meaning in a fundamental reality comprehending all individuals—the reality which is the moral and spiritual basis of the realm of human values. This belongs to our religion. As science is the liberation of our knowledge in the universal reason, which cannot be other than human reason, religion is the liberation of our individual personality in the uni-versal Person who is human all the same.

The ancient explorers in psychology in India who declare that our emancipation can be carried still further into a realm where infinity is not bounded by human limitations, are not content with advancing this as a doctrine; they advocate its pur-suit for the attainment of the highest goal of man. And for its sake the path of dis-cipline has been planned which should be opened out across our life through all its stages, helping us to develop our humanity to perfection, so that we may surpass it in a finality of freedom.

Perfection has its two aspects in man, which can to some extent be separated, the perfection in being and perfection in doing. It can be imagined that, through some training or compulsion, good works may possibly be extorted from a man who personally may not be good. Activities that have fatal risks are often under-taken by cowards even though they are conscious of the danger. Such works may be useful and may continue to exist beyond the lifetime of the individual who pro-duced them. And yet, where the question is not that of utility but of moral perfec-tion, we hold it important that the individual should be true in his goodness. His outer good work may continue to produce good results, but the inner perfection of his personality has its own immense value, which for him is spiritual freedom and for humanity is an endless asset though we may not know it. For goodness represents the detachment of our spirit from the exclusiveness of our egoism; in goodness we identify ourselves with the universal humanity. Its value is not merely in some benefit for our fellow beings, but in its truth itself through which we realize within us that man is not merely an animal, bound by his individual passions and appetites, but a spirit that has its unfettered perfection. Goodness is the freedom of our self in the world of man, as is love. We have to be true within, not for worldly duties, but for that spiritual fulfilment, which is in harmony with the Perfect, in union with the Eternal. If this were not true, then mechanical perfection would be considered to be of higher value than the spiritual. In order to realize his unity with the universal, the individual man must live his perfect life which alone gives him the freedom to transcend it.

Doubtless Nature, for its own biological purposes, has created in us a strong faith in life, by keeping us unmindful of death. Nevertheless, not only our physical existence, but also the environment which it builds up around itself, may desert us in the moment of triumph; the greatest prosperity comes to its end, dissolving into emptiness; the mightiest empire is overtaken by stupor amidst the flicker of its festival lights. All this is none the less true because its truism bores us to be reminded of it.

And yet it is equally true that, though all our mortal relationships have their end, we cannot ignore them with impunity while they last. If we behave as if they do not exist, merely because they will not continue for ever, they will all the same exact their dues, with a great deal over by way of penalty. Trying to ignore bonds that are real, albeit temporary, only strengthens and prolongs their bondage. The soul is great, but the self has to be crossed over in order to reach it. We do not attain our goal by destroying our path.

Our teachers in ancient India realized the soul of man as something very great indeed. They saw no end to its dignity, which found its consummation in Brahma himself. Any limited view of man would therefore be an incomplete view. He could not reach his finality as a mere Citizen or Patriot, for neither City nor Country, nor the bubble called the World, could contain his eternal soul.

Bhartrihari, who was once a king, has said: "What if you have secured the fountain-head of all desires; what if you have put your foot on the neck of your enemy, or by your good fortune gathered friends around you? What, even, if you have succeeded in keeping mortal bodies alive for ages—*tatah kim,* what then?"

That is to say, man is greater than all these objects of his desire. He is true in his freedom.

But in the process of attaining freedom one must bind his will in order to save its forces from distraction and wastage, so as to gain for it the velocity which comes from the bondage itself. Those also, who seek liberty in a purely political plane, constantly curtail it and reduce their freedom of thought and action to that narrow limit which is necessary for making political power secure, very often at the cost of liberty of conscience.

India had originally accepted the bonds of her social system in order to transcend society, as the rider puts reins on his horse and stirrups on his own feet in order to ensure greater speed towards his goal.

The Universe cannot be so madly conceived that desire should be an interminable song with no finale. And just as it is painful to stop in the middle of the tune, it should be as pleasant to reach its final cadence.

India has not advised us to come to a sudden stop while work is in full swing. It is true that the unending procession of the world has gone on, through its ups and downs, from the beginning of creation till today; but it is equally obvious that each individual's connection therewith *does* get finished. Must he necessarily quit it without any sense of fulfilment?

So, in the division of man's world-life which we had in India, work came in the middle, and freedom at the end. As the day is divided into morning, noon, afternoon and evening, so India had divided man's life into four parts, following the requirements of his nature. The day has the waxing and waning of its light; so has man the waxing and waning of his bodily powers. Acknowledging this, India gave a connected meaning to his life from start to finish.

First came *brahmacharya,* the period of discipline in education; then *garhasthya,* that of the world's work; then *vanaprasthya,* the retreat for the loosening of bonds; and finally *pravrajya,* the expectant awaiting of freedom across death.

We have come to look upon life as a conflict with death—the intruding enemy, not the natural ending—in impotent quarrel with which we spend every stage of it. When the time comes for youth to depart, we would hold it back by main force. When the fervour of desire slackens, we would revive it with fresh fuel of our own devising. When our sense organs weaken, we urge them to keep up their efforts. Even when our grip has relaxed we are reluctant to give up possession. We are not trained to recognize the inevitable as natural, and so cannot give up gracefully that which has to go, but needs must wait till it is snatched from us. The truth comes as conqueror only because we have lost the art of receiving it as guest.

The stem of the ripening fruit becomes loose, its pulp soft, but its seed hardens with provision for the next life. Our outward losses, due to age, have likewise corresponding inward gains. But, in man's inner life, his will plays a dominant part, so that these gains depend on his own disciplined striving; that is why, in the case of undisciplined man, who has omitted to secure such provision for the next stage, it is so often seen that his hair is grey, his mouth toothless, his muscles slack, and yet his stem-hold on life has refused to let go its grip, so much so that he is anxious to exercise his will in regard to worldly details even after death.

But renounce we must, and through renunciation gain—that is the truth of the inner world.

The flower must shed its petals for the sake of fruition, the fruit must drop off for the re-birth of the tree. The child leaves the refuge of the womb in order to achieve the further growth of body and mind in which consists the whole of the child life; next, the soul has to come out of this self-contained stage into the fuller life, which has varied relations with kinsman and neighbour, together with whom it forms a larger body; lastly comes the decline of the body, the weakening of desire. Enriched with its experiences, the soul now leaves the narrower life for the universal life, to which it dedicates its accumulated wisdom and itself enters into relations with the Life Eternal, so that, when finally the decaying body has come to the very end of its tether, the soul views its breaking away quite simply and without regret, in the expectation of its own entry into the Infinite.

From individual body to community, from community to universe, from universe to Infinity—this is the soul's normal progress.

Our teachers, therefore, keeping in mind the goal of this progress, did not, in life's first stage of education, prescribe merely the learning of books or things, but *brahmacharya,* the living in discipline, whereby both enjoyment and its renunciation would come with equal ease to the strengthened character. Life being a pilgrimage, with liberation in Brahma as its object, the living of it was as a spiritual exercise to be carried through its different stages, reverently and with a vigilant determination. And the pupil, from his very initiation, had this final consummation always kept in his view.

Once the mind refuses to be bound by temperate requirements, there ceases to be any reason why it should cry halt at any particular limit; and so, like trying to extinguish fire with oil, its acquisitions only make its desires blaze up all the fiercer. That is why it is so essential to habituate the mind, from the very beginning, to be conscious of, and desirous of, keeping within the natural limits; to cultivate the spirit of enjoyment which is allied with the spirit of freedom, the readiness for renunciation.

After the period of such training comes the period of world-life—the life of the householder. Manu tells us:

It is not possible to discipline ourselves so effectively if out of touch with
the world, as while pursuing the world-life with wisdom.

That is to say, wisdom does not attain completeness except through the living of life; and discipline divorced from wisdom is not true discipline, but merely the meaningless following of custom, which is only a disguise for stupidity.

Work, especially good work, becomes easy only when desire has learnt to discipline itself. Then alone does the householder's state become a centre of welfare for all the world, and instead of being an obstacle, helps on the final liberation.

The second stage of life having been thus spent, the decline of the bodily powers must be taken as a warning that it is coming to its natural end. This must not be taken dismally as a notice of dismissal to one still eager to stick to his post, but joyfully as maturity may be accepted as the stage of fulfilment.

After the infant leaves the womb, it still has to remain close to its mother for a time, remaining attached in spite of its detachment, until it can adapt itself to its new freedom. Such is the case in the third stage of life, when man though aloof from the world still remains in touch with it while preparing himself for the final stage of complete freedom. He still gives to the world from his store of wisdom and accepts its support; but this interchange is not of the same intimate character as in the stage of the householder, there being a new sense of distance.

Then at last comes a day when even such free relations have their end, and the emancipated soul steps out of all bonds to face the Supreme Soul.

Only in this way can man's world-life be truly lived from one end to the other, without being engaged at every step in trying conclusions with death, not being overcome, when death comes in due course, as by a conquering enemy.

For this fourfold way of life India attunes man to the grand harmony of the universal, leaving no room for untrained desires of a rampant individualism to pursue their destructive career unchecked, but leading them on to their ultimate modulation in the Supreme.

If we really believe this, then we must uphold an ideal of life in which everything else—the display of individual power, the might of nations—must be counted as subordinate and the soul of man must triumph and liberate itself from the bond of personality which keeps it in an ever-revolving circle of limitation.

If that is not to be, *tatah kim,* what then?

But such an ideal of the utter extinction of the individual separateness has not a universal sanction in India. There are many of us whose prayer is for dualism, so that for them the bond of devotion with God may continue for ever. For them religion is a truth which is ultimate and they refuse to envy those who are ready to sail for the further shore of existence across humanity. They know that human imperfection is the cause of our sorrow, but there is a fulfilment in love within the range of our limitation which accepts all sufferings and yet rises above them.

In the Sanskrit language the bird is described as "twice-born"—once in its limited shell and then finally in the freedom of the unbounded sky. Those of our community who believe in the liberation of man's limited self in the freedom of the spirit retain the same epithet for themselves. In all departments of life man shows this dualism—his existence within the range of obvious facts and his transcendence of it in a realm of deeper meaning.

Having this instinct inherent in his mind which ever suggests to him the crossing of the border, he has never accepted what is apparent as final, and his incessant struggle has been to break through the shell of his limitations. In this attempt he often goes against the instincts of his vital nature, and even exults in his defiance of the extreme penal laws of the biological kingdom. The best wealth of his civilization has been achieved by his following the guidance of this instinct in his ceaseless adventure of the Endless Further. His achievement of truth goes far beyond his needs and the realization of his self strives across the frontier of its individual interest. This proves to him his infinity and makes his religion real to him by his own manifestation in truth and goodness. Only for man can there be religion, because his evolution is from efficiency in nature towards the perfection of spirit.

According to some interpretations of the Vedanta doctrine Brahman is the absolute Truth, the impersonal It, in which there can be no distinction of this and that, the good and the evil, the beautiful and its opposite, having no other quality except its ineffable blissfulness in the eternal solitude of its consciousness utterly devoid of all things and all thoughts. But as our religion can only have its significance in this phenomenal world comprehended by our human self, this absolute conception of Brahman is outside the subject of my discussion. What I have tried to bring out in this book is the fact that whatever name may have been given to the divine Reality it has found its highest place in the history of our religion owing to its human character, giving meaning to the idea of sin and sanctity, and offering an eternal background to all the ideals of perfection which have their harmony with man's own nature.

We have the age-long tradition in our country, as I have already stated, that through the process of *yoga* a man can transcend the utmost bounds of his humanity and find himself in a pure state of consciousness of his undivided unity with Parabrahman. There is none who has the right to contradict this belief; for it is a matter of direct experience and not of logic. It is widely known in India that there are individuals who have the power to attain temporarily the state of *Samadhi*, the complete merging of the self in the infinite, a state which is indescribable. While accepting their testimony as true, let us at the same time have faith in the testimony of others who have felt a profound love, which is the intense feeling of union, for a Being who comprehends in himself all things that are human in knowledge, will, and action. And he is God, who is not merely a sum total of facts, but the goal that lies immensely beyond all that is comprised in the past and the present.

I Am But a Seeker After Truth
Mahatma Gandhi

Mahatma ("great soul") is a title of rare respect; it may have been his friend Tagore who first addressed it to Gandhi. In any event, the people of India and then of the world soon adopted it by common consent. Born Mohandas Karamchand Gandhi in 1869, in Porbandar, India, he was a spiritual and political leader who fought (nonviolently) against racial discrimination in South Africa and British rule in India, and he led the campaign for the abolition of "untouchability." A friend once described him as a "combination of sacred cow and ferocious tiger."* In 1948, in the midst of turmoil over the formation of the state of Pakistan, Gandhi was fatally shot by a Hindu fanatic.

Gilbert Murray wrote a tribute to Gandhi as early as 1914: "Be careful in dealing with a man who cares nothing for sensual pleasures, nothing for comfort or praise or promotion, but is simply determined to do what he believes is right."**

You must watch my life, how I live, eat, sit, talk, behave in general. The sum total of all those in me is my religion.

. . .

My Religion Is Hinduism

I have been asked by Sir S. Radhakrishnan to answer the following three questions:

1. What is your religion?
2. How are you led to it?
3. What is its bearing on social life?

My religion is Hinduism which, for me, is the religion of humanity and includes the best of all the religions known to me.

*Ragavan Iyer (ed.), *The Moral and Political Writings of Mahatma Gandhi* (Oxford: Clarendon Press, 1986), Vol. 1, pp. 28–29.

**Quoted in Louis Fischer, *Gandhi: His Life and Message for the World* (New York: New American Library, 1954), p. 49.

I take it that the present tense in the second question has been purposely used instead of the past. I am being led to my religion through Truth and Non-violence, i.e., love in the broadest sense. I often describe my religion as religion of Truth. Of late, instead of saying God is Truth I have been saying Truth is God, in order more fully to define my religion. I used at one time to know by heart the thousand names of God which a booklet in Hinduism gives in verse form and which perhaps tens of thousands recite every morning. But nowadays nothing so completely describes my God as Truth. Denial of God we have known. Denial of Truth we have not known. The most ignorant among mankind have some truth in them. We are all sparks of Truth. The sum total of these sparks is indescribable, as-yet-Unknown Truth, which is God. I am being daily led nearer to it by constant prayer.

The bearing of this religion on social life is, or has to be, seen in one's daily social contact. To be true to such religion one has to lose oneself in continuous and continuing service of all life. Realization of Truth is impossible without a complete merging of oneself in and identification with this limitless ocean of life. Hence, for me, there is no escape from social service; there is no happiness on earth beyond or apart from it. Social service here must be taken to include every department of life. In this scheme there is nothing low, nothing high. For all is one, though we *seem* to be many.

. . .

The deeper I study Hinduism the stronger becomes the belief in me that Hinduism is as broad as the Universe and it takes in its fold all that is good in this world. And so I find that with Mussalmans I can appreciate the beauties of Islam and sing its praises. And so simultaneously with the professors of other religions, and still something within me tells me that, for all that deep veneration I show to these several religions, I am all the more a Hindu, none the less for it.

. . .

Believing as I do in the influence of heredity, being born in a Hindu family, I have remained a Hindu. I should reject it, if I found it inconsistent with my moral sense or my spiritual growth. On examination, I have found it to be the most tolerant of all religions known to me. Its freedom from dogma makes a forcible appeal to me inasmuch as it gives the votary the largest scope for self-expression. Not being an exclusive religion, it enables the followers of that faith not merely to respect all the other religions, but it also enables them to admire and assimilate whatever may be good in the other faiths. Non-violence is common to all religions, but it has found the highest expression and application in Hinduism.

. . .

I want to realize brotherhood or identity not merely with the beings called human, but I want to realize identity with all life, even with such beings as crawl on earth. I want, if I don't give you a shock, to realize identity with even the crawling things upon earth, because we claim common descent from the same God, and that being so, all life in whatever form it appears must be essentially one.

. . .

It is an arrogant assumption to say that human beings are lords and masters of the lower creation. On the contrary, being endowed with greater things in life, they are trustees of the lower animal kingdom.

. . .

I am not opposed to the progress of science as such. On the contrary the scientific spirit of the West commands my admiration and if that admiration is qualified, it is because the scientist of the West takes no note of God's lower creation. I abhor vivisection with my whole soul: I detest the unpardonable slaughter of innocent life in the name of science and humanity so-called, and all the scientific discoveries stained with innocent blood I count as of no consequence. If the circulation of blood theory could not have been discovered without vivisection, the human kind could well have done without it. And I see the day clearly dawning when the honest scientist of the West will put limitations upon the present methods of pursuing knowledge.

. . .

This unity of *all* life is a peculiarity of Hinduism which confines salvation not to human beings alone but says that it is possible for all God's creatures. It may be that it is not possible, save through the human form, but that does not make man the Lord of creation. It makes him the servant of God's creation. Now when we talk of brotherhood of man, we stop there, and feel that all other life is there for man to exploit for his own purposes. But Hinduism excludes all exploitation. There is no limit whatsoever to the measure of sacrifice that one may make in order to realize this oneness with all life, but certainly the immensity of the ideal sets a limit to your wants. That, you will see, is the antithesis of the position of the modern civilization which says: "Increase your wants." Those who hold that belief think that increase of wants means an increase of knowledge whereby you understand the Infinite better. On the contrary Hinduism rules out indulgence and multiplication of wants as these hamper one's growth to the ultimate identity with the Universal Self.

. . .

ll Religions Are Divinely Inspired

A curriculum of religious instruction should include a study of the tenets of faiths other than one's own. For this purpose the students should be trained to cultivate the habit of understanding and appreciating the doctrines of various great religions of the world in a spirit of reverence and broad-minded tolerance. This, if properly done, would help to give them a spiritual assurance and a better appreciation of their own religion. There is one rule, however, which should always be kept in mind while studying all great religions and that is that one should study them only through the writings of known votaries of the respective religions. For instance, if one wants to study the Bhagavata one should do so not through a translation of it made by a hostile critic but through one prepared by a lover of the Bhagavata. Similarly to study the Bible one should study it through the commentaries of devoted Christians. This study of other religions besides one's own will give one a grasp of the rock-bottom unity of all religions and afford a glimpse also of that universal and absolute truth which lies beyond the "dust of creeds and faiths."

.   .   .

We must not, like the frog in the well who imagines that the universe ends with the wall surrounding his well, think that our religion alone represents the whole Truth and all the others are false.

.   .   .

If we had attained the full vision of Truth, we would no longer be mere seekers, but would have become one with God, for Truth is God. But being only seekers, we prosecute our quest, and are conscious of our imperfection. And if we are imperfect ourselves, religion as conceived by us must also be imperfect.

We have not realized religion in its perfection, even as we have not realized God. Religion of our conception, being thus imperfect, is always subject to a process of evolution and reinterpretation. Progress towards Truth, towards God, is possible only because of such evolution. And if all faiths outlined by men are imperfect, the question of comparative merit does not arise. All faiths constitute a revelation of Truth, but all are imperfect and liable to error. Reverence for other faiths need not blind us to their faults. We must be keenly alive to the defects of our own faith also, yet not leave it on that account, but try to overcome those defects. Looking at all religions with an equal eye, we would not only not hesitate, but would think it our duty, to blend into our faith every acceptable feature of other faiths.

The question then arises: why should there be so many different faiths? The soul is one, but the bodies which she animates are many. We cannot reduce the number of bodies; yet we recognize the unity of the soul. Even as a tree has a single trunk, but many branches and leaves, so is there one true and perfect Religion, but it becomes many as it passes through the human medium.

All religions are divinely inspired, but they are imperfect because they are products of the human mind and taught by human beings. The one Religion is beyond all speech. Imperfect men put it into such language as they can command and their words are interpreted by other men equally imperfect. Whose interpretation is to be held to be the right one? Everybody is right from his own standpoint, but it is not impossible that everybody may be wrong. Hence the necessity for tolerance, which does not mean indifference towards one's own faith, but a more intelligent and purer love for it. Tolerance gives us spiritual insight, which is as far from fanaticism as the north pole is from the south. True knowledge of religion breaks down the barriers between faith and faith. Cultivation of tolerance for other faiths will impart to us a truer understanding of our own.

.   .   .

I do not believe in people telling others of their faith, especially with a view to conversion. Faith does not admit of telling. It has to be lived and then it becomes self-propagating.

. . .

My effort should never to be undermine another's faith but to make him a better follower of his own faith. This implies belief in the truth of all religions and therefore respect for them. It again implies true humility, a recognition of the fact that the divine light having been vouchsafed to all religions through an imperfect medium of flesh, they must share in more or less degree the imperfection of the vehicle.

. . .

As regards taking our message to the aborigines, I do not think I should go and give my message out of my own wisdom. Do it in all humility, it is said. Well, I have been an unfortunate witness of arrogance often going in the garb of humility. If I am perfect, I know that my thought will reach others. It taxes all my time to reach the goal I have set to myself. What have I to take to the aborigines and the Assamese hillmen except to go in my nakedness to them? Rather than ask them to join my prayer, I would join their prayer. We were strangers to this sort of classification—"animists," "aborigines," etc.,—but we have learnt it from English rulers.

. . .

Jesus Belongs to the World

Although I have devoted a large part of my life to the study of religion and to discussion with religious leaders of all faiths, I know very well that I cannot but seem presumptuous in writing about Jesus Christ and trying to explain what He means to me. I do so only because my Christian friends have told me on more than a few occasions that for the very reason that I am not a Christian and that (I shall quote their words exactly) "I do not accept Christ in the bottom of my heart as the only Son of God," it is impossible for me to understand the profound significance of His teachings, or to know and interpret the greatest source of spiritual strength that man has ever known.

Although this may or may not be true in my case, I have reasons to believe that it is an erroneous point of view. I believe that such an estimate is incompatible with the message that Jesus Christ gave to the world. For He was, certainly, the highest example of one who wished to give everything asking nothing in return, and not caring what creed might happen to be professed by the recipient. I am sure that if He were living here now among men, He would bless the lives of many who perhaps have never even heard His name, if only their lives embodied the virtues of which He was a living example on earth; the virtues of loving one's neighbour as oneself and of doing good and charitable works among one's fellow-men.

What, then, does Jesus mean to me? To me He was one of the greatest teachers humanity has ever had. To His believers He was God's only begotten Son. Could the fact that I do or do not accept this belief make Jesus have any more or less influence in my life? Is all the grandeur of His teaching and of His doctrine to be forbidden to me? I cannot believe so.

To me it implies a spiritual birth. My interpretation, in other words, is that in Jesus' own life is the key of His nearness to God; that He expressed, as no other could, the spirit and will of God. It is in this sense that I see Him and recognize Him as the Son of God.

.   .   .

I believe that it is impossible to estimate the merits of the various religions of the world, and moreover I believe that it is unnecessary and harmful even to attempt it. But each one of them, in my judgment, embodies a common motivating force: the desire to uplift man's life and give it purpose.

And because the life of Jesus has the significance and the transcendency to which I have alluded, I believe that He belongs not solely to Christianity, but to the entire world; to all races and people, it matters little under what flag, name or doctrine they may work, profess a faith, or worship a god inherited from their ancestors.

.   .   .

God, Mammon, and America

In so far as we have made the modern materialistic craze our goal, in so far are we going downhill in the path of progress. I hold that economic progress in the sense I have put it is antagonistic to real progress. Hence the ancient ideal has been the limitation of activities promoting wealth. This does not put an end to all material ambition. We should still have, as we have always had, in our midst people who make the pursuit of wealth their aim in life. But we have always recognised that it is a fall from the ideal. It is a beautiful thing to know that the wealthiest among us have often felt that to have remained voluntarily poor would have been a higher state for them. That you cannot serve God and Mammon is an economic truth of the highest value. We have to make our choice. Western nations today are groaning under the heel of the monster-god of materialism. Their moral growth has become stunted. They measure their progress in £.s.d. American wealth has become standard. She is the envy of the other nations. I have heard many of our countrymen say that we will gain American wealth but avoid its methods. I venture to suggest that such an attempt if it were made is foredoomed to failure.

.   .   .

Prayer Is a Cry of the Heart

I am glad that you all want me to speak to you on the meaning of and the necessity for prayer. I believe that prayer is the very soul and essence of religion, and therefore prayer must be the very core of the life of man, for no man can live without religion.

.   .   .

Prayer is either petitional or in its wider sense is inward communion. In either case the ultimate result is the same. Even when it is petitional, the petition should be for the cleansing and purification of the soul, for freeing it from the layers of ignorance and darkness that envelop it. He therefore who hungers for the awakening of the divine in him must fall back on prayer. But prayer is no mere exercise of words or of the ears, it is no mere repetition of empty formula. Any amount of repetition of *Ramanama* is futile if it fails to stir the soul. It is better in prayer to have a heart without word than words without a heart. It must be in clear response to the spirit which hungers for it. And even as a hungry man relishes a hearty meal, a hungry soul will relish a heartfelt prayer. And I am giving you a bit of my experience and that of my companions when I say that he who has experienced the magic of prayer may do without food for days together but not a single moment without prayer. For without prayer there is no inward peace.

.   .   .

Begin therefore your day with prayer, and make it so soulful that it may remain with you until the evening. Close the day with prayer so that you may have a peaceful night free from dreams and nightmares. Do not worry about the form of prayer. Let it be any form, it should be such as can put us into communion with the divine. Only, whatever be the form, let not the spirit wander while the words of prayer run on out of your mouth.

.   .   .

Prayer is a cry of the heart. It can be fruitful if it comes from within. But those who pray for an object do not know the meaning of prayer at all.

.   .   .

God Is Truth

God is certainly One. He has no second. He is unfathomable, unknowable, and unknown to the vast majority of mankind. He is everywhere. He sees without eyes, and hears without ears. He is formless and indivisible. He is uncreated, has no father, mother, or child; and yet He allows Himself to be worshipped as father, mother, wife, and child. He allows himself even to be worshipped as stock and stone, although He is none of these things. He is the most elusive. He is the nearest to us if we would but know the fact. But He is farthest from us when we do not want to realize His omnipresence.

.   .   .

To me God is truth and love; God is ethics and morality; God is fearlessness. God is the source of Light and Life and yet He is above and beyond all these. God is conscience. He is even the atheism of the atheist. For in His boundless love God permits the atheist to live. He is the searcher of hearts. He transcends speech and reason. He knows us and our hearts better than we do ourselves. He does not take us at our word for He knows that we often do not mean it, some knowingly and others unknowingly. He is a personal God to those who need His personal presence. He is embodied to those who need His touch. He is the purest essence. He simply

Is to those who have faith. He is all things to all men. He is in us and yet above and beyond us.

.   .   .

If you ask reason for proof of the existence of God, what proof can reason give since God is above all reason? For, if you say that nothing is beyond rational explanation, you will certainly run into difficulties. If we give the highest place to reason, we shall be faced with serious difficulties. Our own *atman* is beyond reason. People have indeed tried to prove its existence with logical arguments, as they have tried to prove the existence of God. But he who knows God and the *atman* with his intellect only does not know them at all. Reason may be a useful instrument of knowledge at one stage. But anybody who stops there will never enjoy the benefits of true spiritual knowledge, in the same way that intellectual knowledge of the benefits of eating food does not by itself help one to enjoy those benefits. God or the *atman* is not an object of knowledge. He Himself is the Knower. That is why we say that He is above reason.

There are two stages of knowledge of God. The first is faith, and the second and the last is first-hand experience to which faith leads. All great teachers of the world have testified to their having had such experience, and people whom the world would ordinarily dismiss as fools have also demonstrated their faith. If we have faith, like theirs, one day we may have first-hand experience too. If a person sees somebody with his eyes but, being deaf, cannot hear him and then complains that he had not heard him, he would not be justified. Similarly, to say that reason cannot know God betrays ignorance. Just as hearing is not the function of the eyes, so also knowing God is not the function of the senses or of reason. To know Him a different kind of faculty is required, and this is unshakeable faith. We know from experience that reason can be all too easily deceived. But we have not known anybody, howsoever mighty he may be, who could deceive true faith.

Further Reading

Roy C. Amore and Larry D. Shinn, *Lustful Maidens and Ascetic Kings: Buddhist and Hindu Stories of Life* (1981). The title is irresistible and the stories, drawn from the *Mahabharata* and other traditional sources, are a pleasant introduction to the atmosphere of India. In the stories, however, there are pitifully few lustful maidens.

A. L. Basham's *The Wonder That Was India* (1954) is universally admired. It is a survey of Indian civilization up to about the year 1000 C.E.

Thomas J. Hopkins, *The Hindu Religious Tradition* (1971). Very likely the best brief introduction to Hinduism.

Translations can differ considerably: some strive to be more literal, some more literary, and so forth. It is informative to compare them. Look, for example, at Juan Mascaro, *The Upanishads* (1965); Sarvepalli Radhakrishnan, *The Principal Upanishads* (1953); Robert E. Hume, *The Thirteen Principal Upanishads* (2d ed., 1931); and Swami Nikhilananda, *The Upanishads* (1949).

Notable translations of the Gita are those by Juan Mascaro, *The Bhagavad Gita* (1962); Franklin Edgerton, *The Bhagavad Gita* (1944); Sarvepalli Radhakrishnan, *The Bhagavadgita* (1948); Swami Nikhilananda, *The Bhagavad Gita* (1944); and Swami Prabhavananda and Christopher Isherwood, *The Song of God: Bhagavad-Gita* (1945).

Eric J. Sharpe, *The Universal Gita: Western Images of the Bhagavadgita* (1985). Since the first English translation in 1785, the reputation of the Gita in the West has risen steadily, and this has, in turn, caused Hindus to raise their own estimations of its value.

Sri Aurobindo Ghosh (1872–1950) is revered as one of the most important spiritual leaders of modern India. His *The Mind of Light* (1953) is recommended as an introduction.

Useful collections of source materials are those by Kenneth Morgan (ed.), *The Religion of the Hindus* (1953); Sarvepalli Radhakrishnan and Charles A. Moore (eds.), *A Sourcebook in Indian Philosophy* (1957); Wm. Theodore deBary et al. (eds.), *Sources of Indian Tradition* (1958); and Ainslie T. Embree (ed.), *The Hindu Tradition* (1966).

Robert Charles Zaehner, *Hinduism* (1962). The Spaulding Professor of Eastern Religions and Ethics at Oxford University and Fellow of All Souls College, Zaehner (1913–74) was one of the leading scholars of his generation.

II

BUDDHISM
Enlightenment, Compassion, Nirvana

The path to the Deathless is awareness;
Unawareness, the path of death.
They who are aware do not die;
They who are unaware are as dead.   Dhammapada

To become a Buddhist is to follow the way of a man named Siddhartha Gautama. It is to resolve to do what he did—to become a Buddha, an Enlightened One. This is the path that leads from *dukkha*, the irremediable suffering that is the most fundamental condition of life, to Nirvana, a state of ineffable bliss.

The religion begins, then, with Siddhartha. Stated in barest outline, the traditions hold that he was born a prince in Northern India about 560 B.C.E., and that he lived amid luxuries, married, and had a son. At the age of twenty-nine, deeply disturbed by questions about life and death, he left his palace and family to seek answers. A six-year period of arduous searching finally resulted in an ecstatic awakening. Tempted to enter Nirvana, he determined instead to help others understand the way, and thereby was Buddhism born. He taught for forty-five years, dying at the age of eighty in 480 B.C.E.

The heart of the Buddha's teaching is contained in the Four Noble Truths, described in this chapter by Heinrich Zimmer. That description is framed in psychological terms, as it should be, because the Buddha's analysis of the human predicament was a masterpiece of insight into the nature of the self and its "pathological blend of unfulfilled cravings, vexing longings, fears, regrets, and pains." Man is, in effect, mentally and emotionally ill; the Eightfold Path of Buddhism is a prescription.

Dukkha, the aforementioned out-of-jointedness that Buddhists posit as the First Noble Truth about our existential predicament, is variously described by scholars. In a memorable passage, Edward Conze understood it to be a *basic* or *original* anxiety:

> If one has felt it, one will never forget, however much one may try. It may come upon you when you have been asleep . . .; you wake up in the middle of the night and feel a kind of astonishment at being there, which then gives way to a fear and horror at the mere fact of being there. It is then that you catch yourself by yourself, just for a moment, against the background of a

kind of nothingness all around you, and with a gnawing sense of your powerlessness, your utter helplessness.[1]

This, then, or something very close to it, is the starting point of Buddhism. It is a religion that attempts to understand and minister to an ailment that seems built into the world. Begin by becoming aware, the Buddha said. Wake up.

Early divisions of thought developed among the followers of the Buddha, a circumstance that should surprise no observer of human affairs. The result was two camps that can be loosely characterized as conservative and liberal. The conservative wing spread across southern Asia and came to be known as Theravada Buddhism[2] ("The Way of the Elders"); its ideal was the world-renouncing *Arahat*. The liberal school was Mahayana Buddhism ("The Great Raft"). Theravadins stressed self-mastery, wisdom, the solitary way of the monk. Mahayanists, whose portrait is drawn later in these pages by Ananda Coomaraswamy, emphasized compassion for others and the way of the bodhisattva. Mahayana was "the overflowing of Buddhism from the limits of the Order [the Sangha] into the life of the world."

Buddhist Scriptures are a challenge. First, it is not always clear what should be counted as scripture and what should not. There was no early "fixing of a canon," that is, no authoritative determination of the texts that would thereafter be accepted as genuine accounts of the Buddha's life and teachings. In fact, for at least five centuries after the death of the Buddha, there were no texts at all, only an oral tradition. Then, when the writing began, it seemed never to stop, at least in some corners of the Buddhist world: in an edition published in Tokyo in 1924, a Chinese version filled 100 volumes, each of 1,000 pages. A Tibetan version runs to 325 volumes.

A second source of perplexity is that there finally came into being *two* canons, which overlap. There is the Pali Canon, named for the language in which it is composed, which is prized by Theravada Buddhists. The Mahayanists have a Canon preserved in part in Sanskrit, and there are Chinese and Tibetan translations that are important because, in some cases, the Pali and Sanskrit originals on which they are based are lost.

The meditational practices of Buddhism are designed to lead the individual to Enlightenment. Of some forty standard subjects for meditation, two are especially recommended: friendliness and death. The latter meditation is described in this chapter by Buddhaghosa.

The chapter concludes with excerpts from a recent autobiography by the Dalai Lama. Tibetan Buddhists[3] accept as the basis of their religion the Four Noble Truths and other basic doctrines shared by Theravadins and Mahayanists. Meditation is practiced, compassion is essential, and the final goal is Nirvana, as it is for all Buddhists. But from that foundation there rises a superstructure of beliefs as breathtaking as those peaks and plateaus of Tibet itself.

---

1. *Buddhism: Its Essence and Development* (New York: Harper Toorchbook, 1959), p. 23.

2. Theravada Buddhism is sometimes termed Hinayana Buddhism, but Hinayana means "Little Raft," which is thought to be uncomplimentary.

3. Tibetan Buddhism is also known as *Tantrayana*, a name that emphasizes the role played in the religion by those scriptures known as the *Tantras. Lamaism* is sometimes used but is misleading. "Lama" is a title of distinction given to some monks in Tibet.

The Roar of Awakening

Heinrich Zimmer (translator)

"The Roar of Awakening" is an old and popular fable in India. It is one of those entirely impossible stories that we promptly want to believe, and then we do believe, because there really is a lot of truth in them.

Recorded in the works of Sri Ramakrishna,[1] "The Roar of Awakening" is here retold by Heinrich Zimmer. It is about a tiger cub brought up among goats. . . .

Its mother had died in giving it birth. Big with young, she had been prowling for many days without discovering prey, when she came upon this herd of ranging wild goats. The tigress was ravenous at the time, and this fact may account for the violence of her spring; but in any case, the strain of the leap brought on the birth throes, and from sheer exhaustion she expired. Then the goats, who had scattered, returned to the grazing ground and found the little tiger whimpering at its mother's side. They adopted the feeble creature out of maternal compassion, suckled it together with their own offspring, and watched over it fondly. The cub grew and their care was rewarded; for the little fellow learned the language of the goats, adapted his voice to their gentle way of bleating, and displayed as much devotion as any kid of the flock. At first he experienced some difficulty when he tried to nibble thin blades of grass with his pointed teeth, but somehow he managed. The vegetarian diet kept him very slim and imparted to his temperament a remarkable meekness.

One night, when this young tiger among the goats had reached the age of reason, the herd was attacked again, this time by a fierce old male tiger, and again they scattered; but the cub remained where he stood, devoid of fear. He was of course surprised. Discovering himself face to face with the terrible jungle being, he gazed at the apparition in amazement. The first moment passed; then he began to fell self-conscious. Uttering a forlorn bleat, he plucked a thin leaf of grass and chewed it, while the other stared.

Suddenly the mighty intruder demanded: "What are you doing here among these goats? What are you chewing there?" The funny little creature bleated. The

1. Swami Nikhilananda (trans.), *The Gospel of Sri Ramakrishna* (New York: Ramakrishna-Vivekanada Center, 1942), pp. 232–33, 359–60.

old one became really terrifying. He roared, "Why do you make this silly sound?" and before the other could respond, seized him roughly by the scruff and shook him, as though to knock him back to his senses. The jungle tiger then carried the frightened cub to a nearby pond, where he set him down, compelling him to look into the mirror surface, which was illuminated by the moon. "Now look at those two faces. Are they not alike? You have the pot-face of a tiger; it is like mine. Why do you fancy yourself to be a goat? Why do you bleat? Why do you nibble grass?"

The little one was unable to reply, but continued to stare, comparing the two reflections. Then it became uneasy, shifted its weight from paw to paw, and emitted another troubled, quavering cry. The fierce old beast seized it again and carried it off to his den, where he presented it with a bleeding piece of raw meat remaining from an earlier meal. The cub shuddered with disgust. The jungle tiger, ignoring the weak bleat of protest, gruffly ordered: "Take it! Eat it! Swallow it!" The cub resisted, but the frightening meat was forced between his teeth, and the tiger sternly supervised while he tried to chew and prepared to swallow. The toughness of the morsel was unfamiliar and was causing some difficulty, and he was just about to make his little noise again, when he began to get the taste of the blood. He was amazed; he reached with eagerness for the rest. He began to feel an unfamiliar gratification as the new food went down his gullet, and the meaty substance came into his stomach. A strange, glowing strength, starting from there, went out through his whole organism, and he commenced to feel elated, intoxicated. His lips smacked; he licked his jowls. He arose and opened his mouth with a mighty yawn, just as though he were waking from a night of sleep—a night that had held him long under its spell, for years and years. Stretching his form, he arched his back, extending and spreading his paws. The tail lashed the ground, and suddenly from his throat there burst the terrifying, triumphant roar of a tiger.

The grim teacher, meanwhile, had been watching closely and with increasing satisfaction. The transformation had actually taken place. When the roar was finished he demanded gruffly: "Now do you know what you really are?" and to complete the initiation of his young disciple into the secret lore of his own true nature, added: "Come, we shall go now for a hunt together in the jungle."

Buddhahood

Heinrich Zimmer

One of the notable scholars of Indian philosophy and art, German-born Heinrich Zimmer (1890–1943) studied at the universities of Munich and Berlin. He was a professor of philology at Heidelberg, worked with Carl Jung at the University of Zurich, and, leaving Germany on the eve of World War II, taught briefly at Balliol College, Oxford. Coming to the United States in 1940, he lectured at Columbia until shortly before his death. His books include The Art of Indian Asia, The King and the Corpse, Myths and Symbols in Indian Art and Civilization, *and* Philosophies of India, *a posthumous volume edited by Joseph Campbell.*

———————

Buddhism was the only religious and philosophical message of India to spread far beyond the borders of its homeland. Conquering Asia to the north and east, it became in those vast areas the creed of the masses and shaped the civilization for centuries. This tends to conceal the fact that in essence Buddhism is meant only for the happy few. The philosophical doctrine at the root of the numerous fascinating popular features is not the kind of teaching that one would have expected to see made readily accessible to all. In fact, of the numerous answers that have been offered, during the millenniums, in all quarters of the world, as solutions to life's enigmas, this one must be ranked as the most uncompromising, obscure, and paradoxical.

. . .

From the beginning, by the nature of the problem, the doctrine had been meant only for those prepared to hear. It was never intended to interfere with either the life and habits of the multitude or the course of civilization. In time it might even vanish from the world, becoming incomprehensible and meaningless—for the lack of anyone capable of treading the path to understanding; and this, too, would be right. In contrast, in other words, to the other great teachers of mankind (Zarathustra preaching the religious law of Persia; Confucius commenting on the restored system of early Chinese thought: Jesus announcing Salvation to the world) Gautama, the prince of the royal Śākya clan, is known properly as Śākya-muni: the

Heinrich Zimmer, "The Roar of Awakening" and "Buddhahood" from *Philosophies of India* edited by Joseph Campbell, copyright © 1957, renewed 1979, by Princeton University Press. Reprinted by permission of the publisher.

"silent sage *(muni)* of the Śākyas"; for in spite of all that has been said and taught about him, the Buddha remains the symbol of something beyond what can be said and taught.

In the Buddhist texts there is no word that can be traced with unquestionable authority to Gautama Śākyamuni. We glimpse only the enlightening shadow of his personality; yet this suffices to merge us in a spiritual atmosphere that is unique. For though India in his time, half a millennium before Christ, was a veritable treasure-house of magical-religious lore—to our eyes a jungle of mythological systems—the teaching of the Enlightened One offered no mythological vision, either of the present world or of a world beyond, and no tangible creed. It was presented as a therapy, a treatment or cure, for those strong enough to follow it—a method and a process of healing. Apparently Gautama, at least in his terminology, broke from all the popular modes and accepted methods of Indian religious and philosophical instruction. He offered his advice in the practical manner of a spiritual physician, as though, through him, the art of Indian medicine were entering the sphere of spiritual problems—that grand old arena where, for centuries, magicians of every kind had been tapping powers by which they and their disciples lifted themselves to the heights of divinity.

Following the procedure of the physician of his day inspecting a patient, the Buddha makes four statements concerning the case of man. These are the so-called "Four Noble Truths" which constitute the heart and kernel of his doctrine. The first, *All life is sorrowful,* announces that we members of the human race are spiritually unhealthy, the symptom being that we carry on our shoulders a burden of sorrow; the disease is endemic. No discussion of any question of guilt goes with this matter-of-fact diagnosis; for the Buddha indulged in no metaphysical or mythological dissertations. He inquired into the cause of the practical, psychological level, however, hence we have, as the second of the "Four Noble Truths," *The cause of suffering is ignorant craving* (*tṛṣṇā*).

As in the teaching of the Sāṅkhya, an involuntary state of mind common to all creatures is indicated as the root of the world-disease. The craving of nescience, not-knowing-better *(avidyā),* is the problem—nothing less and nothing more. Such ignorance is a natural function of the life-process, yet not necessarily ineradicable; no more ineradicable than the innocence of a child. It is simply that we do not know that we are moving in a world of mere conventions and that our feelings, thoughts, and acts are determined by these. We imagine that our ideas about things represent their ultimate reality, and so we are bound in by them as by the meshes of a net. They are rooted in our own consciousness and attitudes; mere creations of the mind; conventional, involuntary patterns of seeing things, judging, and behaving; yet our ignorance accepts them in every detail, without question, regarding them and their contents as the facts of existence. This—this mistake about the true essence of reality—is the cause of all the sufferings that constitute our lives.

The Buddhist analysis goes on to state that our other symptoms (the familiar incidents and situations of our universal condition of non-well being) are derivatives, one and all, of the primary fault. The tragedies and comedies in which we get ourselves involved, which we bring forth from ourselves and in which we act, develop spontaneously from the impetus of our innermost condition of nonknowing. This sends us forth in the world with restricted senses and conceptions. Unconscious wishes and expectations, emanating from us in the shape of subjectively determined decisions and acts, transcend the limits of the present; they precipitate for us the future, being themselves determined from the past. Inherited from former births, they cause future births, the endless stream of life in which we are carried along being greater far than the bounds of individual birth and death. In other words, the ills of the individual cannot be understood in terms of the individual's mistakes; they are rooted in our human way of life, and the whole content of this way of life is a pathological blend of unfulfilled cravings, vexing longings, fears, regrets, and pains. Such a state of suffering is something from which it would be only sensible to be healed.

This radical statement about the problems that most of us take for granted as the natural concomitants of existence, and decide simply to endure, is balanced in the doctrine of the Buddha by the third and fourth of the "Four Noble Truths." Having diagnosed the illness and determined its cause, the physician next inquires whether the disease can be cured. The Buddhist prognostication is that a cure is indeed possible; hence we hear: *The suppression of suffering can be achieved;* and the last of the Four Truths prescribes the way: *The way is the Noble Eightfold Path*—Right View, Right Aspiration, Right Speech, Right Conduct, Right Means of Livelihood, Right Endeavor, Right Mindfulness, and Right Contemplation.

The Buddha's thoroughgoing treatment is guaranteed to eradicate the cause of the sickly spell and dream of ignorance, and thus to make possible the attainment of a state of serene, awakened perfection. No philosophical explanation of man or the universe is required, only this spiritual physician's program of psycho-dietetics. And yet the doctrine can hardly appeal to the multitude; for these are not convinced that their lives are as unwholesome as they obviously are. Only those few who not only would like to try, but actually feel acutely a pressing need to undertake some kind of thoroughgoing treatment, would have the will and stamina to carry to the end such an arduous, self-ordained discipline as that of the Buddhist cure.

The way of Gautama Śākyamuni is called the "middle path"; for it avoids extremes. One pair of extremes is that of the outright pursuit of worldly desires, on the one hand, and the severe, ascetic, bodily discipline of such contemporaries of the Buddha as the Jainas, on the other, whose austerity was designed to culminate in annihilation of the physical frame. Another pair of extremes is that of skepticism, denying the possibility of transcendental knowledge, and the argumentative assertion of undemonstrable metaphysical doctrines. Buddhism eschews the blind alleys to either side and conduces to an attitude that will of itself lead one to the transcendental experience. It rejects explicitly *all* of the contending formulae of the intellect, as inadequate either to lead to or to express the paradoxical truth, which reposes far, far beyond the realm of cerebral conceptions.

A conversation of the Buddha, recorded among the so-called "Long Dialogues," enumerates an extended list of the practical and theoretical disciplines by which people master various skills, crafts, and professions, or seek some understanding of their own nature and the meaning of the universe. All are described and then dismissed without criticism, but with the formula: "Such knowledge and opinions, if thoroughly mastered, will lead inevitably to certain ends and produce certain

results in one's life. The Enlightened One is aware of all these possible consequences, and also of what lies behind them. But he does not attach much importance to this knowledge. For within himself he fosters another knowledge—the
knowledge of cessation, of the discontinuance of worldly existence, of utter repose
by emancipation. He has perfect insight into the manner of the springing into existence of our sensations and feelings, and into the manner of their vanishing again
with all their sweetness and bitterness, and into the way of escape from them altogether, and into the manner in which, by non-attachment to them through right
knowledge of their character, he has himself won release from their spell."[1]

Buddhism attaches no serious importance to such knowledge as entangles men
more tightly in the net of life, knowledge that adds a comfortable material or interesting spiritual background to existence and thereby only contributes additional
substance to the maintenance of the personality. Buddhism teaches that the value
attributed to a thing is determined by the particular pattern of life from which it is
regarded and the personality concerned. The weight of a fact or idea varies with the
unenlightenment of the observer—his spontaneous commitment to certain spheres
of phenomena and ranges of human value. The atmosphere, nay the world, surrounding and overpowering him, is continually being produced from his own
unconscious nature, and affects him in terms of his commitment to his own imper-
fections. Its traits are the phenomenal projections of his inner state of ignorance
sent out into the realm of sense-perception and there, as it were, discovered by an
act of empirical experience. Hence Buddhism denies, finally, the force and validity
of everything that can be known.

A Tibetan author—a Buddhist Dalai-Lama—puts it this way: The one substance, which fundamentally is devoid of qualities, appears to be of various, completely differing flavors, according to the kind of being who tastes it. The same beverage which for the gods in their celestial realm will be the delightful drink of
immortality, for men on earth will be mere water, and for the tormented inmates
of hell a vile, disgusting liquid which they will be loath to swallow even though tortured with intolerable pangs of thirst. The three qualities of, or ways of experiencing, the one substance are here nothing more than the normal effects of three orders
of karma. The senses themselves are conditioned by the subjective forces that
brought them into being and hold them under strict control. The world without is
no mere illusion—it is not to be regarded as nonexistent; yet it derives its enchanting or appalling features from the involuntary inner attitude of the one who sees it.
The alluring hues and frightening shadows that form its very tissue are projected
reflexes of the tendencies of the psyche.

One lives, in other words, enveloped by the impulses of the various layers of
one's own nature, woven in the spell of their specific atmosphere, to which one submits as to an outside world. The goal of the techniques of the Buddhist therapy is
to bring this process of self-envelopment to a stop. The living process is likened to
a fire burning. Through the involuntary activity of one's nature as it functions in
contact with the outer world, life as we know it goes on incessantly. The treatment
is the extinction *(nirvāna)* of the fire, and the Buddha, the Awake, is the one no

1. *Dīgha-nikāya* 1.

longer kindled or enflamed. The Buddha is far from having dissolved into non-being; it is not He who is extinct but the life illusion—the passions, desires, and normal dynamisms of the physique and psyche. No longer blinded, he no longer feels himself to be conditioned by the false ideas and attendant desires that normally go on shaping individuals and their spheres, life after life. The Buddha realizes himself to be void of the characteristics that constitute an individual subject to a destiny. Thus released from karma, the universal law, he reposes beyond fate, no longer subject to the consequences of personal limitations. What other people behold when they look upon his physical presence is a sort of mirage; for he is intrinsically devoid of the attributes that they venerate and are themselves striving to attain.

. . .

The Buddha's doctrine is called *yāna*. The word means "a vehicle," or, more to the point, "a ferryboat." The "ferryboat" is the principal image employed in Buddhism to render the sense and function of the doctrine. The idea persists through all the differing and variously conflicting teachings of the numerous Buddhist sects that have evolved in many lands, during the long course of the magnificent history of the widely disseminated doctrine. Each sect describes the vehicle in its own way, but no matter how described, it remains always the ferry.

To appreciate the full force of this image, and to understand the reason for its persistence, one must begin by realizing that in everyday Hindu life the ferryboat plays an extremely prominent role. It is an indispensable means of transportation in a continent traversed by many mighty rivers and where bridges are practically nonexistent. To reach the goal of almost any journey one will require a ferry, time and time again, the only possible crossing of the broad and rapid streams being by boat or by a ford. The Jainas called their way of salvation the ford *(tīrtha)*, and the supreme Jaina teachers were . . . *Tīrthaṅkaras,* "those making, or providing, a ford." In the same sense, Buddhism, by its doctrine, provides a ferryboat across the rushing river of *saṁsāra* to the distant bank of liberation. Through enlightenment *(bodhi)* the individual is transported.

The gist of Buddhism can be grasped more readily and adequately by fathoming the main metaphors through which it appeals to our intuition than by a systematic study of the complicated superstructure, and the fine details of the developed teaching. For example, one need only think for a moment about the actual, everyday experience of the process of crossing a river in a ferryboat, to come to the simple idea that inspires and underlies all of the various rationalized systematizations of the doctrine. To enter the Buddhist vehicle—the boat of the discipline—means to begin to cross the river of life, from the shore of the common-sense experience of non-enlightenment, the shore of spiritual ignorance *(avidyā),* desire *(kāma),* and death *(māra),* to the yonder bank of transcendental wisdom *(vidyā),* which is liberation *(mokṣa)* from this general bondage. Let us consider, briefly, the actual stages involved in any crossing of a river by ferry, and see if we can experience the passage as a kind of initiation-by-analogy into the purport of the stages of the Buddhist pilgrim's progress to his goal.

Standing on the nearer bank, this side the stream, waiting for the boat to put in, one is a part of its life, sharing in its dangers and opportunities and in whatever may come to pass on it. One feels the warmth or coolness of its breezes, hears the rustle of its trees, experiences the character of its people, and knows that its earth is underfoot. Meanwhile the other bank, the far bank, is beyond reach—a mere optical image across the broad, flowing waters that divide us from its unknown world of forms. We have really no idea what it will be like to stand in that distant land. How this same scenery of the river and its two shorelines will appear from the other side we cannot imagine. How much of these houses will be visible among the trees? What prospects up and down the river will unfold? Everything over here, so tangible and real to us at present—these real, solid objects, these tangible forms—will be no more than remote, visual patches, inconsequential optical effects, without power to touch us, either to help or to harm. This solid earth itself will be a visual, horizontal line beheld from afar, one detail of an extensive scenic view, beyond our experience, and of no more force for us than a mirage.

The ferryboat arrives; and as it comes to the landing we regard it with a feeling of interest. It brings with it something of the air of that yonder land which will soon be our destination. Yet when we are entering it we still feel like members of the world from which we are departing, and there is still that feeling of unreality about our destination. When we lift our eyes from the boat and boatman, the far bank is still only a remote image, no more substantial than it was before.

Softly the ferryboat pushes off and begins to glide across the moving waters. Presently one realizes that an invisible line has been recently, imperceptibly passed, beyond which the bank left behind is assuming gradually the unsubstantially of a mere visual impression, a kind of mirage, while the farther bank, drawing slowly nearer, is beginning to turn into something real. The former dim remoteness is becoming the new reality and soon is solid ground, creaking under keel—real earth—the sand and stone on which we tread in disembarking; whereas the world left behind, recently so tangible, has been transmuted into an optical reflex devoid of substance, out of reach and meaningless, and has forfeited the spell that it laid upon us formerly—with all its features, all its people and events—when we walked upon it and ourselves were a portion of its life. Moreover, the new reality, which now possesses us, provides an utterly new view of the river, the valley, and the two shores, a view very different from the other, and completely unanticipated.

Now while we were in the process of crossing the river in the boat, with the shore left behind becoming gradually vaguer and more meaningless—the streets and homes, the dangers and pleasures, drawing steadily away—there was a period when the shoreline ahead was still rather far off too; and during that time the only tangible reality around us was the boat, contending stoutly with the current and precariously floating on the rapid waters. The only details of life that then seemed quite substantial and that greatly concerned us were the various elements and implements of the ferryboat itself: the contours of the hull and gunwales, the rudder and the sail, the various ropes, and perhaps a smell of tar. The rest of existence, whether out ahead or left behind, signified no more than a hopeful prospect and a fading recollection—two poles of unrealistic sentimental association affiliated with certain clusters of optical effects far out-of-hand.

In the Buddhist texts this situation of the people in a ferryboat is compared to that of the good folk who have taken passage in the vehicle of the doctrine. The boat is the teaching of the Buddha, and the implements of the ferry are the various details of Buddhist discipline: meditation, yoga-exercises, the rules of ascetic life, and the practice of self-abnegation. These are the only things that disciples in the vehicle can regard with deep conviction; such people are engrossed in a fervent belief in the Buddha as the ferryman and the Order as their bounding gunwale (framing, protecting, and defining their perfect ascetic life) and in the guiding power of the doctrine. The shoreline of the world has been left behind but the distant one of release not yet attained. The people in the boat, meanwhile, are involved in a peculiar sort of middle prospect which is all their own.

Among the conversations of the Buddha known as the "Medium-length Dialogues," there appears a discourse on the value of the vehicle of the doctrine. First the Buddha describes a man who, like himself or any of his followers, becomes filled with a loathing of the perils and delights of secular existence. That man decides to quit the world and cross the stream of life to the far land of spiritual safety. Collecting wood and reeds, he builds a raft, and by this means succeeds in attaining the other shore. The Buddha confronts his monks, then, with the question.

"What would be your opinion of this man," asks the Buddha, "would he be a clever man, if, out of gratitude for the raft that has carried him across the stream to safety, he, having reached the other shore, should cling to it, take it on his back, and walk about with the weight of it?"

The monks reply. "No, certainly the man who would do that would not be a clever man."

The Buddha goes on. "Would not the clever man be the one who left the raft (of no use to him any longer) to the current of the stream, and walked ahead without turning back to look at it? Is it not simply a tool to be cast away and forsaken once it has served the purpose for which it was made?"

The disciples agree that this is the proper attitude to take toward the vehicle, once it has served its purpose.

The Buddha then concludes. "In the same way the vehicle of the doctrine is to be cast away and forsaken, once the other shore of Enlightenment *(nirvāna)* has been attained."[2]

The rules of the doctrine are intended for beginners and advanced pupils, but become meaningless for the perfect. They can be of no service to the truly enlightened, unless to serve him, in his role of teacher, as a convenient medium by which to communicate some suggestion of the truth to which he has attained. It was by means of the doctrine that the Buddha sought to express what he had realized beneath the tree as inexpressible. He could communicate with the world through his doctrine and thus help his unprepared disciples when they were at the start, or somewhere in the middle, of the way. Talking down to the level of relative or total ignorance, the doctrine can move the still imperfect yet ardent mind; but it can say nothing any more, nothing ultimately real, to the mind that has cast away darkness. Like the raft, it must be left behind, therefore, once the goal has been attained; for it can thenceforth be no more than an inappropriate burden.

Moreover, not the raft only, but the stream too, becomes void of reality for the

2. *Majjhima-Nikāya* 3. 2. 22. 135.

one who has attained the other shore. When such a one turns around to look again at the land left behind, what does he see? What *can* one see who has crossed the horizon beyond which there is no duality? He looks—and there *is* no "other shore"; there is no torrential separating river; there is no raft; there is no ferryman; there can have been no crossing of the nonexistent stream. The whole scene of the two banks and the river between is simply gone. There can be no such thing for the enlightened eye and mind, because to see or think of anything as something "other" (a distant reality, different from one's own being) would mean that full Enlightenment had not yet been attained. There can be an "other shore" only for people still in the spheres of dualistic perception; those this side of the stream or still inside the boat and heading for the "other shore"; those who have not yet disembarked and thrown away the raft. Illumination means that the delusory distinction between the two shores of a worldly and a transcendental existence no longer holds. There *is* no stream of rebirths flowing between two separated shores: no saṁsāra and no nir-vāna.

Thus the long pilgrimage to perfection through innumerable existences, moti-vated by the virtues of self-surrender and accomplished at the cost of tremendous sacrifices of ego, disappears like a landscape of dreams when one awakes. The long-continued story of the heroic career, the many lives of increasing self-purification, the picture-book legend of detachment won through the long passion, the saintly epic of the way to become a savior—enlightened and enlightening—vanishes like a rainbow. All becomes void; whereas once, when the dream was coming to pass step by step, with ever-recurrent crises and decisions, the unending series of dra-matic sacrifices held the soul completely under its spell. The secret meaning of Enlightenment is that this titan-effort of pure soul-force, this ardent struggle to reach the goal by acts, ever-renewed, of beautiful self-surrender, this supreme, long strife through ages of incarnations to attain release from the universal law of moral causation *(karma)*—is without reality. At the threshold of its own realization it dis-solves, together with its background of self-entangled life, like a nightmare at the dawn of day.

For the Buddha, therefore, even the notion of nirvana is without meaning. It is bound to the pairs-of-opposites and can be employed only in opposition to saṁ-sāra—the vortex where the life-force is spellbound in ignorance by its own polarized passions of fear and desire.

The Buddhist way of ascetic training is designed to conduce to the understand-ing that there is no substantial ego—nor any object anywhere—that lasts, but only spiritual processes, welling and subsiding: sensations, feelings, visions. These can be suppressed or set in motion and watched at will. The idea of the extinction of the fire of lust, ill will, and ignorance becomes devoid of meaning when this psy-chological power and point of view has been attained; for the process of life is no longer experienced as a burning fire. To speak seriously, therefore, of nirvāna as a goal to be attained is simply to betray the attitude of one still remembering or expe-riencing the process as the burning of the fire. The Buddha himself adopts such an attitude only for the teaching of those still suffering, who feel that they would like to make the flames extinct. His famous Fire Sermon is an accommodation, not by any means the final word of the sage whose final word is silence. From the perspective of the Awake, the Illumined One, such opposed verbalizations as nirvāna, saṁsāra, enlightenment and ignorance, freedom and bondage, are without reference, void of content. That is why the Buddha refused to discuss nirvāna. The pointlessness of the connotations that would inevitably seem to be intended by his words would confuse those trying to follow his mysterious way. They being still in the ferryboat framed of these conceptions and requiring them as devices of transport to the shore of understanding, their teacher would not deny before them the practical function of such convenient terms; and yet would not give the terms weight, either, by discussion. Words like "enlightenment," "ignorance," "freedom," and "entanglement" are preliminary helps, referring to no ultimate reality, mere hints or signposts for the traveler, which serve to point him to the goal of an attitude beyond their own suggestions of a contrariety. The raft being finally left behind, and the vision lost of the two banks and the separating river, then there is in truth neither the realm of life and death nor that of release. Moreover, there is no Buddhism—no boat, since there are neither shores nor waters between. There is no boat, and there is no boatman—no Buddha.

elections, *Buddhist Scriptures*
Edward Conze (translator)

Born in London in 1904, Edward Conze studied at German universities before receiving a doctorate from the University of Cologne. A prolific author and esteemed translator of ancient Buddhist literature, he also taught at the Universities of London, Oxford, Wisconsin, Washington (Seattle), and California (Berkeley and Santa Barbara). He died in 1979.

The Five Precepts

"I undertake to observe the rule

to abstain from taking life;
to abstain from taking what is not given;
to abstain from sensuous misconduct;
to abstain from false speech;
to abstain from intoxicants as tending to cloud the mind."

The first four precepts are explained by Buddhaghosa as follows:

1. "Taking life" means to murder anything that lives. It refers to the striking and killing of living beings. "Anything that lives"—ordinary people speak here of a "living being," but more philosophically we speak of "anything that has the life-force." "Taking life" is then the will to kill anything that one perceives as having life, to act so as to terminate the life-force in it, in so far as the will finds expression in bodily action or in speech. With regard to animals it is worse to kill large ones than small. Because a more extensive effort is involved. Even where the effort is the same, the difference in substance must be considered. In the case of humans the killing is the more blameworthy the more virtuous they are. Apart from that, the extent of the offence is proportionate to the intensity of the wish to kill. Five factors are involved: a living being, the perception of a living being, a thought of murder, the action of carrying it out, and death as a result of it. And six are the ways in which the offence may be carried out: with one's own hand, by instigation, by missiles, by slow poisoning, by sorcery, by psychic power.

2. "To take what is not given" means the appropriation of what is not given. It

refers to the removing of someone else's property, to the stealing of it, to theft. "What is not given" means that which belongs to someone else. "Taking what is not given" is then the will to steal anything that one perceives as belonging to someone else, and to act so as to appropriate it. Its blameworthiness depends partly on the value of the property stolen, partly on the worth of its owner. Five factors are involved: someone else's belongings, the awareness that they are someone else's, the thought of theft, the action of carrying it out, the taking away as a result of it. This sin, too, may be carried out in six ways. One may also distinguish unlawful acquisition by way of theft, robbery, underhand dealings, stratagems, and the casting of lots.

3. "Sensuous misconduct"—here "sensuous" means "sexual," and "misconduct" is extremely blameworthy bad behaviour. "Sensuous misconduct" is the will to transgress against those whom one should not go into, and the carrying out of this intention by unlawful physical action. By "those one should not go into," first of all men are meant. And then also twenty kinds of women. Ten of them are under some form of protection, by their mother, father, parents, brother, sister, family, clan, co-religionists, by having been claimed from birth onwards, or by the king's law. The other ten kinds are: women bought with money, concubines for the fun of it, kept women, women bought by the gift of a garment, concubines who have been acquired by the ceremony which consists in dipping their hands into water, concubines who once carried burdens on their heads, slave girls who are also concubines, servants who are also concubines, girls captured in war, temporary wives. The offence is the more serious, the more moral and virtuous the person transgressed against. Four factors are involved: someone who should not be gone into, the thought of cohabiting with that one, the actions which lead to such cohabitation, and its actual performance. There is only one way of carrying it out: with one's own body.

4. "False"—this refers to actions of the voice, or actions of the body, which aim at deceiving others by obscuring the actual facts. "False speech" is the will to deceive others by words or deeds. One can also explain: "False" means something which is not real, not true. "Speech" is the intimation that that is real or true. "False speech" is then the volition which leads to the deliberate intimation to someone else that something is so when it is not so. The seriousness of the offence depends on the circumstances. If a householder, unwilling to give something, says that he has not got it, that is a small offence; but to represent something one has seen with one's own eyes as other than one has seen it, that is a serious offence. If a mendicant has on his rounds got very little oil or ghee, and if he then exclaims, "What a magnificent river flows along here, my friends," that is only a rather stale joke, and the offence is small; but to say that one has seen what one has not seen, that is a serious offence. Four factors are involved: something which is not so, the thought of deception, an effort to carry it out, the communication of the falsehood to someone else. There is only one way of doing it: with one's own body.

"To abstain from"—one crushes or forsakes sin. It means an abstention which is associated with wholesome thoughts. And it is threefold: (I) one feels obliged to abstain, (II) one formally undertakes to do so, (III) one has lost all temptation not to do so.

I. Even those who have not formally undertaken to observe the precepts may have the conviction that it is not right to offend against them. So it was with Cakkana, a Ceylonese boy. His mother was ill, and the doctor prescribed fresh rabbit meat for her. His brother sent him into the field to catch a rabbit, and he went as he was bidden. Now a rabbit had run into a field to eat of the corn, but in its eagerness to get there had got entangled in a snare, and gave forth cries of distress. Cakkana followed the sound, and thought: "This rabbit has got caught there, and it will make a fine medicine for my mother!" But then he thought again: "It is not suitable for me that, in order to preserve my mother's life, I should deprive someone else of his life." And so he released the rabbit, and said to it: "Run off, play with the other rabbits in the wood, eat grass and drink water!" On his return he told the story to his brother, who scolded him. He then went to his mother, and said to her: "Even without having been told, I know quite clearly that I should not deliberately deprive any living being of life." He then fervently resolved that these truthful words of his might make his mother well again, and so it actually happened.

II. The second kind of abstention refers to those who not only have formally undertaken not to offend against the precepts, but who in addition are willing to sacrifice their lives for that. This can be illustrated by a layman who lived near Uttaravarddhamana. He had received the precepts from Buddharakkhita, the Elder. He then went to plough his field, but found that his ox had got lost. In his search for the ox he climbed up the mountain, where a huge snake took hold of him. He thought of cutting off the snake's head with his sharp knife, but on further reflection he thought to himself: "It is not suitable that I, who have received the Precepts from the venerable Guru, should break them again." Three times he thought, "My life I will give up, but not the precepts!" and then he threw his knife away. Thereafter the huge viper let him go, and went somewhere else.

III. The last kind of abstention is associated with the holy Path. It does not even occur to the Holy Persons to kill any living being.

The Advantages of Meditation

Secluded meditation has many virtues. All the Tathagatas have won their all-knowledge in a state of secluded meditation, and, even after their enlightenment, they have continued to cultivate meditation in the recollection of the benefits it brought to them in the past. It is just as a man who has received some boon from a king, and who would, in recollection of the benefits he has had, remain also in the future in attendance on that king.

There are, in fact, twenty-eight advantages to be gained from secluded meditation, and they are the reason why the Tathagatas have devoted themselves to it. They are as follows: secluded meditation guards him who meditates, lengthens his life, gives him strength, and shuts out faults; it removes ill-fame, and leads to good repute; it drives out discontent, and makes for contentment; it removes fear, and gives confidence; it removes sloth and generates vigour; it removes greed, hate, and delusion; it slays pride, breaks up preoccupations, makes thought one-pointed, softens the mind, generates gladness, makes one venerable, gives rise to much profit, makes one worthy of homage, brings exuberant joy, causes delight, shows the own-being of all conditioned things, abolishes rebirth in the world of becoming, and it bestows all the benefits of an ascetic life. These are the twenty-eight advantages of meditation which induce the Tathagatas to practice it.

And it is because the Tathagatas wish to experience the calm and easeful delight of meditational attainments that they practise meditation with this end in view. Four are the reasons why the Tathagatas tend meditation: so that they may dwell at ease; on account of the manifoldness of its faultless virtues; because it is the road to all holy states without exception; and because it has been praised, lauded, exalted, and commended by all the Buddhas.

The Questions of King Milinda

The Chariot

And King Milinda asked him: "How is your Reverence known, and what is your name, Sir?" "As Nagasena I am known, O great king, and as Nagasena do my fellow religious habitually address me. But although parents give such names as Nagasena, or Surasena, or Virasena, or Sihasena, nevertheless this word "Nagasena" is just a denomination, a designation, a conceptual term, a current appellation, a mere name. For no real person can here be apprehended." But King Milinda explained: "Now listen, you 500 Greeks and 80,000 monks, this Nagasena tells me that he is not a real person! How can I be expected to agree with that!" And to Nagasena he said: "If, most reverend Nagasena, no person can be apprehended in reality, who then, I ask you, gives you what you require by way of robes, food, lodging, and medicines? Who is it that consumes them? Who is it that guards morality, practises meditation, and realizes the [four] Paths and their Fruits, and thereafter Nirvana? Who is it that kills living beings, takes what is not given, commits sexual misconduct, tells lies, drinks intoxicants? Who is it that commits the five Deadly Sins? For, if there were no person, there could be no merit and no demerit; no doer of meritorious or demeritorious deeds, and no agent behind them; no fruit of good and evil deeds, and no reward or punishment for them. If someone should kill you, O Venerable Nagasena, he would not commit any murder. And you yourself, Venerable Nagasena, would not be a real teacher, or instructor, or ordained monk! You just told me that your fellow religious habitually address you as "Nagasena." What then is this 'Nagasena'? Are perhaps the hairs of the head "Nagasena"?—"No, great king!" "Or perhaps the hairs of the body?"—"No, great king!" "Or perhaps the nails, teeth, skin, muscles, sinews, bones, marrow, kidneys, heart, liver, serous membranes, spleen, lungs, intestines, mesentery, stomach, excrement, the bile, phlegm, pus, blood, grease, fat, tears, sweat, spittle, snot, fluid of the joints, urine, or the brain in the skull—are they this 'Nagasena'?"—"No, great king!"—"Or is form this 'Nagasena,' or feeling, or perceptions, or impulses, or consciousness?"— "No, great king!"—"Then is it the combination of form, feelings, perceptions, impulses, and consciousness?"—"No, great king!"—"Then, ask as I may, I can discover no Nagasena at all. Just a mere sound is this "Nagasena," but who is the real Nagasena? Your Reverence has told a lie, has spoken a falsehood! There really is no Nagasena!"

Thereupon the Venerable Nagasena said to King Milinda: "As a king you have been brought up in great refinement and you avoid roughness of any kind. If you would walk at midday on this hot, burning, and sandy ground, then your feet would have to tread on the rough and gritty gravel and pebbles, and they would hurt you, your body would get tired, your mind impaired, and your awareness of your body would be associated with pain. How then did you come—on foot, or on a mount?"

"I did not come, Sir, on foot, but on a chariot."—"If you have come on a chariot, then please explain to me what a chariot is. Is the pole the chariot?"—"No, reverend Sir!"—"Is then the axle the chariot?"—"No, reverend Sir!"—"Is it then the wheels, or the framework, or the flag-staff, or the yoke, or the reins, or the goad-stick?"—"No, reverend Sir!"—"Then is it the combination of pole, axle, wheels, framework, flagstaff, yoke, reins, and goad which is the 'chariot'?"—"No, reverend Sir!"—"Then is this 'chariot' outside the combination of pole, axle, wheels, framework, flagstaff, yolk, reins, and goad?"—"No, reverend Sir!"—"Then , ask as I may, I can discover no chariot at all. Just a mere sound is this 'chariot.' But what is the real chariot? Your Majesty has told a lie, has spoken a falsehood! There really is no chariot! Your Majesty is the greatest king in the whole of India. Of whom then are you afraid, that you do not speak the truth?" And he exclaimed: "Now listen, you 500 Greeks and 80,000 monks, this king Milinda tells me that he has come on a chariot. But when asked to explain to me what a chariot is, he cannot establish its existence. How can one possibly approve of that?"

The five hundred Greeks thereupon applauded the Venerable Nagasena and said to king Milinda: "Now let your Majesty get out of that if you can!"

But king Milinda said to Nagasena: "I have not, Nagasena, spoken a falsehood. For it is in dependence on the pole, the axle, the wheels, the framework, the flagstaff, etc., that there takes place this denomination 'chariot,' this designation, this conceptual term, a current appellation and a mere name."—"Your Majesty has spoken well about the chariot. It is just so with me. In dependence on the thirty-two parts of the body and the five Skandhas there takes place this denomination 'Nagasena,' this designation, this conceptual term, a current appellation and a mere name. In ultimate reality, however, this person cannot be apprehended. And this has been said by our Sister Vajira when she was face to face with the Lord:

> Where all constituent parts are present,
> The word 'a chariot' is applied.
> So likewise where the skandhas are,
> The term a 'being' commonly is used."

"It is wonderful, Nagasena, it is astonishing, Nagasena! Most brilliantly have these questions been answered! Were the Buddha himself here, he would approve what you have said. Well spoken, Nagasena, well spoken!"

Personal Identity and Rebirth

The king asked: "When someone is reborn, Venerable Nagasena, is he the same as the one who just died, or is he another?"—The Elder replied: "He is neither the same nor another."—"Give me an illustration!"—"What do you think, great king: when you were a tiny infant, newly born and quite soft, were you then the same as the one who is now grown up?"—"No, that infant was one, I, now grown up, am another."—"If that is so, then, great king, you have had no mother, no father, no teaching, and no schooling! Do we then take it that there is one mother for the embryo in the first stage, another for the second stage, another for the third, another for the fourth, another for the baby, another for the grown-up man? Is the school-boy one person, and the one who has finished school another? Does one commit a crime, but the hands and feet of another are cut off?"—"Certainly not! But what would you say, Reverend Sir, to all that?"—The Elder replied: "I was neither the tiny infant, newly born and quite soft, nor am I now the grown-up man; but all these are comprised in one unit depending on this very body."—"Give me a simile!"— "If a man were to light a lamp, could it give light throughout the whole night?"— "Yes, it could."—"Is now the flame which burns in the first watch of the night the same as the one which burns in the second?"—"It is not the same."—"Or is the flame which burns in the second watch the same as the one which burns in the last one?"—"It is not the same."—"Do we then take it that there is one lamp in the first watch of the night, another in the second, and another again in the third?"—"No, it is because of just that one lamp that the light shines throughout the night."— "Even so must we understand the collocation of a series of successive dharmas. At rebirth one dharma arises, while another stops; but the two processes take place almost simultaneously (i.e., they are continuous). Therefore the first act of consciousness in the new existence is neither the same as the last act of consciousness in the previous existence, nor is it another."—"Give me another simile!"—"Milk, once the milking is done, turns after some time into curds; from curds it turns into fresh butter, and from fresh butter into ghee. Would it now be correct to say that the milk is the same thing as the curds, or the fresh butter, or the ghee?"—"No, it would not. But they have been produced because of it."—"Just so must be understood the collocation of a series of successive dharmas."

Personal Identity and Karma

The king asked: "Is there, Nagasena, any being which passes on from this body to another body?"—"No, your majesty!"—"If there were no passing on from this body to another, would not one then in one's next life be freed from the evil deeds committed in the past?"—"Yes, that would be so if one were not linked once again with a new organism. But since, your majesty, one is linked once again with a new organism, therefore one is not freed from one's evil deeds."—"Give me a simile!"—"If a man should steal another man's mangoes, would he deserve a thrashing for that?"—"Yes, of course!"—"But he would not have stolen the very same mangoes as the other one had planted. Why then should he deserve a thrashing?"—"For the reason that the stolen mangoes had grown because of those that were planted."—"Just so, your majesty, it is because of the deeds one does, whether pure or impure, by means of this psycho-physical organism, that one is once again linked with another psycho-physical organism, and is not freed from one's evil deeds."— "Very good, Nagasena!"

Problems of Nirvana

The king asked: "Is cessation Nirvana?"—"Yes, your majesty!"—"How is that, Nagasena?"—"All the foolish common people take delight in the senses and their objects, are impressed by them, are attached to them. In that way they are carried away by the flood, and are not set free from birth, old age, and death, from grief, lamentation, pain, sadness, and despair—they are, I say, not set free from suffering. But the well-informed holy disciples do not take delight in the senses and their objects, are not impressed by them, are not attached to them, and in consequence their craving ceases; the cessation of craving leads successively to that of grasping, of becoming, of birth, of old age and death, of grief, lamentation, pain, sadness, and despair—that is to say to the cessation of all this mass of ill. It is thus that cessation is Nirvana."—"Very good, Nagasena!"

The king asked: "Do all win Nirvana?"—"No, they do not. Only those win Nirvana who, progressing correctly, know by their superknowledge those dharmas which should be known by superknowledge, comprehend those dharmas which should be comprehended, forsake those dharmas which should be forsaken, develop those dharmas which should be developed, and realize those dharmas which should be realized."—"Very good, Nagasena!"

The king asked: "Do those who have not won Nirvana know how happy a state it is?"—"Yes, they do."—"But how can one know this about Nirvana without having attained it?"—"Now what do you think, your majesty? Do those who have not had their hands and feet cut off know how bad it is to have them cut off?"—"Yes, they do."—"And how do they know it?"—"From hearing the sound of the lamentations of those whose hands and feet have been cut off."—"So it is by hearing the words of those who have seen Nirvana that one knows it to be a happy state."—"Very good, Nagasena!"

The Nature of Nirvana

King Milinda said: "I will grant you, Nagasena, that Nirvana is absolute Ease, and that nevertheless one cannot point to its form or shape, its duration or size, either by simile or explanation, by reason or by argument. But is there perhaps some quality of Nirvana which it shares with other things, and which lends itself to a metaphorical explanation?"—"Its form, O king, cannot be elucidated by similes, but its qualities can."—"How good to hear that, Nagasena! Speak then, quickly, so that I may have an explanation of even one of the aspects of Nirvana! Appease the fever of my heart! Allay it with the cool sweet breezes of your words!"

"Nirvana shares one quality with the lotus, two with water, three with medicine, ten with space, three with the wishing jewel, and five with a mountain peak. As the lotus is unstained by water, so is Nirvana unstained by all the defilements.—As cool water allays feverish heat, so also Nirvana is cool and allays the fever of all the passions. Moreover, as water removes the thirst of men and beasts who are exhausted, parched, thirsty, and overpowered by heat, so also Nirvana removes the craving for sensuous enjoyments, the craving for further becoming, the craving for the cessation of becoming.—As medicine protects from the torments of poison, so Nirvana from the torments of the poisonous passions. Moreover, as medicine puts an end to sickness, so Nirvana to all sufferings. Finally, Nirvana and medicine both give security.—And these are the ten qualities which Nirvana shares with space. Neither is born, grows old, dies, passes away, or is reborn; both are unconquerable, cannot be stolen, are unsupported, are roads respectively for birds and Arhats to journey on, are unobstructed and infinite.—Like the wishing jewel, Nirvana grants all one can desire, brings joy, and sheds light.—As a mountain peak is lofty and exalted, so is Nirvana. As a mountain peak is unshakeable, so is Nirvana. As a mountain peak is inaccessible, so is Nirvana inaccessible to all the passions. As no seeds can grow on a mountain peak, so the seeds of all the passions cannot grow in Nirvana. And finally, as a mountain peak is free from all desire to please or displease, so is Nirvana."—"Well said, Nagasena! So it is, and as such I accept it."

Selections, The Dhammapada

John Ross Carter and Mahinda Palihawadana (translators)

"Dhammapada" is variously translated as "The Path of Truth," "The Way of Righteousness," or "The Path of Virtue." The book entitled The Dhammapada *consists of 423 aphoristic statements of the Buddha, all in verse and grouped in twenty-six chapters. The date of its composition was probably not later than the third century* B.C.E.

Enormously popular through the ages, frequently memorized, The Dhammapada is here translated by John Ross Carter, professor of philosophy and religion at Colgate University; and Mahinda Palihawadana, professor of Sanskrit at Sri Jayawardhanapura University in Sri Lanka.

---

13. As rain penetrates
    The poorly thatched dwelling,
    So passion penetrates
    The untended mind.

14. As rain does not penetrate
    The well-thatched dwelling,
    So passion does not penetrate
    The well-tended mind.

19. If one, though reciting much of texts,
    Is not a doer thereof, a heedless man;
    He, like a cowherd counting others' cows,
    Is not a partaker in the religious quest.

20. If one, though reciting little of texts,
    Lives a life in accord with dhamma,
    Having discarded passion, ill will, and unawareness,
    Knowing full well, the mind well freed,
    He, not grasping here, neither hereafter,
    Is a partaker of the religious quest.

21. The path to the Deathless is awareness;
    Unawareness, the path of death.

They who are aware do not die;
They who are unaware are as dead.

29. Among those unaware, the one aware,
Among the sleepers, the wide-awake,
The one with great wisdom moves on,
As a racehorse who leaves behind a nag.

35. Commendable is the taming
Of mind, which is hard to hold down,
Nimble, alighting wherever it wants.
Mind subdued brings ease.

41. Soon indeed
This body on the earth will lie,
Pitched aside, without consciousness,
Like a useless chip of wood.

50. Let one regard
Neither the discrepancies of others,
Nor what is done or left undone by others,
But only the things one has done oneself or left undone.

60. Long is the night for one awake,
Long is a league to one exhausted,
Long is samsara to the childish ones
Who know not dhamma true.

79. One who drinks of dhamma sleeps at ease,
With mind calmly clear.
In dhamma made known by noble ones,
The wise one constantly delights.

81. Even as a solid rock
Does not move on account of the wind,
So are the wise not shaken
In the face of blame and praise.

82. Even as a deep lake
Is very clear and undisturbed,
So do the wise become calm,
Having heard the words of dhamma.

85. Few are they among humans,
The people who reach the shore beyond.
But these other folk
Only run along the [hither] bank.

90. To one who has gone the distance,
Who is free of sorrows, freed in every respect;
To one who has left behind all bonds,
Fever there exists not.

103. He, truly, is supreme in battle,
     Who would conquer himself alone,
     Rather than he who would conquer in battle
     A thousand, thousand men.

112. And should one live a hundred years
     Indolent, of inferior enterprise;
     Better still is one day lived
     Of one initiating enterprise, firm.

121. Think not triflingly of wrong,
     "It will not come to me!"
     With falling drops of water,
     Even a waterpot is filled.
     A childish one is filled with wrong,
     Acquiring bit by bit.

122. Think not triflingly of good,
     "It will not come to me!"
     With falling drops of water

127. That spot in the world is not found,
     Neither in the sky nor in the ocean's depths,
     Nor having entered into a cleft in mountains,
     Where abiding, one would be released from the bad deed.

128. That spot one does not find,
     Neither in the sky nor in the ocean's depths,
     Nor having entered into a cleft in mountains,
     Where abiding, death would not overwhelm one.

148. Quite wasted away is this form,
     A nest for disease, perishable.
     This putrid accumulation breaks up.
     For life has its end in death.

165. By oneself is wrong done,
     By oneself is one defiled.
     By oneself wrong is not done,
     By oneself, surely, is one cleansed.
     One cannot purify another;
     Purity and impurity are in oneself [alone].

171. Come ye, look at this world—
     Like an adorned royal chariot—
     Wherein childish ones are immersed;
     No clinging there is among those who really know.

188. Many for refuge go
     To mountains and to forests,

To shrines that are groves or trees—
Humans who are threatened by fear.

189. This is not a refuge secure,
This refuge is not the highest.
Having come to this refuge,
One is not released from all misery.

190. But who to the Buddha, Dhamma,
And Sangha as refuge has gone,
Sees with full insight
The four noble truths;

191. Misery, the arising of misery,
And the transcending of misery,
The noble Eightfold Path
Leading to the allaying of misery.

192. This, indeed, is a refuge secure.
This is the highest refuge.
Having come to this refuge,
One is released from all misery.

193. Hard to come by is a person of nobility;
Not everywhere is he born.
Wherever that wise one is born,
That family prospers in happiness.

201. Winning, one engenders enmity;
Miserably sleeps the defeated.
The one at peace sleeps pleasantly,
Having abandoned victory and defeat.

235. Like a yellow leaf are you now;
And even Yama's men have appeared for you;
And at the threshold of departure you stand;
But even the journey's provisions you do not have.

251. There is no fire like passion.
There is no grip like ill will.
There is no snare like delusion.
There is no river like craving.

258. One is not a learned one
Merely because one speaks much.
The one secure, without enmity, without fear,
Is called a "learned one."

287. That man of entangled mind,
Inebriated by sons and cattle,

Death carries away
Like a great flood, a sleeping village.

322. Excellent are tamed mules,
     Thoroughbreds and horses of Sindh,
     Also tuskers, great elephants.
     But better than them is one who has subdued oneself.

334. The craving of a person who lives heedlessly
     Grows like a *māluvā* creeper.
     He moves from beyond to beyond,
     Like a monkey, in a forest, wishing for fruit.

338. As long as the roots are unharmed, firm,
     A tree, though topped, grows yet again.
     Just so, when the latent craving is not rooted out,
     This suffering arises again and again.

348. Let go in front, let go behind, let go in between!
     Gone to the further shore of existence,
     With mind released as to "everything,"
     You shall not again come upon birth and old age.

354. The gift of dhamma prevails over every gift,
     The flavor of dhamma prevails over every flavor,
     The delight in dhamma prevails over every delight,
     The dissolution of craving subdues all suffering.

355. Possessions strike down one deficient in wisdom,
     But not those seeking the beyond.
     Through craving for possessions, one deficient in wisdom
     Strikes oneself down as one would the others.

358. For fields, grasses are the bane,
     For humankind, confusion is the bane.
     Hence, to those free from confusion
     What is given yields much fruit.

360. Restraint with the eye is commendable,
     Commendable is restraint with the ear.
     Restraint with the nose is commendable,
     Commendable is restraint with the tongue.

361. Restraint with the body is commendable,
     Commendable is restraint with speech.
     Restraint with the mind is commendable,
     Commendable is restraint in all [the senses].
     The bhikkhu who is restrained in all [the senses],
     Is freed from all suffering.

362. The one restrained in hand, restrained in foot,
     Restrained in speech, the one of best restraint,
     Having delight in introspection, composed, solitary, contented—
     That one they call a bhikkhu.

369. O bhikkhu, bail out this boat.
     Bailed out, it shall go quickly for you.
     Having cut away both lust and hate,
     You shall then reach Nibbāna.

378. A bhikkhu, with body pacified, speech pacified,
     Who is possessed of peace, well composed,
     Who has thrown out the world's material things,
     Is called the "one at peace."

382. Truly, a young bhikkhu
     Who engages in the Buddha's instruction
     This world illumines,
     Like the moon set free from a cloud.

385. For whom the farther shore or the nearer shore
     Or both does not exist,
     Who is free of distress, unyoked,
     That one I call a *brāhmaṇa.*

393. Not by matted hair, or by clan,
     Or by birth does one become a *brāhmaṇa.*
     In whom is truth and dhamma,
     He is the pure one, and he is the *brāhmaṇa.*

394. What's the use of your matted hair, O you of poor insight?
     What's the use of your deerskin garment?
     Within you is the jungle;
     The exterior you groom.

402. Who comes to understand, even here,
     The destruction of sorrow,
     Who has put aside the burden, who is free of the bonds,
     That one I call a *brāhmaṇa.*

411. In whom are not found attachments,
     Who is without doubts due to understanding,
     Who has attained the plunge into the Deathless,
     That one I call a *brāhmaṇa.*

416. Who, here, having renounced craving,
     Would go forth, a homeless one,
     In whom is extinct craving and existence,
     That one I call a *brāhmaṇa.*

Buddhaghosa on the Recollection of Death

Edward Conze (translator)

Buddhaghosa was a great Indian scholar of the fifth century C.E. *He is believed to have been the compiler of most of the ancient commentaries on the Pali Canon, which are second in importance only to the Canon itself, and he was the author of a treatise on Buddhist doctrine entitled* The Path of Purity *(the* Visuddhimagga*), from which the following selection is taken.*

The translator is again Edward Conze, introduced earlier as the translator of Buddhist Scriptures.

In "the recollection of death," the word "death" refers to the cutting off of the life-force which lasts for the length of one existence. Whoso wants to develop it, should in seclusion and solitude wisely set up attention with the words: "Death will take place, the life-force will be cut off," or (simply), "Death, death." But if somebody takes up an unwise attitude (to this problem of death), then sorrow will arise in him when he recalls the death of a loved person, like the grief of a mother when she thinks of the death of the dear child whom she has borne; and joy will arise when he recalls the death of an unloved person, like the rejoicing of a foe who thinks of an enemy's death; and when he recalls the death of an indifferent person, no perturbation will arise in him, just as the man who all day long burns corpses looks on dead bodies without perturbation; when, finally, he recalls his own death, violent trembling arises in him, as in a frightened man who sees before him a murderer with his sword drawn. And all this is the result of a lack in mindfulness, (reasonable) perturbation, and cognition.

Therefore the Yogin should look upon beings killed or dead here and there, and advert to the death of beings who died after having first seen prosperity. To this (observation) he should apply mindfulness, perturbation and cognition, and set up attention with the words, "Death will take place," and so on. When he proceeds thus, he proceeds wisely, i.e., he proceeds expediently. For only if someone proceeds in this way will his hindrances be impeded, will mindfulness be established with death for its object, and will some degree of concentration be achieved.

If this is not enough (to produce access), he should recall death from the following eight points of view:

1. As a murderer, standing in front of him.
2. From the (inevitable) loss of (all) achievement.
3. By inference.
4. Because one's body is shared with many others.
5. From the weakness of the stuff of life.
6. From the absence of signs.
7. Because the life-span is limited.
8. From the shortness of the moment.

1. *"As a murderer standing in front of him"* means, "as if a murderer were standing in front of him." One should recall that death stands in front of us just like a murderer, who confronts us with his drawn sword raised to our neck, intending to cut off our head. And why? Because death comes together with birth, and deprives us of life.

(a) As a budding mushroom shoots upwards carrying soil on its head, so beings from their birth onwards carry decay and death along with them. For death has come together with birth, because everyone who is born must certainly die. Therefore this living being, from the time of his birth onwards, moves in the direction of death, without turning back even for a moment; (b) just as the sun, once it has arisen, goes forward in the direction of its setting, and does not turn back for a moment on the path it traverses in that direction; (c) or as a mountain stream rapidly tears down on its way, flows and rushes along, without turning back even for a moment. To one who goes along like that, death is always near; (d) just as brooks get extinguished when dried up by the summer heat; (e) as fruits are bound to fall from a tree early one day when their stalks have been rotted away by the early morning mists; (f) as earthenware breaks when hit with a hammer; (g) and as dewdrops are dispersed when touched by the rays of the sun. Thus death, like a murderer with a drawn sword, has come together with birth. Like the murderer who has raised his sword to our neck, so it deprives us of life. And there is no chance that it might desist.

2. *"By the failure of achievement,"* which means: Here in this world achievement prospers only so long as it is not overwhelmed by failure. And there is no single achievement that stands out as having transcended the (threat of) failure.

Moreover, all health ends in sickness, all youth in old age, all life in death; wherever one may dwell in the world, one is afflicted by birth, overtaken by old age, oppressed by sickness, struck down by deat... Through realizing that the achievements of life thus end in the failure of death, he should recollect death from the failure of achievement.

3. *"By inference,"* means that one draws an inference for oneself from others. And it is with seven kinds of person that one should compare oneself: those great in fame, great in merit, great in might, great in magical power, great in wisdom, Pratyekabuddhas, and fully enlightened Buddhas.

In what manner? This death has assuredly befallen even those (kings) like Mahasammata, Mandhatu, Mahasudassana, Dalhanemin, and Nimippabhuti, who possessed great fame, a great retinue, and who abounded in treasures and might. How then could it be that it will not befall also me?

> The greatly famous, noble kings,
> Like Mahasammata and others,
> They all fell down before the might of death.
> What need is there to speak of men like us?

(And so for the other kinds of distinction.)

In this way he draws from others, who have achieved great fame, and so on, and inference as to himself, i.e., that death is common to himself and to them. When he recalls that, "as for those distinguished beings so also for me death will take place," then the subject of meditation attains to access.

4. *"Because one's body is shared with many others"*: This body is the common property of many. It is shared by the eighty classes of parasitic animals, and it incurs death as a result of their turbulence. Likewise it belongs to the many hundreds of diseases which arise within it, as well as to the outside occasions of death, such as snakes, scorpions, and so on.

For just as, flying from all directions, arrows, spears, lances, stones, and so on, fall on a target placed at the cross roads, so on the body also all kinds of misfortune are bound to descend. And through the onslaught of these misfortunes it incurs death. Hence the Lord has said: "Here, monks, a monk, when the day is over and night comes round, thinks to himself: many are, to be sure, for me the occasions of death: a snake, or a scorpion, or a centipede may bite me; thereby I may lose my life, and that may act as an obstacle (to my spiritual progress). Or I may stumble and fall, or the food I have eaten may upset me, or the bile may trouble me, or the phlegm, or the winds which cut like knives; and thereby I may lose my life, and that may act as an obstacle" (Anguttara III, 306).

5. *"From the weakness of the stuff of life"*: This life-force is without strength and feeble. For the life of beings is bound up with (a) breathing in and out, (b) the postures, (c) heat and cold, (d) the (four) great primaries, and (e) with food.

(a) It goes on only as long as it can obtain an even functioning of breathing in and out; as soon, however, as air issues from the nose without re-entering, or enters without going out again, one is considered dead. (b) Again, it goes on only as long as it can obtain an even functioning of the four postures; but through the preponderance of one or the other of these the vital activities are cut off. (c) Again, it goes on as long as it can obtain the even functioning of heat and cold; but it fails when oppressed by excessive heat or cold. (d) Again, it goes on as long as it can obtain the even functioning of the (four) great primaries; but through the disturbance of one or the other of them (i.e.) of the solid, fluid, etc., element, the life of even a strong person is extinguished, be it by the stiffening of his body, or because his body has become wet and putrid from dysentery, and so on, or because it is overcome by a high temperature, or because his sinews are torn. (e) Again, life goes on only as long as one obtains solid food, at suitable times; when one cannot get food, it gets extinguished.

6. *"From the absence of signs,"* because one cannot determine (the time of

death, etc.), "From the absence of a definite limit," that is the meaning. For one says with regard to the death of beings:

(a) Life's duration, (b) sickness, (c) time,
(d) The place where the body is cast off, (e) the future destiny.
These are five things about this animate world,
Which never can be known for certain, for no sign exists.

(a) There is no sign (i.e., no clear indication) of the duration of life, because one cannot determine that so long will one live, and no longer. For beings may die in the first embryonic state, or in the second, third, or fourth, or after one month, or two, three, four, five, or ten months, at the time when they issue from the womb, and further still at any time within or beyond one hundred years.

(b) There is also no sign of the (fatal) sickness, insofar as one cannot determine that beings will die of this or that sickness, and no other; for beings may die from a disease of the eyes, or the ears, or any other.

(c) There is also no sign of the time, insofar as one cannot determine that one will have to die just at this time of day and no other; for beings may die in the morning, or at midday, or at any other time.

(d) There is also no sign as to the laying down of the body; for, when one is dying, one cannot determine that the body should be laid down just here and not anywhere else. For the body of those born within a village may fall away outside the village; and those born outside a village may perish inside one; those born on land may perish in water, those born in water may perish on land; and so this might be expanded in various ways.

(e) There is also no sign of the future destiny, insofar as one cannot determine that one who has deceased there will be reborn here. For those who have deceased in the world of the gods may be reborn among men, and those deceased in the world of men may be reborn in the world of the gods, or anywhere else. In this way the world revolves round the five kinds of rebirth like an ox yoked to an oil-pressing mill.

7. *"Because the life-span is limited."* Brief is the life of men at present; he lives long who lives for a hundred years, or a little more. Hence the Lord has said: "Short, oh monks, is the life-span of men, transient, having its sequel elsewhere; one should do what is wholesome, one should lead a holy life, no one who is born can escape death; he lives long who lives for a hundred years, or a little more.

> Short is the life of men, the good must scorn it,
> And act as if their turban were ablaze.
> For death is surely bound to come." (Samyutta I, 108)

Furthermore, the whole Araka-Sutta (Anguttara IV, 136–38) with its seven similes should be considered in detail: (i.e., Life is fleeting, and passes away quickly, (a) like dewdrops on the tips of blades of grass, which soon dry up when the sun rises; (b) or like the bubbles which rain causes in water, and which burst soon; (c) or like the line made by a stick in water, which vanishes soon; (d) or like a mountain brook, which does not stand still for a moment; (e) or like a gob of spittle spat out with ease; (f) or like a lump of meat thrown into a hot iron pot, which does not last long;

(g) or like a cow about to be slaughtered; each time she raises her foot she comes nearer to death).

Furthermore, He said: "If, oh monks, a monk develops the recollection of death in such a way that he thinks—'may I just live for one day and night—for one day—for as long as it takes to eat an alms-meal—for as long as it takes to chew and swallow four or five lumps of food—and I will then attend to the Lord's religion, and much surely will still be done by me'—then such monks are said to lead heedless lives, and they develop in a sluggish way the recollection of death which aims at the extinction of the outflows. But if, oh monks, a monk develops the recollection of death in such a way that he thinks—'may I just live for so long as it takes to chew and swallow one lump of food—were I to live just long enough to breathe in after breathing out, or to breathe out after breathing in'—then such monks are said to lead watchful lives, and they develop keenly the recollection of death which aims at the extinction of the outflows" (Anguttara III, 305–6). And the span of life is brief like a mere swallowing of four or five lumps of food, and it cannot be trusted.

8. *"From the shortness of the moment."* In ultimate reality beings live only for an exceedingly brief moment, for it (life) lasts just as long as one single moment of thought. Just as a cart-wheel, whether it rolls along or stands still, always rests on one single spot of the rim; just so the life of beings lasts for one single moment of thought. As soon as that thought has ceased, the being also is said to have ceased. As it has been said: "In the past thought-moment one has lived, but one does not live and one will not live in it; in the future thought-moment one has not lived, but one does live, and one will live; in the present thought-moment one has not lived, but one does live, and one will not live in it.

> Our life and our whole personality,
> All our joys and all our pains,
> Are bound up with one single thought,
> And rapidly that moment passes.
> And those skandhas which are stopped,
> For one who's dying, or one remaining here,
> They all alike have gone away,
> And are no longer reproduced.
> Nothing is born from what is unproduced;
> One lives by that which is at present there.
> When thought breaks up, then all the world is dead.
> So't is when final truth the concept guides."
> (Nidessa I, 42)

Result: When he recollects (death) from one or the other of these eight points of view, his mind by repeated attention becomes practised therein, mindfulness with death for its object is established, the hindrances are impeded, the Jhana-limbs become manifest. But, because of the intrinsic nature of the object and the agitation it produces, the Jhana only reaches access and not full ecstasy.

Benefits: And the monk who is devoted to this recollection of death is always watchful, he feels disgust for all forms of becoming, he forsakes the hankering after life, he disapproves of evil, he does not hoard up many things, and with regard to the necessities of life he is free from the taint of stinginess. He gains familiarity with the notion of impermanence, and, when he follows that up, also the notions of ill and not-self will stand out to him. At the hour of death, beings who have not developed the recollection of death, feel fear, fright and bewilderment, as if they were suddenly attacked by wild beasts, ghosts, snakes, robbers or murderers. He, on the contrary, dies without fear and bewilderment. If in this very life he does not win deathlessness, he is, on the dissolution of his body, bound for a happy destiny.

The Mahayana and the Ideal of the Bodhisattva

Ananda Coomaraswamy

Born in Ceylon of an English mother and a Ceylonese father, Ananda Coomaraswamy (1877–1947) was raised and educated in England, receiving a Doctor of Science degree (in geology) from the University of London. Circumstances, however, led to an interest in art and then to wide-ranging scholarly research in art history, philology, religion, and philosophy. From 1917 until his death he was Fellow for Research in Indian, Persian, and Muhammadan Art at the Museum of Fine Arts in Boston. He lectured widely on art and wrote over a dozen books, his pen "an instrument of precision."* His titles include Hinduism and Buddhism, A New Approach to the Vedas, Myths and Legends of the Hindus and Buddhists, *and* Buddha and the Gospel of Buddhism, *from which the following selection is taken. Coomaraswamy's* Selected Papers *have been collected in two volumes as Bollingen Series LXXXIX; a third volume is* His Life and Work *by Roger Lipsy.*

The Mahāyāna or Great Vessel is so-called by its adherents, in contradistinction to the Hīnayāna or Little Vessel of primitive Buddhism, because the former offers to all beings in all worlds salvation by faith and love as well as by knowledge, while the latter only avails to convey over the rough sea of Becoming to the farther shore of Nibbāna those few strong souls who require no external spiritual aid nor the consolation of Worship. The Hīnayāna, like the 'unshown way' of those who seek the *'nirguna Brahman,'* is exceeding hard;[1] whereas the burden of the Mahāyāna is light, and does not require that a man should immediately renounce the world and all the affections of humanity. The manifestation of the Body of the Law, says the Mahāyāna, is adapted to the various needs of the children of the Buddha; whereas the Hīnayāna is only of avail to those who have left their spiritual childhood far behind them. The Hīnayāna emphasizes the necessity of saving knowledge, and aims at the salvation of the individual, and refuses to develop the mystery of Nib-

---

*Robert Allerton Parker, in Ananda Coomaraswamy, *Am I My Brother's Keeper* (Freeport, N.Y.: Books for Libraries Press, 1967), p. ix.

1. In the words of Behmen (*Supersensual Life,* Dialogue 2): "But, alas how hard it is for the Will to sink into nothing, to attract nothing, to imagine nothing."

From Amanda Coomaraswamy, *Buddha and the Gospel of Buddhism,* 1916.

bāna in a positive sense; the Mahāyāna lays as much or greater stress on love, and aims at the salvation of every sentient being, and finds in Nirvāna the One Reality, which is 'Void' only in the sense that it is free from the limitations of every phase of the limited or contingent experience of which we have empirical knowledge. The Buddhists of the primitive school, on the other hand, naturally do not accept the name of the 'Lesser Vessel,' and as true Protestants they raise objection to the theological and aesthetic accommodation of the true doctrine to the necessities of human nature.

Opinions thus differ as to whether we may regard the Mahāyāna as a development or a degeneration. Even the professed exponents of the Hīnayāna have their doubts. Thus in one place Professor Rhys Davids speaks of the Bodhisattva doctrine as the *bīrana*-weed which "drove out the doctrine of the Ariyan path," and the weed "is not attractive":[2] while in another, Mrs. Rhys Davids writes of the cool detachment of the Arahat, that perhaps "a yet more saintly Sāriputta would have aspired yet further, even to an infinite series of rebirths, wherein he might, with evergrowing power and self-devotion, work for the furtherance of the religious evolution of his fellows," adding that "social and religious ideals evolve out of, yea, and even beyond the finished work and time-straitened vision of the Arahants of old."[3] Perhaps we need not determine the relative value of either school: the way of knowledge will ever appeal to some, and the way of love and action to others, and the latter the majority. Those who are saved by knowledge stand apart from the world and its hopes and fears, offering to the world only that knowledge which shall enable others to stand aside in the same way: those others who are moved by their love and wisdom to perpetual activity—in whom the will to life is dead, but the will to power yet survives in its noblest and most impersonal forms—attain at last the same goal, and in the meanwhile effect a reconciliation of religion with the world, and the union of renunciation with action.

The development of the Mahāyāna is in fact the overflowing of Buddhism from the limits of the Order into the life of the world; into whatever devious channels Buddhism may have ultimately descended, are we to say that that identification with the life of the world, with all its consequences in ethic and aesthetic, was a misfortune? Few who are acquainted with the history of Asiatic culture would maintain any such thesis.

Mahāyānists do not hesitate to describe the Hīnayāna ideal as selfish; and we have indicated in several places to what extent it must in any case be called narrow. But the Mahāyānists—not to speak of Christian critics of the Hīnayāna—do not sufficiently realize that a selfish being could not possibly become an Arahat, who must be free from even the conception of an ego, and still more from every form of ego-assertion. The selfishness of the would-be Arahat is more apparent than real. The ideal of self-culture is not opposed to that of self-sacrifice: in any perfectly harmonious development these seemingly opposite tendencies are reconciled. To achieve this reconciliation, to combine renunciation with growth, knowledge with love, stillness with activity, is the problem of all ethics. Curiously enough, though

2. Dialogues of the Buddha, ii, p. 1.

3. *Psalms of the Brethren*, p. xlviii.

its solution has often been attempted by oriental religions, it has never been so clearly enunciated in the west as by the 'irreligious' Nietzsche—the latest of the mystics—whose ideal of the Superman combines the Will to Power . . . with the Bestowing Virtue. . . .

If the ideal of the Private Buddha seems to be a selfish one, we may reply that the Great Man can render to his fellows no higher service than to realize the highest possible state of his being. From the Unity of life we cannot but deduce the identity of (true) self-interest with the (true) interest of others. While therefore the Mahāyānists may justly claim that their system is indeed a greater vessel of salvation in the sense of greater convenience, or better adaptation to the needs of a majority of voyagers, they cannot on the other hand justly accuse the captain and the crew of the smaller ship of selfishness. Those who seek to the farther shore may select the means best suited to their own needs: the final goal is one and the same.

The most essential part of the Mahāyāna is its emphasis on the Bodhisattva ideal, which replaces that of Arahatta, or ranks before it. Whereas the Arahat strives most earnestly for Nirvāna, the Bodhisattva as firmly refuses to accept the final release. "Forasmuch as there is the will that all sentient beings should be altogether made free, I will not forsake my fellow creatures."[4] The Bodhisattva is he in whom the Bodhicitta or heart of wisdom is fully expanded. In a sense, we are all Bodhisattvas, and indeed all Buddhas, only that in us by reason of ignorance and imperfection in love the glory of the Bodhi-heart is not yet made manifest. But those are specially called Bodhisattvas who with specific determination dedicate all the activities of their future and present lives to the task of saving the world. They do not merely contemplate, but feel, all the sorrow of the world, and because of their love they cannot be idle, but expend their virtue with supernatural generosity. It is said of Gautama Buddha, for example, that there is no spot on earth where he has not in some past life sacrificed his life for the sake of others, while the whole story of his last incarnation related in the *Vessantara Jātaka* relates the same unstinting generosity, which does not shrink even from the giving away of wife and children. But Buddhahood once attained, according to the old school, it remains for others to work out their salvation alone: "Be ye lamps unto yourselves," in the last words of Gautama. According to the Mahāyāna, however, even the attainment of Buddhahood does not involve indifference to the sorrow of the world; the work of salvation is perpetually carried on by the Bodhisattva emanations of the supreme Buddhas, just as the work of the Father is done by Jesus.

The Bodhisattvas are specially distinguished from the Srāvakas (Arahats) and Pacceka-Buddhas or 'Private Buddhas,' who have become followers of the Buddha 'for the sake of their own complete Nirvāna':[5] for the Bodhisattvas enter upon their course "out of compassion to the world, for the benefit, weal, and happiness of the

---

4. *Avatamsaka Sūtra.*

5. Hindus would express this by saying that Srāvakas and Pacceka-Buddhas choose the path of Immediate Salvation: Bodhisattvas, that of Ultimate Salvation. "The deferred path of Liberation is the path of all Bhaktas. It is the path of compassion or service."—P. N. Sinha, *Commentary on the Bhāgavata Purāna,* p. 359.

world at large, both gods and men, for the sake of the complete Nirvāna of all beings. . . . Therefore they are called Bodhisattva Mahāsattva."[6]

A doctrine specially associated with the Bodhisattva ideal is that of the *parivarta* or turning over of ethical merit to the advantage of others, which amounts very nearly to the doctrine of vicarious atonement. Whereas in early Buddhism it is emphasized that each life is entirely separate from every other (also a Jaina doctrine, and no doubt derived from the Sāmkhya conception of a plurality of Purushas), the Mahāyāna insists on the interdependence and even the identity of all life; and this position affords a logical basis for the view that the merit acquired by one may be devoted to the good of others. This is a peculiarly amiable feature in late Buddhism; we find, for example, that whoever accomplishes a good deed, such as a work of charity or a pilgrimage, adds the prayer that the merit may be shared by all sentient beings.

.   .   .

The Mahāyānist doctors recognize ten stations in the spiritual evolution of the Bodhisattva, beginning with the first awakening of the Wisdom-heart (Bodhicitta) in the warmth of compassion (karuna) and the light of divine knowledge *(prajñā).* These stations are those of 'joy,' 'purity,' 'effulgence,' 'burning,' 'hard to achieve,' 'showing the face,' 'going afar off,' 'not moving to and fro,' 'good intelligence,' and 'dharma-cloud.' It is in the first station that the Bodhisattva makes those pregnant resolutions *(pranidhāna)* which determine the course of his future lives. An example of such a vow is the resolution of Avalokitesvara not to accept salvation until the least particle of dust shall have attained to Buddhahood before him.

It may be mentioned that the course *(cariyā)* of the Bodhisattva has this advantage, that he never comes to birth in any purgatory, nor in any unfavourable condition on earth. Nor is the Bodhisattva required to cultivate a disgust for the conditions of life; he does not practise a meditation of Foul Things, like the aspirant for Arahatta. The Bodhisattva simply recognizes that the conditions of life have come to be what they are, that it is in the nature *(tattva, bhutathā,* suchness) of things to be so, and he takes them accordingly for what they are worth. This position is nowhere more tersely summed up than in the well-known Japanese verselet—

> Granted this dewdrop world be but a dewdrop world,
>   This granted, yet . . .

Thus the new Buddhist law was in no way puritanical, and did not inculcate an absolute detachment. Pleasure indeed is not to be sought as an end in itself, but it need not be rejected as it arises incidentally. The Bodhisattva shares in the life of the world; for example, he has a wife, that his supernatural generosity may be seen in the gift of wife and children, and for the same reason he may be the possessor of power and wealth. If by reason of attachment and this association with the world some venial sins are unavoidably committed, that is of little consequence, and such sins are wiped away in the love of others: the cardinal sins of hatred and self-think-

6. *Saddharmapundarīka Sūtra.*

ing cannot be imagined in him in whom the heart of wisdom has been awakened. It must not, however, be supposed that the Mahāyāna in any way relaxes the rule of the Order; and even in the matter of the remission of sins of the laity it is only minor and inevitable shortcomings that are considered, and not deliberate deeds of evil. And if the Mahāyāna doctors preach the futility of remorse and discouragement, on the other hand they are by no means quietists, but advocate a mysticism fully as practical as that of Ruysbroeck.

The idea of the Bodhisattva corresponds to that of the Hero, the Superman, the Saviour, and the Avatār of other systems. In this connexion it is interesting to note that legitimate pride—the will to power, conjoined with the bestowing virtue—is by no means alien to the Bodhisattva character, but on the contrary, "In respect of three things may pride be borne—man's works, his temptations, and his power," and the exposition follows: "The pride of works lies in the thought 'for me alone is the task.'[7] This world, enslaved by passion, is powerless to accomplish its own weal; then must I do it for them, for I am not impotent like them. Shall another do a lowly task while I am standing by? If I in my pride will not do it, better it is that my pride perish. . . . Then with firm spirit I will undo the occasions of undoing; if I should be conquered by them, my ambition to conquer the threefold world would be a jest. I will conquer all; none shall conquer me. This is the pride that I will bear, for I am the son of the Conqueror Lions![8] . . . Surrounded by the troop of the passions man should become a thousand times prouder, and be as unconquerable to their hordes as a lion to flocks of deer . . . so, into whatever straits he may come, he will not fall into the power of the Passions. He will utterly give himself over to whatever task arrives, greedy for the work . . . how can he whose happiness is work itself be happy in doing no work? He will hold himself in readiness, so that even before a task comes to him he is prepared to turn to every course. As the seed of the cotton-tree is swayed at the coming and going of the wind, so will he be obedient to his resolution; and thus divine power is gained."[9]

We may remark here an important distinction between the Mahāyāna and the Hīnayāna lies in the fact that the former is essentially mythical and unhistorical; the believer is, indeed, warned—precisely as the worshipper of Krishna is warned in the Vaishnava scriptures that the Krishna Līlā is not a history, but a process for ever unfolded in the heart of man—that matters of historical fact are without religious significance. On this account, notwithstanding its more popular form, the Mahāyāna has been justly called 'more philosophical' than the Hīnayāna, "because under the forms of religious or mystical imagery it expresses the universal, whereas the Hīnayāna cannot set itself free from the domination of the historical fact."

7. Cf. Blake:

> But when Jesus was crucified,
> Then was perfected His galling pride.

8. Buddha is often spoken of as Conqueror (Jina—a term more familiar in connexion with the followers of Mahāvīra, the 'Jainas') and as Lion (Sākyasinha, the lion of the Sākya race).

9. From the *Bodhicaryāvatāra* of Shānti Deva, translated by L. D. Barnett, 1902.

Buddhism as a Way of Life
Walpola Rahula

One of the first points made by Heinrich Zimmer in his essay "Buddhahood," the introductory essay for this chapter, was that "in essence Buddhism is meant only for the happy few." In the light of the severe demands it places upon the individual, Buddhism "was never intended to interfere with either the life or the habits of the multitude." In contrast, the present essay, by a distinguished Buddhist and scholar, asserts Buddhism is meant for everyone.

Walpola Rahula may be addressed as the "Reverend Doctor" Rahula: he has had the education and training of a Buddhist monk in Ceylon, and he held positions of responsibility in monastic institutions in that country. He holds also a doctorate from Ceylon University and was for years on the faculty at the Sorbonne. He is the author of History of Buddhism in Ceylon *and* The Heritage of the Buddha. *The following essay is from his* What the Buddha Taught.

There are some who believe that Buddhism is so lofty and sublime a system that it cannot be practised by ordinary men and women in this workaday world of ours, and that one has to retire from it to a monastery, or to some quiet place, if one desires to be a true Buddhist.

This is a sad misconception, due evidently to a lack of understanding of the teaching of the Buddha. People run to such hasty and wrong conclusions as a result of their hearing, or reading casually, something about Buddhism written by someone, who, as he has not understood the subject in all its aspects, gives only a partial and lopsided view of it. The Buddha's teaching is meant not only for monks in monasteries, but also for ordinary men and women living at home with their families. The Noble Eightfold Path, which is the Buddhist way of life, is meant for all, without distinction of any kind.

. . .

It may be agreeable for certain people to live a retired life in a quiet place away from noise and disturbance. But it is certainly more praiseworthy and courageous to practise Buddhism living among your fellow beings, helping them and being of service to them. It may perhaps be useful in some cases for a man to live in retirement for a time in order to improve his mind and character, as preliminary moral, spiritual, and intellectual training, to be strong enough to come out later and help others. But if a man lives all his life in solitude, thinking only of his own happiness and "salvation," without caring for his fellows, this surely is not in keeping with the Buddha's teaching which is based on love, compassion, and service to others.

One might now ask: If a man can follow Buddhism while living the life of an ordinary layman, why was the Sangha, the Order of monks, established by the Buddha? The Order provides opportunity for those who are willing to devote their lives not only to their own spiritual and intellectual development, but also to the service of others. An ordinary layman with a family cannot be expected to devote his whole life to the service of others, wheras a monk, who has no family responsibilities or any other worldly ties, is in a position to devote his whole life "for the good of the many, for the happiness of the many" according to the Buddha's advice. That is how in the course of history, the Buddhist monastery became not only a spiritual centre, but also a centre of learning and culture.

The *Sigāla-sutta* (No. 31 of the *Dīgha-nikāya*) shows with what great respect the layman's life, his family, and social relations are regarded by the Buddha.

A young man named Sigala used to worship the six cardinal points of the heavens—east, south, west, north, nadir, and zenith—in obeying and observing the last advice given him by his dying father. The Buddha told the young man that in the "noble discipline" *(ariyassa vinaye)* of his teaching the six directions were different. According to his "noble discipline" the six directions were: east: parents; south: teachers; west: wife and children; north: friends, relatives, and neighbours; nadir: servants, workers and employees; zenith: religious men.

"One should worship these six directions," said the Buddha. Here the word "worship" *(namasseyya)* is very significant, for one worships something sacred, something worthy of honour and respect. These six family and social groups mentioned above are treated in Buddhism as sacred, worthy of respect and worship. But how is one to "worship" them? The Buddha says that one could "worship" them only by performing one's duties towards them. These duties are explained in his discourse to Sigala.

First: Parents are sacred to their children. The Buddha says: "Parents are called Brahma" *(Brahmāti mātāpitaro).* The term *Brahma* denotes the highest and most sacred conception in Indian thought, and in it the Buddha includes parents. So in good Buddhist families at the present time children literally "worship" their parents every day, morning and evening. They have to perform certain duties towards their parents according to the "noble discipline": they should look after their parents in their old age; should do whatever they have to do on their behalf; should maintain the honour of the family and continue the family tradition; should protect the wealth earned by their parents; and perform their funeral rites after their death. Parents, in their turn, have certain responsibilities towards their children: they should keep their children away from evil courses; should engage them in good and profitable activities; should give them a good education; should marry them into good families; and should hand over the property to them in due course.

Second: The relation between teacher and pupil: a pupil should respect and be obedient to his teacher; should attend to his needs if any; should study earnestly. And the teacher, in his turn, should train and shape his pupil properly; should teach him well; should introduce him to his friends; and should try to procure him security or employment when his education is over.

Third: The relation between husband and wife: love between husband and wife is considered almost religious or sacred. It is called *sadāra-Brahmacariya* "sacred family life." Here, too, the significance of the term *Brahma* should be noted: the highest respect is given to this relationship. Wives and husbands should be faithful, respectful, and devoted to each other, and they have certain duties towards each other: the husband should always honour his wife and never be wanting in respect to her; he should love her and be faithful to her; should secure her position and comfort; and should please her by presenting her with clothing and jewellery. (The fact that the Buddha did not forget to mention even such a thing as the gifts a husband should make to his wife shows how understanding and sympathetic were his humane feelings towards ordinary human emotions.) The wife, in her turn, should supervise and look after household affairs; should entertain guests, visitors, friends, relatives and employees; should love and be faithful to her husband; should protect his earnings; should be clever and energetic in all activities.

Fourth: The relation between friends, relatives and neighbours: they should be hospitable and charitable to one another; should speak pleasantly and agreeably; should work for each other's welfare; should be on equal terms with one another; should not quarrel among themselves; should help each other in need; and should not forsake each other in difficulty.

Fifth: The relation between master and servant: the master or the employer has several obligations towards his servant or his employee: work should be assigned according to ability and capacity; adequate wages should be paid; medical needs should be provided; occasional donations or bonuses should be granted. The servant or employee, in his turn, should be diligent and not lazy; honest and obedient and not cheat his master; he should be earnest in his work.

Sixth: The relation between the religious (lit. recluses and brāhmaṇas) and the laity: lay people should look after the material needs of the religious with love and respect; the religious with a loving heart should impart knowledge and learning to the laity, and lead them along the good path away from evil.

We see then that the lay life, with its family and social relations, is included in the "noble discipline," and is within the framework of the Buddhist way of life, as the Buddha envisaged it.

So in the *Saṃyutta-nikāya,* one of the oldest Pali texts, Sakka, the king of the gods *(devas),* declares that he worships not only the monks who live a virtuous holy life, but also "lay disciples *(upāsaka)* who perform meritorious deeds, who are virtuous, and maintain their families righteously."

If one desires to become a Buddhist, there is no initiation ceremony (or baptism) which one has to undergo. (But to become a *bhikkhu,* a member of the Order of the *Sangha,* one has to undergo a long process of disciplinary training and education.) If one understands the Buddha's teaching, and if one is convinced that his teaching is the right Path and if one tries to follow it, then one is a Buddhist. But according to the unbroken age-old tradition in Buddhist countries, one is considered a Buddhist if one takes the Buddha, the *Dhamma* (the Teaching), and the *Sangha* (the Order of Monks)—generally called "the Triple-Gem"—as one's refuges, and undertakes to observe the Five Precepts *(Pañca-sīla)*—the minimum moral obligations of a lay Buddhist. . . .

There are no external rites or ceremonies which a Buddhist has to perform. Buddhism is a way of life, and what is essential is following the Noble Eightfold Path. Of course there are in all Buddhist countries simple and beautiful ceremonies on religious occasions. There are shrines with statues of the Buddha, *stūpas* or *dāgābas* and Bo-trees in monasteries where Buddhists worship, offer flowers, light lamps, and burn incense. This should not be likened to prayer in theistic religions; it is only a way of paying homage to the memory of the Master who showed the way. These traditional observances, though inessential, have their value in satisfying the religious emotions and needs of those who are less advanced intellectually and spiritually, and helping them gradually along the Path.

Those who think that Buddhism is interested only in lofty ideals, high moral and philosophical thought, and that it ignores the social and economic welfare of people, are wrong. The Buddha was interested in the happiness of men. To him happiness was not possible without leading a pure life based on moral and spiritual principles. But he knew that leading such a life was hard in unfavourable material and social conditions.

Buddhism does not consider material welfare as an end in itself: it is only a means to an end—a higher and nobler end. But it is a means which is indispensable, indispensable in achieving a higher purpose for man's happiness. So Buddhism recognizes the need of certain minimum material conditions favourable to spiritual success—even that of a monk engaged in meditation in some solitary place.

The Buddha did not take life out of the context of its social and economic background; he looked at it as a whole, in all its social, economic, and political aspects. His teachings on ethical, spiritual, and philosophical problems are fairly well known. But little is known, particularly in the West, about his teaching on social, economic, and political matters. Yet there are numerous discourses dealing with these scattered throughout the ancient Buddhist texts. Let us take only a few examples.

The *Cakkavattisīhanāda-sutta* of the *Dīgha-nikāya* (No. 26) clearly states that poverty *(dāḷiddiya)* is the cause of immorality and crimes such as theft, falsehood, violence, hatred, cruelty, etc. Kings in ancient times, like governments today, tried to suppress crime through punishment. The *Kūṭadanta-sutta* of the same *Nikāya* explains how futile this is. It says that this method can never be successful. Instead the Buddha suggests that, in order to eradicate crime, the economic condition of the people should be improved: grain and other facilities for agriculture should be provided for farmers and cultivators; capital should be provided for traders and those engaged in business; adequate wages should be paid to those who are employed. When people are thus provided for with opportunities for earning a sufficient income, they will be contented, will have no fear or anxiety, and consequently the country will be peaceful and free from crime.

Because of this, the Buddha told lay people how important it is to improve their economic condition. This does not mean that he approved of hoarding wealth with desire and attachment, which is against his fundamental teaching, nor did he approve of each and every way of earning one's livelihood. There are certain trades like the production and sale of armaments, which he condemns as evil means of livelihood.

. . .

The Buddha was just as clear on politics, on war and peace. It is too well known to be repeated here that Buddhism advocates and preaches non-violence and peace as its universal message, and does not approve of any kind of violence or destruction of life. According to Buddhism there is nothing that can be called a "just war"— which is only a false term coined and put into circulation to justify and excuse hatred, cruelty, violence, and massacre. Who decides what is just or unjust? The mighty and the victorious are "just," and the weak and the defeated are "unjust." Our war is always "just," and your war is always "unjust." Buddhism does not accept this position.

. . .

[The Buddha advocated the "Ten Duties of the King," which applies to all those who are involved in governing others.]

The first of the "Ten Duties of the King" is liberality, generosity, charity *(dāna)*. The ruler should not have craving and attachment to wealth and property, but should give it away for the welfare of the people.

Second: A high moral character *(sīla)*. He should never destroy life, cheat, steal, and exploit others, commit adultery, utter falsehood, and take intoxicating drinks. That is, he must at least observe the Five Precepts of the layman.

Third: Sacrificing everything for the good of the people *(pariccāga)*, he must be prepared to give up all personal comfort, name and fame, and even his life, in the interest of the people.

Fourth: Honesty and integrity *(ajjava)*. He must be free from fear or favour in the discharge of his duties, must be sincere in his intentions, and must not deceive the public.

Fifth: Kindness and gentleness *(maddava)*. He must possess a genial temperament.

Sixth: Austerity in habits *(tapa)*. He must lead a simple life, and should not indulge in a life of luxury. He must have self-control.

Seventh: Freedom from hatred, ill-will, enmity *(akkodha)*. He should bear no grudge against anybody.

Eighth: Non-violence *(avihiṃsā)*, which means not only that he should harm nobody, but also that he should try to promote peace by avoiding and preventing war, and everything which involves violence and destruction of life.

Ninth: Patience, forbearance, tolerance, understanding *(khanti)*. He must be able to bear hardships, difficulties, and insults without losing his temper.

Tenth: Non-opposition, non-obstruction *(avirodha)*, that is to say that he should not oppose the will of the people, should not obstruct any measures that are conducive to the welfare of the people. In other words he should rule in harmony with his people.

.   .   .

Buddhism aims at creating a society where the ruinous struggle for power is renounced; where calm and peace prevail away from conquest and defeat; where the persecution of the innocent is vehemently denounced; where one who conquers oneself is more respected than those who conquer millions by military and economic warfare; where hatred is conquered by kindness, and evil by goodness; where enmity, jealousy, ill-will, and greed do not infect men's minds; where compassion is the driving force of action; where all, including the least of living things, are treated with fairness, consideration, and love; where life in peace and harmony, in a world of material contentment, is directed towards the highest and noblest aim, the realization of the Ultimate Truth, Nirvāṇa.

Holder of the White Lotus

The Dalai Lama

By any normal means of reckoning, his birth in 1935 could not have looked auspicious. The place of birth—Takster, a village of twenty families in far northeastern Tibet—by the standards of the modern world had few amenities. His parents were farmers; the family house was constructed of stone and mud. The ninth child (of sixteen, of whom seven survived childhood), he was named Lhamo Thondup, and all was quiet until he was two years of age. It was then that an official Tibetan search party identified him as the Fourteenth Dalai Lama.

Jumping ahead to 1959 in this unlikely story, we find him and some 100,000 followers forced by Chinese troops to flee Tibet. He has since traveled the world seeking support for his people and for Tibet's freedom; in 1989 he was awarded the Nobel Peace prize. His shaven head, claret robe, and warm smile have made him one of the most readily recognized people in the world.

Modest and unassuming, the Dalai Lama (the title is loosely translated as "Ocean of Wisdom") prefers to think of himself as a "simple Buddhist monk." On airline flights he refuses the luxury of first-class seating. There is evident in his books and lectures deep learning in Buddhist philosophy and a resolute commitment to principle.

His books include My Land and My People, Universal Responsibility and the Good Heart, Ocean of Wisdom, The Buddhism of Tibet and the Key to the Middle Way, Kindness, Clarity, and Insight, *and* The Opening of the Wisdom-Eye. *The reading selection that follows is from* Freedom in Exile *(1990).*

Even in the late twentieth century, Tibet is still a "mysterious" country, isolated and remote. It has been hazily associated with the "Shangri-la" of James Hilton's novel Lost Horizon *by a generation or two of readers (and moviegoers) in the West. Buddhism was introduced to Tibet in the seventh century C.E., and it gradually assimilated and superceded the ancient, indigenous Bon religion. One of the Tibetan Buddhist sects (for there were divisions) is the Gelukpa. This is the Yellow-Hat School, in contrast to a rival sect, the Kagyupa, or Red-Hat School. It was the third Grand Lama of the Gelukpa who was given the title* Dalai.

I am held to be the reincarnation of each of the previous thirteen Dalai Lamas of Tibet (the first having been born in A.D. 1351), who are in turn considered to be

Excerpts from *Freedom in Exile: The Autobiography of the Dalai Lama* by Tenzin Gyatso. Copyright © 1990 by Tenzin Gyatso, His Holiness, The Fourteenth Dalai Lama of Tibet. Reprinted by permission of HarperCollins Publishers and Hodder and Stoughton Limited.

manifestations of Avalokiteshvara, or Chenrezig, Bodhisattva of Compassion, holder of the White Lotus. Thus I am believed also to be a manifestation of Chenrezig, in fact the seventy-fourth in a lineage that can be traced back to a Brahmin boy who lived in the time of Buddha Shakyamuni. I am often asked whether I truly believe this. The answer is not simple to give. But as a fifty-six year old, when I consider my experiences during this present life, and given my Buddhist beliefs, I have no difficulty accepting that I am spiritually connected both to the thirteen previous Dalai Lamas, to Chenrezig, and to the Buddha himself.

.   .   .

The Search Party

When I was not quite three years old, a search party that had been sent out by the Government to find the new incarnation of the Dalai Lama arrived at Kumbum monastery. It had been led there by a number of signs. One of these concerned the embalmed body of my predecessor, Thupten Gyatso, the Thirteenth Dalai Lama, who had died aged fifty-seven in 1933. During its period of sitting in state, the head was discovered to have turned from facing south to north-east. Shortly after that the Regent, himself a senior lama, had a vision. Looking into the waters of the sacred lake, Lhamoi Lhatso, in southern Tibet, he clearly saw the Tibetan letters *Ah, Ka,* and *Ma* float into view. These were followed by the image of a three-storeyed monastery with a turquoise and gold roof and a path running from it to a hill. Finally, he saw a small house with strangely shaped guttering. He was sure that the letter *Ah* referred to Amdo, the north-eastern province, so it was there that the search party was sent.

By the time they reached Kumbum, the members of the search party felt that they were on the right track. It seemed likely that if the letter *Ah* referred to Amdo, then *Ka* must indicate the monastery at Kumbum—which was indeed three storeyed and turquoise roofed. They now only needed to locate a hill and a house with peculiar guttering. So they began to search the neighbouring villages. When they saw the gnarled branches of juniper wood on the roof of my parents' house, they were certain that the new Dalai Lama would not be far away. Nevertheless, rather than reveal the purpose of their visit, the group asked only to stay the night. The leader of the party, Kewtsang Rinpoché, then pretended to be a servant and spent much of the evening observing and playing with the youngest child in the house.

The child recognised him and called out "Sera Lama, Sera Lama." Sera was Kewtsang Rinpoché's monastery. Next day they left—only to return a few days later as a formal deputation. This time they brought with them a number of things that had belonged to my predecessor, together with several similar items that did not. In every case, the infant correctly identified those belonging to the Thirteenth Dalai Lama saying, "It's mine. It's mine." This more or less convinced the search party that they had found the new incarnation. However, there was another candidate to be seen before a final decision could be reached. But it was not long before the boy from Taktser was acknowledged to be the new Dalai Lama. I was that child.

.   .   .

My Religious Practice

As for my own religious practice, I try to live my life pursuing what I call the Bodhisattva ideal. According to Buddhist thought, a Bodhisattva is someone on the path to Buddhahood who dedicates themselves entirely to helping all other sentient beings towards release from suffering. The word Bodhisattva can best be understood by translating the *Bodhi* and *Sattva* separately: *Bodhi* means the understanding or wisdom of the ultimate nature of reality, and a *Sattva* is someone who is motivated by universal compassion. The Bodhisattva ideal is thus the aspiration to practise infinite compassion with infinite wisdom. As a means of helping myself in this quest, I choose to be a Buddhist monk. There are 253 rules of Tibetan monasticism (364 for nuns) and by observing them as closely as I can, I free myself from many of the distractions and worries of life. Some of these rules mainly deal with etiquette, such as the physical distance a monk should walk behind the abbot of his monastery; others are concerned with behaviour. The four root vows concern simple prohibitions: namely that a monk must not kill, steal, or lie about his spiritual attainment. He must also be celibate. If he breaks any one of these, he is no longer a monk.

I am sometimes asked whether this vow of celibacy is really desirable and indeed whether it is really possible. Suffice to say that its practice is not simply a matter of suppressing sexual desires. On the contrary, it is necessary fully to accept the existence of these desires and to transcend them by the power of reasoning. When successful, the result on the mind can be very beneficial. The trouble with sexual desire is that it is a blind desire. To say "I want to have sex with this person" is to express a desire which is not intellectually directed in the way that "I want to eradicate poverty in the world" is an intellectually directed desire. Furthermore, the gratification of sexual desire can only ever give temporary satisfaction. Thus as Nagarjuna, the great Indian scholar, said:

> When you have an itch, you scratch.
> But not to itch at all
> Is better than any amount of scratching.

Regarding my actual daily practice, I spend, at the very least, five and a half hours per day in prayer, meditation, and study. On top of this, I also pray whenever I can during odd moments of the day, for example over meals and whilst travelling. In this last case, I have three main reasons for doing so: firstly, it contributes towards fulfilment of my daily duty; secondly, it helps to pass the time productively; thirdly, it assuages fear! More seriously though, as a Buddhist, I see no distinction between religious practice and daily life. Religious practice is a twenty-four-hour occupation. In fact, there are prayers prescribed for every activity from waking to washing, eating and even sleeping. For Tantric practitioners, those exercises which are undertaken during deep sleep and in the dream state are the most important preparation for death.

However, for myself, early morning is the best time for practice. The mind is at its freshest and sharpest then. I therefore get up at around four o'clock. On waking, I begin the day with the recitation of *mantras.* I then drink hot water and take my medicine before making prostrations in salutation of the Buddhas for about half an hour. The purpose of this is twofold. Firstly, it increases one's own merit (assuming proper motivation) and secondly, it is good exercise. After my prostrations, I wash—saying prayers as I do so. Then I generally go outside for a walk, during which I make further recitations, until breakfast at around 5:15A.M. I allow about half an hour for this meal (which is quite substantial) and whilst eating read scriptures.

From 5:45A.M. until around 8:00A.M., I meditate, pausing only to listen to the 6:30 news bulletin of the BBC World Service. Then, from 8:00 A.M. until noon, I study Buddhist philosophy. Between then and lunch at 12:30, I might read either official papers or newspapers, but during the meal itself I again read scripture. At 1:00 P.M., I go to my office, where I deal with government and other matters and give audiences until 5:00 P.M. This is followed by another short period of prayer and meditation as soon as I get back home. If there is anything worthwhile on television, I watch it now before having tea at 6:00 P.M. Finally, after tea, during which I read scripture once more, I say prayers until 8:30 or 9:00 P.M., when I go to bed. Then follows very sound sleep.

Of course, there are variations to this routine. Sometimes during the morning I will participate in a *puja* or, in the afternoon, I will deliver a teaching. But, all the same, I very rarely have to modify my daily practice—that is my morning and evening prayers and meditation.

The rationale behind this practice is quite simple. During the first part of it when I make prostrations, I am "taking refuge" in the Buddha, the *Dharma,* and the *Sangha.* The next stage is to develop *Bodhichitta* or a Good Heart. This is done firstly by recognising the impermanence of all things and secondly by realising the true nature of being which is suffering. On the basis of these two considerations, it is possible to generate altruism.

To engender altruism, or compassion, in myself, I practise certain mental exercises which promote love towards all sentient beings, including especially my so-called enemies. For example, I remind myself that it is the actions of human beings rather than human beings themselves that make them my enemy. Given a change of behaviour, that same person could easily become a good friend.

The remainder of my meditation is concerned with *Sunya* or Emptiness, during which I concentrate on the most subtle meaning of Interdependence. Part of this practice involves what is termed "deity yoga," *lhai naljor,* during which I use different *mandalas* to visualise myself as a succession of different "deities." (This should not, however, be taken to imply belief in independent external beings.) In so doing, I focus my mind to the point where it is no longer preoccupied with the data produced by the senses. This is not a trance, as my mind remains fully alert; rather it is an exercise in pure consciousness. What exactly I mean by this is hard to explain: just as it is difficult for a scientist to explain in words what is meant by the term "space-time." Neither language nor every-day experience can really communicate the meaning experience of "pure mind." Suffice to say that it is not an easy practice. It takes many years to master.

One important aspect of my daily practice is its concern with the idea of death. To my mind, there are two things that, in life, you can do about death. Either you can choose to ignore it, in which case you may have some success in making the idea of it go away for a limited period of time, or you can confront the prospect of your own death and try to analyse it and, in so doing, try to minimise some of the inevitable suffering that it causes. Neither way can you actually overcome it. However, as a Buddhist, I view death as a normal process of life, I accept it as a reality that will occur while I am in *Samsara*. Knowing that I cannot escape it, I see no point in worrying about it. I hold the view that death is rather like changing one's clothes when they are torn and old. It is not an end in itself. Yet death is unpredictable—you do not know when and how it will take place. So it is only sensible to take certain precautions before it actually happens.

. . .

Oracles

I must stress that the purpose of oracles is not, as might be supposed, simply to foretell the future. This is only part of what they do. In addition, they can be called upon as protectors and in some cases they are used as healers. But their principal function is to assist people in their practice of the *Dharma*. Another point to remember is that the word "oracle" is itself misleading. It implies that there are people who possess oracular powers. This is wrong. In the Tibetan tradition there are merely certain men and women who act as mediums between the natural and the spiritual realms, the name for them being *kuten,* which means, literally, "the physical basis." Also, I should point out that whilst it is usual to speak of oracles as if they were people, this is done for convenience. More accurately, they can be described as "spirits" which are associated with particular things (for example a statue), people, and places. This should not be taken to imply belief in the existence of external, independent entities, however.

In former times there must have been many hundred oracles throughout Tibet. Few survive, but the most important—those used by the Tibetan Government—still exist. Of these, the principal one is known as the Nechung oracle. Through him manifests Dorje Drakden, one of the protector divinities of the Dalai Lama.

Nechung originally came to Tibet with a descendant of the Indian sage Dharmapala, settling at a place in Central Asia called Bata Hor. During the reign of King Trisong Dretsen in the eighth century A.D., he was appointed protector of Samye monastery by the Indian Tantric master and supreme spiritual guardian of Tibet, Padmasambhava. (Samye was in fact the first Buddhist monastery to be built in Tibet and was founded by another Indian scholar, the abbot Shantarakshita.) Subsequently, the second Dalai Lama developed a close relationship with Nechung—who had by this time become closely associated with Drepung monastery—and thereafter Dorje Drakden was appointed personal protector of succeeding Dalai Lamas.

For hundreds of years now, it has been traditional for the Dalai Lama, and the Government, to consult Nechung during the New Year festivals. In addition, he might well be called upon at other times if either have specific queries. I myself have dealings with him several times a year. This may sound far-fetched to twentieth-century western readers. Even some Tibetans, mostly those who consider themselves "progressive," have misgivings about my continued use of this ancient method of intelligence gathering. But I do so for the simple reason that as I look back over the many occasions when I have asked questions of the oracle, on each one of them time has proved that his answer was correct. This is not to say that I rely solely on the oracle's advice. I do not. I seek his opinion in the same way as I seek the opinion of my Cabinet and just as I seek the opinion of my own conscience. I consider the gods to be my "upper house." The *Kashag* constitutes my lower house. Like any other leader, I consult both before making a decision on affairs of state. And sometimes, in addition to Nechung's counsel, I also take into consideration certain prophecies.

.   .   .

I well remember a particular incident that occurred when I was about fourteen. Nechung was asked a question about China. Rather than answer it directly, the *kuten* turned towards the East and began bending forward violently. It was frightening to watch, knowing that this movement combined with the weight of the massive helmet he wore on his head would be enough to snap his neck. He did it at least fifteen times, leaving no one in any doubt about where the danger lay.

Dealing with Nechung is by no means easy. It takes time and patience during each encounter before he will open up. He is very reserved and austere, just as you would imagine a grand old man of ancient times to be. Nor does he bother with minor matters: his interest is only in the larger issues, so it pays to frame questions accordingly. He also has definite likes and dislikes, but he does not show them very readily.

Nechung has his own monastery in Dharamsala, but usually he comes to me. On formal occasions, the *kuten* is dressed in an elaborate costume consisting of several layers of clothing topped by a highly ornate robe of golden silk brocade, which is covered with ancient designs in red and blue and green and yellow. On his chest he wears a circular mirror which is surrounded by clusters of turquoise and amethyst, its polished steel flashing with the Sanskrit *mantra* corresponding to Dorje Drakden. Before the proceedings begin, he also puts on a sort of harness, which supports four flags and three victory banners. Altogether, this outfit weighs more than seventy pounds and the medium, when not in trance, can hardly walk in it.

.   .   .

Other Religions

I look on religion as medicine. For different complaints, doctors will prescribe different remedies. Therefore, because not everyone's spiritual "illness" is the same, different spiritual medicines are required.

. . .

Religion should never become a source of conflict, a further factor of division within the human community. For my own part, I have even, on the basis of my deep respect for the contribution that other faiths can make towards human happiness, participated in the ceremonies of other religions. And, following the example of a great many Tibetan lamas both ancient and modern, I continue to take teachings from as many different traditions as possible. For whilst it is true that some schools of thought felt it desirable for a practitioner to stay within his or her own tradition, people have always been free to do as they think fit. Furthermore, Tibetan society has always been highly tolerant of other people's beliefs. Not only was there a flourishing Muslim community in Tibet, but also there were a number of Christian missions which were admitted without hindrance. I am therefore firmly in favour of a liberal approach. Sectarianism is poison.

. . .

What is religion? As far as I am concerned, any deed done with good motivation is a religious act. On the other hand, a gathering of people in a temple or church who do not have good motivation are not performing a religious act when they pray together.

. . .

The present Pope is a man I hold in high regard. To begin with, our somewhat similar backgrounds give us an immediate common ground. The first time we met, he struck me as a very practical sort of person, very broad-minded and open. I have no doubt that he is a great spiritual leader. Any man who can call out "Brother" to his would-be assassin, as Pope John Paul did, must be a highly evolved spiritual practitioner.

Mother Teresa, whom I met at Delhi airport on my way back from a conference at Oxford, England, during 1988 (which she had also attended), is someone for whom I have the deepest respect. I was at once struck by her demeanour of absolute humility. From the Buddhist point of view she could be considered to be a Bodhisattva.

Further Reading

Kenneth K. Inada and Nolen P. Jacobson (eds.), *Buddhism and American Thinkers* (1983). Essays by Charles Hartshorne, David L. Hall, Robert C. Neville, Hajime Nakamura, and others, trace Buddhist influence on American thought. East and West have met.

David J. and Indrani Kalupahana's *The Way of Siddhartha* (1982) and Hajime Nakamura's *Gotama Buddha* (1977) are both authoritative biographies.

Nancy Wilson Ross, *Buddhism: A Way of Life and Thought* (1980) and *Three Ways of Asian Wisdom* (1966). Pleasant introductions, the latter volume offering Hinduism, Buddhism, and Zen as the "three ways." Both books are enhanced by reproductions of works of Asian art, in which the Buddhist author had a special interest.

Bhikshu Sangharakshita's *A Survey of Buddhism* (1957) is thorough and scholarly. See also his *The Three Jewels: An Introduction to Modern Buddhism* (1967). The three jewels (and the three parts of this book) are the Buddha, the Dharma, and the Sangha.

Open Secrets: A Western Guide to Tibetan Buddhism (1979) by Walter T. Anderson is a clear-headed and inviting introduction to a formidable topic.

Chogyam Trungpa, who died in 1987, told of his early life and much about Tibetan Buddhism in his fascinating *Born in Tibet* (1966).

Because Buddhist scriptures are so extensive, anthologies that draw from them may vary widely. Among the best such collections are those by E.A. Burtt (ed.), *The Teachings of the Compassionate Buddha* (1955); Wm. Theodore de Bary (ed.), *The Buddhist Tradition* (1969); Lucien Stryk (ed.), *The World of the Buddha* (1968); Dwight Goddard (ed.), *A Buddhist Bible* (1938); Clarence Hamilton (ed.), *Buddhism: A Religion of Infinite Compassion* (1952); and, especially, Edward Conze (ed.), *Buddhist Scriptures* (1959), *Buddhist Texts Through the Ages* (1954), and *Buddhist Wisdom Books* (1958).

Widely adopted as a textbook, Richard H. Robinson and Willard L. Johnson's *The Buddhist Religion* (3d ed., 1982) is both an introduction to and history of its subject.

III

ZEN BUDDHISM
The Sound of One Hand

In walking, just walk.
In sitting, just sit.
Above all, don't wobble.

Yun-men

If religion could be called a kind of poetry, Zen might be *haiku,* that delightful form of poetry upon whose development in Japan Zen had a decisive influence. And those who are familiar with these simple, suggestive poems already know something of Zen. A good *haiku,* like Zen itself,

> is a hand beckoning, a door half-opened, a mirror wiped clean. It is a way
> of returning to nature, our moon nature, our cherry blossom nature, our
> falling leaf nature, in short to our Buddha nature. It is a way in which the
> cold winter rain, the swallows of evening, even the very day in its hotness,
> and the length of the night become truly alive, share in our humanity, speak
> their own silent and expressive language.[1]

In Zen and in *haiku* the sights and sounds of the everyday world are vivid and real, but they are also imbued with a sense of wonder: the concrete Here and Now is permeated with the Miraculous. Historically speaking, it is a blending of the visions of Taoist China and Indian Buddhism.

The name by which we know the religion is itself a thumbnail history: the Sanskrit term for meditation, *dhyana,* became *ch'an* in China[2] and *zen* in Japan; and it was from Japan that Zen came to the West. Zen's origins, then, are in India, but the details of its history there are speculative. Although Buddhist meditational practices were widespread, there seems to be no evidence of a distinctively Zen-type school in primitive Buddhism. The *traditional* history of Zen, nevertheless, begins with Gautama Buddha and claims an unbroken succession to the Twenty-eighth Patriarch, the Indian monk Bodhidharma, who brought Zen to China in the sixth century. (Scholars now believe that he had precursors in preceding centuries.) In

---

1. R. H. Blyth, quoted in Nancy Wilson Ross, *The World of Zen* (New York: Random House, 1960), p. 120.

2. Hence accounts of what we usually think of as Zen is called Ch'an Buddhism when the setting is China.

China Bodhidharma became known as the First Patriarch, and with him appeared some of the signs of things to come. Later portraits of Bodhidharma convey a tiger-like disposition, and it is reported that he sat meditating before the wall of a cave for nine years. A disciple, Shen-kuang, is said to have cut off his left arm with a sword in order to demonstrate to Bodhidharma his sincerity. In time, Shen-kuang became the Second Patriarch.

Of special note is the Sixth Patriarch, Hui-neng (638–713), who (in spite of those exact dates for his life) may have been entirely legendary. The story of his enlight-enment and of the nature of enlightenment itself is told in *The Platform Sutra of the Sixth Patriarch,* one of the most highly regarded of all Zen writings.[3] That it is called a *sutra* (a "discourse") is significant: the term is normally reserved for the teachings of the Buddha, and the *Platform Sutra* is the only Chinese work honored with that designation. Hui-neng was the last of the Patriarchs: in order to avoid jealousy and strife among his disciples, he did not name a successor.

The Golden Age of Zen followed Hui-neng, whether he existed or not, and lasted until the beginning of the tenth century. Zen literature concerning this period abounds with stories of great Zen masters and their eccentricities. Ma-tsu (707–786) once suddenly twisted the nose of a disciple, who was abruptly enlightened. A deafening shout at another disciple left him stunned for three days—and precipi-tated his *satori* (awakening). Huang-po (d. 850) wrote *Treatise on the Essentials of the Transition of Mind* and had among his disciples I-hsuan (d. 867), founder of the Lin-chi (Rinzai, in Japanese) school. Zen continued to thrive in China until about the seventeenth century, after which there began a long and steady decline.

In the twelfth and thirteenth centuries, however, two Japanese masters, Eisai (1141–1215) and Dogen (1200–1253), firmly established Zen in Japan, where over the centuries it has prospered and exerted a vast influence upon the thought and culture of that land. Eisai had studied Rinzai Zen in China, and he brought those teachings back to Japan. Dogen had also learned his Zen in China, but his wander-ings there had led him to Soto teachings (the origins of which go back to one of the disciples of Hui-neng).

These two sects, the Rinzai and the Soto, are today the strongest of several in Japan. Both employ *zazen* (seated meditation), but the Rinzai more rigorously, particularly with its use of the *koan* (a paradoxical, mind-snapping problem assigned to a student for meditation), which is the subject of Ruth Fuller Sasaki's essay. Hakuin Ekaku (1686–1769), from whose writings a selection appears in this chapter, was a major contributor to the *koan* system. The most widely known *koan* of all, "The Sound of the Single Hand," is his. (You know the sound of two hands clapping. What is the sound of one hand?)

D. T. Suzuki, author of the introductory essay for this chapter, is a follower of the Rinzai school and the leading interpreter of Zen in this century. Rinzai is the "sudden awakening" school; in contrast (though not too much should be made of these differences), Soto Zen, for which Shunryu Suzuki is the representative in these

---

3. Recommended is the translation by Phillip B. Yampolsky, *The Platform Sutra of the Sixth Patri-arch* (New York: Columbia University Press, 1967).

pages, holds that one's awakening might come more naturally and spontaneously. This is, then, the "gradual awakening" school.

Of Han-shan's *Cold Mountain* poems, perhaps all that need be said is that "Cold Mountain" is not so much a *place* as it is a *quest*. Han-shan is here translated by Gary Snyder, who is himself a lover and climber of mountains, both real and metaphorical.

The Essence of Zen

D. T. Suzuki

It may be said (and in fact always is said) that it was the writings of one Japanese scholar, Daisetz Teitaro Suzuki, that opened up Zen to the West. Alan Watts described Suzuki as

> unofficial lay master of Zen Buddhism, humorous offbeat scholar, and about the most gentle and enlightened person I have ever known; for he combined the most complex learning with utter simplicity. He was versed in Japanese, English, Chinese, Sanskrit, Tibetan, French, Pali, and German, but while attending a meeting . . . he would play with a kitten.*

Born in 1870, Suzuki lived most of his years in Japan, but he also traveled the world during his long lifetime. He came to the United States as early as 1897, working with Paul Carus and the Open Court Publishing Company as a writer and translator. In the late 1930s he lectured on Zen at Cambridge, Oxford, and other English universities. Under the auspices of the Rockefeller Foundation he toured American universities, and he spent several years during the 1950s as a professor at Columbia University. Returning to Japan in 1958, he continued to work vigorously until his death in 1966.

Over the years he had published some 130 books and countless articles. His first book on Zen in English was Essays in Zen Buddhism (First Series), *published in 1927. He began that volume with the memorable statement, "Zen in its essence is the art of seeing into the nature of one's own being, and it points the way from bondage to freedom." Other works on Zen included* Essays, Second Series *and* Essays, Third Series, The Training of the Zen Buddhist Monk, *and* Zen and Japanese Culture.

———

What Is Zen?

Before proceeding to expound the teaching of Zen at some length in the following pages, let me answer some of the questions which are frequently raised by critics concerning the real nature of Zen.

In My Own Way (New York: Vintage Books, 1973), pp. 89–90.

Is Zen a system of philosophy, highly intellectual and profoundly metaphysical, as most Buddhist teachings are?

. . . We find in Zen all the philosophy of the East crystallized, but this ought not to be taken as meaning that Zen is a philosophy in the ordinary application of the term. Zen is decidedly not a system founded upon logic and analysis. If anything, it is the antipode to logic, by which I mean the dualistic mode of thinking. There may be an intellectual element in Zen, for Zen is the whole mind, and in it we find a great many things; but the mind is not a composite thing that is to be divided into so many faculties, leaving nothing behind when the dissection is over. Zen has nothing to teach us in the way of intellectual analysis; nor has it any set doctrines which are imposed on its followers for acceptance. In this respect Zen is quite chaotic if you choose to say so. Probably Zen followers may have sets of doctrines, but they have them on their own account, and for their own benefit; they do not owe the fact to Zen. Therefore, there are in Zen no sacred books or dogmatic tenets, nor are there any symbolic formulae through which an access might be gained into the signification of Zen. If I am asked, then, what Zen teaches, I would answer, Zen teaches nothing. Whatever teachings there are in Zen, they come out of one's own mind. We teach ourselves; Zen merely points the way. Unless this pointing is teaching, there is certainly nothing in Zen purposely set up as its cardinal doctrines or as its fundamental philosophy.

Zen claims to be Buddhism, but all the Buddhist teachings as propounded in the sutras and sastras are treated by Zen as mere waste paper whose utility consists in wiping off the dirt of intellect and nothing more. Do not imagine, however, that Zen is nihilism. All nihilism is self-destructive, it ends nowhere. Negativism is sound as method, but the highest truth is an affirmation. When it is said that Zen has no philosophy, that it denies all doctrinal authority, that it casts aside all so-called sacred literature as rubbish, we must not forget that Zen is holding up in this very act of negation something quite positive and eternally affirmative. This will become clearer as we proceed.

Is Zen a religion? It is not a religion in the sense that the term is popularly understood; for Zen has no God to worship, no ceremonial rites to observe, no future abode to which the dead are destined, and, last of all, Zen has no soul whose welfare is to be looked after by somebody else and whose immortality is a matter of intense concern with some people. Zen is free from all these dogmatic and "religious" encumbrances.

When I say there is no God in Zen, the pious reader may be shocked, but this does not mean that Zen denies the existence of God; neither denial nor affirmation concerns Zen. When a thing is denied, the very denial involves something not denied. The same can be said of affirmation. This is inevitable in logic. Zen wants to rise above logic. Zen wants to find a higher affirmation where there are no antitheses. Therefore, in Zen, God is neither denied nor insisted upon; only there is in Zen no such God as has been conceived by Jewish and Christian minds. For the same reason that Zen is not a philosophy, Zen is not a religion.

As to all those images of various Buddhas and Bodhisattvas and Devas and other beings that one comes across in Zen temples, they are like so many pieces of wood or stone or metal; they are like the camellias, azaleas, or stone lanterns in my garden. Make obeisance to the camellia now in full bloom, and worship it if you like, Zen would say. There is as much religion in so doing as in bowing to the various Buddhist gods, or as sprinkling holy water, or as participating in the Lord's Supper. All those pious deeds considered to be meritorious or sanctifying by most so-called religiously minded people are artificialities in the eyes of Zen. It boldly declares that "the immaculate Yogins do not enter Nirvana and the precept-violating monks do not go to hell." This, to ordinary minds, is a contradiction of the common law of moral life, but herein lies the truth and life of Zen. Zen is the spirit of a man. Zen believes in his inner purity and goodness. Whatever is superadded or violently torn away, injures the wholesomeness of the spirit. Zen, therefore, is emphatically against all religious conventionalism.

Its irreligion, however, is merely apparent. Those who are truly religious will be surprised to find that after all there is so much of religion in the barbarous declaration of Zen. But to say that Zen is a religion, in the sense that Christianity or Mohammedanism is, would be a mistake. To make my point clearer, I quote the following. When Sakyamuni was born, it is said that he lifted one hand toward the heavens and pointed to the earth with the other, exclaiming, "Above the heavens and below the heavens, I alone am the Honoured One!" Ummon (Yun-men), founder of the Ummon School of Zen, comments on this by saying, "If I had been with him at the moment of his uttering this, I would surely have struck him dead with one blow and thrown the corpse into the maw of a hungry dog." What unbelievers would ever think of making such raving remarks over a spiritual leader? Yet one of the Zen masters following Ummon says: "Indeed, this is the way Ummon desires to serve the world, sacrificing everything he has, body and mind! How grateful he must have felt for the love of Buddha!"

Zen is not to be confounded with a form of meditation as practised by "New Thought" people, or Christian Scientists, or Hindu Sannyasins, or some Buddhists. Dhyana, as it is understood by Zen, does not correspond to the practice as carried on in Zen. A man may meditate on a religious or philosophical subject while disciplining himself in Zen, but that is only incidental; the essence of Zen is not there at all. Zen purposes to discipline the mind itself, to make it its own master, through an insight into its proper nature. This getting into the real nature of one's own mind or soul is the fundamental object of Zen Buddhism. Zen, therefore, is more than meditation and Dhyana in its ordinary sense. The discipline of Zen consists in opening the mental eye in order to look into the very reason of existence.

To meditate, a man has to fix his thought on something; for instance, on the oneness of God, or his infinite love, or on the impermanence of things. But this is the very thing Zen desires to avoid. If there is anything Zen strongly emphasizes it is the attainment of freedom; that is, freedom from all unnatural encumbrances. Meditation is something artificially put on; it does not belong to the native activity of the mind. Upon what do the fowl of the air meditate? Upon what do the fish in the water meditate? They fly; they swim. Is not that enough? Who wants to fix his mind on the unity of God and man, or on the nothingness of this life? Who wants to be arrested in the daily manifestations of his life-activity by such meditations as the goodness of a divine being or the everlasting fire of hell?

We may say that Christianity is monotheistic, and the Vedanta pantheistic; but we cannot make a similar assertion about Zen. Zen is neither monotheistic nor pantheistic; Zen defies all such designations. Hence there is no object in Zen upon which to fix the thought. Zen is a wafting cloud in the sky. No screw fastens it, no string holds it; it moves as it lists. *No amount of meditation will keep Zen in one place.* Meditation is not Zen. Neither pantheism nor monotheism provides Zen with its subjects of concentration. If Zen is monotheistic, it may tell its followers to meditate on the oneness of things where all differences and inequalities, enveloped in the all-illuminating brightness of the divine light, are obliterated. If Zen were pantheistic it would tell us that every meanest flower in the field reflects the glory of God. But what Zen says is "After all things are reduced to oneness, where would that One be reduced?" Zen wants to have one's mind free and unobstructed; even the idea of oneness or allness is a stumbling-block and a strangling snare which threatens the original freedom of the spirit.

Zen, therefore, does not ask us to concentrate our thought on the idea that a dog is God, or that three pounds of flax are divine. When Zen does this it commits itself to a definite system of philosophy, and there is no more Zen. Zen just feels fire warm and ice cold, because when it freezes we shiver and welcome fire. The feeling is all in all, as Faust declares; all our theorization fails to touch reality. But "the feeling" here must be understood in its deepest sense or in its purest form. Even to say that "This is the feeling" means that Zen is no more there. Zen defies all concept-making. That is why Zen is difficult to grasp.

Whatever meditation Zen may propose, then, will be to take things as they are, to consider snow white and the raven black. When we speak of meditation we in most cases refer to its abstract character; that is, meditation is known to be the concentration of the mind on some highly generalized proposition, which is, in the nature of things, not always closely and directly connected with the concrete affairs of life. Zen perceives or feels, and does not abstract nor meditate. Zen penetrates and is finally lost in the immersion. Meditation, on the other hand, is outspokenly dualistic and consequently inevitably superficial.

·   ·   ·

The basic idea of Zen is to come in touch with the inner workings of our being, and to do this in the most direct way possible, without resorting to anything external or superadded. Therefore, anything that has the semblance of an external authority is rejected by Zen. Absolute faith is placed in a man's own inner being. For whatever authority there is in Zen, all comes from within. This is true in the strictest sense of the word. Even the reasoning faculty is not considered final or absolute. On the contrary, it hinders the mind from coming into the directest communication with itself. The intellect accomplishes its mission when it works as an intermediary, and Zen has nothing to do with an intermediary except when it desires to communicate itself to others. For this reason all the scriptures are merely tentative and provisory; there is in them no finality. The central fact of life as it is lived is what Zen aims to grasp, and this in the most direct and most vital manner. Zen professes itself to be the spirit of Buddhism, but in fact it is the spirit of all religions and philosophies. When Zen is thoroughly understood, absolute peace of mind is attained, and a man lives as he ought to live. What more may we hope?

Some say that as Zen is admittedly a form of mysticism it cannot claim to be unique in the history of religion. Perhaps so; but Zen is a mysticism of its own order. It is mystical in the sense that the sun shines, that the flower blooms, that I hear at this moment somebody beating a drum in the street. If these are mystical facts, Zen is brim-full of them. When a Zen master was once asked what Zen was, he replied, "Your everyday thought." Is this not plain and most straightforward? It has nothing to do with any sectarian spirit. Christians as well as Buddhists can practise Zen just as big fish and small fish are both contentedly living in the same ocean. Zen is the ocean, Zen is the air, Zen is the mountain, Zen is thunder and lightning, the spring flower, summer heat, and winter snow; nay, more than that, Zen is the man. With all the formalities, conventionalisms, and superadditions that Zen has accumulated in its long history, its central fact is very much alive. The special merit of Zen lies in this: that we are still able to see into this ultimate fact without being biased by anything.

As has been said before, what makes Zen unique as it is practised in Japan is its systematic training of the mind. Ordinary mysticism has been too erratic a product and apart from one's ordinary life; this Zen has revolutionized. What was up in the heavens, Zen has brought down to earth. With the development of Zen, mysticism has ceased to be mystical; it is no more the spasmodic product of an abnormally endowed mind. For Zen reveals itself in the most uninteresting and uneventful life of a plain man of the street, recognizing the fact of living in the midst of life as it is lived. Zen systematically trains the mind to see this; it opens a man's eye to the greatest mystery as it is daily and hourly performed; it enlarges the heart to embrace eternity of time and infinity of space in its every palpitation; it makes us live in the world as if walking in the garden of Eden; and all these spiritual feats are accomplished without resorting to any doctrines but by simply asserting in the most direct way the truth that lies in our inner being.

Whatever else Zen may be, it is practical and commonplace and at the same time most living. An ancient master, wishing to show what Zen is, lifted one of his fingers, another kicked a ball, and a third slapped the face of his questioner. If the inner truth that lies deep in us is thus demonstrated, is not Zen the most practical and direct method of spiritual training ever resorted to by any religion? And is not this practical method also a most original one? Indeed, Zen cannot be anything else but original and creative because it refuses to deal with concepts but deals with living facts of life. When conceptually understood, the lifting of a finger is one of the most ordinary incidents in everybody's life. But when it is viewed from the Zen point of view it vibrates with divine meaning and creative vitality. So long as Zen can point out this truth in the midst of our conventional and concept-bound existence we must say that it has its reason of being.

Satori

The essence of Zen Buddhism consists in acquiring a new viewpoint of looking at life and things generally. By this I mean that if we want to get into the inmost life of Zen, we must forgo all our ordinary habits of thinking which control our everyday life, we must try to see if there is any other way of judging things, or rather if our ordinary way is always sufficient to give us the ultimate satisfaction of our spiritual needs. If we feel dissatisfied somehow with this life, if there is something in our ordinary way of living that deprives us of freedom in its most sanctified sense, we must endeavour to find a way somewhere which gives us a sense of finality and contentment. Zen proposes to do this for us and assures us of the acquirement of a new point of view in which life assumes a fresher, deeper, and more satisfying aspect. This acquirement, however, is really and naturally the greatest mental cataclysm one can go through with in life. It is no easy task, it is a kind of fiery baptism, and one has to go through the storm, the earthquake, the overthrowing of the mountains, and the breaking in pieces of the rocks.

This acquiring of a new point of view in our dealings with life and the world is popularly called by Japanese Zen students 'satori' (*wu* in Chinese). It is really another name for Enlightenment *(annuttara-samyak-sambodhi),* which is the word used by the Buddha and his Indian followers ever since his realization under the Bodhi-tree by the River Nairañjanā. There are several other phrases in Chinese designating this spiritual experience, each of which has a special connotation, showing tentatively how this phenomenon is interpreted. At all events there is no Zen without satori, which is indeed the Alpha and Omega of Zen Buddhism. Zen devoid of satori is like a sun without its light and heat. Zen may lose all its literature, all its monasteries, and all its paraphernalia; but as long as there is satori in it it will survive to eternity. I want to emphasize this most fundamental fact concerning the very life of Zen; for there are some even among the students of Zen themselves who are blind to this central fact and are apt to think when Zen has been explained away logically or psychologically, or as one of the Buddhist philosophies which can be summed up by using highly technical and conceptual Buddhist phrases, Zen is exhausted, and there remains nothing in it that makes it what it is. But my contention is, the life of Zen begins with the opening of satori (*kai wu* in Chinese).

Satori may be defined as an intuitive looking into the nature of things in contradistinction to the analytical or logical understanding of it. Practically, it means the unfolding of a new world hitherto unperceived in the confusion of a dualistically-trained mind. Or we may say that with satori our entire surroundings are viewed from quite an unexpected angle of perception. Whatever this is, the world for those who have gained a satori is no more the old world as it used to be; even with all its flowing streams and burning fires, it is never the same one again. Logically stated, all its opposites and contradictions are united and harmonized into a consistent organic whole. This is a mystery and a miracle, but according to the Zen masters such is being performed every day. Satori can thus be had only through our once personally experiencing it.

Zen Dust: The Koan
Ruth Fuller Sasaki

Raised in a strict Presbyterian family, Ruth Fuller became a Buddhist while still in her twenties. She studied under a Zen master in Japan and, in the United States, eventually married one: Sokei-an Sasaki, who had a temple in New York. After his death in 1945—his health perhaps having been impaired by time spent in an intern-ment camp during World War II—she returned to Japan to become Abbess of Ryosen-an, Daitoku-ji, Kyoto, and Director of the First Zen Institute of America in Japan.

She is the author of Zen: A Method for Religious Awakening *(1959), which began as a lecture delivered at MIT. With others, she translated* A Man of Zen: The Recorded Sayings of Layman P'ang, *but she is probably best known for her work with Isshu Miura,* The Zen Koan, *which was later expanded into* Zen Dust *(1966). That latter title she explained as having been chosen by Isshu Roshi, "all words about Zen being but dust to be gotten rid of, or, from a deeper standpoint, having no real existence at all."* *

The origin of the koan and the method of using it lie in the nature of Zen itself. The masters of earliest Zen discerned that the source of the dynamic power of Buddhism was not in the sutras and the voluminous commentaries upon them, but in the enlightenment of Shakyamuni and in his teaching that every man has the potenti-ality of attaining this enlightenment for himself. Supported by faith in this teaching, these early masters forged ahead with indomitable courage to gain this realization for themselves through the method Shakyamuni had used and advocated, that is, meditation. Having attained the realization and comprehended its deepest mean-ing as well as its implications for human life, out of the compassionate heart born of their enlightenment they sought ways and means of assisting others to achieve the same experience. Meditation certainly remained the basic practice. Though methods of meditation were developed in Zen that differed from those in other Buddhist sects, whether of Indian or Chinese origin, we have no evidence that med-itation itself was ever abandoned or even neglected. Nor is it neglected today. The

Zen Dust (New York: Harcourt, Brace & World, 1966), p. xiv.

Excerpts from *Zen Dust, The History of the Koan, & Koan Study in Rinzai (Lin-Chi) Zen* by Isshu Miura and Ruth Sasaki, copyright © 1966 by Ruth Fuller Sasaki, reprinted by permission of Harcourt Brace Jovanovich, Inc. and the Bank of California, N.A.

different schools of Zen developed somewhat different ways of handling the mind during meditation, but in all schools the main road to the attainment of satori is still that of practicing meditation in the posture in which Shakyamuni Buddha was sitting when he attained his enlightenment.

In China

The earliest Chinese masters seem to have attained their enlightenment with little instruction. The histories of their lives indicate that most had been Buddhist monks, many from a young age, and as such were steeped in the doctrines of the Buddhist scriptures. Many had studied the classics of Confucianism and Taoism as well. Their inability to attain the enlightenment they sought through the study of written words caused them to seek out meditation masters. When these monks had reached some profound insight through their meditation practice they went to the master to have their insight verified by his. Or, if they were beset by doubts, they went to him to have these doubts resolved. Many times the master's one word at this point brought them to satori. If the master seemed to be *their* master, they remained with him for a number of years; if not, they went on to other masters until they found the one they recognized to be their own. When their enlightenment had been attested to and confirmed, they retired to the mountains to spend long years in ripening it. Only gradually did other seekers find them out and come to live with or near them. From such a group a new temple might arise, or, if the master's fame had reached the capital, a command might come to take charge of one already established.

The satori or enlightenment that the old masters experienced was ineffable and incommunicable. It had not come about as the result of thinking or reasoning. It was, indeed, an experience beyond and above the intellect. Understanding this only too well, they did not, on the whole, attempt to describe their experiences in words. They knew that verbal explanations were useless as a means of leading their students to the realization itself. They had to devise other means.

In the mountain monasteries where they preferred to live, the early Chinese masters were in intimate contact with their disciples, sharing all phases of their daily life and work. While master and monks were picking tea, planting trees, or sitting around the fire together, the master, by means of a seemingly simple question about something in the immediate situation, would indicate to the disciple some aspect of the immutable Principle, bringing him to a deeper realization, or test the depth of understanding he had already achieved.

From time to time the masters took the high seat in the main hall of the monastery and gave lectures to the assembly of monks. On such occasions they did not expound the sutras or scriptures as did the clerics of other sects of Buddhism. Though, on the whole, Zen masters were conversant with the teachings of other schools—and many of these teachings undoubtedly underlie Zen thought and doctrines—from the first Zen had prided itself on *not* being founded on any scripture. Zen was concerned only with Absolute Mind. Absolute Mind was the masters' one theme, pure, original, basic Mind, and their every word and action was a pointing to and a manifesting of Absolute Mind. In energetic and vivid language, much of it the colloquial idiom of the time, interspersed with quotations from the sutras and other Buddhist writings, the old masters relentlessly drove their message home. When they gave their own views, these were apt to be expressed in cryptic statements and formulas. At such times members of the community and any visiting monks and laymen who might be present were free to ask the master for further elucidation. They were also free to ask him questions of their own, or to bring up one of the numerous stereotyped questions that Zen adherents seemed always to have at hand when they had nothing else to inquire about.

The master took advantage of all such opportunities to demonstrate the principle, to awaken the questioner to deeper levels of understanding, or to destroy his pretensions. The answer the master gave, whether in word or in action, though always pointing to the Principle, was invariably adapted to the particular occasion. Thus it often came about that at different times the same master gave different answers to the same question. Furthermore, since these early masters were men of great originality and creative ability, their ways of demonstrating the profound Principle, their questions, and even their answers to the stock questions asked them, invariably bore the stamp of their own individual genius.

As the number of students around the famous masters grew larger, the personal contacts of the earlier days could not be maintained except with immediate disciples. Then a master might give to a number of students a certain question that he had already found effectual. Though the question originally had arisen in response to an immediate situation and was the immediate and personal problem of the individual disciple to whom it had been addressed, since the principle the master was making manifest through it was the immutable Principle and therefore valid for all men, the question also was valid for other students. Such questions performed the function of koans, and there is some evidence that by the end of T'ang (618–907) the masters themselves were referring to them as koans. But they were not koans in the full sense of the word, for they were questions being used by the masters who had originally created them. However, when Nan-yüan Hui-yung (Nan'in Egyō, d. 930), a descendant of Lin-chi I-hsüan (Rinzai Gigen, d. 866) in the third generation, questioned a disciple about certain of Lin-chi's formulas, Koan Zen, or the use of the words of earlier masters in a fixed and systematized form to instruct or test a student, may be said to have truly begun.

From that time on, the most illustrious masters, though they did not entirely cease creating their own koans, depended in large part on the "words of the ancients" in instructing their students, and the less talented masters relied upon them entirely. We may suppose that there were at least two reasons for this: the decline in the high level of creative genius with which the earlier masters had been endowed, and the great increase in the number, with a corresponding decrease in the quality, of the monks and lay students who were now flocking to individual monasteries by the hundreds, even thousands, to be instructed by the more reputable masters.

What were the "words of the ancients" now being used as "public records" or koans? Briefly, they consisted of questions the early masters had asked individual students, together with the answers given by the students; questions put to the masters by students in personal talks or in the course of the masters' lectures, together with the masters' answers; statements of formulas in which the masters had pointed to the profound Principle; anecdotes from the daily life of the masters in which their attitudes or actions illustrated the functioning of the Principle; and occasionally a phrase from a sutra in which the Principle or some aspect of it was crystallized in words. By presenting a student with one or another of these koans and observing his reaction to it, the degree or depth of his realization could be judged. The koans were the criteria of attainment.

Thus a unique method had been evolved for assisting men to attain religious awakening, a method of teaching in which there was no stated creed to be believed or precepts to be followed, no instruction in doctrines or discussions about them, no wordy descriptions of the stages on the way to enlightenment. Nor did the masters examine their students by asking them to state their views and beliefs in words. The koan was the examination. If the student had attained the understanding of the Principle as embodied in the koan, he would reply in such a fashion as clearly to indicate this. If not, then he must take the koan and wrestle with it, in the meditation hall and in the course of carrying out his daily tasks, until such time as he and it became one. The master gave him no further help or instruction.

.   .   .

In Japan

In the curriculum of the monastery, koan study unquestionably held first place. Every monk studied koans under the personal supervision of the master of the monastery. When a monk entered the sodo the master gave him his first koan; he did not choose it himself, as would seem to have been the general custom previously. On this koan the monk meditated until he had attained a satori deep enough to satisfy the master that he was ready to begin his "practice after satori." The attainment of the first satori, or *kenshō,* was expected to take two or three years, the full training after satori, from ten to fifteen years more.

The master or roshi met his student-monks individually at stated times for a private interview called *sanzen.* This might take place several times a day during the weeks especially devoted to meditation and known as *sesshin,* or only once or twice a day at other times. The etiquette for such an interview was definitely prescribed and extremely formal. The monk entered the master's room after a series of deep bows outside and inside the entrance to it, sat down facing the master, stated his koan immediately, and gave the answer he had arrived at. If the master was convinced that the student's insight tallied with the koan, he might accept the answer, then ask him to bring a jakugo for it at the next regular time for sanzen. If not, the master might give the student a word of encouragement or drop a hint to let him know that he was on the wrong path. Most often, however, the master did not utter a single word; he merely rang a little bell at his right hand, indicating that the interview was over and he was ready to receive the next student. Etiquette demanded that the monk leave the room at once after making the usual bows. Thus there was little or no opportunity for the student to ask a question or even to open his mouth after his first words.

On certain fixed days the roshi gave a *teishō,* or lecture, to the monks. For this lecture he took a high seat facing the altar in the center of the main hall of the monastery, and discoursed, in the fashion set by Hakuin, on one of the old koan collections, taking up one "case" or a part of a case at each lecture successively until he had covered the entire collection.

Such is the manner of koan study that has prevailed in Japanese Rinzai Zen from the time of Hakuin and his disciples to the present day.

. . .

Enlightenment, the personal experience of Reality, is man's ultimate experience. The quest for this experience is the most difficult quest upon which he can embark. It demands of him faith, determination, sacrifice, and, above all, passion. Without the sustained sense of urgency which passion imparts, the goal cannot be achieved. All the great men of Zen have understood this. The koans were in part devised to keep the sense of urgency sustained during the intervals when the heat of passion subsided. The seemingly unsolvable problem goads the disciple on mercilessly; when at last it is solved, the assurance that the insight attained tallies with the insight of enlightened men before him renews the disciple's faith in himself and his determination to press on. The koans are indeed peerless aids in the quest for the experience of enlightenment.

Han-shan and Cold Mountain

Gary Snyder (translator)

Gary Snyder is a poet and essayist of distinction; in 1974 his Turtle Island *won the Pulitzer Prize for poetry. A San Franciscan by birth (1930) and a graduate of Reed College, Snyder did graduate work in anthropology and linguistics, but came upon the writings of D. T. Suzuki and turned toward the East. He studied Chinese with Shih-hsiang Chen at the University of California, Berkeley, and practiced Zen for several years in Japan. (His essay "Spring* Sesshin *at Shokoku-ji" is a description of life in a Rinzai Zen temple.*)*

Since 1969 Snyder's home has been a house he built in the woods on the western slope of the Sierra Nevada in northern California. He cuts firewood, grows the crops that thin soil permits, and otherwise keeps his feet on the ground—much of this a reflection of his long-time interest in Native American culture.

Of note also is Snyder's prominent role in the Beat Generation: he was among the poets reading from their work the evening in 1955 when Allan Ginsberg read "Howl" at the Six Gallery in San Francisco. Jack Kerouac was there and described the scene in his novel The Dharma Bums *(1958), in which the central character, Japhy Ryder, is a portrayal of Snyder. Early in the novel, in fact, Ryder-Snyder is shown working on his translation of the Cold Mountain poems; the novel is dedicated to Han-shan.*

Among his recent titles are The Real Work: Interviews and Talks *(1980);* Passage Through India *(1983),* Axe Handles *(1983, poetry);* Left Out in the Rain: Poems 1947–1984 *(1986); and a book of essays,* The Practice of the Wild *(1990).*

1

The path to Han-shan's place is laughable,
A path, but no sign of cart or horse.
Converging gorges—hard to trace their twists

*Reprinted in Snyder, *Earth House Hold* (New York: New Directions, 1969).

Selections from "Cold Mountain Poems" translated by Gary Snyder in *Anthology of Chinese Literature, Vol. I* edited by Cyril Burch. Copyright © 1965 by Grove Press, Inc. Used by permission of Grove Press, Inc.

Jumbled cliffs—unbelievably rugged.
A thousand grasses bend with dew,
A hill of pines hums in the wind.
And now I've lost the shortcut home,
Body asking shadow, how do you keep up?

2

In a tangle of cliffs I chose a place—
Bird-paths, but no trails for men.
What's beyond the yard?
White clouds clinging to vague rocks.
Now I've lived here—how many years—
Again and again, spring and winter pass.
Go tell families with silverware and cars
"What's the use of all that noise and money?"

6

Men ask the way to Cold Mountain
Cold Mountain: there's no through trail.
In summer, ice doesn't melt
The rising sun blurs in swirling fog.
How did I make it?
My heart's not the same as yours.
If your heart was like mine
You'd get it and be right here.

7

I settled at Cold Mountain long ago,
Already it seems like years and years.
Freely drifting, I prowl the woods and streams
And linger watching things themselves.
Men don't get this far into the mountains,
White clouds gather and billow.
Thin grass does for a mattress,
The blue sky makes a good quilt.
Happy with a stone underhead
Let heaven and earth go about their changes.

8

Clambering up the Cold Mountain path,
The Cold Mountain trail goes on and on:
The long gorge choked with scree and boulders,
The wide creek, the mist-blurred grass.
The moss is slippery, though there's been no rain
The pine sings, but there's no wind.
Who can leap the world's ties
And sit with me among the white clouds?

10

I have lived at Cold Mountain
These thirty long years.
Yesterday I called on friends and family:
More than half had gone to the Yellow Springs.
Slowly consumed, like fire down a candle;
Forever flowing, like a passing river.
Now, morning, I face my lone shadow:
Suddenly my eyes are bleared with tears.

15

There's a naked bug at Cold Mountain
With a white body and a black head.
His hand holds two book-scrolls,
One the Way and one its Power.
His shack's got no pots or oven,
He goes for a walk with his shirt and pants askew.
But he always carries the sword of wisdom:
He means to cut down senseless craving.

20

Some critic tried to put me down—
"Your poems lack the Basic Truth of Tao"
And I recall the old-timers
Who were poor and didn't care.
I have to laugh at him,
He misses the point entirely,
Men like that
Ought to stick to making money.

24

When men see Han-shan
They all say he's crazy
And not much to look at—
Dressed in rags and hides.
They don't get what I say
& I don't talk their language.
All I can say to those I meet:
"Try and make it to Cold Mountain."

Hakuin: Poor Hole-Dwelling Devil

Philip B. Yampolsky (translator)

Born in 1686 in Japan, in a village at the base of Mt. Fuji, Hakuin Ekaku* so revived and restructured the practice of Japanese Rinzai Zen that he is acclaimed as its pivotal historical figure. He focused on the use of the koan as a means to satori, and he urged a lifetime of effort toward repeated and ever-deepening satori experiences: there are, he taught, major and minor awakenings, and one must persist. After an exceedingly energetic life, well illustrated in the following excerpt from his autobiographical writings, Hakuin died at the age of eighty-three in 1769. In addition to extensive writings in both Japanese and Chinese, he left over a thousand paintings, drawings, and examples of his calligraphy.

The translator, Philip B. Yampolsky, a professor in the Department of East Asian Languages and Cultures at Columbia University, has also translated The Platform Sutra of the Sixth Patriarch.

When I was seven or eight years old my mother took me to a temple for the first time and we listened to a sermon on the hells as described in the *Mo-ho-chih-kuan*. The priest dwelt eloquently on the torments of the Hells of Wailing, Searing Heat, Incessant Suffering, and the Red Lotus. So vivid was the priest's description that it sent shivers down the spines of both monks and laymen and made their hair stand on end in terror. Returning home, I took stock of the deeds of my short life and felt that there was but little hope for me. I did not know which way to turn and I was gooseflesh all over. In secret I took up the chapter on Kannon from the Lotus Sūtra and the *dhāraṇī* on Great Compassion and recited them day and night,

One day when I was taking a bath with my mother, she asked that the water be made hotter and had the maid add wood to the fire. Gradually my skin began to prickle with the heat and the iron bath-cauldron began to rumble. Suddenly I recalled the descriptions of the hells that I had heard and I let out a cry of terror that resounded through the neighborhood.

From this time on I determined to myself that I would leave home to become a monk. To this my parents would not consent, yet I went constantly to the temple

---

*"Hakuin" was a name he took for himself; "Ekaku" was given to him when he was a boy by a temple priest.

to recite the sutras and to study the works of Confucianism. At fifteen I left home to become a monk and at that time I vowed to myself: "Even if I should die I will not cease my efforts to gain the power of one whom fire will not burn and water will not drown." Day and night I recited the sutras and made obeisance to the Buddhas, but I noticed that when I was ill or taking acupuncture or moxa treatment, the pain I felt was just as it had been before. I was greatly depressed and said to myself: "I became a monk against my parents' wishes and have yet to make the slightest progress. I have heard that the Lotus is the king of all sutras, venerated even by ghosts and spirits. People who are suffering in the lower worlds, when they rely on others in their efforts to be saved, always ask that the Lotus Sūtra be recited for them. When one considers that recitation by others can save a person from suffering, how much more effective must be recitation by oneself! There must indeed be profound and mysterious doctrines in this Sūtra."

Thereupon I picked up the Lotus Sūtra and in my study of it found that, other than the passages that explain that there is only One Vehicle and that all phenomena are in the state of Nirvana, the text was concerned with parables relating to cause and effect. If this Sūtra had all these virtues, then surely the six Confucian classics and the books of all the other schools must be equally effective. Why should this particular sutra be so highly esteemed? My hopes were completely dashed. At this time I was sixteen years of age.

When I was nineteen I happened to read the [*Wu-chia*] *cheng-tsung tsan*,[1] in which the story of how the Master Yen-t'ou was killed by bandits and how his cries at the time resounded for over three *li* is described. I wondered why such an enlightened monk was unable to escape the swords of thieves. If such a thing could happen to a man who was like a unicorn or phoenix among monks, a dragon in the sea of Buddhism, how was I to escape the staves of the demons of hell after I died? What use was there in studying Zen? What a fraud Buddhism! How I regretted that I had cast myself into this band of strange and evil men. What was I to do now? So great was my distress that for three days I could not eat and for a long time my faith in Buddhism was completely lost. Statues of the Buddha and the sacred scriptures looked like mud and dirt to me. It seemed much better to read lay works, to amuse myself with poetry and prose, and thus to a small degree to alleviate my distress.

When I was twenty-two I went to the province of Wakasa, and while attending lectures on the *Hsü-t'ang lu*, I gained an awakening. Later, when I was in the province of Iyo, I read the *Fo-tsu san-ching* and achieved an intense awakening. I concentrated night and day on the *Mu* koan without a moment's rest, but to my great disappointment I was unable to achieve a pure and uninvolved state of undistracted meditation. Equally disappointing to me was the fact that I could not achieve the state where waking and sleeping are the same.

The spring of my twenty-fourth year found me in the monk's quarters of the Eigan-ji in Echigo, pursuing my strenuous studies. Night and day I did not sleep; I forgot both to eat and rest. Suddenly a great doubt manifested itself before me. It was as though I were frozen solid in the midst of an ice sheet extending tens of

---

1. A collection of seventy-four biographies of famous monks, with verses in their praise attached. Completed in 1254.

thousands of miles. A purity filled my breast and I could neither go forward nor retreat. To all intents and purposes I was out of my mind and the *Mu* alone remained. Although I sat in the Lecture Hall and listened to the Master's lecture, it was as though I were hearing a discussion from a distance outside the hall. At times it felt as though I were floating through the air.

This state lasted for several days. Then I chanced to hear the sound of the temple bell and I was suddenly transformed. It was as if a sheet of ice had been smashed or a jade tower had fallen with a crash. Suddenly I returned to my senses. I felt then that I had achieved the status of Yen-t'ou, who through the three periods of time encountered not the slightest loss [although he had been murdered by bandits]. All my former doubts vanished as though ice had melted away. In a loud voice I called: "Wonderful, wonderful. There is no cycle of birth and death through which one must pass. There is no enlightenment one must seek. The seventeen hundred koans handed down from the past have not the slightest value whatsoever." My pride soared up like a majestic mountain, my arrogance surged forward like the tide. Smugly I thought to myself: "In the past two or three hundred years no one could have accomplished such a marvelous breakthrough as this."

Shouldering my glorious enlightenment, I set out at once for Shinano. Calling on Master Shōju, I told of my experience and presented him with a verse. The Master, holding my verse up in his left hand, said to me: "This verse is what you have learned from study. Now show me what your intuition has to say," and he held out his right hand.

I replied: "If there were something intuitive that I could show you, I'd vomit it out," and I made a gagging sound.

The Master said: "How do you understand Chao-chou's *Mu*?"

I replied: "What sort of place does *Mu* have that one can attach arms and legs to it?"

The Master twisted my nose with his fingers and said: "Here's someplace to attach arms and legs." I was nonplussed and the Master gave a hearty laugh. "You poor hole-dwelling devil!" he cried. I paid him no attention and he continued: "Do you think somehow that you have sufficient understanding?"

I answered: "What do you think is missing?"

Then the Master began to discuss the koan that tells of Nanch'üan's death. I clapped my hands over my ears and started out of the room. The Master called after me: "Hey, monk!" and when I turned to him he added: "You poor hole-dwelling devil!" From then on, almost every time he saw me, the Master called me a "poor hole-dwelling devil."

One evening the Master sat cooling himself on the veranda. Again I brought him a verse I had written. "Delusions and fancies," the Master said. I shouted his words back at him in a loud voice, whereupon the Master seized me and rained twenty or thirty blows with his fists on me, and then pushed me off the veranda.

This was on the fourth day of the fifth month after a long spell of rain. I lay stretched out in the mud as though dead, scarcely breathing and almost unconscious. I could not move; meanwhile the Master sat on the veranda roaring with laughter. After a short while I regained consciousness, got up, and bowed to the

Master. My body was bathed in perspiration. The Master called out to me in a loud voice: "You poor hole-dwelling devil!"

After this I devoted myself to an intensive study of the koan on the death of Nan-ch'üan, not pausing to sleep or eat. One day I had a kind of awakening and went to the Master's room to test my understanding, but he would not approve it. All he did was call me a "poor hole-dwelling devil."

I began to think that I had better leave and go somewhere else. One day when I had gone to town to beg for food I encountered a madman who tried to beat me with a broom. Unexpectedly I found that I had penetrated the koan on the death of Nan-ch'üan. Then the other koans that had puzzled me, Su-shan's Memorial Tower and Ta-hui's verse on the Roundness of the Lotus Leaf, fell into place of themselves and I penetrated them all. After I returned to the temple I spoke of the understanding I had gained. The Master neither approved nor denied what I said, but only laughed pleasantly. But from this time on he stopped calling me a "poor hole-dwelling devil." Later I experienced enlightenment two or three times, accompanied by a great feeling of joy. At times there are words to express such experiences, but to my regret at other times there are none. It was as though I were walking about in the shadow cast by a lantern. I returned then and attended on my old teacher Nyoka, who had fallen ill.

One day I read in the verse given by Hsi-keng to his disciple Nampo as they were parting, the passage: "As we go to part a tall bamboo stands by the gate; its leaves stir the clear breeze for you in farewell." I was overcome with a great joy, as though a dark path had suddenly been illumined. Unconsciously I cried aloud: "Today for the first time I have entered into the *samādhi* of words." I arose and bowed in reverence.

After this I set out on a pilgrimage. One day when I was passing through southern Ise I ran into a downpour and the waters reached to my knees. Suddenly I gained an even deeper understanding of the verse on the Roundness of the Lotus Leaf by Ta-hui. I was unable to contain my joy. I lost all awareness of my body, fell headlong into the waters, and forgot completely to get up again. My bundles and clothing were soaked through. Fortunately a passer-by, seeing my predicament, helped me to get up. I roared with laughter and everyone there thought I was mad. That winter, when I was sitting at night in the monk's hall at Shinoda in Izumi, I gained an enlightenment from the sound of snow falling. The next year, while practicing walking meditation at the monk's hall of the Reishō-in in Mino, I suddenly had an enlightenment experience greater than any I had had before, and was overcome by a great surge of joy.

I came to this dilapidated temple when I was thirty-two. One night in a dream my mother came and presented me with a purple robe made of silk. When I lifted it, both sleeves seemed very heavy, and on examining them I found an old mirror, five or six inches in diameter, in each sleeve. The reflection from the mirror in the right sleeve penetrated to my heart and vital organs. My own mind, mountains and rivers, the great earth seemed serene and bottomless. The mirror in the left sleeve, however, gave off no reflection whatsoever. Its surface was like that of a new pan that had yet to be touched by flames. But suddenly I became aware that the luster of the mirror from the left sleeve was innumerable times brighter than the other. After this, when I looked at all things, it was as though I were seeing my own face. For the first time I understood the meaning of the saying, "The Tathāgata sees the Buddha-nature within his eye."

Later I happened to read the *Pi-yen lu* again, and my understanding of it differed completely from what it had been before. One night, some time after, I took up the Lotus Sūtra. Suddenly I penetrated to the perfect, true, ultimate meaning of the *Lotus*. The doubts I had held initially were destroyed and I became aware that the understanding I had obtained up to then was greatly in error. Unconsciously I uttered a great cry and burst into tears.

I wish that everyone would realize that studying Zen under a teacher is not such a simple matter after all. Although I am old and dissipated, and have nothing of which I can be proud, I am aware that at least I have not spent forty years in vain. Was it not for this reason that Chang Wu, when he was in Yang-chou, let go of his gold and engaged in his painful struggles [toward success]? As in the example I gave you, if you shoulder the one-sided understanding you have gained and spend your whole life vainly polishing and purifying it, how are you any different from Chang Lu, who guarded his piece of gold throughout his life, starving himself and bringing only harm to his body?

In India such a person is called a poor son of a rich man, [a follower] of the Two Vehicles.[2] In China he is spoken of as belonging to the group that practices the heretical silent-illumination Zen. None of these knows the dignity of the bodhisattva, nor does he reach the understanding that illuminates the cause for entrance to a Buddha land. Nowadays people go about carrying on their shoulders a single empty principle and with it "understand the Buddha, understand the Patriarchs, understand the old koans." Then they all say: "Like the stick, like the *dhāraṇī*, like the *katsu*."[3] How laughable this is! Exert yourselves, students, for the Buddha Way is deep and far. Let everyone know that the farther you enter the sea the deeper it becomes and the higher you climb a mountain the taller it gets.

If you wish to test the validity of your own powers, you must first study the koan on the death of Nan-ch'üan.

A long time ago San-sheng had the head monk Hsiu go to the Zen Master Tsen of Ch'ang-sha and ask him: "What happened to Nan-ch'üan after he passed away?"

Ch'ang-sha replied: "When Shih-t'ou became a novice monk he was seen by the Sixth Patriarch."

Hsiu replied: "I didn't ask you about when Shih-t'ou became a novice monk; I asked you what happened to Nanch'uan after he passed away."

Ch'ang-sha replied: "If I were you I would let Nan-ch'üan worry about it himself."

---

2. "The Two Vehicles" refers here to the two kinds of Hinayana practitioners, the *śrāvaka* and the *Pratyeka-buddha*. The *śrāvaka* is working toward or has gained Nirvana in Hinayana terms only. The *Pratyeka-buddha* has gained enlightenment through his own efforts, but gives no thought to aiding others.

3. This passage is unclear. Presumably these people, who bear a single empty principle on their shoulders, and claim to understand the Buddha, Patriarchs, and koans, equate the stick with the Buddha, the *dhāraṇī* with the koans, and the shout *(katsu)* with the Patriarchs.

Hsiu replied: "Even though you had a thousand-foot winter pine, there is no bamboo shoot to rise above its branches."

Ch'ang-sha had nothing to say. Hsiu returned and told the story of his conversation to San-sheng. San-sheng unconsciously stuck out his tongue [in surprise] and said: "He has surpassed Lin-chi by seven paces."

If you are able to understand and make clear these words, then I will acknowledge that you have a certain degree of responsiveness to the teachings. Why is this so? If you speak to yourself while no one is around, you behave as meanly as a rat. What can anyone possibly prove [about your understanding]?

I may have been hitting a dangerous animal in the teeth three times. I join my palms together and say: "Let's leave it at that for today."

Be Like a Frog

Shunryu Suzuki

A year or two before his death in 1971, Shunryu Suzuki was interviewed by Jacob Needleman, who drew this portrait of him:

> Short and slight, he appears to be in his early sixties; his head is shaved, and he wears the robes of a priest. One's overwhelming first impression is of openness and warmth. He laughs often, noiselessly—and when I was with him, trying to discuss "profound questions," I found myself laughing with him throughout the interview. Beneath the lightness and gentleness, however, one feels as well his tremendous rigor.[1]

A Zen master in Japan (and the son of a Zen master), Suzuki came to this country in 1959 to head the Zen Center in San Francisco. In 1966 he founded the Zen Mountain Center at Tassajara Springs, a Soto Zen monastery in the mountains near Carmel on the California coast and the first Zen monastery in the United States.

Zen Mind, Beginner's Mind, *from which the following selections are taken, is composed of talks given by Suzuki and taped by Marian Derby. The tapes were edited by Trudy Dixon.*

Zen and Excitement

It is necessary for us to keep the constant way. Zen is not some kind of excitement, but concentration on our usual everyday routine. If you become too busy and too excited, your mind becomes rough and ragged. This is not good. If possible, try to be always calm and joyful and keep yourself from excitement. Usually we become busier and busier, day by day, year by year, especially in our modern world. If we revisit old, familiar places after a long time, we are astonished by the changes. It cannot be helped. But if we become interested in some excitement, or in our own change, we will become completely involved in our busy life, and we will be lost. But if your mind is calm and constant, you can keep yourself away from the noisy world even though you are in the midst of it. In the midst of noise and change, your mind will be quiet and stable.

1. Needleman, *The New Religions* (New York: Doubleday, 1970), p. 50.

Zen is not something to get excited about. Some people start to practice Zen just out of curiosity, and they only make themselves busier. If your practice makes you worse, it is ridiculous. I think that if you try to do zazen once a week, that will make you busy enough. Do not be too interested in Zen. When young people get excited about Zen they often give up schooling and go to some mountain or forest in order to sit. That kind of interest is not true interest.

Just continue in your calm, ordinary practice and your character will be built up. If your mind is always busy, there will be no time to build, and you will not be successful, particularly if you work too hard on it. Building character is like making bread—you have to mix it little by little, step by step, and moderate temperature is needed. You know yourself quite well, and you know how much temperature you need. You know exactly what you need. But if you get too excited, you will forget how much temperature is good for you, and you will lose your own way. This is very dangerous.

Buddha said the same thing about the good ox driver. The driver knows how much load the ox can carry, and he keeps the ox from being overloaded. You know your way and your state of mind. Do not carry too much! Buddha also said that building character is like building a dam. You should be very careful in making the bank. If you try to do it all at once, water will leak from it. Make the bank carefully and you will end up with a fine dam for the reservoir.

Our unexciting way of practice may appear to be very negative. This is not so. It is a wise and effective way to work on ourselves. It is just very plain. I find this point very difficult for people, especially young people, to understand. On the other hand it may seem as if I am speaking about gradual attainment. This is not so either. In fact, this is the sudden way, because when your practice is calm and ordinary, everyday life itself is enlightenment.

To Polish a Tile

Zen stories, or *koans,* are very difficult to understand before you know what we are doing moment after moment. But if you know exactly what we are doing in each moment, you will not find *koans* so difficult. There are so many *koans.* I have often talked to you about a frog, and each time everybody laughs. But a frog is very interesting. He sits like us, too, you know. But he does not think that he is doing anything so special. When you go to a zendo and sit, you may think you are doing some special thing. While your husband or wife is sleeping, you are practicing zazen! You are doing some special thing, and your spouse is lazy! That may be your understanding of zazen. But look at the frog. A frog also sits like us, but he has no idea of zazen. Watch him. If something annoys him, he will make a face. If something comes along to eat, he will snap it up and eat, and he eats sitting. Actually that is our zazen—not any special thing.

Here is a kind of frog *koan* for you. Baso was a famous Zen master called the Horse-master. He was the disciple of Nangaku, one of the Sixth Patriarch's disciples. One day while he was studying under Nangaku, Baso was sitting, practicing zazen. He was a man of large physical build; when he talked, his tongue reached to his nose; his voice was loud; and his zazen must have been very good. Nangaku saw him sitting like a great mountain or like a frog. Nangaku asked, "What are you doing?" "I am practicing zazen," Baso replied. "Why are you practicing zazen?" "I want to attain enlightenment; I want to be a Buddha," the disciple said. Do you know what the teacher did? He picked up a tile, and he started to polish it. In Japan, after taking a tile from the kiln, we polish it to give it a beautiful finish. So Nangaku picked up a tile and started to polish it. Baso, his disciple, asked, "What are you doing?" "I want to make this tile into a jewel," Nangaku said. "How is it possible to make a tile a jewel?" Baso asked. "How is it possible to make a tile a jewel?" Baso asked. "How is it possible to become a Buddha by practicing zazen?" Nangaku replied. "Do you want to attain Buddhahood? There is no Buddhahood besides your ordinary mind. When a cart does not go, which do you whip, the cart or the horse?" the master asked.

Nangaku's meaning here is that whatever you do, that is zazen. True zazen is beyond being in bed or sitting in the zendo. If your husband or wife is in bed, that is zazen. If you think, "I am sitting here, and my spouse is in bed," then even though you are sitting here in the cross-legged position, that is not true zazen. You should be like a frog always. That is true zazen.

Dogen-zenji commented on this *koan*. He said, "When the Horse-master becomes the Horse-master, Zen becomes Zen." When Baso becomes Baso, his zazen becomes true zazen, and Zen becomes Zen. What is true zazen? When you become you! When you are you, then no matter what you do, that is zazen. Even though you are in bed, you may not be you most of the time. Even though you are sitting in the zendo, I wonder whether you are you in the true sense.

Here is another famous *koan*. Zuikan was a Zen master who always used to address himself. "Zuikan?" he would call. And then he would answer. "Yes!" "Zuikan?" "Yes!" Of course he was living all alone in his small zendo, and of course he knew who he was, but sometimes he lost himself. And whenever he lost himself, he would address himself, "Zuikan?" "Yes!"

If we are like a frog, we are always ourselves. But even a frog sometimes loses himself, and he makes a sour face. And if something comes along, he will snap at it and eat it. So I think a frog is always addressing himself. I think you should do that also. Even in zazen you will lose yourself. When you become sleepy, or when your mind starts to wander about, you lose yourself. When your legs become painful— "Why are my legs so painful?"—you lose yourself. Because you lose yourself, your problem will be a problem for you. If you do not lose yourself, then even though you have difficulty, there is actually no problem whatsoever. You just sit in the midst of the problem; when you are a part of the problem, or when the problem is a part of you, there *is* no problem, because you are the problem itself. The problem is you yourself. If this is so, there is no problem.

When your life is always a part of your surroundings—in other words, when you are called back to yourself, in the present moment—then there is no problem. When you start to wander about in some delusion which is something apart from you yourself, then your surroundings are not real anymore, and your mind is not real anymore. If you yourself are deluded, then your surroundings are also a misty, foggy delusion. Once you are in the midst of delusion, there is no end to delusion.

You will be involved in deluded ideas one after another. Most people live in delusion, involved in their problem, trying to solve their problem. But just to live is actually to live in problems. And to solve the problem is to be a part of it, to be one with it.

So which do you hit, the cart or the horse? Which do you hit, yourself or your problems? If you start questioning which you should hit, that means you have already started to wander about. But when you actually hit the horse, the cart will go. In truth, the cart and the horse are not different. When you are you, there is no problem of whether you should hit the cart or the horse. When you are you, zazen becomes true zazen. So when you practice zazen, your problem will practice zazen, and everything else will practice zazen too. Even though your spouse is in bed, he or she is also practicing zazen—when *you* practice zazen! But when you do not practice true zazen, then there is your spouse, and there is yourself, each quite different, quite separate from the other. So if you yourself have true practice, then everything else is practicing our way at the same time.

That is why we should always address ourselves, checking up on ourselves like a doctor tapping himself. This is very important. This kind of practice should be continued moment after moment, incessantly. We say, "When the night is here, the dawn comes." It means there is no gap between the dawn and the night. Before the summer is over, autumn comes. In this way we should understand our life. We should practice with this understanding, and solve our problems in this way. Actually, just to work on the problem, if you do it with single-minded effort, is enough. You should just polish the tile; that is our practice. The purpose of practice is not to make a tile a jewel. Just continue sitting; that is practice in its true sense. It is not a matter of whether or not it is possible to attain Buddhahood, whether or not it is possible to make a tile a jewel. Just to work and live in this world with this understanding is the most important point. That is our practice. That is true zazen. So we say, "When you eat, eat!" You should eat what is there, you know. Sometimes you do not eat it. Even though you are eating, your mind is somewhere else. You do not taste what you have in your mouth. As long as you can eat when you are eating, you are all right. Do not worry a bit. It means you are you yourself.

When you are you, you see things as they are, and you become one with your surroundings. There is your true self. There you have true practice; you have the practice of a frog. He is a good example of our practice—when a frog becomes a frog, Zen becomes Zen. When you understand a frog through and through, you attain enlightenment; you are Buddha. And you are good for others, too: husband or wife or son or daughter. This is zazen!

Naturalness

There is a big misunderstanding about the idea of naturalness. Most people who come to us believe in some freedom or naturalness, but their understanding is what we call *jinen ken gedo,* or heretical naturalness. *Jinen ken gedo* means that there is no need to be formal—just a kind of "let-alone policy" or sloppiness. That is naturalness for most people. But that is not the naturalness we mean. It is rather difficult to explain, but naturalness is, I think, some feeling of being independent from everything, or some activity which is based on nothingness. Something which comes out of nothingness is naturalness, like a seed or plant coming out of the ground. The seed has no idea of being some particular plant, but it has its own form and is in perfect harmony with the ground, with its surroundings. As it grows, in the course of time it expresses its nature. Nothing exists without form and color. Whatever it is, it has some form and color, and that form and color are in perfect harmony with other beings. And there is no trouble. That is what we mean by naturalness.

For a plant or stone to be natural is no problem. But for us there is some problem, indeed a big problem. To be natural is something which we must work on. When what you do just comes out from nothingness, you have quite a new feeling. For instance, when you are hungry, to take some food is naturalness. You feel natural. But when you are expecting too much, to have some food is not natural. You have no new feeling. You have no appreciation for it.

The true practice of zazen is to sit as if drinking water when you are thirsty. There you have naturalness. It is quite natural for you to take a nap when you are very sleepy. But to take a nap just because you are lazy, as if it were the privilege of a human being to take a nap, is not naturalness. You think, "My friends, all of them, are napping; why shouldn't I? When everyone else is not working, why should I work so hard? When they have a lot of money, why don't I?" This is not naturalness. Your mind is entangled with some other idea, someone else's idea, and you are not independent, not yourself, and not natural. Even if you sit in the cross-legged position, if your zazen is not natural, it is not true practice. You do not have to force yourself to drink water when you are thirsty; you are glad to drink water. If you have true joy in your zazen, that is true zazen. But even though you have to force yourself to practice zazen, if you feel something good in your practice, that is zazen. Actually it is not a matter of forcing something on you or not. Even though you have some difficulty, when you want to have it, that is naturalness.

This naturalness is very difficult to explain. But if you can just sit and experience the actuality of nothingness in your practice, there is no need to explain. If it comes out of nothingness, whatever you do is natural, and that is true activity. You have the true joy of practice, the true joy of life in it. Everyone comes out from nothingness moment after moment. Moment after moment we have true joy of life. So we say *shin ku myo u,* "from true emptiness, the wondrous being appears." *Shin* is "true"; *ku* is "emptiness"; *myo* is "wondrous"; *u* is "being": from true emptiness, wondrous being.

Without nothingness, there is no naturalness—no true being. True being comes out of nothingness, moment after moment. Nothingness is always there, and from it everything appears. But usually, forgetting all about nothingness, you behave as if you have something. What you do is based on some possessive idea or some concrete idea, and that is not natural. For instance, when you listen to a lecture, you should not have any idea of yourself. You should not have your own idea when you listen to someone. Forget what you have in your mind and just listen to what he says. To have nothing in your mind is naturalness. Then you will understand what he says. But if you have some idea to compare with what he says, you will not hear everything; your understanding will be one-sided; that is not naturalness. When you do something, you should be completely involved in it. You should devote yourself to it completely. Then you have nothing. So if there is no true emptiness in your activity, it is not natural.

Most people insist on some idea. Recently the younger generation talks about love. Love! Love! Love! Their minds are full of love! And when they study Zen, if what I say does not accord with the idea they have of love, they will not accept it. They are quite stubborn, you know. You may be amazed! Of course not all, but some have a very, very hard attitude. That is not naturalness at all. Even though they talk about love, and freedom or naturalness, they do not understand these things. And they cannot understand what Zen is in that way. If you want to study Zen, you should forget all your previous ideas and just practice zazen and see what kind of experience you have in your practice. That is naturalness.

Whatever you do, this attitude is necessary. Sometimes we say *nyu nan shin,* "soft or flexible mind." *Nyu* is "soft feeling"; *nan* is "something which is not hard"; *shin* is "mind." *Nyu nan shin* means a smooth, natural mind. When you have that mind, you have the joy of life. When you lose it, you lose everything. You have nothing. Although you think you have something, you have nothing. But when all you do comes out of nothingness, then you have everything. Do you understand? That is what we mean by naturalness.

Further Reading

Shundo Aoyama is the chief priest of Aichi Semmon Niso-do, a Soto Zen training temple for women priests. Her *Zen Seeds* (1991) is composed of fifty-eight very short reflections on everyday topics. (On aging: "In the life that is left me, I am right now at my youngest.")

Stephen Addiss, *The Art of Zen: Paintings and Calligraphy by Japanese Monks, 1600–1925* (1989). Included are both traditional and nontraditional works, from a smiling frog to Nantembo's "Procession of Monks."

Kenneth Kraft (ed.), *Zen: Tradition and Transition* (1988). Eleven contemporary essays by authors particularly informed on their topics. Burton Watson, for example, writes here about Zen poetry; Morinaga Soko, Roshi of Daishuin temple in Kyoto, relates "My Struggle to Become a Zen Monk."

Helen Tworkov, *Zen in America: Profiles of Five Teachers* (1989). Zen with an American flavor: Robert Aiken, Bernard Glassman, Maurine Stuart, Jakusho Kwong, and Richard Baker are the subjects.

Paul Rep's *Zen Flesh, Zen Bones* (1957) includes the wonderful "101 Zen Stories," which convey much of the spirit (and fun) of Zen.

Alan Watts was an exceptionally talented writer with a great interest in Zen and Eastern thought, and for years he was one of the most popular interpreters of Zen; his *The Way of Zen* (1960) remains a fine introduction.

Heinrich Dumoulin's *A History of Zen Buddhism* (1963) is a standard history of the religion.

William Johnston, an Irish Catholic priest, noted author, and director of the Institute of Oriental Religions of Sophia University in Tokyo, had lived in Japan for twenty years at the time he wrote *Christian Zen* (1971). He found his contact with Zen "tremendously enriching; it has deepened and broadened my Christian faith more than I can say.... So this is a personal book about what I have gained."

Connections to another religion are made by several authors in *Zen and Hasidism* (1978), edited by Harold Heifetz. Contributors include Gary Snyder, Martin Buber, Christmas Humphreys, Kennett Roshi, John Blofeld, and Zalman Schacter.

Robert Aitken was a student under and friend of D. T. Suzuki and is a Zen master himself. Recommended especially are *Taking the Path of Zen* (1982) and *The Mind of Clover: Essays in Zen Buddhist Ethics* (1984).

IV

CONFUCIANISM
An Ideal of Moral Order

The superior man understands what is right,
The inferior man understands what will sell.   The Analects

The story of the life of Confucius is remarkable for its lack of those dramatic events one might have expected in the career of the man who became the "First Teacher" of China and whose influence has extended to this day. No "voices" spoke to him, no miracles are claimed. He never walked on red-hot coals. No visions. Instead, he was only a teacher, and to make matters worse, he talked a great deal about the necessity of our being *good*. Good fathers and mothers, good sons and daughters, good citizens, good brothers and sisters and friends. . . . Compounding the problem, he had the audacity to lay down rules.

Although Confucius[1] occasionally held minor posts in government, he mostly taught, and he excelled at it: students became disciples. He had, he said, a great love of learning and considered himself a diligent student, but he made no claim to wisdom nor even to high moral character. His ambition was to attain a significant position in government through which he could put into practice the ideas and ideals he taught. That ambition was never realized. After a long teaching career, he retired, spent his last years studying, and died, in Arthur Waley's phrase, " a disappointed itinerant tutor."

The substance of his teaching, described in the following essay by H. G. Creel, dealt with those moral qualities that comprise the *chun tzu,* the superior man or "true gentleman." The *chun tzu* was a model of modest strength and decorum: gentle, poised, kind, sincere, dutiful, and trustworthy. He was not, however, an "individual." He was, of course, a person in his own right, but he was primarily a member of a family and of society—and it was this network of responsibilities that concerned Confucius.

The society in which Confucius lived had disintegrated into feuding states, and there were sporadic outbursts of devastating warfare. What was required first, therefore, was order, but Confucius knew that an inflexible, strong-armed regime of "law

---

1. His family name was K'ung and given name Chung-ni; but as his reputation grew, he became known as K'ung Fu-tzu ("Master" K'ung). In the Latin of Jesuit missionaries, "K'ung Fu-tzu" came out "Confucius."

and order" was not the answer. Hence the great Confucian virtue of *li* (the principle of propriety; the proper, structured way of doing things) was to be accompanied by *jen* (goodness, human-heartedness, kindness). Orderliness and ceremony were to be observed, in other words, but they were to be balanced by a feeling for "humanity."

The preponderance of ethical and social content in the teachings of Confucius has often prompted two different responses. On the one hand, Confucianism is sometimes termed a philosophy or, more specifically, "Chinese Humanism," rather than a religion. On the other hand, laborious attempts have been made to ferret out in Confucian literature those indications of "conventional" religious behavior and conviction that would prove Confucianism a legitimate member of the world's family of religions. But each of these responses appears to rest on categories of thought more appropriate to Western than to Far Eastern religion.

Confucius was undeniably preoccupied with "down-to-earth" moral issues, but the term "humanism" implies a dualism foreign to Chinese thought. Confucianism is perhaps best understood as an expression of that older and larger conception in China of a cosmic harmony. The Confucian ideal of social order—of the rules of propriety observed by all, of tradition and ritual enhancing our lives—was a reflection of that Ultimate Order.[2] Heaven, earth, and humankind were, in China, a continuum: the ruler, for example, was the "Son of Heaven" and he ruled only by "decree" of Heaven. To restore harmony to human society was to return to Tao, the Way. In ancient China, Joseph Kitagawa has written,

> the world of man and the world of nature constitute a seamless whole, governed by reciprocal relationships. . . . Chinese religion never made a distinction between sacred and secular. . . . The religious ethos of the Chinese must be found in the midst of their everyday life. . . . The meaning of life was sought in the whole of life, and not confined to any section of it called specifically "religious."[3]

The readings of this chapter, apart from the introductory essay by Creel, include selections from three of the *Four Books* of Confucianism, all of which are products of the followers of Confucius. (Confucius said that he was "a transmitter and not a creator." It is not certain what, if anything, we have from his own hand.) *The Analects* is the most important source of the "sayings" and life of Confucius. *The Book of Mencius* is a collection of the teachings of the "Second Sage" of China. *The Great Learning,* a brief summary of moral and social doctrines, is presented in its entirety.

Tu Wei-ming explains in "Confucian Self-realization" that the fully realized self is essentially *communal,* "an open and communicating center of relationships," and those relationships, it turns out, are with everything from our families to the cosmos.

---

2. This is a theme rarely explicit in early Confucian literature, with the exception of *The Doctrine of the Mean* ("Equilibrium is the great foundation of the world, and harmony its universal path," etc.). Neo-Confucianists later pursued the subject extensively.

3. *Religions of the East* (Philadelphia: Westminster Press, 1960), pp. 49–50.

In the Preface to his *Confucius—The Secular as Sacred,* Herbert Fingarette, whose essay concludes this chapter, wrote

> When I began to read Confucius, I found him to be a prosaic and parochial moralizer. . . . Later, and with increasing force, I found him a thinker with profound insight and with an imaginative vision of man equal in its grandeur to any I know. Increasingly, I have become convinced that Confucius can be a teacher to us today. . . . He tells us things not being said elsewhere; things needing to be said. He has a new lesson to teach.

Confucius and the Struggle for Human Happiness

H. G. Creel

A native of Chicago, Herrlee G. Creel (1905–   ) received his doctorate from, and spent most of his career at, the University of Chicago. When he retired in 1974, he was the Martin A. Ryerson Distinguished Service Professor of Chinese History. During World War II he served as a lieutenant colonel in Military Intelligence, and over the years was honored with fellowships from the American Council of Learned Societies and the Harvard-Yenching Institute.

Creel's books have been published in England, France, Japan, Italy, and Spain, as well as in the United States; his many titles include Confucius: The Man and the Myth *(later reprinted as* Confucius and the Chinese Way) *and* What Is Taoism? Chinese Thought: From Confucius to Mao Tse-tung, *from which the following selection is taken, was published in 1953.*

Confucius was one of the handful of men who have deeply influenced human history by the force of their personal and intellectual gifts and achievements. The fact that such men appear upon the scene can never be completely explained; but, by examining the circumstances of their lives, we can at least increase our ability to understand them.

Our attempt to understand Confucius is made difficult by the large mass of legend and tradition that has accumulated about his name so thickly, over the centuries, that it becomes very hard to see the truth. These elaborations, not to say distortions, spring from two quite different motives. On the one hand, the faithful have wished to exalt him and have therefore performed such pious acts as building up an elaborate genealogy that traces his ancestry back to emperors. On the other, those whose interests were menaced by this revolutionary thinker have sought, and with partial success, to nullify his attacks upon intrenched privilege by distorting and misrepresenting what he had to say. Our only safe course, therefore, is completely to disregard the elaborate traditional story of his life and thought and trust only the more meager testimony that can be gleaned from documents that can be proved to be early and reliable.[1]

1. See Creel, *Confucius, the Man and the Myth,* (New York, 1949) pp. 7–11, 291–94.

Confucius was born in 551 B.C. in the small state of Lu, which was located in what is now Shantung Province. What his ancestry was we cannot be certain, but it is probable that there were aristocrats among his forebears. As a young man he was, however, by his own testimony, "without rank and in humble circumstances."[2] He had to make his own living, at tasks that were more or less menial. He was able to study, but seems to have been largely self-taught.

These experiences undoubtedly gave him a close view of the sufferings of the common people, about which he became deeply concerned. He felt that the world was sadly out of joint and that it was vital that drastic changes be made. He had opportunity not only to know the people but also to become familiar with the aristocrats, who were the hereditary lords of creation. Of most of the aristocrats he had a very poor opinion. He was undoubtedly speaking of the parasitic nobles of his time when he said: "It is difficult to expect anything from men who stuff themselves with food the whole day, while never using their minds in any way at all. Even gamblers do *something,* and to that degree are better than these idlers."[3]

Unfortunately, however, the aristocrats were not always idle. They used considerable ingenuity in devising ever more expensive adjuncts to luxurious living, for which the people paid with taxes and forced labor. Above all, the nobles practiced the art of war. In China, as perhaps in most other nations, the nobility was military in origin. In an earlier day these military officers had performed a useful function in protecting society, but as a class they had largely outlived their usefulness, and now they preyed on the people and on one another. Most of them felt that the arts of war were theonly occupations worthy of the serious attention of a gentleman, and they made fun of those, even among their own numbers, who concerned themselves with the need for good government and orderly administration.

Confucius was not a pacifist. He believed that, regrettably, there are times when force must be used by moral men, in order to prevent themselves and the world from being enslaved by those for whom force is the only argument and the only sanction. But he considered force a last resort and one that must always be subordinate, not only ideally but as a matter of hard fact, to the power of justice. On the ideal and personal level he said: "If I feel in my heart that I am wrong, I must stand in fear even though my opponent is the least formidable of men. But if my own heart tells me that I am right, I shall go forward even against thousands and tens of thousands."[4] On the more practical level, he believed that an army could not fight effectively unless even its common soldiers knew why they were fighting and were convinced of the justice of their cause. He believed that morale is dependent on moral conviction. He said: "To lead a people who have not been educated to war, is to throw them away."[5]

Confucius was aware that such ideas were completely at variance with those of the nobility. He not only realized it but tried to do something about it. Up to his time the term *chün tzŭ,* "gentleman," had almost universally had a significance

2. *Analects* 9.6.3.

3. Ibid. 17.22.

4. *Mencius* 2(1)2.7.

5. *Analects* 13.30; see also 13.29.

somewhat like the original meaning of our word "gentleman." It denoted, that is, a man of good birth, whose ancestors had belonged to a stratum above that of the common herd. Such a person was a gentleman by birth; no one not born so could become a gentleman, and no gentleman could ever become less than one, no matter how vile his conduct might be. Confucius changed this usage completely. He asserted that any man might be a gentleman, if his conduct were noble, unselfish, just, and kind. On the other hand, he asserted that no man could be considered a gentleman on the ground of birth; this was solely a question of conduct and character.

Confucius was always markedly contemptuous of eloquence and of ornate language, and there is no record that he ever delivered a public lecture. Nevertheless, he must have been an unusually persuasive speaker to one person or to small groups. Even today, as we read the things he said, we can feel the magnetism of his personality. He talked about his ideas for reforming the world, which were many and bold, to those with whom he came in contact, and gradually there were attracted to him a number of men who became his students, or, as we commonly call them, his disciples. At the beginning some of them were only a little younger than himself.

In so far as we know, this group, composed of Confucius and those who studied with him, formed the first private school devoted to higher education in Chinese history. The sons of rulers and aristocrats had long had tutors; and men who were destined to be minor officials in the courts had studied, as apprentices of officials, with their superiors. That kind of teaching seems to have consisted chiefly of training in techniques, to enable men to carry on certain traditional functions. Confucius, however, was not concerned merely to train his charges, but to *educate* them, in the sense of, as one dictionary definition explains the word, "to develop and cultivate mentally or morally, to expand, strengthen, and discipline."

.   .   .

Since he was undertaking to make men of humble background into "gentlemen," able to hold their own in the halls of state with the most polished courtiers, he had to teach them court etiquette. He did so; but here again he profoundly altered the character of an ancient institution, in a manner that was to have the most important consequences. The Chinese term by which such etiquette is known is *li;* it is commonly translated, even as Confucius uses it, as "ritual" or "the rules of propriety." These translations will do well enough, no doubt, for this institution as Confucius found it, but they are hopelessly inadequate to express what he made of it.

The original meaning of *li* was "to sacrifice"; it still has this sense in modern Chinese. It was extended to denote the ritual used in sacrifice and then to cover every sort of ceremony and the "courtesy" that characterized the conduct of those who made up a ruler's court.

Confucius started from there. If rulers were gravely serious in sacrificing to their ancestors, why should they not be equally so in attending to the government of the realm? If ministers treated one another with courtesy, in the daily intercourse of the court, why should they not be equally considerate toward the common people, who were the backbone of the state? Thus he said to one of his disciples that, wherever he went in the world, he should treat all those with whom he came in contact as if he were "receiving an important guest"; and if he became an official of the government, he should deal with the people as if he were "officiating at a great sacrifice."[6] Such conduct would, of course, contrast sharply with the careless conduct of most of the aristocrats.

Court etiquette was then, as it has been in most times and places, conceived as a more or less well-defined body of fixed rules. Even in some of the so-called Confucian "classics" we find the most minute directions for behavior, which tell one exactly where each finger should be placed in picking up a ritual object. But Confucius himself conceived of *li* quite differently. It was the spirit that counted, and he was contemptuous of those who believed that, by mere ostentatious display of costly trappings and sedulous aping of the behavior of others, they could excel in *li*.

·   ·   ·

His whole system of ethics and, indeed, most of his philosophy seem to have been based upon a consideration of what is the nature of the human being. He did not make either of two mistakes that have sometimes been made in this connection. On the one hand, he did not think of the individual as existing quite separately from society. On the other, he did not think of society as a kind of metaphysical entity that is so completely prior to the individual that the individual can hardly be said to exist, except as he is wholly absorbed in it.

Confucius believed that men are essentially social beings. They are to a very considerable extent (though by no means totally) made what they are by society. On the other hand, since society is nothing more than the interaction of men, society is made what it is by the individuals who compose it. Confucius believed that the conscience of the individual must equally forbid him either to withdraw from society or to surrender his moral judgment to it. It is equally wrong, then, either to become a recluse or to "follow the crowd." The moral man must not be a cipher in, but a co-operating member of, society. Wherever the conventional practices seem to him immoral or harmful, he not only will refrain from conforming with them but will try to persuade others to change the convention. Necessarily, however, the areas in which he does this will be limited. As a sensible and social man, he will accord with convention wherever the common practice seems reasonable or harmless.

It goes without saying that convention is the cement of society. If each of us ate, slept, and worked when and where we pleased and used words that we individually invented to mean what we individually desired them to mean, the world would be a difficult place to live in. Confucius used the term *li* to stand for the whole complex of conventional and social usage, which he endowed with a *moral* connotation. Thus combined, the sanctions of morality and courtesy reinforced each other. We consider it courteous, but not necessarily a moral duty, to be polite to everyone with whom we come in contact. We consider it a moral duty, but not necessarily an obligation of courtesy, to return property we find to the loser, even though we may not

6. Ibid. 12.2.

know him. But the whole range of the obligations imposed by the highest conceptions of both courtesy and moral duty were included in *li*. To say "it is *li*" was equivalent to our "it is done," which is often far more persuasive than the most detailed argument.

This conception of *li* was extremely important in Confucius' program of education. Psychiatrists say that our education, although it cultivates the intellect to a high degree, often fails signally to discipline the emotions. For this reason it is sometimes unable to produce a well-adjusted individual, capable of taking his place as a happy and useful member of society. Confucius considered intellectual cultivation to be of little worth if it were not accompanied by emotional balance; to produce such balance he depended upon education in *li*. The learning of the gentleman, he said, must be "disciplined by means of *li*"; one thus prepared to meet the world is strengthened, he believed, to hold true to his principles through any crisis and in the face of every temptation.[7]

. . .

The problem of Confucius' relationship to religion is a difficult one. Certainly he was not primarily, as has sometimes been supposed, a religious prophet or teacher. In fact, it is easy to cite passages from the *Analects* that show that he was reluctant to discuss religious questions. Although he talked a great deal about the way that men should follow, one of his disciples said that he did not discuss "the way [that is, the *tao*] of Heaven."[8] Another disciple asked how one should serve spirits; Confucius told him: "You are not yet able to serve men; how can you serve spirits?" The disciple asked about death; the Master told him: "You do not yet understand life; how can you understand death?"[9]

From these and certain other passages it has sometimes been concluded that Confucius was insincere. Some have thought that he was, in fact, skeptical or even atheistic but that, for lack of courage or for some other reason, he refrained from telling his disciples the truth. This seems to resolve a difficult problem too simply.

There are several passages in which Confucius speaks of Heaven, the principal deity of the Chinese. He seems, in fact, to have felt that he had been intrusted by Heaven with a mission to cure the ills of the Chinese world, and he hoped that Heaven would not permit him to fail.[10] Once when he cried out in despair that there was no one who understood him, he added, "But Heaven understands me!"[11]

What did Confucius understand by the term "Heaven"? Not an anthropomorphic being. Heaven was seldom so conceived in his time, and there is explicit reason for rejecting this idea in connection with Confucius. If we examine the ways in which Confucius refers to Heaven, it appears that this term stood, in his thinking, for a vaguely conceived moral force in the universe. He placed the utmost emphasis on striving by the individual, but he seems to have hoped that Heaven would, as we

7. Ibid. 6.25; see also 4.5.

8. Ibid. 5.12.

9. Ibid. 11.11.

10. Ibid. 9.5.

11. Ibid. 14.37.

say, "help those who help themselves." Yet even this could not be counted on, for, as he sadly observed, the wicked often prosper and the efforts of the good sometimes come to nought. Nevertheless, the idea of Heaven gave him the feeling that some-how, somewhere, there was a power that stood on the side of the lonely man who struggles for the right.

The religion of the day said little about life after death and made little or no use of it as a deterrent to wickedness or a stimulus to virtue. Confucius, as we have seen, would not discuss this topic. In numerous respects he broke sharply with the tra-ditional religion. In accord with his usual practice, however, he did not call atten-tion to these departures from precedent, so that they are sometimes overlooked. In general, sacrifice was considered a barter transaction, in which so much goods was sacrificed to the ancestors and other spirits in the expectation of receiving so many blessings. Confucius condemned this attitude. He believed that the traditional sac-rifices should be made, but in the same spirit in which one is courteous to one's friends: not because of what one expects to get from them, but because it is the right thing to do. Did he believe that the spirits conferred blessings? We simply do not know; it is possible that he did not.

· · ·

Although Confucius had certain religious convictions, he does not seem to have used them as the basis of his philosophy. Here his attitude seems to have had some resemblance to that of the modern scientist. Probably no scientist would say that the existence of God can be proved by scientific technique; even theologians have asserted that this cannot be done. On the other hand, it is doubtful that any careful scientist would say that God can be scientifically proved *not* to exist. For science is not concerned with the ultimate nature of the universe but with making certain observations from experience and formulating these into principles that represent preponderant probabilities. By foregoing the right to speak of ultimate truth, sci-ence gains the ability to help us act practically and fruitfully.

Confucius operated in much the same way. He made no claim to the possession of the ultimate truth. He was groping toward the truth, by the method of observa-tion and analysis. He said that one should "hear much, leave to one side that which is doubtful, and speak with due caution concerning the remainder. . . . See much, but leave to one side that of which the meaning is not clear, and act carefully with regard to the rest."[12] He said nothing about attaining the truth through a sudden flash of mystical enlightenment; on the contrary, he stated flatly that meditation alone does not lead to wisdom.[13] He also said: "To hear much, select what is good, and follow it; to see much and remember it; these are the steps by which under-standing is attained."[14]

Thus it is clear enough that, however religious Confucius may have been, he was far from feeling assured of his own omniscience or infallibility concerning the ulti-

12. Ibid. 2.18.

13. Ibid. 15.30.

14. Ibid. 7.27. Concerning this translation, see Creel, *Confucius, the Man and the Myth,* p. 311, n. 24.

mate nature of the universe. He was trying to set up a structure of ideas that would last, and be strong enough to serve as a foundation upon which to build the freedom and happiness of the human race. For this he had to build with materials which he not merely hoped, but which as nearly as possible he knew, to be sound. He took as his basis, therefore, neither theological dogma nor religious hope but the nature of man and society as he observed them.

. . .

Confucius based his ethics, we have said, upon the nature of man and society. But what is the nature of man and society? Obviously this is the crucial question, and if Confucius had tried to answer it hastily or dogmatically his empirical approach would have been little more than pretense. He did not. Unlike Mencius, the great Confucian philosopher of the fourth century B.C., Confucius did not say that human nature is "good." Nor did he, like another slightly later Confucian, Hsun Tzu, say that human nature is "bad." . . .

Confucius stayed closer to the concrete. Perhaps his most important observation about men was that they are essentially equal. Probably the fact that he had himself been born into depressed circumstances, from which he wished to rise, had much to do with this. He saw, too, that men who were born with every hereditary claim to exalted rank and noble character often behaved like beasts or clods, while others without these advantages often conducted themselves in a manner far more worthy of respect.

He also made the simple observation that all men, however differently they may define it, desire happiness. Since there was not in his background any religious or philosophical dogma that branded happiness, or the desire for it, as bad, he believed that in so far as possible men should have what they wanted. All about him, however, he saw that people in general were anything but happy. The masses were in want, sometimes starving, oppressed by war and by the aristocrats; and even the aristocrats did not always derive much pleasure from their irregular and often precarious way of life. Here, then, was an obvious goal: to make men happy. Thus we find him defining a good government as one that makes its people happy.[15]

Since happiness is the good and man is normally a social being, it was only a short step to Confucius' principle of reciprocity. Obviously, if everyone worked for the happiness of all, we should have a situation more likely to bring about general happiness than any other. Confucius once defined reciprocity as "not doing to others what one does not wish them to do to one's self."[16] He stated the same idea more positively as follows: "The truly virtuous man, desiring to be established himself, seeks to establish others; desiring success for himself, he strives to help others succeed. To find in the wishes of one's own heart the principle for his conduct toward others is the method of true virtue."[17]

Yet Confucius was not so naïve as to suppose that the mere recognition of these principles would solve men's problems. All men want happiness, and most of us

15. *Analects* 13.16.

16. Ibid. 15.23.

17. Ibid. 6.28.

like to see those about us happy. But most of us will act unwisely, choosing a lesser immediate pleasure instead of a greater, deferred one. And we commonly act unsocially, preferring to secure our own happiness even at the expense of that of others. To correct these tendencies and to enlighten men and socialize them, Confucius clearly recognized and constantly insisted upon the necessity of some degree of universal education. He considered an enlightened citizenry the necessary foundation for the state. Punishment may temporarily compel men to do what they should, but it is at best a poor and unreliable substitute for education. He said: "If one tries to guide the people by means of rules, and keep order by means of punishments, the people will merely seek to avoid the penalties without having any sense of moral obligation. But if one leads them with virtue [both by precept and by example], and depends upon *li* to maintain order, the people will then feel their moral obligation to correct themselves."[18]

.   .   .

No concise statement of the political philosophy of Confucius has come down to us, but it is possible to reconstruct its main outlines. Clearly, he believed that government should be aimed at bringing about the welfare and happiness of the whole people. This, he thought, could be done only when the government was administered by the most capable men in the country. Such capability has nothing to do with birth, or wealth, or position, but is solely a matter of character and knowledge. These are produced by proper education. Education should therefore be widely diffused, so that the most talented men in the whole population might be prepared for the business of government. And the administration of the government should be handed over to such men, without regard to their origin.

Confucius did not, however, demand that the hereditary rulers vacate their thrones. If he had, it is doubtful that he would have accomplished anything by it, and his teaching would probably have been suppressed. Instead, he tried to persuade the hereditary rulers that they should "reign but not rule," handing over all administrative authority to ministers chosen for their qualifications.

Confucius attributed to the minister the highest degree of moral responsibility. Thus, while a minister ought to be loyal to his ruler, "can there be loyalty," Confucius asked, "which does not lead to the instruction of its object?"[19] When one of his disciples asked Confucius how a minister ought to behave toward his ruler, he replied: "He should not deceive him, but when necessary he should take issue with him openly."[20] Confucius once told the Duke of Lu that if a ruler's policies are bad, and yet none of those about him oppose them, such spinelessness is enough to ruin a state.[21]

.   .   .

Confucius spent the last years of his life in teaching in Lu. He was deeply disappointed, but not embittered; if he ever whined, we have no record of it. Once,

18. Ibid. 2.3.

19. Ibid. 14.8.

20. Ibid. 14.23.

21. Ibid. 13.15.

when he was seriously ill, one of his disciples wished to offer prayers that he might recover. But Confucius smiled and told him: "My kind of praying was done long ago."[22] When he was so ill that he was unconscious, some of his disciples dressed themselves up in court robes and stood about his bed in the attitude of the ministers he would have had if he had realized his ambition to be a high official. Regaining consciousness and seeing this pantomime, Confucius said to them: "By making this pretence of having ministers when in fact I have none, whom do you think I am going to deceive? Heaven? And is it not better that I should die in the hands of you, my friends, than in the hands of ministers?"[23]

When he died, in 479 B.C., there were probably very few who did not think that this rather pathetic old man had died a failure. Certainly he himself thought so. Yet few human lives have influenced history more profoundly than that of Confucius. The appeal of his thought has been perennial. In China, generation after generation has made him its own; today, even some of the Chinese Communists claim him for their own revolutionary tradition. In the West his influence has been greater than we sometimes realize. This was particularly the case during the seventeenth and eighteenth centuries, so that Reichwein says that "Confucius became the patron saint of eighteenth-century Enlightenment."[24]

If we look for the secret of his appeal, it seems probable that it lies in his insistence upon the supremacy of human values. Wisdom, he said, is to know men; virtue is to love men.[25]

Perhaps even more important than this, because it is still more rare, is what might be called his "intellectual democracy." A great many men have been willing that the people should govern themselves, but relatively few philosophers have been willing to trust men in general to think for themselves—unless, that is, they are willing to think for themselves along the line which the philosopher graciously points out for their own good. Confucius was not only willing that men should think for themselves; he insisted upon it. He was willing to help them and to teach them *how* to think, but the answers they must find for themselves. He frankly admitted that he himself did not know the truth, but only a way to look for it.

He believed that humanity could find happiness only as a co-operative community of free men. But men cannot be free while forever following a star pointed out by another. And he believed that to give them, under the guise of the immutable truth, a dogma that represented only the imperfect insight of one individual would be to betray their trust. He never did so. He said: "If a man does not constantly ask himself, 'What is the right thing to do?' I really don't know what is to be done about him."[26]

22. Ibid. 7.34.

23. Ibid. 9.11.

24. Reichwein, *China and Europe,* (translated by J. C. Powell, New York, 1925). p.77.

25. *Analects* 12.22.1.

26. Ibid. 15.15.

Selections, *The Analects*

Arthur Waley (translator)

Arthur Waley (1889–1966) was a translator, poet, and all-round scholar, particularly of Chinese and Japanese classics. Born in London and educated at Cambridge, Waley read a dozen or more languages, including "some Hebrew and Sanskrit," as well as Greek and Latin, which he had studied at Cambridge. As a young man, in the course of work in a minor position in the British Museum, he taught himself ancient Chinese and Japanese. He wrote some forty books and scores of articles and reviews. He read everything, loved music, wrote articles on anthropology, art, and archeology, and was an avid skier and cyclist. A quiet man, he avoided organizations, groups, and movements. Asked once whether he might accept a position at Cambridge, he answered, "I would rather be dead." He cared nothing for honors, though he received many, and he lived simply and frugally.

Waley's principal titles in Eastern philosophy and religion are Three Ways of Thought in Ancient China, Zen Buddhism and Its Relation to Art, The Analects of Confucius, *and* The Way and Its Power: A Study of the Tao Te Ching.

The Master said, High office filled by men of narrow views, ritual performed without reverence, the forms of mourning observed without grief—these are things I cannot bear to see! (Book III, 26)

The Master said, Without Goodness a man

> Cannot for long endure adversity,
> Cannot for long enjoy prosperity.

The Good Man rests content with Goodness; he that is merely wise pursues Goodness in the belief that it pays to do so. (Book IV, 2)

Of the adage "Only a Good Man knows how to like people, knows how to dislike them," the Master said, He whose heart is in the smallest degree set upon Goodness will dislike no one. (Book IV, 3, 4)

---

*Ivan Morris (ed.), *Madly Singing in the Mountains: An Appreciation and Anthology of Arthur Waley* (New York: Walker and Company, 1970), p. 85.

From *The Analects of Confucius,* translated by Arthur Waley, copyright © 1938 George Allen and Unwin Ltd. Reprinted by permission of HarperCollins Publishers.

Wealth and rank are what every man desires; but if they can only be retained to the detriment of the Way he professes, he must relinquish them. Poverty and obscurity are what every man detests; but if they can only be avoided to the detriment of the Way he professes, he must accept them. The gentleman who ever parts company with Goodness does not fulfil that name. Never for a moment does a gentleman quit the way of Goodness. He is never so harried but that he cleaves to this; never so tottering but that he cleaves to this. (Book IV, 5)

The Master said, I for my part have never yet seen one who really cared for Goodness, nor one who really abhorred wickedness. One who really cared for Goodness would never let any other consideration come first. One who abhorred wickedness would be so constantly doing Good that wickedness would never have a chance to get at him. Has anyone ever managed to do Good with his whole might even as long as the space of a single day? I think not. Yet I for my part have never seen anyone give up such an attempt because he had not the *strength* to go on. It may well have happened, but I for my part have never seen it. (Book IV, 6)

The Master said, A Knight whose heart is set upon the Way, but who is ashamed of wearing shabby clothes and eating coarse food, is not worth calling into counsel. (Book IV, 9)

The Master said, Those[1] whose measures are dictated by mere expediency will arouse continual discontent. (Book IV, 12)

The Master said, He[2] does not mind not being in office; all he minds about is whether he has qualities that entitle him to office. He does not mind failing to get recognition; he is too busy doing the things that entitle him to recognition. (Book IV, 14)

The Master said, A gentleman takes as much trouble to discover what is right as lesser men take to discover what will pay. (Book IV, 16)

The Master said, In the presence of a good man, think all the time how you may learn to equal him. In the presence of a bad man, turn your gaze within! (Book IV, 17)

The Master said, In serving his father and mother a man may gently remonstrate with them. But if he sees that he has failed to change their opinion, he should resume an attitude of deference and not thwart them; may feel discouraged, but not resentful. (Book IV, 18)

The Master said, If for the whole three years of mourning a son manages to carry on the household exactly as in his father's day, then he is a good son indeed. (Book IV, 20)

1. The rulers and upper classes in general.
2. The gentleman. But we might translate "I do not mind," etc.

The Master said, Those who err on the side of strictness are few indeed! (Book IV, 23)

The Master said, A gentleman covets the reputation of being slow in word but prompt in deed. (Book IV, 24)

The Master said Moral force *(tê)* never dwells in solitude; it will always bring neighbours.[3] (Book IV, 25)

The Master said, I have never yet seen a man who was truly steadfast.[4] Someone answered saying, "Ch'êng." The Master said, Ch'êng! He is at the mercy of his desires. How can *he* be called steadfast? (Book V, 10)

Tzu-kung said, Our Master's views concerning culture and the outward insignia of goodness, we are permitted to hear; but about Man's nature and the ways of Heaven[5] he will not tell us anything at all. (Book V, 12)

Of Tzu-ch'an the Master said that in him were to be found four of the virtues that belong to the Way of the true gentleman. In his private conduct he was courteous, in serving his master he was punctilious, in providing for the needs of the people he gave them even more than their due; in exacting service from the people, he was just. (Book V, 15)

Chi Wên Tzu used to think thrice before acting. The Master hearing of it said, Twice is quite enough.[6] (Book V, 19)

The Master said, How can we call even Wei-shêng Kao upright? When someone asked him for vinegar he went and begged it from the people next door, and then gave it as though it were his own gift.[7] (Book V, 23)

The Master said, Clever talk, a pretentious manner and a reverence that is only of the feet—Tso Ch'iu Ming was incapable of stooping to them, and I too could never stoop to them. Having to conceal one's indignation and keep on friendly terms with the people against whom one feels it—Tso Ch'iu Ming was incapable of stooping to such conduct, and I too am incapable of stooping to such conduct. (Book V, 24)

3. Whenever one individual or one country substitutes *te* for physical compulsion; other individuals or other countries inevitably follow suit.

4. Impervious to outside influences, intimidations, etc.

5. T'ien Tao. The Tao taught by Confucius only concerned human behavior ("the ways of man"); he did not expound a corresponding Heavenly Tao, governing the conduct of unseen powers and divinities.

6. Ch'êng Hao (A.D. 1032–85) says that if one thinks more than twice, self-interest begins to come into play.

7. Wei-shêng Kao . . . is the legendary paragon of truthfulness. . . . How rare, how almost non-existent a quality uprightness must be, Confucius bitterly says, if even into the legend of the most upright of all men there has crept an instance of falsity!

Once when Yen Hui and Tzu-lu were waiting upon him the Master said, Suppose each of you were to tell his wish. Tzu-lu said, I should like to have carriages and horses, clothes and fur rugs, share them with my friends and feel no annoyance if they were returned to me the worse for wear. Yen Hui said, I should like never to boast of my good qualities nor make a fuss about the trouble I take on behalf of others. Tzu-lu said, A thing I should like is to hear the Master's wish. The Master said, In dealing with the aged, to be of comfort to them; in dealing with friends, to be of good faith with them; in dealing with the young, to cherish them. (Book V, 25)

The Master said. In vain I have looked for a single man capable of seeing his own faults and bringing the charge home against himself. (Book V, 26)

The Master said, In an hamlet of ten houses you may be sure of finding someone quite as loyal and true to his word as I. But I doubt if you would find anyone with such a love of learning.[8] (Book V, 27)

The Master said, Hui is capable of occupying his whole mind for three months on end with no thought but that of Goodness. The others can do so, some for a day, some even for a month; but that is all.[9] (Book VI, 5)

The Master said, Incomparable indeed was Hui! A handful of rice to eat, a gourdful of water to drink, living in a mean street—others would have found it unendurably depressing, but to Hui's cheerfulness it made no difference at all. Incomparable indeed was Hui! (Book VI, 9)

The Master said, Mêng Chih-fan is no boaster. When his people were routed he was the last to flee; but when they neared the city-gate, he whipped up his horses, saying, It was not courage that kept me behind. My horses were slow. (Book VI, 13)

The Master said, Who expects to be able to go out of a house except by the door? How is it then that no one follows this Way of ours?[10] (Book VI, 15)

The Master said, When natural substance prevails over ornamentation,[11] you get the boorishness of the rustic. When ornamentation prevails over natural substance, you get the pedantry of the scribe. Only when ornament and substance are duly blended do you get the true gentleman. (Book VI, 16)

---

8. I.e., self-improvement in the most general sense. Not book-learning.

9. On the strength of sayings such as this, the Taoists claimed Yen Hui as an exponent of *tso-wang* ("sitting with blank mind"), the Chinese equivalent of *yoga.*

10. Though it is the obvious and only legitimate way out of all our difficulties.

11. I.e., when nature prevails over culture.

The Master said, To men who have risen at all above the middling sort, one may talk of things higher yet. But to men who are at all below the middling sort it is useless to talk of things that are above them.[12] (Book VI, 19)

The Master said, A gentleman who is widely versed in letters and at the same time knows how to submit his learning to the restraints of ritual is not likely, I think, to go far wrong. (Book VI, 25)

The Master said, How transcendent is the moral power of the Middle Use![13] That it is but rarely found among the common people is a fact long admitted. (Book VI, 27)

The Master said, I have "transmitted what was taught to me without making up anything of my own." I have been faithful to and loved the Ancients. In these respects, I make bold to think, not even our old P'eng[14] can have excelled me. The Master said, I have listened in silence and noted what was said, I have never grown tired of learning nor wearied of teaching others what I have learnt. These at least are merits which I can confidently claim. The Master said, The thought that "I have left my moral power *(tê)* untended, my learning unperfected, that I have heard of righteous men, but been unable to go to them; have heard of evil men, but been unable to reform them"—it is these thoughts that disquiet me. (Book VII, 1, 2, 3)

The Master said, From the very poorest upwards—beginning even with the man who could bring no better present than a bundle of dried flesh—none has ever come to me without receiving instruction. (Book VII, 7)

The Master said, Only one who bursts with eagerness do I instruct; only one who bubbles with excitement, do I enlighten. If I hold up one corner and a man cannot come back to me with the other three, I do not continue the lesson. (Book VII, 8)

The Master said to Yen Hui, The maxim

> When wanted, then go;
> When set aside; then hide.

is one that you and I could certainly fulfil. Tzu-lu said, Supposing you had command of the Three Hosts,[15] whom would you take to help you? The Master said, The man who was ready to "beard a tiger or rush a river" without caring whether he lived or died—that sort of man I should not take. I should certainly take someone who approached difficulties with due caution and who preferred to succeed by strategy. (Book VII, 10)

---

12. That belong to a higher stage of learning.

13. Confucius's Way was essentially one of moderation: "to exceed is as bad as to fall short." . . .

14. The Chinese Nestor. It is the special business of old men to transmit traditions.

15. I.e., the whole army.

The Master said, He who seeks only coarse food to eat, water to drink and bent arm for pillow, will without looking for it find happiness to boot. Any thought of accepting wealth and rank by means that I know to be wrong is as remote from me as the clouds that float above. (Book VII, 15)

The "Duke of Shê" asked Tzu-lu about Master K'ung (Confucius). Tzu-lu did not reply. The Master said, Why did you not say "This is the character of the man: so intent upon enlightening the eager that he forgets his hunger, and so happy in doing so, that he forgets the bitterness of his lot and does not realize that old age is at hand.[16] That is what he is." (Book VII, 18)

The Master said, I for my part am not one of those who have innate knowledge. I am simply one who loves the past and who is diligent in investigating it. (Book VII, 19)

The Master never talked of prodigies, feats of strength, disorders,[17] or spirits. (Book VII, 20)

The Master said, Even when walking in a party of no more than three I can always be certain of learning from those I am with. There will be good qualities that I can select for imitation and bad ones that will teach me what requires correction in myself. (Book VII, 21)

The Master took four subjects for his teaching: culture, conduct of affairs, loyalty to superiors, and the keeping of promises. (Book VII, 24)

The Master said, A Divine Sage I cannot hope ever to meet; the most I can hope for is to meet a true gentleman. The Master said, A faultless man I cannot hope ever to meet; the most I can hope for is to meet a man of fixed principles. Yet where all around I see Nothing pretending to be Something, Emptiness pretending to be Fullness, Penury pretending to be Affluence, even a man of fixed principles will be none too easy to find. (Book VII, 25)

The Master said, There may well be those who can do without knowledge; but I for my part am certainly not one of them. To hear much, pick out what is good and follow it, to see much and take due note of it, is the lower[18] of the two kinds of knowledge. (Book VII, 27)

The Master said, Is Goodness indeed so far away? If we really wanted Goodness, we should find that it was at our very side. (Book VII, 29)

16. According to the traditional chronology Confucius was sixty-two at the time when this was said.

17. Disorders of nature; such as snow in summer, owls hooting by day, or the like.

18. The higher being innate knowledge, which Confucius disclaims above, VII, 19. He thus (ironically) places himself at two removes from the hypothetical people who can dispense with knowledge, the three stages being, (1) those who do not need knowledge; (2) those who have innate knowledge; (3) those who accumulate it by hard work.

The Master said, As to being a Divine Sage or even a Good Man, far be it from me to make any such claim. As for unwearying effort to learn and unflagging patience in teaching others, those are merits that I do not hesitate to claim. Kung-hsi Hua said, The trouble is that we disciples cannot learn! (Book VII, 33)

The Master said, Just as lavishness leads easily to presumption, so does frugality to meanness. But meanness is a far less serious fault than presumption. (Book VII, 35)

The Master said, A true gentleman is calm and at ease; the Small Man is fretful and ill at ease. (Book VII, 36)

The Master's manner was affable yet firm, commanding but not harsh, polite but easy. (Book VII, 37)

The Master said, Courtesy not bounded by the prescriptions of ritual becomes tiresome. Caution not bounded by the prescriptions of ritual becomes timidity, daring becomes turbulence, inflexibility becomes harshness.
The Master said, When gentlemen deal generously with their own kin, the common people are incited to Goodness. When old dependents are not discarded, the common people will not be fickle. (Book VIII, 2)

When Master Tsêng was ill, Mêng Ching Tzu came to see him. Master Tsêng spoke to him saying, When a bird is about to die its song touches the heart. When a man is about to die, his words are of note. There are three things that a gentleman, in following the Way, places above all the rest: from every attitude, every gesture that he employs he must remove all trace of violence or arrogance; every look that he composes in his face must betoken good faith; from every word that he utters, from every intonation, he must remove all trace of coarseness or impropriety. As to the ordering of ritual vessels and the like, there are those whose business it is to attend to such matters. (Book VIII, 4)

Master Tsêng said, Clever, yet not ashamed to consult those less clever than himself; widely gifted, yet not ashamed to consult those with few gifts; having, yet seeming not to have; full, yet seeming empty; offended against, yet never contesting—long ago I had a friend whose ways were such as this. (Book VIII, 5)

Master Tsêng said, The man to whom one could with equal confidence entrust an orphan not yet fully grown or the sovereignty of a whole State, whom the advent of no emergency however great could upset—would such a one be a true gentleman? He I think would be a true gentleman indeed. (Book VIII, 6)

Master Tsêng said, The true Knight of the Way must perforce be both broad-shouldered and stout of heart; his burden is heavy and he has far to go. For Goodness is the burden he has taken upon himself; and must we not grant that it is a heavy one to bear? Only with death does his journey end; then must we not grant that he has far to go? (Book VIII, 7)

The Master said, Let a man be first incited by the *Songs,* then given a firm footing by the study of ritual, and finally perfected by music. (Book VIII, 8)

The Master said, The common people can be made to follow it;[19] they cannot be made to understand it. (Book VIII, 9)

The Master said, One who is by nature daring and is suffering from poverty will not long be law-abiding. Indeed, any men, save those that are truly Good, if their sufferings are very great, will be likely to rebel. (Book VIII, 10)

The Master said, If a man has gifts as wonderful as those of the Duke of Chou, yet is arrogant and mean, all the rest is of no account. (Book VII, 11)

The Master said:

> One who will study for three years
> Without thought of reward[20]
> Would be hard indeed to find.
>
> (Book VIII, 12)

The Master said, Learn as if you were following someone whom you could not catch up, as though it were someone you were frightened of losing. (Book VIII, 17)

The Master said, In Yü I can find no semblance of a flaw. Abstemious in his own food and drink, he displayed the utmost devotion in his offerings to spirits and divinities.[21] Content with the plainest clothes for common wear, he saw to it that his sacrificial apron and ceremonial head-dress were of the utmost magnificence. His place of habitation was of the humblest, and all his energy went into draining and ditching. In him I can find no semblance of a flaw. (Book VIII, 21)

There were four things that the Master wholly eschewed: he took nothing for granted, he was never over-positive, never obstinate, never egotistic. (Book IX, 4)

The Master said, Do I regard myself as a possessor of wisdom? Far from it. But if even a simple peasant comes in all sincerity and asks me a question, I am ready to thrash the matter out, with all its pros and cons, to the very end. (Book IX, 7)

Whenever he was visited by anyone dressed in the robes of mourning or wearing ceremonial head-dress, with gown and skirt, or a blind man, even if such a one were younger than himself, the Master on seeing him invariably rose to his feet, and if compelled to walk past him always quickened his step.[22] (Book IX, 9)

19. I.e. the Way.
20. I.e. of obtaining a paid appointment.
21. To ancestors, and spirits of hill, stream, etc.
22. A sign of respect.

The Master wanted to settle among the Nine Wild Tribes of the East. Someone said, I am afraid you would find it hard to put up with their lack of refinement. The Master said, Were a true gentleman to settle among them there would soon be no trouble about lack of refinement. (Book IX, 13)

The Master said, I have never yet seen anyone whose desire to build up his moral power was as strong as sexual desire. (Book IX, 17)

The Master said, The words of the *Fa Yü* (Model Sayings) cannot fail to stir us; but what matters is that they should change our ways. The words of the Hsüan Chü cannot fail to commend themselves to us; but what matters is that we should carry them out. For those who approve but do not change, I can do nothing at all. (Book IX, 23)

The Master said, First and foremost, be faithful to your superiors, keep all promises, refuse the friendship of all who are not like you; and if you have made a mistake, do not be afraid of admitting the fact and amending your ways. (Book IX, 24)

The Master said, "Wearing a shabby hemp-quilted gown, yet capable of standing unabashed with those who wore fox and badger." That would apply quite well to Yu, would it not?

> Who harmed none, was foe to none,
> Did nothing that was not right.

Afterwards Tzu-lu (Yu) kept on continually chanting those lines to himself. The Master said, Come now, the wisdom contained in them is not worth treasuring to that extent! (Book IX, 26)

The Master said, he that is really Good can never be unhappy. He that is really wise can never be perplexed. He that is really brave is never afraid.[23] (Book IX, 28)

> The flowery branch of the wild cherry
> How swiftly it flies back![24]
> It is not that I do not love you;
> But your house is far away.

The Master said, He did not really love her. Had he done so, he would not have worried about the distance.[25] (Book IX, 30)

---

23. Goodness, wisdom and courage are the Three Ways of the true gentleman. Cf. XIV, 30. Confucius always ranks courage below wisdom and wisdom below Goodness. . . .

24. When one pulls it to pluck the blossom. Cf. *Songs*, 268, I. Image of things that are torn apart after a momentary union. . .

25. Men fail to attain to Goodness because they do not care for it sufficiently, not because Goodness "is far away." . . .

Selections, *The Book of Mencius*

W. A. C. H. Dobson (translator)

Mencius (the Latinized form of Meng Tzu, "Master Meng") was the most important of the early followers of Confucius; he later became known as the "Second Sage" of China. Born c. 390 B.C.E., Mencius revered Confucius and sought to emulate him. And, indeed, his career paralleled rather closely that of Confucius: he, too, was a teacher who tried without success to influence the rulers of his day.

One of his central ideas was that human beings are by nature good, that the crucial virtues of "Humanity" (jen) and "Justice" (yi) were innate qualities. For the full development and expression of that goodness there was required effort by the individual, but it was only when the individual was stunted or otherwise coerced by the environment that there occurred improper behavior.

Though Mencius taught with eloquence and courage, his message—particularly his call for a government that exemplified humane principles—was too idealistic for those hardened rulers to whom he had to appeal for a position. "[He] remained, as he began, an obscure teacher with a teaching that was out of joint with the times."* He died c. 305 B.C.E.

Of his translation of Mencius, W. A. C. H. Dobson (1913–) noted that he had "tried to render an Archaic Chinese original in a modern and unadorned prose" for the general reader, without attempting to imitate, for effect, "the idiosyncracies of Chinese word order."** Dobson, born in London and educated at Oxford (BA, MA, D.Litt.), was Professor of Chinese and Head of the Department of East Asiatic Studies at the University of Toronto. He is also the author of Early Archaic Chinese, Late Archaic Chinese, Late Han Chinese, The Language of the Book of Songs, *and* A Dictionary of Chinese Particles.

Mencius was received in audience by King Hui of Liang. The King said, "Aged Sir! You have come, with no thought for so long a journey, to see me. You have, no doubt, some teaching by which I might profit my state?" Mencius replied, "Why must your Majesty use that word 'profit'? There is after all just Humanity and Justice, nothing more. If your Majesty asks 'How can I profit my state?' your nobles

*W. A. C. H. Dobson (trans.), *Mencius* (University of Toronto Press, 1963), p. xvii.

**Ibid.

will ask 'How can we profit our estates?' and knights and commoners will ask 'How can we profit ourselves?' All ranks in society will be competing for profits. Such would undermine the state. In a 'ten-thousand-chariot state' [a major state] he who slew his prince might gain a 'thousand-chariot estate' [a large estate], and in a 'thousand-chariot state' he who slew his prince might gain a 'hundred-chariot estate.' A thousand in ten thousand, a hundred in a thousand is no small profit. If indeed you put profit first and relegate justice to a minor place, no one will be happy unless they are forever grabbing something. There has never been a Humane man abandoned by his kin. There has never been a Just man who turned his back upon his prince. The king should speak of Justice and Humanity; why must he speak about profit?" (I.A. 1)

King Hui of Liang said, "No state, at one time, was greater than Tsin, and that, Sir, you know full well. But in my time we have been defeated by Ch'i in the east; my oldest son died in that campaign. We have lost seven hundred miles of territory to Ch'in in the west. Ch'u has humiliated us to the south. I feel the disgrace of this keenly, and hope before I die to expunge this disgrace in one fell swoop. What should I do to bring this about?" Mencius replied, "One could rule as a True King with a kingdom a hundred miles square. If the people saw your policies to be Humane, if you were to lighten the penal code, reduce taxes, encourage intensive ploughing and clearing of waste land, then the able bodied would have leisure to cultivate filial and fraternal duty, loyalty, and trust. On the one hand they could serve the elders of their families, and on the other serve their seniors in the state. They could oppose the stout mail and sharp weapons of Ch'in and Ch'u with sharpened sticks. Those great states deprive their people of labour in the farming seasons so that they can neither sow nor reap in season to feed their families. Parents freeze and starve to death. Brothers, wives, and children are separated. Those princes ensnare their people. If the King were to set out and punish them, who would dare oppose him? For this reason it is said, 'None can oppose the man of Humanity.' Let not your Majesty doubt this." (1A. 5)

He who properly might be called a great man is one who dwells in the broad mansion of the world, takes his place in its seat of rectitude, pursues the Great Way of the world, who, gaining his ambition, shares it with the common people, but who, failing to gain his ambition, pursues his principles in solitude. He is one whom riches and honours cannot taint, poverty and lowly station cannot shift, majesty and power cannot bend. Such a one I call a great man." (3B. 2)

Only men of Humanity ought properly to occupy high position. To lack Humanity and to be highly placed is to spread abroad evil among the populace. When the prince has no principles by which to measure, his subordinates have no standards to maintain. If the Court does not remain true to principles, the workmen will not keep true to standards. If the ruler contravenes Justice, lesser men will contravene the penal code. It will then be a matter of sheer luck that the state survives. Truly it is said, 'It is not the imperfection of defensive walls, or the paucity of arms, that constitutes disaster for the state. It is neither a failure to increase the acreage of arable land, nor an inadequate accumulation of goods and wealth, that constitutes the losses of a state. . . . (4A. 1)

Mencius said, "People commonly speak of 'the Empire, the state, and the family.' The Empire lies rooted in the state, the state lies rooted in the family, and the family lies rooted in the individual." (4A. 5)

Mencius said, "The great man seeks no assurance that his words will be believed or that his course of action will get results. He is concerned only that in his words and actions Justice resides." (4B.11)

The great man is one who never loses his child-like touch. (4B. 12)

Mencius said, "It is by what he guards in his thoughts that the True Gentleman differs from other men. He guards Humanity and propriety in his thoughts. The man of Humanity loves others. The man of propriety respects others. He who loves others is in turn loved by others. He who respects others is in turn respected by others. Suppose someone treats us badly. The True Gentleman will look for the reason within himself, feeling that he must have failed in Humanity or propriety, and will ask himself how such a thing could in fact have happened to him. If after examination he finds that he has acted Humanely and with propriety, and the bad treatment continues, he will look within himself again, feeling that he must have failed to do his best. But if on examination he finds that he has done his best, and the bad treatment continues, he will say, 'This person, after all, is an utter reprobate; I will have done with him. If he behaves like this, how does he differ from an animal? Why should I be put out by an animal?'

"Therefore the True Gentleman spends a lifetime of careful thought, but not a day in worrying. There are things to which he does give careful thought. 'Shun,' he says, 'was a man. I too am a man. But Shun became an examplar to the whole world, an example that has been passed down to us who come after, while I, as it were, am still a mere villager.' This is a matter about which he might take careful thought—taking careful thought only that he might be like Shun. As to those things about which the True Gentleman worries—they do not exist. What is contrary to Humanity he would not be. What is contrary to propriety he would not do. As to 'spending the day worrying,' the True Gentleman simply does not worry." (4B.28)

Kao Tzu said, "The nature of man is comparable to water trapped in a whirlpool. Open a channel for it on the east side and it will flow away to the east. Open a channel for it on the west side and it will flow away to the west. This is because man's nature is neither inherently good nor bad, just as it is not inherently in the nature of water to flow to the east or to the west."

Mencius replied, "It is assuredly not in the nature of water to flow to the east or to the west, but can one say that it is not in the nature of water to flow upwards or downwards? Man's nature is inherently good, just as it is the nature of water to flow downwards. As there is no water that flows upwards, so there are no men whose natures inherently are bad. Now you may strike forcefully upon water, and it will splash above your head. With a series of dams, you may force it uphill. But this is surely nothing to do with the nature of water; it happens only after the intrusion of some exterior force. A man can be made to do evil, but this is nothing to do with his nature. It happens only after the intrusion of some exterior force." (6A.2)

Kung-tu Tzu said, "Kao Tzu says, 'Man's nature is neither good nor bad.' Others say man's nature may tend in either direction. They say in the reigns of the good kings Wen and Wu the people were disposed to do good. In the reigns of the bad kings Yu and Li the people were disposed to do evil. Still others say some men's natures are good while others are bad. These say that, under a good sovereign like Yao, a bad man like Hsiang appeared; and that, to a bad father like Ku-sou, a good son Shun was born; that, with a nephew of a senior branch as evil as Chou on the throne, such good uncles as Ch'i, Lord of Wei, and Prince Pi Kan lived.

"Now, Sir, you say, 'Man's nature is good.' I suppose that these others are wrong?"

Mencius said, "It is of the essence of man's nature that he do good. That is what I mean by good. If a man does what is evil he is guilty of the sin of denying his natural endowment. Every man has a sense of pity, a sense of shame, a sense of respect, a sense of right and wrong. From his sense of pity comes *jen* (Humanity); from his sense of shame comes *yi* (Justice); from his sense of respect, *li* (the observance of rites); from his sense of right and wrong, *chih* (wisdom). *Jen, yi, li,* and *chih* do not soak in from without; we have them within ourselves. It is simply that we are not always consciously thinking about them. So I say, 'Seek them and you have them. Disregard them and you lose them.' Men differ, some by twice, some by five times, and some by an incalculable amount, in their inability to exploit this endowment. The *Book of Sons* says.

> Heaven gave birth to all mankind
> Gave them life and gave them laws,
> In their holding to them
> They lean towards the virtue of excellence.

Confucius said, 'This poet really understood the Way,' Thus, to possess life is to possess laws. There are to be laid hold upon by the people, and thus they will love the virtue of excellence." (6A.6)

Mencius said, "I am fond of fish, but, too, I am fond of bear's paws. If I cannot have both, then I prefer bear's paws. I care about life, but, too, I care about Justice. If I cannot have both, then I choose Justice. I care about life, but then there are things I care about more than life. For that reason I will not seek life improperly. I do not like death, but there there are things I dislike more than death. For that reason there are some contingencies from which I will not escape.

"If men are taught to desire life above all else, then they will seize it by all means in their power. If they are taught to hate death above all else, then they will avoid all contingencies by which they might meet it. There are times when one might save one's life, but only by means that are wrong. There are times when death can be avoided, but only by means that are improper. Having desires above life itself and having dislikes greater than death itself is a type of mind that all men possess—it is not only confined to the worthy. What distinguishes the worthy is that he ensures that he does not lose it.

"Even though it be a matter of life or death to him, a traveller will refuse a basket of rice or a dish of soup if offered in an insulting manner. But food that has been trampled upon, not even a beggar will think fit to eat. And yet a man will accept emoluments of ten thousand *chung* regardless of the claims of propriety and Justice. And what does he gain by that? Elegant palaces and houses, wives and concubines to wait on him, and the allegiance of the poor among his acquaintance! I was previously speaking of matters affecting life and death, where even there under certain conditions one will not accept relief, but this is a matter of palaces and houses, of wives and concubines, and of time-serving friends. Should we not stop such things? This is what I mean by 'losing the mind with which we originally were endowed.'" (6A.10)

Mencius said, "There are patents of nobility bestowed by Heaven, and those bestowed by man. Such things as Humanity and Justice, loyalty and trustworthiness, and a tireless delight in the good—these are Heaven's patents of nobility. 'Duke,' 'minister,' 'noble'—these are noble ranks bestowed by man. In antiquity, men cultivated Heaven's titles, and the titles of man followed in due course. Today, men cultivate Heaven's titles as a means of gaining man's titles, and, once they obtain them, Heaven's titles are abandoned. This is the height of self-delusion. It ends only in the loss of all title." (6A. 16)

Mencius replied, "The Way is like a great road; it is surely not difficult to understand. The sickness of men is that they do not seek it. If you, Sir, return to your home and seek for it, there will be teachers enough." (6B.2)

Mencius said, "If a True Gentleman has not integrity, by what will he be governed?" (6B. 12)

It was proposed in the State of Lu to put Yo-cheng Tzu in charge of its government. Mencius said, "When I heard about the proposal, I was so delighted I could not sleep." Kung-sun Ch'ou said, "But is he forceful enough?" Mencius replied, "No." "But is he thoughtful enough?" Mencius replied, "No." "Then is he experienced enough?" Mencius replied, "No" "Then," said Kung-sun Ch'ou, "why were you so delighted that you could not sleep?" Mencius replied, "As a man he inclines towards the good." Kung-sun Ch'ou asked, "But is that enough?" Mencius replied, "In inclining towards the good, he would be adequate to govern the whole world, much less the State of Lu! For if he really inclines towards the good, all within the four seas will report to him, regarding a journey of one thousand miles as a light matter. But if it transpires that he does not incline towards the good, then men will say 'an upstart!' 'He thinks he knows everything.' The sight and sound of an upstart will drive men a thousand miles away. When True Gentlemen stay a thousand miles away, gossip-mongers and toadies gather. Can those who associate with gossip-mongers and toadies help to govern the state?" (6B. 13)

Mencius said, "Most people do things without knowing what they do, and go on doing them without any thought as to what they are doing. They do this all their lives without ever understanding the Way." (7A. 5)

Mencius said to Kou Chien of Sung, "You, Sir, like to travel from court to court. Let me tell you my views on this subject. If in doing so you gain recognition, then be content, but if you fail to gain recognition, then too be content."

Kou Chien said, "How can one always 'be content'?"

Mencius replied, "Honour virtue, delight in Justice; then you may be content. For a knight in financial straits does not lose sight of Justice, and in success he does not depart from the Way. In financial straits without losing sight of Justice—that is his satisfaction. In succcess and not departing from the Way—thus the people never lose their sense of expectation from him. In antiquity, when a man attained his goal, his beneficence flowed down to the common people; when he failed to attain it, he cultivated his person and so became famous in his generation. So that if you meet with financial straits, ensure that you are good yourself, and if you meet with success ensure that you do good to the whole world." (7A.9)

Mencius said, "He who, rising at cock-crow, exerts every effort to be good is a disciple of Shun. He who, rising at cock-crow, exerts every effort in the pursuit of gain is a disciple of the brigand Ch'ih. If you wish to know what separates Shun from the brigand Ch'ih, it is no other than this: it is the margin that lies between making profits and being good." (7A. 25)

Prince Tien, son of King Hsüan, asked, "What are the duties of a knight?" Mencius replied, "To exalt his ideals." The Prince said, "What does that mean?" Mencius replied, "It means to exalt Justice and Humanity—nothing more. The murder of a single innocent man is contrary to Humanity. Taking things to which one has no right is contrary to Justice. Where is the knight to be found? Wherever Humanity is present. What road does he travel? The road that leads to Justice. In dwelling in Humanity and in the pursuit of Justice the duties of the great man are fulfilled." (7A. 33)

Kung-sun Ch'ou said, "As far as your teaching is concerned, it is lofty and admirable; indeed, it is like an ascent to Heaven—something one cannot quite attain to. Why not make it a little more attainable by daily unremitting effort?"

Mencius replied, "The Master Craftsman does not accommodate the inept workman by tampering with the measuring line. Yi the Archer did not accommodate an inept pupil by changing the target or the rules. The true gentleman leads. He does not turn aside. He leaps forward as it were, placing himself squarely in the centre of the Way. Those who can, follow him." (7A. 41)

Humanity *(jen)* is man *(jen)*. Put together, the words spell out "the Way." (7B. 16)

Huo-sheng Pu-hai asked, "What sort of a man is Yo-cheng Tzu?"

Mencius replies, "He is good and reliable."

Huo-sheng said, "What do you mean 'good' and 'reliable'?"

Mencius replied, "By 'good,' I mean 'that which we properly may wish for'; by 'reliable' I mean 'having it within himself.' When goodness and reliability are fully realized in a man, I call him 'excellent'; when so realized as to dazzle the beholder, I call him 'a great man'; but when realized in such measure as to change the life of the beholder, I call him 'a sage.' One with the attributes of a Sage, but who is unknowable, I call 'a god.' Yo-cheng Tzu I place among the 'good and reliable' but below the next four ['excellent,' 'great,' 'sage' and 'divine']." (7B. 25)

Mencius said, "In the nurturing of the mind, there is no better method than that of cutting down the number of desires. A man who has few desires, though he may have things in his mind which he should not have, will have but few of them. A man who has many desires, though he may have things in his mind which he should have, will have but few of them." (7B.35)

The Great Learning
Wing-tsit Chan (translator)

"The importance of this little Classic is far greater than its small size would suggest," states Wing-tsit Chan, its translator in these pages. "It gives the Confucian educational, moral, and political programs in a nutshell."*

It was in the twelfth century that the Neo-Confucian scholar Chu Hsi grouped together The Analects, The Book of Mencius, The Great Learning, *and* The Doctrine of the Mean *to form the* Four Books, *the basic documents of Confucianism, and since that time the role of* The Great Learning *in the life of China has been immeasurable: until the present century, it was with this essay that all Chinese children began their studies.***

The theme of The Great Learning *is that the health and well-being of individuals, the family, and the state are inextricably connected. There is, in fact, no distinction to be made between ethics and politics: both private conduct and the affairs of state are similarly moral issues. Moral behavior is dependent upon the proper "cultivation" of the young in the family—but the family cannot function as it ought unless the affairs of state are conducted in a moral manner.*

Appearing throughout The Great Learning *are editorial comments by Chu Hsi. He explains in one of his notes that he thought the first portion of the book was in the words of Confucius, as recorded by his disciple Tsang, and that the following chapters of commentary were by Tsang, as recorded by his followers. It is now considered unlikely that Confucius and Tsang were the sources of the book.* The Great Learning *was originally a chapter of the* Li Chi (The Book of Rites) *and possibly dates from the third century* B.C.E.; *the author is not known.*

Wing-tsit Chan (1901–) has had a long and notable career as a professor, author, and translator. Raised in South China, he received a Confucian education there and then a doctorate from Harvard in 1929. He was Professor of Chinese Thought and Culture at Dartmouth College and held similar positions at the University of Hawaii and Columbia University. He has published some twenty books and over a hundred articles in English and Chinese.

**Source Book of Chinese Philosophy* (Princeton University Press, 1963), p. 84.

**Yin Yutang, *The Wisdom of Confucius* (New York: Random House, 1938), p. 135.

The Great Learning

Chu Hsi's Remark. Master Ch'eng I said, "The *Great Learning* is a surviving work of the Confucian school and is the gate through which the beginning student enters into virtue. It is only due to the preservation of this work that the order in which the ancients pursued their learning may be seen at this time. The *Analects* and the *Book of Mencius* are next to it. The student should by all means follow this work in his effort to learn, and then he will probably be free from mistakes."

The Text

The Way of learning to be great (or adult education) consists in manifesting the clear character, loving the people, and abiding *(chih)* in the highest good.

Only after knowing what to abide in can one be calm. Only after having been calm can one be tranquil. Only after having achieved tranquility can one have peaceful repose. Only after having peaceful repose can one begin to deliberate. Only after deliberation can the end be attained. Things have their roots and branches. Affairs have their beginnings and their ends. To know what is first and what is last will lead one near the Way.

The ancients who wished to manifest their clear character to the world would first bring order to their states. Those who wished to bring order to their states would first regulate their families. Those who wished to regulate their families would first cultivate their personal lives. Those who wished to cultivate their personal lives would first rectify their minds. Those who wished to rectify their minds would first make their wills sincere. Those who wished to make their wills sincere would first extend their knowledge. The extension of knowledge consists in the investigation of things. When things are investigated, knowledge is extended; when knowledge is extended, the will becomes sincere; when the will is sincere, the mind is rectified; when the mind is rectified, the personal life is cultivated; when the personal life is cultivated, the family will be regulated; when the family is regulated, the state will be in order; and when the state is in order, there will be peace throughout the world. From the Son of Heaven down to the common people, all must regard cultivation of the personal life as the root or foundation. There is never a case when the root is in disorder and yet the branches are in order. There has never been a case when what is treated with great importance becomes a matter of slight importance or what is treated with slight importance becomes a matter of great importance.

Chu Hsi's Remark. The above is the text in one chapter. It is the words of Confucius, handed down by Tseng Tzu. The ten chapters of commentary which follow are the views of Tseng Tzu and were recorded by his pupils. In the traditional version there have been some mistakes in its arrangement. Now follows the new version fixed by Master Ch'eng I, and in addition, having examined the contents of the text, I (Chu Hsi) have rearranged it as follows:

Chapters of Commentary

1. In the "Announcement of K'ang" it is said, "He was able to manifest his clear character." In the "T'ai-chia" it is said, "He contemplated the clear Mandates of Heaven." In the "Canon of Yao" it is said, "He was able to manifest his lofty character." These all show that the ancient kings manifested their own character.

Chu Hsi's Remark. The above first chapter of commentary explains manifesting the clear character.

2. The inscription on the bath-tub of King T'ang read, "If you can renovate yourself one day, then you can do so every day, and keep doing so day after day." In the "Announcement of K'ang," it is said, "Arouse people to become new." The *Book of Odes* says, "Although Chou is an ancient state, the mandate it has received from Heaven is new." Therefore, the superior man tries at all times to do his utmost [in renovating himself and others].

Chu Hsi's Remark. The above second chapter of commentary explains the renovating of the people.

3. The *Book of Odes* says, "The imperial domain of a thousand *li* is where the people stay *(chih)*." The *Book of Odes* also says, "The twittering yellow bird rests *(chih)* on a thickly wooded mount." Confucius said, "When the bird rests, it knows where to rest. Should a human being be unequal to a bird?" The *Book of Odes* says, "How profound was King Wen! How he maintained his brilliant virtue without interruption and regarded with reverence that which he abided *(chih)*." As a ruler, he abided in humanity. As a minister, he abided in reverence. As a son, he abided in filial piety. As a father, he abided in deep love. And in dealing with the people of the country, he abided in faithfulness.

The *Book of Odes* says, "Look at that curve in the Ch'i River. How luxuriant and green are the bamboo trees there! Here is our elegant and accomplished prince. [His personal life is cultivated] as a thing is cut and filed and as a thing is carved and polished. How grave and dignified! How majestic and distinguished! Here is our elegant and accomplished prince. We can never forget him!" "As a thing is cut and filed" refers to the pursuit of learning. "As a thing is carved and polished" refers to self-cultivation. "How grave and how dignified" indicates precaution. "How majestic and distinguished" expresses awe-inspiring appearance. "Here is our elegant and accomplished prince. We can never forget him" means that the people cannot forget his eminent character and perfect virtue. The *Book of Odes* says, "Ah! the ancient kings are not forgotten." [Future] rulers deemed worthy what they deemed worthy and loved what they loved, while the common people enjoyed what they enjoyed and benefited from their beneficial arrangements. That was why they are not forgotten even after they passed away.

Chu Hsi's Remark. The above third chapter of commentary explains abiding in the highest good.

4. Confucius said, "In hearing litigations, I am as good as anyone. What is necessary is to enable people not to have litigations at all." Those who would not tell the truth will not dare to finish their words, and a great awe would be struck into people's minds. This is called knowing the root.

Chu Hsi's Remark. The above fourth chapter of commentary explains the root and the branches.

5. This is called knowing the root. This is called the perfecting of knowledge.

Chu Hsi's Remark. The above fifth chapter of commentary explains the meaning of the investigation of things and the extension of knowledge, which is now lost. I have ventured to take the view of Master Ch'eng I and supplement it as follows: The meaning of the expression "The perfection of knowledge depends on the investigation of things *(ko-wu)*" is this: If we wish to extend our knowledge to the utmost, we must investigate the principles of all things we come into contact with, for the intelligent mind of man is certainly formed to know, and there is not a single thing in which its principles do not inhere. It is only because all principles are not investigated that man's knowledge is incomplete. For this reason, the first step in the education of the adult is to instruct the learner, in regard to all things in the world, to proceed from what knowledge he has of their principles, and investigate further until he reaches the limit. After exerting himself in this way for a long time, he will one day achieve a wide and far-reaching penetration. Then the qualities of all things, whether internal or external, the refined or the coarse, will all be apprehended, and the mind, in its total substance and great functioning, will be perfectly intelligent. This is called the investigation of things. This is called the perfection of knowledge.

6. What is meant by "making the will sincere" is allowing no self-deception, as when we hate a bad smell or love a beautiful color. This is called satisfying oneself. Therefore the superior man will always be watchful over himself when alone. When the inferior man is alone and leisurely, there is no limit to which he does not go in his evil deeds. Only when he sees a superior man does he then try to disguise himself, concealing the evil and showing off the good in him. But what is the use? For other people see him as if they see his very heart. This is what is meant by saying that what is true in a man's heart will be shown in his outward appearance. Therefore the superior man will always be watchful over himself when alone. Tseng Tzu said, "What ten eyes are beholding and what ten hands are pointing to—isn't it frightening?" Wealth makes a house shining and virtue makes a person shining. When one's mind is broad and his heart generous, his body becomes big and is at ease. Therefore the superior man always makes his will sincere.

Chu Hsi's Remark. The above sixth chapter of commentary explains the sincerity of the will.

7. What is meant by saying that cultivation of the personal life depends on the rectification of the mind is that when one is affected by wrath to any extent, his mind will not be correct. When one is affected by fear to any extent, his mind will not be

correct. When he is affected by fondness to any extent, his mind will not be correct. When he is affected by worries and anxieties, his mind will not be correct. When the mind is not present, we look but do not see, listen but do not hear, and eat but do not know the taste of the food. This is what is meant by saying that the cultivation of the personal life depends on the rectification of the mind.

Chu Hsi's Remark. The above seventh chapter of commentary explains the rectification of the mind in order to cultivate the personal life.

8. What is meant by saying that the regulation of the family depends on the cultivation of the personal life is this: Men are partial toward those for whom they have affection and whom they love, partial toward those whom they despise and dislike, partial toward those whom they fear and revere, partial toward those whom they pity and for whom they have compassion, and partial toward those whom they do not respect. Therefore there are few people in the world who know what is bad in those whom they love and what is good in those whom they dislike. Hence it is said, "People do not know the faults of their sons and do not know (are not satisfied with) the bigness of their seedlings." This is what is meant by saying that if the personal life is not cultivated, one cannot regulate his family.

Chu Hsi's Remark. The above eighth chapter of commentary explains the cultivation of the personal life in order to regulate the family.

9. What is meant by saying that in order to govern the state it is necessary first to regulate the family is this: There is no one who cannot teach his own family and yet can teach others. Therefore the superior man (ruler) without going beyond his family, can bring education into completion in the whole state. Filial piety is that with which one serves his ruler. Brotherly respect is that with which one serves his elders, and deep love is that with which one treats the multitude. The "Announcement of K'ang" says, "Act as if you were watching over an infant." If a mother sincerely and earnestly looks for what the infant wants, she may not hit the mark but she will not be far from it. A young woman has never had to learn about nursing a baby before she marries. When the individual families have become humane, then the whole country will be aroused toward humanity. When the individual families have become compliant, then the whole country will be aroused toward compliance. When one man is greedy or avaricious, the whole country will be plunged into disorder. Such is the subtle, incipient activating force of things. This is what is meant by saying that a single word may spoil an affair and a single man may put the country in order. (Sage-emperors) Yao and Shun led the world with humanity and the people followed them. (Wicked kings) Chieh and Chou led the world with violence and the people followed them. The people did not follow their orders which were contrary to what they themselves liked. Therefore the superior man must have the good qualities in himself before he may require them in other people. He must not have the bad qualities in himself before he may require others not to have them. There has never been a man who does not cherish altruism *(shu)* in himself and yet can teach other people. Therefore the order of the state depends on the regulation of the family.

The *Book of Odes* says, "How young and pretty is that peach tree! How luxuriant is its foliage! This girl is going to her husband's house. She will rightly order her household." Only when one has rightly ordered his household can he teach the people of the country. The *Book of Odes* says, "They were correct and good to their elder brothers. They were correct and good to their younger brothers." Only when one is good and correct to one's elder and younger brothers can one teach the people of the country. The *Book of Odes* says, "His deportment is all correct, and he rectifies all the people of the country." Because he served as a worthy example as a father, son, elder brother, and younger brother, therefore the people imitated him. This is what is meant by saying that the order of the state depends on the regulation of the family.

> *Chu Hsi's Remark.* The above ninth chapter of commentary explains regulating the family to bring order to the state.

10. What is meant by saying that peace of the world depends on the order of the state is this: When the ruler treats the elders with respect, then the people will be aroused toward filial piety. When the ruler treats the aged with respect, then the people will be aroused toward brotherly respect. When the ruler treats compassionately the young and the helpless, then the common people will not follow the opposite course. Therefore the ruler has a principle with which, as with a measuring square, he may regulate his conduct.

What a man dislikes in his superiors, let him not show it in dealing with his inferiors; what he dislikes in those in front of him, let him not show it in preceding those who are behind; what he dislikes in those behind him, let him not show it in following those in front of him; what he dislikes in those on the right, let him not apply it to those on the left; and what he dislikes in those on the left, let him not apply it to those on the right. This is the principle of the measuring square.

The *Book of Odes* says, "How much the people rejoice in their prince, a parent of the people!" He likes what the people like and dislikes what the people dislike. This is what is meant by being a parent of the people. The *Book of Odes* says, "Lofty is the Southern Mountain! How massive are the rocks! How majestic is the Grand Tutor Yin (of Chou)! The people all look up to you!" Thus rulers of states should never be careless. If they deviate from the correct path, they will be cast away by the world. The *Book of Odes* says, "Before the rulers of the Yin (Shang) dynasty lost the support of the people, they could have been counterparts of Heaven. Take warning from the Yin dynasty. It is not easy to keep the Mandate of Heaven." This shows that by having the support of the people, they have their countries, and by losing the support of the people, they lose their countries. Therefore the ruler will first be watchful over his own virtue. If he has virtue, he will have the people with him. If he has the people with him, he will have the territory. If he has the territory, he will have wealth. And if he has wealth, he will have its use. Virtue is the root, while wealth is the branch. If he regards the root as external (or secondary) and the branch as internal (or essential), he will compete with the people in robbing each other. Therefore when wealth is gathered in the ruler's hand, the people will scatter away from him; and when wealth is scattered [among the people], they will gather round him. Therefore if the ruler's words are uttered in an evil way, the same words will be uttered back to him in an evil way; and if he acquires wealth in an evil way, it will be taken away from him in an evil way. In the "Announcement of K'ang" it is said, "The Mandate of Heaven is not fixed or unchangeable." The good ruler gets it and the bad ruler loses it. In the *Book of Ch'u* it is said, "The State of Ch'u does not consider anything as treasure; it considers only good [men] as treasure. Uncle Fan (maternal uncle to a prince of Chin in exile) said, 'Our exiled prince has no treasure; to be humane toward his parents is his only treasure.'" In the "Oath of Ch'in" it is said, "Let me have but one minister, sincere and single-minded, not pretending to other abilities, but broad and upright of mind, generous and tolerant toward others. When he sees that another person has a certain kind of ability, he is as happy as though he himself had it, and when he sees another man who is elegant and wise, he loves him in his heart as much as if he said so in so many words, thus showing that he can really tolerate others. Such a person can preserve my sons, and grandsons and the black-haired people (the common people). He may well be a great benefit to the country. But when a minister sees another person with a certain kind of ability, he is jealous and hates him, and when he sees another person who is elegant and wise, he blocks him so he cannot advance, thus showing that he really cannot tolerate others. Such a person cannot preserve my sons, grandsons, and the black-haired people. He is a danger to the country." It is only a man of humanity who can send away such a minister and banish him, driving him to live among the barbarian tribes and not allowing him to exist together with the rest of the people in the Middle Kingdom (China). This is what is meant by saying that it is only the man of humanity who can love or who can hate others. To see a worthy and not be able to raise him to office, or to be able to raise him but not to be the first one to do so—that is negligence. To see bad men and not be able to remove them from office, or to be able to remove them but not to remove them as far away as possible—that is a mistake. To love what the people hate and to hate what the people love—that is to act contrary to human nature, and disaster will come to such a person. Thus we see that the ruler has a great principle to follow. He must attain it through loyalty and faithfulness and will surely lose it through pride and indulgence.

There is a great principle for the production of wealth. If there are many producers and few consumers, and if people who produce wealth do so quickly and those who spend it do so slowly, then wealth will always be sufficient. A man of humanity develops his personality by means of his wealth, while the inhumane person develops wealth at the sacrifice of his personality. There has never been a case of a ruler who loved humanity and whose people did not love righteousness. There has never been a case where the people loved righteousness and yet the affairs of the state have not been carried to completion. And there has never been a case where in such a state the wealth collected in the national treasury did not continue in the possession of the ruler.

The officer Meng-hsien said, "He who keeps a horse [one who has just become an official] and a carriage does not look after poultry and pigs. [The higher officials] who use ice [in their sacrifices] do not keep cattle and sheep. And the nobles who can keep a hundred carriages do not keep rapacious tax-gathering ministers under them. It is better to have a minister who robs the state treasury than to have such a tax-gathering minister. This is what is meant by saying that in a state financial profit is not considered real profit whereas righteousness is considered to be the real profit.

He who heads a state or a family and is devoted to wealth and its use must have been under the influence of an inferior man. He may consider this man to be good, but when an inferior man is allowed to handle the country or family, disasters and injuries will come together. Though a good man may take his place, nothing can be done. This is what is meant by saying that in a state financial profit is not considered real profit whereas righteousness is considered the real profit.

Chu Hsi's Remark. The above tenth chapter of commentary explains ordering the state to bring peace to the world. There are altogether ten commentary chapters. The first four generally discuss the principal topics and the basic import. The last six chapters discuss in detail the items and the required effort involved. Chapter five deals with the essence of the understanding of goodness and chapter six deals with the foundation of making the personal life sincere. These two chapters, especially, represent the immediate task, particularly for the beginning student. The reader should not neglect them because of their simplicity.

Confucian Self-Realization

Tu Wei-ming

Tu Wei-ming (1940–) was born in Kunming, China, and came to the United States in 1962. He received his doctorate from Harvard University and has taught at Tunghai University (Taiwan); Princeton; the University of California, Berkeley; and Harvard, where he became chair of the Department of East Asian Languages and Civilizations. Among his books in English are Neo-Confucian Thought in Action: Wang Yang-ming's Youth, Centrality and Commonality: An Essay on Confucian Religiousness, Humanity and Self-Cultivation: Essays in Confucian Thought, Confucian Ethics Today: The Singapore Challenge, *and* Confucian Thought: Selfhood as Creative Transformation.

Professor Tu has stated that his concentration on the Confucian tradition "is not only the academic commitment of a professional intellectual historian but also the personal quest of a reflective human being." Widely acclaimed for his scholarly work on Confucianism, he lists that religion as his own.

Personality, in the Confucian perception, is an achieved state of moral excellence rather than a given human condition. An implied distinction is made between what a person is by temperament and what a person has become by self-conscious effort. A person's natural disposition—whether introverted or extroverted, passive or aggressive, cold or warm, contemplative or active, shy or assertive—is what the Confucians refer to as that aspect of human nature which is composed of *ch'i-chih* (vital energy and raw stuff). For the sake of convenience, we may characterize the human nature of vital energy and raw stuff as our psychophysiological nature, our physical nature, or simply the body.

The Confucian tradition—in fact, the Chinese cultural heritage as a whole— takes our physical nature absolutely seriously. Self-cultivation, as a form of mental and physical rejuvenation involving such exercises as rhythmic bodily movements and breathing techniques, is an ancient Chinese art. The classical Chinese conception of medicine is healing in the sense not only of curing disease or preventing sickness but also of restoring the vital energy essential for the wholeness of the body. Since the level of vital energy required for health varies according to sex, age, weight, height, occupation, time, and circumstance, the wholeness of the body is situationally defined as a dynamic process rather than a static structure. The maintenance of health, accordingly, is a fine art encompassing a wide range of environmental, dietary, physiological, and psychological factors. The delicate balance attained and sustained is the result of communal as well as personal effort. To become well and sound is therefore an achievement.

However, the centrality of the physical nature (the body) in the Confucian conception of the person is predicated not only on the irreducibility of the vital energy and raw stuff for personal growth but also on the potentiality of the body to become an aesthetic expression of the self. The wholeness of the body, often understood as allowing the vital energy to flow smoothly, is not only a measuring standard but also a unique accomplishment. Indeed, the idea is laden with ethico-religious as well as psychophysiological implications. When Mencius defines the sage (who has attained the highest moral excellence in the human community) as the person who has brought the bodily form to fruition, he assumes that the body is where the deepest human spirituality dwells. Yet, it is important to note that the Mencian conception of sagehood involves much more than our physical nature.

It seems that the conscious refusal to accept, rather than the lack of conceptual apparatus to perceive, the exclusive dichotomy between body and mind prompts the Confucians to endow rich resources to the idea of the body as the proper home for human flourishing. The ascetic rigor deemed necessary for reaching a higher spiritual state in virtually all major religions is practiced in the Confucian tradition, but the attention is not focused on self-denial, let alone immolation of the body. The Confucians do not take the body as, by nature, an impediment to full self-realization. To them, the body provides the context and the resources for ultimate self-transformation.

Understandably, Confucian education takes the "ritualization of the body" as the point of departure in the development of the person.[1] Lest the purpose be misconstrued as the imposition of well-established societal norms of behavior upon the innocent youth, "ritualization" as a dynamic process of interpersonal encounter and personal growth is not passive socialization but active participation in recognizing, experiencing, interpreting, and representing the communicative rationality that defines society as a meaningful community. In other words, through ritualization we learn not only the form of the accepted behavior but the grammar of action underlying the form as well. Surely, on the surface at least, it seems that we are socialized unsuspectingly, if not totally against our will, to become members of a linguistic and cultural community. We really do not have much choice in adopting the linguistic specificities of our mother tongue and the cultural particularities of our fatherland. Nevertheless, the Confucians believe that if we make a conscientious effort to actively incorporate the societal norms and values in our own conduct, we will be able to transcend the linguistic and cultural constraints of our society by transforming them into instruments of self-realization. Like poets who have

1. For a general discussion on ritualization as humanization, see Tu Wei-ming, "Li as Process of Humanization," *Philosophy East and West*, 22, no. 2 (April 1972): 187–201.

mastered the subtleties of the language, articulating their innermost thoughts through them, Confucians who have become thoroughly proficient in the nuances of the ritual are said to be able to establish and enlarge others as well as themselves by bringing this personal knowledge to bear on daily practical living. The seeming naïveté of the Confucians in accepting their own linguistic and cultural universe as intrinsically meaningful and valuable is based on the collective judgment that the survival and continuation of their civilization is not a given reality but a communal attainment. This judgment is itself premised on a fundamental faith in the transformability and perfectibility of the human condition through communal self-effort.

Actually, for the Confucians, the intellectual recognition and experiential acceptance of the body as the point of departure for personal growth are the result of a strong commitment to a holistic view of self-realization. The body, as our physical nature, must be transformed and perfected so that it can serve as a vehicle for realizing that aspect of our nature known as the nature of *i-li* (rightness and principle), the moral nature, or simply the heart-mind *(hsin)*.[2] Even though the body is a constitutive part of our nature, it is the heart-mind that is truly human.

A person's temperament may significantly determine his natural disposition in a social environment. Whether he is introverted, passive, cold, contemplative, and shy, or extroverted, aggressive, warm, active, and assertive may very well be a reflection of his native endowments. Quite a few Chinese thinkers, for pragmatic and bureaucratic considerations as well as for social and aesthetic ones, have been fascinated by the classification and evaluation of distinctive character traits. A third-century treatise on the categorization of human beings according to talent and disposition remains to this day a comprehensive treatment and sophisticated analysis of personality types.[3] However, despite the importance and irreducibility of the vital energy and raw stuff (the physical nature or the body) that we are endowed with, the main concern of Confucian education is the process through which we realize ourselves by transforming and perfecting what we are born with.

The Heart-Mind and Human Sensitivity

As Mencius notes, in regard to physical nature, the difference between humans and animals (birds or beasts) is quite small. What truly distinguishes human beings from animals is not the body but the heart-mind. Since the body is the proper home in which the heart-mind dwells, it is perhaps more appropriate to say that the heart-mind (in addition to the body or the body fully informed by the heart-mind) specifically defines the uniqueness of being human. Learning to be human means that the self-consciousness of the heart-mind initiates a process by which the body is transformed and perfected. The ritualization of the body can thus be understood as the active participation of the heart-mind to help the body to become a fitting expression of the self in a social context. To be sure, an act of the will or an existen-

2. Mencius 6A:7.

3. Unfortunately, Liu Shao's *Treatise on Personalities (Jen-u-u chih)* is still not yet available in English translation.

tial decision is required when the heart-mind becomes fully aware of its role and function in bringing this process to fruition. For Confucius, the critical juncture occurred when he "set his heart upon learning" at fifteen.[4] However, even the very young, when involved in simple rituals such as sprinkling water for the adults to sweep the floor or giving answers of yes or no to easy questions, exercise their hearts and minds in ritualizing their bodies. It is precisely because the heart-mind is housed in the body (although in practice it can be absent from it) that the human body takes on the profound spiritual significance that distinguishes it from the physical nature of birds and beasts. As a corollary, the body devoid of the heart-mind, is, strictly speaking, no longer human and can easily degenerate into a state of unreflexivity indistinguishable from the physical nature of birds and beasts.

The most prominent feature of the heart-mind is sympathy, the ability to share the suffering of others. This is why the Chinese character *hsin*—like the French word *conscience,* which involves both cognitive and affective dimensions of consciousness—must be rendered as "heart-mind": For *hsin* signifies both intellectual awareness and moral awakening. By privileging sympathy as the defining characteristic of true humanity, Confucians underscore feeling as the basis for knowing, willing, and judging. Human beings are therefore defined primarily by their sensitivity and only secondarily by their rationality, volition, or intelligence.

Expanding Sensitivity: The Perfection of the Self

Learning to be human, in this sense, is to learn to be sensitive to an ever-expanding network of relationships. It may appear to be a consciousness-raising proposition, but it entails the dynamic process of transforming the body as a private ego to the body as an all-encompassing self. To use the Confucian terminology of Master Ch'eng Hao (1032–85), the whole enterprise involves the realization of the authentic possibility of "forming one body with Heaven, Earth, and the myriad things."[5] Concretely, for Confucians, in learning to be human beings by cultivating the capacity to empathize with the negative feelings of one's closest kin—namely, by directly referring to our own hearts and minds—we should understand the reasonableness of the following dictum: "Do not do unto others what I would not want others to do unto me"[6]

The ability to feel the suffering of others or the inability to endure their suffering empowers us to establish an experiential connection with another human being. This provides a great resource for realizing our moral nature (the nature of rightness and principle). The Confucians believe that our sympathetic bonding to our parents is not only biologically natural but morally imperative, for it is the first step in learning to appreciate ourselves not in isolation but in communication. Indeed, since the Confucians perceive the self as a center of relationships rather than as an isolable

4. *Analects* 2:4.

5. See his essay on "Understanding the Nature of *Jen* (Humanity)." in *A Source Book in Chinese Philosophy,* trans. and comp. Wing-tsit Chan (Princeton: Princeton University Press, 1963): 523.

6. *Analects* 15:23.

individuality, the ability to show intimacy to those who are intimate is vitally important for allowing the closed private ego to acquire a taste for the open communicating self so that the transformation of the body can start on a concrete experiential basis.

But if we extend sympathy only to our parents, we take no more than the initial step toward self-realization. By embodying our closest kin in our sensitivity, we may have gone beyond egoism, but without the learned ability to enter into fruitful communication outside the immediate family, we are still confined to nepotism. Like egoism, nepotism fails to extend our sensitivity to embody a larger network of human relationships and thus limits our capacity for self-realization. Similarly, parochialism, ethnocentrism, and chauvinistic nationalism are all varying degrees of human insensitivity. In the dynamic process of self-realization, they are inertia or limitation. In either case, they are detrimental to the human capacity for establishing a community encompassing humanity as a whole.

Confucian communitarianism, far from being a romantic utopian assertion about equality, unity, and universality, takes as its theoretical and practical basis the natural order of things in human society: the family, neighborhood, kinship, clan, state, and world. In fact, it recognizes the necessity and legitimacy of these structures, both as historically evolved institutions and socially differentiated organizations. They are natural to the human community not only because they enable us to define ourselves in terms of the breadth and depth of human-relatedness but also because they provide both material and spiritual resources for us to realize ourselves. The Confucians do not accept the status quo as necessarily rational. Actually their main mission is to improve on the current situation by bridging the gap between what the status quo is and what it can and ought to be. Confucians are in the world but not of the world. They take an active role in changing the world by managing it from within; instead of adjusting themselves to the status quo, they try to transform it according to their moral idealism.

A salient feature of Confucians' moral idealism is their commitment to the efficacy of education as character building. The Confucian faith in the transformability and perfectibility of the human condition through communal self-effort implies that personal growth has not only ethical value but political significance. The ritualization of the body is relevant to political leadership as well as to social harmony in the family, neighborhood, and clan. Since Confucians believe that exemplary teaching is an integral part of political leadership, the personal morality of those involved is a precondition for good politics. Politics and morality are inseparable. What political leaders do at home is closely linked not only to their styles of leadership but also to the very nature of their politics. Self-realization, in this sense, is not a lonely quest for one's inner spirituality but a communicative act empowering one to become a responsible householder, an effective community worker, and a conscientious public servant. Confucians may not be successful in their political careers or may choose not to seek office, but they can never abandon their vocation as concerned intellectuals.

A concerned intellectual, the modern counterpart of the Confucian *chün-tzu* (nobleman or profound person), does not seek a spiritual sanctuary outside the world. He is engaged in this world, for total withdrawal from society and politics is not an option. Yet, although to be part of the "secular" world is the Confucian vocation, the Confucian calling is not to serve the status quo but to transform the "secular" world of wealth and power into a "sacred" community in which, despite egoistic drives, the quest for human flourishing in moral, scientific, and aesthetic excellence continuously nourishes our bodies and uplifts our hearts and minds.

The Ceaseless Process of Human Flourishing

Understandably, to become a mature person (an adult), in the Confucian sense, is not to attain a limited professional or personal goal but to open oneself up to the ceaseless process of human flourishing. The becoming process, rather than an attained state of being, defines the Confucian personality. One's critical self-awareness in the later stages of one's maturation (e.g., at the age of fifty, when Confucius confessed to have known the Mandate of Heaven)[7] ought to be directed to the authentic possibilities of further growth in moral development. Unlike scientific and aesthetic talents, sensitivity in ethics never declines and, properly cultivated, it becomes more subtle and refined.

Nevertheless, a person becomes a personality not by conscientiously obeying conventional rules of conduct but by exemplifying a form of life worth living; indeed by establishing a standard of self-transformation as a source of inspiration for the human community as a whole. The interchange between an exemplary teacher and the students aspiring to become householders, community workers, or public servants is never one-way. As fellow travelers on the Way, they form a community of the like-minded so that the project of human flourishing becomes a joint venture, mutually admonishing and mutually encouraging. The exemplary teacher as an achieved personality in the eyes of the students must continue to cultivate his inner resources for self-transformation. Confucians do not believe in fixed personalities. While they regard personalities as accomplishments, they insist that the strength of one's personality lies not in its past glories but in its future promises. Real personalities are always evolving. This is why fundamental improvement in the quality of existence is possible for even a human being a breath away from death: "Thou shall not judge the person conclusively before the coffin is sealed!"[8]

This faith in and commitment to the transformability and perfectibility of the human condition through communal self-effort enables Confucians to perceive each person as a center of relationships who is in the process of *ultimate* transformation as a communal act. The "ultimacy" in this seemingly humanistic enterprise is premised on the ability of the human heart-mind, without departing from its proper home (the body), to have the sensitivity to establish an internal resonance with Heaven by fully comprehending its Mandate. Sensitivity so conceived is a

---

7. *Analects* 2:4.

8. This common expression is still widely used in China. Although it is a popular idiom rather than an assertion in the Confucian classics, it vividly captures the Confucian spirit that self-realization never completes and that, as long as a person lives, he is still redeemable.

"silent illumination." It is neither a gift from an external source nor a knowledge acquired through empirical learning. Rather, it is an inner quality of the heart-mind, the shining wisdom that a ritualized body emits for its own aesthetic expression. Such an expression is neither private nor individualistic, but communal.

As mentioned, for the Confucian to bring self-transformation to fruition (to its ultimacy), he must transcend not merely egoism but nepotism, parochialism, eth-nocentrism, and chauvinistic nationalism. These undesirable habits of thought, perceived as varying degrees of human insensitivity, limit the full potential of the silent illumination of the human heart-mind to manifest itself. The Confucian insistence that we must work through our families, communities, and nations to realize ourselves is not at all incompatible with the Confucian injunction that we must go beyond nepotism, parochialism, and chauvinistic nationalism to fully embody our humanity. Actually, the seemingly contradictory assertions signify a dynamic process that defines the richness of the Confucian way of learning to be human.

On the one hand, Confucians, in contrast to individuals, take the communal path by insisting that, as a center of relationships, a personality comes into being by fruitfully interacting with its natural human environment—the family, kin, community, and the state. This process of continuously communicating with an ever-expanding network of human relationships enables the self to embody an increasingly widening circle of inclusiveness in its own sensitivity. On the other hand, Confucians, as opposed to collectivists, firmly establish the "subjectivity" of the person as sui generis. No social program, no matter how lofty, can undermine the centrality of selfhood in Confucian learning. After all, Confucians see learning for the sake of the self as the authentic purpose of education. To be sure, the self as an open and communicating center of relationships is intimately connected with other selves; far from being egoistic, it is communal. However, by stressing the centrality of the self in learning to be human, the Confucians advocate ultimate self-transformation, not only as social ethics but also as the flourishing of human nature with profound religious significance.

Forming One Body with Earth and Myriad Things

For Confucians to fully realize themselves, it is not enough to become a responsible householder, effective social worker, or conscientious political servant. No matter how successful one is in the sociopolitical arena, the full measure of one's humanity cannot be accommodated without a reference to Heaven. The highest Confucian ideal is the "unity of Man and Heaven," which defines humanity not only in anthropological terms but also in cosmological terms. In the *Doctrine of the Mean (Chung-yung)*, the most authentic manifestation of humanity is characterized as "forming a trinity with Heaven and Earth."[9]

9. *Chung-yung (Doctrine of the Mean)* XXII. For a discussion of this idea in the perspective of Con-fucian "moral metaphysics," see Tu Wei-ming, *Centrality and Commonality: An Essay on Chung-yung* (Honolulu: University Press of Hawaii, 1976 pp. 100–111.

Yet, since Heaven does not speak and the Way in itself cannot make human beings great—which suggests that although Heaven is omnipresent and may be omniscient, it is certainly not omnipotent—our understanding of the Mandate of Heaven requires that we fully appreciate the rightness and principle inherent in our heart-minds. Our ability to transcend egoism, nepotism, parochialism, ethnocentrism, and chauvinistic nationalism must be extended to anthropocentrism as well. To make ourselves deserving partners of Heaven, we must be constantly in touch with that silent illumination that makes the rightness and principle in our heart-minds shine forth brilliantly. If we cannot go beyond the constraints of our own species, the most we can hope for is an exclusive, secular humanism advocating man as the measure of all things. By contrast, Confucian humanism is inclusive; it is predicated on an "anthropocosmic" vision. Humanity in its all-embracing fullness "forms one body with Heaven, Earth, and the myriad things." Self-realization, in the last analysis, is ultimate transformation, that process which enables us to embody the family, community, nation, world, and cosmos in our sensitivity.

A Confucian Metaphor—The Holy Vessel

Herbert Fingarette

Born in New York, Herbert Fingarette (1921–) earned his doctorate from the University of California, Los Angeles, and taught philosophy at the University of California, Santa Barbara. His books include The Self in Transformation, On Responsibility, Self-Deception, The Meaning of Criminal Responsibility, *and with his daughter, Anne Fingarette Hasse,* Mental Disability and Criminal Responsibility.

It is one of Fingarette's contentions that Confucius was not as earthbound, so to speak, as has so often been thought in the past. The main thesis of Confucius—The Secular as Sacred, *from which the following selection is taken, is that Confucius's great insight was into the "holiness in human existence" and that "the truly, distinctively human powers have, characteristically, a magical quality." Confucius found the means to capture and reveal this dimension of humanity in his doctrine of* li *("holy rite," "sacred ceremony" in its earliest meaning).*

What is it that distinguishes man from the beasts and the inanimate? In what do man's peculiar dignity and power reside? Confucius offers an amazingly apt and generative image: Rite *(li)*. But Rite and Ceremony would seem, offhand, to deemphasize the individual, whereas the tendency in much modern criticism is to stress the "discovery of the individual"[1] by Confucius. It is true that Hughes, who uses this particular phrase, adds a qualifying clause "man's ability to look at himself in relation to his fellows and in that light to integrate himself."

Wing-tsit Chan summarizes in a similar formula "the entire Confucian philosophy: . . . the realization of the self and the creation of a social order."[2] Although Hughes and Chan bring out the two poles "individual"—"society," Liu Wu-chi emphasizes even more the "individual" pole: "No matter from which angle we view it, the individual man is, after all, the hub of the universe. . . . Master K'ung discovered by a happy stroke of genius the ethical individual. . . . Individual man was

1. E. R. Hughes (ed.), *The Individual in East and West* (London: Oxford University Press, 1937), p. 94.

2. Wing-tsit Chan, "The Story of Chinese Philosophy," *Philosophy—East and West,* edited by C. A. Moore (Princeton: Princeton University Press, 1944), p. 27.

now exalted to his new position as a social entity. . . . Thus for the first time in the history of man, the dignity of the individual was asserted. . . . The flowering of the individual is to be one's ultimate aim."[3] Creel, although he too elaborates on the social orientation of Confucius, nevertheless emphasizes in various contexts the "primacy and worth of the individual" in Confucius's thought.[4] And Lin Yutang, while stressing the social, says. ". . . the kingdom of God is truly within man himself."[5]

In short, in these passages from a representative sample of modern writers we see a broadly recurring pattern of interpretation. In citing such brief phrases, one wrenches the remarks from contexts in which there is essential qualification and amplification. My aim in quoting, however, is not to provide a rounded report of the commentaries, but rather to note that when a brief and summary formula is finally required, the formula often tends to be formulated in terms of "society" and the "individual," with relative emphasis on the "individual" as primary. Self-realization, self-integrity, "self-flowering," the "ultimate worth of the individual"— these are supposed to reflect the characteristic discovery of Confucius. It is the thesis of the present remarks that we would do better to think of Confucius as concerned with the nature of "humanity" rather than with the polar terms "individual" and "society." The formulation in terms of individual and society reflects Western preoccupations and categories—and perhaps Taoist, Buddhist, and neo-Confucian concerns.

Rather than arguing this point in the abstract, we cannot do better than to learn from Confucius himself, and more particularly from reflection on one of the illuminating images he presents to us.

> Tzu-Kung asked: "What would you say about me as a person?"
> The Master said: "You are a utensil."
> "What sort of utensil?"
> "A sacrificial vase of jade." (5:3)

This passage is usually read in the light of another passage in the *Analects* (2:II): "A noble man is not a utensil."

The general opinion among commentators, in the light of 2:II, seems to have

---

3. Liu Wu-chi, *Confucius, His Life and Times* (New York: Philosophical Library, 1955), pp. 155–56.

4. H. G. Creel, *Confucius and the Chinese Way* (New York: Harper & Row, Torchbook No. 63, 1960), pp. 136, 138. My own interpretation follows Creel (and in some ways Kaizuka) [S. Kaizuka, *Confucius,* translated by G. Bournes (London: George Allen & Unwin, Ltd., 1956)] more than most in the way they stress the inseparability of man from society and the role of *li*. Without wishing to minimize this similarity or to enter into detailed comparative commentary, I might simply say that I have attempted to draw the philosophical and psychological implications of this view more stringently and more fully. I think that doing this puts Confucius's position in a new light. For one thing it helps to bring out the close logical connection between this view of man and the magical-reverential dimension of Confucius's thought—a dimension that I believe is seriously understated by Creel and "rationalized" (in spite of his evident *feeling* for it). See also H. G. Creel, *Chinese Thought: From Confucius to Mao Tse-Tung* (New York: New American Library, 1960), pp. 33–34.

5. Lin Yutang, *The Wisdom of Confucius* (New York: Random House, Modern Library, 1938), p. 17.

been that Confucius is first putting Tzu-Kung in his place, and then, in his next response, softening the blow. These interpreters (whom I believe to be mistaken) might be supposed to read the cryptic passage along the lines of the following paraphrase.

"Master," we may suppose Tzu-Kung to be saying, "tell me where I stand with regard to the ideal." The Master replies, "You are still only a utensil, useful only for specific purposes. You are not the morally self-realized man, the man with broad (moral) capacities who is capable of governing or using the special (technical) capacities of others." Tzu-Kung, his eagerness and optimism shaken, does not give up. "But, Master, how do you mean that? Don't you have some qualifying or softening word with which you can give me more hope?" And the Master replies, in a paternalistic, encouraging tone: "Tzu-Kung, don't feel too bad about it. Even if you are still a man to be used and not yet one who is perfected and capable of using others, at least you are a very fine utensil of your kind. Indeed you are among the most handsome and valuable."

In my own opinion, as I have indicated, a reading along such lines is quite wrong. The only element of it that is acceptable is that Confucius does initially intend to dash cold water on Tzu-Kung's too-ready optimism. Confucius wants to bring him up short, to shake him, disturb him, puzzle him; Tzu-Kung must be made to feel the necessity to *think* his way through to a new insight. Confucius puts his answer in a manner best calculated to accomplish this end with a man of Tzu-Kung's character. It seems that this disciple was the most facilely successful and worldly of Confucius's disciples. With his learning and his worldly success, he might well feel pride in his personal achievement, might well be surprised and shaken at Confucius's initial response. For Tzu-Kung is well aware of the metaphor of the utensil and of the saying that a noble man is *not* a utensil. Confucius's initial response, like others he makes, is the first element, then, in a pedagogically effective paradox.[6]

However, the second statement by Confucius—"You are a sacrificial vessel of jade"—is not a mere sentimental softening of the blow. It both completes and resolves the paradox. It contains in a highly condensed image the central teaching which Confucius wishes to get across to the glib and self-satisfied Tzu-Kung. What is this central teaching?

Consider the sacrificial vessel: in the original text Confucius merely names a certain type of jade sacrificial vessel used for holding grain in connection with ceremonies for a bounteous harvest. Such a vessel is holy, sacred. Its outer appearance—the bronze, the carving, the jade—is elegant. Its content, the rich grain, expresses abundance.

Yet the vessel's sacredness does not reside in the preciousness of its bronze, in the beauty of its ornamentation, in the rarity of its jade or in the edibility of the grain. Whence does its sacredness come? It is sacred not because it is useful or handsome but because it is a constitutive element in the ceremony. It is sacred by virtue

---

6. For examples of Confucius's readiness to let an ironic comment stand without softening if irony is his intent and for his use of challenging, puzzling, or paradoxical statements, see, for example, 3:8; 5:3; 6:1; 6:10; 6:22; 6:23; 7:10; 7:29; 10:26; 11:17; 11:21.

of its participation in rite, in holy ceremony. In isolation from its role in the ceremony, the vessel is merely an expensive pot filled with grain.

It is therefore a paradox as utensil, for unlike utensils in general, this has no (utilitarian) use external to ceremony itself but only a ritual function. (Indeed some ceremonial pots had holes in them in order to emphasize their ritual rather than utilitarian value.)

By analogy, Confucius may be taken to imply that the individual human being, too, has ultimate dignity, sacred dignity by virtue of his role in rite, in ceremony, in *li*. We must recall that Confucius expanded the sense of the word *li*, originally referring to religious ceremonial, in such a way as to envision society itself on the model of *li*. If the teaching about *li* is thus generalized, it is reasonable to follow through and generalize the analogy between Tzu-Kung and the ceremonial vessel. We will then see how this image deepens our understanding of Confucius's teaching about man and human relations.

Social etiquette in general, the father-son relation, the brother-brother relation, the prince-subject relation, the friend-friend relation and the husband-wife relation—persons and their relationships are to be seen as ultimately sanctified by virtue of their place in *li*. Society, at least insofar as regulated by human convention and moral obligations, becomes in the Confucian vision one great ceremonial performance, a ceremony with all the holy beauty of an elaborate religious ritual carried out with that combination of solemnity and lightness of heart that graces the inspired ritual performance. It is not individual existence per se, nor is it the existence of a group per se that is the condition sufficient to create and sustain the ultimate dignity of man. It is the ceremonial aspect of life that bestows sacredness upon persons, acts, and objects which have a role in the performance of ceremony.

Confucius does not see the individual as an ultimate atom nor society on the analogy of animal or mechanism, nor does he see society as a proving ground for immortal souls or a contractual or utilitarian arrangement designed to maximize individual pleasure. He does not talk in the *Analects* of society and the individual. He talks of what it is to be man, and he sees that man is a special being with a unique dignity and power deriving from and embedded in *li*.

Is it enough merely to be born, to eat, breathe, drink, excrete, enjoy sensual gratification and avoid physical pain and discomfort? Animals do this. To become civilized is to establish relationships that are not merely physical, biological, or instinctive; it is to establish *human* relationships, relationships of an essentially symbolic kind, defined by tradition and convention and rooted in respect and obligation.

"Merely to feed one's parents well" . . . "even dogs and horses are fed" (2:7). To be devoted to one's parents is far more than to keep the parents alive physically. To serve and eat in the proper way, with the proper respect and appreciation, in the proper setting—this is to transform the act of mere nourishment into the human ceremony of dining. To obey the whip is to be not much more than a domestic animal; but to be loyal and faithful to those who rightly govern, to serve them and thus to serve *in* the human community, to do this out of one's own heart and nature—this is to be a true citizen of one's community.

Man's dignity, as does the dignity of things, lies in the ceremony rather than in individual biological existence, and this is evident in the fact that we understand a man who sacrifices his biological existence, his "life" in the biological but not the spiritual sense, if the "rite" demands it. Confucius makes the point succinctly when he responds to his disciple's concern over killing a sheep as an element in a sacrificial rite: "You love the sheep, but I love the ceremony," says Confucius (3:17).

"Virtue does not exist in isolation; there must be neighbors," says Confucius. (4:25) Man is transformed by participation with others in ceremony which is communal. Until he is so transformed he is not truly man but only potentially so—the new-born infant, the wolf-boy of the forests, or the "barbarian." Ceremony is justified when we see how it transforms the barbarian into what we know as man at his best. And, from the opposite direction, man at his best is justified when we see that his best is a life of holy ceremony rather than of appetite and mere animal existence. Whichever standpoint we take, we get a perspective on man and society which illuminates and deepens our vision of man's distinctive nature and dignity. When we see man as participant in communal rite rather than as individualistic ego, he takes on to our eyes a new and holy beauty just as does the sacrificial vessel.

Thus, in the *Analects,* man as individual is not sacred. However, he is not therefore to be thought of as a mere utensil to serve "society." For society is no more an independent entity than is ceremony independent of the participants, the holy vessels, the altar, the incantations. Society is men treating each other as men *(jen),* or to be more specific, according to the obligations and privileges of *li,* out of the love *(ai)* and loyalty *(chung)* and respect *(shu)* called for by their human relationships to each other. The shapes of human relationships are not imposed on man, not physically inevitable, not an instinct or reflex. They are rites learned and voluntarily participated in. The rite is self-justifying. The beings, the gestures, the words are not subordinate to rite, nor is rite subordinate to them. To "be self-disciplined and ever turning to *li*" (12:1) is to be no longer at the mercy of animal needs and demoralizing passion, it is to achieve that freedom in which the human spirit flowers; it is not, as Waley's translation may lead one to think, a matter of "submission" but of the triumph of the human spirit.

Confucius's theme, then, is not the "discovery of the individual" or of his ultimate importance. The *mere* individual is a bauble, malleable and breakable, a utensil transformed into the resplendent and holy as it serves in the ceremony of life. But then this does not deny *ultimate* dignity to men and to each man; he is not a meaningless ant serving the greater whole. His participation in divinity is as real and clearly visible as is that of the sacrificial vessel, for it *is* holy. And unlike the way he appears in the Christian view, man is not holy by virtue of his absolute possession, within himself and independently of other men, of a "piece" of the divine, the immortal soul. Nor is the "flowering" of the individual the central theme; instead it is the flowering of humanity in the ceremonial acts of men.

Although the individual must cultivate himself, just as the temple vessel must be carved and chiseled and polished, this self-cultivation is no more *central* to man's dignity, in Confucius's views, than the preparation of the vessel is central. Preparation and training are essential, but it is the ceremony that is central, and *all* the elements and relationships and actions in it are sacred though each has its special characteristics.

Nor should we suppose that Nature is cast out unless shaped into artifact for ritual use. The raiment of holiness is cast upon Nature as well as man, upon the river and the air as well as upon youth and song, when these are seen through the image of a ceremonial Rain Dance (11:25).

The noble man is the man who most perfectly having given up self, ego, obstinacy, and personal pride (9:4) follows not profit but the Way. Such a man has come to fruition as a person; he is the consummate Man. He is a Holy Vessel.

Further Reading

Lawrence G. Thompson presents both an overview and insight in *Chinese Religion: An Introduction* (4th ed., 1989), and does so in a concise 184 pages. His *The Chinese Way in Religion* (1973) is an accompanying anthology.

The Doctrine of the Mean (the *Chung-yung:* the title is sometimes translated as *The Central Harmony*) is one of the Four Books of Confucianism and of enormous importance to Chinese thought and life. Wing-tsit Chan's translation is recommended; it can be found in Chan (ed. and trans.), *A Sourcebook in Chinese Philosophy* (1963).

Still another very helpful anthology is *Sources of Chinese Tradition* (1960), edited by Wm. Theodore de Bary, et al.

"At the age of 40 Lin Yutang was already an ancient Chinese sage," wrote Joseph Wood Krutch. Some of Lin's work may be dated now, but his *My Country and My People* (1935; rev. ed., 1939) is an enjoyable and still valuable portrait of the China of the recent past. He also edited and translated *The Wisdom of Confucius* (1938) and *The Wisdom of China and India* (1942).

In his *Socrates, Buddha, Confucius, Jesus* (1957), the philosopher Karl Jaspers wrote of Confucius: "He had no fundamental religious experience, no revelation; he achieved no inner rebirth, he was not a mystic. . . . He was guided by the idea of an encompassing community through which man becomes man. His passion was for beauty, order, truthfulness, and happiness in the world."

The Story of Chinese Philosophy (1961) by Ch'u Chai and Winberg Chai is a popular treatment of its subject. The same father-and-son team collaborated on *The Humanist Way in Ancient China: Essential Works of Confucianism* (1965). (The latter volume was entitled *The Sacred Books of Confucius* in another edition.)

David L. Hall and Roger T. Ames, *Thinking Through Confucius* (1987). Two leading scholars here offer an interpretation of Confucius based upon a detailed study of key concepts in early Confucian thought and make it relevant to the late twentieth century.

Arthur Waley's *Three Ways of Thought in Ancient China* (1939) is a delight from cover to cover. One of the "three ways" is that of Mencius.

V

TAOISM
The Way To Do Is To Be

Miraculous power and marvelous activity—
Drawing water and hewing wood!   P'ang-yun

As with the Hindu's *Brahman,* there can perhaps be some sort of intuitive awareness of the nature of *Tao,* but no words are adequate to describe either the experience or *Tao* itself.

> Those who know do not speak;
> Those who speak do not know.[1]

The word "Tao" means Way, and here it refers most fundamentally to that
inexpressible Way of Reality of which no one can speak. This is the Ground of
Being, the Absolute. *Tao* is also manifested in nature, in those sublime rhythms of
the seasons and in the perennial processes of growth and decay, creation and death.
Tao, says Arthur Waley, refers to "the way the universe works," and "ultimately,
something very like God, in the more abstract and philosophical use of that term."[2]
It is the *Tao* of nature that can be the guide for those not too distracted or confused
to see the path. To know nature and to live an uncomplicated life in harmony with
it is the *Tao* of the wise.

Intellectuality, on the other hand, is a sad irrelevance: an excessive reliance
upon ideas and words clutters up the mind. "To be always talking is against nature"
is one of the blunt admonitions of the *Tao Te Ching.* The chatter of "progress" and

---

1. Arthur Waley, *The Way and Its Power* (London: George Allen & Unwin, Ltd., 1934), chap. LVI,
p. 210.
   Another translation of the same lines is that by Ho-shang Kung: "To know Tao and say you do not
know is the best. Not to know Tao and say you know is a disease." Quoted in Wing-tsit Chan, *The Way
of Lao Tzu* (Indianapolis: The Library of Liberal Arts, 1963), p. 225.

2. Waley, *The Way and Its Power,* p. 30. Because of the theistic connotations of the word "God," it
is probably not helpful to stress the comparison of that term with *Tao,* but one further reference is too
interesting to omit. A translation of the Gospel of John into Chinese juxtaposed the two terms in this
manner: "In the beginning was the *Tao,* and the *Tao* was with God, and the *Tao* was God." Quoted in
Chung-yuan Chang, "The Concept of Tao in Chinese Culture," *The Review of Religion,* 17 (March 1953):
116.

of civilization is likewise nonsense. No "salvation" is sought by the Taoist, no liberation from this world.[3] We are children of nature, and we can follow and trust its ways. The *Tao Te Ching,* Huston Smith has commented, is "a testament to humanity's at-homeness in the universe."[4]

The Taoist way of life is epitomized in the concept of *wu-wei.* Defined variously as "actionless activity," "creative quietude," and "yielding to win," it means possessing such empathy with nature that its powers become one's own. The lightest touch, then, at the proper time and place, will do what heavy and forceful blows cannot. Movement can be so effortless that it seems not to be movement. This is neither a matter of mere technique nor even of knowledge: ultimately, it is accomplishing everything by *becoming* a certain type of person. The way to *do* is to *be.*

Frederic Spiegelberg's essay, in the pages that follow, reviews what little is known of Lao Tzu, the "Old Master," who is held by tradition (and doubted by scholars) to have been the author of the *Tao Te Ching* and hence the "founder" of Taoism. It is typical of the spirit of the Taoist that it does not really matter whether Lao Tzu was in fact the author of that work or not—or even whether he was a historical figure or not. In the world of Taoism nothing should be fussed about, much less an academic question of authorship or distant detail of history. But the subtle themes of the *Tao Te Ching* do matter, and these are the subject of Spiegelberg's essay.

Then there are presented selections from the primary sources for Taoism, the *Tao Te Ching* and *Chuang Tzu.* The former books consists of eighty-one poems that could easily be printed on half that number of pages. Terse, paradoxical, epigrammatic, suggestive of mystery, the *Tao Te Ching* fits perfectly the Western image of the Wisdom of the East. It has prompted more translations than any other Chinese work. *Chuang Tzu* is the "second" book of Taoism, chronologically speaking. There is reflected in its tone and humor a truly liberated mind and spirit.

Comparisons of China's two indigenous religions are inevitable: Confucianism and Taoism are so different and yet so complementary. Lin Tung-chi's approach in his "The Chinese Mind: Its Taoist Substratum" is to describe them as they are manifested as character traits in the individual. The Confucian impulse is social and politely aggressive; the Taoist is private and "yielding." The Confucian concern about the business of state is countered by the indifferent anarchism of the Taoist. The conformity and orderliness of the Confucianist stand in contrast to the casualness of the Taoist.

"Tao Now," as it is presented here, constitutes about half of the original essay. Subtitled "An Ecological Testament," the essay in its entirety deals with the emphasis that grew in the West upon scientific objectivity and which led to a degree of useful mastery of and control over nature. But that very attitude of detachment also

---

3. Not discussed in this chapter is "popular" Taoism, which evolved in the course of time and featured belief in many deities, Heaven and Hell, magical practices, great concern about longevity and immortality, astrology, fortune-telling, and the like.

4. *The World's Religions* (San Francisco: HarperSanFrancisco, 1991), p. 197.

resulted in an estrangement from nature—the dire ecological consequences of which plague us today. In contrast, there is the Taoist, whose world is, among other things, "a realm of interpenetration and interdependence." In the process of explaining this, Smith provides an analysis of Taoism that summarizes and balances this chapter. ("Now yin, now yang: that is the Tao.")

The Old Master and His Book

Frederic Spiegelberg

Frederic Spiegelberg (1897–) was born and educated in Germany, earning a doctorate from the University of Tubingen, but fled Germany and the Nazis in the 1930s. He taught at a number of schools: Columbia University; Union Theological Seminary; University of California, Berkeley; the Pacific School of Religion; and, principally, Stanford University, where he lectured variously on Indian, Tibetan, and Chinese philosophy to the delight of students, who one year voted him the best professor on the faculty. His publications include The Religion of No Religion, Spiritual Practices of India, Living Religions of the World, *and* Zen, Rocks, and Waters.

The content of religious experience, he has written, is the Miracle of Being. Not miracles (in the plural), but the miracle, which is "the simple fact that we are, that the whole complex that we call the world is and has being." And "awakening to the Miracle of Being is the one and only true subject of all religions."* In China, the name for this is Tao.

Lao Tse, which is not a proper name, but merely means Old Master, is generally considered to have been born circa 604 B.C. Sinologists place the date two or three hundred years either way, but 604 is the traditional date.[1] According to legend, Lao Tse was carried in his mother's womb not for ten months, as in the case of the Buddha, but for eighty two years. One way or another, some fable of miraculous birth gathers about any great religious leader. It is, however, the longest parturition on record. Lao Tse was thus born as an old man with a long white beard and a wrinkled face. Despite this appearance, he immediately went down on the floor and began to perform in the manner of a small child. He was carrying out the great Chinese principle of filial piety. He did not do so for long, but nonetheless, he conformed to the pattern society demanded. But having been born at the age of eighty two, when he began to grow older, he aged very rapidly and lived to a vast age. Since old men were rare in those days, as such he was exceptional and was considered a great sage. No doubt the legend about his age reflects an outward aspect of his wisdom. In China an old man is not merely a person who by chance has survived the ravages

---

**Living Religions of the World* (Englewood Cliffs, N.J.: Prentice-Hall, 1956), pp. 8–9, 17.

1. Modern scholars question whether he lived at all, a few claiming him to have been invented by Chuang-Tzu, his supposed disciple.

From Frederic Spiegelberg, *Living Religions of the World.* Reprinted by permission of the author.

of time, disease, and his own offspring, and who no longer fulfills any useful social function. On the contrary, he is regarded as a person who, by reason of his longer experience, has much to teach.

We are told very little about Lao Tse. We learn that he was a librarian in the Court service, and legend would have it that in his old age he left China to travel westward, either to India, or to the glorious Buddhist paradise of Sukhavati. Clearly he went west in search of further wisdom, but since we do not know the exact date of the legends, we cannot say where this wisdom was thought to be located.

It is stated that the Chinese frontier officials would not allow Lao Tse to leave China without an export license for his possessions. Lao Tse had nothing with him, and explained that all he possessed was his philosophy, and that was in his mind. The customs inspector said that in that case he would have to leave his wisdom in China before departing, so Lao Tse sat at the border for three days and wrote down the *Tao te King*. The book is so succinct that it could easily have been written in three days, and could be read in half an hour. On the other hand, one could also spend a year on it, depending upon how thoroughly one read it. The *Tao te King* deals with the highest word concept of the Chinese language, the word tao.

It is not of importance that we know the doubtful English phonetic rendering of the word, but it is important that we know the Chinese ideogram and its meaning. Tao is, so to speak, the course of nature, or what we might call seasonableness; the agreement of circumstances with the needs of the hour. It might therefore just as well be placed in the center of the yang-yin hexagram of the *Yi-Ching*.

The ideogram is supposedly a picture of a head. The other part of the ideogram is an abbreviation of the walking-man sign, so tao is a head-walking, or headway, or mainroad. There are several hundred translations of the expression tao in various European languages. The ramifications of any Chinese ideogram are so diverse, and the ramifications of its relation with other ideograms in a certain order so multiform, that no one translation can ever deal with all of them. It is as though we were to try to compress the twenty-four simple meanings of the French verb "garder," not to mention their cognate meanings, into one word, together with the twenty-one meanings, let us say, of the word "eau" to which it might be found in as many multiple relations. It is like that, but it is also worse. Thus one sees that even in a book as brief as the *Tao te King* the possibilities are almost infinite. Even in China the reading of ideograms, let alone the translation of them, is a great art. For that matter, to take an Occidental symbol at random, what does a cross with equidistant arms mean? It may mean any one of a hundred different things, or all of them, even though we understand it quite differently when it is a silent symbol than when we connect it with the word for which it stands. The difference between an original and a translation is always great. But when we are translating things that are both words *and* visual symbols, the difference is all the greater. The first sentence of the *Tao te King* may make this matter clear:

Tao ko Tao Fei Chang Tao

We find the word tao itself three times. Ko is something like a genitive participle or relative pronoun, and means relation. Tao, insofar as it is termed tao is not the real tao, in other words. Fei means not. Chang; the real, eternal, or basically existent. So this sentence means that the Being of Being, insofar as it is expressed in terms of existence, is not the Being of Being that we really mean as the light that stands behind all things. Or, in the words of Meister Eckhart, "Our mind does not want God insofar as He is God. Why not? Because there He has names, and even if there would be a thousand, our mind penetrates them all more and more because it wants Him there where He has no names."

The very fact that tao is reflected in the mind means that the conception fails to be even the projection of the light we are talking about:

The name that can be named is not the enduring and unchanging name.[2]

Lao Tse goes on with his metaphysical exposition to prove that tao cannot be expressed in human terms or discussed, because once we try to do so, we lose it. As long as we do not try to conceive of it, however, it is there all the time. Thus we interpret the opening sentence of the *Tao te King*. But it could be interpreted in many other ways, for it is an arrangement of negatives and positives with no concrete root or externalized and specific statement.

There was something undefined and complete, coming into existence before Heaven and Earth. How still it was and formless, standing alone, and undergoing no change, reaching everywhere and in no danger [of being exhausted]! It may be regarded as the Mother of all things.

I do not know its name, and I give it the designation of the Tao [the Way or Course]. Making an effort [further] to give it a name I call it The Great.

Great, it passes on [in constant flow]. Passing on, it becomes remote. Having become remote, it returns. Therefore the Tao is great; Heaven is great; Earth is great; and the [sage] king is also great. In the universe there are four that are great, and the [sage] king is one of them.

Man takes his law from the Earth; the Earth takes its law from Heaven; Heaven takes its law from the Tao. The law of the Tao is its being what it is.[3]

Nonetheless Lao Tse has written an entire book about the inexpressibility of tao. He endeavors to exposit this inexpressibility by means of parables, showing what Tao could be called if one wished to explain it, though it is better not to do so. The Buddha also used examples, in exactly the same way, in discussing nirvana without defining it, because he believed it to be undefinable. The Buddha says only that nirvana is like sparks that fly from the anvil when the hammer strikes it; like the oil lamp that burns out because one forgot to refuel it. Lao Tse uses the same technique:

There is nothing in the world more soft and weak than water, and yet for attacking things that are firm and strong there is nothing that can take precedence of it;—for there is nothing [so effectual] for which it can be changed.

2. James Legge (trans.), *The Sacred Books of China, The Texts of Confucianism*, p. 47.

3. Ibid., pp. 67–68.

Every one in the world knows that the soft overcomes the hard, and the weak the strong, but no one is able to carry it out in practice.

Therefore the sage has said:

> He who accepts his state's reproach.
> Is hailed therefore its altars' lord;
> To him who bears men's direful woes
> They all the name of King accord.

Words that are strictly true seem to be paradoxical.[4]

and:

> The highest excellence is like [that of] water. The excellence of water appears in its benefiting all things, and in its occupying, without striving [to the contrary], the low place which all men dislike. Hence [its way] is near to [that of] the Tao.

It is necessary to speak of Tao in parabolic terms, for:

> The Tao, considered as unchanging, has no name. As soon as it proceeds to action, it has a name.[5]

So he uses the simile of water. Tao is not water, but it is like water because it seeks the lowest places and never stands high: that is, it is humble, insofar as it knows and finds its own place, and does not aspire to be higher than it is. Also, like water, it is the strongest and most powerful element on earth, for through yielding, like water, you achieve success.

We all know some of the thousands of Taoist, Zen, and Buddhist brush paintings of a waterfall cascading down over rocks. Such pictures are not meant to be depictive. They have a quality that we sense, apart from what they show, for they are visible sermons and aids to meditation. They are designed to say that water tumbling over rocks yields entirely to the shape of the rocks, as it would to a vessel into which it might be poured. It takes the shape it is allowed, at least for a time; yet if you look again after a lapse of geologic time you would see that the rocks have taken on the shape of the water-flow, their corners are rounded off. Pictures of waterfalls are frequently given as wedding presents in the Orient, for what happens when a man (yang) and a woman (yin) live together? The man sets the pattern of living and the woman yields, but the more she yields, the more interesting and unexpected will be the outcome. This attitude of not actually struggling to perform any action, out of conformity to passing circumstances, is the highest ethical principle of Taoism and is called the wu-wei. Usually, wu-wei is translated inaccurately as "not doing," giving the impression that Taoism is a doctrine of passive inactivity.

This is not the true meaning, for the word wu does not mean not in the sense of pure negation, as it does in English. The ideogram for wu originally meant: "forty men disappear in the woods." If you ask what happens to forty men who disappear in the woods, the answer is, nothing at all, they are merely no longer visible. So it

4. Ibid., p. 120.

5. Ibid., pp. 52, 74.

is with wu as a negative. It does not mean a total negation, but rather an absence from the immediate scene. Wu-wei is therefore an imperative: act in such a way as forty men who disappear into the woods do. In other words, to translate the matter into the terms of Kant's categorical imperative, to act in such way that your action and the results of your actions are not noticeable, either to yourself or to others, for they should fit so smoothly into the surroundings and circumstances that they will not be egregious. If so:

He who does not fail in the requirements of his position continues long."[6]

On this matter Lao Tse is extremely explicit:

The skilful traveller leaves no traces of his wheels or footsteps; the skilful speaker says nothing that can be found fault with or blamed; the skilful reckoner uses no tallies; the skilful closer needs no bolts or bars, while to open what he has shut will be impossible.[7]

It is perhaps interesting that even when we discuss tao, we have to use such words as improper, proper, egregious, which are hardly ever used in current speech to define correct behavior. They were so used in the eighteenth century, when an appropriate and unostentatious conduct was emphasized by the social compact as highly as it has ever been in the Anglo-Saxon-American cultural stream.

Such conduct, to which nothing need be added, and from which nothing can be taken away without changing its nature, we found enunciated in the *Bhagavad-Gita,* or *Song of the Lord.* The God Krishna tells the hero, Arjuna, not to choose either akarma, or inactivity, or karma, which was vigorous action for the sake of specific ends, but to seek Nishkama karma, the kind of action that is gratuitous, performed for no goal of the self, but as an instrument of the divine force that acts through us, if we do not impede it with our personal selfishness.

In the literature that touches more or less directly upon any possible expression of the Being of Being by means of words, the book of tao stands as one of the best metaphysics. Unfortunately like all such pure sources, tao hardens with the passage of time into an -ism, the colloidal suspension of its approach to the ineffable precipitating out into dogma and ritual. Mystical insight into the Being of Being is a personal, and not a social matter. So when such an insight is adjusted to the needs of those who cluster round the original master, very odd things are apt to happen. In the case of the system of Lao Tse, what happened was that his original insight solidified into a system of necromancy. Today most of the light-blue gowned Taoist monks and priests of China, far from being infallible philosophers, are sorcerers, soothsayers, and magicians of the lowest kind. Consequently there are very few enlightened persons who call themselves Taoists, and as Taoists, they are not appreciated as serious scholars. The hexagram of the *I-Ching,* from the form of a parable of the greater nature forces, deteriorated into a dream and magic book, and so too, did Tao.

6. Ibid., p. 75.
7. Ibid., p. 70.

A Chinese friend of the author's once took him to see a Taoist scholar, who lived in a tiny hermitage in the mountain ranges north of Hong Kong, in a condition of utmost simplicity. When asked if he thought the great spirit of the ancient tradition of tao was still alive, the scholar, who was fat, began to laugh until his belly shook. That was his only answer. Whether he was laughing at the impertinence of the question or at the irony of the answer was not clear. It is for the reader to decide. But no matter what Taoism is now, the book of tao remains. It is really a series of meditations upon the nature of tao, which, as we know from the first sentence of the *Tao te King,* cannot be the great tao if it can be expressed, the great tao being inexpressible. The second chapter of the *Tao te King* is particularly celebrated:

> All in the world know the beauty of the beautiful, and in doing this they have [the idea of] what ugliness is; they all know the skill of the skilful, and in doing this they have [the idea of] what the want of skill is.
>
> So it is that existence and non-existence give birth the one to [the idea of] the other; that difficulty and ease produce the one [the idea of] the other. . . .
>
> Therefore the sage manages affairs without doing anything, and conveys his instructions without the use of speech.[8]

In other words, by overemphasizing one quality, we only serve to evoke its opposite. Or perhaps, as in all things, beauty in this sense is not the norm, but an extreme, on the eternal teeter-totter of yang and yin, so that by bearing all emphasis upon it, we only serve to drag it down and to make its opposite rise. In the last line, "teaching without words," is literally "not speaking talk," which is not quite the same thing. However, since we have seen that wu-wei does not mean without action, but acting in such a way that neither the action nor the result of the action is glaringly visible, we might reconsider the role of the sage. Emerson mentions somewhere that Socrates said: "All my good is magnetic; and I educate not by lessons, but by going about my business." We also have the old saw about education consisting of Mark Hopkins at one end of a log and the pupil at the other. For education is not only an instruction in opinion and fact. It also deals with the transmission of a good deal of ineffable material that can only be conveyed by a form of osmosis. The Chinese sage, and in particular the sage envisioned by Lao Tse, did not only teach by example. He also taught by presence. This, clearly, was also the great strength of the Buddha, as it is of any revealed personality. When we read the great and momentous political speeches of the past, even of the immediate past, they make no impression on us at all. We wonder how they made their effect. If we have ever seen a first-rate actress in a fifth-rate play we would know how instantly. A great sage or teacher actually transmits, not information, except incidentally, but his personality, more or less intact. But this personality is not his personal ego, so much as it is a living mind modified by a special type of or series of experiences. Like a great artist, his skill consists in being able to transmit the insights he has received, which usually have little or nothing to do with the form in which he wraps them, so to speak, or even with his own ego. The artist, like the teacher, if inspired,

---

8. Ibid., pp. 47–48.

has not only his own personal ego, but also an impersonal persona. It is the insights impressed upon this that he transmits. Rembrandt's *"Side of Beef"*; Chardin's pots and pans; Winslow Homer's trout streams, and Milton's *Paradise Lost* deal with matters far different than their subject matter. Thus, we can conjecture, the Buddha, though never describing nirvana, managed to convey its nature very well to his immediate disciples, for though we do not find the matter in his recorded texts, he had at his disposal the eighty four principal mudras, or hand and body postures that, when we see them, still convey something to us, even if we do not know their precise symbolic meaning.

In this regard, it is not without interest that Buddhist sculpture in China, with the exception of the lotus postures, favored more than any other position "the posture of heavenly ease" of Kwannon.

In the *Tao te King,* Lao Tse mentions the god concept only once, in Section four:

> The Tao is [like] the emptiness of a vessel; and in our employment of it we must be on our guard against all fulness. How deep and unfathomable it is, as if it were the Honoured Ancestor of all things!
>
> . . . .
>
> How pure and still the Tao is, as if it would ever so continue.[9]

This is very much like the hymn to creation in the *Rig Veda:*

> Who verily knows and who can here declare it, whence it was
>   born and whence comes this creation?
> The gods are later than this world's production. Who knows
>   then whence it first came into being?[10]

The *Tao te King* is extremely sparse and laconic, much more succinct than anything to be found in the *Vedas*. Also, the general impression is one of more impersonality and detachment. Even the parables and similes are fleetingly brief.

> The highest excellence is like [that of] water. The excellence of water appears in its benefiting all things, and in its occupying, without striving, [to the contrary], the low place which all men dislike. Hence [its way] is near to [that of] the Tao.[11]
>
> .   .   .
>
> Clay is fashioned into vessels; but it is on their empty hollowness that their use depends.[12]

You don't want the glass or the brass or the clay, when you buy a vessel, you want the empty space, or capacity to carry liquid. The thing itself is worth nothing,

9. Ibid., p. 50.

10. Ralph T. H. Griffith, trans., *Hymns of the Rig-Veda* (Benares: E.J. Lazarus and Co., 1896), p. 129.

11. *The Sacred Books of China,* p. 52.

12. Ibid., p. 55.

but its ability, or emptiness, to receive is what is worth having. Man is worth nothing. His ability to receive insight is worth everything.

> The door and windows are cut out [from the walls] to form an apartment;
> but it is on the empty space [within], that its use depends.[13]

This sentence has been applied to Chinese and Japanese art, with their emphasis upon what is not to be seen in the picture, usually considered as more important than the actual lines the painter draws. Watch what he has left out, instead of concentrating on what he has drawn, and it usually becomes apparent that what he has drawn is there only so that what he left out may be noticed by contrast. Thus Hia Kouei's famous landscape of a storm in autumn shows only a man bending under an umbrella, a tree blowing in the wind, and grasses blowing on the edge of a cliff. The rest of the paper is bare. Ying Yu-Kien's "Fog Parting From A Village in the Mountains" consists of six rocks, three rooftops, and two bled-edge washes, plus two small figures each drawn with not more than three brushstrokes apiece; yet the picture is vast. The same is true of music. It is the interval, not the note, that is important there. Psychologically this idea is akin to some of the ideas behind the Yoga practices of India, in particular the attempt to abolish the personal ego, to act in an average way, and not to be noticed any longer insofar as one's work is no more worthy of notice than one is oneself.

. . .

In the last entry of the *Tao te King* Lao Tse pokes fun at himself. After three days of writing, when he presents his written wisdom to the frontier official so that he may be permitted to leave China, what can he say but:

> Sincere words are not fine; fine words are not sincere. Those who are skilled
> [in the Tao] do not dispute [about it]; the disputatious are not skilled in it.
> Those who know [the Tao] are not extensively learned; the extensively
> learned do not know it.[14]

So Lao Tse laughs and mocks like the elderly Taoist scholar north of Hong Kong, for when one talks of profound matters, by talking one only makes them the more elusive. Such is the wisdom of Lao Tse.

13. Ibid., p. 55.
14. Ibid., p. 123.

Selections, *Tao Te Ching*
Gia-fu Feng and Jane English (translators)

Gia-fu Feng (1919–1985) was born in Shanghai and received his bachelor degree from Peking University. He came to the United States in 1947 to study comparative religion; his masters is from the University of Pennsylvania. He taught at Esalen (Big Sur, California) and directed the Stillpoint Foundation (a Taoist community in Colorado). His collaborator, Jane English, with whom he also worked on Chuang Tzu/Inner Chapters, *was born in Boston in 1942 and is a graduate of Mount Holyoke College. She holds a doctorate in physics from the University of Wisconsin and has taught Oriental thought and modern physics at Colorado College.*

The difficulties of translating the Tao Te Ching, *commented upon by Spiegelberg, extend even to its title, which has been rendered as variously as* The Way and Its Power *(Arthur Waley) and*The Canon of Reason and Virtue *(D. T. Suzuki and Paul Carus).*

One

The Tao that can be told is not the eternal Tao.
The name that can be named is not the eternal name.
The nameless is the beginning of heaven and earth.
The named is the mother of ten thousand things.
Ever desireless, one can see the mystery.
Ever desiring, one can see the manifestations.
These two spring from the same source but differ in name; this appears as
    darkness.
Darkness within darkness.
The gate to all mystery.

Two

Under heaven all can see beauty as beauty only because there is ugliness.
All can know good as good only because there is evil.

Therefore having and not having arise together.
Difficult and easy complement each other.
Long and short contrast each other;
High and low rest upon each other;
Voice and sound harmonize each other;
Front and back follow one another.

Therefore the sage goes about doing nothing, teaching no-talking.
The ten thousand things rise and fall without cease,
Creating, yet not possessing,
Working, yet not taking credit.
Work is done, then forgotten.
Therefore it lasts forever.

Eight

The highest good is like water.
Water gives life to the ten thousand things and does not strive.
It flows in places men reject and so is like the Tao.

In dwelling, be close to the land.
In meditation, go deep in the heart.
In dealing with others, be gentle and kind.
In speech, be true.
In ruling, be just.
In business, be competent.
In action, watch the timing.

No fight: No blame.

Nineteen

Give up sainthood, renounce wisdom,
And it will be a hundred times better for everyone.

Give up kindness, renounce morality.
And men will rediscover filial piety and love.

Give up ingenuity, renounce profit.
And bandits and thieves will disappear.

These three are outward forms alone; they are not sufficient in themselves.
It is more important
To see the simplicity,
To realize one's true nature,
To cast off selfishness
And temper desire.

Twenty-Two

Yield and overcome;
Bend and be straight;
Empty and be full;
Wear out and be new;
Have little and gain;
Have much and be confused.

Therefore wise men embrace the one
And set an example to all.
Not putting on a display,
They shine forth.
Not justifying themselves,
They are distinguished.
Not boasting,
They receive recognition.
Not bragging,
They never falter.
They do not quarrel,
So no one quarrels with them.
Therefore the ancients say, "Yield and overcome."
Is that an empty saying?
Be really whole,
And all things will come to you.

Twenty-Four

He who stands on tiptoe is not steady.
He who strides cannot maintain the pace.
He who makes a show is not enlightened.
He who is self-righteous is not respected.
He who boasts achieves nothing.
He who brags will not endure.
According to followers of the Tao,
    "These are extra food and unnecessary luggage."
They do not bring happiness.
Therefore followers of the Tao avoid them.

Twenty-Nine

Do you think you can take over the universe and improve it?
I do not believe it can be done.

The universe is sacred.
You cannot improve it.
If you try to change it, you will ruin it.
If you try to hold it, you will lose it.

So sometimes things are ahead and sometimes they are behind;
Sometimes breathing is hard, sometimes it comes easily;
Sometimes there is strength and sometimes weakness;
Sometimes one is up and sometimes down.

Therefore the sage avoids extremes, excesses, and complacency.

Thirty-Three

Knowing others is wisdom;
Knowing the self is enlightenment.
Mastering others requires force;
Mastering the self needs strength.

He who knows he has enough is rich.
Perseverance is a sign of will power.
He who stays where he is endures.
To die but not to perish is to be eternally present.

Thirty-Five

All men will come to him who keeps to the one,
For there lie rest and happiness and peace.

Passersby may stop for music and good food,
But a description of the Tao
Seems without substance or flavor.
It cannot be seen, it cannot be heard,
And yet it cannot be exhausted.

Forty

Returning is the motion of the Tao.
Yielding is the way of the Tao.
The ten thousand things are born of being.
Being is born of not being.

Forty-Three

The softest thing in the universe.
Overcomes the hardest thing in the universe.
That without substance can enter where there is no room.
Hence I know the value of non-action.

Teaching without words and work without doing
Are understood by very few.

Forty-Six

When the Tao is present in the universe,
The horses haul manure.
When the Tao is absent from the universe,
War horses are bred outside the city.

There is no greater sin than desire,
No greater curse than discontent,
No greater misfortune than wanting something for oneself.
Therefore he who knows that enough is enough will always have enough.

Forty-Seven

Without going outside, you may know the whole world.
Without looking through the window, you may see the ways of heaven.
The farther you go, the less you know.

Thus the sage knows without traveling;
He sees without looking;
He works without doing.

Forty-Eight

In the pursuit of learning, every day something is acquired.
In the pursuit of Tao, every day something is dropped.

Less and less is done.
Until non-action is achieved.
When nothing is done, nothing is left undone.

The world is ruled by letting things take their course.
It cannot be ruled by interfering.

Forty-Nine

The sage has a mind of his own.
He is aware of the needs of others.

I am good to people who are good.
I am also good to people who are not good.
Because Virtue is goodness.
I have faith in people who are faithful.
I also have faith in people who are not faithful.
Because Virtue is faithfulness.

The sage is shy and humble—to the world he seems confusing.
Men look to him and listen.
He behaves like a little child.

Fifty-Seven

Rule a nation with justice.
Wage war with surprise moves.
Become master of the universe without striving.
How do I know that this is so?
Because of this!

The more laws and restrictions there are,
The poorer people become.
The sharper men's weapons,
The more trouble in the land.
The more ingenious and clever men are,
The more strange things happen.
The more rules and regulations,
The more thieves and robbers.

Therefore the sage says:
    I take no action and people are reformed.
    I enjoy peace and people become honest.
    I do nothing and people become rich.
    I have no desires and people return to the good and simple life.

Seventy-Six

A man is born gentle and weak.
At his death he is hard and stiff.
Green plants are tender and filled with sap.
At their death they are withered and dry.

Therefore the stiff and unbending is the disciple of death.
The gentle and yielding is the disciple of life.

Thus an army without flexibility never wins a battle.
A tree that is unbending is easily broken.

The hard and strong will fall.
The soft and weak will overcome.

Eighty-One

Truthful words are not beautiful.
Beautiful words are not truthful.
Good men do not argue.
Those who argue are not good.
Those who know are not learned.
The learned do not know.

The sage never tries to store things up.
The more he does for others, the more he has.
The more he gives to others, the greater his abundance.
The Tao of heaven is pointed but does no harm.
The Tao of the sage is work without effort.

Selections, *Chuang Tzu*

Arthur Waley (translator)

*"Chuang Tzu" is used to refer to either the book by that title or the man, but of the man nothing is known except that he was a contemporary of Mencius in the fourth century **B.C.E.** Chuang Tzu himself did not write the book (which probably dates from the third century **B.C.E.**); it bears his name because he is the subject of or inspiration for its stories.*

The Chuang Tzu *pursues the themes of the* Tao Te Ching *but adds its own personality; the author of the* Chuang Tzu *is delightfully light-hearted. The later development of Ch'an (Zen) Buddhism in China owed much to Taoism in general and to Chuang Tzu in particular.*

The selections that follow were translated by Arthur Waley and are taken from his Three Ways of Thought in Ancient China. *Waley appeared earlier in this volume as the translator of* The Analects *of Confucius.*

Hui Tzu said to Chuang Tzu, "Your teachings are of no practical use." Chuang Tzu said, "Only those who already know the value of the useless can be talked to about the useful. This earth we walk upon is of vast extent, yet in order to walk a man uses no more of it than the soles of his two feet will cover. But suppose one cut away the ground round his feet till one reached the Yellow Springs,[1] would his patches of ground still be of any use to him for walking?" Hui Tzu said, "They would be of no use." Chuang Tzu said, "So then the usefulness of the useless is evident."

·   ·   ·

When Chuang Tzu's wife died, Hui Tzu came to the house to join in the rites of mourning. To his surprise he found Chuang Tzu sitting with an inverted bowl on his knees, drumming upon it and singing a song. "After all," said Hui Tzu, "she lived with you, brought up your children, grew old along with you. That you should not mourn for her is bad enough; but to let your friends find you drumming and singing—that is going too far!" "You misjudge me," said Chuang Tzu. "When she died, I was in despair, as any man well might be. But soon, pondering on what had happened, I told myself that in death no strange new fate befalls us. In the beginning

---

1. The world of the dead.

we lack not life only, but form. Not form only, but spirit. We are blended in the one great featureless indistinguishable mass. Then a time came when the mass evolved spirit, spirit evolved form, form evolved life. And now life in its turn has evolved death. For not nature only but man's being has its seasons, its sequence of spring and autumn, summer and winter. If some one is tired and has gone to lie down, we do not pursue him with shouting and bawling. She whom I have lost has lain down to sleep for a while in the Great Inner Room. To break in upon her rest with the noise of lamentation would but show that I knew nothing of nature's Sovereign Law. That is why I ceased to mourn."

. . .

"Take the case of some words," Chuang Tzu says, parodying the logicians, "I do not know which of them are in any way connected with reality or which are not at all connected with reality. If some that are so connected and some that are not so connected are connected with one another, then as regards truth or falsehood the former cease to be in any way different from the latter. However, just as an experiment, I will now say them: If there was a beginning, there must have been a time before the beginning began, and if there was a time before the beginning began, there must have been a time before the time before the beginning began. If there is being, there must also be not-being. If there was a time before there began to be any not-being, there must also have been a time before the time before there began to be any not-being. But here am I, talking about being and not-being and still do not know whether it is being that exists and not-being that does not exist, or being that does not exist and not-being that really exists! I have spoken, and do not know whether I have said something that means anything or said nothing that has any meaning at all."

. . .

[Translator's note: To be worked up about the difference between things that are really the same is called Three in the morning.]

What is meant by Three in the morning? In Sung there was a keeper of monkeys. Bad times came and he was obliged to tell them that he must reduce their ration of nuts. "It will be three in the morning and four in the evening," he said. The monkeys were furious. "Very well then," he said, "you shall have four in the morning and three in the evening." The monkeys accepted with delight.

. . .

When Confucius was in the West, he wanted to present copies of his works to the Royal House of Chou. A disciple advised him, saying, "I have heard that there is a former Royal Librarian called Lao Tzu, who now lives in retirement at his home. If you, Sir, want to get your books accepted at the Library, you had better see if you can secure his recommendation." "A good idea," said Confucius, and went to see Lao Tzu, who received the project very coldly. Whereupon Confucius unrolled a dozen treatises and began to expound them. Lao Tzu interrupted him, saying, "This is going to take too long. Tell me the gist of the matter." "The gist of the matter," said Confucius, "is goodness and duty." "Would you pray tell me," said Lao Tzu, "are these qualities natural to man?" "Indeed these are," said Confucius. "We have a saying that gentlemen

> Without goodness cannot thrive,
> Without duty cannot live.

Goodness and duty are indeed natural to man. What else should they be?" "And what pray, do you mean by goodness and duty?"

> "To have a heart without guile,
> To love all men without partiality,

that," said Confucius, "is the true state of goodness and duty."

"Hum," said Lao Tzu, "the second saying sounds to me dangerous. To speak of "loving all men" is a foolish exaggeration, and to make up one's mind to be impartial is in itself a kind of partiality. If you indeed want the men of the world not to lose the qualities that are natural to them, you had best study how it is that Heaven and Earth maintain their eternal course, that the sun and moon maintain their light, the stars their serried ranks, the birds and beasts their flocks, the trees and shrubs their station. Thus you too shall learn to guide your steps by Inward Power, to follow the course that the Way of Nature sets; and soon you will reach a goal where you will no longer need to go round laboriously advertising goodness and duty, like the town-crier with his drum, seeking for news of a lost child. No, Sir! What you are doing is to disjoint men's natures!"

Confucius visited Lao Tzu and began talking about goodness and duty. "Chaff from the winnower's fan," said Lao Tzu, "can so blear our eyes that we do not know if we are looking north, south, east, or west; at heaven or at the earth. One gnat or mosquito can be more than enough to keep us awake a whole night. All this talk of goodness and duty, these perpetual pin-pricks, unnerve and irritate the hearer; nothing, indeed, could be more destructive of his inner tranquility. . . . The swan does not need a daily bath in order to remain white; the crow does not need a daily inking in order to remain black."

. . .

Confucius said to Lao Tzu, "I have edited the Songs, the Book of History, the Rites, the Canon of Music, the Book of Changes, the Chronicle of Springs and Autumns—six scriptures in all—and I think I may say that I have thoroughly mastered their import. Armed with this knowledge I have faced seventy-two rulers, expounding the Way of former kings, the achievements of Chou and Shao; but there was not one ruler who made the slightest use of my teaching. It seems that either my hearers must have been singularly hard to convince, or the Way of the former kings is exceedingly difficult to understand."

"It is a lucky thing," said Lao Tzu, "that you did not meet with a prince anxious to reform the world. Those six scriptures are the dim footprints of ancient kings. They tell us nothing of the force that guided their steps. All your lectures are concerned with things that are no better than footprints in the dust. Footprints are made by shoes; but they are far from being shoes."

. . .

Tzu-lai fell ill. He was already at the last gasp; his wife and children stood weeping and wailing round his bed. "Pst," said Tzu-li, who had come to call, "stand back! A great Change is at work; let us not disturb it." Then, leaning against the door, he said to Tzu-lai, "Mighty are the works of the Changer! What is he about to make of you, to what use will he put you? Perhaps a rat's liver, perhaps a beetle's claw!" "A child," said Tzu-lai, "at its parents' bidding must go north and south, east or west; how much the more when those parents of all Nature, the great powers Yin and Yang command him, must he needs go where they will. They have asked me to die, and if I do not obey them, shall I not rank as an unmanageable child? I can make no complaint against them. These great forces housed me in my bodily frame, spent me in youth's toil, gave me repose when I was old, will give me rest at my death. Why should the powers that have done so much for me in life, do less for me in death?"

. . .

How do I know that wanting to be alive is not a great mistake? How do I know that hating to die is not like thinking one has lost one's way, when all the time one is on the path that leads to home? Li Chi was the daughter of the frontier guardsman at Ai. When first she was captured and carried away to Chin, she wept till her dress was soaked with tears. But when she came to the king's palace, sat with him on his couch and shared with him the dainties of the royal board, she began to wonder why she had wept. How do I know that the dead do not wonder why they should ever have prayed for long life?

. . .

Once Chuang Chou[2] dreamt that he was a butterfly. He did not know that he had ever been anything but a butterfly and was content to hover from flower to flower. Suddenly he woke and found to his astonishment that he was Chuang Chou. But it was hard to be sure whether he really was Chou and had only dreamt that he was a butterfly, or was really a butterfly, and was only dreaming that he was Chou.

. . .

It was the time when the autumn floods come down. A hundred streams swelled the River, that spread and spread till from shore to shore, nay from island to island so great was the distance that one could not tell horse from bull. The god of the River felt extremely pleased with himself. It seemed to him that all lovely things under heaven had submitted to his power. He wandered down-stream, going further and further to the east, till at last he came to the sea. He gazed eastwards, confidently expecting to see the further shore. He could discern no end to the waters. Then the god of the River began to turn his head, peering this way and that; but still he could see no shore. At last, addressing the ocean, he said with a deep sigh: "There is a proverb which says,

2. I.e., Chuang Tzu.

None like me
Proves none so blind as he.

I fear it applies very well to myself . . . as I realize only too well when I gaze at your limitless immensity. Had I not this day enrolled myself as your disciple, I might well have made myself the laughing-stock of all who take the Wider View."

. . .

There are those whose thoughts are sublime without being strained; who have never striven after goodness, yet are perfect. There are those who win no victories for their State, achieve no fame, and yet perfect its policies; who find quietness, though far from streams and lakes; who live to great old age, though they have never practised Induction (tao-yin). They have divested themselves of everything, yet lack nothing. They are passive, seek no goal; but all lovely things attend them. Such is the way of Heaven and Earth, the secret power of the Wise. Truly is it said, "Quietness, stillness, emptiness, not-having, inactivity—these are the balancers of Heaven and Earth, the very substance of the Way and its Power." Truly is it said, "The Wise Man rests therein, and because he rests, he is at peace. Because he is at peace, he is quiet." One who is at peace and is quiet no sorrow or harm can enter, no evil breath can invade. Therefore his inner power remains whole and his spirit intact.

Truly is it said, "For the Wise Man life is conformity to the motions of Heaven, death is but part of the common law of Change. At rest, he shares the secret powers of Yin; at work, he shares the rocking of the waves of Yang. He neither invites prosperity nor courts disaster. Only when incited does he respond, only when pushed does he move, only as a last resort will he rise. He casts away all knowledge and artifice, follows the pattern of Heaven. Therefore Heaven visits him with no calamity, the things of the world do not lay their trammels upon him, no living man blames him, no ghost attacks him. His life is like the drifting of a boat, his death is like a lying down to rest. He has no anxieties, lays no plans."

. . .

King Hui of Wei had a carver named Ting. When this carver Ting was carving a bull for the king, every touch of the hand, every inclination of the shoulder, every step he trod, every pressure of the knee, while swiftly and lightly he wielded his carving-knife, was as carefully timed as the movements of a dancer in the *Mulberry Wood.* . . . "Wonderful," said the king. "I could never have believed that the art of carving could reach such a point as this." "I am a lover of Tao," replied Ting, putting away his knife, "and have succeeded in applying it to the art of carving. When I first began to carve I fixed my gaze on the animal in front of me. After three years I no longer saw it as a whole bull, but as a thing already divided into parts. Nowadays I no longer see it with the eye; I merely apprehend it with the soul. My sense-organs are in abeyance, but my soul still works. Unerringly my knife follows the natural markings, slips into the natural cleavages, finds its way into the natural cavities. And so by conforming my work to the structure with which I am dealing, I have arrived at a point at which my knife never touches even the smallest ligament or tendon, let alone the main gristle.

"A good carver changes his knife once a year; by which time the blade is dented. An ordinary carver changes it once a month; by which time it is broken. I have used my present knife for nineteen years, and during that time have carved several thousand bulls. But the blade still looks as though it had just come out of the mould."

.   .   .

"Do not seek precision," says Chuang Tzu, speaking of the realm of Tao ... "I myself have traversed it this way and that; yet still know only where it begins. I have roamed at will through its stupendous spaces. I know how to get to them, but I do not know where they end."

.   .   .

When Chuang Tzu was angling in the river P'u, the king of Ch'u sent two high officers of state, who accosting Chuang Tzu announced that the king wished to entrust him with the management of all his domains. Rod in hand and eyes still fixed upon his line, Chuang Tzu replied, "I have been told that in Ch'u there is a holy tortoise that died three thousand years ago. The king keeps it in the great hall of his ancestral shrine, in a casket covered with a cloth. Suppose that when this tortoise was caught, it had been allowed to choose between dying and having its bones venerated for centuries to come or going on living with its tail draggling in the mud, which would it have preferred?" "No doubt," said the two officers, "it would have preferred to go on living with its tail draggling in the mud." "Well then, be off with you," said Chuang Tzu, "and leave me to drag my tail in the mud."

The Chinese Mind:
Its Taoist Substratum

Lin Tung-chi

As Lin Tung-chi suggests in the pages that follow, Confucianism and Taoism may be looked upon as the yang *and* yin *of China. Confucianism turns outward toward community and duty; Taoism thrives in solitude and freedom. The Confucianist shoulders responsibilities and stands on ceremony, while the Taoist philosophy is that of "an artist, of a rustic and vagabond"; the cool reasonableness of the one is offset by the poetical intuitiveness of the other.*

Certainly, these are not and ought not be rival religions. They are, as Burton Watson has written, "complementary doctrines, an ethical and political system for the conduct of public and family life, and a mystical philosophy for the spiritual nourishment of the individual, with the metaphysical teachings of the Book of Changes *acting as a bridge between the two."**

I

Are Chinese Confucian? Yes, indeed. Every Chinese, if tutored at all, cannot help being Confucian, more or less.

And yet, there is necessarily the other side—the counterpoise. For every Chinese is likewise a Taoist, and the definition of a Taoist is, normally, what a Confucianist is not!

Most Westerners are at a loss in understanding Chinese personality. Not a little of the difficulty, I suggest, has come from ignoring this dual nature of the Chinese.

The fact is: we are socially Confucian and individually Taoist. For all the imposing superstructures of our society, with its intricate family ties and relations and its myriad conventions and mannerisms to which we submit as good Confucianists, we as individuals per se are irreducibly Taoists.

There is such a thing as personality in solitude as distinguished from personality in association—the intimate self that we feel at home with and are ever inclined to be, as distinguished from the public self that we will to be or have to be. The psychologist has perhaps a word for it—the subconscious. Consciously we are Confu-

**Chuang Tzu: Basic Writings* (New York: Columbia University Press, 1964), pp. 10–11.

Lin Tung-chi, "The Chinese Mind: Its Taoist Substratum" from the *Journal of the History of Ideas,* Vol. 8, No. 3 (June 1947). Reprinted by permission of the publisher.

cianists, but deep in the obscure subconscious we feel with alternate fear and joy the blatant Taoist in us all. We fear because we believe we *should be* Confucian in toto. We rejoice because we know we *are* not.

Confucianism is a practical, prosaic affair. Society, social control, gregarious-ness, and reciprocity of action guided by accepted rules and expressed through a code of decorum—these are but elemenetary requirements for any decent com-munal living. The underlying spirit is Duty—namely, the duty of the individual towards his fellowmen and society.

Taoism, on the other hand, is not concerned with society and social order. In direct antithesis to these and other man-made institutions, the Taoist upholds Nature and the State of Nature, wherein the individual and his free expression become the end and justification of everything. What Taoism represents is mani-festly a spirit of Freedom—freedom to behave as one pleases irrespective of what society may say and how it may be affected. We are here speaking of Taoism as that subtle but abiding psychic mood in an educated Chinese, and not of the supersti-tious hodgepodge of the same name with its bewildering hierarchy of gods and fair-ies concocted and spread by the magician-priests. The latter is a form of popular religion, and hence a social institution. The former is a philosophic attitude or even an aesthetic temperament which, while perpetually seeking expression, ever refuses to actualize itself in any institutional form, religious or otherwise.

Confucianism, with its command of duty, calls for cooperation and conformity; socially speaking, it unites, conserves and perpetuates. Taoism, as an embodiment of individual free will, ever tends toward dissent and dissociation. The contrast between the two is glaring indeed. Yet, like so many paradoxes of life, opposites dwell closest together. The combination of these two modes of thought in one cul-ture, nay, in one person, is not an unhappy mixture in many ways. They supply, shall we say, the positive and the negative elements in Chinese life—the *yin* and the *yang* which complement each other and operate dialectically to lead life out of its periodic impasse; and thanks to them, China is no nation of monomaniacs and monotones.

II

One should be on one's guard against confounding Taoism facilely with Western individualism. True, both advocate individual freedom. But it would be sheer naïveté to assume that they mean the same thing. Taoist freedom is the freedom of a pre-social or an asocial being, while the libertarian freedom of the West is the freedom of a socially conscious man.

Broadly speaking, the gulf that separates the two is perhaps one that separates romanticism from realism in general. There was a time in Europe when the first romantic flush of the Rousseauean indictment against civilization carried with it an advocacy of freedom à la Taoiste—idyllic, abstract, and generalized. But that stage was an effervescence; it soon gave way to something organically different. Lib-ertarian individualism of post-Rousseauean days smacks less of romanticism than of practical levelheadedness. The actual question at issue has never been generalized freedom as such, which concept the consensus of Western opinion, even among theoreticians, has long abandoned as untenable. The real issue in each case has always been freedom from something specific and for something specific. Hence, freedom of speech, freedom of assemblage, freedom of belief and worship and, characteristically enough, freedom of contract. There is an unerring move to a definition of position and a specification of concrete objectives which makes the libertarian individualism of the West a realistic and calculated drive almost from the very start. . . .

In Taoism, however, specific objectives do not exist. Taoism postulates generalized freedom without giving it content; it proposes wholesale destruction of civilization without offering an attainable substitute. Freedom to a Taoist does not mean the struggle to free oneself from somebody or something specific; it means freedom of all from all.

.   .   .

Western individualism is essentially the battling creed of a social group in pursuit of power, a rising bourgeoisie demanding liberties to undo the ancien régime in order to bring about its reconstruction. Taoism is the philosophy of an artist, of a rustic and vagabond, who feels physiologically incompatible with the congested and sordid atmosphere of over-urbanized life and who impatiently shouts "Air! air!" simply because air is the immediate relief he needs. If he proposes to abandon a stuffy room for deep breathing in the open, he has not the slightest intention of building a sanitorium with scientific ventilation and contrivances for himself or for his fellow-sufferers. Western individualism is born of a new unfolding technology, irresistibly oriented toward a new order. Taoism, impelled by no technological changes, derives its inspiration purely from a retrospective glance over the enchanting simplicities of societies which are either non-existent or have, technologically speaking, been more or less irrevocably superseded. The one is pregnant with an urge for social action; the other remains a lyrical note, expressive of private likes and dislikes, which, however intense, operates basically within the frame of a single individual.

This brings us to a fundamental point: Western individualism is a faith and Taoism is scepticism par excellence.

The impulse to social action makes every Western individualist forever conscious of the need of a following. He craves an audience. He is out for converts. Not only is he obliged to demonstrate how profitable and workable his schemes are, but he must of necessity become a zealous missionary, bearing a new standard of revealed truth. Here, the law of psychic action operates. Intent upon hypnotizing, the zealot becomes self-hypnotized. Practically motivated, he soon comes to be convinced of the righteousness of his cause. Interests are transformed into rights and rights are further sanctified as eternal verities. Despite its hard-headed utilitarian origin, libertarian individualism is destined to become a faith, a new faith enthroned to displace an old idol. The average Western individualist can hardly doubt for a moment that God is on his side. He is dead certain—certain of his moral superiority and of his inevitable triumph.

A Taoist is anything but certain. In the last analysis, a Taoist is a sceptic—by temperamental necessity. Basically an artist, he has little use for a faith. The motivation of group interests is absent in him. Nor is he prone to view things in terms of moral significance. Freed from social considerations such as these, he is left with a lone, detached eye which, "seeing through things," as the favorite Taoist phrase has it, does seem to possess the devilish faculty of divesting faith of its staunchness and reducing social symbols to mere shams. A Taoist is persistently tempted to question the ultimate values of things. Suspicious as an old fox, he looks behind and beneath every object he comes upon. He mistrusts, especially where trust is taken for granted. There gleams a native mischievousness in his sidelong glances that makes him forever an uncomfortable companion to the credulous and the faithful.

III

Taoism may be defined as romantic individualism baptized in the fire of what Nietzsche calls "the grand distrust." It is the natural and necessary counterpart to the complacent gregariousness of Confucianism. Come what may, the first prompting of a Taoist is to "debunk," so much folly and ill taste does he see in this all-too-human world.

The urge to debunk is probably the most basic of Taoist traits. Yet, to debunk just the world would make but half a Taoist. A mature Taoist will start with a debunking of humanity and end with a thorough debunking of *himself*.

One can perhaps best describe the working of the Taoist mentality in terms of a psychic curve.

It begins with an ascending movement, whereby the discharging energy of debunking is directed outward to the external objects around until it reaches a point where the fire of debunking turns into a white flame of defiance. Here, one sees the Taoist rise to the full stature of a man as the West commonly conceives it. He looks the world straight in the eye, with the aroused strength of an ego entrenched for battle. It is the moment most surcharged with possibility of action, the juncture at which a Chinese intellectual may most readily turn a revolutionary if ever his defiant mood finds the way to combine with the popular discontent of his age.

A typical Taoist nature does not, however, become a revolutionary as a rule. He does not easily mix with the populace. A proud artist, he stands alone, contemplating no comrades. His predestined fight is of one against all and one against everything. And a more exalted and tense state of mind cannot be imagined.

Yet, there is no vent. Totally unable to view the impending battle in terms of practical interests and concrete issues, he is at a loss as to where and on whom to deal his blows. The intensity of his charged feeling, thus blocked, soon recoils upon itself. A mental crisis develops when an involuntary repression compresses the rising temper on a narrow plateau, which, foundering at this tremulous height, quickly turns into a state of Dionysian drunkenness. The Taoist revolt at this stage takes on the character of an emotional self-abandonment. He gives himself up to himself, having lost sight of the non-ego world and then of the ego itself. He no longer defies, he simply disregards. A sort of ecstasy takes place, in which the half-conscious bitterness and the half-felt rapture combine to produce a vent peculiarly Taoist—the devastating laugh of the intoxicated.

But this blessed stage cannot stay long. A mental numbness born of helpless desperation is foredoomed to come to a *dénouement*;—the beginning of the descending curve.

The effects of intoxication clearing away, the last possibility of action disappears. The tension between the ego and the non-ego drops as his facial muscles resume their normal expression. He cannot but question, now, the worth of it all. "Why excitement and fury?" asks the erstwhile rebel. If the Dionysian drunkenness still suggests faintly the pride of one who thinks himself the wisest, this ensuing sobriety of mind brings him to doubts. *Que sais-je?* And he begins to debunk *himself.* He discovers the folly of it all and the fool in himself. With a chuckle, he drops the gauntlet and retires to the mountains. The boisterous rebel becomes the saintly recluse. After the tempest, the serene sunset.

IV

It is important not to confuse Taoist retirement with Buddhist resignation. The Buddhist becomes resigned out of pity for the sufferings of life; he does so with a laden heart. The Taoist retires out of scorn for all; but it is a scorn without bitterness, a departure in high spirits. The one is Gravity personified, heavy, dead serious, full of pathos and tragic forebodings. The other is Emancipation achieved through a whirling dance and celebrated with perfumed wine. For the Taoist fairies are light-footed immortals who tread bird-like on the undulant surface of floating clouds—laughing as they move on, sleeves in the wind, carefree, nonchalant, and altogether oblivious of humanity swarming below.

Unlike the Buddhist with Nirvana as his last hope and belief, a true Taoist neither hopes nor believes. He retires from the world with no Paradise in view, no Finality to attain. He retires simply because he sees the folly of quibbling about anything. He will live and let live the remainder of his life—wishing nothing and doing nothing, a disbeliever at heart to the last, but a disbeliever who, having found the limitations of everything on earth, decides to leave them as they are. And he will not dogmatize on his disbelief. There is in him something of the Pyrrhonian imperturbability which denies knowledge even as regards one's own ignorance or doubt. Thus, between believing and disbelieving, he rests in equilibrium. In this non-committal silence, he has found his Freedom.

A Taoist recluse has all the ease and gracefulness of the truly free. He is truly free because he is so thoroughly the Child of the Present. He lives from moment to moment, taking life as it comes and giving it up as it passes. So completely is his spirit of the Here-and-Now that he escapes altogether the crushing weight of Time and Space which, for all the salvation devices of transmigrations and redemptions of the world-famed religions, persists in hanging heavily on the waking consciousness of man. It is left to the Taoist to achieve the strange spirituality of ethereal diffuseness, which seems to envelop the silhouettes of Time and Space, not by vainly reaching for eternity and infinitude, but by breaking them into myriad atomic bits and fusing himself with these one by one as he chances upon them. The result is the attainment of a *pantheistic repose,* at once immanent and transcendental—like a fish lying listlessly on the surface of undulating waves, or a bird resting its wings on the air currents, rising and falling as the atmospheric pressure changes. There is an elasticity of adjustment in the apparent stillness of position, which definitely makes the word "static" altogether inadequate to describe the subtle relations involved.

It is here that one divines the spiritual fountain-head of Chinese landscape painting.

Chinese landscape painting is the world-feeling of the Taoist recluse, expressed in a form providential in its fitness and with instruments that permit of no substitutes. Take up, if you will, any of the existent masterpieces by the Sung and Ming artists. As the scroll unfolds, one is instantaneously transported body and soul, as it were, to a sphere where Man and Nature palpably merge. What pre-eminently satisfies is the pantheistic repose which the art affords. It is the repose of one who, having debunked everything, realizes debunking itself is vain, and who therefore, while withdrawing from all, will yet diffuse into all. In thus diffusing, he is able to obliterate in his art as in his soul the awareness of the finite ego and, hence, the tension of Time and Space.

Tao Now

Huston Smith

Huston Smith is the author of the enormously popular The Religions of Man *(1958; revised as* The World's Religions *in 1991), the most readable and helpful introduction to the subject.*

Born in 1919 in Soochow, China, of missionary parents, Smith lived there for seventeen years. Coming to the United States, he progressed from a small Methodist college in Missouri to a doctorate from the University of Chicago. He has since taught at a number of universities—principally the University of Denver, Washington University, the Massachusetts Institute of Technology, and Syracuse University; and he has guest-lectured at many others.

Smith began, in those years in China, with ministerial plans, but his personal philosophy has evolved. He ran into the Upanishads, so to speak, and for a time in St. Louis was both an associate minister for a Methodist Church and *president of a local Vedanta Society. He team-taught a course with a Zen priest and spent a summer in a Zen monastery in Japan (with "dharma brother" Gary Snyder). Along the way he has written a dozen books, including the recent* Beyond the Post-Modern Mind *(1982) and (with David Ray Griffen)* Primordial Truth and Postmodern Theology *(1989). He has done "The Religions of Man" and "Science and Human Responsibility" for National Educational Television, and he is the producer of award-winning films on Tibetan Buddhism and Sufism.*

The Tao cannot be objectively described . . . in the sense of being depicted in a way that is logically consistent and intuitively plausible to all. To assume the contrary would be to continue in the Western objectivist mistake. The only approaches to it are the way of letters and the way of life. The way of letters is the poet's way: by verbal wizzardry to trigger an astral projection of our moods and imaginings to another plane. The way of life is different. It requires long years of cultivation, for it requires altering not one's imagination but one's self; transforming one's sentiments, attitudes, and outlook until, a new perceptual instrument having been forged, a new world swings into view.

This world of the accomplished Taoist, of the man whose psychic integration has progressed to the point where not only are his inner forces harmonized but the sum of these are attuned to his enveloping surround—what is this world of the perfected Taoist like?

It is the Realm of the Great Infinite. Here too let us acknowledge that even the accomplished Taoist can have only the slightest sense of what this realm is really like. We approach it as men, with minds and senses that suffice for our needs but fall as far short in their capacity to discern reality's ultimate nature as an amoeba's intelligence founders before Einstein; if physicists like David Bohm and Phillip Morrison can suspect that the levels of size in the universe—transstellar, mega, macro, micro, subquantum—are infinite, a sage may be pardoned his hunch that its value-reaches are comparably beyond our ken. To be in any way manageable our question must be modified to read: What is the profoundest view of the Realm of the Great Infinite available to man?

1. *It is a realm of relativity.* Perhaps, as Kierkegaard put the matter, existence *is* a system—for God; for man, who is within it, system it can never be. Within it, all is perspectival. The flower, in front of the candle to me, is behind it to my wife. One stone is light compared to a second, heavy compared to a third. The pitch of a locomotive's whistle is constant for the engineer; to a bystander it falls. Nothing can be absolutely positioned, for we lack the absolute framework such positioning would require. If this is true of perception and thought, it must also hold of course for language. It being impossible to say everything at once, every statement is perforce partial; it is one-sided. But the world itself, being in us and around us, is never one-sided. All this holds, of course, for the present statement. Naturally I shall try to make my account of the Tao as cogent as possible, for if I begin to fail glaringly, I shall myself lose interest as quickly as will you. Still, somewhere in my words there will be a flaw—that's a priori; somewhere in my depiction is a value counterpart of the surd Goedel spotted in mathematics: a point that contradicts something I say elsewhere or collides with a piece of your considered experience. We should not bemoan this buckle in our logic, for it keeps us moving, keeps us from settling down, insists on an extension in our horizons if it is to be smoothed out. If it doesn't show itself today, it will tomorrow.

2. *It is a realm of interpenetration and interdependence.* It is not one in a simple sense that excludes distinctions and could be visualized as the clear light of the void, a sky unflecked with clouds, or the sea without a wave. Distinctions abound, but the domains they establish cohere. "Heaven and Earth and I live together, and therein all things and I are one" (Chuang Tzu).

Thirty spokes joined at the hub.
From their non-being [i.e., the point at which their distinctnesses disappear in the hub itself]
Comes the function of the wheel. (Lao Tzu)

Multiplicity is itself a unity. As nothing exists by itself, all things being in fact interdependent, no phenomenon can be understood by divorcing it from its surround. Indeed, it is the underlying unity that provides the possibility *for* distinctions. Thus even parts that appear discordant unite at some level to form a whole: "Tweedledum and Tweedledee/*Agreed* to have a battle." Or like elderly chess players who, having done their utmost to vanquish each other, at game's end push back the board, light up cigarettes, and review the moves as friends. Being is organic. Peculiarities dissolve, parts fuse into other parts. Each individual melds into other individuals and through this melding makes its contribution, leaves its mark.

This complementary interpenetration is symbolized in many ways in China. One of the best-known ways is the *yin-yang,* a circle divided into black and white halves, not be a straight line but by one that meanders, leading white into black domain and allowing black to lap back into the white. Moreover, a white dot stakes its claim in the deepest recesses of black, while a black dot does likewise in the central citadel of the white. All things do indeed carry within themselves the seeds of their own antitheses. And the opposites are bonded; banded together by the encompassing circle that locks both black and white in inseparable embrace.

On a two-dimensional surface, no symbol can rival the yang-yin in depicting the Great Infinite's complementing interpenetration, but because it remains to the end two-dimensional, it needs supplementing. Our two cats when they sleep lapped over one another are a three-dimensional yin-yang, and indeed when they fight they form a four-dimensional one. But man needs to feel the play of these forces in himself kinesthetically, not just observe them in others. So the Chinese created *Tai Chi,* the Great Polarity, a discipline that cuts right across our disparate categories of calisthenics, dance, martial arts, and meditation. In lieu of a film strip I insert here some notes I once jotted down at a Tai Chi class:

> Everything a little curved; nothing extended or pushed to the limit. Expansive gestures (out and up) are yang, ingathering gestures (down and in) are yin. No side of the body exclusively one or the other. Yang dissolves at once into yin, yin gathers strength to become yang. Down becomes up, up down. All is lightness and freedom. As soon as it's done, stop; no sooner heavy than grows light. Strong, then immediately release. Energy reserved, highly volatile, capable of being deployed in any direction, at any point. So finely balanced that a fly cannot alight nor feather be added.

Apocryphal like all such stories, yet making its point, is the account of the great master, Yang Chien Ho. Birds were unable to take off from his palm because as their feet pushed down to spring, his hand dropped concomitantly. Drawing a cocoon thread is another image; if there is no pressure the thread isn't drawn, but the instant there is too much the thread snaps.

3. *Viewed extrovertively, under the aspect of yang, the interrelatedness of existence shows forth as the Great Creativity.* From a single primordial atom the entire universe derives: galaxies, nebulae, island universes, pushing forward faster and faster. Potentiality explodes into actuality, infinitely. Every possibility must be exploited, each nook and cranny filled. Thereby diversity is accomplished. When attention shifts from this multiplicity to its relatedness, the Great Sympathy comes into view. As sympathy, Tao synthesizes; as creativity it proliferates. The two movements complement; creativity flows from one to all, sympathy from all to one. Without sympathy multiplicity would be chaos, whereas without creativity sympathy would lack province. They proceed together, hand in hand, partners in the Tao's sublime ecology. Chuang Tzu's illustration, characteristically homey, is the centipede. At the points at which they touch the earth its legs are a hundred or so,

but on a higher level such orchestration! It is through the many that the one enacts its versatility.

Perceived thus in the context of the Tao, nature to the Chinese was no disenchanted causal mechanism floating on the foundation of nothingness. It was undergirded by an eternal numinous reality from which life proceeds and which inclines it towards harmony. Underlying the visible—our phenomenal world, the "realm of the ten thousand things"—is something of immense importance that is invisible. The essential relation between the two is nonduality. Life's dependability, mingling with nature's, betokens a hidden oneness in the bosom of the multiple, a total interdependence at the heart of the spheres. A rhythm falls upon the visible, breaking it into day and night, summer and winter, male and female, but these divisions are caught up and ordered in a superior integration that resolves the tensions and reconciles the irreconcilable. Heaven and earth agree. They are united in a hymn for a double choir, an antiphony on a cosmic scale. It is a concentric vision, the vision of society set like a stone in nature, and nature set similarly in the deep repose of eternity.

The Ladder of Ascent

To experience reality as just described results in sensing a friendly continuity between one's own life and the Tao, and a willingness to blend with its ways. There comes also a shift toward *yes* and away from *no* where the claims of the nonego are concerned and a consequent freedom and elation as the boundaries of confining selfhood melt down. A generalized sense of life's enlargement and well-being commences. How to get into this state—the question of method—lies outside the scope of this paper, but I will note five stages through which the aspirant is said to pass.[1]

1. *He begins with the world as it appears to men generally,* composed of discrete and apparently self-subsisting entities that are related only in such ways as empirical observation discloses.

2. *The second stage involves a dramatic awakening in which the world's undifferentiated aspect is realized.* This is the world known to mystics and a good many artists. Individual selfhood vanishes; one becomes merged with the Great Self, Emptiness, or the Void.

3. *But we live in the everyday world, the world of relativity and separate things.* So the next step is to realize that noumena and phenomena, the relative and absolute worlds of stages one and two respectively, are but two aspects of one reality. With feet planted in the absolute the aspirant is directed to look anew at the relative world that he previously took to be the only world. He must come to see that the phenomenal is in truth but the aspect under which the noumenon is perceived. Absolute and relative completely interpenetrate without obstruction or hindrance. They are one and the same thing. With this realization the aspirant discovers that

---

1. The first four steps are taken from the *Hua-yen* school, which, building on Buddhism and hence indirectly on India's willingness to attempt to conceptualize positions the Chinese would have left intuitive, articulated the doctrine of "perfect mutual unimpeded solution" more explicitly than did any other school in East Asia. The fifth step is added by the Ch'an school.

everything in the world about him, every tree and rock, every hill and star, every bit of dust and dirt, as well as every insect, plant, and animal, himself included, are manifestations of the Tao and their movements are functionings of the Tao. Everything, just as it is, is in essence holy.

4. *But more lies ahead.* One must come to see that the things that have already come to be recognized as manifestations of the Tao together form one complete and total whole by means of harmonious and unobstructed penetration, interconvertibility, and identification with each other. Everything in the universe is realized to be constantly and continuously, freely and harmoniously interpenetrating, interconverting itself with every other thing. A favorite symbol here is Indra's net, each intersection of which lodges a jewel that reflects all the other jewels in the net together with the reflections each of them contained. The problem with this symbol is the same as that which we encountered in connection with the yin-yang; a net, too, is static, whereas the point is to grasp dynamically the Tao whose nature is always to move on. This requires that the grasper himself be forever in the mood of moving, this being the character of life itself. Taoist terms are, for the most part, dynamic rather than static, terms like 'entering-into' and 'being-taken-in,' or 'taking-in,' 'embracing-and-pervading,' and 'simultaneous-unimpeded-diffusion.'

5. *Finally, and characteristically Chinese, there is 'the return to the natural.'* Having come to recognize every element in the world and every act as holy and indispensable to the total universe, as this realization deepens and grows increasingly profound, it is no longer necessary to think explicitly about such things. It is enough for things to be affirmed in their own right; each moment can be responded to naturally and spontaneously as sufficient in itself. It is in this culminating state that one realizes with Master Nansen that "the everyday mind is Tao." Trudging through the snow a master and disciple were surprised by a rabbit that sprang out of nowhere and bounded across their path. "What would you say of that?" the master asked. "It was like a god!" the disciple answered. As the master seemed unimpressed with the answer, the disciple returned the question: "Well, what would you say it was?" "It was a rabbit!"

Quietism: The Test of the Theory

Every position has its problematic, a shoal that, navigated or foundered upon, determines whether the system stands or falls. For Taoism the danger is quietism, the reading of its pivotal *wu wei* (no action) doctrine as admonishing us to do as little as possible or in any case nothing contrary to natural impulse. If everything is an aspect of Tao and thereby holy exactly as it is, why change it? Or to put the question another way: Since, although the Tao's parts are always in flux, its balance of forces is constant, why try to shift its parts from one place to another?

The path that winds past this precipice is a narrow one, and time and again China fell off it. Indeed, one can read the entire history of philosophical Taoism, as well as Buddhism in its Taoist variant (Ch'an), as one long struggle to keep from reading Chuang Tzu's "Do nothing, and everything will be done" as counselling sloth and rationalizing privilege. What other reading is possible? If the answer is "none," the jig's up. If Taoism ends up admonishing us to lounge around while tsetse flies bite us, to sink back in our professional settees, handsomely upholstered by endowments amassed from exhorbitant rents in ghetto slums; if Taoism suggests that we rest on our oars while our nation mashes peasant countrysides in Southeast Asia, the sooner it is forgotten the better.

The doctrine cannot be stated to preclude such misreading, but the misreading itself can, with care, be avoided. Helpful to doing so is the realization that Taoist assertions are made from the far side of the self/other divide, being in this respect the Orient's equivalent of "Love God and do what you please." *Wu wei* can be read unequivocally only after one has attained Tao-identification. At that point one will continue to act—the Tao, we recall, is never static; to be in it is to be always in the mood of moving—but the far shore attained, one need do nothing save what comes naturally, for what needs doing will claim one's will directly. Unobscured by attachment to ones own perquisites, the suffering of the dispossessed will draw one spontaneously to their side. Until that point is reached there must be labors that are not wholly spontaneous as we try to act our way into right thinking while concomitantly thinking our way into right action.

The Tao is not unilateral yin. Sensing that even in China when the Tao hits man's mind it tends to enter a yang phase, Taoism sought to redress the balance, but the balance itself was its true concern. "Now yin, now yang: that is the Tao" (*The Great Commentary*). The formulation is exact; countering man's disposition to put yang first, Taoism throws its ounces on the side of yin, but to recover the original wholeness. That emphasis is what we need as well. "Heroic materialism" is the phrase Kenneth Clark used on the concluding program of his *Civilization* series to characterize our Western achievement; pointing to the Manhattan skyline he noted that it had been thrown up in a century, about a third of the time it took the Middle Ages to build a cathedral. With an impunity Asia would not have believed possible, we have indulged ourselves in a yang trip the likes of which was never before essayed. And we are still here; we haven't capsized. But if we have arrived at a point where taste as well as prudence counsels a redressing, the Tao stands waiting in the wings with "now yin" as its first suggestion. It doesn't ask us to dismantle our machines; civilization needn't be de-yanged. Its call is simply to open the sluice gates of our Great Sympathy to let it catch up with our Great Creativity. The virtues of mastery and control we have developed to near perfection, but life can't proceed on their terms alone.

To enter a friendship, to say nothing of marriage, with an eye to control is to sully the relationship from the start. Complementing the capacity to control is the capacity to surrender—to others in love and friendship, to duty in conscience, to life itself in some sustaining way. The same holds for possessions and complexity; we know well the rewards that they can bestow, while knowing less well the complementing rewards that derive from simplicity. When a Western musicologist was seeking help in deciphering the score of certain Tibetan chants, he was informed by the Karmapa that they "could only be understood by a perfect being, there being so much to hear in a single note." And fronting Eiheiji is Half-Dipper bridge, so-called because whenever Dogen dipped water from the river he used only half a dipperful, returning the rest to the river. Such sayings and behavior are difficult for us to understand; they tend to be beyond our comprehension. But if we were to feel the beauty of the river and a oneness with the water, might we not feel its claims on us and do as Dogen did? It is our own true nature, our natural 'uncarved block' as the Taoist would say, to do so.

Simplicity and surrender can appear as high-ranking values only in a world one trusts and to which one feels at deepest level attuned. If the Taoist approach to nature was not based on reasoned strategy and well-planned attack, it was because such stratagems appeared unneeded. Western civilization has tended to regard the world either as mystery to be entered through religious initiation or as antagonist to be opposed with technological adroitness or stoical courage. Greek tragedy and philosophy set the tone for this; modern science and technology have amplified it a hundredfold. Western man has been at heart Promethian; therein lie both his greatness and his absurdity. Taoism does not try to beat or cajole the universe or the gods; it tries to join them. The Western stoic tries this tack too, but from the premise of antagonistic wills to be reconciled by obedience or overcome by dogged refusal. To Asia the problem is a matter of ignorance and enlightenment. If seventeenth-to-nineteenth-century science saw the world as mechanism and twentieth-century science is seeing it (with its holism, reciprocity, and growth) as resembling more an organism, is it possible that the twenty-first century will see it as—what? Is the savingly indefinite word "spirit" appropriate? "If I could say impersonal person, it would be that" (Sokei-an).

> There is a being, wonderful, perfect;
> It existed before heaven and earth.
> How quiet it is!
> How spiritual it is!
> It stands alone and it does not change.
> It moves around and around, but does not on this account suffer.
> All life comes from it.
> It wraps everything with its love as in a garment, and yet it
>   claims no honor, it does not demand to be Lord.
> I do not know its name, and so I call it Tao, the Way, and I
>   rejoice in its power.[2]

---

2. Adapted from K. L. Reichelt's translation of the Twenty-fifth Chapter of the *Tao Teh Ching,* in his *Meditation and Piety in the Far East* (New York: Harper & Row, Publishers, 1954), p. 41.

Further Reading

It is often observed that every translation is also an interpretation. This is especially true of works as difficult to translate as those of ancient China, which makes comparisons of those translations a revealing exercise. Notable attempts to convey the meaning and spirit of the *Tao Te Ching* include those by D. T. Suzuki and Paul Carus, *The Canon of Reason and Virtue* (1913); Arthur Waley, *The Way and Its Power* (1934); Witter Bynner, *The Way of Life According to Lao Tzu* (1944); John C. H. Wu, *Lao Tzu/Tao Te Ching* (1961); Wing-tsit Chan, *The Way of Lao Tzu* (1963); D. C. Lau, *Tao Te Ching* (1982); and Robert G. Henricks, *Lao-tzu: Te-tao ching* (1989). The Lau and Henricks translations are based on the Ma-wang-tui texts.

Thomas Merton's *The Way of Chuang Tzu* (1965) was one of Merton's own favorites among his many titles. An introductory essay is followed by his "renderings" of selections from the ancient classic. For more of Chuang Tzu, see Burton Watson (trans.), *The Complete Works of Chuang Tzu* (1968).

A. C. Graham, also an outstanding translator of Chuang Tzu, offers a scholarly study of the whole range of thought in the Classical period of China (500–200 B.C.E.) in his *Disputers of the Tao* (1989).

Chang Chung-yuan, *Creativity and Taoism: A Study of Chinese Philosophy* (1963). Topics include "Invisible Ground of Sympathy," Immeasurable Potentialities of Creativity," and "Processes of Self-Realization."

Holmes Welch, *Taoism: The Parting of the Way* (1957; rev. ed., 1965). A popular and successful introduction. Its final chapter compares Taoism and the American way of life.

Herrymon Maurer's *The Old Fellow* (1943) is an early "non-fiction novel": Maurer elaborates on the traditions about Lao Tzu in telling the story of the Old Fellow and borrows from the *Tao Te Ching* for portions of his dialogue.

"Blake the Taoist" by Arthur Waley sheds light on both the English poet and on Taoism. It is reprinted in Ivan Morris (ed.), *Madly Singing in the Mountains: An Appreciation and Anthology of Arthur Waley* (1970).

VI

SHINTO
The Way of the Kami

There seems to be a sense of divine magic in the very atmosphere, through all the luminous day, brooding over the vapory land, over the ghostly blue of the flood—a sense of Shinto.   Lafcadio Hearn

Shinto is the old religion of Japan, the indigenous[1] religion, which has been there since the beginning, so to speak, though for centuries it was nameless. It is as though Shinto *was* the natural order, and thus required no name. But then, when Buddhism came to Japan from China in the sixth century C.E., an identifying label was needed to distinguish the old Way from the new Butsudo, the Way of the Buddha.

Oddly enough, the name that came into use for this Japanese religion was a name drawn from the Chinese: "Shinto" is from *shen do (dao, tao),* which is commonly translated as the Way of the Gods. But the connotations of "Gods" for Western eyes and ears are misleading. Shinto is not an Eastern variety of polytheism. Shinto is better rendered as the Way of the Kami.[2] And it is with the kami that we come to the heart of the religion.

Unfortunately, with the kami we also come up against one of those fundamental concepts that can be so difficult. Explaining the kami is a task comparable to that of explaining God. "I do not yet understand the meaning of the term *kami*," wrote Motoori Norinaga, the man who many think was the greatest of Shinto scholars:

> Speaking in general, however, it may be said that *kami* signifies, in the first place, the deities of heaven and earth that appear in the ancient records and also the spirits of the shrines where they are worshipped.
>
> It is hardly necessary to say that it includes human beings. It also includes such objects as birds, beasts, trees, plants, seas, mountains, and so forth. In ancient usage, anything whatsoever which was outside the ordinary, which possessed superior power, or which was awe-inspiring was

---

1. "Strictly speaking, . . . Shinto was not an indigenous religion, for the Japanese were not the first inhabitants of the islands, and their religion apparently came with them from elsewhere." Wm. Theodore de Bary, *et al.* (eds.), *Sources of Japanese Tradition* (New York: Columbia University Press, 1958), p. 23. (But this is indeed to be very strict about it.)

2. Some sources use the Japanese *kami no michi.*

called *kami*. Eminence here does not refer merely to the superiority of nobility, goodness, or meritorious deeds. Evil and mysterious things, if they are extraordinary and dreadful, are called *kami*. It is needless to say that among human beings who are called *kami* the successive generations of sacred emperors are all included. The fact that emperors are also called "distant kami" is because, from the standpoint of common people, they are far-separated, majestic, and worthy of reverence. In a lesser degree we find, in the present as well as in ancient times, human beings who are *kami*. Although they may not be accepted throughout the whole country, yet in each province, each village, and each family there are human beings who are *kami*, each one according to his own proper position. The *kami* of the divine age were for the most part human beings of that time and, because the people of that time were all *kami*, it is called the Age of the Gods (*kami*).[3]

Is there anything *not* "signified" by the kami or the action of kami? In the last analysis, perhaps not. This is a world created, ruled, and inhabited by kami. On one level the kami have to do with what is sacred or mysterious, with power and fate, with life and death. They are the Japanese version of "the idea of the holy."[4] On another level, although no hard lines are drawn, human beings are kami. There are degrees through all this, the upper reaches and the lower reaches, but nothing is finally excluded. "Heaven and earth are one; there is no barrier between them," said Motoori. After all, given its divine origins and governance, all of life must share in that divinity. First from the great primal Kami, then from the great lands and shrines of Japan there radiates divinity. The universe of Shinto is a sacred universe.

Another approach to the kami, employing different images, is offered by Mircea Eliade. In Shinto, he has written,

> everything in the cosmos can be transfigured, no one is unworthy to receive the visit of a god: a flower, a stone, a pillar of wood. The universe is constantly being sanctified by an infinity of instant epiphanies. The gods do not settle down anywhere in the world. The spirit descends any time, anywhere, but it does not remain; it does not allow itself to be caught by temporal duration. Epiphany is especially lightninglike.[5]

There is no Shinto "Bible" that can be quoted on this or any other question. The closest that Shinto comes to "sacred scripture" are two ancient histories, the *Kojiki* ("Records of Ancient Matters") and the *Nihongi* ("Chronicles of Japan"), both written in the eighth century C.E., though the myths and history they relate existed earlier as oral traditions. Neither is there in Shinto an explicit system of beliefs or ethical code, as Edwin Reischauer observes in his introductory essay.

3. Quoted in D. C. Holtom, *The National Faith of Japan* (New York: E. P. Dutton & Company, 1938), p. 23.

4. See Rudolf Otto, *The Idea of the Holy,* translated by J. W. Harvey (London: Oxford University Press, 1923), chaps. III–VI, much of which is relevant to Shinto (as it is, of course, to many other religions).

5. *No Souvenirs: Journal, 1957–1969* (New York: Harper & Row, 1977), p. 35.

Instead, there are habits of thought and feeling, various ritual practices, and "an attitude of joyful acceptance of life."

Even without the sanctions, however, of a clearly identified or otherwise "certified" revelation, much is made of the mythology of Shinto. Professor Sokyo Ono recounts in "The Kami and Mythology" a small part of that myth and notes that it "amounts to something like a simple constitution for the country." More of that myth is cited by Motoori in "The True Way": he was convinced that it was literally and absolutely true. He quotes the *Kojiki* and *Nihongi* as though there could be no higher authority.

Lafcadio Hearn, who loved Japan—his "land of dreams"—and lived the last and happiest years of his life there, concludes this chapter. Written a century ago, "Glimpses of Shinto" draws together various observations and reflections, but he cautioned that

> the reality of Shintō lives not in books, nor in rites, nor in commandments, but in the national heart, of which it is the highest emotional religious expression, immortal and ever young. Far underlying all the surface crop of quaint superstitions and artless myths and fantastic magic there thrills a mighty spiritual force, the whole soul of a race with all its impulses and powers and intuitions.

Shinto and Japan: An Overview

Edwin O. Reischauer

Edwin O. Reischauer was born in Tokyo in 1910 and lived there until 1927. A graduate of Oberlin College, he studied at the Universities of Paris, Tokyo, and Kyoto, and received his doctorate from Harvard in 1939. He was for decades a professor of Japanese history at Harvard, and he served as president of the Association for Asian Studies and as director of the Harvard-Yenching Institute. From 1961 to 1966 he was United States ambassador to Japan. Reischauer wrote several books about U.S. policy in Asia and on Japanese history and culture; he also translated Chinese and Japanese works. Of particular interest are his memoirs, My Life Between Japan and America *(1986) and* The Japanese Today: Continuity and Change *(1988). He died in 1990.*

It would be hard to imagine Japan without Shinto or Shinto anywhere but in Japan. The two of course are not synonymous. Japan is Shinto and a great deal more. But no element in Japanese culture has run so persistently through the whole history of the Japanese people from their earliest beginnings right up to the present day or so consistently colored their attitudes toward life and the world around them. Shinto has been an unchanging warp on which a rich and varied woof of other threads has been woven into the constantly changing patterns of Japanese civilization. These patterns can be brilliantly diverse and confusingly complex, but they are always subtly influenced by the constant, continuing threads of Shinto.

Our earliest knowledge of the Japanese shows Shinto to have been already at that time their religion, or rather their way of life. It was their way of understanding the natural world around them and their relationship to it and to one another. To them nature was beautiful and bountiful. They were awed by its fertility and wonder. They reveled in the richness and luxuriance of their island home. They felt a oneness with nature, seeking to merge with it rather than struggling to overcome it. That which was particularly wondrous, whether in nature or among people, they accepted as a superior object of worship, called *kami*. In fact, they traced their origin to the manifold *kami* of nature, as in the case of the imperial family, descended from the supreme Sun Goddess.

Worship of the *kami* and the ordering of human affairs were seen as part of the same activity, and were supervised by hereditary sacred leaders, in early times apparently feminine shamans. What we would call government and religion were one and the same. *Miya,* an early word for a Shinto shrine, became the word for a palace. *Matsuri,* the term for a Shinto festival, and the ancient word for government, *matsurigoto,* are both derived from the verb *matsuru,* "to worship."

Shinto in those early times had no clear philosophy or ethics, and it still does not today. It expressed an attitude of joyful acceptance of life and a feeling of closeness to nature. Life and death were seen as part of the normal processes of nature. There was no struggle between good and evil. The only concern was with ritual purity, perhaps originating in part from sanitary measures and certainly contributing to the Japanese love of bathing and their record of being undoubtedly the world's cleanest people throughout history. *Kami* were felt to be everywhere and were worshiped and prayed to as beneficent forces. These were the simple beliefs of Shinto in earliest times, and they remain the heart of Shinto today.

Our first clear picture of Shinto goes back more than a millennium and a half. The early Japanese histories, written down at a relatively early period in the eighth century, start with the mythology of Shinto and gradually develop from mythology into the story of the predominance of one family of tribal sacred leaders, which was to become the imperial line that still occupies the Japanese throne. Chinese records, derived from persons who had obviously visited the islands, date back some five centuries earlier but give a picture that fits in well with the Japanese accounts. Archaeology reinforces the story. There are the great tumuli of leaders of the future imperial line as well as of their rivals and many examples of what were to become the Three Imperial Regalia of the emperors—the sacred bronze mirror, representing their ancestress, the Sun Goddess; sacred curved "jewels" of still unknown significance; and the sacred sword.

.   .   .

The wave of culture from China that started in full force in the sixth century came at first largely by way of Korea. It seems surprising that Chinese civilization did not sweep Shinto completely away or swallow it whole by incorporating elements of it into its own religions, as Christianity did with the native cults of northern Europe. Japan was still a primitive land, while China had had a high civilization for at least two millennia and was just entering on an extended period of clear leadership among the civilizations of the world. But this did not happen, and Shinto lived on.

Chinese Confucianism brought with it a fully developed and extremely complex concept of political organization and a social and ethical system to match it. These the Japanese accepted with enthusiasm, devoting amazing effort and skill to transferring their loose association of tribelike *uji,* under the supreme Yamato group, into a bureaucratic, centralized "empire" on the Chinese model. The Chinese political system eroded over time in Japan until it consisted merely of meaningless titles and a theory of government, but Confucian ethics became steadily more ingrained in Japan, reaching their heyday from the seventeenth to the early nineteenth centuries under the rule of the Tokugawa shoguns. Though subsequently rejected as Japan's political philosophy and supplanted by Western political ideas and to some extent by ethical concepts derived from Christianity, Confucianism still remains a strong ethical foundation for contemporary Japan. And yet Shinto practices have persisted during all this time relatively unchanged; Shinto attitudes toward nature and life have retained their validity; and the sacred nature of the emperors as the chief performers of the Shinto cults has continued unchanged for almost a thousand years after the emperors lost their temporal power as Chinese-type rulers and more than a century after the Meiji Restoration of 1868 returned secular power to them in theory even if not in reality.

Buddhism, starting around the fifth century B.C., in India and developing into an extraordinarily diverse and complex religion over time as it spread from India to China and Korea, might more easily than Confucianism have swallowed Shinto whole. It did this to other religions elsewhere in Asia, and in Japan it soon developed the concept that Shinto beliefs and *kami* were simply the local manifestation of universal Buddhist principles and deities. This doctrine, elaborated by Buddhist monks of the Shingon sect, was known as *ryōbu* Shinto, or "Dual Shinto." It persisted through the whole premodern history of Japan, and the two religions became institutionally very much intertwined. It took forceful action by the Meiji government in the second half of the nineteenth century to pull them apart. And yet, throughout, Shinto retained its distinctiveness and strength. While Buddhism tended to lose its intellectual vigor in recent centuries, Shinto took on new life, contributing to the anti-Tokugawa movement which resulted in a new political beginning in 1868 under the unifying symbol of the imperial line. Shinto also spawned the bulk of the "new religions," such as Tenrikyō, which rose during the past century and a half to answer the spiritual needs of the common man in the changing environment of the modern world.

Perhaps Shinto has survived so strongly in Japan because it had its own secure niche in the Japanese way of life. Confucianism dealt with political organization, ethical precepts, and a rational view of the universe. Concepts derived from the West provided these same things for the modern Japanese. Buddhism was concerned with the relation of the individual soul to the limitless cosmos and the afterlife, stressing either escape from the unending cycle of painful existences through enlightenment or salvation by faith into paradise. Christianity, too, addressed these same problems. But Shinto was focused on adapting to life in this world and on a simple merging of man into the natural environment around him.[1] There was room for all three levels of understanding. A person could be a Buddhist in his ideas about the other world, a Confucianist in his ideas about government and society, but at the same time a believer in the Shinto *kami* and the Shinto attitudes toward nature in his everyday life. This is the way it has been for most Japanese throughout history, and this is the way it still is for many today. They feel no sense of conflict between these different philosophies and religions. Each has its own place and its own validity.

Shinto pervades the sophisticated, highly developed society of contemporary

---

1. *Editor's note:* "When people think of death, they feel closer to Buddhism. . . . When people think of life, they feel drawn to Shinto." Hisako Matsubara, in her novel *Cranes at Dusk* (New York: Dial Press, 1985), pp. 5–6.

Japan, but it remains very much what it was as we first know of it from history. Efforts to distort it into something else have always failed in the long run. The attempt to graft the political system of China onto archaic Shinto Japan faded, turning into the very different system of feudalism and finally into democracy, but the Shinto roots persisted with little change. Buddhism sought to incorporate Shinto into its all-embracing theology, but in the process was probably more influenced by Shinto than Shinto was by it. The nineteenth-century modernizers of Japan and the twentieth-century imperial expansionists both tried to shape Shinto to fit their needs, but they and their ideas have passed into history, while Shinto continues to be what it has always been, an unassertive but powerful current flowing below the surface turmoil of political and social change.

It is amazing how true Shinto remains to its early beginnings. The shrines of Shinto are to be found everywhere throughout the land—the great Ise Shrines of the Sun Goddess, unchanged from prehistoric times through continual faithful reproductions of their original form; the equally moving and magnificent shrine in Tokyo built in this century to the memory of Emperor Meiji; the village shrines dedicated to the progenitors of some long-vanished tribal *uji;* the shrines that celebrate the spirit of some great waterfall or mountain; the tiny boxlike shrines in front of gnarled old trees; the shrines tucked into tiny corners of the busy downtown sections of cities or placed on the roofs of many-storied buildings; and the *kami-dana,* or "god shelves," for worship of the ancestors within private homes. The *kami* are still to be found everywhere throughout the islands of Japan, and Shinto ways still permeate life.

The *matsuri,* or Shinto festivals, with all their color and gay bustle, still loom large in rural life and have helped shape the historical parades and public festivities of urban Japan. Shinto lies behind most of the seasonal holidays, with their distinctive activities, special foods, traditional clothing, New Year calls, visits to shrines, remembrance of ancestors, and gathering of the family again at the old farm homestead or in the old home town. People still pray to the *kami* in private or at their local shrines, and Shinto rituals are still seen as appropriate for many occasions from marriages to the dedications of skyscrapers. Most important of all, people still maintain the original Shinto sense of closeness to nature and awe before its beauty, its creativeness, and its power.

The Kami and Mythology
Sokyo Ono

"The Kami and Mythology" was first published under the auspices of the International Institute for the Study of Religions, Tokyo, of which Sokyo Ono served as executive director. Dr. Ono held the same position with the Japan Religious Co-operative Council and was a professor at the Shinto university, Kokugakuin Daigaku, engaged in the training of Shinto priests and scholars. He has also been a lecturer for the National Association of Shinto Shrines.

The Japanese people, Ono has written, "are aware of the kami intuitively at the depth of their consciousness and communicate with the kami directly without having formed the kami-idea conceptually or theologically. Therefore, it is impossible to make explicit and clear that which fundamentally by its very nature is vague."*

Unlike Buddhism, Christianity, and Islam, Shinto has neither a founder, such as Gautama the Enlightened One, Jesus the Messiah, or Mohammed the Prophet. . . .

In its personal aspects "Shinto" implies faith in the kami, usages practiced in accordance with the mind of the kami, and spiritual life attained through the worship of and in communion with the kami. To those who worship kami, "Shinto" is a collective noun denoting all faiths. It is an all-inclusive term embracing the various faiths which are comprehended in the kami-idea. Its usage by Shintoists, therefore, differs from calling Buddha's teaching "Buddhism" and Christ's teaching "Christianity."

In its general aspects Shinto is more than a religious faith. It is an amalgam of attitudes, ideas, and ways of doing things that through two milleniums and more have become an integral part of the *way* of the Japanese people. Thus, Shinto is both a personal faith in the kami and a communal way of life according to the mind of the kami, which emerged in the course of the centuries as various ethnic and cultural influences, both indigenous and foreign, were fused, and the country attained unity under the Imperial Family.

**Shinto: The Kami Way* (Rutland, Vt.: Charles E. Tuttle Company, 1962), p. 8.

From Sokyo Ono, *Shinto.* Copyright © 1962 by Charles E. Tuttle Co. Reprinted by permission of the publisher.

Mythology

The Age of the Kami, the mythological age, sets the Shinto pattern for daily life and worship. In the mythology the names and order of appearance of the kami differ with the various records. According to the *Kojiki* the Kami of the Center of Heaven (Ame-no-minaka-nushi-no-kami) appeared first and then the kami of birth and growth (Taka-mimusubi-no-mikoto and Kami-musubi-no-mikoto). However, it is not until the creative couple, Izanagi-no-mikoto and Izanami-no-mikoto, appear that the mythology really begins. These two, descending from the High Plain of Heaven, gave birth to the Great Eight Islands, that is, Japan, and all things, including many kami. Three of the kami were the most august: the Sun Goddess (Ama-terasu-ō-mikami), the kami of the High Plain of Heaven, her brother (Susa-no-o-no-mikoto), who was in charge of the earth, and the Moon Goddess, (Tsuki-yomi-no-mikoto), who was the kami of the realm of darkness.

The brother, however, according to the *Kojiki,* behaved so very badly and committed so many outrages that the Sun Goddess became angry and hid herself in a celestial cave, which caused the heavens and earth to become darkened. Astonished at this turn of events, the heavenly kami put on an entertainment, including dancing, which brought her out of the cave; and thus light returned to the world. For his misdemeanor the brother was banished to the lower world, where by his good behavior he returned to the favor of the other kami, and a descendant of his, the Kami of Izumo (Ōkuni-nushi-no-kami), became a very benevolent kami, who ruled over the Great Eight Islands and blessed the people. Little is said in the mythology of the Moon Kami.

Subsequently, the grandson of the Sun Goddess, Ninigi-no-mikoto, received instructions to descend and rule Japan. To symbolize his authority he was given three divine treasures: a mirror, a sword, and a string of jewels. Moreover, he was accompanied on his journey by the kami that had participated in the entertainment outside the celestial cave. However, to accomplish his mission it was necessary to negotiate with the Kami of Izumo, who after some discussion agreed to hand over the visible world, while retaining the invisible. At the same time, the Kami of Izumo pledged to protect the heavenly grandson. Ninigi-no-mikoto's great grandson, Emperor Jimmu, became the first human ruler of Japan.

This, in very simple form, is the basic myth which explained for primitive Japanese their origin and the basis of their social structure. It is a description of the evolution of Japanese thought in regard to the origin of life, the birth of the kami and all things out of chaos, the differentiation of all phenomena, and the emergence and evolution of order and harmony. In a *sense* the myth amounts to something like a simple constitution for the country.

. . .

Kami

Kami are the object of worship in Shinto. What is meant by "kami"? Fundamentally, the term is an honorific for noble, sacred spirits, which implies a sense of adoration for their virtues and authority. All beings have such spirits, so in a sense all beings can be called kami or be regarded as potential kami. However, because the term is an honorific, it is not customary to apply it to ordinary individuals or beings. We do not use honorifics in referring to ourselves, or to persons of our own group, whether that group be large or small. Thus, while Shinto teaches that people should be worshipped as kami, they are not in fact usually called *kami.*

Among the objects or phenomena designated from ancient times as kami are the qualities of growth, fertility, and production; natural phenomena, such as wind and thunder; natural objects, such as the sun, mountains, rivers, trees, and rocks; some animals; and ancestral spirits. In the last-named category are the spirits of the Imperial ancestors, the ancestors of noble families, and in a sense all ancestral spirits. Also regarded as kami are the guardian spirits of the land, occupations, and skills; the spirits of national heroes, men of outstanding deeds or virtues, and those who have contributed to civilization, culture, and human welfare; those who have died for the state or the community; and the pitiable dead. Not only spirits superior to man, but even some that are regarded as pitiable and weak have nonetheless been considered to be kami.

. . .

In Shinto there is no absolute deity that is the creator and ruler of all. The creative function of the world is realized through the harmonious cooperation of the kami in the performance of their respective missions. Even the progenitor of the Imperial Family, the Sun Goddess, the kami who brightens the world with the virtue of the sun and is commonly regarded as the supreme kami of Shinto, consults the opinion of other kami, calls upon them for help, and at times makes concessions to them.

. . .

Guardian Kami

Each kami may be said to have its own special characteristics, capacity, and mission; and in a sense each is worshipped as the founder or guardian of some definite object or phenomenon. For example, one is concerned with the distribution of water, another with the manufacture of medicine, and still another with the healing process. Then there are ancestral kami that are the protectors of a given group, and those that are the patrons of a given territory or of clans, that is, social groups based on kinship. It is quite proper to ask what almost any kami protects, but a clear answer cannot always be given.

Prominent among the kami are the guardians of the clans (*uji*). These are generally called *ujigami,* and are always worshipped in shrines. Throughout the country there are many shrines of this origin. But with the increasing mobility of the people and the gradual break-up of the clans the term *ujigami* was also applied to the guardians of the residents of a given area as well as the area itself. Thus, while in the past lineal descent was a primary factor, today the common community relationship has come to assume greater importance. Nevertheless, in many cases the consciousness of lineal descent from a clan is still strong and some persons regularly return to their native places to take part in the festivals of their guardian kami.

Scriptures

Shinto does not possess sacred scriptures, such as are found in many other religions,—a fact which is a significant indication of the character of the Shinto faith itself. Nevertheless, there are certain ancient records that are regarded as authoritative and provide its historical as well as its spiritual basis.

The earliest of these were compiled by Imperial order and contain the mythology and early history of the Japanese people. The *Kojiki* ("Record of Ancient Matters") is the oldest extant Japanese historical record. Its date is 712 of the Christian era. It provides an account of events down to the year 628. Though written in Chinese ideographs the style is ancient, pure Japanese and through it we can know something of the style of the earlier oral transmission from generation to generation. Consequently it is especially valued. The *Nihongi* or *Nihon Shoki* ("Chronicles of Japan"), which appeared eight years later and brings the record down to the year 697, was written in Chinese and thus changed the form of transmission. However, it is more detailed than the *Kojiki;* and because several mythologies or versions are given of some events, it has a special value in matters in which the *Kojiki* is lacking.

.   .   .

It must be stressed, however, that none of these writings are regarded as holy writ in the sense that the term is used in Christianity and Islam. They are primarily historical records which, in addition to their political or dynastic interest, embody the ancient forms of the kami-faith.

Shinto did not develop a canon because, in the first place, the shrine and its ritual mediated the kami-faith to the people; and in the second place, the acceptance of the shrine as the symbol of their communal faith made it unnecessary to guide the people by means of doctrine and instruction. In the course of history very few people have evaded their communal obligation with respect to Shrine worship.

The True Way

Motoori Norinaga

Motoori Norinaga (1730–1801) was one of the greatest scholars of Shinto, if not the greatest. A major figure in a movement to "revive" what was conceived to have been an original and pristine "Pure Shinto," Motoori threw himself into an effort to remove the dust of centuries from the records. His approach was philological: he spent much of his lifetime, over thirty years, studying the ancient history of Shinto, the Kojiki *in particular, sifting its language to rediscover that "true way," which had been obscured by foreign influence and native neglect. "In short," writes the modern historian of Shinto, Masaharu Anesaki, "his contention was that the Japanese and their Shinto . . . represented the pure, and therefore the best, inheritance of humanity from the divine ages."**

The True Way is one and the same, in every country and throughout heaven and earth. This Way, however, has been correctly transmitted only in our Imperial Land. Its transmission in all foreign countries was lost long ago in early antiquity, and many and varied ways have been expounded, each country representing its own way as the Right Way. But the ways of foreign countries are no more the original Right Way than end-branches of a tree are the same as its root. They may have resemblances here and there to the Right Way, but because the original truth has been corrupted with the passage of time, they can scarcely be likened to the original Right Way. Let me state briefly what that one original Way is. One must understand, first of all, the universal principle of the world. The principle is that Heaven and earth, all the gods and all phenomena, were brought into existence by the creative spirits of two deities—Takami-musubi and Kami-musubi. The birth of all humankind in all ages and the existence of all things and all matter have been the result of that creative spirit. It was the original creativity of these two august deities which caused the deities Izanagi and Izanami to create the land, all kinds of phenomena, and numerous gods and goddesses at the beginning of the Divine Age. This spirit of creativity [*musubi,* lit., "union"] is a miraculously divine act the reason for which is beyond the comprehension of the human intellect.

**History of Japanese Religion* (Rutland, Vt.: Charles E. Tuttle Company, 1963), p. 308.

From Motoori Noringa, "The True Tradition of the Sun Goddess," in William Theodore de Bary (ed.), *Sources of Japanese Tradition.* Copyright © 1958 by Columbia University Press, New York. Used by permission of the publisher.

But in the foreign countries where the Right Way has not been transmitted this act of divine creativity is not known. Men there have tried to explain the principle of Heaven and earth and all phenomena by such theories as the yin and yang, the hexagrams of the Book of Changes, and the Five Elements. But all of these are fallacious theories stemming from the assumptions of the human intellect and they in no wise represent the true principle.

Izanagi, in deep sorrow at the passing of his goddess, journeyed after her to the land of death. Upon his return to the upper world he bathed himself at Ahagiwara in Tachibana Bay in Tsukushi in order to purify himself of the pollution of the land of death, and while thus cleansing himself, he gave birth to the Heaven-Shining Goddess who by the explicit command of her father-God, came to rule the Heavenly Plain for all time to come. This Heaven-Shining Goddess is none other than the sun in heaven which today casts its gracious light over the world. Then, an Imperial Prince of the Heaven-Shining Goddess was sent down from heaven to the middle kingdom of Ashihara. In the Goddess' mandate to the Prince at that time it was stated that his dynasty should be coeval with Heaven and earth. It is this mandate which is the very origin and basis of the Way. Thus, all the principles of the world and the way of humankind are represented in the different stages of the Divine Age. Those who seek to know the Right Way must therefore pay careful attention to the stages of the Divine Age and learn the truths of existence. These aspects of the various stages are embodied in the ancient traditions of the Divine Age. No one knows with whom these ancient traditions began, but they were handed down orally from the very earliest times and they refer to the accounts which have since been recorded in the *Kojiki* and the *Nihongi*. The accounts recorded in these two scriptures are clear and explicit and present no cause for doubt. Those who have interpreted these scriptures in a later age have contrived oracular formulae and have expounded theories which have no real basis. Some have become addicts of foreign doctrines and have no faith in the wonders of the Divine Age. Unable to understand that the truths of the world are contained in the evolution of the Divine Age, they fail to ascertain the true meaning of our ancient tradition. As they base their judgment on the strength of foreign beliefs, they always interpret at their own discretion and twist to their own liking anything they encounter which may not be in accord with their alien teachings. Thus, they say that the High Heavenly Plain refers to the Imperial Capital and not to Heaven, and that the Sun Goddess herself was not a goddess nor the sun shining in the heavens but an earthly person and the forebear of the nation. These are arbitrary interpretations purposely contrived to flatter foreign ideologies. In this way the ancient tradition is made to appear narrow and petty, by depriving it of its comprehensive and primal character. This is counter to the meaning of the scriptures.

Heaven and earth are one; there is no barrier between them. The High Heavenly Plain is the high heavenly plain which covers all the countries of the world, and the Sun Goddess is the goddess who reigns in that heaven. Thus, she is without a peer in the whole universe, casting her light to the very ends of heaven and earth and for all time. There is not a single country in the world which does not receive her beneficent illuminations, and no country can exist even for a day or an hour bereft of her grace. This goddess is the splendor of all splendors. However, foreign countries, having lost the ancient tradition of the Divine Age, do not know the meaning of revering this goddess. Only through the speculations of the human intelligence have they come to call the sun and the moon the spirit of yang and yin. In China and other countries the "Heavenly Emperor" is worshiped as the supreme divinity. In other countries there are other objects of reverence, each according to its own way, but their teachings are based, some on the logic of inference, and some on arbitrary personal opinions. At any rate, they are merely man-made designations and the "Heavenly Ruler" or the "Heavenly Way" have no real existence at all. That foreign countries revere such nonexistent beings and remain unaware of the grace of the Sun Goddess is a matter of profound regret. However, because of the special dispensation of our Imperial Land, the ancient tradition of the Divine Age has been correctly and clearly transmitted in our country, telling us of the genesis of the great goddess and the reason for her adoration. The "special dispensation of our Imperial Land" means that ours is the native land of the Heaven-Shining Goddess who casts her light over all countries in the four seas. Thus our country is the source and fountainhead of all other countries, and in all matters it excels all the others. It would be impossible to list all the products in which our country excels, but foremost among them is rice, which sustains the life of man, for whom there is no product more important. Our country's rice has no peer in foreign countries, from which fact it may be seen why our other products are also superior. Those who were born in this country have long been accustomed to our rice and take it for granted, unaware of its excellence. They can enjoy such excellent rice morning and night to their heart's content because they have been fortunate enough to be born in this country. This is a matter for which they should give thanks to our shining deities, but to my great dismay they seem to be unmindful of it.

Our country's Imperial Line, which casts its light over this world, represents the descendants of the Sky-Shining Goddess. And in accordance with that Goddess' mandate of reigning "forever and ever, coeval with Heaven and earth," the Imperial Line is destined to rule the nation for eons until the end of time and as long as the universe exists. That is the very basis of our Way. That our history has not deviated from the instructions of the divine mandate bears testimony to the infallibility of our ancient tradition. It can also be seen why foreign countries cannot match ours and what is meant by the special dispensation of our country. Foreign countries expound their own ways, each as if its way alone were true. But their dynastic lines, basic to their existence, do not continue; they change frequently and are quite corrupt. Thus one can surmise that in everything they say there are falsehoods and that there is no basis in fact for them.

Objection: You are obstinate in insisting that the Sun Goddess is the sun in heaven. If this is so, perpetual darkness must have reigned everywhere before her birth. The sun must have been in heaven since the beginning of the universe [before the birth of the Goddess].

Motoori: First of all, I cannot understand why you say that I am obstinate. That the Sun Goddess is the sun in heaven is clear from the records of the *Kojiki* and the *Nihongi.* If it is so beyond any doubt, is not the person who raises an objection the one who is obstinate? This Sun Goddess casts her light to the very extremities of the universe, but in the beginning it was in our Imperial Land that she made her appearance, and as the sovereign of the Imperial Line, that is, of the Imperial Land, she has reigned supreme over the Four Seas until now. When this Goddess hid herself in a cave in heaven, closing its doors, darkness fell over the countries of the world. You ask why darkness did not reign everywhere before her birth, a question a child might well ask. It seems childish indeed when a question which might spring from the doubts of a child is asked with such insistence by you. But this very point proves that the ancient happenings of the Divine Age are facts and not fabrications. Some say that the records are the fabrication of later sovereigns, but who would fabricate such shallow sounding, incredible things? This is a point you should reflect upon seriously.

The acts of the gods cannot be measured by ordinary human reasoning. Man's intellect, however wise, has its limits. It is small, and what is beyond its confines it cannot know. The acts of the gods are straightforward. That they appear to be shallow and untrue is due to the limitation of what man can know. To the human mind these acts appear to be remote, inaccessible, and difficult of comprehension and belief. Chinese teachings, on the other hand, were established within the reach of human intelligence; thus, to the mind of the listener, they are familiar and intimate and easy of comprehension and belief. The Chinese, because they believe that the wisdom of the Sage [Confucius] was capable of comprehending all the truths of the universe and of its phenomena, pretend to the wisdom of the Sage and insist, despite their small and limited minds, that they know what their minds are really incapable of knowing. But at the same time they refuse to believe in the inscrutability of the truth, for this, they conclude, is irrational. This sounds clever, but on the contrary, it betrays the pettiness of their intelligence. If my objector would rid himself of such a habit and reflect seriously, such a doubt as he has just expressed would disappear of itself.

It will be recalled that when Izanagi made his way to the nether region, he carried a light because of the darkness there, but while he lived in the actual world, he did not. The nether world is dark because it has to be dark; the actual world is clear because it has to be clear. Thus, there was light in the actual world before the birth of the Sun Goddess, although the reason why it is so cannot be fathomed. In the commentaries on the *Nihongi* there are references to luminous human beings of the days of creation who cast light about them, but these references were derived from the Buddhist scriptures. There is also mention of a deity of firefly light, but this was an evil deity, and his case cannot be taken as a typical one. There are otherwise no traditions about deities of light, and thus we have no way of knowing what light there was for illumination. But presumably there was light for reasons beyond the reach of human intelligence. Why then did darkness prevail when the Sun Goddess hid herself behind the door of the rocky cave? It was because it had been determined that with the birth of the Sun Goddess the whole space of the universe should come within her illumination, and that henceforth there would be no light without her illumination. This is the same sort of inscrutable truth as the case of the descent of the Imperial Grandchild from Heaven after which communication between Heaven and earth was completely severed. There are many other strange and inscrutable happenings in the Divine Age, which should be accepted in the same way. The people of antiquity never attempted to reason out the acts of the gods with their own intelligence, but the people of a later age, influenced by the Chinese, have become addicts of rationalism. Such people appear wise, but in reality are quite foolish in their suspicion and skepticism about the strange happenings of the Divine Age which are quite different from the happenings of the human age. The fact is that even the things of the human age are, in reality, strange and wondrous, but because we are accustomed to their present form and have always lived in their midst, we cease to be aware of their wondrous quality. Consider, for example, how this universe goes on. Is the earth suspended in the sky or attached to something else? In either instance it is a wondrous thing. Suppose it is attached to something else, what is there under it to support it? This is something which cannot be understood.

Glimpses of Shinto

Lafcadio Hearn

Born in 1850 on an Ionian island to a Greek mother and British Army surgeon father, Lafcadio Hearn had to endure a difficult childhood and youth. By the age of four he had been left with relatives in Ireland and had seen his mother for the last time. His father he recalled seeing on no more than five occasions, and the Irish relatives sent him off to schools to be rid of him. Then an accident added cruelly to his woes: he lost the sight of one eye and was disfigured; his vision in the other eye was poor. In 1869, nineteen years old, he was given a one-way ticket to Cincinnati and yet another relative, who gave him five dollars and put him back out on the street. He struggled with odd jobs and drifted into journalism and, in time, remarkable success. Commissioned to write articles by Harper's Magazine, *he went to Japan in 1890, and there he found a home. He married a Japanese woman, fathered three children, taught school, and continued to write, becoming celebrated both in Japan and America. By 1896 he was a professor of English literature at the Imperial University, Tokyo, and a naturalized citizen of Japan. He died in 1904, only fifty-four years of age. He had published twenty books, twelve of them about Japan.*

Among the most highly regarded are Glimpses of an Unfamiliar Japan, Out of the East, Kokuro, Exotics and Retrospectives, In Ghostly Japan, Shadowings, A Japanese Miscellany, Kwaidan, *and* Japan, An Attempt at Interpretation.

The Kami

The term "Kami," although translated by the term "deity," "divinity," or "god," has really no such meaning as that which belongs to the English words: it has not even the meaning of those words as referring to the antique beliefs of Greece and Rome. It signifies that which is "above," "superior," "upper," "eminent," in the non-religious sense; in the religious sense it signifies a human spirit having obtained supernatural power after death. The dead are the "powers above," the "upper ones"—the Kami. . . . The Kami are ghosts of greatly varying dignity and power—belonging to spiritual hierarchies like the hierarchies of ancient Japanese society. Although essentially superior to the living in certain respects, the living are, nevertheless, able to give them pleasure or displeasure, to gratify or to offend them—even sometimes to ameliorate their spiritual condition. Wherefore posthumous

Excerpts from *Out of the East* (1895), *Kokuro* (1896), and *Japan: An Attempt at Interpretation* (1904).

254

honors are never mockeries, but realities, to the Japanese mind. During the present year [1895], for example, several distinguished statesmen and soldiers were raised to higher rank immediately after their death; and I read only the other day, in the official gazette, that "His Majesty has been pleased to posthumously confer the Second Class of the Order of the Rising Sun upon Major-General Baron Yamane, who lately died in Formosa." Such imperial acts must not be regarded only as formalities intended to honor the memory of brave and patriotic men; neither should they be thought of as intended merely to confer distinction upon the family of the dead. They are essentially of Shintō, and exemplify that intimate sense of relation between the visible and invisible worlds which is the special religious characteristic of Japan among all civilized countries. To Japanese thought the dead are not less real than the living. They take part in the daily life of the people—sharing the humblest sorrows and the humblest joys. They attend the family repasts, watch over the well-being of the household, assist and rejoice in the prosperity of their descendants. They are present at the public pageants, at all the sacred festivals of Shintō, at the military games, and at all the entertainments especially provided for them. And they are universally thought of as finding pleasure in the offerings made to them or the honors conferred upon them.

For the purpose of this little essay, it will be sufficient to consider the Kami as the spirits of the dead—without making any attempt to distinguish such Kami from those primal deities believed to have created the land. With this general interpretation of the term Kami, we return, then, to the great Shintō idea that all the dead still dwell in the world and rule it; influencing not only the thoughts and the acts of men, but the conditions of nature. "They direct," wrote Motowori, "the changes of the seasons, the wind and the rain, the good and the bad fortunes of states and of individual men." They are, in short, the viewless forces behind all phenomena.

Shrines

Besides temples to deities presiding over industries and agriculture—or deities especially invoked by the peasants, such as the Goddess of Silkworms, the Goddess of Rice, the Gods of Wind and Weather—there are to be found in almost every part of the country what I may call propitiatory temples. These latter Shintō shrines have been erected by way of compensation to spirits of persons who suffered great injustice or misfortune. In these cases the worship assumes a very curious character, the worshiper always appealing for protection against the same kind of calamity or trouble as that from which the apotheosized person suffered during life. In Izumo, for example, I found a temple dedicated to the spirit of a woman, once a prince's favorite. She had been driven to suicide by the intrigues of jealous rivals. The story is that she had very beautiful hair; but it was not quite black, and her enemies used to reproach her with its color. Now mothers having children with brownish hair pray to her that the brown may be changed to black; and offerings are made to her of tresses of hair and Tōkyō colored prints, for it is still remembered that she was fond of such prints. In the same province there is a shrine erected to the spirit of a young wife who pined away for grief at the absence of her lord. She used to climb a hill to watch for his return, and the shrine was built upon the place where she waited; and wives pray there to her for the safe return of absent husbands. . . . An almost similar kind of propitiatory worship is practiced in cemeteries. Public pity seeks to apotheosize those urged to suicide by cruelty, or those executed for offenses which, although legally criminal, were inspired by patriotic or other motives commanding sympathy. Before their graves offerings are laid and prayers are murmured. Spirits of unhappy lovers are commonly invoked by young people who suffer from the same cause. . . . And among other forms of propitiatory worship I must mention the old custom of erecting small shrines to spirits of animals—chiefly domestic animals—either in recognition of dumb service rendered and ill-rewarded, or as a compensation for pain unjustly inflicted.

Yet another class of tutelar divinities remains to be noticed—those who dwell within or about the houses of men. Some are mentioned in the old mythology, and are probably developments of Japanese ancestor-worship; some are of alien origin; some do not appear to have any temples. . . .

Suijin-Sama, the God of Wells; Kojin, the God of the Cooking-Range (in almost every kitchen there is either a tiny shrine for him, or a written charm bearing his name); the Gods of the Cauldron and Saucepan, Kudo-no-Kami and Kobé-no-Kami (anciently called Okitsuhiko and Okitsuhimé); the Master of Ponds, Iké-no-Nushi, supposed to make apparition in the form of a serpent; the Goddess of the Rice-Pot, O-Kama-Sama; the Gods of the Latrina, who first taught men how to fertilize their fields (these are commonly represented by little figures of paper, having the forms of a man and a woman, but faceless); the Gods of Wood and Fire and Metal; the Gods likewise of Gardens, Fields, Scarecrows, Bridges, Hills, Woods, and Streams; and also the Spirits of Trees (for Japanese mythology has its dryads): most of these are undoubtedly of Shintō. On the other hand, we find the roads under the protection of Buddhist deities chiefly.

. . .

Certain occupations assume a religious character even to-day. For example, the carpenter still builds according to Shintō tradition: he dons a priestly costume at a certain stage of the work, performs rites, and chants invocations, and places the new house under the protection of the gods. But the occupation of the swordsmith was in old days the most sacred of crafts: he worked in priestly garb, and practiced Shintō rites of purification while engaged in the making of a good blade. Before his smithy was then suspended the sacred rope of rice-straw (shiménawa), which is the oldest symbol of Shintō: none even of his family might enter there, or speak to him; and he ate only of food cooked with holy fire.

. . .

Worship and Purification

We have seen that, in Old Japan, the world of the living was everywhere ruled by the world of the dead—that the individual, at every moment of his existence, was under ghostly supervision. In his home he was watched by the spirits of his fathers;

without it, he was ruled by the god of his district. All about him, and above him, and beneath him were invisible powers of life and death. In his conception of nature all things were ordered by the dead—light and darkness, weather and season, winds and tides, mist and rain, growth and decay, sickness and health. The viewless atmosphere was a phantom-sea, an ocean of ghost; the soil that he tilled was pervaded by spirit-essence; the trees were haunted and holy; even the rocks and the stones were infused with conscious life. . . . How might he discharge his duty to the infinite concourse of the invisible?

. . .

In Izumo, the oldest Shintō province, the customary morning worship offers perhaps the best example of the ancient rules of devotion. Immediately upon rising, the worshiper performs his ablutions; and after having washed his face and rinsed his mouth, he turns to the sun, claps his hands, and with bowed head reverently utters the simple greeting: "Hail to thee this day, August One!" In thus adoring the sun he is also fulfilling his duty as a subject—paying obeisance to the Imperial Ancestor. . . . The act is performed out of doors, not kneeling, but standing; and the spectacle of this simple worship is impressive. I can now see in memory—just as plainly as I saw with my eyes many years ago, off the wild Oko coast—the naked figure of a young fisherman erect at the prow of his boat, clapping his hands in salutation to the rising sun, whose ruddy glow transformed him into a statue of bronze. Also I retain a vivid memory of pilgrim figures poised upon the topmost crags of the summit of Fuji, clapping their hands in prayer, with faces to the east.[2] . . . Perhaps ten thousand—twenty thousand—years ago all humanity so worshiped the Lord of Day. . . .

After having saluted the sun, the worshiper returns to his house, to pray before the Kamidana and before the tables of the ancestors. Kneeling, he invokes the great gods of Isé or of Izumo, the gods of the chief temples of his province, the god of his parish-temple also (Ujigami), and finally all the myriads of the deities of Shintō. These prayers are not said aloud. The ancestors are thanked for the foundation of the home; the higher deities are invoked for aid and protection. . . .

The nature of the public rites varied according to the rank of the gods. Offerings and prayers were made to all; but the greater deities were worshiped with exceeding ceremony. To-day the offerings usually consist of food and rice-wine, together with symbolic articles representing the costlier gifts of woven stuffs presented by ancient custom. The ceremonies include processions, music, singing, and dancing. At the very small shrines there are few ceremonies—only offerings of food are presented. But at the great temples there are hierarchies of priests and priestesses (miko)— usually daughters of priests; and the ceremonies are elaborate and solemn. It is particularly at the temples of Isé (where, down to the fourteenth century, the high priestess was a daughter of emperors), or at the great temple of Izumo, that the archaic character of the ceremonial can be studied to most advantage. There, in

---

2. *Editor's note:* Hearn wrote an account of his own ascent of Fuji. See "Fuji-no-Yama" in his *Exotics and Retrospectives* (Boston: Little, Brown, and Co., 1898). Hearn was not much of a mountain climber, and Fuji, the highest peak in Japan, rises to 12,388 feet.

spite of the passage of that huge wave of Buddhism, which for a period almost sub-merged the more ancient faith, all things remain as they were a score of centuries ago;—Time, in those haunted precincts, would seem to have slept, as in the enchanted palaces of fairy-tale. The mere shapes of the buildings, weird and tall, startle by their unfamiliarity. Within, all is severely plain and pure: there are no images, no ornaments, no symbols visible—except those strange paper-cuttings (gohei), suspended to upright rods, which are symbols of offerings and also tokens of the viewless. By the number of them in the sanctuary, you know the number of the deities to whom the place is consecrate. There is nothing imposing but the space, the silence, and the suggestion of the past. The innermost shrine is veiled: it con-tains, perhaps, a mirror of bronze, an ancient sword, or other object enclosed in multiple wrappings: that is all. For this faith, older than icons, needs no images: its gods are ghosts; and the void stillness of its shrines compels more awe than tangible representation could inspire.

. . .

As a matter of fact, the most important of all Shintō ceremonies is the ceremony of purification—"o-harai," as it is called, which term signifies the casting-out or expul-sion of evils. . . . In ancient Athens a corresponding ceremony took place every year; in Rome, every four years. The o-harai is performed twice every year—in the sixth month and the twelfth month by the ancient calendar. It used to be not less obligatory than the Roman lustration; and the idea behind the obligation was the same as that which inspired the Roman laws on the subject. . . . So long as men believe that the welfare of the living depends upon the will of the dead—that all happenings in the world are ordered by spirits of different characters, evil as well as good—that every bad action lends additional power to the viewless forces of destruction, and therefore endangers the public prosperity—so long will the neces-sity of a public purification remain an article of common faith. The presence in any community of even one person who has offended the gods, consciously or unwill-ingly, is a public misfortune, a public peril. Yet it is not possible for all men to live so well as never to vex the gods by thought, word, or deed—through passion or ignorance or carelessness. "Every one," declares Hirata, "is certain to commit acci-dental offenses, however careful he may be. . . . Evil acts and words are of two kinds: those of which we are conscious, and those of which we are not conscious. . . . It is better to assume that we have committed such unconscious offenses." . . .

From the earliest period Shintō exacted scrupulous cleanliness—indeed, we might say that it regarded physical impurity as identical with moral impurity, and intolerable to the gods. It has always been, and still remains, a religion of ablutions. The Japanese love of cleanliness—indicated by the universal practice of daily bath-ing, and by the irreproachable condition of their homes—has been maintained, and was probably initiated, by their religion. Spotless cleanliness being required by the rites of ancestor-worship—in the temple, in the person of the officiant, and in the home—this rule of purity was naturally extended by degrees to all the conditions of existence.

Further Reading

H. Byron Earhart, *Japanese Religion: Unity and Diversity* (3d ed., 1982). "The panorama of religion in Japan is truly bewildering," Earhart writes, but he surveys it with skill and insight. See also his collection of source materials, *Religion in the Japanese Experience* (1974).

Shinto, Landon Warner has observed, "has always been the artist's way of life." See Chapter 2 of his *The Enduring Art of Japan* (1952).

In 1991 Donald Keene received a National Book Critics Circle Award for his "lifetime achievements" as a translator and scholar of Japanese literature. *The Pleasures of Japanese Literature* (1988) is an elegant introduction to both the subject at hand and to Keene.

Ryusaku Tsunoda, Wm. Theodore de Bary, and Donald Keene (eds.), *Sources of Japanese Tradition* (1958). An extensive anthology with very helpful background and commentary by expert editors.

G. B. Sansom, *Japan: A Short Cultural History* (rev. ed., 1962) and *History of Japan* (3 vols., 1958–1963). (The author's name appears as George Sansom in the latter volumes.) By common consensus, authoritative works.

In his *History of Japanese Religion* (1930), Masaharu Anesaki notes that when the world began, "men and animals were gods, and plants and animals had speech; but even now, according to the Shinto conception, it is not entirely otherwise." Anesaki also wrote *Religious Life of the Japanese People* (1936), which has been revised by Kishimoto Hideo (4th rev. ed., 1970).

The eminent University of Chicago scholar Joseph M. Kitagawa examined the intertwined religious traditions of Japan in *On Understanding Japanese Religion* (1987), a collection of twenty articles. His *Religion in Japanese History* (1966) has long been highly regarded. Writing about Shinto in the 1966 volume, Kitagawa noted that "Japanese myths mention the existence of eight hundred myriads of kami, a metaphor employed to express belief in the sacredness of the whole universe."

-

VII

JUDAISM
The Sanctification of Life

What is hateful unto you,
do not do unto your neighbor.
The rest is commentary—
now go and study.

Hillel

Judaism is the hallowing of life for the glory of God, and it is God's covenant with a chosen people. It is a history of God's revelation through great prophets and events; it is the Torah and the Talmud and a profound love of learning. Mordecai Kaplan called it a civilization. It is a religion rich in tradition and ritual, but the prophet Micah was able to ask so very simply, "What does the Lord require of you but to do justice, and to love kindness, and to walk humbly with your God?"

Nicholas de Lange, in this chapter's opening essay, pursues the question of the nature of Judaism, noting that Judaism, Christianity, and Islam, so close in beliefs and sharing so much history (as well as the Bible and Jerusalem), are clearly a family of religions. But, as in all families, the relationships are not as simple as they may at first appear. Even the word "religion" is understood differently by each of the three religions, and this of course has significant bearing on how Judaism is to be defined.[1]

That Judaism for many Jews is more a way of life than a system of beliefs is another of de Lange's points, and this is the theme of Louis Finkelstein's essay. The Jewish way of life is a discipline "so rigorous . . . that it may be compared to those specified for members of religious orders in other faiths." But there is no *creed* to which all Jews subscribe: this is a religion taken on somewhat different terms than is Christianity.

While keeping in mind that Judaism is not a credal religion, it is nevertheless of interest to look at the best known statement of the basic dogmas of Judaism. As formulated by Maimonides,[2] and debated ever since, they are:

1. The belief in God's existence.
2. The belief in His unity.

1. For a seminal study of the word "religion," see Wilfred Cantwell Smith, *The Meaning and End of Religion* (New York: Macmillan, 1963).

2. Moses Maimonides (1135–1204), the outstanding Jewish philosopher of the Middle Ages, was the author of *The Guide for the Perplexed* and other works.

3. The belief in His incorporeality.
4. The belief in His timelessness.
5. The belief that He is approachable through prayer.
6. The belief in prophecy.
7. The belief in the superiority of Moses to all other prophets.
8. The belief in the revelation of the Law, and that the Law as contained in the Pentateuch is that revealed by Moses.
9. The belief in the immutability of the Law.
10. The belief in Divine providence.
11. The belief in Divine justice.
12. The belief in the coming of the Messiah.
13. The belief in the resurrection and human immortality.

But the *real* statement of creed for Jews, the complete one, is *The Holy Scriptures,* some selections from which appear in the following pages. "We have preserved the Book, and the Book has preserved us," said David Ben-Gurion.

Of *The Talmud* Adin Steinsaltz states that "no other work has had a comparable influence on the theory and practice of Jewish life." Steinsaltz finds a key to the meaning of that work in its very title, which means "study, learning."

Jewish mystical tales, a number of which are recounted in these pages by Howard Schwartz, typically express wonder at life and its daily miracles: God is always close at hand. The tale entitled "The Precious Prayer" expresses a favorite theme—that a good heart is more important than anything else. Two of the tales, "The Master Key" and "The Cave of Mattathias," are of Hasidic origin, the former of these featuring the eighteenth century founder of Hasidism, the Baal Shem Tov. Hasidism is a variety of Jewish mysticism that exalts God by exalting life. In Elie Wiesel's words, it is "a smiling Judaism...a resounding call to joy."[3]

> What cannot but astound us is that Hasidim [the pious ones] remained Hasidim inside ghetto walls, inside the death camps. In the shadow of the executioner, they celebrated life. Startled Germans whispered to each other of Jews dancing in the cattle cars rolling toward Birkenau.[4]

The faith of Jews has been challenged through the centuries by calamity after calamity and relentless persecution, but what happened to them at the hands of Nazi Germany in this century is incomprehensible. Jews throughout Europe were systematically herded into "work camps" and subjected to unspeakable horrors. Some six million of them—men, women, children—were methodically murdered for no other reason than that they were Jews. Emil Fackenheim writes of this "Holocaust" and of "Auschwitz," one of the more notorious camps, the very name of which has come to represent all the camps and the attendant agony.

---

3. *Souls on Fire* (New York: Random House, 1972), p. 209.
4. Ibid., p. 38.

What Is Judaism?

Nicholas de Lange

Born in England, Nicholas de Lange (1944–) holds a doctorate in philosophy from Christ Church, Oxford, and is a lecturer in Rabbinics at the University of Cambridge. He is the author of A Woman in Israel, Origen and the Jews, Apocrypha: Jewish Literature of the Hellenistic Age, *and* Atlas of the Jewish World, *as well as scores of articles and reviews. The translator of several of the works of the noted Israeli author Amos Oz, he is particularly interested in the art of translation. Insofar as over a third of the reading selections in the present volume are translations, his views on that art are pertinent:*

> I used to think, as many people think, that translation consists of exchanging one word for another, like changing money. I have learned through experience that a faithful translation is not necessarily a literal one. A translator's loyalty is not to words. He has to be faithful to his author, to himself, to his readers. He has to interpret ideas, longings, moods. He has to absorb them, make them his own, and pass them on. The words help, but sometimes they get in the way.

The term "Judaism" is commonly used in a number of different ways. One of the commonest is to refer to a religion, one of the major religions of the world, and a member (together with Christianity and Islam) of what is known as the "monotheistic family" of religions.

This usage raises several problems, which we shall consider presently, but it is worth beginning by pointing out some of its positive merits.

In the first place it accurately indicates an important historical reality. Judaism, Christianity, and Islam do belong together. They all began in the same part of the world, the Middle East. (The honoured place thay all ascribe, in their different ways, to the city of Jerusalem is a living reminder of this.) From here they spread out in broadly similar directions. In the specific case of Judaism this historical aspect is particularly important. Since the advent of Christianity and Islam, Judaism has rarely spread, and it has never flourished, beyond the confines of what may be called the Christian-Muslim world. Judaism, Christianity, and Islam have developed in close contact with one another, and each religion has influenced the development of the others in important respects. Historically, then, the metaphor of a family is not inappropriate.

Theologically, too, it makes sense to speak of a family relationship. The fundamental beliefs of the three religions are, if not identical, remarkably similar. They all begin from the belief in a single, unique God: this is what we mean by the term "monotheistic religions." This God is perfect and incorporeal, the creator of the world and of mankind, existing beyond the world yet active within it. He is just yet compassionate, cares for his creatures and their welfare, makes his will known to mankind through direct revelation, demands and rewards righteousness and punishes wrongdoing. The actual details of the code of behaviour which God demands of man are also very similar in all three religions. Perhaps because of the close family relationship there has been a constant and often hostile internal debate between the three members which has had the effect of bringing to prominence those elements which divide rather than those which unite. But even a superficial comparison between these three religions and the other major religions of the world will immediately reveal that the common ground between Judaism, Christianity, and Islam is not accidental or incidental but essential, fundamental and unique.

The precise place of Judaism within the "monotheistic family" is an interesting and debatable question. Judaism is often described as the parent of the other two religions, and here we meet the first major ambiguity in the use of the term "Judaism." Christianity and Islam are both religions with an obvious beginning in time, even though both recognize that they have an important "prehistory." Thus the terms "pre-Christian" and "pre-Islamic" both have a recognizable meaning, and both terms are in fact in current use. But Judaism has no obvious starting-point, and the term "pre-Jewish" is not used. Judaism and Christianity both share a body of ancient sacred scriptures (indeed they constitute one of the most important areas of common ground between the two religions): Jews call them the Bible whereas for Christians they are only part of the Bible—the "Old Testament." Judaism has evolved by gradual stages, and Jews, even though they recognize later developments, tend to consider the religion of the Bible as essentially the same religion as the Judaism that has existed ever since. But Christians, while considering the Old Testament as an important source of their religion, tend to see it as a "pre-Christian," and more particularly as a "Jewish" document. In Christian usage, therefore, the term "Judaism" often refers to the biblical "prehistory" of Christianity, or to the Jewish religion as it existed at the time of Christ. It is in this sense that Judaism is described as the parent-religion of Christianity. And similarly in the case of Islam: as Christianity presents itself as a new revelation superseding the earlier Judaism, so Islam presents itself as a new revelation superseding both Judaism and Christianity.

All this belongs to the mutual polemic between the three religions, and each claim has some historical justification. But it must be emphasized that this way of looking at the relationship between the three religions has little or no bearing on their individual character or mutual relationship today. Perhaps it would be more realistic to view the three as brothers or sisters rather than as parent and children, or as three branches of the same tree rather than two branches deriving from the same Jewish trunk. But all such images are inadequate and they fail to do justice to the complexity of the relationship. . . .

Having considered some of the positive merits of the conception of Judaism as one of the monotheistic religions, it is time to consider some of its shortcomings. And it must be admitted that, from a Jewish point of view, they are real and serious. What the objections boil down to is a feeling that Judaism is misrepresented as being essentially the same kind of thing as Christianity or Islam, and a particular source of difficulty here is the concept of a religion. Judaism is often described by Jews as being "not so much a religion, more a way of life," and what this saying reveals is a deep-seated unease about the definition of Judaism as a religion. This widely felt unease, which may well appear paradoxical at first sight, deserves deeper scrutiny.

The use of the word "religion" to mean primarily a system of beliefs can be fairly said to be derived from a Christian way of looking at Christianity. The comparative study of religions is an academic discipline which has been developed within Christian theology faculties, and it has a tendency to force widely differing phenomena into a kind of strait-jacket cut to a Christian pattern. The problem is not only that other "religions" may have little or nothing to say about questions which are of burning importance for Christianity, but that they may not even see themselves as religions in precisely the way in which Christianity sees itself as a religion. At the heart of Christianity, of Christian self-definition, is a creed, a set of statements to which the Christian is required to assent. To be fair, this is not the only way of looking at Christianity, and there is certainly room for, let us say, a historical or sociological approach. But within the history of Christianity itself a crucial emphasis has been placed on belief as a criterion of Christian identity. It has been plausibly argued that the Christian creeds originated as tests of authentic Christian allegiance, and the great divisions within Christendom, whatever may have been their underlying social, cultural, or political causes, have tended to be articulated as theological differences. In fact it is fair to say that theology occupies a central role in Christianity which makes it unique among the "religions" of the world.

It is not necessary here to consider the implications of all this for the study of religions in general, but it is certainly necessary to ponder the implications for the study of Judaism. And in the first place it must be pointed out that the very term "religion" has been foreign to Judaism until relatively recently, when the dialogue with Christianity has compelled Jews to recognize and use it. Indeed the Hebrew language does not really have a word for "religion." In modern Hebrew the word *dat* has been pressed into service to translate "religion," but it is a word which properly belongs to the realm of law, not belief. A more obvious contender might be the word *emunah,* but *emunah,* which is a key word in the Jewish religious vocabulary, properly means "trust": belief *in,* rather than belief *that.*

Even the word "Judaism," it might be added, is a relative newcomer to the Jewish vocabulary in the sense of the religion of the Jews. This word, like so much of the Jewish religious terminology in English (we may think of such words as "pentateuch," "prophet," "phylactery," "proselyte," even "Bible" and "synagogue"), is of Greek origin; it is an abstract noun formed from the word for "Jew." In its original use it does not refer to belief but rather means something like "Jewish identity." Hebrew for a long time had no equivalent for the usual Christian meaning of "Judaism." The abstract noun *Yahadut* meant Jewish identity, the condition of being a Jew, until in modern times it was given the normal meaning of Judaism, which had by now been adopted by Jews speaking English and other western languages.

This history of the word "Judaism" brings us face to face with a phenomenon which is of the utmost importance in understanding Judaism. To be a Jew means first and foremost to belong to a group, the Jewish people, and the religious beliefs are secondary, in a sense, to this corporate allegiance. The contrast with Christianity is self-evident. The Christian also belongs to a corporate entity, the Christian Church, but the Church is defined as the body of Christian believers, and the Christian is defined in turn by his beliefs. Religious belief is only one ingredient in the makeup of the Jew, and it may not be the most important ingredient at that. Indeed there are many people in the world who consider themselves to be loyal Jews in every respect and who would deny that they have any religion at all. And, however strange it may appear to the Christian who is used to thinking of religions in theological terms, the role of theology in Judaism has been distinctly secondary, and some leading Jews, both in the past and today, have viewed it with the deepest suspicion. This in itself makes Judaism something very different from Christianity.

If Judaism cannot, without unacceptable sacrifice, be reduced to a system of beliefs, there is another approach to the study of religions which may produce more helpful results. This is the sociological approach which concentrates in the first instance not on statements of belief but on observable phenomena such as worship and ritual. The strength of this approach is that it can be applied to any society, whether or not it considers itself a "religious" community and even if it does not explicitly articulate its theological ideas. In this way we may study, for example, the "religion" of the Greeks or Romans, and from observing the phenomena we may argue to the underlying religious beliefs of the society. In the case of Judaism there is abundant material in the form of institutions, public and private worship, ritual observances, and so forth. What is more, this material would be acknowledged by many Jews as being far more central to Judaism than religious beliefs or theological doctrines.

Nevertheless, valuable though the sociological approach can be, it is doubtful whether it can really help us to an understanding of what Judaism is, let alone provide us with a realistic description or analysis of it. There are two main reasons for this. The first is the problem of scale. The sociological approach works best with a small and localized society. If we try to apply it to Jews worldwide, living under very different conditions and for the most part not forming distinct groups but scattered among a non-Jewish majority, we shall first have enormous difficulty in collecting and collating our material, and we may well end up by wondering whether we are studying a single phenomenon or an apparently infinite variety of different "Judaisms." It is certainly true, and generally accepted, that Judaism (particularly in terms of observance) takes different forms in different places, or indeed even in the same place; but it is also strongly felt that there is a single thing called "Judaism," which is not just the lowest common denominator of Jewish observance worldwide.

The second problem, which is perhaps even more intractable, is the difficulty of deciding which phenomena to study. In addition to worship and related activities, which would qualify as "religious" under any definition, there are many other aspects of Jewish life whose status is more equivocal. For many Jews the food they eat, even the clothes they wear, are an expression of their Jewish identity. How is the observer to select the elements which are relevant to his investigation without producing results which would be, to say the least, bizarre? For some selection, when faced with such a wealth of possible material, is inevitable. The danger is that we may be tempted, once again, to import definitions which derive from Christianity, and to seek out in Judaism the familiar elements of Christian religion, or their close equivalents. This can be misleading. It is tempting, for example, to see the synagogue as the Jewish equivalent of a church, and the rabbi as the equivalent of the Christian priest or minister. Now, it is true that in Christian countries the synagogue has come to resemble a church and the rabbi has assumed many of the functions of a minister of religion. But the traditional roles of the synagogue and the rabbi contain important elements which are not precisely religious in the Christian sense of the word. Conversely, there are institutions in traditional Judaism, such as the bathhouse or the abattoir, which probably deserve to be classified as religious even though they have no obvious Christian equivalent. The non-Jewish student of Judaism, particularly if he is accustomed to thinking in terms of Christianity, must be constantly on his guard against his own preconceptions.

Nothing Is Ordinary

Louis Finkelstein

Rabbi Louis Finkelstein (1895–1991) was born in Ohio, the son of a rabbi. He received a doctorate from Columbia University and was ordained by the Jewish Theological Seminary of America, to which he returned for over fifty years as (successively) instructor, professor, provost, president, and chancellor (1951–72). The recipient of many honorary degrees, he also served as religious advisor to the president of the United States during World War II.

Among the many books he wrote are The Beliefs and Practices of Judaism *and* Akiba: Scholar, Saint, and Martyr. *The present essay is drawn from a volume he edited,* The Jews: Their Religion and Culture.

A Way of Life

Judaism is a way of life that endeavors to transform virtually every human action into a means of communion with God. Through this communion with God, the Jew is enabled to make his contribution to the establishment of the Kingdom of God and the brotherhood of men on earth. So far as its adherents are concerned, Judaism seeks to extend the concept of right and wrong to every aspect of their behavior. Jewish rules of conduct apply not merely to worship, ceremonial, and justice between man and man, but also to such matters as philanthropy, personal friendships and kindnesses, intellectual pursuits, artistic creation, courtesy, the preservation of health, and the care of diet.[1]

So rigorous is this discipline, as ideally conceived in Jewish writings, that it may be compared to those specified for members of religious orders in other faiths. A casual conversation or a thoughtless remark may, for instance, be considered a grave violation of Jewish Law. It is forbidden, as a matter not merely of good form but of religious law, to use obscene language, to rouse a person to anger, or to display unusual ability in the presence of the handicapped. The ceremonial observances are equally detailed. The ceremonial Law expects each Jew to pray thrice

---

1. Without desiring to ascribe to them any responsibility for this statement, the author records with deep gratitude the assistance in its preparation given by colleagues from different schools of Jewish thought. These include Rabbis Max Arzt, Ben Zion Bokser, Samuel S. Cohon, Judah Goldin, Israel M. Goldman, Simon Greenberg, David de Sola Pool, Samuel Schulman, and Aaron J. Tofield.

every day, if possible at the synagogue; to recite a blessing before and after each meal; to thank God for any special pleasure, such as a curious sight, the perfume of a flower, or the receipt of good news; to wear a fringed garment about his body; to recite certain passages from Scripture each day; and to don *tephillin* (cubical receptacles containing certain biblical passages) during the morning prayers.

Decisions regarding right and wrong under given conditions are not left for the moment, but are formulated with great care in the vast literature created by the Jewish religious teachers. At the heart of this literature are the Hebrew Scriptures, usually described as the Old Testament, consisting of the Five Books of Moses (usually called the *Torah*), the Prophets, and the Hagiographa. These works, particularly the Five Books of Moses, contain the prescriptions for human conduct composed under Divine inspiration. The ultimate purpose of Jewish religious study is the application of the principles enunciated in the Scriptures, to cases and circumstances the principles do not explicitly cover.

Because Judaism is a way of life, no confession of faith can by itself make one a Jew. Belief in the dogmas of Judaism must be expressed in the acceptance of its discipline rather than in the repetition of a verbal formula. But no failure either to accept the beliefs of Judaism or to follow its prescriptions is sufficient to exclude from the fold a member of the Jewish faith. According to Jewish tradition, the covenant between God and Moses on Mt. Sinai included all those who were present and also all their descendants. This covenant was reaffirmed in the days of Ezra and Nehemiah, when the people together with their leaders made "a sure covenant to walk in God's law, which was given to Moses the servant of God, and to observe and do all the commandments of the Lord our Lord, and His ordinances and His statutes" (Neh. 10:30). To apply the words used by Scripture in another connection, this covenant has thus been made binding upon the Jews, "and upon their seed, and upon all such as joined themselves unto them" (Esth. 9:27). There is therefore no need for any ceremony to admit a Jewish child into the faith of Judaism. Born in a Jewish household, he becomes at once "a child of the covenant." The fact that the child has Jewish parents involves the assumption of the obligations that God has placed on these parents and their descendants.

This concept of the inheritance of religious traditions does not imply any sense of racial differentiation. The concept derives simply from the belief that a person may assume binding obligations not only for himself, but also for his descendants. Thus anyone who is converted to Judaism assumes the obligation to observe its discipline, and makes this obligation binding on his descendants forever, precisely as if he had been an Israelite, standing with Moses, before Mt. Sinai on the day of the Revelation.

The ancestry of the proselyte, and therefore his "race," are quite irrelevant. Whether he be of Arabic background like Queen Helene, or Roman like Aquila, or Khazar like the members of the south Russian kingdom that became converted to Judaism in the eighth century of the Common Era, or like Obadiah, the well-known Moslem who became a proselyte, or Polish like the famous Count Valentine Potocki of the eighteenth century, his descendants, from the point of view of Judaism, would all be bound by his obligation to follow the laws and customs of Judaism.

On the other hand, in view of the Jewish attitude toward other monotheistic faiths, it is considered improper for a Jew to urge a member of another faith to become a Jew. Indeed, a person who desires to adopt Judaism must be told of all the difficulties inherent in affiliation with the faith. Only a person who persists in his desire to become a Jew, and demonstrates that his desire is based on no mundane motive, may be accepted into the Jewish fold.

Because of the special place that the home occupies in Judaism as a center of religious life and worship, almost co-ordinate with the synagogue itself, Judaism holds it essential that both parties to a Jewish marriage be members of the Jewish faith. There is, of course, no objection to marriage with a sincere convert to Judaism. But it is not possible for the home to function in the manner prescribed by Jewish law unless both husband and wife are of the Jewish faith.

In the case of a mixed marriage, the status of the children is determined by the faith of the mother, as the greatest influence in their lives. The children of a Christian mother are considered Christians; the children of a Jewish mother are considered Jews. The Jewish partner in such a mixed marriage is considered living in continual transgression of Jewish law, but remains, like those who deviate from the Law in other respects, within the fold of Judaism, entirely subject to the duties and obligations placed on other Jews.

.   .   .

Ethics

Judaism lays great stress on the importance of personal ethical relations between friends. The last of the Ten Commandments is a prohibition against "coveting" the blessings of a neighbor. Other regulations warn against talebearing, gossip, envy, and dislike of a neighbor. Any form of vengeance also is prohibited. If a persons says to another, "Lend me your hatchet," and the second replies, "I will not lend you my hatchet today, because yesterday you refused to lend me your sickle," the second transgresses the commandment, "Thou shalt not take vengeance" (Lev. 19:18). If the second replies, "I will lend you my hatchet, despite the fact that yesterday you refused to lend me your sickle," he transgresses the second half of the verse, "nor bear any grudge." The importance of these commandments in Judaism is such that one of the most distinguished Jewish scholars of the eleventh century, Bahya ibn Pakudah, devoted a whole book to their analysis, the *Book of the Duties of the Heart.* In our own generation, the famous Rabbi Israel Meir Kahan (better known by the title of his book, *Chofetz Chayyim,* first publiched anonymously) devoted his life to warning against the transgression of these laws of ethical conduct. During the nineteenth century, there developed under the influence of Rabbi Israel Salanter (1810–83) a whole group of students who refrained from conversation over long periods, in order to discipline themselves against the sin of "evil speech."

In accordance with the precept of Lev. 19:17, Judaism considers every member of the faith responsible for the moral conduct of those neighbors over whom he is able to exert influence. To see injustice done without protesting against it is to participate in the injustice. To provoke a man to anger is to partake of the sin of unjust anger. To permit an opposing litigant to take a false oath is to share in the transgression of perjury; just as to listen to blasphemy, gossip, or talebearing is to be a party to them. The concept is summarized in the teaching of Rabbi Jacob that "a person, on whose account God has to inflict punishment on another, will not be admitted into the presence of God" (*Shabbat* 149b). The underlying principle of this teaching is the doctrine that a victim of injustice falls short of the ideal of Judaism to the extent that he fails to obtain Divine forgiveness for the person who acted unjustly toward him.

.   .   .

Bible, Scroll, Talmud

It is impossible to understand Judaism without an appreciation of the place it assigns to the study and practice of the talmudic Law. Doing the Will of God is the primary spiritual concern of the Jew. Therefore, to this day, he must devote considerable time not merely to the mastery of the content of the Talmud, but also to training in its method of reasoning. The study of the Bible and the Talmud is thus far more than a pleasing intellectual exercise, and is itself a means of communion with God. According to some teachers, this study is the highest form of such communion imaginable.[2]

Because the preservation of the Divine will regarding human conduct is basic to all civilization, none of the commandments is more important than that of studying and teaching the Law. The most sacred object in Judaism is the Scroll containing the Five Books of Moses. Every synagogue must contain at least one copy of it. The Scroll must be placed in a separate Ark, before which burns an eternal light. The position of this Ark in the synagogue is in the direction of Jerusalem; everyone turns toward the Ark in prayer. When the Scroll is taken from the Ark for the purpose of reading, all those present must rise. No irreverent or profane action may be performed in a room which contains a Scroll, nor may a Scroll be moved from place to place except for the performance of religious rites. From time to time the Scroll must be examined to ascertain that its writing is intact.

The preparation of the Scroll is a task requiring much care, erudition, and labor. It is usually done by a professional copyist called a *sofer* (scribe). The test is written on sheets of parchment, especially prepared for the purpose. Only skins of animals permitted for food, in accordance with Lev. 11:1–9 and Deut. 14:3–9, are used. The whole work is then attached at the beginning and at the end to wooden rods, so that it can be rolled in the form of a scroll.

The ink used in writing must be black, and should be indelible. Before beginning to copy the text, the scribe must say, "I am about to write this book as a sacred Scroll of the Law." He must repeat a similar formula every time he is about to copy the Divine Name, saying, "I am writing this word as the sacred Name."

Like other Semitic languages, Hebrew requires only a consonantal text for reading: the vowels are omitted in classical texts. Hence the Scroll of the Five Books of

2. Cf. the essay on "Study as a Mode of Worship" by Professor Nathan Isaacs, in *The Jewish Library*, edited by Rabbi Leo Jung, 1928, pp. 51–70.

Moses contains only the consonantal text. This text is fixed by tradition, almost to the last detail. Even such matters as division into paragraphs and sections, and the special size of certain letters, which are particularly large or particularly small, is determined. The texts of all the extant Scrolls are thus virtually identical. Any significant deviation from the traditional text makes a Scroll unfit for use, and must be corrected as soon as it is discovered. No decorations or illuminations are permitted in the Scrolls intended for the public service. Tradition prescribes, however, that certain poetic portions are to be written in verse form and that certain letters shall have little coronets adorning them.

No less important than this homage paid to the Scroll as symbol of the Law, is that paid to the living Law itself. Fully three-fourths of the Hebrew literature produced within the first nineteen centuries of the Common Era, is devoted to the elucidation of the Law. Many of the best minds in Judaism have been devoted to its study. Every parent is required to teach his child its basic elements. Its study is considered vital not only for the guidance it offers in the practice of Judaism, but for liberation from the burden of secular ambition and anxieties. The study of the Law is believed to be a foretaste of the immortal life, for the Sages of the Talmud believed that Paradise itself could offer men no nearer communion with God than the opportunity of discovering His will in the study of the Law.

The Talmud derives its authority from the position held by the ancient academies. The teachers of those academies, both of Babylonia and of Palestine, were considered the rightful successors of the older *Sanhedrin,* or Supreme Court, which before the destruction of Jerusalem (in the year 70 of the Common Era) was the arbiter of Jewish Law and custom. The Sanhedrin derived its authority from the statement in Deut. 17:8–13, that whenever a question of interpretation of the Law arises, it is to be finally decided by the Sages and priests in Jerusalem.

At the present time, the Jewish people have no living central authority comparable in status to the ancient Sanhedrin or the later academies. Therefore any decision regarding the Jewish religion must be based on the Talmud, as the final résumé of the teachings of those authorities when they existed. The right of an individual to decide questions of religious Law depends entirely on his knowledge of the Bible, the Talmud, and the later manuals based on them, and upon his fidelity to their teachings. Those who have acquired this knowledge are called *rabbis.* There is no sharp distinction in religious status between the rabbi and the layman in Judaism. The rabbi is simply a layman especially learned in Scripture and Talmud. Nor is there any hierarchical organization or government among the rabbis of the world. Yet some rabbis, by virtue of their special distinction in learning, by common consent come to be regarded as superior authorities on questions of Jewish Law. Difficult and complicated issues are referred to them for clarification.

To be recognized as a rabbi, a talmudic student customarily is ordained. Traditionally, the authority to act as rabbi may be conferred by any other rabbi. It is usual, however, for students at various theological schools to receive this authority from their teachers. In America, there are several rabbinical schools, each of which ordains its graduates in the manner in which degrees are conferred on graduates of other institutions of learning.

.   .   .

God

The central doctrine of Judaism is the belief in the One God, the Father of all mankind. The first Hebrew words a Jewish child learns are the confession of faith contained in the verse "Hear, O Israel, the Lord is our God, the Lord is One," and every believing Jew hopes that as he approaches his end in the fullness of time he will be sufficiently conscious to repeat this same confession. This monotheistic belief is subject to no qualification or compromise.

We owe this monotheism to some of the earliest teachers of Israel who, having discovered that the Lord is One and His name One, devoted their lives to the propagation of this teaching. But the prophets proceeded a step further. To whom shall you compare God, they exclaimed, and what manner of likeness shall you set up alongside Him? This served as a cue to sages and philosophers who pondered over the meaning of God. Through their insight the Jew learned that at most every description of God was a metaphor, due to the limited idiom of man. God is not to be compressed into physical form (He is incorporeal), He is not subject to the boundaries of time, of beginning and end (He is eternal), He cannot be confined by space (He is omnipresent). As one of the talmudic Sages put it, "In God is the universe fixed, not He in it."

True enough, not only the simple but the learned, not only the average but the saintly, have described God as wise, just, long-suffering, merciful; and, depending on the occasion, have appealed to Him because preeminently these attributes are His. When our motives are questioned we call upon Him for support, for in His wisdom He knows the deepest stirrings of our hearts. When we suffer, we invoke His justice. When in haste we sin, we plead for sufferance on His part. Where we have been exacting or rebellious, we cry for His mercy. What, however, does such language suggest? That man in his dependence and helplessness employs as best he may, to the stretching point if necessary, the sounds and vocabulary at his disposal. These terms, and others like them, are the finest human beings have developed. But even at their finest they will not do; they cannot be precise; they are a stammering to which we have simply grown accustomed. God, the nature of God, rises higher than our discourse. As He is the source of wisdom, we call Him wise; as He is the fullness of mercy, we call Him merciful. But the words fall short of His being.

Put thus, monotheism may strike us with the chill of an intellectual premise, necessary for an adequate interpretation of the universe but inaccessible to man, who is matter, transient and earth-bound. Indeed, these are the qualities that forever interfere with our ambition to understand the meaning of God in full. Fragments, approximations of this understanding, have been the privilege of the saintly in every age. Yet the more they beheld the more they saw that their ignorance was endless. It was as though one filled his cup once and again and once more and still again with water from the ocean; the sea was not diminished.

God's uniqueness and transcendence, however, have not discouraged the Jew from the effort to understand Him and cleave to His ways, for Judaism has also told him that the Lord is near unto them that call upon Him; to all that call upon Him in truth, God's proximity and majesty form a speculative paradox only if they are regarded as categories unrelated to man's own awareness of his shortcomings, to his perennial urge to supersede his status quo of deed and thought. To the self-satisfied, it is probably true, God is not nigh; otherwise, how could such a one be content? His charity is niggardly, his justice expedient, his patience mannered, when weighed against Him Whose qualities are a contradiction of the imperfect.

The very surpassing nature of God has taught the Jew that God is not only to be revered, but loved, that the Creator of the heavens and earth, and all that in them is, is also his Rock, his Father, his Shepherd, his Beloved. And in order to escape being remote from God he utilizes every phenomenon and occasion to remind him of the Creator and Father of all. This his prayers accomplish for him. A new morning begins; God has created this light, his morning liturgy reminds him. An evening arrives; and the prayers force upon him the realization that God's activity is once more manifest. For every occasion, experience, event, the Rabbis declared, man ought to pray. The sight of the rainbow, the new moon, a shooting star, the sea, a wise man; deliverance from peril; a visit to historic scenes, particularly those related to biblical history; good fortune, tragedy—each has its proper blessing, and these Rabbinic formulations are the Jew's memoranda. Nothing happens but that his thoughts are at once directed to God. Nothing is taken for granted, nothing is ordinary. Everything is alive with the reality of God, at once man's support and dwelling on high.

Selections, The Holy Scriptures

The Jewish Publication Society

A team of scholars, including Orthodox, Reform, and Conservative rabbis, worked together to translate Tanakh: The Holy Scriptures *(1985), from which the following selections are taken.* Tanakh *is the Hebrew term for the Holy Scriptures, the writings that Christians know as the Old Testament. Needless to say, the "Old Testament" title is entirely inappropriate as far as Jews are concerned.* *

The concept of revelation—the idea that God reveals his will to humankind through prophets and through history—attaches an enormous significance to the Holy Scriptures, which chronicle that revelation and the Hebrews' response to it. Jews today may differ over matters of interpretation, but to all Jews these are inspired writings and they guide the life of Judaism. "We Jews have no holy mountains, monuments, or cathedrals," Abraham Heschel once said, "only holy words."

Genesis

1 When God began to create[a] heaven and earth—[2]the earth being unformed and void, with darkness over the surface of the deep and a wind from[b] God sweeping over the water—[3]God said, "Let there be light"; and there was light. [4] God saw that the light was good, and God separated the light from the darkness. [5]God called the light Day, and the darkness He called Night. And there was evening and there was morning, a first day.[c]

[6]God said, "Let there be an expanse in the midst of the water, that it may separate water from water." [7]God made the expanse, and it separated the water which was below the expanse from the water which was above the expanse. And it was so. [8]God called the expanse Sky. And there was evening and there was morning, a second day.

*Responding to Christian use of the "Old Testament" title, Harold Bloom has proposed that Jews refer to their Scriptures as the "Original Testament" and to the Christian work as the "Belated Testament." *The Book of J* (New York: Grove Weidenfeld, 1990), p. 3.

[a]Others "In the beginning God created."

[b]Others "the spirit of."

[c]Others "one day."

⁹God said, "Let the water below the sky be gathered into one area, that the dry land may appear." And it was so. ¹⁰God called the dry land Earth, and the gathering of waters He called Seas. And God saw that this was good. ¹¹And God said, "Let the earth sprout vegetation: seed-bearing plants, fruit trees of every kind on earth that bear fruit with the seed in it." And it was so. ¹²The earth brought forth vegetation: seed-bearing plants of every kind, and trees of every kind bearing fruit with the seed in it. And God saw that this was good. ¹³And there was evening and there was morning, a third day.

¹⁴God said, "Let there be lights in the expanse of the sky to separate day from night; they shall serve as signs for the set times—the days and the years; ¹⁵and they shall serve as lighs in the expanse of the sky to shine upon the earth." And it was so. ¹⁶God made the two great lights, the greater light to dominate the day and the lesser light to dominate the night, and the stars. ¹⁷And God set them in the expanse of the sky to shine upon the earth, ¹⁸to dominate the day and the night, and to separate light from darkness. And God saw that this was good. ¹⁹And there was evening and there was morning, a fourth day.

²⁰God said, "Let the waters bring forth swarms of living creatures, and birds that fly above the earth across the expanse of the sky." ²¹God created the great sea monsters, and all the living creatures of every kind that creep, which the waters brought forth in swarms, and all the winged birds of every kind. And God saw that this was good. ²²God blessed them, saying, "Be fertile and increase, fill the waters in the seas, and let the birds increase on the earth." ²³And there was evening and there was morning, a fifth day.

²⁴God said, "Let the earth bring forth every kind of living creature: cattle, creeping things, and wild beasts of every kind." And it was so. ²⁵God made wild beasts of every kind and cattle of every kind, and all kinds of creeping things of the earth. And God saw that this was good. ²⁶And God said, "Let us make man in our image, after our likeness. They shall rule the fish of the sea, the birds of the sky, the cattle, the whole earth, and all the creeping things that creep on earth." ²⁷And God created man in His image, in the image of God He created him; male and female He created them. ²⁸God blessed them and God said to them, "Be fertile and increase, fill the earth and master it; and rule the fish of the sea, the birds of the sky, and all the living things that creep on earth."

²⁹God said, "See, I give you every seed-bearing plant that is upon all the earth, and every tree that has seed-bearing fruit; they shall be yours for food. ³⁰And to all the animals on land, to all the birds of the sky, and to everything that creeps on earth, in which there is the breath of life, [I give] all the green plants for food." And it was so. ³¹And God saw all that He had made, and found it very good. And there was evening and there was morning, the sixth day.

2 The heaven and the earth were finished, and all their array. ²On the seventh day God finished the work that He had been doing, and He ceased[a] on the seventh day from all the work that He had done. ³And God blessed the seventh day and declared

---

[a]Or "rested."

it holy, because on it God ceased from all the work of creation that He had done. [4]Such is the story of heaven and earth when they were created.

When the LORD God made earth and heaven—[5]when no shrub of the field was yet on earth and no grasses of the field had yet sprouted, because the LORD God had not sent rain upon the earth and there was no man to till the soil, [6]but a flow would well up from the ground and water the whole surface of the earth—[7]the LORD God formed man[b] from the dust of the earth.[c] He blew into his nostrils the breath of life, and man became a living being.

[8]The LORD God planted a garden in Eden, in the east, and placed there the man whom He had formed. [9]And from the ground the LORD God caused to grow every tree that was pleasing to the sight and good for food, with the tree of life in the middle of the garden, and the tree of knowledge of good and bad.

[10]A river issues from Eden to water the garden, and it then divides and becomes four branches. [11]The name of the first is Pishon, the one that winds through the whole land of Havilah, where the gold is. ([12]The gold of that land is good; bdellium is there, and lapis lazuli.[d]) [13]The name of the second river is Gihon, the one that winds through the whole land of Cush. [14]The name of the third river is Tigris, the one that flows east of Asshur. And the fourth river is the Euphrates.

[15]The LORD God took the man and placed him in the garden of Eden, to till it and tend it. [16]And the LORD God commanded the man, saying, "Of every tree of the garden you are free to eat; [17]but as for the tree of knowledge of good and bad, you must not eat of it; for as soon as you eat of it, you shall die."

[18]The LORD God said, "It is not good for man to be alone; I will make a fitting helper for him." [19]And the LORD God formed out of the earth all the wild beasts and all the birds of the sky, and brought them to the man to see what he would call them; and whatever the man called each living creature, that would be its name. [20]And the man gave names to all the cattle and to the birds of the sky and to all the wild beasts; but for Adam no fitting helper was found. [21]So the LORD God cast a deep sleep upon the man; and, while he slept, He took one of his ribs and closed up the flesh at that spot. [22]And the LORD God fashioned the rib that He had taken from the man into a woman; and He brought her to the man. [23]Then the man said,

> "This one at last
> Is bone of my bones
> And flesh of my flesh.
> This one shall be called Woman,[e]
> For from man[f] was she taken."

[24]Hence a man leaves his father and mother and clings to his wife, so that they become one flesh.

[b]Heb. *'adam.*

[c]Heb. *'adamah.*

[d]Others "onyx"; meaning of Heb. *shoham* uncertain.

[e]Heb. *'ishshah.*

[f]Heb. *'ish.*

Exodus

19 On the third new moon after the Israelites had gone forth from the land of Egypt, on that very day, they entered the wilderness of Sinai. [2]Having journeyed from Rephidim, they entered the wilderness of Sinai and encamped in the wilderness. Israel encamped there in front of the mountain, [3]and Moses went up to God. The Lord called to him from the mountain, saying, "Thus shall you say to the house of Jacob and declare to the children of Israel: [4]'You have seen what I did to the Egyptians, how I bore you on eagles' wings and brought you to Me. [5]Now then, if you will obey Me faithfully and keep My covenant, you shall be My treasured possession among all the peoples. Indeed, all the earth is Mine, [6]but you shall be to Me a kingdom of priests and a holy nation.' These are the words that you shall speak to the children of Israel."

[7]Moses came and summoned the elders of the people and put before them all that the Lord had commanded him. [8]All the people answered as one, saying, "All that the Lord has spoken we will do!" And Moses brought back the people's words to the Lord. [9]And the Lord said to Moses, "I will come to you in a thick cloud, in order that the people may hear when I speak with you and so trust you ever after." Then Moses reported the people's words to the Lord, [10]and the Lord said to Moses, "Go to the people and warn them to stay pure[a] today and tomorrow. Let them wash their clothes. [11]Let them be ready for the third day; for on the third day the Lord will come down, in the sight of all the people, on Mount Sinai. [12]You shall set bounds for the people round about, saying, 'Beware of going up the mountain or touching the border of it. Whoever touches the mountain shall be put to death: [13]no hand shall touch him, but he shall be either stoned or shot; beast or man, he shall not live.' When the ram's horn[b]–sounds a long blast,[b] they may go up on the mountain."

[14]Moses came down from the mountain to the people and warned the people to stay pure, and they washed their clothes. [15]And he said to the people, "Be ready for the third day: do not go near a woman."

[16]On the third day, as morning dawned, there was thunder, and lightning, and a dense cloud upon the mountain, and a very loud blast of the horn; and all the people who were in the camp trembled. [17]Moses led the people out of the camp toward God, and they took their places at the foot of the mountain.

[18]Now Mount Sinai was all in smoke, for the Lord had come down upon it in fire; the smoke rose like the smoke of a kiln, and the whole mountain[c] trembled violently. [19]The blare of the horn grew louder and louder. As Moses spoke, God answered him in thunder. [20]The Lord came down upon Mount Sinai, on the top of the mountain, and the Lord called Moses to the top of the mountain and Moses

[a]Cf. v. 15.

[b-b]Meaning of Heb. uncertain.

[c]Some Hebrew manuscripts and the Greek read "all the people"; cf. v. 16.

went up. [21]The LORD said to Moses, "Go down, warn the people not to break through to the LORD to gaze, lest many of them perish. [22]The priests also, who come near the LORD, must stay pure, lest the LORD break out against them." [23]But Moses said to the LORD, "The people cannot come up to Mount Sinai, for You warned us saying, 'Set bounds about the mountain and sanctify it.'" [24]So the LORD said to him, "Go down, and come back together with Aaron; but let not the priests or the people break through to come up to the LORD, lest He break out against them." [25]And Moses went down to the people and spoke to them.

20 God spoke all these words,[a] saying:
[2]I the LORD am your God who brought you out of the land of Egypt, the house of bondage: [3]You shall have no other gods besides Me.

[4]You shall not make for yourself a sculptured image, or any likeness of what is in the heavens above, or on the earth below, or in the waters under the earth. [5]You shall not bow down to them or serve them. For I the LORD your God am an impassioned God, visiting the guilt of the parents upon the children, upon the third and upon the fourth generations of those who reject Me, [6]but showing kindness to the thousandth generation of those who love Me and keep My commandments.

[7]You shall not[b]-swear falsely by-[b] the name of the LORD your God; for the LORD will not clear one who swears falsely by His name.

[8]Remember the sabbath day and keep it holy. [9]Six days you shall labor and do all your work, [10]but the seventh day is a sabbath of the LORD your God: you shall not do any work—you, your son or daughter, your male or female slave, or your cattle, or the stranger who is within your settlements. [11]For in six days the LORD made heaven and earth and sea, and all that is in them, and He rested on the seventh day; therefore the LORD blessed the sabbath day and hallowed it.

[12]Honor your father and your mother, that you may long endure on the land that the LORD your God is assigning to you.

[13]You shall not murder.

You shall not commit adultery.

You shall not steal.

You shall not bear false witness against your neighbor.

[14]You shall not covet your neighbor's house: you shall not covet your neighbor's wife, or his male or female slave, or his ox or his ass, or anything that is your neighbor's.

Deuteronomy

6 And this is the Instruction—the laws and the rules—that the LORD your God has commanded [me] to impart to you, to be observed in the land that you are about to cross into and occupy, [2]so that you, your children, and your children's children

---

[a]Tradition varies as to the division of the Commandments in vv. 2–14, and as to the numbering of the verses from 13 on.

[b–b]Others "take in vain."

may revere the LORD your God and follow, as long as you live, all His laws and commandments that I enjoin upon you, to the end that you may long endure. ³Obey, O Israel, willingly and faithfully, that it may go well with you and that you may increase greatly [in] ᵃa land flowing with milk and honey,⁻ᵃ as the LORD, the God of your fathers, spoke to you.

⁴Hear, O Israel! The LORD is our God, the LORD alone.ᵇ ⁵You shall love the LORD your God with all your heart and with all your soul and with all your might. ⁶Take to heart these instructions with which I charge you this day. ⁷Impress them upon your children. Recite them when you stay at home and when you are away, when you lie down and when you get up. ⁸Bind them as a sign on your hand and let them serve as a symbolᶜ on your forehead;ᵈ ⁹inscribe them on the doorposts of your house and on your gates.

¹⁰When the LORD your God brings you into the land that He swore to your fathers, Abraham, Isaac, and Jacob, to assign to you—great and flourishing cities that you did not build, ¹¹houses full of all good things that you did not fill, hewn cisterns that you did not hew, vineyards and olive groves that you did not plant— and youe at your fill, ¹²take heed that you do not forget the LORD who freed you from the land of Egypt, the house of bondage. ¹³Revere only the LORD your God and worship Him alone, and swear only by His name. ¹⁴Do not follow other gods, any gods of the peoples about you ¹⁵—for the LORD your God in your midst is an impassioned God—lest the anger of the LORD your God blaze forth against you and He wipe you off the face of the earth.

¹⁶Do not try the LORD your God, as you did at Massah.ᵉ ¹⁷Be sure to keep the commandments, decrees, and laws that the LORD your God has enjoined upon you. ¹⁸Do what is right and good in the sight of the LORD, that it may go well with you and that you may be able to possess the good land that the LORD your God promised on oath to your fathers, ¹⁹and that all your enemies may be driven out before you, as the LORD has spoken.

²⁰When, in time to come, your children ask you, "What mean the decrees, laws, and rules that the LORD our God has enjoined upon you?"ᶠ ²¹you shall say to your children, "We were slaves to Pharaoh in Egypt and the LORD freed us from Egypt with a mighty hand. ²²The LORD wrought before our eyes marvelous and destructive signs and portents in Egypt, against Pharaoh and all his household; ²³and us He freed from there, that He might take us and give us the land that He had promised on oath to our fathers. ²⁴Then the LORD commanded us to observe all these laws, to revere the LORD our God, for our lasting good and for our survival, as is now the case. ²⁵It will be therefore to our merit before the LORD our God to observe faithfully this whole Instruction, as He has commanded us."

ᵃ⁻ᵃAccording to Ibn Ezra, this phrase connects with the end of v. 1.

ᵇCf. Rashbam and Ibn Ezra; see Zech. 14.9. Others "The LORD our God, the LORD is one."

ᶜOthers "frontlet"; cf. Exod. 13.16.

ᵈLit. "between your eyes"; cf. Exod. 13.9.

ᵉCf. Exod. 17.1–7.

ᶠSeptuagint and rabbinic quotations read "us."

Psalms

Book One

1

Happy is the man who has not followed the counsel of the wicked,
  or taken the path of sinners,
  or joined the company of the insolent;
  [2]rather, the teaching of the LORD is his delight,
  and he studies[a] that teaching day and night.
[3]He is like a tree planted beside streams of water,
  which yields its fruit in season,
  whose foliage never fades,
  and whatever [b–]it produces thrives.[–b]

[4]Not so the wicked;
  rather, they are like chaff that wind blows away.
[5]Therefore the wicked will not survive judgment,
  nor will sinners, in the assembly of the righteous.
[6]For the LORD cherishes the way of the righteous,
  but the way of the wicked is doomed.

96

[a]Sing to the LORD a new song,
  sing to the LORD, all the earth.
[2]Sing to the LORD, bless His name,
  proclaim His victory day after day.
[3]Tell of His glory among the nations,
  His wondrous deeds, among all peoples.
[4]For the LORD is great and much acclaimed,
  He is held in awe by all divine beings.
[5]All the gods of the peoples are mere idols,
  but the LORD made the heavens.
[6]Glory and majesty are before Him;
  strength and splendor are in His temple.

[7]Ascribe to the LORD, O families of the peoples,
  ascribe to the LORD glory and strength.
[8]Ascribe to the LORD the glory of His name,
  bring tribute and enter His courts.
[9]Bow down to the LORD majestic in holiness;
  tremble in His presence, all the earth!
[10]Declare among the nations, "The LORD is king!"

[a]Or "recites"; lit. "utters."

[b–b]Or "he does prospers."

The world stands firm; it cannot be shaken;
He judges the peoples with equity.
[11]Let the heavens rejoice and the earth exult;
    let the sea and all within it thunder,
    [12]the fields and everything in them exult;
    then shall all the trees of the forest shout for joy
    [13]at the presence of the LORD, for He is coming,
    for He is coming to rule the earth;
    He will rule the world justly
    and its peoples in faithfulness.

Proverbs

3

[13]Happy is the man who finds wisdom,
The man who attains understanding.
[14]Her value in trade is better than silver,
Her yield, greater than gold.
[15]She is more precious than rubies;
All of your goods cannot equal her.
[16]In her right hand is length of days,
In her left, riches and honor.
[17]Her ways are pleasant ways,
And all her paths, peaceful.
[18]She is a tree of life to those who grasp her,
And whoever holds on to her is happy.

6

[6]Lazybones, go to the ant;
Study its ways and learn.
[7]Without leaders, officers, or rulers,
[8]It lays up its stores during the summer,
Gathers in its food at the harvest.
[9]How long will you lie there, lazybones;
When will you wake from your sleep?
[10]A bit more sleep, a bit more slumber,
A bit more hugging yourself in bed,
[11]And poverty will come [a-]calling upon you,[-a]
And want, like a man with a shield.
[12]A scoundrel, an evil man
Lives by crooked speech,

[a-a]Meaning of Heb. uncertain.

¹³Winking his eyes,
Shuffling his feet,
Pointing his finger.
¹⁴Duplicity is in his heart;
He plots evil all the time;
He incites quarrels.
¹⁵Therefore calamity will come upon him without warning;
Suddenly he will be broken beyond repair.

¹⁶Six things the LORD hates;
Seven are an abomination to Him:
¹⁷A haughty bearing,
A lying tongue,
Hands that shed innocent blood,
¹⁸A mind that hatches evil plots,
Feet quick to run to evil,
¹⁹A false witness testifying lies,
And one who incites brothers to quarrel.

8

It is Wisdom calling,
Understanding raising her voice.
²She takes her stand at the topmost heights,
By the wayside, at the crossroads,
³Near the gates at the city entrance;
At the entryways, she shouts,
⁴"O men, I call to you;
My cry is to all mankind.
⁵O simple ones, learn shrewdness;
O dullards, instruct your minds.
⁶Listen, for I speak noble things;
Uprightness comes from my lips;
⁷My mouth utters truth;
Wickedness is abhorrent to my lips.
⁸All my words are just,
None of them perverse or crooked;
⁹All are straightforward to the intelligent man,
And right to those who have attained knowledge.
¹⁰Accept my discipline rather than silver,
Knowledge rather than choice gold.
¹¹For wisdom is better than rubies;
No goods can equal her.

12

¹⁵The way of a fool is right in his own eyes;
But the wise man accepts advice.

¹⁶A fool's vexation is known at once,
But a clever man conceals his humiliation.
¹⁷He who testifies faithfully tells the truth,
But a false witness, deceit.
¹⁸There is blunt talk like sword-thrusts,
But the speech of the wise is healing.
¹⁹Truthful speech abides forever,
A lying tongue for but a moment.

14

¹⁰ The heart alone knows its bitterness,
And no outsider can share in its joy.

¹³The heart may ache even in laughter,
And joy may end in grief.

¹⁵A simple person believes anything;
A clever man ponders his course.

15

A gentle response allays wrath;
A harsh word provokes anger.
²The tongue of the wise produces much knowledge,
But the mouth of dullards pours out folly.

⁴A healing tongue is a tree of life,
But a devious one makes for a broken spirit.

16

¹⁶How much better to acquire wisdom than gold;
To acquire understanding is preferable to silver.
¹⁷The highway of the upright avoids evil;
He who would preserve his life watches his way.
¹⁸Pride goes before ruin,
Arrogance, before failure.

17

¹²Sooner meet a bereaved she-bear
Than a fool with his nonsense.

¹⁶What good is money in the hand of a fool
To purchase wisdom, when he has no mind?

²⁷A knowledgeable man is sparing with his words;
A man of understanding is reticent.

²⁸Even a fool, if he keeps silent, is deemed wise;
Intelligent, if he seals his lips.

27

⁵An endless dripping on a rainy day
And a contentious wife are alike;
¹⁶As soon repress her as repress the wind,
Or declare one's right hand to be oil.

Ecclesiastes

1 The words of Koheleth[a] son of David, king in Jerusalem!

²Utter futility!—said Koheleth—
Utter futility! All is futile!
³What real value is there for a man
In all the gains[b] he makes beneath the sun?

⁴One generation goes, another comes,
But the earth remains the same forever.
⁵The sun rises, and the sun sets—
And glides[c] back to where it rises.
⁶Southward blowing,
Turning northward,
Ever turning blows the wind;
On its rounds the wind returns.
⁷All streams flow into the sea,
Yet the sea is never full;
To the place [from] which they flow
The streams flow back again.[d]
⁸All such things are wearisome:
No man can ever state them;
The eye never has enough of seeing,
Nor the ear enough of hearing.
⁹Only that shall happen
Which has happened,
Only that occur
Which has occurred;
There is nothing new
Beneath the sun!

[a]Probably "the Assembler," i.e., of hearers or of sayings; cf. 12.9–11.

[b]So Rashbam. Heb. *'amal* usually has this sense in Ecclesiastes; cf. Ps. 105.44.

[c]So Targum; cf. Bereshith Rabbah on Gen. 1.17.

[d]According to popular belief, through tunnels; so Targum and Rashi.

[10]Sometimes there is a phenomenon of which they say, "Look, this one is new!"—
it occurred long since, in ages that went by before us. [11]The earlier ones are not
remembered; so too those that will occur later ᵉwill no more be remembered thanᵉ
those that will occur at the very end.

[12]I, Koheleth, was king in Jerusalem over Israel. [13]I set my mind to study and to
probe with wisdom all that happens under the sun.—An unhappy business, that,
which God gave men to be concerned with! [14]I observed all the happenings beneath
the sun, and I found that all is futile and pursuitᶠ of wind:

> [15]A twisted thing that cannot be made straight,
> A lack that cannot be made good.

[16]I said to myself: "Here I have grown richer and wiser than any that ruled before
me over Jerusalem, and my mind has zealously absorbed wisdom and learning."
[17]And so I set my mind to appraise wisdom and to appraise madness and folly. And
I learned—that this too was pursuit of wind:

> [18]For as wisdom grows, vexation grows;
> To increase learning is to increase heartache.

.   .   .

3 A season is set for everything, a time for every experience under heaven:ᵃ
> [2]A time for ᵇ⁻being bornᵇ and a time for dying,
> A time for planting and a time for uprooting the planted;
> [3]A time for ᶜ⁻slaying and a time for healing,⁻ᶜ
> A time for tearing down and a time for building up;
> [4]A time for weeping and a time for laughing,
> A time for wailing and a time for dancing;
> [5]A time for throwing stones and a time for gathering stones,
> A time for embracing and a time for shunning embraces;
> [6]A time for seeking and a time for losing,
> A time for keeping and a time for discarding;
> [7]A time for ripping and a time for sewing,
> A time for silence and a time for speaking;
> [8]A time for loving and a time for hating;
> A time for war and a time for peace.

ᵉ⁻ᵉLit. "will not be remembered like . . ." For *'im* meaning "like," cf. 2.16; ;7.11; Job 9.26.

ᶠLit. "tending," from root *ra'ah,* "to shepherd."

ᵃI.e., all human experiences are preordained by God; see v. 11.

ᵇ⁻ᵇLit. "giving birth."

ᶜ⁻ᶜEmendation yields "wrecking . . . repairing"; cf. 1 Kings 18.30.

The Essential Talmud

Adin Steinsaltz

By all accounts, Adin Steinsaltz is one of the great scholars of the century. Israeli-born, he has lived there all of his life and is considered a national treasure. He won the 1988 Israel Prize, the highest honor awarded by that nation. His monumental work—a project that will occupy him for years to come—is a translation of the sixty-four volume Babylonian Talmud into modern Hebrew, with extensive notes and commentary. Some twenty volumes have been published to date. Translation of that work into English (The Talmud—The Steinsaltz Edition) *has begun, the initial volumes having been published in 1989.*

Rabbi Steinsaltz has also written a number of other books: The Thirteen Petalled Rose *is an interpretation of the meaning of Judaism;* Beggars and Prayers *retells and comments upon six tales of Rabbi Nahman of Bratslav;* The Long Shorter Way *discusses Hasidic thought;* The Strife of the Spirit *is a collection of essays and includes three interviews of the rabbi.* The Essential Talmud *is an introduction to the Talmud.*

If the Bible is the cornerstone of Judaism, then the Talmud is the central pillar, soaring up from the foundations and supporting the entire spiritual and intellectual edifice. In many ways the Talmud is the most important book in Jewish culture, the backbone of creativity and of national life. No other work has had a comparable influence on the theory and practice of Jewish life, shaping spiritual content and serving as a guide to conduct. The Jewish people have always been keenly aware that their continued survival and development depend on study of the Talmud, and those hostile to Judaism have also been cognizant of this fact. The book was reviled, slandered, and consigned to the flames countless times in the Middle Ages and has been subjected to similar indignities in the recent past as well. At times, talmudic study has been prohibited because it was abundantly clear that a Jewish society that ceased to study this work had no real hope of survival.

The formal definition of the Talmud is the summary of oral law that evolved after centuries of scholarly effort by sages who lived in Palestine and Babylonia until the beginning of the Middle Ages. It has two main components: the Mishnah, a book of *balakhah* (law) written in Hebrew; and the commentary on the Mishnah, known as the Talmud (or Gemarah), in the limited sense of the word, a summary of discussion and elucidations of the Mishnah written in Aramaic-Hebrew jargon.

This explanation, however, though formally correct, is misleading and imprecise. The Talmud is the repository of thousands of years of Jewish wisdom, and the oral law, which is as ancient and significant as the written law (the Torah), finds expression therein. It is a conglomerate of law, legend, and philosophy, a blend of unique logic and shrewd pragmatism, of history and science, anecdotes and humor. It is a collection of paradoxes: its framework is orderly and logical, every word and term subjected to meticulous editing, completed centuries after the actual work of composition came to an end; yet it is still based on free association, on a harnessing together of diverse ideas reminiscent of the modern stream-of-consciousness novel. Although its main objective is to interpret and comment on a book of law, it is, simultaneously, a work of art that goes beyond legislation and its practical application. And although the Talmud is, to this day, the primary source of Jewish law, it cannot be cited as an authority for purposes of ruling.

The Talmud treats abstract and totally unrealistic problems in the same manner in which it refers to the most prosaic facts of everyday life, yet succeeds in avoiding abstract terminology. Though based on the principles of tradition and the transmission of authority from generation to generation, it is unparalleled in its eagerness to question and reexamine convention and accepted views and to root out underlying causes. The talmudic method of discussion and demonstration tries to approximate mathematical precision, but without having recourse to mathematical or logical symbols.

The Talmud is best understood through analysis of the basic objectives of its authors and compilers. What were they aiming at, those thousands of sages who spent their lives in debate and discussion in hundreds of large and small centers of learning? The key is to be found in the name of the work: Talmud (that is, study, learning). The Talmud is the embodiment of the great concept of *mitzvat talmud Torah*—the positive religious duty of studying Torah, of acquiring learning and wisdom, study which is its own end and reward. A certain talmudic sage who has left us nothing but his name and this one dictum had this to say on the subject: "Turn it and turn it again, for everything is contained in the Torah. Regard it and grow old in it and never abandon it, for there is no greater virtue."

Study of Torah undoubtedly serves numerous practical purposes, but these are not the crucial objectives. Study is not geared to the degree of importance or the practical potential of the problems discussed. Its main aim is learning itself. Likewise, knowledge of Torah is not an aid to observance of law but an end in itself. This does not mean that the Talmud is not concerned with the values contained in the material studied. On the contrary, it is stated emphatically that he who studies Torah and does not observe what he studies would better never have been born. A true scholar serves as a living example by his way of life and conduct. But this is part of the general outlook of the Talmud; for the student poring over the text, study has no other end but knowledge. Every subject pertaining to Torah, or to life as related to Torah, is worthy of consideration and analysis, and an attempt is always made to delve into the heart of the matter. In the course of study, the question of whether these analyses are of practical use is never raised. We often encounter in the Talmud protracted and vehement debates on various problems that try to examine the structure of the method and to elucidate the conclusions deriving from it. The scholars invested all this effort despite the fact that they knew the source itself had been rejected and was of no legislative significance. This approach also explains why we find debates on problems that were relevant in the distant past and were unlikely ever to arise again.

It sometimes occurs, of course, that problems or debates once thought impractical or irrelevant gain practical significance in some later age. This is a familiar phenomenon in the sphere of pure science. But this development is of little consequence to the talmudic student, as, from the outset, his sole objective has been to solve theoretical problems and to seek the truth.

The Talmud is ostensibly constructed along the lines of a legal tract, and many people commit the error of thinking that it is legal in essence. It treats the subjects with which it deals—basic *balakhah,* biblical verses, or traditions handed down by sages—as natural phenomena, components of objective reality. When a man has dealings with nature, he cannot claim that the subject does not appeal to him or is unworthy of perusal. There are, of course, varying degrees of importance to issues, but all are alike in that they *are*—they exist and note must be paid to them. When the talmudic sage examined an ancient tradition, he perceived it, above all, as a reality in itself, and whether binding on him or not, it was part of his world and could not be dismissed. When the scholars discuss a rejected idea or source, their attitude resembles that of the scientist contemplating an organism that has become extinct because of its inability to adapt itself to changing conditions. This organism has, in a manner of speaking, "failed" and died out, but this fact does not detract from its interest for the scientist as a subject of study.

One of the greatest historical controversies was that between the methods of the "houses" (schools) of Shammai and Hillel, which lasted for more than a century. It was eventually resolved in the famous dictum: "Both are the words of the living God, and the decision is in accordance with the House of Hillel." The fact that one method is preferred does not mean that the other is based on a misconception. It, too, is an expression of creativity and of "the words of the living God." When one of the sages ventured to say a certain theory was not to his liking, he was scolded by his colleagues, who informed him that it was wrong to say of Torah, "This is good and this is not." Such a view is analogous to the case of the scientist who is not permitted to say that a certain creature seems to him "unappealing." This does not mean to imply that evaluations (even of appeal) should never be made; they should, however, be based on consciousness of the fact that no man has the right to judge or to determine that a certain object lacks beauty from the purely objective point of view.

This analogy between the natural world and Torah is ancient and was developed at length by the sages. One of its earliest expressions is the theory that just as an architect builds a house according to a blueprint, so the Holy One, Blessed be He, scanned his Torah in creating the world. According to this viewpoint, it follows that there must be a certain correlation between the world and Torah, the latter forming part of the essence of the natural world and not merely constituting external speculation on it. This way of thinking also engendered the view that no subject is too strange, remote, or bizarre to be studied.

The Talmud reflects so wide a range of interests because it is not a homogeneous work composed by a single author. When several people collaborate on a book, they have in mind a certain specific aim which lends the work character and direction. But the Talmud is the end result of the editing of the thoughts and sayings of many scholars over a long period, none of whom envisaged a final written work at the time. Their remarks were inspired by life, growing out of the problems submitted to them and the exchange of views between the various sages and their disciples. This is why we cannot discern a clear trend or a specific objective in the Talmud. Each debate is, to a large extent, independent of others and unique, and each subject is the focus of interest at the time it is being discussed. At the same time, the Talmud has an unmistakable and striking character of its own, which does not bear the imprint of an individual, or of the editors, but is collective, reflecting the quality of the Jewish people over a given period. Not only where the thousands of anonymous views are concerned, but also in cases where the identity of the author or proponent is known, the differences between individuals are blurred and the general spirit prevails. However violently two sages may differ, their shared traits and likemindedness must eventually become evident to the reader, who then discerns the overall unity that overcomes all differences.

Since the Talmud is concerned with subjects, ideas, and problems, there evolved over the centuries the custom of quoting various views in the present tense: "Abbaye says, Rabba says." This stylistic habit reflects the belief that the work is not merely a record of the opinions of the scholars of past ages, and it should not be judged by historical criteria. The talmudic sages themselves distinguished between personalities and periods (clarification of such questions is, in fact, an integral part of study), but the distinctions are only cited when strictly relevant and are not employed for evaluation and discussion. For these scholars time is not an everflowing stream in which the present always obliterates the past; it is understood organically as a living and developing essence, present and future being founded on the living past. Within this wide-ranging process, certain elements take on more stable form, while others, pertaining to the present, are flexible and much more changeable; the process as such, however, is based on faith in the vitality of each element, ancient as it may be, and the importance of its role in the never-ending, self-renewing work of creation.

This process of renewal is closely connected to the centrality of the query in the talmudic debate. To a certain extent, the entire Talmud is framed by questions and answers, and even when not explicitly formulated, questions constitute the background to every statement and interpretation. One of the most ancient methods of studying the Talmud attempted to reconstruct the question on the basis of the statement that served as a response. It is no coincidence that the Talmud contains so many words denoting questions, ranging from queries aimed at satisfying curiosity to questions that attempt to undermine the validity of the debated issue. The Talmud also differentiates between a fundamental query and a less basic inquiry, a question of principle and a marginal query. Voicing doubts is not only legitimate in the Talmud, it is essential to study. To a certain degree, the rule is that any type of query is permissible and even desirable; the more the merrier. No inquiry is regarded as unfair or incorrect as long as it pertains to the issue and can cast light on some aspect of it. This is true not only of the Talmud itself but also of the way in which it is studied and perused. After absorbing the basic material, the student is expected to pose questions to himself and to others and to voice doubts and reservations. From this point of view, the Talmud is perhaps the only sacred book in all of world culture that permits and even encourages the student to question it.

This characteristic leads us to another aspect of the composition and study of the Talmud. It is impossible to arrive at external knowledge of this work. Any description of its subject matter or study methods must, inevitably, be superficial because of the Talmud's unique nature. True knowledge can only be attained through spiritual communion, and the student must participate intellectually and emotionally in the talmudic debate, himself becoming, to a certain degree, a creator.

Jewish Mystical Tales

Howard Schwartz

Born and educated in St. Louis, Howard Schwartz (1945–) is a professor of English at the University of Missouri and a distinguished (and prolific) poet, essayist, translator, editor, and author of works of fiction. One rich source of his work is the Jewish tradition—particularly the mystical-Hasidic tradition—of story-telling. Schwartz variously collects and retells parables and folktales and fairy tales old and new. He has explained that he is of that largely assimilated generation of Jews in America who "looks back and cries, 'Look what you've lost! Look what you've traded away!'"
(Judaica Book News).

The stories that follow, drawn from Gabriel's Palace: Jewish Mystical Tales *(1993), are among those given new life by Schwartz. But he has seen to it that they have not lost that comfortable feeling of old tales polished by many tellings, time-honored and valued. Such is art.*

Schwartz's many titles include Gathering the Sparks: Poems 1965–1979, Midrashim: Collected Jewish Parables, Elijah's Violin and Other Jewish Fairy Tales, The Captive Soul of the Messiah: New Tales about Reb Nachman, *and* The Dream Assembly: Tales of Rabbi Zalman Schachter-Shalomi.

The Precious Prayer

Long ago, in the city of Safed in the land of Israel, there lived a great rabbi who was known as the Ari, which mean "the Lion." The Ari prayed with all his heart and all his soul, and his prayers were dear to God. In fact, there was only one other whose prayers were more precious. And one Yom Kippur God decided to reveal this other one, so that the Ari might understand what is precious to God in prayer.

While the Ari was praying in the synagogue, an angel came to him and whispered in his ear the existence of this one whose prayers had reached the highest heavens. The angel told him the name of the man, and the city in which he lived, which was Tiberias. And when Yom Kippur was over, the Ari went to that city to seek out that man. For he wanted to learn the secret of his praying.

When the Ari reached that city, he first looked for the man in the House of

Study. But he was not to be found among any of the men there. Then he sought him in the market. And there he was told that the only man by that name in Tiberias was a poor farmer who lived in the mountains.

So the Ari climbed into the mountains to find that man. When he reached his house, he was surprised to see that it was just a hut, for he was very poor. The poor farmer greeted him and invited the Ari to come in. And when they were together at last, the Ari did not waste any time. He asked the man to tell him the secret of his prayer. The man was very surprised by this, and said: "But, rabbi, I am afraid that I cannot pray. For I cannot read. All I know are the letters of the alphabet from Aleph to Yod."

The Ari was astonished to hear this, for had not the angel said that the prayers of this man were precious to God? Then the Ari said: "What did you do on Yom Kippur?" The man replied: "I went to the synagogue, of course. And when I saw how intently everyone around me was praying, my heart broke. And I began to recite all that I know of the alphabet. And I said in my heart: 'Dear God, take these letters and form them into prayers for me, that will rise up like the scent of hon-eysuckle. For that is the most beautiful scent that I know. And that is what I said with all my strength, over and over.'"

When the Ari heard this, he understood at once that God had sent him to learn that secret: that while man sees what is before his eyes, God looks into the heart. And that is why the prayers of the simple farmer were so precious. (Palestine: Six-teenth Century)

The Cottage of Candles

There once was a Jew who went out into the world to seek justice. He looked in the streets and the markets of cities but could not find it. He traveled to villages and he explored distant fields and farms, but still justice eluded him. At last he came to an immense forest, and he entered it, for he was certain that justice must exist some-where. He wandered there for many years and he saw many things—the hovels of the poorest peasants, the hideaways of thieves, and the huts of witches in the darkest part of the forest. And he stopped in each of these, despite the danger, and sought clues. But no one was able to help him in his quest.

One day, just as dusk was falling, he arrived at a small clay hut that looked as if it were about to collapse. Now there was something strange about this hut, for many flickering flames could be seen through the window. The man who sought justice wondered greatly about this and knocked on the door. There was no answer. He pushed the door open and entered.

Before him was a small room crowded with many shelves. And on the shelves were a multitude of lighted candles, burning oil. Together their flames seem to beat like wings, and the flickering light made him feel as if he were standing in the center of a quivering flame. He held up his hand, and it seemed to be surrounded with an aura, and all the candles were like a constellation of stars.

Stepping closer, he saw that some of the flames burned with a very pure fire, while others were dull, and still others were sputtering, about to go out. So too did he now notice that some of the wicks were in golden vessels, while others were in silver or marble ones, and many burned in simple vessels of clay or tin. These plain vessels had thin wicks, which burned quickly, while those made of gold or silver had wicks that lasted much longer.

While he stood there, marveling at that forest of candles, an old man in a white robe came out of one of the corners and said: "*Shalom Aleichem,* my son, what are you looking for?"

"*Aleichem Shalom,*" the man answered. "I have traveled everywhere searching for justice, but never have I seen anything like all these candles. Why are they burning?"

The old man spoke softly: "Know that these are soul-candles. Each candle is the soul of one of the living. As long as it burns, the person remains alive. But when the flame burns out, he departs from this life."

Then the man who sought justice turned to the old man and asked: "Can I see the candle of my soul?"

The old man led him into a corner and showed him a line of tins on a low shelf. He pointed out a small, rusty one that had very little oil left. The wick was smoking and had tilted to one side. "This is your soul," said the old man.

Then a great fear fell upon the man and he started to shiver. Could it be that the end of his life was so near and he did not know it?

Then the man noticed that next to his tin there was another, filled with oil. Its wick was straight, burning with a clear, pure light.

"And this one, who does it belong to?" asked the man, trembling. "That is a secret that cannot be revealed," answered the old man. "I only reveal each man's candle to himself alone."

Suddenly the old man vanished from sight, and the room seemed empty except for the candles burning on every shelf.

While the man stood there, he saw a candle on another shelf sputter and go out. For a moment there was a wisp of smoke rising in the air and then it was gone. One soul had just left the world.

The man's eyes returned to his own tin. He saw that only a few drops of oil remained, and he knew that the flame would soon burn out. At that instant he saw the candle of his neighbor, burning brightly, the tin full of oil.

All at once an evil thought entered his mind. He looked around and saw that no one else was in the room. The old man had disappeared. He looked closely in the corner from which he had come, and then in the other corners, but there was no sign of him there. At that moment he reached out and took hold of the full tin and raised it above his own. But suddenly a strong hand gripped his arm and the old man stood beside him.

"Is this the kind of justice you are seeking?" he asked. His grip was like iron, and the pain caused the man to close his eyes.

And when the fingers released him, he opened his eyes and saw that everything had disappeared: the old man, the cottage, the shelves and all the candles. And the man stood alone in the forest and heard the trees whispering his fate. (Eastern Europe: Oral Tradition)

Gabriel's Palace

In the city of Worms there is an ancient Torah inscribed on parchment of deerskin. It is said that this scroll was written by Rabbi Meir of Rottenberg, known as the Maharam, while he was imprisoned. No possession of the Jews of the city is more precious, for its origin was miraculous. Rabbi Meir had been libeled and cast into jail and a huge ransom of twenty thousand gold coins had been placed on his head. Nevertheless, the Jews of that generation decided to raise the sum. They sent a delegation to Rabbi Meir, but he rejected their offer, saying: "I regret to deprive you of the *mitzvah* of redeeming a captive. Still, I prefer to remain in prison rather than to encourage this kind of extortion. All I ask is that you bring me the tools of a scribe so that I may write down my thoughts about the Torah. For, as you know, I have been forbidden to have any books." With no other choice, the delegation respected his wishes, and saw to it that he received a scribe's quill, ink, and pieces of parchment.

So Rabbi Meir remained imprisoned, much to the disappointment of those who had expected to receive the ransom. And even though he had been deprived of every book, he had long since memorized not only the Torah, but both Talmuds, and many other holy texts as well, so that he lacked for nothing. Indeed, all that he truly needed was a scroll of the Torah to read on the Sabbath, since it is written that the Torah must be studied on that day from a text.

One Friday evening Rabbi Meir fell asleep, and while he slept his soul took wings and ascended on high. When he opened his eyes, he was blinded by a bright light. And when his eyes began to grow accustomed to that light, he found himself in a palace chamber, and there was a glowing figure standing before him, an angel. Just then the angel spoke and said: "Welcome, Rabbi Meir. I am the angel Gabriel, and you have ascended to my palace. The heavenly hosts are aware of how distressed you are, because you lack a scroll of the Torah. You have been brought here to receive one. This is one of the thirteen scrolls that Moses himself wrote before his death. One scroll was given to each of the twelve tribes, and the thirteenth was brought to the heavenly academy. This is that Torah. Now it is to remain with you. All that we ask is that you read loud enough that it can be heard here. For the sages on high will be listening to every word, since it is their Torah that you will be reading." And with awe and wonder Rabbi Meir received that celestial Torah from the arms of the angel Gabriel, and then he awoke.

When Rabbi Meir opened his eyes, it was the first crack of dawn. He looked around, still in a daze, and it was then that he saw the scroll of the Torah lying upon the table—and he knew that the dream had been true. Then Rabbi Meir washed and dressed and stood near the table, staring with amazement at the Torah that had been brought to him from on high. For a long time he did not dare to touch it, lest it all be a dream.

Then he began to recite the Sabbath prayers, and when the time came to read the weekly portion, the scroll of the Torah rolled open to the right place. And as Rabbi Meir began to read, the room filled with a holy light, and he felt the presence of all of the Tzaddikim on high. He read slowly and clearly, taking his time with every word. And he read loud enough that not even a single one would be lost. And when he finished reading, the scroll of the Torah rolled closed on its own, and the light vanished from the room.

So it was that Rabbi Meir lived in the presence of that sacred scroll, reading the Sabbath portion from it every week, and studying it night and day. And during that time he discovered many truths that could only be discerned by one who read in that celestial scroll.

One day it occurred to Rabbi Meir to copy that scroll of the Torah for the generations to come, for all of the other scrolls that Moses had written had been lost over the ages. So it was that every day he sat at the table transcribing every word from the sacred parchment, counting out every letter as if it were a golden coin. He worked on it for twelve months, and at last he completed transcribing it without a single error. And when he reread what he had written, he discovered that heaven had assisted him in creating a perfect replica of the celestial Torah.

The next morning, on waking, Rabbi Meir discovered that the scroll of Moses was gone, and he knew that Gabriel must have descended during the night to take it back. And Rabbi Meir knew that this meant that heaven had agreed that the Torah he had written was indeed perfect and would now serve as a model for the scribes of the future generations.

Now Rabbi Meir remained imprisoned for six more years. During that time he fashioned a wooden ark to hold the scroll of the Torah, and covered it with pitch to make it waterproof. When he felt the end of his life drawing near, he sealed the ark with the scroll inside it, and lowered it from his window into the Rhine River, and consigned it to its fate.

In the days that followed, the ark floated down the river until at last it approached the city of Worms. Some gentile fishermen tried to catch it in their nets, but it always eluded them. Word spread about this elusive box. It became the talk of the city, and many tried their luck at capturing it, but no one succeeded.

Among the Jews of the city there was also an intense debate about the box. Some said that it had a demon inside, while others insisted it was being guided by the Holy Spirit, which is why it eluded all the gentiles who had tried to ensnare it. At last the Jews decided to see if they would have any better luck. They rented a boat and set out near the last place where the box had been sighted. And sure enough, a current soon carried the box in their direction, and they were quickly able to pull it into the boat.

When they returned to shore, however, the gentile owner of the boat claimed the box as his own, since it was caught with his boat. The Jews were forced to give it up, but when the gentiles tried to take it out of the boat, they could not. Even when a dozen men tried to pick it up, they could not budge it an inch. At this they became frightened, and ran away. Then the Jews had no difficulty in lifting the box and carrying it into the synagogue. There they opened it with fear and trepidation. Inside they found the scroll of the Torah, inscribed on deerskin. And along with it was a message, also on parchment, from Rabbi Meir, giving it as a gift to the community of Worms.

When the Jews of the city learned of this miracle, they celebrated and gave thanks to God. And that Torah has remained there for many generations, guarding them from danger, and serving as a great blessing in their lives.

As for Rabbi Meir, he died in jail soon after he lowered the ark into the river, and his soul ascended directly to Gabriel's palace. There he made his home in the World to Come, serving every Sabbath as the reader of the celestial Torah that had been returned to its place in the ark on high. (Germany: Oral Tradition)

Rabbi Shimon's Escape

Among the prisoners of the Inquisition on the island of Majorca was Rabbi Shimon ben Duran. Many of his fellow Jews were also confined in that prison, where they were often tortured because they were unwilling to abandon their faith. At last they were condemned to death, for the inquisitors saw that they would never turn their back on the Torah.

As they awaited the day of execution, which was to take place in thirty days, Rabbi Shimon drew a ship on the wall of the jail. Now Rabbi Shimon had never been known as an artist, and the others marveled at his skill. For he drew every detail as if he had sailed for many years, while, as far as they knew, he had never set foot in a ship.

For three weeks, as the days until the date of the execution approached, his cell-mates watched him at work on the drawing. Once they asked him why he was so exacting, and he answered: "I intend to escape on this ship. Who among you would like to accompany me?" And all of them announced their readiness at once, for they knew that Rabbi Shimon was a master of miracles.

Before the drawing of the ship was completed, Rabbi Shimon added himself and all of the others, so that they could be seen standing on the deck, looking out to sea. Every prisoner recognized himself at once, for the resemblance was uncanny.

Then, on the very day of their execution, when they heard the keys of the soldiers turning in the lock, Rabbi Shimon told them it was time to go. And he turned to the ship and pronounced the Holy Name. At that instant all of them found themselves on the deck of a great ship in the middle of the ocean, sailing by itself to the beaches of North Africa. And, indeed, they were. (North Africa: Oral Tradition)

The Master Key

Once the Baal Shem Tov dreamed that he was walking outside his hut, and he saw that one of the trees that grew there had the shape of a shofar, twisting in and out of the earth, as if a giant ram's horn had taken root. The sight of that great shofar took the Baal Shem's breath away. And in the dream the Baal Shem gathered all of his Hasidim together by that tree, and told them to see who among them could sound it. So one by one they approached the mouth of that mighty shofar, but none of them could bring forth a single sound. At last Reb Wolf Kitzes approached it, and this time a deep and long-sustained blast came forth, like a voice from deep in the earth. And he only blew that one note, but it rose up into heaven.

When the Baal Shem awoke, he was still being borne by that long note, and he sighed because there was no such shofar in this world, only in the world of dreams.

The next day the Baal Shem called upon Wolf Kitzes and told him that he wanted to teach him the secret meanings of the blasts of the shofar, so that he could serve as the *Baal tekiah* for the High Holy Days. Of course Wolf Kitzes relished this chance to delve into the mysteries with the Besht. So it was that he learned, over many months, that every blast of the shofar is a branch of the Tree of Life, and that there are great powers residing in the shofar. So mighty is its blessing that a note blown with the right meaning and intensity could rise on a single breath all the way to the Throne of Glory.

Now Wolf Kitzes listened carefully to the words of the Baal Shem, and wrote down the secret meaning of each and every sound, so that he could remember it precisely as he blew on the shofar.

Then it happened that on the day of Rosh Hashanah, when he was about to blow on the shofar before the Ark for the first time, the notes with all the secret meanings vanished. He frantically searched for them everywhere, but to no avail.

Then, weeping bitter tears, he blew on the shofar with his broken heart, without concentrating on the secret meanings. And the sound of the shofar rose up in long and short blasts, and carried all of their prayers with it into the highest heavens. And everyone who heard him blow the shofar that day knew that for one moment heaven and earth had been brought together in the same place.

Afterward, the Baal Shem said to Wolf Kitzes: "In the palace of the king there are many chambers, and every one has a lock of its own. But the master key is a broken heart. When a man truly breaks his heart before the Holy One, blessed be He, he can pass through each and every gate." (Eastern Europe: Nineteenth Century)

The Cave of Mattathias

There once was a Hasid whose custom it was to take newly made oil from his village to the rabbi in the nearby city of Romanov, and the rabbi would light the first candle of Hanukah in his presence. One winter the land was covered with deep snow and few ventured out of their homes. But on the eve of Hanukah, the Hasid was still planning to deliver the oil. His family pleaded with him not to go, but he was determined, and in the end he set forth.

The moment he entered the forest that separated his village from Romanov, more snow began to fall. It soon covered every landmark, and when it finally stopped, the Hasid realized he was lost.

Now the Hasid began to regret not listening to his family. Surely the rabbi would have forgiven his absence. The wind rose, and the Hasid was so cold he feared he might freeze. Worse yet, if he died there in the forest, he might not be taken to a Jewish grave. That is when he remembered the oil he was carrying. In order to save his life, he would have to use it. There was no other choice.

His fingers were numb, but he managed to tear some of the lining out of his coat to make a wick. And he put that wick in the snow. Then he poured oil on it and prayed with great intensity. Finally he lit the first candle of Hanukah, and the flame seemed to light up the whole forest. And when the wild animals saw that light, they ran away and hid.

The exhausted Hasid lay down on the snow. He fell asleep and dreamed he was walking in a warm land, and before him he saw a great mountain, and next to that mountain he saw a palm tree. He dreamed there was a cave at the foot of that mountain and near its entrance a candle was burning. He picked up the candle, and it lit his way to a great cavern where he saw a man with a long white beard making wicks. There were bales of wicks piled high all around. The old man looked up and said: "Blessed be you in the Name of God."

The Hasid returned the old man's blessing and asked him who he was. "I am Mattathias, father of the Maccabees. During my lifetime I lit a big torch. I hoped that all of Israel would join me, but only a few obeyed my call. Now heaven has sent me to watch for the little candles in the houses of Israel to come together to form a very big flame. And that flame will announce the Redemption and the End of Days.

"Meanwhile, I prepare wicks for the day when everyone will contribute his candle to this great flame. And now, there is something you must do for me—when you reach the Rabbi of Romanov, tell him that the wicks are ready, and he should do whatever he can to light the flame that we have awaited so long."

Amazed at all he had heard, the Hasid promised to give the message to his the Rabbi. As he turned to leave the cave, he awoke, and found himself standing before the Rabbi's house. The Rabbi opened the door and his face was glowing. He said: "Now you know just how great is the power of lighting the Hanukah candles. Whoever dedicates his soul to this deed brings the time of Redemption that much closer." (Eastern Europe: Oral Tradition)

Holocaust

Emil L. Fackenheim

Emil L. Fackenheim has been called the philosopher of the Holocaust; he was nearly one of its victims. Born in 1916 in Germany, he was educated there and ordained a rabbi in Berlin in 1939. Fleeing the Nazis, he went to Canada in 1940 and received a doctorate in 1945 from the University of Toronto. He returned to that school to teach for over thirty years as a professor of philosophy. In 1983 he immigrated to Israel and was named a Fellow of the Institute of Contemporary Jewry at the Hebrew University of Jerusalem. His more recent books include To Mend the World *(1982),* What Is Judaism? *(1987), and* The Jewish Bible After the Holocaust *(1991).*

Deeply affected by the Holocaust, Fackenheim has written passionately and eloquently about it, as he does in the essay which follows. Elsewhere he has written that "Auschwitz is a unique descent into hell." He formulated the "614th commandment" (adding one, that is, to the 613 of the Torah): there must be no slackening of Jewish faith because that would be to grant Hitler a posthumous victory.

Holocaust is the term currently most widely employed for the persecution of the Jewish people by Nazi Germany from 1933 to 1945, first in Germany itself and subsequently in Nazi-occupied Europe, culminating in "extermination" camps and resulting in the murder of nearly six million Jews. However, the Hebrew term *Shoah* (total destruction) would be more fitting, since *Holocaust* also connotes "burnt sacrifice." It is true that, like ancient Moloch worshipers, German Nazis and their non-German henchmen at Auschwitz threw children into the flames alive. These were not, however, their own children, thrown in acts of sacrifice, but those of Jews, thrown in acts of murder.

Is the Holocaust unique? The concept *unprecedented* is preferable, as it refers to the same facts but avoids not only well-known difficulties about the concept of *uniqueness* but also the temptation of taking the event out of history and thus mystifying it.[1] To be sure, Auschwitz was "like another planet," in the words of "Katz-

---

1. See the warning voiced by Yehuda Bauer.

etnik 135683," the pen name of the novelist Yechiel Dinur, that is, a world of its own, with laws, modes of behavior, and even a language of its own. Even so, as *unprecedented,* rather than *unique,* it is placed firmly into history. Historians are obliged, so far as possible, to search for precedents; and thoughtful people, by no means historians only, are obliged to ask if the Holocaust itself may become a precedent for future processes, whether as yet only possible or already actual. Manès Sperber, for example, has written: "Encouraged by the way Hitler had practiced genocide without encountering resistance, the Arabs [in 1948] surged in upon the nascent Israeli nation to exterminate it and make themselves its immediate heirs."[2]

The most obvious recent precedent of the Holocaust is the Turkish genocide of the Armenians in World War I. Like the Nazi genocide of the Jews in World War II, this was an attempt to destroy a whole people, carried out under the cover of a war with maximum secrecy, and with the victims being deported to isolated places prior to their murder, all of which provoked few countermeasures or even verbal protests on the part of the civilized world. Doubtless the Nazis both learned from, and were encouraged by, the Armenian precedent.

But unlike the Armenian genocide, the Holocaust was intended, planned, and executed as the "final solution" of a "problem." Thus, whereas, for example, the roundup of Armenians in Istanbul, the very heart of the Turkish empire, was discontinued after a while, Nazi Germany, had it won the war or even managed to prolong it, would have succeeded in murdering every Jew. North American Indians have survived in reservations; Jewish reservations in a victorious Nazi Empire are inconceivable. Thus the Holocaust may be said to belong, with other catastrophes, to the species *genocide.* Within the species, defined as intended, planned, and largely executed extermination, it is without precedent and, thus far at least, without sequel. It is—here the term really must be employed—unique.

Equally unique are the means without which this project could not have been planned or carried out. These include: a scholastically precise definition of the victims; juridical procedures, enlisting the finest minds of the legal profession, aimed at the total elimination of the victims' rights; a technical apparatus, including murder trains and gas chambers, and, most importantly, a veritable army not only of actual murderers but also of witting and unwitting accomplices—clerks, lawyers, journalists, bank managers, army officers, railway conductors, entrepreneurs, and an endless list of others.

All these means and accomplices were required for the *how* of the "Final Solution." Its *why* required an army of historians, philosophers, and theologians. The historians rewrote history. The philosophers refuted the idea that mankind is human before it is Aryan or non-Aryan. And the theologians were divided into Christians who made Jesus into an Aryan and neo-pagans who rejected Christianity itself as non-Aryan. (Their differences were slight compared to their shared commitments.) Such were the shock troops of this army. Equally necessary, however, were its remaining troops: historians, philosophers, and theologians who knew differently but betrayed their calling by holding their peace.

What was the *why* of the Holocaust? Even the shock troops never quite faced it,

2. ... *Than a Tear in the Sea* (1967), p. xiii.

although they had no reason or excuse for not doing so. As early as 1936 Julius Streicher was on record to the effect that "who fights the Jew fights the devil," and "who masters the devil conquers heaven."[3] Streicher was only expressing more succinctly Hitler's assertion in *Mein Kampf* that "if the Jew will be victorious" in his cosmic struggle with mankind, his "crown" will be the "funeral wreath of humanity, and this planet will, as it did millions of years ago, move through the ether devoid of human beings."[4]

Planet Auschwitz was as good as Streicher's word. When the Third Reich was at the height of its power, the conquest of heaven seemed to lie in the apotheosis of the master race; even then, however, the mastery of the Jewish devil was a necessary condition of the conquest. When the Third Reich collapsed and the apocalypse was at hand, Planet Auschwitz continued to operate until the end, and Hitler's last will and testament made the fight against the Jewish people mandatory for future generations. The mastery of the Jewish devil, it seems, had become the sufficient condition for the "conquest of heaven," if indeed not identical with it.

To be sure, this advent of salvation in the Auschwitz gas chambers was but for relatively few eyes to see. What could be heard by all, however, was the promise of it years earlier, when the streets of Germany resounded to the stormtroopers' hymn: "When Jewish blood spurts from our knives, our well-being will redouble."

Never before in history had a state attempted to make a whole country—indeed, as in this case, a whole continent—*rein* (free) of every member of a whole people, man, woman, and child. Never have attempts resembling the Holocaust been pursued with methods so thorough and with such unswerving goal-directedness. It is difficult to imagine, and impossible to believe that, this having happened, world history can ever be the same. The Holocaust is not only an unprecedented event. It is also of an unfathomable magnitude. It is world historical.

As a world-historical event, the Holocaust poses new problems for philosophical thought. To begin with reflections on historiography, if, by near-common philosophical consent, to explain an event historically is to show how it was possible, then, to the philosopher, the Holocaust historian emerges sooner or later as asserting the possibility of the Holocaust solely because it was actual. He thus exposes the historian's explanation as being, in fact, circular. This impasse, to be sure, is often evaded, most obviously when, as in many histories of World War II, the Holocaust is relegated to a few footnotes. An impasse is even explicitly denied when, as in Marxist ideological history, Nazism-equals-facism-equals-the-last-stage-of-capitalism, or when, as in liberalistic ideological history, the Holocaust is flattened out into man's-inhumanity-to-man-especially-in-wartime. (Arnold Toynbee, for example, considered that "what the Nazis did was nothing peculiar."[5]) The philosopher, however, must penetrate beyond these evasions and ideological distortions. And when such a philosopher finds a solid historian who states, correctly enough, that "the extermination grew out of the biologistic insanity of Nazi ideology, and for

3. Quoted in *The Yellow Spot: The Extermination of the Jews in Germany* (1936), p. 47.

4. Hitler, *Mein Kampf*, translated by R. Manheim (1943), p. 60.

5. In a debate with Yaacov Herzog. See Yaacov Herzog, *A People That Dwells Alone* (1975), p. 31.

that reason is completely unlike the terrors of revolutions and wars of the past,"[6] he must ponder whether "biologistic insanity" has explanatory force or is rather a metaphor whose chief significance is that explanation has come to an end. As he ponders this, he may well be led to wonder "whether even in a thousand years people will understand Hitler, Auschwitz, Maidanek, and Treblinka better than we do now. . . . Posterity may understand it even less than we do."[7]

Such questions turn philosophical thought from methodological to substantive issues, and above all to the subject of man. Premodern philosophy was prepared to posit a permanent human nature that was unaffected by historical change. More deeply immersed in the varieties and vicissitudes of history, modern philosophy generally has perceived, in abstraction from historical change, only a human condition, which was considered permanent only insofar as beyond it was the humanly impossible. At Auschwitz, however, "more was real than is possible,"[8] and the impossible was done by some and suffered by others. Thus, prior to the Holocaust, the human condition, while including the necessity of dying, was seen as also including at least one inalienable freedom—that of each individual's dying his own death.[9] "With the administrative murder of millions" in the death camps, however, "death has become something that was never to be feared in this way before. . . . The individual is robbed of the last and poorest that until then still remained his own. In the camps it was no longer the individual that died; he was made into a specimen."[10]

As well as a new way of dying, the Auschwitz administrators also manufactured a new way of living. Prior to the Holocaust no aspect of the human condition could make so strong a claim to permanency as the distinction between life and death, between still-being-here and being-no-more. The Holocaust, however, produced the *Muselmann* (Muslim; pl., *Musclmänner)*—camp slang for a prisoner near death—the skin-and-bone walking corpse, or living dead, the vast "anonymous mass, continuously renewed and always identical, of non-men who march and labor in silence, the divine spark dead within them, already too empty really to suffer. One hesitates to call them living. One hesitates to call their death death."[11] The *Muselmann* may be called the most truly original contribution of the Third Reich to civilization.

From these new ways of being human—those of the victims—philosophical thought is turned to another new way of being human, that of the victimizers. Philosophy has all along been acquainted with the quasi-evil of sadism (a mere sickness), the semievil of moral weakness, the superficial evil of ignorance, and even—hardest to understand and, therefore, often ignored or denied—the radical or

6. K. D. Bracher, *The German Dictatorship* (1971), p. 430.

7. Isaac Deutscher, *The Non-Jewish Jew* (1968), pp. 163 ff.

8. A statement by Hans Jonas, made to Ernst Simon as reported in the latter's "Revisionist History of the Jewish Catastrophe," *Judaism* 12, no. 4 (Summer 1963): 395.

9. See especially Martin Heidegger's *Sein und Zeit* (1935), section II, chap. 1.

10. Theodor Adorno, *Negative Dialektik* (1966), pp. 354 ff.

11. Primo Levi, *Survival in Auschwitz,* translated by Stuart Woolf (1959), p. 82.

demonic evil that is done and celebrated for its own sake. Prior to the Holocaust, however, it was unacquainted with the "banality of evil"[12] practiced by numberless individuals who, having been ordinary or even respected citizens, committed at Auschwitz crimes on a scale previously unimaginable, only to become, in the Holocaust's aftermath, ordinary and respectable once more—without showing signs of any moral anguish.

The evil banal by dint not of the nature of the crimes but of the people who committed them: these, it is said, were made to do what they did by the system. This, however, is only half a philosophical thought, for who made the system—conceived, planned, created, perpetuated, and escalated it—if not such as Himmler and Eichmann, Stangl and Hoess, to say nothing of the unknown-soldier-become-S.S.-murderer? Already having difficulty with radical or demonic evil, philosophical thought is driven by the "banal" evil of the Holocaust from the operators to the system, and from the system back to the operators. In this circular movement, to be sure, banal evil, except for ceasing to be banal, does not become intelligible. Yet the effort to understand is not without result, for from it the Holocaust emerges as a world or, rather, as the antiworld par excellence. The human condition does not dwell in a vacuum. It "always-already-is" within a world, that is, within a structured whole that exists at all because it is geared to life and that is structured because it is governed by laws of life. Innocent so long as they obey the law, the inhabitants of a world have a right to life, and forfeit it, if at all, only by an act of will—the breach of the law. The Holocaust anti-world, while structured, is governed by a law of death. For some—Jews—existence itself was a capital crime (a hitherto unheard-of proposition) and the sole *raison d'être* of the others was to mete out their punishment. In this world, the degradation, torture, and eventual murder of some human beings at the hands of others was not a by-product of, or means to, some higher, more ultimate purpose. They were its whole essence.

Modern philosophers, we have said previously, were able to conceive of a human condition because not all things were considered humanly possible. Even so, some of their number, possibly with modern history in mind, have not hesitated to ascribe to man a "perfectibility" that is infinite. Auschwitz exacts a new concession from future philosophy: whether or not man is infinitely perfectible, he is in any case infinitely depravable. The Holocaust is not only a world-historical event. It is also a "watershed,"[13] or "caesura,"[14] or "rupture"[15] in man's history on earth.

Is the Holocaust a rupture in the sight of theology? This question requires a separate inquiry. Theology, to be sure, at least if it is Jewish or Christian, is bound up with history. But it can be, and has been, argued that this is a *Heilgeschichte* immune to all merely secular historical events. Thus, for Franz Rosenzweig nothing crucial could happen for Jews between Sinai and the Messianic days. And for

12. See, e.g., Hannah Arendt, *Eichmann in Jerusalem: A Report on the Banality of Evil* (1977), passim.

13. Franklin Littell, *The Crucifixion of the Jews* (1975), passim.

14. Arthur A. Cohen, *The Tremendum* (1981), passim.

15. Emil L. Fackenheim, *To Mend the World: Foundations of Future Jewish Thought* (1982), passim.

Karl Barth it was "always Good Friday *after* Easter," the implication being that the crucial saving event of Christianity has already occurred and is unassailable ever after.

Is the Holocaust a rupture for Christianity? German Christians, and possibly Christians as a whole, "can no longer speak evangelically to Jews."[16] They cannot "get behind" Auschwitz; they can get "beyond it" if at all only "in company with the victims," and this latter only if they identify with the State of Israel as being a Jewish "house against death" and the "last Jewish refuge."[17] Christians must relate "positively" to Jews, not "despite" Jewish nonacceptance of the Christ but "because" of it.[18] Even to go only this far and no further with their theologians (it seems fitting here to cite only German theologians) is for Christians to recognize a post-Holocaust rupture in their faith, for the step demanded—renunciation of Christian missions to the Jews, as such and in principle—is, within Christian history, unprecedented. (Of the Christian theologians who find it necessary to go much further A. Roy Eckardt is, perhaps, the most theologically oriented.) To refuse even this one step, that is, for Christians to stay with the idea of mission to the Jews in principle, even if suspending it altogether in practice, is either to ignore the Holocaust, or else sooner or later to reach some such view as that mission to the Jews "is the sole possibility of a genuine and meaningful restitution *(Wiedergutmachung)* on the part of German Christendom."[19] Can Christians view such a stance as other than a theological obscenity? The Jewish stance toward Christian missionizing attempts directed at them, in any case, cannot be what it once was. Prior to the Holocaust, Jews could respect such attempts, although of course considering them misguided. After the Holocaust, they can only view them as trying in one way what Hitler undertook in another.

It would seem, then, that for Christians Good Friday can no longer be *always* after Easter. As for Jews, was the Holocaust a crucial event, occurring though it did between Sinai and the Messianic days? Franz Rosenzweig's Jewish truth, it emerges in our time, was a truth not of Judaism but of *Galut* (exile) Judaism only, albeit its most profound modern statement. *Galut* Judaism, however, has ceased to be tenable.

Galut Judaism may be characterized as follows:

1. A Jew can appease or bribe, hide or flee from an enemy and, having succeeded, can thank God for having been saved.
2. When *in extremis* such salvation is impossible, when death can be averted only through apostasy, he can still choose death, thus becoming a martyr; and then he is secure in the knowledge that, while no Jew should seek death,

---

16. Dietrich Bonhoeffer as quoted in *The German Church Struggle and the Holocaust,* Franklin H. Littell and Hubert G. Locke, eds. (1974), p. 288.

17. Johann Baptist Metz in *Gott Nach Auschwitz* (1979), pp. 124 ff., 139 ff.

18. H. H. Henrix, F. M. Marquardt, M. Stoehr, all in personal conversation with this writer. The formulation is Henrix's.

19. The German Lutheran theologian Martin Wittenberg, as quoted in *Auschwitz als Herausforderung für Juden und Christen,* G. B. Ginzel, ed. (1980), p. 566.

kiddush ha-Shem (sanctifying God's name by dying for it) is the highest stage of which he can be worthy.[20]

3. Exile, though painful, is bearable, for it is meaningful, whether its meaning consists in punishment for Jewish sins, vicarious suffering for the sins of others, or whether it is simply inscrutable, a meaning known only to God.

4. *Galut* will not last forever. If not he himself or even his children's children, at any rate some Jews' distant offspring will live to see the Messianic end.

These are the chief conditions and commitments of *Galut* Judaism. Existing in the conditions and armed by the commitments, a Jew in past centuries was able to survive the poverty of the eastern European ghetto; the slander, ideologically embellished and embroidered, of anti-Semitism in modern Germany and France; the medieval expulsions; the Roman Emperor Hadrian's attempt once and for all to extirpate the Jewish faith; and, of course, the fateful destruction of the Jerusalem Temple in 70 C.E., to which *Galut* Judaism was the normative and epoch-making response. All these *Galut* Judaism was able to survive. The Holocaust, however, already shown by us to be unprecedented simply as an historical event, is unprecedented also as a threat to the Jewish faith, and *Galut* Judaism is unable to meet it.

1. The Holocaust was not a gigantic pogrom from which one could hide until the visitation of the drunken Cossacks had passed. This enemy was coldly sober, systematic rather than haphazard; except for the lucky few, there was no hiding.

2. The Holocaust was not a vast expulsion, causing to arise the necessity, but also the possibility, of once again resorting to wandering, with the Torah as "portable fatherland."[21] Even when the Third Reich was still satisfied with expelling Jews there was, except for the fortunate or prescient, no place to go; and when the Reich became dissatisfied with mere expulsions, a place of refuge, had such been available, would have been beyond reach.

3. The Holocaust was not an assault calling for bribing or appeasing the enemy. This enemy was an "idealist" who could not be bribed, and he remained unappeasable until the last Jew's death.

4. The Holocaust was not a challenge to Jewish martyrdom but, on the contrary, an attempt to destroy martyrdom forever. Hadrian had decreed death for the crime of practicing Judaism and thereby inspired the martyrdom of such as Rabbi Akiva, which in turn inspired countless Jewish generations. Hitler, like Hadrian, sought to destroy Jews but, unlike Hadrian, was too cunning to repeat the ancient emperor's folly. He decreed death for Jews, not for doing or even believing, but rather for being—for the crime of possessing Jewish ancestors. Thus, Jewish martyrdom was made irrelevant. Moreover, no effort was spared to make martyrdom impossible as well, and the supreme effort in this direction was the manufacture of *Muselmänner*. A martyr

---

20. See Maimonides in his *Responsum on Martyrdom.*

21. A celebrated and much-quoted dictum by the German Jewish poet Heinrich Heine.

chooses to die; as regards the *Muselmänner*, "one hesitates to call them living. One hesitates to call their death death."[22]

It cannot be stressed enough that, despite these unprecedented, super-human efforts to murder Jewish martyrdom, countless, nameless Akivas managed to sanctify God's name by choosing how to die, even though robbed of the choice of whether to die; their memory must have a special sacredness to God and man. Such memory is abused, however, if it is used to blot out, minimize, or even divert attention from the death of the children as yet unable to choose and the death of the *Muselmänner* who could choose no more.

That these four *nova* have made *Galut* Judaism untenable has found admirable expression in an ancient midrash that was originally intended to expound the then-new form of Judaism. In this midrash God, at the beginning of the great exile initiated by the destruction of the Temple in 70 C.E., exacts three oaths, one from the Gentiles and two from the Jews. The Gentiles are made to swear not to persecute the Jews, now stateless and helpless, excessively. The Jews are made to swear not to resist their persecutors, and not to "climb the wall," that is, prematurely to return to Jerusalem.

But what, one must ask, if not Auschwitz, is "excessive persecution"? In response, some have said that the Jews broke their oath by climbing the wall, that is, by committing the sin of Zionism, and that in consequence God at Auschwitz released the Gentiles from obligation. Any such attempt to save *Galut* Judaism, however, reflects mere desperation, for it lapses into two blasphemies: toward the innocent children and the guiltless *Muselmänner*, and toward a God who is pictured as deliberately, callously, consigning them to their fate. There remains, therefore, only a bold and forthright taking leave from *Galut* Judaism. It was the Gentiles at Auschwitz who broke their oath, and the Jews in consequence are now released from theirs.

A "post-*Galut*" Judaism is, unmistakably, in the making in our time. Its most obvious aspects are that "resisting" the persecutors and "climbing the wall" have become not only rights but also ineluctable duties. After the Holocaust, Jews owe anti-Semites, as well as, of course, their own children, the duty of not encouraging murderous instincts by their own powerlessness. And after the absolute homelessness of the twelve Nazi years that were equal to a thousand, they owe the whole world, as well as, of course, their own children, the duty to say no to Jewish wandering, to return home, to rebuild a Jewish state.

These aspects of the Judaism in the making are moral and political. Their inner source is spiritual and religious. In the Warsaw ghetto Rabbi Isaac Nissenbaum, a famous and respected orthodox rabbi, made the statement—much quoted by Jews of all persuasions in their desperate efforts to defend, preserve, and hallow Jewish life against an enemy sworn to destroy it all—that this was a time not for *kiddush ha-Shem* (martyrdom) but rather for *kiddush ha-hayyim* (the sanctification of life). It is a time for *kiddush ha-hayyim* still. The Jewish people have passed through the Nazi antiworld of death; thereafter, by any standard, religious or secular, Jewish life

22. See above, note 11.

ranks higher than Jewish death, even if it is for the sake of the divine name. The Jewish people have experienced exile in a form more horrendous than ever dreamt of by the apocalyptic imagination; thereafter, to have ended exile bespeaks a fidelity and a will to live that, taken together, give a new dimension to piety. The product of this fidelity—the Jewish state—is fragile still, and embattled wherever the world is hostile or does not understand. Yet Jews both religious and secular know in their hearts that Israel—the renewed people, the reborn language, the replanted land, the rebuilt city, the state itself—is a new and unique celebration of life. There are many reasons why Israel has become the center of the Jewish people in our time; not least is that it is indispensable to a future Judaism. If a Jewish state had not arisen in the wake of the Holocaust, it would be a religious necessity—although, one fears, a political near-impossibility—to create it now.

Further Reading

The torrent of books about the Jews and Judaism requires special guides, and one of the best is *The Book of Jewish Books: A Reader's Guide to Judaism* (1986) by Ruth S. Frank and William Wollheim. The listings are under twelve headings ("History," "Holocaust," "Women," etc.), and each title is amply annotated.

Rabbi Joseph Telushkin, *Jewish Literacy: The Most Important Things to Know About the Jewish Religion, Its People, and Its History* (1991). The 346 entries average two pages in length and are written with care and style. This is much more than a collection of facts and figures.

Elie Wiesel spent part of his youth in the camps at Auschwitz and Buchenwald: his autobiographical *Night* (1964) is an unforgettable account of that experience. For another eyewitness, see Primo Levi, *Survival in Auschwitz* (originally *If This Is a Man,* 1947) and *The Drowned and the Saved* (1988), his last book before his suicide. Hugh Nissenson wrote of Levi, "He is our Dante."

Herman Wouk, *This Is My God* (rev. ed., 1970). The best-selling author of fiction (*The Caine Mutiny, Marjorie Morningstar, The Winds of War*) here turns to his own Orthodox faith and describes it with great feeling.

Herbert Weiner's *9 1/2 Mystics: The Kabbala Today* (1969) is a wonderful introduction to the difficult subject of Jewish mysticism. Gershon Scholem is an outstanding scholar of the topic: see his *Major Trends in Jewish Mysticism* (3d ed., 1954).

Cecil Roth's *A History of the Jews: From Earliest Times to the Six-Day War* (rev. ed., 1970) combines scholarship and readability and is widely regarded as one of the best one-volume histories.

Judah Goldin, *The Living Talmud* (1957). Selections from the Talmud, which he describes as not only a vast body of commentary on the Law, but also "legends, folklore, . . . theosophical and theological speculation, homilies, parables, prayers, gnomic sayings, historical reminiscence."

Nathan Glazer, *American Judaism* (rev. ed., 1972). A volume in the prestigious History of American Civilization Series from the University of Chicago Press.

VIII

CHRISTIANITY
Taking Up the Cross

In the Cross is salvation, in the Cross is life. . . . Take up therefore thy Cross and
follow Jesus: and thou shalt go into life eternal.

Thomas à Kempis

There is really just one topic for the student of Christianity: the life and teaching of
Jesus of Nazareth—a life and teaching that have been the subject of centuries of
loving study, extraordinary research, and contentious disputation, too. It is that last
matter that must concern us for a moment. Along with its great themes of love and
forgiveness and redemption, there has been acrimonious debate and worse about
who Jesus was and what he asked of humankind.

It will shock no one to read that Christians do not all agree on what it means to
be a Christian. Every other street corner church in America is testimony to the
diversity of Christian thought in this country alone. In a great number of cases,
moreover, Christians believe that the differences among them are important differences. It is a postulate of Christianity that it is the one true religion, from which it
follows (in the minds of many Christians) that there must be one true understanding of that religion: Episcopalians and Baptists and Methodists cannot all be on the
right path. From the earliest centuries of the Christian era, creeds have been formulated—the Nicene, Athanasian, and others—in attempts to define correct belief
(and heresy). Wars have been fought, inquisitions have been conducted, and heretics have been burned at the stake.

One possible reason for the many schools of Christian thought lies within the
New Testament. Jesus wrote nothing; the New Testament is the primary source of
information about Jesus, and it is an anthology—a gathering of materials by a variety of authors writing at different times and places and with diverse purposes in
mind.[1] Matthew, Mark, and Luke are "major theologians in their own right, with
viewpoints every bit as distinctive as those of John and Paul," Norman Perrin has
written. Thus the New Testament itself

---

1. Some Christian conservatives will protest this position immediately, saying that the New Testament speaks clearly and consistently in one voice.

311

represents the whole spectrum of possibilities of what it means to be a Christian in the world, and either anticipates or inspires every subsequent development within the Christian churches. The Roman Catholic and the Lutheran, the liberal protestant and the fundamentalist, the contemplative mystic and the apocalyptic visionary, all find themselves at home in one part or another of this collection from the literature of the earliest Christianity.[2]

The first reading selection in the following pages is a summary outline of five major ways of interpreting Christianity, all based (if Perrin is correct) on the New Testament.

What all this comes down to, for present purposes, is the rather commonplace observation that Christianity has been many different things to different people. The approach to Christianity in this chapter, accordingly, will be to present authors from the past and present who represent some of the those varied streams of Christian experience. Following some excerpts from the New Testament (drawn from each of the four Gospels, three of Paul's Letters, and the Letter of James) are the great Bishop of Hippo, St. Augustine; the Danish existentialist Christian Søren Kierkegaard; the liberal Christian scholar John Hick; the Catholic contemplative Thomas Merton; and the American poet Rita Dove.

One of the concerns of Augustine's *Confessions,* written in the last years of the fourth century, is the story of a lost soul—Augustine himself—finding its way back to God. It is the classic pilgrimage of the sinner seeking redemption.

Rigorously and sternly Protestant, Søren Kierkegaard spent his brief life grappling with the challenge of becoming an authentic Christian. That goal was for him absolutely crucial ("Christianity is the frightful earnestness that your eternity is decided in this life"), and it was an almost unbearably difficult undertaking. "To be a Christian," he wrote, "is the most appalling of all agonies." He was infuriated by those around him who contentedly accepted an easy, watered-down Christianity. Kierkegaard said that they were merely "playing at Christianity," and he thought that kind of hypocrisy so unspeakably vile that it should not even be listed with the other heresies.

John Hick, in a phrase not designed to please everyone, explains that though he began as a very conservative Christian, "I have grown out of that": he became a decidedly liberal Christian. A conservative like C. S. Lewis, for example, states that when "Christianity differs from other religions, Christianity is right and they are wrong."[3] Hick, in contrast, declines even to claim that Christianity provides "a better framework for the religious life than is provided by Rabbinic Judaism, or Islam, or Hinduism. . . . "

Thomas Merton, a Trappist monk—a contemplative—has the unusual distinction of being the best-known monk in the world. In his "New Seeds of Contemplation" he describes contemplation, a spiritual practice to which he was himself com-

---

2. *The New Testament: An Introduction* (New York: Harcourt Brace Jovanovich, 1974), pp. v, 19.

3. *Mere Christianity* (London: Fontana Books, 1952), p. 39.

mitted and which he considered the focal point of his life. It was also the subject of his last book, *Contemplative Prayer.*

Rita Dove, in her essay "On the Road to Damascus," writes of being in a villa in Italy and of vivid childhood memories of an African Methodist Episcopal Zion church in Ohio. Along the way there emerges the figure of the apostle Paul, around whom gravitate Dove's reflections on doubt and the mystery of grace.

Ways of Being Religious in the New Testament

Norman Perrin

Born in England in 1920, Norman Perrin served in the Royal Air Force during the years of World War II and then went to the University of Manchester for his undergraduate degree. Ordained a Baptist minister, he briefly served churches in London and South Wales before returning to school for a Bachelor of Divinity degree from the University of London. At the University of Gottingen he earned a Doctor of Theology degree, and in 1956 he came to the United States to teach at Emory University. His last position was with the University of Chicago as professor of the New Testament. He died in 1976.

Among his honors was a Guggenheim memorial scholarship; his best-known book is Rediscovering the Teaching of Jesus. *The present reading selection is drawn from his* The New Testament: An Introduction.

———————

No one can read the New Testament without being impressed by its immense variety, and especially by the variety of ways of being religious it exhibits. Although the New Testament is a unity in that all of its books accept the centrality of Jesus Christ, nonetheless it is diverse in that both the understanding of Jesus as the Christ and the understanding of what it means to accept him as the Christ are almost infinitely varied. What is more, the variations are such as almost to run the gamut of ways of being religious in the world. Ascetic and mystic, warrior priest and worker priest, apocalyptic visionary and social revolutionary, ecclesiastical dignitary and street-corner pamphleteer—all these and many more have taken their inspiration from the New Testament or from some part of it. . . .

Apocalypticism

The Christian movement began as an apocalyptic sect and apocalypticism is a major element in the synoptic gospel source Q,[1] in the gospel of Mark and, of

1. *Editor's note:* The gospels of Matthew and Luke have material common to both which is worded so similarly that it is believed by many scholars that Matthew and Luke must have had the same source: hence Q, for the German *Quelle,* "a source."

course, in the book of Revelation, itself an apocalypse. The apocalyptic visionary is one caught up in the drama of a history hurrying to its close, preparing himself for the imminent future in which all will be different. Christian apocalypticism developed the concept of Jesus as the Son of Man, the powerful redeemer who would descend to the earth on the clouds of heaven to judge and redeem, destroy and remake. But it did more than that, because not only was Jesus the Son of Man; the Son of Man was Jesus. That meant that characteristics of the redeemer figure were always subject to the control of the lineaments of Jesus. (So the evangelist Mark was able to blend together the elements of power and authority and the necessity of suffering.) In many respects, Christian apocalyptic was indistinguishable from Jewish, and certainly Christian apocalyptic writers made extensive use of Jewish apocalyptic literature. But the central feature of their visions was always Jesus. Nonetheless, the movement was apocalyptic, with its sense of a world being caught up in the throes of catastrophic change and its belief in the imminence of the final intervention of God that would make all things new and different. Like all apocalypticists, the Christian apocalypticist despaired of the world and its history but had faith in God who was about to change it. As a Christian he believed that Jesus would be the means of that change, and he prepared himself for the imminent coming of Jesus as Son of Man by obeying the teaching that was given in the name of Jesus.

The Apostle Paul

"For the good that I would I do not: but the evil that I would not, that I do" (Rom 7:19, KJV). With this cry from the heart of religious humanity we reach one of the classical options of New Testament religion—Paul and his search for justification. Haunted by the sense of stain, of guilt, of defilement, Paul searches for the means of cleansing, of expiation, of redemption, and he finds it in Christ and his cross. That which he could not do for himself, that which the Law could not help him to do, Christ has done for him. He can now stand in the presence of God, from which presence he would before have had to flee, for he now bears not his own righteousness but Christ's. He now lives in the world not the life of guilt and fear but of freedom and power, and this life is Christ's gift to him. Here we recognize a classical form of the Christian experience of religious reality. It is the quest for justification in the sight of God, and the discovery that it can be received only as a gift. Central to this understanding is a concentration on the cross of Christ, interpreting it as a means of reconciling man to God. This understanding of religion is loaded with the symbolism of evil and focuses attention on the means whereby that evil is overcome and a quality of life free from it can be known.

The Evangelist Matthew

With the evangelist Matthew we reach another of the classical options of New Testament religion. Here the central point is the concept of a verbal revelation authoritatively interpreted. The essence of religion is obedience to the revealed truth, and such obedience is possible because the world and life are ordered by the God who has revealed this truth to man. There is order and stability to be experienced; there is the firm basis of a revealed truth on which to build; there are appointed means both to make possible the necessary understanding and also to help attain the necessary level of obedience. These means are present in the church, in the structure and organization of the community of which the individual is a member and in which the risen and glorified Christ is present. In this understanding of what it means to be religious in the world the essential elements are those of revelation and of obedience to revelation, and the conviction that there is a correspondence between the revealed truth and the experienced reality of life in the world such that life in the world can be successfully organized on the basis of obedience to the revelation, and only on that basis.

The Author of Luke–Acts

The author of Luke–Acts is also concerned with revelation but with revelation in the form of a sacred person and a sacred time, and with a structured means of relating to that time. That person is Jesus and his time is that between the descent of the Spirit upon him at his baptism and the return of the Spirit to the Father at the cross. One relates to him and to his time by means of the Spirit, which returned to the church and the believer at the baptism of Pentecost. In his own life Jesus was a paradigm of the possibilities for human existence in the world and the model of what it means to be religious in the world. The presence of the spirit of Jesus in the world, linking the believer with the sacred life and sacred time of Jesus, empowers the believer to exhibit the same quality of life in the world that Jesus did. This is borne out by the heroes of the church whose lives paralleled Jesus' in many respects. To be religious in the world is to imitate Jesus, an imitation made possible by the presence and work of his spirit in the world. To imitate Jesus means to care for the outcast, to concern oneself for the neighbor, to live the life of love in the world and for the world.

The Evangelist John

In the case of the evangelist John we have a concentration on the cross of Christ almost as strong as that in the case of the apostle Paul. In John, however, the context is not the symbolism of evil but rather the symbolism of glory. The Christ of John's gospel is the descending/ascending redeemer, and the cross is the moment of his glorious return whence he came—having achieved that for which he was sent. While the cross itself is the moment of supreme glorification, there is a series of earlier majestic "signs" by means of which the Christ also manifests his glory. Moreover, a series of solemn discourses explores the glory of this Christ by using primary symbols of life-giving power—water, light, bread—and by claiming explicitly that he gives life and "eternal life" to those who believe in him. Further, he does the Father's work; he is at one with God. Combined with this emphasis on glory and power and on the Christ's oneness with God is an emphasis on the concern of the Christ for the believer—for example, by the use of shepherd and sheep symbolism—and on the believer's oneness with him.

This last point is the key to the Johannine understanding of what it means to be religious in the world. The believer contemplates the glorious majesty of the Christ and of the Christ's oneness with the Father, and then finds himself at one with the Christ in a mystical union by means of which he experiences the life of love in the world. But the emphasis now is on the rapture of love as experienced in the world through knowledge of Christ, whereas in Luke–Acts the emphasis is on the manifestation of love in human relationships. Of course, neither excludes the other (see 1 John 1:9–11), but the emphasis is different.

The gospel and letters of John are the charter of Christian mysticism.

The Other Ways

There are other understandings of what it means to be religious in the world in the New Testament, but they are all variations, sometimes very important variations, on the themes we have already established. So, for example, the gospel of Mark reshapes the apocalyptic way of being religious in the world by systematizing the apocalyptic drama, by developing the theme of the Son of Man who "must" suffer, and by showing what these things mean to faith and discipleship. Similarly, the writers of the period of "emergent Catholicism" develop, systematize—and further institutionalize—the "way" of the gospel of Matthew. But we have said enough, we believe, to indicate something of the classical options the New Testament presents.

Selections, *The New Testament*
New Revised Standard Version

The New Revised Standard Version (1989) of the New Testament is a revision of the Revised Standard Version (1952), which, as its title announces, was itself a revision of still earlier revisions going back to the King James Version of 1611. The first revision of the King James Version appeared in 1613.

The King James Version, the most familiar and beloved of all English versions, came to be called the Authorized Version (which sounds like Divine sanction but had only to do with King James I authorizing its publication in England). The King James Version was, in its turn, based upon still earlier English versions, notably that of William Tyndale. It is estimated that 80 percent of the King James Version retained Tyndale's phraseology.*

The work of the translators of the Bible goes on continuously for three reasons. First, our own language changes constantly; the meanings and connotations of words do not sit still. Second, the work of recovering the Greek and Hebrew texts of the Old and New Testaments is an ongoing project. There is no original "first edition" of either Testament. The earliest complete New Testament dates from the fourth century; there are fragments from the second and third centuries. Third, more is learned all the time about the Greek and Hebrew languages of the Bible as linguistic and philological studies advance. Discoveries of ancient manuscripts, such as those of the Nag Hammadi Library (1945) and the Dead Sea Scrolls (1947), are of tremendous importance: found among the Dead Sea Scrolls, for example, were copies in Hebrew of almost all of the books of the Old Testament—copies perhaps a thousand years older than anything previously held.

Thus it is that the more recent translations of the Bible, if based upon current scholarship, are to be preferred if one is looking for accuracy of translation.**

Matthew

5 When Jesus saw the crowds, he went up the mountain; and after he sat down, his disciples came to him. [2]Then he began to speak, and taught them, saying:

---

*Tyndale (1484–1536) did his work of translation in spite of the disapproval of Church and civil authorities. He was eventually convicted of heresy and was accordingly strangled and then burned at the stake.

**Not all new editions of the Bible are new translations. Anyone can rewrite the Bible into "modern English" without knowing a word of Greek or Hebrew.

3 "Blessed are the poor in spirit, for theirs is the kingdom of heaven.

4 "Blessed are those who mourn, for they will be comforted.

5 "Blessed are the meek, for they will inherit the earth.

6 "Blessed are those who hunger and thirst for righteousness, for they will be filled.

7 "Blessed are the merciful, for they will receive mercy.

8 "Blessed are the pure in heart, for they will see God.

9 "Blessed are the peacemakers, for they will be called children of God.

10 "Blessed are those who are persecuted for righteousness' sake, for theirs is the kingdom of heaven.

11 "Blessed are you when people revile you and persecute you and utter all kinds of evil against you falsely on my account. [12]Rejoice and be glad, for your reward is great in heaven, for in the same way they persecuted the prophets who were before you.

13 "You are the salt of the earth; but if salt has lost its taste, how can its saltiness be restored? It is no longer good for anything, but is thrown out and trampled under foot.

14 "You are the light of the world. A city built on a hill cannot be hid. [15]No one after lighting a lamp puts it under the bushel basket, but on the lampstand, and it gives light to all in the house. [16]In the same way, let your light shine before others, so that they may see your good works and give glory to your Father in heaven.

17 "Do not think that I have come to abolish the law or the prophets; I have come not to abolish but to fulfill. [18]For truly I tell you, until heaven and earth pass away, not one letter, not one stroke of a letter, will pass from the law until all is accomplished. [19]Therefore, whoever breaks one of the least of these commandments, and teaches others to do the same, will be called least in the kingdom of heaven; but whoever does them and teaches them will be called great in the kingdom of heaven. [20]For I tell you, unless your righteousness exceeds that of the scribes and Pharisees, you will never enter the kingdom of heaven.

21 "You have heard that it was said to those of ancient times, 'You shall not murder'; and 'whoever murders shall be liable to judgement.' [22]But I say to you that if you are angry with a brother or sister, you will be liable to judgment; and if you insult a brother or sister, you will be liable to the council; and if you say, 'You fool,' you will be liable to the hell of fire. [23]So when you are offering your gift at the altar, if you remember that your brother or sister has something against you, [24]leave your gift there before the altar and go; first be reconciled to your brother or sister, and then come and offer your gift. [25]Come to terms quickly with your accuser while you are on the way to court with him, or your accuser may hand you over to the judge, and the judge to the guard, and you will be thrown into prison. [26]Truly I tell you, you will never get out until you have paid the last penny.

27 "You have heard that it was said, 'You shall not commit adultery.' [28]But I say to you that everyone who looks at a woman with lust has already committed adultery with her in his heart. [29]If your right eye causes you to sin, tear it out and throw it away; it is better for you to lose one of your members than for your whole body to be thrown into hell. [30]And if your right hand causes you to sin, cut if off and throw it away; it is better for you to lose one of your members than for your whole body to go into hell.

31 "It was also said, 'Whoever divorces his wife, let him give her a certificate of divorce.' ³²But I say to you that anyone who divorces his wife, except on the ground of unchastity, causes her to commit adultery; and whoever marries a divorced woman commits adultery.

33 "Again, you have heard that it was said to those of ancient times, 'You shall not swear falsely, but carry out the vows you have made to the Lord.' ³⁴But I say to you, Do not swear at all, either by heaven, for it is the throne of God, ³⁵or by the earth, for it is his footstool, or by Jerusalem, for it is the city of the great King. ³⁶And do not swear by your head, for you cannot make one hair white or black. ³⁷Let your word be 'Yes, Yes' or 'No, No'; anything more than this comes from the evil one.

38 "You have heard that it was said, 'An eye for an eye and a tooth for a tooth.' ³⁹But I say to you, Do not resist an evildoer. But if anyone strikes you on the right cheek, turn the other also; ⁴⁰and if anyone wants to sue you and take your coat, give your cloak as well; ⁴¹and if anyone forces you to go one mile, go also the second mile. ⁴²Give to everyone who begs from you, and do not refuse anyone who wants to borrow from you.

43 "You have heard that it was said, 'You shall love your neighbor and hate your enemy.' ⁴⁴But I say to you, Love your enemies and pray for those who persecute you, ⁴⁵so that you may be children of your Father in heaven; for he makes his sun rise on the evil and on the good, and sends rain on the righteous and on the unrighteous. ⁴⁶For if you love those who love you, what reward do you have? Do not even the tax collectors do the same? ⁴⁷And if you greet only your brothers and sisters, what more are you doing than others? Do not even the Gentiles do the same? ⁴⁸Be perfect, therefore, as your heavenly Father is perfect.

6 "Beware of practicing your piety before others in order to be seen by them; for then you have no reward from your Father in heaven.

2 "So whenever you give alms, do not sound a trumpet before you, as the hypocrites do in the synagogues and in the streets, so that they may be praised by others. Truly I tell you, they have received their reward. ³But when you give alms, do not let your left hand know what your right hand is doing, ⁴so that your alms may be done in secret; and your Father who sees in secret will reward you.

5 "And whenever you pray, do not be like the hypocrites; for they love to stand and pray in the synagogues and at the street corners, so that they may be seen by others. Truly I tell you, they have received their reward. ⁶But whenever you pray, go into your room and shut the door and pray to your Father who is in secret; and your Father who sees in secret will reward you.

7 "When you are praying, do not heap up empty phrases as the Gentiles do; for they think that they will be heard because of their many words. ⁸Do not be like them, for your Father knows what you need before you ask him.

9 Pray then in this way:
Our Father in heaven,
    hallowed be your name.
¹⁰Your kingdom come.
Your will be done,
    on earth as it is in heaven.
¹¹Give us this day our daily bread.

¹²And forgive us our debts,
    as we also have forgiven our debtors.
¹³And do not bring us to the time of trial
    but rescue us from the evil one.

¹⁴For if you forgive others their trespasses, your heavenly Father will also forgive you; ¹⁵but if you do not forgive others, neither will your Father forgive your trespasses.

16 "And whenever you fast, do not look dismal, like the hypocrites, for they disfigure their faces so as to show others that they are fasting. Truly I tell you, they have received their reward. ¹⁷But when you fast, put oil on your head and wash your face, ¹⁸so that your fasting may be seen not by others but by your Father who is in secret; and your Father who sees in secret will reward you.

19 "Do not store up for yourselves treasures on earth, where moth and rust consume and where thieves break in and steal; ²⁰but store up for yourselves treasures in heaven, where neither moth nor rust consumes and where thieves do not break in and steal. ²¹For where your treasure is, there your heart will be also.

22 "The eye is the lamp of the body. So, if your eye is healthy, your whole body will be full of light; ²³but if your eye is unhealthy, your whole body will be full of darkness. If then the light in you is darkness. If then the light in you is darkness, how great is the darkness!

24 "No one can serve two masters; for a slave will either hate the one and love the other, or be devoted to the one and despise the other. You cannot serve God and wealth.

25 "Therefore I tell you, do not worry about your life, what you will eat or what you will drink, or about your body, what you will wear. Is not life more than food, and the body more than clothing? ²⁶Look at the birds of the air, they neither sow nor reap nor gather into barns, and yet your heavenly Father feeds them. Are you not of more value than they? ²⁷And can any of you by worrying add a single hour to your span of life? ²⁸And why do you worry about clothing? Consider the lilies of the field, how they grow; they neither toil nor spin, ²⁹yet I tell you, even Solomon in all his glory was not clothed like one of these. ³⁰But if God so clothes the grass of the field, which is alive today and tomorrow is thrown into the oven, will he not much more clothe you—you of little faith? ³¹Therefore do not worry, saying, 'What will we eat?' or 'What will we drink?' or 'What will we wear?' ³²For it is the Gentiles who strive for all these things; and indeed your heavenly Father knows that you need all these things. ³³But strive first for the kingdom of God and his righteousness, and all these things will be given to you as well.

34 "So do not worry about tomorrow, for tomorrow will bring worries of its own. Today's trouble is enough for today.

7 "Do not judge, so that you may not be judged. ²For with the judgment you make you will be judged, and the measure you give will be the measure you get. ³Why do you see the speck in your neighbor's eye, but do not notice the log in your own eye? ⁴Or how can you say to your neighbor, 'Let me take the speack out of your eye,'

while the log is in your own eye? [5]You hypocrite, first take the log out of your own eye, and then you will see clearly to take the speck out of your neighbor's eye.

6 "Do not give what is holy to dogs; and do not throw your pearls before swine, or they will trample them under foot and turn and maul you.

7 "Ask, and it will be given you; search, and you will find; knock, and the door will be opened for you. [8]For everyone who asks receives, and everyone who searches finds, and for everyone who knocks, the door will be opened. [9]Is there anyone among you who, if your child asks for bread, will give a stone? [10]Or if the child asks for a fish, will give a snake? [11]If you then, who are evil, know how to give good gifts to your children, how much more will your Father in heaven give good things to those who ask him!

12 "In everything do to others as you would have them do to you; for this is the law and the prophets.

13 "Enter through the narrow gate; for the gate is wide and the road is easy that leads to destruction, and there are many who take it. [14]For the gate is narrow and the road is hard that leads to life, and there are few who find it.

15 "Beware of false prophets, who come to you in sheep's clothing but inwardly are ravenous wolves. [16]You will know them by their fruits. Are grapes gathered from thorns, or figs from thistles? [17]In the same way, every good tree bears good fruit, but the bad tree bears bad fruit. [18]A good tree cannot bear bad fruit, nor can a bad tree bear good fruit. [19]Every tree that does not bear good fruit is cut down and thrown into the fire. [20]Thus you will know them by their fruits.

21 "Not everyone who says to me, 'Lord, Lord,' will enter the kingdom of heaven, but only the one who does the will of my Father in heaven. [23]On that day many will say to me, 'Lord, Lord, did we not prophesy in your name, and cast out demons in your name, and do many deeds of power in your name?' [23]Then I will declare to them, 'I never knew you; go away from me, you evil-doers.'

24 "Everyone then who hears these words of mine and acts on them will be like a wise man who built his house on rock. [25]The rain fell, the floods came, and the winds blew and beat on that house, but it did not fall, because it had been founded on rock. [26]And everyone who hears these words of mine and does not act on them will be like a foolish man who built his house on sand. [27]The rain fell, and the floods came, and the winds blew and beat against that house, and it fell—and great was its fall!"

28 Now when Jesus had finished saying these things, the crowds were astounded at his teaching, [29]for he taught them as one having authority, and not as their scribes.

Mark

10:17–27 17 As he was setting out on a journey, a man ran up and knelt before him, and asked him, "Good Teacher, what must I do to inherit eternal life?" [18]Jesus said to him, "Why do you call me good? No one is good but God alone. [19]You know the commandments: 'You shall not murder; You shall not commit adultery; You shall not steal; You shall not bear false witness; You shall not defraud; Honor your father and mother.'" [20]He said to him, "Teacher, I have kept all these since my youth." ²¹Jesus, looking at him, loved him and said, "You lack one thing; go, sell what you own, and give the money to the poor, and you will have treasure in heaven; then come, follow me." ²²When he heard this, he was shocked and went away grieving, for he had many possessions.

23 Then Jesus looked around and said to his disciples, "How hard it will be for those who have wealth to enter the kingdom of God!" ²⁴And the disciples were perplexed at these words. But Jesus said to them again, "Children, how hard it is to enter the kingdom of God! ²⁵It is easier for a camel to go through the eye of a needle than for someone who is rich to enter the kingdom of God." ²⁶They were greatly astounded and said to one another, "Then who can be saved?" ²⁷Jesus looked at them and said, "For mortals it is impossible, but not for God; for God all things are possible."

12:28–34 28 One of the scribes came near and heard them disputing with one another, and seeing that he answered them well, he asked him, "Which commandment is the first of all?" ²⁹Jesus answered, "The first is, 'Hear, O Israel: the Lord our God, the Lord is one; ³⁰you shall love the Lord your God with all your heart, and with all your soul, and with all your mind, and with all your strength.' ³¹The second is this, 'You shall love your neighbor as yourself.' There is no other commandment greater than these." ³²Then the scribe said to him, "You are right, Teacher; you have truly said that 'he is one, and besides him there is no other'; ³³and 'to love him with all the heart, and with all the understanding, and with all the strength', and 'to love one's neighbor as oneself,'—this is much more important than all whole burnt offerings and sacrifices." ³⁴When Jesus saw that he answered wisely, he said to him, "You are not far from the kingdom of God." After that no one dared to ask him any question.

Luke

10:25–37 25 Just then a lawyer stood up to test Jesus." "Teacher," he said, "what must I do to inherit eternal life?" ²⁶He said to him, "What is written in the law? What do you read there?" ²⁷He answered, "You shall love the Lord your God with all your heart, and with all your soul, and with all your strength, and with all your mind; and your neighbor as yourself." ²⁸And he said to him, "You have given the right answer; do this, and you will live."

29 But wanting to justify himself, he asked Jesus, "And who is my neighbor?" ³⁰Jesus replied, "A man was going down from Jerusalem to Jericho, and fell into the hands of robbers, who stripped him, beat him, and went away, leaving him half dead. ³¹Now by chance a priest was going down that road; and when he saw him, he passed by on the other side. ³²So likewise a Levite, when he came to the place and saw him, passed by on the other side. ³³But a Samaritan while traveling came near him; and when he saw him, he was moved with pity. ³⁴He went to him and bandaged his wounds, having poured oil and wine on them. Then he put him on his own animal, brought him to an inn, and took care of him. ³⁵The next day he took out two denarii, gave them to the innkeeper, and said, 'Take care of him; and

when I come back, I will repay you whatever more you spend.' ³⁶Which of these three, do you think, was a neighbor to the man who fell into the hands of the robbers?" ³⁷He said, "The one who showed him mercy." Jesus said to him, "Go and do likewise."

John

1 In the beginning was the Word, and the Word was with God, and the Word was God. ²He was in the beginning with God. ³All things came into being through him, and without him not one thing came into being. 'What has come into being ⁴in him was life, and the life was the light of all people. ⁵The light shines in the darkness, and the darkness did not overcome it.

6 There was a man sent from God, whose name was John. ⁷He came as a witness to testify to the light, so that all might believe through him. ⁸He himself was not the light, but he came to testify to the light. ⁹The true light, which enlightens everyone, was coming into the world.

10 He was in the world, and the world came into being through him; yet the world did not know him. ¹¹He came to what was his own and his own people did not accept him. ¹²But to all who received him, who believed in his name, he gave power to become children of God, ¹³who were born, not of blood or of the will of the flesh or of the will of man, but of God.

14 And the Word became flesh and lived among us, and we have seen his glory, the glory as of a father's only son, full of grace and truth. ¹⁵(John testified to him and cried out, "This was he of whom I said, 'He who comes after me ranks ahead of me because he was before me.'") ¹⁶From his fullness we have all received, grace upon grace. ¹⁷The law indeed was given through Moses; grace and truth came through Jesus Christ. ¹⁸No one has ever seen God. It is God the only Son who is close to the Father's heart, who has made him known.

Romans

3:21–28 21 But now, apart from law, the righteousness of God has been disclosed, and is attested by the law and the prophets, ²²the righteousness of God through faith in Jesus Christ for all who believe. For there is no distinction, ²³since all have sinned and fall short of the glory of God; ²⁴they are now justified by his grace as a gift, through the redemption that is in Christ Jesus, ²⁵whom God put forward as a sacrifice of atonement by his blood, effective through faith. He did this to show his righteousness, because in his divine forbearance he had passed over the sins previously committed; ²⁶it was to prove at the present time that he himself is righteous and that he justifies the one who has faith in Jesus.

27 Then what becomes of boasting? It is excluded. By what law? By that of works? No, but by the law of faith. ²⁸For we hold that a person is justified by faith apart from works prescribed by the law.

1 Corinthians

1:18–31 18 For the message about the cross is foolishness to those who are perishing, but to us who are being saved it is the power of God. [19]For it is written,

> "I will destroy the wisdom of the wise
> and the discernment of the discerning I will thwart."

[20]Where is the one who is wise? Where is the scribe? Where is the debater of this age? Has not God made foolish the wisdom of the world? [21]For since, in the wisdom of God, the world did not know God through wisdom, God decided, through the foolishness of our proclamation, to save those who believe. [22]For Jews demand signs and Greeks desire wisdom, [21]but we proclaim Christ crucified, a stumbling block to Jews and foolishness to Gentiles, [24]but to those who are the called, both Jews and Greeks, Christ the power of God and the wisdom of God. [25]For God's foolishness is wiser than human wisdom, and God's weakness is stronger than human strength.

26 Consider your own call, brothers and sisters not many of you were wise by human standards not many were powerful, not many were of noble birth. [27]But God chose what is foolish in the world to shame the wise; God chose what is weak in the world to shame the strong; [28]God chose what is low and despised in the world, things that are not, to reduce to nothing things that are, [29]so that no one might boast in the presence of God. [30]He is the source of your life in Christ Jesus, who became for us wisdom from God, and righteousness and sanctification and redemption, [31]in order that, as it is written, "Let the one who boasts, boast in the Lord."

. . .

13 If I speak in the tongues of mortals and of angels, but do not have love, I am a noisy gong or a clanging cymbal. [2]And if I have prophetic powers, and understand all mysteries and all knowledge, and if I have all faith, so as to remove mountains, but do not have love, I am nothing. [3]If I give away all my possessions, and if I hand over my body so that I may boast, but do not have love, I gain nothing.

4 Love is patient; love is kind; love is not envious or boastful or arrogant [5]or rude. It does not insist on its own way; it is not irritable or resentful; [6]it does not rejoice in wrongdoing, but rejoices in the truth. [7]It bears all things, believes all things, hopes all things, endures all things.

8 Love never ends. But as for prophecies, they will come to an end; as for tongues, they will cease; as for knowledge, it will come to an end. [9]For we know only in part, and we prophesy only in part; [10]but when the complete comes, the partial will come to an end. [11]When I was a child, I spoke like a child, I thought like a child, I reasoned like a child; when I became an adult, I put an end to childish ways. [12]For now we see in a mirror, dimly, but then we will see face to face. Now I know only in part; then I will know fully, even as I have been fully known. [13]And now faith, hope, and love abide, these three; and the greatest of these is love.

. . .

15 Now I would remind you, brothers and sisters, of the good news that I proclaimed to you, which you in turn received, in which also you stand, [2]through which also you are being saved, if you hold firmly to the message that I proclaimed to you—unless you have come to believe in vain.

3 For I handed on to you as of first importance what I in turn had received: that Christ died for our sins in accordance with the scriptures, ⁴and that he was buried, and that he was raised on the third day in accordance with the scriptures, ⁵and that he appeared to Cephas, then to the twelve. ⁶Then he appeared to more than five hundred brothers and sisters at one time, most of whom are still alive, though some have died. ⁷Then he appeared to James, then to all the apostles. ⁸Last of all, as to one untimely born, he appeared also to me. ⁹For I am the least of the apostles, unfit to be called an apostle, because I persecuted the church of God. ¹⁰But by the grace of God I am what I am, and his grace toward me has not been in vain. On the contrary, I worked harder than any of them—though it was not I, but the grace of God that is with me. ¹¹Whether then it was I or they, so we proclaim and so you have come to believe.

12 Now if Christ is proclaimed as raised from the dead, how can some of you say there is not resurrection of the dead? ¹³If there is no resurrection of the dead, then Christ has not been raised; ¹⁴and if Christ has not been raised, then our proclamation has been in vain and your faith has been in vain. ¹⁵We are even found to be misrepresenting God, because we testified of God that he raised Christ—whom he did not raise if it is true that the dead are not raised. ¹⁶For if the dead are not raised, then Christ has not been raised. ¹⁷If Christ has not been raised, your faith is futile and you are still in your sins. ¹⁸Then those also who have died in Christ have perished. ¹⁹If for this life only we have hoped in Christ, we are of all people most to be pitied.

Ephesians

2 You were dead through the trespasses and sins ²in which you once lived, following the course of this world, following the ruler of the power of the air, the spirit that is now at work among those who are disobedient. ³All of us once lived among them in the passions of our flesh, following the desires of flesh and senses, and we were by nature children of wrath, like everyone else. ⁴But God, who is rich in mercy, out of the great love with which he loved us ⁵even when we were dead through our trespasses, made us alive together with Christ—by grace you have been saved—⁶and raised us up with him and seated us with him in the heavenly places in Christ Jesus, ⁷so that in the ages to come he might show the immeasurable riches of his grace in kindness toward us in Christ Jesus. ⁸For by grace you have been saved through faith, and this is not your own doing; it is the gift of God—⁹not the result of works, so that no one may boast. ¹⁰For we are what he has made us, created in Christ Jesus for good works, which God prepared beforehand to be our way of life.

James

2:14–26 14 What good is it, my brothers and sisters, if you say you have faith but do not have works? Can faith save you? ¹⁵If a brother or sister is naked and lacks daily food, [16]and one of you says to them, "Go in peace; keep warm and eat your fill," and yet you do not supply their bodily needs, what is the good of that? [17]So faith by itself, if it has no works, is dead.

18 But someone will say, "You have faith and I have works." Show me your faith apart from your works, and I by my works will show you my faith. [19]You believe that God is one; you do well. Even the demons believe—and shudder. [20]Do you want to be shown, you senseless person, that faith apart from works is barren? [21]Was not our ancestor Abraham justified by works when he offered his son Isaac on the altar? [22]You see that faith was active along with his works, and faith was brought to completion by the works. [23]Thus the scripture was fulfilled that says, "Abraham believed God, and it was reckoned to him as righteousness," and he was called the friend of God. [24]You see that a person is justified by works and not by faith alone. [25]Likewise, was not Rahab the prostitute also justified by works when she welcomed the messengers and sent them out by another road? [26]For just as the body without the spirit is dead, so faith without works is also dead.

Selections, *The Confessions*

St. Augustine

It has been observed by others that the painters of the Middle Ages chose the perfect image when they portrayed Augustine with his heart in flames. One need read only a few pages of The Confessions *to grow conscious of that heart: Augustine was aflame with moral concern, with faith, and with intellect, too, if the metaphor will hold. He was the first great Christian philosopher and the greatest until the thirteenth century and Thomas Aquinas.*

Augustine was born in Tagaste, North Africa, in 354 c.e., of a nonreligious father and a Christian mother. After much soul-searching and moral anguish, he was converted to Christianity in 386. He became Bishop of Hippo and before his death in 430 had completed a body of work that left an indelible impression on Christianity. He brought together diverse strands of Classical and Hellenistic thought and wove them into Christian fabric. He placed vital emphasis on the role of the Church, but he also stressed faith *in the life of the individual Christian, and through it all there was his abiding moral sense.*

BOOK II

i

I intend to remind myself of my past foulnesses and carnal corruptions, not because I love them but so that I may love you, my God. It is from love of your love that I make the act of recollection. The recalling of my wicked ways is bitter in my memory, but I do it so that you may be sweet to me, a sweetness touched by no deception, a sweetness serene and content. You gathered me together from the state of disintegration in which I had been fruitlessly divided. I turned from unity in you to be lost in multiplicity.

At one time in adolescence I was burning to find satisfaction in hellish pleasures. I ran wild in the shadowy jungle of erotic adventures. "My beauty wasted away and

Reprinted from St. Augustine's *Confessions,* translated by Henry Chadwick, by permission of Oxford University Press. Copyright © 1991 Henry Chadwick.

in your sight I became putrid" (Dan. 10: 8), by pleasing myself and by being ambitious to win human approval.

ii

The single desire that dominated my search for delight was simply to love and to be loved. But no restraint was imposed by the exchange of mind with mind, which marks the brightly lit pathway of friendship. Clouds of muddy carnal concupiscence filled the air. The bubbling impulses of puberty befogged and obscured my heart so that it could not see the difference between love's serenity and lust's darkness. Confusion of the two things boiled within me. It seized hold of my youthful weakness sweeping me through the precipitous rocks of desire to submerge me in a whirlpool of vice. Your wrath was heavy upon me and I was unaware of it. I had become deafened by the clanking chain of my mortal condition, the penalty of my pride. I travelled very far from you, and you did not stop me. I was tossed about and spilt, scattered and boiled dry in my fornications. And you were silent. How slow I was to find my joy! At that time you said nothing, and I travelled much further away from you into more and more sterile things productive of unhappiness, proud in my self-pity, incapable of rest in my exhaustion.

. . .

BOOK III

i

I came to Carthage and all around me hissed a cauldron of illicit loves. As yet I had never been in love and I longed to love; and from a subconscious poverty of mind I hated the thought of being less inwardly destitute. I sought an object for my love; I was in love with love, and I hated safety and a path free of snares (Wisd. 14: II; Ps. 90: 3).[1] My hunger was internal, deprived of inward food, that is of you yourself, my God. But that was not the kind of hunger I felt. I was without any desire for incorruptible nourishment, not because I was replete with it, but the emptier I was, the more unappetizing such food became. So my soul was in rotten health. In an ulcerous condition it thrust itself to outward things, miserably avid to be scratched by contact with the world of the senses. Yet physical things had no soul. Love lay outside their range. To me it was sweet to love and to be loved, the more so if I could also enjoy the body of the beloved. I therefore polluted the spring water of friendship with the filth of concupiscence. I muddied its clear stream by the hell of lust, and yet, though foul and immoral, in my excessive vanity, I used to carry on in the manner of an elegant man about town. I rushed headlong into love, by which I was

1. *Translator's note:* References are to Augustine's Latin Bible, so that from Psalm 10 to 148 the reader must add one to find the corresponding passage in an English Bible.

longing to be captured. "My God, my mercy" (Ps. 58: 18) in your goodness you mixed in much vinegar with that sweetness. My love was returned and in secret I attained the joy that enchains. I was glad to be in bondage, tied with troublesome chains, with the result that I was flogged with the red-hot iron rods of jealousy, suspicion, fear, anger, and contention.

. . .

xi

"You put forth your hand from on high" (Ps. 143: 7), and from this deep darkness "you delivered my soul" (Ps. 85: 13). For my mother, your faithful servant, wept for me before you more than mothers weep when lamenting their dead children. By the "faith and spiritual discernment" (Gal. 5: 5) which she had from you, she perceived the death which held me, and you heard her, Lord. You heard her and did not despise her tears which poured forth to wet the ground under her eyes in every place where she prayed. You heard her. Hence she was granted the dream by which you encouraged her to allow me to live with her and to have me at the same table in the house. She had begun by refusing me, in her revulsion from and detestation of the blasphemies of my error. Her vision was of herself standing on a rule made of wood. A young man came to her, handsome, cheerful, and smiling to her at a time when she was sad and "crushed with grief" (Lam. I: 13). He asked her the reasons why she was downcast and daily in floods of tears—the question being intended, as is usual in such visions, to teach her rather than to learn the answer. She had replied that she mourned my perdition. He then told her to have no anxiety and exhorted her to direct her attention and to see that where she was, there was I also. When she looked, she saw me standing beside her on the same rule. How could this vision come to her unless "your ears were close to her heart" (Ps. 9B: 38/10A: 17)? You are good and all-powerful, caring for each one of us as though the only one in your care, and yet for all as for each individual.

Moreover, what was the source of the fact that when she had recounted the vision to me, I tried to twist its meaning to signify that she should not despair of becoming what I was? But she instantly replied, without a moment's hesitation: "The word spoken to me was not 'Where he is, there will you be also,' but 'Where you are, there will he be also.'" I confess to you Lord that to the best of my memory (and it is a matter which I have frequently discussed) I was more moved by your answer through my vigilant mother than by the dream itself. My misinterpretation seemed very plausible. She was not disturbed and quickly saw what was there to be seen, and what I certainly had not seen before she spoke. By the dream the joy of this devout woman, to be fulfilled much later, was predicted many years in advance to give consolation at this time in her anxiety. For almost nine years then followed during which I was "in the deep mire" (Ps. 68: 3) and darkness of falsehood. Despite my frequent efforts to climb out of it, I was the more heavily plunged back into the filth and wallowed in it. During this time this chaste, devout, and sober widow, one of the kind you love, already cheered by hope but no less constant in prayer and weeping, never ceased her hours of prayer to lament about me to you. Her "prayer entered into your presence" (Ps. 87: 3). Nevertheless you still let me go on turning over and over again in that darkness.

. . .

BOOK IV

i

During this same period of nine years, from my nineteenth to my twenty-eighth year, our life was one of being seduced and seducing, being deceived and deceiving (2 Tim. 3: 13), in a variety of desires. Publicly I was a teacher of the arts which they call liberal,[2] privately I professed a false religion—in the former role arrogant, in the latter superstitious, in everything vain. On the one side we pursued the empty glory of popularity, ambitious for the applause of the audience at the theatre when entering for verse competitions to win a garland of mere grass, concerned with the follies of public entertainments and unrestrained lusts. On the other side, we sought to purge ourselves of that filth by supplying food to those whose title was the Elect and Holy, so that in the workshop of their stomach they could manufacture for us angels and gods to bring us liberation. This was how my life was spent, and these were the activities of myself and my friends who had been deceived through me and with me.

Proud people may laugh at me. As yet they have not themselves been prostrated and brought low for their soul's health by you, my God. But I shall nevertheless confess to you my shame, since it is for your praise (Ps. 105: 47). Allow me, I pray you, grant me leave to run through my memory, as it is in the present, of the past twistings of my mistaken life and to sacrifice to you "a victim of jubilation" (Ps. 26: 6). Without you, what am I to myself but a guide to my own self-destruction? When all is well with me, what am I but an infant sucking your milk and feeding on you, "the food that is incorruptible" (John 6: 27)? What is a human being (name anyone you may please) when he is merely a man? So let the mighty and powerful laugh at our expense. In our weakness and indigence (Ps. 73: 21), we may make our confession to you.

ii

In those years I used to teach the art of rhetoric. Overcome by greed myself, I used to sell the eloquence that would overcome an opponent. Nevertheless, Lord, as you know (Ps. 68: 6), I preferred to have virtuous students (virtuous as they are commonly called). Without any resort to a trick I taught them the tricks of rhetoric, not that they should use them against the life of an innocent man, but that sometimes they might save the life of a guilty person. God, from far off you saw me falling about on slippery ground and in the midst of much smoke (Isa. 42: 3) discerned the

---

2. Literature, rhetoric and dialectic, leading on to the mathematical studies of arithmetic, geometry, music, and astronomy; called 'liberal' because they were the mark of a cultivated gentleman.

spark of my integrity which in my teaching office I manifested to people who 'loved vanity and sought after a lie' (Ps. 4: 3).

In those years I had a woman. She was not my partner in what is called lawful marriage. I had found her in my state of wandering desire and lack of prudence. Nevertheless, she was the only girl for me, and I was faithful to her. With her I learnt by direct experience how wide a difference there is between the partnership of marriage entered into for the sake of having a family and the mutual consent of those whose love is a matter of physical sex, and for whom the birth of a child is contrary to their intention—even though, if offspring arrive, they compel their parents to love them.

.   .   .

BOOK VIII

vii

. . . Many years of my life had passed by—about twelve—since in my nineteenth year I had read Cicero's *Hortensius,* and had been stirred to a zeal for wisdom. But although I came to despise earthly success, I put off giving time to the quest for wisdom. For "it is not the discovery but the mere search for wisdom which should be preferred even to the discovery of treasures and to ruling over nations and to the physical delights available to me at a nod." But I was an unhappy young man, wretched as at the beginning of my adolescence when I prayed you for chastity and said: "Grant me chastity and continence, but not yet." I was afraid you might hear my prayer quickly, and that you might too rapidly heal me of the disease of lust which I preferred to satisfy rather than suppress. I had gone along "evil ways" (Ecclus. 2: 10) with a sacrilegious superstition, not indeed because I felt sure of its truth but because I preferred it to the alternatives, which I did not investigate in a devout spirit but opposed in an attitude of hostility.

I supposed that the reason for my postponing "from day to day" (Ecclus. 5: 8) the moment when I would despise worldly ambition and follow you was that I had not seen any certainty by which to direct my course. But the day had now come when I stood naked to myself, and my conscience complained against me: "Where is your tongue? You were saying that, because the truth is uncertain, you do not want to abandon the burden of futility. But look, it is certain now, and the burden still presses on you. Yet wings are won by the freer shoulders of men who have not been exhausted by their searching and have not taken ten years or more to meditate on these matters."

viii

Then in the middle of that grand struggle in my inner house, which I had vehemently stirred up with my soul in the intimate chamber of my heart, distressed not only in mind but in appearance, I turned on Alypius[3] and cried out: "What is wrong with us? What is this that you have heard? Uneducated people are rising up and capturing heaven (Matt. II: 12), and we with our high culture without any heart—see where we roll in the mud of flesh and blood. Is it because they are ahead of us that we are ashamed to follow? Do we feel no shame at making not even an attempt to follow?" That is the gist of what I said, and the heat of my passion took my attention away from him as he contemplated my condition in astonished silence. For I sounded very strange. My uttered words said less about the state of my mind than my forehead, cheeks, eyes, colour, and tone of voice.

Our lodging had a garden. We had the use of it as well as of the entire house, for our host, the owner of the house, was not living there. The tumult of my heart took me out into the garden where no one could interfere with the burning struggle with myself in which I was engaged, until the matter could be settled. You knew, but I did not, what the outcome would be. But my madness with myself was part of the process of recovering health, and in the agony of death I was coming to life. I was aware how ill I was, unaware how well I was soon to be. So I went out into the garden. Alypius followed me step after step. Although he was present, I felt no intrusion on my solitude. How could he abandon me in such a state? We sat down as far as we could from the buildings. I was deeply disturbed in spirit, angry with indignation and distress that I was not entering into my pact and covenant with you, my God, when all my bones (Ps. 34: 10) were crying out that I should enter into it and were exalting it to heaven with praises. But to reach that destination one does not use ships or chariots or feet. It was not even necessary to go the distance I had come from the house to where we were sitting. The one necessary condition, which meant not only going but at once arriving there, was to have the will to go—provided only that the will was strong and unqualified, not the turning and twisting first this way, then that, of a will half-wounded, struggling with one part rising up and the other part falling down.

.   .   .

xi

Such was my sickness and my torture, as I accused myself even more bitterly than usual. I was twisting and turning in my chain until it would break completely: I was now only a little bit held by it, but I was still held. You, Lord, put pressure on me in my hidden depths with a severe mercy wielding the double whip of fear and shame, lest I should again succumb, and lest that tiny and tenuous bond which still remained should not be broken, but once more regain strength and bind me even more firmly. Inwardly I said to myself: Let it be now, let it be now. And by this phrase I was already moving towards a decision; I had almost taken it, and then I did not do so. Yet I did not relapse into my original condition, but stood my ground very close to the point of deciding and recovered my breath. Once more I made the attempt and came only a little short of my goal; only a little short of it—yet I did

---

3. *Editor's note:* Alypius was a former student who had become a close friend. In the *Confessions,* see Book VI (chapters 7–10 in particular) for an account of his role in Augustine's life.

not touch it or hold on to it. I was hesitating whether to die to death and to live to life. Ingrained evil had more hold over me than unaccustomed good. The nearer approached the moment of time when I would become different, the greater the horror of it struck me. But it did not thrust me back nor turn me away, but left me in a state of suspense.

Vain trifles and the triviality of the empty-headed, my old loves, held me back. They tugged at the garment of my flesh and whispered: "Are you getting rid of us?" And "from this moment we shall never be with you again, not for ever and ever." And "from this moment this and that are forbidden to you for ever and ever." What they were suggesting in what I have called "this and that"—what they were suggesting, my God, may your mercy avert from the soul of your servant! What filth, what disgraceful things they were suggesting! I was listening to them with much less than half my attention. They were not frankly confronting me face to face on the road, but as it were whispering behind my back, as if they were furtively tugging at me as I was going away, trying to persuade me to look back. Nevertheless they held me back. I hesitated to detach myself, to be rid of them, to make the leap to where I was being called. Meanwhile the overwhelming force of habit was saying to me: "Do you think you can live without them?"

Nevertheless it was now putting the question very half-heartedly. For from that direction where I had set my face and towards which I was afraid to move, there appeared the dignified and chaste Lady Continence, serene and cheerful without coquetry, enticing me in an honourable manner to come and not to hesitate. To receive and embrace me she stretched out pious hands, filled with numerous good examples for me to follow. There were large numbers of boys and girls, a multitude of all ages, young adults and grave widows and elderly virgins. In every one of them was Continence herself, in no sense barren but "the fruitful mother of children" (Ps. 112: 9), the joys born of you, Lord, her husband. And she smiled on me with a smile of encouragement as it to say "Are you incapable of doing what these men and women have done? Do you think them capable of achieving this by their own resources and not by the Lord their God? Their Lord God gave me to them. Why are you relying on yourself, only to find yourself unreliable? Cast yourself upon him, do not be afraid. He will not withdraw himself so that you fall. Make the leap without anxiety; he will catch you and heal you."

I blushed with embarrassment because I was still listening to the mutterings of those vanities, and racked by hesitations I remained undecided. But once more it was as if she said: "'Stop your ears to your impure members on earth and mortify them' (Col. 3: 5). They declare delights to you, but 'not in accord with the law of the Lord your God'" (Ps. 118: 85). This debate in my heart was a struggle of myself against myself. Alypius stood quite still at my side, and waited in silence for the outcome of my unprecedented state of agitation.

xii

From a hidden depth a profound self-examination had dredged up a heap of all my misery and set it "in the sight of my heart" (Ps. 18: 15). That precipitated a vast storm bearing a massive downpour of tears. To pour it all out with the accompanying groans, I got up from beside Alypius (solitude seemed to me more appropriate for the business of weeping), and I moved further away to ensure that even his presence put no inhibition upon me. He sensed that this was my condition at that moment. I think I may have said something which made it clear that the sound of my voice was already choking with tears. So I stood up while in profound astonishment he remained where we were sitting. I threw myself down somehow under a certain figtree, and let my tears flow freely. Rivers streamed from my eyes, a sacrifice acceptable to you (Ps. 50: 19), and (though not in these words, yet in this sense) I repeatedly said to you: "How long, O Lord? How long, Lord, will you be angry to the uttermost? Do not be mindful of our old iniquities." (Ps. 6: 4). For I felt my past to have a grip on me. It uttered wretched cries: "How long, how long is it to be?" "Tomorrow, tomorrow. Why not now? Why not an end to my impure life in this very hour?"

As I was saying this and weeping in the bitter agony of my heart, suddenly I heard a voice from the nearby house chanting as if it might be a boy or a girl (I do not know which), saying and repeating over and over again "Pick up and read, pick up and read." At once my countenance changed, and I began to think intently whether there might be some sort of children's game in which such a chant is used. But I could not remember having heard of one. I checked the flood of tears and stood up. I interpreted it solely as a divine command to me to open the book and read the first chapter I might find. For I had heard how Antony happened to be present at the gospel reading, and took it as an admonition addressed to himself when the words were read: "Go, sell all you have, give to the poor, and you shall have treasure in heaven; and come, follow me" (Matt. 19: 21). By such an inspired utterance he was immediately "converted to you" (Ps. 50: 15). So I hurried back to the place where Alypius was sitting. There I had put down the book of the apostle when I got up. I seized it, opened it and in silence read the first passage on which my eyes lit: "Not in riots and drunken parties, not in eroticism and indecencies, not in strife and rivalry, but put on the Lord Jesus Christ and make no provision for the flesh in its lusts" (Rom. 13: 13–14).

I neither wished nor needed to read further. At once, with the last words of this sentence, it was as if a light of relief from all anxiety flooded into my heart. All the shadows of doubt were dispelled.

Then I inserted my finger or some other mark in the book and closed it. With a face now at peace I told everything to Alypius. What had been going on in his mind, which I did not know, he disclosed in this way. He asked to see the text I had been reading. I showed him, and he noticed a passage following that which I had read. I did not know how the text went on; but the continuation was "Receive the person who is weak in faith" (Rom. 14: I). Alypius applied this to himself, and he made that known to me. He was given confidence by this admonition. Without any agony of hesitation he joined me in making a good resolution and affirmation of intention, entirely congruent with his moral principles in which he had long been greatly superior to me. From there we went in to my mother, and told her. She was filled with joy. We told her how it had happened. She exulted, feeling it to be a triumph, and blessed you who "are powerful to do more than we ask or think" (Eph. 3: 20). She saw that you had granted her far more than she had long been praying for in her unhappy and tearful groans.

The effect of your converting me to yourself was that I did not now seek a wife and had no ambition for success in this world. I stood firm upon that rule of faith on which many years before you had revealed me to her. You "changed her grief into joy" (Ps. 29: 12) far more abundantly than she desired, far dearer and more chaste than she expected when she looked for grandchildren begotten of my body.

The Anguish of Being a Christian
Søren Kierkegaard

Søren Kierkegaard (1813–55) was born and lived almost all of his life in Copenhagen. Physically, he was "slight, spindly, and with so pronounced a stoop that he was regarded as a hunchback. The curvature of his spine . . . made him lean back as he walked, and gave him a dislocated, mechanical, crab-like gait."* Intellectually, he was brilliant, and socially he could be witty, charming, and a fascinating conversationalist.

Privately, he was a complex and often enigmatic man who was subject to periods of melancholy and despair. Dark crises were precipitated by his relationship with his father, a dourly religious man tormented by a sense of guilt, and by his engagement to Regina Olsen. Kierkegaard broke that engagement, possibly because he felt such renunciation was necessary for his religious quest. He agonized over the decision and his love for Regina for the rest of his life. Thus he led a solitary life, set apart by both a malformed body and an endlessly reflective and deliberative mind. There are 10,000 pages in his journal, twice the number he published. He died at the age of only forty-two. "My whole life," he wrote in 1848, "is an epigram calculated to make people aware."

It is the same with Christianity or with becoming a Christian as it is with all radical cures. One postpones it as long as possible. (1835)

There is a most remarkable saying, I know not where, but one which bears the inward stamp of being the kind of utterance which, so to speak, is spoken with the mouth of a whole people. A desperate sinner wakes up in hell and cries out, "What time is it?" The devil answers, "Eternity." (1836)

What is the nourishment offered one by all the world's knowledge in comparison to what is given by Christianity, which pours out the very body and blood of its founder. (1837)

**The Journal of Kierkegaard*, translated and selected by Alexander Dru (New York: Harper Torchbooks, 1959), p. 8.

From *Søren Kierkegaard's Journal and Papers, Vol. I*, edited and translated by Howard V. Hong and Edna H. Hong. Copyright © 1967 by Howard V. Hong. Reprinted by permission of Indiana University Press.

To need God is man's highest perfection. (1844)

Deep within every human being there still lives the anxiety over the possibility of being alone in the world, forgotten by God, overlooked among the millions and millions in this enormous household. One keeps this anxiety at a distance by looking at the many round about who are related to him as kin and friends, but the anxiety is still there, nevertheless, and one hardly dares think of how he would feel if all this were taken away. (1847)

It is claimed that arguments against Christianity arise out of doubt. This is a total misunderstanding. The arguments against Christianity arise out of insubordination, reluctance to obey, mutiny against all authority. Therefore, until now the battle against objections has been shadow-boxing, because it has been intellectual combat with doubt instead of being ethical combat against mutiny. (1847)

It is easy enough to show how false and basically traitorous, even though unconscious, all this defense of Christianity is—yes, even the very form which discourse about Christianity ordinarily takes. The fact of the matter is that pastors and scholars, etc., do not believe in Christianity at all. If a person himself firmly believes that the good he is discoursing about is the highest good, if he almost sags under the impression of its exceedingly abundant blessedness—how in all the world could he ever come to defend it, to conduct a defense of its really being a good, or even to talk in the following manner: This is a great good for three reasons—this supreme good, this good which makes the wisest of men's understanding dizzy and reduces it to tiny sparrow-like understanding, this is a great good—for three reasons. What an anticlimax! Imagine a lover. Yes, he can keep on talking day in and day out about the gloriousness of his beloved. But if anyone demands him to prove it with three reasons, or even defend it—I wonder if he would not regard this as a demented proposal; or if he were a bit more sagacious, he no doubt would say to the person who suggested this to him: Oho, you do not know what it is to be in love at all, and you half believe that I am not either. (1848)

The fact of the matter is that Christianity is really all too joyous, and therefore really to stick to Christianity a man must be brought to madness by suffering. Most men, therefore, will be able to get a real impression of Christianity only in the moment of their death, because death actually takes away from them what must be surrendered in order to get an impression of Christianity. (1848)

There is something almost cruel about the Christian's being placed in a world which in every way wants to pressure him to do the opposite of what God bids him to do with fear and trembling in his innermost being. It would be something like the cruelty of parents if they were to threaten and sternly order their child to do thus and so—and then place the child together with the kind of children who would pressure him in every way to do just the opposite. (1848)

"Seek first the kingdom of God"—these words could be presented in such a way that one negatively examines everything else and shows that this is what one should not do, or in such a way that one shows that the first manifestation of seeking God's kingdom first is, in a certain sense, to do nothing; for to seek the kingdom of God first is at first the same as to renounce everything. (1848)

Seek first the kingdom of God. But what am I supposed to do? Shall I seek an office in order to be influential? No, first you shall seek God's kingdom. Shall I give all my fortune to the poor? No, first you shall seek God's kingdom and his righteousness. Shall I go out in the world as an apostle and proclaim this? No, first you shall seek God's kingdom. But isn't this in a certain sense doing nothing at all? Yes, to be sure, in a certain sense this is what it is. (1848)

Being a Christian is neither more nor less, without a doubt neither more nor less, than being a martyr; every Christian, that is, every true Christian, is a martyr.

But I hear one of those shabby pastors (by shabby I mean one of those who is shabby enough to accept two or three thousand rix-dollars a year, prestige with decorations, etc.—in order to betray Christianity) say: But, of course, we cannot all be martyrs. To this God would reply: Stupid man, do you not think I know how I have arranged the world. Fear only that it will never happen that all become Christians, that only 1/10, only 1/1000 become Christians.

The point is this—becoming a Christian is an examination given by God. But for this very reason in every age (year 1 and year 1848) it must continually be equally difficult to become a Christian. In a certain sense God has squandered so much upon existence [*Tilvaerelsen*] that at any and every moment there will be thousands upon thousands in abundance to persecute the true Christians—and yet in another sense it continues to be possible for every one of these thousands also to become a Christian.

The purpose (and this will also be the end of the matter) of Christendom's suddenly being called out for inspection is that in a more serious way all the sweat will be tormented out of all those shabby, profusely sweating clergymen.

Let us then once again in a noble Christian sense get shabby pastors, poor men who walk about in poor clothing, despised men whom all ridicule, mock, and spit upon. I hope and believe that with the assistance of God I would be able to preach fearlessly even if someone spat in my face as I climbed the stairs to the pulpit. But if I were to be dressed up in a velvet cloak with stars and ribbons and then name the name of Christ—I would die of shame. (1848)

After all, many people think that the Christian message (i.e., to love one's neighbor as oneself) is purposely a little too rigorous—something like the household alarm clock which runs a half-hour fast so that one does not get up too late in the morning. (1848)

There is only one, and quite rightly pathological, proof of the truth of Christianity—when the anxiety of sin and the burdened conscience constrain a man to cross the narrow line between despair unto madness—and Christianity.

There lies Christianity. (1849)

Humanly speaking, there is an almost mad self-contradiction in Christianity's requirement, which is the anguish of being a Christian. It sets a task and says: In the same degree as you succeed, you will come to suffer more and more. You will continually think: "But, Lord God, if I rightly love men—then. . . ." The Christian answer to this must be: Stupid man, or presumptuous man, did not the Savior of the world rightly love men, and he was mocked, spit upon, etc.; has it not been this way for all true Christians, and if not, it merely indicates that they were not Christians, for the prototype settles everything. (1849).

If you desire, humanly speaking, pleasant and happy days, then never get involved *in earnest* with Christianity.

If you do, there is humanly only one consolation for you: death, for which you will learn to long more impatiently than the most amorous girl longs to see her lover again. Yet death is no consolation either. But truly there is, there is one consolation—the eternal. Love the eternal, then you hate this life—this is Christianity. Love God, then you hate this world—this is Christianity. Love Christ, then you are hated by all men—this is Christianity.

See, this is Christianity. If you are not conscious of being a sinner to the degree that in the anxiety of the anguished conscience you do not dare anything other than to commit yourself to Christ—then you never will become a Christian. Only the agony of the consciousness of sin can explain the fact that a person will submit to this radical cure. To become a Christian is the most fearful operation of all, of all. Just as unlikely as it is for a person who merely feels a little indisposed to think of submitting to the most painful operation, just as unlikely is it for a man to think of getting involved with Christianity if sin did not pain him inordinately—if, note well, he then knows what Christianity is and has not been talked into some nonsense about Christianity's gentle, life-beautifying, and ennobling ground of comfort. (1849)

There are so and so many children baptized every year, so and so many confirmed, so many become theological professors; there are a thousand pastors; there are theological professors, bishops, deans, custodians, subcustodians—everything is as it should be—if only Christianity also existed. (1850)

There was a time when one could almost be afraid to call himself a disciple [*Discipel*] of Christ, because it meant so much. Now one can do it with complete ease, because it means nothing at all. (1851)

It is frequently said that if Christ were to come again now he would once more be slain. This is perfectly true; but qualified more precisely, it would have to be added that he would be sentenced to death and slain because what he proclaimed was *not Christianity* but a lunatic, wicked, blasphemous, misanthropic exaggeration and caricature of that gentle doctrine, Christianity, the true Christianity, which is found in Christendom and whose founder was Jesus Christ. (1850)

Above all, read the N. T. without a commentary. Would it ever occur to a lover to read a letter from his beloved with a commentary!

In connection with everything which qualitatively makes a claim of having purely personal significance to me, a commentary is a most hazardous meddler.

If the letter from the beloved were in a language I do not understand—well, then I learn the language—but I do not read the letter with the aid of commentaries by others. I read it, and since the thought of my beloved is vividly present and my purpose in everything is to will according to her will and wishes, I understand the letter all right. It is the same with the Scriptures. With the help of God I understand it all right. (1850)

As soon as the awakened get together they immediately chatter about nothing else but Christianity.

This is disgusting frivolousness. But didn't the first Christians do it? Indeed. Why was it not frivolousness then? Because the sword of persecution hung over their heads every hour, because it was constantly a matter of life and death, because everything was event and action, so that it was impossible to talk about anything else than that, just as it is impossible to talk about anything else than a fire—as long as it lasts.

But the awakened nowadays suffer nothing, do nothing—and that is why this continual chatter is frivolousness. (1852)

Christianity has become complete nonsense. We are all Christians by birth—in "Christendom" a child is not merely born in sin but also in nonsense. (1853)

Anselm prays in all inwardness that he might succeed in proving God's existence. He thinks he has succeeded, and he flings himself down in adoration to thank God. Amazing. He does not notice that this prayer and this expression of thanksgiving are infinitely more proof of God's existence than—the proof. (1853)

A young girl "16 summers old"—it is her confirmation day. Among various elegant and beautiful gifts she also receives a beautifully bound New Testament.

Look, this is what they call Christianity! Actually they do not expect her to read it, now any more than the others, of course, or read it in any primitive way. She receives this book as a consolation in her life: Here you will find consolation if you should need it. Of course they do not expect her to read it, no more than the other young girls, and above all not primitively, otherwise she would discover that here are all the terrors, compared to which the ordinary terrors found in the world are almost a jest.

But look, this is Christianity. And this, too, is Christianity, this foolishness with Bible societies which distribute New Testaments by the millions.

No, I could be tempted to make another proposal to Christendom. Let us collect all the New Testaments there are and bring them out to an open place or up on a mountain and then, while we all kneel, let someone talk to God in this manner: Take this book back again. We human beings, such as we are, are not fit to involve ourselves with such a thing; it only makes us unhappy. I suggest that we, like those inhabitants (Matt. 8:34), beg Christ "to leave the neighborhood." This would be honest and human talk—something different from this nauseating, hypocritical preacher-prattle about life being worthless to us without this priceless good, which is Christianity. (1854)

To be a Christian in Christendom in plain and simple conformity is just as impossible as doing gymnastics in a straitjacket. (1854)

Whenever I think of the insipid, mawkish, syrupy concept of the Savior of the world which Christendom adores and offers for sale, reading his own words about himself has a strange effect: "I have come to set afire," come to produce a split which can tear the most holy bonds, the bonds God himself has sanctified, the bonds between father and son, wife and husband, parents and children, etc. (1854)

Have you seen people at a fire? How do they look? Is it not true that everyone in death-anxiety thinks only of saving himself.

But according to the Christian view a man lives at every moment in far greater danger than in the most raging fire, in danger of forfeiting an eternity: do they look like it? (1854)

Take 1/10 of the essentially Christian, add this ingredient to what man has invented—and you will find (what thousands and thousands of clergymen and professors of lies have found) that this kind of "Christianity" tastes so sweet to men, so delicious, so indescribably delightful, that they do not know what they should concoct in return as a treat for such a professor or preacher.

Take Christianity whole—and you will find (what you, glorious martyrs and witnesses of the truth, have found!) that even the most good-natured man becomes as if he were infuriated, furiously embittered, by this kind of "Christianity," that it is a matter of life and death.

Alas, but God knows man, and since, according to the New Testament, to love God is to hate the world, God has intentionally established Christianity in such a way that it completely shocks those who, merely humanly speaking, might be called the most good-natured of men, as well as the most obstinate of men. For God wants no man to have direct transition into being a Christian. Men do not, according to Christianity, live in a pretty world which God loves—in such a case to become a Christian could be a direct transition for natural human goodness and kindness. No, born in sin, every man, according to Christianity, lives in a sinful world which God hates, and to become a Christian is anything but direct transition; Christianity, this so-called natural human goodness and kindness is just as bad as defiance, etc., and this shows up, also, as soon as Christianity in its truth is brought into contact with this natural human goodness and kindness, for then it becomes just as infuriated with Christianity as defiance, etc. (1854)

Christianity is the frightful earnestness that your eternity is decided in this life. (1854)

We play at Christianity. We use all the orthodox Christian terminology—but everything, everything without character. Yes, we are not fit at all to shape a heresy or a schism, for which some character is always necessary, after all.

No, the whole thing survives: the Christian sacraments and customs, the Christian terminology—but it is all decoration, a way of speaking, the preacher-actor, the artist.

But then Christianity is nothing but mythology, poetry—and the difference between the orthodox clergyman and the free-thinker is this—the free-thinker comes out and says it, but the orthodox clergyman says: For the sake of God in heaven let's not talk about it, let's just keep our ears open—otherwise the whole thing goes to pot.

There is something frightful in the fact that the most dangerous thing of all, playing at Christianity, is never included in the list of heresies and schisms. Still, of course, it is too frightful to be included this way on a list with other heresies. No, this frightful thing has to have a rubric for itself. The question is whether this is not precisely what the New Testament means by "the fall from Christianity." (1854)

To be a Christian is the most appalling of all agonies; it is, so it must be, to have one's hell here on earth. (1855)

The Christian Message
John Hick

John Hick (1922–) was born in England and educated at Edinburgh, Oxford, and Cambridge. Early in his career he served as a Presbyterian minister in rural Northumberland, England, and then taught at Cornell, Princeton Theological Seminary, Cambridge, the University of Birmingham (England), and Claremont Graduate School. He has served on the editorial boards of Religious Studies *and* The Journal of Religion *and as general editor of Macmillan's Library of Philosophy eand Religion. He was chosen the Gifford lecturer, 1986–87.*

Hick is the author or editor of a score of books. Two of his recent titles are Problems of Religious Pluralism *(1985) and* An Interpretation of Religion *(1988).*

*In the essay that follows, Hick mentions having been a conservative Christian in his younger days, moving to a liberal position over the years. In another of his books, he describes an underlying and unchanging conviction: "I have from almost as early as I can remember had a rather strong sense of the reality of God as the personal and loving lord of the universe, and of life as having a meaning within God's purpose."**

I started out a long time ago as a very conservative Christian—indeed, a fundamentalist Christian, though I have grown out of that. But I think it worthwhile to say that the fundamentalist wing within Christianity does serve an important purpose. Fundamentalism, or extreme conservative evangelicalism, can be an important phase through which to pass, though not a good one in which to get stuck. The conservative evangelicals do have the zeal to sometimes jolt young people out of an unthinking, self-centered materialism, and this can be very good. What is not good, of course, is for people to remain in that mold and become not simply enthusiastic young evangelicals but retarded adult ones.

From the liberal Christian standpoint, which I now occupy, I would like to ask two questions in connection with the subject of Jesus in history and myth. The two questions are: What do the liberal Christian and the secular humanist have in common? And where do we part company? We have in common, first, an opposition

God Has Many Names: Britain's New Religious Pluralism (London: Macmillan Press, 1980), pp. 1–2.

From John Hick, "A Liberal Christian View," *Free Inquiry* (Fall 1985). Copyright © 1985 by CODESH, Inc. Reprinted by permission of CODESH, Inc.

to the so-called creationists who are trying to turn the clock back in the teaching of science in the schools, and also an opposition to the people who are trying to impose Christian worship in the schools. So far as I am concerned, this opposition is in the interests not only of secularists but also of Jews, Muslims, Hindus, Buddhists, Sikhs, et al. This is a pluralistic country, and for that reason, quite apart from any other, there ought not to be required Christian worship in the nation's schools.

I spoke of the creationists. Notice how tricky language is. It seems to me a shame that the word "creationist" has become a label not only for people who believe that the universe is God's creation but also for those who insist that biological evolution has not occurred. I too am a creationist in the sense that I believe that the universe is God's creation, but I believe that God's creative work is progressive and continuous and that biological evolution is a part of it. And so I am sorry that the word *creation* has become linked with the obscurantist rejection of evolution. The kind of creationism that I and other liberal Christians espouse is neither scientific nor antiscientific. The purview of science only goes back some fifteen billion years to the big bang. And, if the big bang should turn out to have been an absolute beginning, then science has nothing to say beyond it, though of course religion does.

Now let us turn to the Jesus of history. Was there a first-century person called Jesus or Joshua ben Joseph who was the founder of the Christian religion? This question of course has the rider that, if there was, he did not *intend* to found the Christian religion, since he believed that the end of the present age and the present order of history was going to come very soon. He could not possibly have had any idea of founding a religion that was to exist for twenty centuries, or indeed for one century. But the idea that there never was such a person goes back, I suppose, some one hundred and fifty years and has not been persuasive to more than a very small minority of those who have studied the matter carefully. Its status among historians is no higher than, and I would think in fact lower than, the theory among Elizabethan historians that Francis Bacon wrote the plays of Shakespeare. And, if I might offer a piece of friendly advice—and it is meant as genuinely friendly advice—to the secular humanist movement, it would be: Don't identify too closely with this kind of eccentric view. For the theory that Jesus never existed is not really a very probable one; and, further, the issue is, to say the least, not today at the cutting edge of research concerning Christian origins.

And I would extend the same advice to seeing the Dead Sea Scrolls as a stick with which to beat Christianity. The Dead Sea Scrolls are enormously important; but primarily, it would seem, in enlarging our understanding of the varieties of first-century Judaism. The idea that they have transformed the understanding of Christianity so as somehow to discredit it is not easy to sustain.

. . .

So I really think that we are stuck, whether we like it or not, with the figure of the historical Jesus. Of course we do not see him directly, but through thick layers of first-, second-, and third-generation Christian faith. Some very interesting papers have appeared that have pointed out the various theological and sociological interests that entered into the growth and transmission of the New Testament tradition. It is clear, I think, that what we have is not just straight reporting but remembering in faith, with all the differences that faith makes to the remembering. But nevertheless it has been possible to give an approximate date to most of the documents, to set them in a probable chronological order, and to observe certain trajectories in the growth of the tradition. And when you have a documented forward trajectory you can to some extent reverse it and extrapolate back to the starting point. You have to do this very cautiously. You can do it only to a limited extent. But the growth of the tradition does seem to point back to a historical person who was Jesus.

We can say that Jesus lived in the first third of the first century and that he was a Jew—inded, his Jewishness is becoming more and more fully recognized. He was evidently a charismatic preacher and healer. And it would seem, from the cluster of stories and parables and sayings that are associated with his name, that he must have had an extraordinarily intense and compelling sense of the reality and presence of God; also that he expected God's kingdom to come very soon on earth, wiping away the whole present order of society. And, furthermore, in the parables and sayings that are attributed to him, there is a very strong emphasis upon self-giving love, agape. Furthermore, it seems clear that some of his disciples had visions of him after his death. And when his followers, going out in the enthusiasm of the transformed life that had come upon them, tried to make his existence meaningful to others they clutched at images that were there—floating, so to speak, in the air of their culture. There was the image of the son of man of Danielic prophecy, who was to come again in clouds of glory, and there was the image of the Messiah. However, it does not seem very probable that Jesus applied either of these images, or any other titles, to himself; rather, other people came to apply them to him.

Negatively—and this is very important—it seems pretty clear that Jesus did not present himself as being God incarnate. He did not present himself as the second person of a divine trinity leading a human life. If in his lifetime he was called "son of God," as is entirely possible, it would be in the metaphorical sense that was familiar in the ancient world. In this sense, kings, emperors, pharaohs, wise men, and charismatic religious leaders were very freely called sons of God, meaning that they were close to God, in the spirit of God, that they were servants and instruments of God. The ancient Hebrew kings were regularly enthroned as son of God in this metaphorical sense.

Now this original, biblical "son of God" language is entirely innocent, so to speak, entirely acceptable and understandable in the context of the ancient Near East. We use the metaphor today in an extended form when we say, for example, that all human beings are children of God. This is a metaphorical way of saying that all human beings are valued by God. But the fateful development that created what was to become orthodox Christian belief for many centuries occurred when this poetry hardened into prose and the metaphorical son of God, with a small s, was transmuted into the metaphysical God the Son, with a capital S. The philosophers then developed the explanatory theory that Jesus had two complete natures, one human and the other divine, and that in his divine nature he was of the same substance as God the Father, while in his human nature he was of the same substance as humanity.

Now I hold, as do many liberal Christians today, that a Christian does not have to accept those philosophical and theological theories of the third and fourth centuries. I think that we can base our Christianity upon Jesus' teachings concerning the reality and love and claim of God, and upon the love ethic that has developed out of it. This provides a framework for life regardless of how much or how little detail we know for sure about Jesus' life.

Christianity has, like every other religion, developed its own mythology. This mythology is at its height in the beautiful imagery that centers around the festivals of Christmas and Easter. And I would suggest that mythology is not necessarily a bad thing; it is not to be scorned. Indeed, there is today a rediscovery of the value of myth in human life. A considerable literature is growing up about its positive uses. Myths are not literally true, but they may nevertheless be mythologically true; that is to say, they may evoke in the hearer practical dispositions that are appropriate to the ultimate subject matter of the myth. They may be a good way of communicating the claim of the transcendent upon us.

Having said that Christianity provides a good framework for the religious life, I do not go on to say that it provides a *better* framework than is provided by Rabbinic Judaism, or Islam, or Hinduism, or Buddhism, and so on. Rather, for many of us it is the framework into which we were born, which has therefore formed us in its own image, and which accordingly suits us better than a framework that is alien to us. Accordingly, I do not seek to convert people of the other great world religions to Christianity, though I would be very happy if I could convert secular humanists to any one of the great world religions—whichever one happened to be most suitable to the particular individual, because they all provide windows onto the transcendent. They all lead to what religion is ultimately all about, namely, the transformation of human existence from self-centeredness to Reality-centeredness.

Having referred to the other great world religions, let me mention a parallel between the historical Jesus, known as the Messiah or the Christ, and the historical Gautama, known as the Buddha. It occurs to me that it would be quite possible for someone to come along and question the existence of the historical Buddha. It would be possible to suggest that maybe there was no such person; certainly one cannot strictly prove that there was. But, just as the trajectories of the physical universe, when you follow them backward, lead to the postulated big bang, so the trajectories of Buddhist development lead back to the spiritual big bang of a man who had attained enlightenment; and so also the trajectories of Christian development point back to the spiritual big bang of a man who was overwhelmingly conscious of the dynamic presence of God. And I think that it is religiously important that we know something, even if something rather general and minimal, about the lives of Gautama and Jesus. It adds something important to the Buddhist message of the transcendence of ego to know that this man Gautama, who attained that total transcendence of ego that is nirvana, did not then retreat from the world to enjoy this bliss but spent the next forty years of his life strenuously traveling around India teaching other people, helping them to attain to that which is beyond the ego state. Thus, if we knew nothing about the man who gave the teaching, we would be impoverished. And, likewise, it seems to me that it adds something important to the Christian message of the reality and love of God, and of the claim of love upon all human life, to know that the person who so powerfully taught this lived, as did

Gautama, in relative poverty, that he gave his time and energies to others, and that he was willing to accept the rather grisly death that came to him.

Reverting now to the role of one giving friendly advice, in which I suggested that secular humanism should not become the last refuge of eccentric theories about Jesus, I also want to suggest that secular humanists should not spend too much time fighting yesterday's battles. It was, for example, back in the eighteenth century that the argument from miracles to the truth of Christianity was flourishing. Today it can no doubt be found among some of our evangelical brethren, but it does not play a large part in the ongoing encounter of Christianity with the modern world. The contemporary issues in the philosophy of religion are very different from those of the eighteenth century. They include such topics as the epistemology and sociology of knowledge, and the place of interpretation, and thus of faith, in all worldviews and also in historical knowledge; the study of interesting developments in contemporary scientific cosmology; the problem of the apparently conflicting truth-claims of the different world religions; the epistemological question of foundationalism; fascinating new forms of the ontological argument; the application of Bayesian probability theory to theism; the encounter between Christianity and Marxism. These are some of the live issues today; and there are so many live issues that there seems to me no need to continue to spend a lot of time on dead ones.

Let me end by asking: If one takes this kind of liberal Christian stance, is one still a Christian? Well, if you see Christianity as a body of propositions that have to be the same in the twentieth century as they were in the fourth century, then probably not. But of course Christianity has never been as unchanging and monolithic as both conservative believers and conservative unbelievers like to think. It has always been an actively developing tradition. And it has always been internally pluralistic. Even in the earliest period there was a plurality of Christologies. There are different trajectories moving out of the New Testament, and today, with the collapse, or partial collapse, of ecclesiastical authority, these differences are flourishing again.

And I end, literally now, with a footnote about the Bishop of Durham, David Jenkins. You may perhaps know, and it is this that makes news about the bishop particularly significant, that he ranks fourth among the Anglican bishops in England, after the archbishops of Canterbury and York and the bishop of London. Of course it is a delightful joke that he said that he did not believe in Christianity. . . . But I imagine that your common sense has already told you that that can't be literally true. What he denied was the physical virgin birth. He said that it has symbolic significance but is not a literal physiological fact. He also denied the bodily resurrection of Jesus, saying that Jesus lived beyond death, but not in a physical sense. Now it takes a fundamentalist, whether a Christian one or an anti-Christian one, to conclude that in saying this the bishop was disavowing Christianity. Personally, I think that he was right in what he said about the virgin birth and the resurrection.

Seeds of Contemplation

Thomas Merton

Thomas Merton (1919–68) was born in France of an American mother and New Zealander father. He attended French schools and Clare College, Cambridge, but received his undergraduate and Master's degrees from Columbia University. He was a convert to Catholicism in 1939; in 1941, twenty-six years of age, he became a Trappist monk, entering Our Lady of Gethsemani Abbey, a monastery in Kentucky. ("Trappist" is the popular name for the austere Order of Cistercians of the Strict Observance. The monks of Gethsemani follow a rigorous routine of prayer and work, and they observe the rule of silence: all conversation is forbidden.)

The Seven Storey Mountain, Merton's best-selling autobiography, was published in 1948, the first of some sixty volumes. Even since his death, new titles have appeared, as his letters (he corresponded with 1800 people) and journals have been published. Late in his short life his interest in the religions of the East resulted in some of his finest work: Mystics and Zen Masters, Zen and the Birds of Appetite, and The Way of Chuang Tzu. He was on an extended trip to the Far East, meeting with Buddhist monks and others, when he suffered a fatal accident: while in Bangkok he was electrocuted by a faultily wired fan in his room.*

Just weeks before Merton's death, the Dalai Lama had meetings with him: "This was the first time that I had been struck by such a feeling of spirituality in anyone who professed Christianity. Since then I have come across others with similar qualities, but it was Merton who introduced me to the real meaning of the word 'Christian.'"*

Contemplation

Contemplation is the highest expression of man's intellectual and spiritual life. It is that life itself, fully awake, fully active, fully aware that it is alive. It is spiritual wonder. It is spontaneous awe at the sacredness of life, of being. It is gratitude for life, for awareness and for being. It is a vivid realization of the fact that life and being in

*Freedom in Exile (New York: HarperCollins, 1990), p. 189.

us proceed from an invisible, transcendent, and infinitely abundant Source. Contemplation is, above all, awareness of the reality of that Source. It *knows* the Source, obscurely, inexplicably, but with a certitude that goes both beyond reason and beyond simple faith. For contemplation is a kind of spiritual vision to which both reason and faith aspire, by their very nature, because without it they must always remain incomplete. Yet contemplation is not vision because it sees "without seeing" and knows "without knowing." It is a more profound depth of faith, a knowledge too deep to be grasped in images, in words or even in clear concepts. It can be suggested by words, by symbols, but in the very moment of trying to indicate what it knows the contemplative mind takes back what it has said, and denies what it has affirmed. For in contemplation we know by "unknowing." Or, better, we know *beyond* all knowing or "unknowing."

Poetry, music, and art have something in common with the contemplative experience. But contemplation is beyond aesthetic intuition, beyond art, beyond poetry. Indeed, it is also beyond philosophy, beyond speculative theology. It resumes, transcends, and fulfills them all, and yet at the same time it seems, in a certain way, to supersede and to deny them all. Contemplation is always beyond our own knowledge, beyond our own light, beyond systems, beyond explanations, beyond discourse, beyond dialogue, beyond ourself. To enter into the realm of contemplation one must in a certain sense die: but this death is in fact the entrance into a higher life. It is a death for the sake of life, which leaves behind all that we can know or treasure as life, as thought, as experience, as joy, as being.

And so contemplation seems to supersede and to discard every other form of intuition and experience—whether in art, in philosophy, in theology, in liturgy, or in ordinary levels of love and of belief. This rejection is of course only apparent. Contemplation is and must be compatible with all these things, for it is their highest fulfillment. But in the actual experience of contemplation all other experiences are momentarily lost. They "die" to be born again on a higher level of life.

In other words, then, contemplation reaches out to the knowledge and even to the experience of the transcendent and inexpressible God. It knows God by seeming to touch Him. Or rather it knows Him as if it had been invisibly touched by Him. . . . Touched by Him Who has no hands, but Who is pure Reality and the source of all that is real! Hence contemplation is a sudden gift of awareness, an awakening to the Real within all that is real. A vivid awareness of infinite Being at the roots of our own limited being. An awareness of our contingent reality as received, as a present from God, as a free gift of love. This is the existential contact of which we speak when we use the metaphor of being "touched by God."

Contemplation is also the response to a call: a call from Him Who has no voice, and yet Who speaks in everything that is, and Who, most of all, speaks in the depths of our own being: for we ourselves are words of His. But we are words that are meant to respond to Him, to answer to Him, to echo Him, and even in some way to contain Him and signify Him. Contemplation is this echo. It is a deep resonance in the inmost center of our spirit in which our very life loses its separate voice and resounds with the majesty and the mercy of the Hidden and Living One. He answers Himself in us and this answer is divine life, divine creativity, making all things new. We ourselves become His echo and His answer. It is as if in creating us God asked a question, and in awakening us to contemplation He answered the question, so that the contemplative is at the same time, question and answer.

The life of contemplation implies two levels of awareness: first, awareness of the question, and second, awareness of the answer. Though these are two distinct and enormously different levels, yet they are in fact an awareness of the same thing. The question is, itself, the answer. And we ourselves are both. But we cannot know this until we have moved into the second kind of awareness. We awaken, not to find an answer absolutely distinct from the question, but to realize that the question is its own answer. And all is summed up in one awareness—not a proposition, but an experience: "I Am."

The contemplation of which I speak here is not philosophical. It is not the static awareness of metaphysical essences apprehended as spiritual objects, unchanging and eternal. It is not the contemplation of abstract ideas. It is the religious apprehension of God, through my life in God, or through "sonship" as the New Testament says. "For whoever are led by the Spirit of God, they are the sons of God. . . . The Spirit Himself gives testimony to our own spirit that we are the sons of God." "To as many as received Him He gave the power to become the sons of God. . . ." And so the contemplation of which I speak is a religious and transcendent gift. It is not something to which we can attain alone, by intellectual effort, by perfecting our natural powers. It is not a kind of self-hypnosis, resulting from concentration on our own inner spiritual being. It is not the fruit of our own efforts. It is the gift of God Who, in His mercy, completes the hidden and mysterious work of creation in us by enlightening our minds and hearts, by awakening in us the awareness that we are words spoken in His One Word, and that Creating Spirit *(Creator Spiritus)* dwells in us, and we in Him. That we are "in Christ" and that Christ lives in us. That the natural life in us has been completed, elevated, transformed and fulfilled in Christ by the Holy Spirit. Contemplation is the awareness and realization, even in some sense *experience,* of what each Christian obscurely believes: "It is now no longer I that live but Christ lives in me."

Hence contemplation is more than a consideration of abstract truths about God, more even than affective meditation on the things we believe. It is awakening, enlightenment, and the amazing intuitive grasp by which love gains certitude of God's creative and dynamic intervention in our daily life. Hence contemplation does not simply "find" a clear idea of God and confine Him within the limits of that idea, and hold Him there as a prisoner to Whom it can always return. On the contrary, contemplation is carried away by Him into His own realm, His own mystery, and His own freedom. It is a pure and a virginal knowledge, poor in concepts, poorer still in reasoning, but able, by its very poverty and purity, to follow the Word "wherever He may go."

Seeds

Every moment and every event of every man's life on earth plants something in his soul. For just as the wind carries thousands of winged seeds, so each moment brings with it germs of spiritual vitality that come to rest imperceptibly in the minds and wills of men. Most of these unnumbered seeds perish and are lost, because men are not prepared to receive them: for such seeds as these cannot spring up anywhere except in the good soil of freedom, spontaneity, and love.

This is no new idea. Christ in the parable of the sower long ago told us that "The seed is the word of God." We often think this applies only to the word of the Gospel as formally preached in churches on Sundays (if indeed it is preached in churches any more!). But every expression of the will of God is in some sense a "word" of God and therefore a "seed" of new life. The ever-changing reality in the midst of which we live should awaken us to the possibility of an uninterrupted dialogue with God. By this I do not mean continuous "talk," or a frivolously conversational form of affective prayer which is sometimes cultivated in convents, but a dialogue of love and of choice. A dialogue of deep wills.

In all the situations of life the "will of God" comes to us not merely as an external dictate of impersonal law but above all as an interior invitation of personal love. Too often the conventional conception of "God's will" as a sphinx-like and arbitrary force bearing down upon us with implacable hostility, leads men to lose faith in a God they cannot find it possible to love. Such a view of the divine will drives human weakness to despair and one wonders if it is not, itself, often the expression of a despair too intolerable to be admitted to conscious consideration. These arbitrary "dictates" of a domineering and insensible Father are more often seeds of hatred than of love. If that is our concept of the will of God, we cannot possibly seek the obscure and intimate mystery of the encounter that takes place in contemplation. We will desire only to fly as far as possible from Him and hide from His Face forever. So much depends on our idea of God! Yet no idea of Him, however pure and perfect, is adequate to express Him as He really is. Our idea of God tells us more about ourselves than about Him.

We must learn to realize that the love of God seeks us in every situation, and seeks our good. His inscrutable love seeks our awakening. True, since this awakening implies a kind of death to our exterior self, we will dread His coming in proportion as we are identified with this exterior self and attached to it. But when we understand the dialectic of life and death we will learn to take the risks implied by faith, to make the choices that deliver us from our routine self and open to us the door of a new being, a new reality.

The mind that is the prisoner of conventional ideas, and the will that is the captive of its own desire cannot accept the seeds of an unfamiliar truth and a supernatural desire. For how can I receive the seeds of freedom if I am in love with slavery and how can I cherish the desire of God if I am filled with another and an opposite desire? God cannot plant His liberty in me because I am a prisoner and I do not even desire to be free. I love my captivity and I imprison myself in the desire for the things that I hate, and I have hardened my heart against true love. I must learn therefore to let go of the familiar and the usual and consent to what is new and unknown to me. I must learn to "leave myself" in order to find myself by yielding to the love of God. If I were looking for God, every event and every moment would sow, in my will, grains of His life that would spring up one day in a tremendous harvest.

For it is God's love that warms me in the sun and God's love that sends the cold rain. It is God's love that feeds me in the bread I eat and God that feeds me also by hunger and fasting. It is the love of God that sends the winter days when I am cold and sick, and the hot summer when I labor and my clothes are full of sweat: but it is God Who breathes on me with light winds off the river and in the breezes out of the wood. His love spreads the shade of the sycamore over my head and sends the water-boy along the edge of the wheat field with a bucket from the spring, while the laborers are resting and the mules stand under the tree.

It is God's love that speaks to me in the birds and streams; but also behind the clamor of the city God speaks to me in His judgments, and all these things are seeds sent to me from His will.

If these seeds would take root in my liberty, and if His will would grow from my freedom, I would become the love that He is, and my harvest would be His glory and my own joy.

And I would grow together with thousands and millions of other freedoms into the gold of one huge field praising God, loaded with increase, loaded with wheat. If in all things I consider only the heat and the cold, the food or the hunger, the sickness or labor, the beauty or pleasure, the success and failure, or the material good or evil my works have won for my own will, I will find only emptiness and not happiness. I shall not be fed, I shall not be full. For my food is the will of Him Who made me and Who made all things in order to give Himself to me through them.

My chief care should not be to find pleasure or success, health or life or money or rest or even things like virtue and wisdom—still less their opposites, pain, failure, sickness, death. But in all that happens, my one desire and my one joy should be to know: "Here is the thing that God has willed for me. In this His love is found, and in accepting this I can give back His love to Him and give myself with it to Him. For in giving myself I shall find Him and He is life everlasting."

By consenting to His will with joy and doing it with gladness I have His love in my heart, because my will is now the same as His love and I am on the way to becoming what He is, Who is Love. And by accepting all things from Him I receive His joy into my soul, not because things are what they are but because God is Who He is, and His love has willed my joy in them all.

How am I to know the will of God? Even where there is no other more explicit claim on my obedience, such as a legitimate command, the very nature of each situation usually bears written into itself some indication of God's will. For whatever is demanded by truth, by justice, by mercy, or by love must surely be taken to be willed by God. To consent to His will is, then, to consent to be true, or to speak truth, or at least to seek it. To obey Him is to respond to His will expressed in the need of another person, or at least to respect the rights of others. For the right of another man is the expression of God's love and God's will. In demanding that I respect the rights of another God is not merely asking me to conform to some abstract, arbitrary law: He is enabling me to share, as His son, in His own care for my brother. No man who ignores the rights and needs of others can hope to walk in the light of contemplation, because his way has turned aside from truth, from compassion, and therefore from God.

The requirements of a work to be done can be understood as the will of God. If I am supposed to hoe a garden or make a table, then I will be obeying God if I am true to the task I am performing. To do the work carefully and well, with love and respect for the nature of my task and with due attention to its purpose, is to unite myself to God's will in my work. In this way I become His instrument. He works through me. When I act as His instrument my labor cannot become an obstacle to contemplation, even though it may temporarily so occupy my mind that I cannot engage in it while I am actually doing my job. Yet my work itself will purify and pacify my mind and dispose me for contemplation.

Unnatural, frantic, anxious work, work done under pressure of greed or fear or any other inordinate passion, cannot properly speaking be dedicated to God, because God never wills such work directly. He may permit that through no fault of our own we may have to work madly and distractedly, due to our sins, and to the sins of the society in which we live. In that case we must tolerate it and make the best of what we cannot avoid. But let us not be blind to the distinction between sound, healthy work and unnatural toil.

In any case, we should always seek to conform to the *logos* or truth of the duty before us, the work to be done, or our own God-given nature. Contemplative obedience and abandonment to the will of God can never mean a cultivated indifference to the natural values implanted by Him in human life and work. Insensitivity must not be confused with detachment. The contemplative must certainly be detached, but he can never allow himself to become insensible to true human values, whether in society, in other men, or in himself. If he does so, then his contemplation stands condemned as vitiated in its very root.

On the Road to Damascus

Rita Dove

Rita Dove (1952–), originally from Akron, Ohio, is a Pulitzer Prize-winning poet (in 1987 for Thomas and Beulah*). She is also a short story writer* (Fifth Sunday), *novelist, and professor of creative writing—first at Arizona State University and most recently at the University of Virginia. Much honored, she has received Fulbright and Guggenheim Fellowships, two National Endowment for the Arts grants, and other awards. In 1993 she was named the nation's poet laureate—the youngest ever.*

On the mysteries of vision, H. D.[1] writes: "We begin with sympathy of thought." One of the last great modern mystics, H. D. scribbled her *Notes on Thoughts and Vision* in a notebook marked "July, Scilly Islands" in 1919, when she retreated to these islands off the coast of Cornwall in order to recuperate—from war, from illness and the breakup of her marriage, from the death of her brother and the hazardous birth of her daughter Perdita. Sea air and salt light to heal a wounded spirit: "The doctor prescribes rest."

I am reading H. D. on a grassy knoll overlooking the grounds of the Villa Serbelloni, the "Study and Conference Center" of the Rockefeller Foundation on Lake Como in northern Italy, trying to ignore a niggling restlessness I've had ever since my arrival. Do I feel displaced in the serenity of this splendid retreat, high above the tourist traffic of the village of Bellagio, here where terraced hills plunge into clear waters and cypresses slope into the mists at evening? Five weeks of hydrangeas and tiger lilies, white-coated butlers and silver candlesticks—what sumptuous reward for all the hours spent hunched in a sixty-watt circle of light, smudging my way through a wilderness of words! At last no meals to cook or phones to answer; little mail, no children; a room of one's own, a study in the woods, and all around, beauty . . . but I'm not writing.

I've told myself it takes time to unwind, and I try to relax by reading afternoons when the *breva* sweeps the fog from the lake, freshening the shore. I read sprawled

---

1. *Editor's note:* H. D. was the pen name of the American poet Hilda Doolittle (1886–1961).

in a rattan chair set up outside, next to my study, hoping the sun will burn off the stress and fill the emptiness with magic.

While browsing in the villa library this morning I talked with a poet from Canada; he was convinced that the jewellike medieval painting of Saul on the way to Damascus that's mounted near the dictionaries is an unsigned Bono. Unsure who Bono was but unwilling to show my ignorance, I scrutinized the canvas for a signature—nothing in the tufted grass, the parched and rutted road, no scrawls in the surreal blue heaven or bright curls of the seraphim—and before I remembered to put on my museum demeanor I was captivated by the wistful sincerity of the scene before me. Saul looked utterly terrified, his horse rearing and his fellow travelers baffled by such strange behavior on an ordinary day. How devastating an experience for a man so certain of his convictions! No wonder he spent three days in darkness afterward, emptied of himself, until Ananias came to claim him in the name of Christianity. No wonder his name changed, the same sound but a different beginning.

H. D.'s *Notes* drop to the grass. A few yards away, three goldfish hidden under the lily pads send up their perky semaphores: I hear this infinitesimal percolation even as wild birds overhead belt out Italian chorales and a speedboat growls across the lake. So that's what's been bothering me: the germ of a poem dealing with religion. But, as if I were a Jewish dyer trading in royal purple, I struggle against the notion of Christianity acquiring a poem from me—just as I struggle against the ideologue who has haunted me since adolescence, whose stony gaze I still feel whenever I rail against the strictures of institutional belief.

Life before Paul was milk and honey, grapes and warm bread, cardboard-and-glitter crèches. In those early Sunday-school years we were fed on floods and famines, raining toads and babies in baskets. Come twelve and the age of accountability, Christ appeared in the Temple and there followed a progression of sun-drenched miracles—Lazarus rising from his shroud, fish gleaming on proliferating hunks of bread. We loved the repetition of blessings, the palms fanning above the stolid head of a donkey, even the thirty pieces of silver. Blood and vinegar on the cross was swept over quickly, and Sunrise Services emphasized the rock rolled away, shining wings, astonishment, and His Glorious Resurrection. That was what a miracle was, after all: absence and light.

I was thirteen when the man who would introduce me to the apostle Paul walked into our senior Sunday-school class. He was tall, dark, and hellishly handsome, severely dressed in a matte-black narrow suit and black shirt from which rose a ring of shocking white, like a slipped halo. Never before had I seen a clerical collar (our minister wore standard suits with striped ties which peeked from his velvet-trimmed "preaching" robe); I thought the collar was his own invention, a kind of symbolic leash worn as a token of his service to God. He was the new assistant minister, straight out of theological school in the South (an exotic country to us in Akron, Ohio), and would take over the twelve-to-fifteen-year-olds, leaving our former teacher with the less unruly high schoolers.

Of course all the girls developed an immediate crush on him. We followed him breathlessly across the hall to a smaller, pale green classroom and without being asked formed a semicircle around the table he leaned against, like a male model from *Ebony* magazine, pin-striped trousers draping elegantly just above the buffed black wing tips. On his left hand glinted, to our disappointment, a large wedding band.

"What do you know of mortal sin?" he asked.

We goggled at him and tittered nervously. "Mortal" sounded all right to us. He frowned, straightening the crease in his pant leg, then patiently unveiled to us the concepts of irretrievable error and purgatory. Since we were past the age of twelve, he explained, we were accountable for our sins against the Ten Commandments, which were inviolable. And our transgressions against any of those laws—whether actual or committed *in thought only*—were unforgivable except through Jesus Christ.

We barely heard the Jesus Christ part. We were doomed, for we had just coveted another woman's husband; we had also disobeyed our parents, stolen, lied, cursed—and if one counted thinking (how can you control your thoughts?) as well, then we committed these transgressions all the time. In an instant, flirting had changed from harmless entertainment to hellfire.

Our church was A.M.E. Zion. The acronym stands for African Methodist Episcopal, an appellation that contains all the contradictions and acclimatizations black Americans have gone through to accommodate both the African memory and the American dream. Basically Methodist, our church believed in a moderate liturgy (responsive readings) but did not tolerate kneeling or chanting; the "Episcopal" distinguished us from the Baptists not only in decorum—we baptized with a few drops of water on a baby's forehead—but in class. Determinedly of the bourgeoisie ("boojy" we called our parents, among them dentists, general practitioners, dry-cleaning moguls), we did not approve of hee-hawing sermons, though the minister was permitted to shout out the last sixth of his text.

"African" meant many things. Sometimes it was the license to wear proud colors and hats piled high, as extravagant as platters—unlike the drab skirt-and-blouse attire of the white Lutherans one street over. "African" also referred to our intimate relationship with God and Christ, the permission to wipe Christ's sweat from our brows and talk to him like a brother, to identify our lot with that of the Israelites under Pharaoh. Martin Luther King, Jr. was our Moses, charged with delivering his people across the Selma bridge. "African" bore the very cadences of nostalgia for our lost homeland, wherever it may have been—though in those turbulent years of Miriam Makeba and Malcolm X there was an edge to that nostalgia as well, a defiant hope from those who wished for mercy but just might choose, if pressed, to prevail by whatever means necessary.

But "African" always meant righteous singing. I particularly loved the "old hundred" hymns, standard oldies sung during the formal catechism of the service, before the sermon, as well as the choral outbursts from the white-clad women in the front pew.

Ah, the deaconesses! Mostly widows with massive bosoms, all ancient, these women put on their blinding white shirtwaists, their chalky nylons, and Shinola-white shoes every Sunday. Some wore tiny starched bonnets, very much like nurses or pilgrims, and others preferred the pure ornament of a scrubbed dark face lifted to the Lord. They were the self-appointed brides of Christ and the acknowledged mothers of the church, the arbiters of the Holy Spirit, and they disapproved of flash and frivolity and black militancy. (Though they never complained about Afros, since several of them had let their hair "go back" to furry halos.) The deaconesses were already seated when the rest of the congregation trickled in. Usually they were bent in prayer, humming vigorously to the mumbled supplications of a deacon, usually the oldest male, who by virtue of his sex and age was permitted to kneel on the first step leading to the altar.

The deaconesses were also intimate with what W.E.B. Du Bois called the Sorrow Songs—older hymns, prehistoric canons that resembled nothing familiar or comforting. They had very few words and were frightening in their near-inarticulate misery. For at least a half hour before the processional signaled the official start of the service, the old women hummed, rocked, wailed these chants as parishioners arrived and drifted into the pews. Unlike gospel, "big/with all the wrongs done done," these songs reeked with unappeasable loss and pain. They were the moans of slavery, the rhythms of an existence dulled by rote and brutality and hopelessness, an isolation so complete there could be no words.

The deaconesses led the congregation in that complex courtship between the Holy Spirit and mortal endeavor; the give and take, the surge and ebb between the minister's sermon and their shouted counterpoint was our clue to how well the minister was doing in bringing us closer to holiness, indeed, bringing us *in Christ,* in Paul's complex, mystical phrase, until heat and pinching waistbands dropped away and the message from the pulpit entered us directly, like an injection.

What is the mystery of grace? What does it mean to be *in* Christ? I watched the older women of the church "get happy"; I could see them gathering steam, pushing out the seams of their composure until it dropped down, the Holy Spirit, falling upon them like a hatchet from heaven. Instead of crumbling they rose up, incandescent, to perform amazing feats—they tightroped the backs of pews, skipped along the aisles, threw off ushers and a half-dozen able-bodied men with every shout. (Men rarely got happy; when they did, theirs was a decorous performance, hardly an experience at all.) A woman "full of the Spirit" was indomitable; one could almost see sunbeams glancing off the breastplate of righteousness, the white wings twinkling on the sandals of faith. And when it was over, they were not diminished but serene, as if they'd been given a tonic.

Why couldn't I be filled, transfused with glory? The most I'd experienced was a "quickening"—a mini-transformation characterized by shortened breath and an intense longing for the indefinite . . . what? I was tongue-tied, hopelessly guilt-ridden, and self-conscious to boot. The most I could do was get teary-eyed. In the face of those bolder ecstasies, I'd fall back into my own ashes, quenched.

Witnessing these transformations usually made me churlish for the rest of the day. I decided God didn't like intelligence. And though we hadn't been meant to sample the Tree of Knowledge, surely we couldn't be blamed for the intelligence we'd been saddled with.

Sunday evenings after *60 Minutes* my father would push off his slippers and shrug into his overcoat, keys jangling. We knew the signal: another trip to Grandma's on the East Side. It was a long way through town, along the gorge and then the slow climb up Market Street, past the defunct oats silos and the Fir Hill Conservatory of Music, then down Arlington and into the purgatorial Furnace Street, where the smoke and brimstone miraculously began, spewing from Plant One of the Goodyear Rubber Company and the smaller infernos of Mohawk and General Tire. This was the part of the journey I waited for. The backlit plumes of smoke and murky variations of exhaust and light were exciting, a negative snapshot of power and hope; the mere sight of a belching smokestack at night made me think of evening gowns and diamond lavaliers.

All across town the accompaniment was radio—the staid ministerial admonitions of a local Presbyterian congregation on the way, and afterward the surging gospels of Shiloh Baptist, my grandmother's own church, whose evening service she attended faithfully via the airwaves, rocking in her armchair in the back bedroom. I was awed by so much fervor: that one could go to church on Sunday morning and still have ardor left over to attend an evening service seemed strange, yet weirdly desirable. How simple life would be if one could believe that much! Later, in bed, I'd tuck my transistor radio under the pillow and tune into the Catholic broadcast at ten—after Shiloh Baptist's creaking ship of lamentations what a relief, a balm, *Hail Mary full of grace Blessed art thou among women and blessed is the fruit of thy womb Jesus* whispered over and over until I dozed off, safe for another night.

Into the intact world of childhood, Paul had introduced Doubt, and I resisted. As far as I was concerned, Saul/Paul was altogether too fervent—his persecution of the Christians too single-minded, his conversion too spectacular, his teachings too humorless. It wasn't the gaudiness of his martyr's life I distrusted (John's vision of the Apocalypse, in contrast, seemed absolute to me and vividly *correct*); rather, it was the contradiction between his life and his words. "Do as I say, not as I do"— we'd learned in Sunday school to nod, straight-faced, when reciting the commandments but to watch as scandals erupted in that orchestrated adult world: a senior usher ogling a pair of fine hips rolling under orange shantung, the occasional girl burgeoning under her choir robes. We waited for public recriminations, but all went on as before. We had a saying: Saints can backslide, but never trust a person who can't dance. Paul couldn't dance, but he shore could talk. Our assistant minister felt it his duty to initiate us into the world of words, the irretrievability of a vow.

I also distrusted the name change, from the Jew Saul to the astringent New Age Paul. Paul—a name without history. Somehow I suspected him of abandoning with his born name the Old Testament, where Sauls and Jeremiahs flourished, and his desert treks and prison tenure had no aura. He was a traveling salesman, his epistles little more than shtick.

And Paul had no music; neither did he make a joyful noise before the Lord. He despised pageantry and silver ornament. His was a ministry of noon—no shadows or respite from the all-reaching rays of righteousness. I could not think of Paul without imagining parched mesas and the emblazoned killing ground of a Colosseum. Even the olives he preferred must have been sharp with rosemary, chewy and bitter.

But the god I knew understood the value of a wink. He was nothing like this Paul with his blind stare, his frozen faith burning in his eyes. Leave such clenched fervor to human beings; gods and angels are casual. No wonder he saw life in terms of architecture, and the body become church, a sacred building you entered silently and where you'd better not spit. And farther up the wine-dark aisle, the path of blood transfixed, this sacrificial artery leading to the plateau where no body lived but Thought reigned, gold and wax and velvet, paltry adornment designed to render palpable to the congregation the ineffable integrity of the spirit. This, then, was Christ presiding over the church, and Man presiding over Wife.

The mystery of Paul's ideology is revealed through his metaphors: comparing the church to a marriage. To be saved, to establish a mystical and *ongoing* spiritual strength, one does not try to become Christ or to identify with Christ; instead, one develops a *relationship to* him. This is a "primitive" concept: the ancient Greeks mingled freely with their gods and goddesses, with sometimes disastrous (poor Leda), sometimes beneficent (Odysseus guided to Ithaca by Pallas Athene) results. African slaves in America transferred their attitudes toward divinities to the abstract figures of Christianity, telling Mary not to weep, exhorting Jonah not to despair, and rejoicing that Christ had personally reached down to lift them up. Black worshipers sat down to talk with God as with an old friend. When I was in my early teens, black disc jockeys favored a popular song that went: "I had a talk with my man last night; / He reassured me everything was all right." It was years before I heard the gospel song that had been its inspiration: "I had a talk with God last night." I was not as shocked by this discovery as perhaps I should have been; I was already on the way to secular humanism. After all, I had been talking to God for several years, bargaining and wheedling from the cave of my pillow, protesting my good intentions.

Human agency. I rolled the phrase around in my mouth as I perched on the curved lip of the pew, willing myself to remember the words through the sermon's climax and the preacher's ecstatic Call to Altar so that I might carry them home and find a use for them. *Human agency* was the key I'd been looking for in the rigid latticework the New Testament had raised around my daily living. Obedient though I was, I could not believe the thoughts that entered my daydreams so easily were forbidden. To hold the mind accountable—surely this wasn't what God had meant. Surely he did not want robots as children; surely a doll's house would be a bore for such a mighty spectator.

The world is protean. Every adolescent knows this, lives this . . . and is astonished at adults' ability to fasten onto the order of things with smug attentions. How can they skim the surface of such stormy oceans? Mother snapping her facial compact shut with a satisfied click, Father Turtle-waxing the Ford on Saturday afternoon: where is the pleasure to be located in these routines when the ultimate pleasure (as every adolescent discovers) is sexual—the disintegrating joy of a French kiss, the utterly selfish desire of the body to *know more?* Of course, we didn't understand the concept of guilt, major guilt—the kind that can't be erased from heart and mind, that distresses even ten, fifteen years later, whenever buried incidents float unbidden to the surface. How could we? We hadn't lived very much.

Saul watched as Stephen was stoned to death; Paul was celibate in order to serve his Christ more ardently. Aren't these flip sides of the same coin? And if not, where did Saul go? Who, if anyone, was in the body that sat three days in darkness in Damascus, who spoke before the crowds, who crouched in that dark prison cell and built up the body of Christian thought into a white and pillared building? Did he remember Saul at all—or had he, as Paul, burned away his past self so completely that with it fled the childhood words for stone and bread? What initially fills the void when the old self is struck down and out—what rushes in before the light, what rides the arrow tip of redemption into the benighted soul?

In the rattan chair beside the lily pond, far above the unspeakably blue waters of Lake Como, the poem for Paul takes shape:

On the Road to Damascus

They say I was struck down by the voice of an angel:
  flames poured through the radiant fabric of heaven
as I cried out and fell to my knees.

My first recollection was of Unbroken Blue,
  but two of the guards have already sworn by
the tip of my tongue set ablaze. As an official,

I recognize the lure of a good story:
  useless to suggest that my mount
had stumbled, that I was pitched into a clump

of wild chamomile, its familiar stink
  soothing even as my palms sprang blisters
under the nicked leaves. I heard shouts,

the horse pissing in terror—but my eyes
  had dropped to my knees, and I saw nothing.
I was a Roman and had my business

among the clouded towers of Damascus.
  I had not counted on earth rearing,
honey streaming down a parched sky,

a spear skewering me to the dust of the road
  on the way to the city I would never
enter now, her markets steaming with vendors

and compatriots in careless armor lifting a hand
  in greeting as they call out my name,
only to find no one home.

Paul's first visit to Ephesus lasted over two years, during which time he argued in the synagogue and converted "divers souls." Afterward he made for Jerusalem, sending back to Ephesus two disciples to keep the flame burning. In Paul's absence, the disciples met resistance from the silversmiths, who had a hefty business in shrines to the goddess Diana and naturally resented the loss in trade the new icon-less religion would occasion. Led by the silversmith Demetrius, the people rose up in defense of their goddess; when the disciples tried to speak, the crowd outshouted them, for two hours chanting "Great *is* Diana of the Ephesians." Forced to retreat, the disciples were recalled by Paul, who "embraced them" and set out himself for Ephesus, where he gave the heretics "much exhortation" (Acts 20:1–2).

Did Paul's harsh words succeed at Ephesus, or did Diana prevail? The Bible is curiously silent on this point. In fact, the authorship of the Epistle to the Ephesians is heavily disputed among theological scholars—and it was almost certainly not written for the Ephesians, though of course we have other testimonies of his ministry there. It hardly matters whether Paul wrote this epistle or not—the spirit of his thought is still intact. We know from Acts that Paul appeared at Ephesus with a bag of tricks, handkerchiefs emerging from his sleeves to heal the sick and raise the dead . . . and yet the artisans with their silver statuettes of Diana were still able to rouse the people: We want Diana, thousand-breasted deity, they told Paul's disciples, who were forced to retreat. Was the light in Paul's eyes too empty? Or was it simply that two mysticisms—the matriarchal vision of fertility and wholeness, the patriarchal vision of order and clarity—were insisting on their separate paths to glory?

When I was a teenager Paul seemed to be a hard man with an unrealistically severe code of sacrifice, a fanatic who devised silly laws of diet, dress codes, and impossible rules of behavior; an ideologue who equated belief with ethics and transformation with institutional rhetoric. This was the world view our assistant minister promulgated; Paul was his boogeyman.

I see now that Paul's proclamations were demanded of him. At that time Christianity was still a heresy within a larger tradition; Saul's persecution of Christians, his conversion, and his consequent wrangles with the priests of the Temple—these events were all in the family, so to speak. At the time when the Pauline Epistles were written, the biggest question for the new religion was whether or not to accept Gentiles; once that quandary was settled, more mundane issues (Can they remain uncircumcised? Must they obey the Judaic rules of diet?) were the order of the day. The disciples attempted to thread a path through the existing Old Testament laws; they sought an extension, and fulfillment, of Judaism. Paul's public needed concrete rules, so he gave them restrictions to hold on to: Wife, obey your husband; husband, love your wife—just as you obey Christ and He loves you. Children, obey your parents. Servants (this is the tricky one), obey your masters—followed by a telling conditional: "according to the flesh, with fear and trembling, in singleness of your heart, as unto Christ" (Ephesians 6:5–6). And because pictures are worth a thousand words, he gave them metaphors: the Church as a bride, Christ as bridegroom, and martial imagery sure to delight a city devoted to the huntress Diana. Gird the loins with truth, slip the feet into the Gospel of peace, take up the breastplate of righteousness and the shield of faith! Blatant theatrics, but it worked.

Yet Paul *was* a mystic. Only a mystic would address the newly converted with "And you *hath he quickened,* who were dead in trespasses and sins." Or: "the fulness of him that filleth all in all." Devising a system for connecting and reflection, a guide for conducting a life of energized joy—this is Paul's abiding light.

Whenever I move to a new place, the first thing I usually do is "cozy up" my study; I throw down rugs, mount marionettes on the walls, place a crystal or a hand-carved elephant on a shelf where my fidgety gaze might fall for a moment and rest. This time, though, it was different. After leaving the Rockefeller Study and Conference Center in Bellagio, I moved into what was easily the most nondescript room I have ever written poetry in—white brick, gray industrial-strength carpet—and yet, six months later I still could not bear to tack up so much as a single poster.

It was as if the photographs and paintings that used to provide companionship in my solitary hours of composition had ceased to serve as windows and begun to block the view. It seemed I required no distraction from the void. To put it less negatively: I no longer felt the need to focus in on an object in order to allow my thoughts free rein, unsupervised—a window had opened in me.

I was nearly finished writing "On the Road to Damascus" before I understood what about the gold-leaf-and-lapis universe in the painting the Canadian poet attributed to Bono had so moved me that morning in the Villa Serbelloni. Saul was terrified because the eyes that had studied the Law and looked calmly on at the slaying of another man had for the first time failed their owner. The Roman world, once as compact and manageable as the toylike apparition of the city of Damascus hovering on the horizon, had split apart, and he was falling into a mystery, bottomless and widening.

Paul's account of his conversion, on the other hand, is essentially the story of a seduction. He has been entered by Christ the Bridegroom and remade in the image of his Love. Then, as in any marriage, one must work at redemption; one must learn to forgive oneself.

H. D. writes: "We must be 'in love' before we can understand the mysteries of vision." This does not mean penetrating the mysterious, nor does it mean being taken by storm. Grace is a state of being, not an assault; and enlightenment, unlike epiphany, is neither brief nor particularly felicitous. The Saul in the painting knew better. Anyone who feels the need to connect the outside world with an interior presence must *absorb* the mysterious into the tangle of contradictions and longings that form each one of us. That's hard, ongoing work, and it never ends.

Further Reading

In Upper Egypt in 1945 Arab peasants by chance dug up a large earthenware jar that contained fifty-two early Christian documents. *The Gnostic Gospels* (1979), by Princeton University professor of religion Elaine Pagels, is a study of those documents and their significance. Pagels won the National Book Award and the National Book Critics Circle Award for this book.

The Nag Hammadi Library (rev. ed., 1988), edited by James M. Robinson, is a translation of the texts mentioned above, with an introductory essay for each. Included are "The Gospel of Truth," "The Gospel to the Egyptians," "The Gospel of Mary," etc. Nag Hammadi was the name of the town near which the discovery of the documents was made.

More on those crucial early centuries may be found in *Pagans and Christians* (1989) by Oxford University historian Robin Lane Fox. This is a detailed and engrossing study of the transition of the ancient world from pagan to Christian.

Jaroslav Pelikan, *Jesus Through the Centuries: His Place in the History of Culture* (1985). Each age has had its own image of Jesus, reflecting the needs and aspirations of that time. Pelikan here presents eighteen such images in their historical settings.

The Oxford Illustrated History of Christianity (1990), edited by John McManners, is a wide-ranging series of nineteen essays: Martin Marty, for example, contributes "North America"; Maurice Wile's topic is "What Christians Believe"; and Jeremy Johns focuses on "Christianity and Islam."

George Marsden is a professor in the Divinity School, Duke University, and a leading authority on Christian fundamentalism. See *Fundamentalism and American Culture* (1980), *Reforming Fundamentalism* (1988), and most recently, *Understanding Fundamentalism and Evangelicalism* (1991).

American Catholicism (rev. ed., 1969), by John Tracy Ellis, is a standard work, lucid and fair-minded. It is a volume in the Chicago History of American Civilization Series.

Two anthologies that offer most of the leading feminists and feminist issues of the last two decades are those by Carol P. Christ and Judith Plasgow (eds.), *Womanspirit Rising: A Feminist Reader in Religion* (1979); and Ann Loades (ed.), *Feminist Theology* (1990).

IX

ISLAM
The Straight Path

In the Name of God, the Merciful, the Compassionate
. . . Thee only we serve; to Thee alone we pray for succour.
Guide us in the straight path. . . .

Qur'an I:5

For most of its followers over the course of the centuries, Islam has been an uncomplicated but profoundly demanding way of life. Its teachings, as the orthodox have understood them, are explicit and comprehensive, and they require total commitment. The word "Islam" itself suggests the dominating theme of the religion: it means *submission* to the will of Allah. A Muslim is one who submits, who surrenders to God. It is as "uncomplicated" as that.

Islam had its origins in the seventh century with a single remarkable man whose life is described in the following pages by John L. Esposito. Muhammad claimed no special powers, no miracles, no extraordinary knowledge. He said only that he had been chosen (to his own amazement) to serve as God's messenger, as a prophet. Through ancient prophets—Abraham, Moses, and Jesus among them—God had spoken to other peoples. Those earlier revelations, however, had been incomplete, and they had been obscured and confused in their passage through time. Now the message was to be clarified and completed: Muhammad was to be the last and the greatest of the prophets.

And thus was the stage set for conflict between Muslims and Christians, which over the centuries has been one of humankind's saddest stories, a tragedy shot through with ignorance, fear, prejudice, hate—indeed, all the evils the two religions abhor.

Islam and Christianity each claim to be the final truth, the true religion; and in spite of the many beliefs the two religions share, each must deny the essential truth of the other. For Muslims, the divinity of Jesus is out of the question; for Christians, Muhammad was a false prophet. Expressing an attitude not untypical, Dante assigned Muhammad to the eighth circle of Hell, which is next to the bottom, horribly wounded (split open) as fitting punishment for one who brought division and discord into religion. The Qur'an, revered by Muslims, was misrepresented by

367

overtly hostile translators and interpretors.[1] Thomas Carlyle's summation of the Qur'an is notorious: "A wearisome, confused jumble, crude, incondite; endless iterations, long windedness, entanglement; . . . insupportable stupidity, in short! . . . One feels it difficult to see how any mortal ever could consider this Koran as a Book written in Heaven."[2]

In "The Qur'ānic Teaching" Fazlur Rahman discusses in some detail the sense in which Muhammad was a "messenger." The critical question has to do with the nature of the revelation Muhammad received—its "verbal character," in Rahman's phrase. The end result, in any event, is of course the Qur'an (the word means "recitation"), the title of which is itself an assertion about the form of the revelation. In Muslim belief, the Qur'an is a standing miracle, "that inimitable symphony, the very sounds of which move men to tears and ecstasy."[3] It is the absolutely infallible word of God: Muslims hold that the Qur'an in Arabic is an exact duplicate of an original Qur'an, also in Arabic, which is with God.

Most of the teachings revealed through Muhammad may have been recorded by scribes during Muhammad's lifetime; certainly all were committed to memory by men who had perfected that art. Shortly after the death of Muhammad in 632 C.E. an effort was initiated to collect and preserve the revelations, and during the Caliphate of Ulthman (644–653) an authorized collection was established.

Two of the readings in this chapter, one from the Middle Ages (al-Ghazali), the other contemporary (Martin Lings), have to do with Islamic mysticism, known as Sufism (probably from a word denoting the coarse woollen garments worn by early Sufi ascetics). The way of the Sufi is long, arduous, lonely, and radical: "Sufism reminds man to seek all that he needs inwardly within himself, to tear his roots from the outer world and plunge them in the Divine nature, which resides at the centre of his heart."[4] Al-Ghazali left a successful career and loved ones in order to have "no other occupation than the cultivation of retirement and solitude, together with religious and ascetic exercises, as I busied myself purifying my soul, improving my character and cleansing my heart for the constant recollection of God most high." The climactic end of the journey is the experience of the Divine, an ecstatic "union" that is utterly beyond words. Al-Ghazali says simply, "I learnt with certainty that it is above all the mystics who walk on the road of God," and later he adds, "in general what [the Sufis] manage to achieve is nearness to God."

Martin Lings, in "The Originality of Sufism," employs especially the striking image of a wave (which flows from the "Ocean of Infinitude," i.e., God) to convey something of the meaning of Sufism and the important sense in which it is "original."

1. Arthur J. Arberry provides an interesting and brief survey of the major translations of the Qur'an into English, in the Preface to his *The Koran Interpreted* (London: George Allen & Unwin, Ltd., 1955), pp. 7–28.

2. "Mohammed and Mohammedanism," in *Sacred Books of the East,* rev. ed. (New York: Colonial Press, 1900), pp. 198–99.

3. Mohammed Marmaduke Pickthall (trans.), *The Meaning of the Glorious Koran* (London: George Allen & Unwin, Ltd., 1930), p. vii.

4. Seyyed Hossein Nasr, *Sufi Essays* (Albany: State University of New York Press, 1972), p. 33.

The Five Pillars of Islam—the confession of faith, worship, wealth sharing, fasting, and the pilgrimage—are described by Ishma'il R. Faruqi in "Moments of the Religious Life." The Five Pillars constitute only a central core of duties, a *minimum*.

The final reading selection of the chapter, Seyyed Hossein Nasr's "Male and Female in Islamic Perspective," presents the point of view of traditional Islam on the roles of men and women. Those roles are decidedly *different* and are so because God intended a division of social and family responsibilities.

Muhammad, Prophet of God

John L. Esposito

John L. Esposito was born in 1940 in Brooklyn, New York, and educated at St. John's University (M.A.), the University of Pennsylvania, the Middle East Center for Arab Studies (Lebanon), and Temple University (Ph.D.). He has since taught or lectured at a number of schools both in the United States and abroad, including the Center for the Study of World Religions (Harvard), St. Anthony's College (Oxford), Tel Aviv University, the Hebrew University of Jerusalem, Haifa University, American University of Cairo, Kuwait University, and still others. At present, he is professor and director of international studies at College of the Holy Cross in Massachusetts, and serves as president of the American Council for Study of Islamic Literature.

Esposito is the author of Women in Muslim Family Law *and* Islam and Politics; *the editor of* Islam in Asia, Voices of Resurgent Islam, Islam and Development; *and the coeditor of* Islam in Transition.

In a concluding passage to Islam: The Straight Path, *from which the following selection is also taken, Esposito noted that "one-fifth of the world's population testifies to the dynamism of Islam and the continued commitment of Muslims to follow 'the straight path, the way of God, to whom belongs all that is in the heavens and all that is on earth' (42:52–53)."*

History, legend, and Muslim belief portray Muhammad as a remarkable man and prophet. While we know a good deal about Muhammad's life after his "call" to be God's messenger, historical records tell us little about Muhammad's early years prior to becoming a prophet at the age of forty in 610 C.E. The Quran has served as a major source for information regarding the life of the Prophet. In addition, Prophetic traditions (reports about what Muhammad said and did) and biographies give us a picture of his meaning and significance in early Islam as do Islamic calligraphy and art, where the names of Allah and Muhammad often occur side by side— God and His Prophet. Muhammad serves both as God's human instrument in bearing His revelation and as the model or ideal whom all believers should emulate. Thus, understanding Muhammad and his role in the early Islamic community is crucial for an appreciation of the development of early Islam as well as contemporary Muslim belief and practice.

Muhammad ibn Abdullah (the son of Abd Allah) was born in 570 c.e. Tradition tells us that he was orphaned at a young age. His father was a trader who died before Muhammad was born; his mother, Amina, died when he was only six years old. As a young man, Muhammad was employed in Mecca's thriving caravan trade. The city was at the crossroads of trade routes between the Indian Ocean and the Mediterranean. Central Arabia was emerging as a major commercial power, sitting astride important trade routes that extended from Africa across the Middle East to China and Malaysia. Muhammad became a steward or business manager for the caravans of a wealthy widow, Khadija, whom he subsequently married. Tradition tells us that at the time, Muhammad was twenty-five years old and Khadija was forty. During their fifteen years of marriage, they enjoyed a very close relationship and had three sons (who died in infancy) and four daughters. The most famous of Muhammad's surviving children was Fatima, who would marry Ali, the revered fourth caliph of Sunni Islam and the first legitimate *Imam* (leader) of Shii Islam.

Mecca was a prosperous center of trade and commerce. Yet it was a society in which traditional tribal ways were strained by Mecca's transition from a semi-Bedouin to a commercial, urban society. This process was accompanied by serious economic and social cleavages. Muhammad, who had become a successful member of Meccan society, was apparently profoundly affected by these changes. He enjoyed great respect for his judgment and trustworthiness, as was reflected by his nickname al-Amin, the trusted one. This rectitude was complemented by a reflective nature that led him to retreat regularly to a cave on Mt. Hira, a few miles north of Mecca. Here, in long periods of solitude, he contemplated his life and the ills of his society, seeking greater meaning and insight. Here, at the age of forty during the month of Ramadan, Muhammad the caravan leader became Muhammad the messenger of God. On the night Muslims call "The Night of Power and Excellence," he received the first of many revelations from God. A heavenly intermediary, later identified by tradition as the angel Gabriel, commanded, "Recite." Muhammad responded that he had nothing to recite. The angel persisted twice more, and each time a frightened and bewildered Muhammad pleaded that he did not know what to say. Finally, the words came to him:

> Recite in the name of your Lord who has created, Created man out of a germ-cell. Recite for your Lord is the Most Generous One Who has taught by the pen, Taught man what he did not know!

With this revelation, Muhammad joined that group of individuals whom Semitic faiths acknowledge as divinely inspired messengers or prophets of God. Muhammad continued to receive divine revelations over a period of twenty-two years (610–632). These messages were finally collected and written down in the Quran ("The Recitation"), Islam's sacred scripture.

Muslim tradition reports that Muhammad reacted to his "call" much the same as the Hebrew prophets. He was both frightened and reluctant. Frightened by the unknown—for surely he did not expect such an experience. Reluctant, at first, because he feared he was possessed and that others would use such grounds and dismiss his claims as inspired by spirits, or *jinns.* Despondent and confused, Muhammad set out to kill himself but was stopped when he again heard the voice say, "O Muhammad! You are the messenger of God and I am Gabriel." This message was reinforced by his wife, Khadija, who reassured him that he was neither mad nor possessed; the messenger was from God and not a demon. Interestingly, according to Muslim tradition a Christian played an important role as well. One of those whom Khadija and Muhammad turned to for advice was her Christian cousin, Waraqa ibn Qusayy. When he heard of Muhammad's experience, Waraqa reassured him:

> Surely, by Him in whose hand is Waraqa's soul, thou art the prophet of this people. There hath come unto thee the greatest Namus (angel or Gabriel) who came unto Moses. Like the Hebrew prophets, Thou wilt be called a liar, and they will use thee despitefully and cast thee out and fight against thee.[1]

For just such reasons, Muhammad, like many of the prophets before him, was initially reluctant to preach God's message. His fears would be realized.

The first ten years of Muhammad's preaching were difficult, marked by Meccan resistance and rejection. While there was a trickle of converts, opposition to Muhammad was formidable. For the powerful and prosperous Meccan oligarchy, the monotheistic message of this would-be reformer, with its condemnation of the socioeconomic inequities of Meccan life, constituted a direct challenge not only to traditional polytheistic religion but also to the power and prestige of the establishment, threatening their economic, social, and political interests. The Prophet denounced false contracts, usury, and the neglect and exploitation of orphans and widows. He defended the rights of the poor and the oppressed, asserting that the rich had an obligation to the poor and dispossessed. This sense of social commitment and responsibility was institutionalized in the form of religious tithes or taxes on wealth and agricultural lands. Like Amos and Jeremiah before him, Muhammad was a "warner" from God who admonished his hearers to repent and obey God, for the final judgment was near:

> Say: "O men, I am only for you a warner." Those who believe, and do deeds of righteousness—theirs shall be forgiveness and generous provision. And those who strive against Our signs to avoid them—they shall be inhabitants of Hell (Quran 22:49–50).

Muhammad's rejection of polytheism undermined the religious prestige of the Meccans (in particular, the Umayyad clan) as keepers of the Kaba, the religious shrine that housed the tribal idols. It threatened the considerable revenues that accrued from the annual pilgrimage and festival to this central sanctuary of Arabian tribal religion. This potential economic loss was coupled with the undermining of Meccan tribal political authority by Muhammad's claim to prophetic authority and leadership and his insistence that all true believers belonged to a single universal community *(umma)* that transcended tribal bonds.

---

1. *The Life of Muhammad,* translated by A. Guillaume (London: Oxford University Press, 1955), p. 107.

Creation of the Islamic Community

For almost ten years, Muhammad struggled in Mecca, preaching God's message and gathering a small band of faithful followers. Among the early converts were Ali, his cousin and son-in-law, and Abu Bakr, his future father-in-law and the first caliph, or successor of the Prophet. The deaths of Khadija and of his uncle and protector, Abu Talib, in 619 C.E. made life especially difficult. Meccan opposition escalated from derision and verbal attacks to active persecution. The core of the opposition came from the Umayyad clan of the Quraysh tribe. As we shall see, their descendants, even after converting to Islam at a later date, would continue to challenge the family of the Prophet. As conditions deteriorated in Mecca, Muhammad sent some of his followers to other areas, such as Christian Abyssinia, for safety. The situation changed significantly in 620. Muhammad was invited by a delegation from Yathrib (later called Medina), a city two hundred miles north of Mecca, to serve as a chief arbitrator or judge in a bitter feud between its Arab tribes. Muhammad and two hundred of his followers quietly emigrated, from July to September 622, to Medina. This migration *(hijra)* marked a turning point in Muhammad's fortunes and a new stage in the history of the Islamic movement. Islam took on political form with the establishment of an Islamic community-state at Medina. The significance of the *hijra* is reflected in its adoption as the beginning of the Islamic calendar. Muslims chose to date their history from neither Muhammad's birth nor his reception of the first revelation in 610, but from the creation of the Islamic community *(umma)*. The community, as much as the individual, was to be the vehicle for realizing God's will on earth.

Muhammad at Medina

At Medina, Muhammad had the opportunity to implement God's governance and message, for he was now the prophet-head of a religiopolitical community. He did this by establishing his leadership in Medina, subduing Mecca, and consolidating Muslim rule over the remainder of Arabia through diplomatic and military means.

Muhammad had come to Medina as the arbiter or judge for the entire community, Muslim and non-Muslim alike. In addition, he was the leader of all the Muslims, the commander of the faithful, both those who had emigrated from Mecca (the *muhajirin,* emigrants) and those raised in Medina (the *ansar,* helpers). While the majority of the Arab tribes came to embrace Islam, the Jewish tribes (that is, those Arabs who had previously converted to Judaism) remained an important minority. Muhammad promulgated a charter, sometimes called the constitution of Medina, that set out the rights and duties of all citizens and the relationship of the Muslim community *(umma)* to other communities. Muslims constituted an *umma* whose primary identity and bond were no longer to be tribal ties but a common religious faith and commitment. Jews were recognized as a separate community allied to the Muslim *umma,* but with religious and cultural autonomy.

As the Medinan state was taking shape, Muhammad also turned his attention to Mecca. Mecca was the religious, political, economic, and intellectual center of

Arabia. Its importance was not diminished by its hostility to Muhammad's preaching. If anything, further revelations to Muhammad, which designated Mecca as the direction *(qibla)* for prayer and the site for Muslim pilgrimage *(hajj),* increased its religious significance. Muslim religious fervor was matched by the power of Meccan tribal mores that branded the Muslims as secessionists and traitors. All the ingredients were there for a formidable battle. Muhammad initiated a series of raids against Meccan caravans, threatening both the political authority and the economic power of the Quraysh. Several important battles ensued. In 624 at Badr, near Medina, Muslim forces, though greatly outnumbered, defeated the Meccan army. For Muslims, then and now, the Battle of Badr has special significance. It was the first and a most decisive victory for the forces of monotheism over those of polytheism, for the army of God over the followers of ignorance and unbelief. God had sanctioned and assisted His soldiers (Quran 3:123, 8:42ff) in victory. Quranic witness to divine guidance and intervention made Badr a sacred symbol, and it was used throughout history, as evidenced most recently in the 1973 Egyptian-Israeli war, whose Egyptian code name was "Operation Badr."

The elation after Badr was dissipated when Muslims were defeated by the Meccans in the Battle of Uhud in 625, where Muhammad himself was wounded. Finally, in 627, frustrated by the growing strength of Muhammad, the Meccans mounted an all-out seige of Medina in order to once and for all crush their opposition. At the Battle of the "Ditch" (so named because the Muslims dug a trench to neutralize the Meccan cavalry), the Muslims held out so successfully against a coalition of Meccans and mercenary Bedouins that the coalition disintegrated. The Meccans withdrew. The failure of the Quraysh enhanced Muhammad's prestige and leadership among the tribes of Arabia, placing him in the ascendant position. He had consolidated his leadership in Medina, extended his influence over other tribal areas in the Hijaz, and asserted his independence of the then dominant tribe in central Arabia. The balance of power had shifted. Muhammad would now initiate, and Mecca would respond.

The final phase in the struggle between Medina and Mecca highlights the method and political genius of Muhammad. He employed both military and diplomatic means, often preferring the latter. Instead of seeking to rout his Meccan opponents, Muhammad sought to gain submission to God and His messenger by incorporating them within the Islamic community-state. A truce was struck in 628 at Hudaybiyah to permit the Muslims to make their pilgrimage to Mecca the following year. In 629, Muhammad established Muslim control over the Hijaz and led the pilgrimage to Mecca, as had been scheduled. Then in 630, Muhammad accused the Quraysh of breaking the treaty, and the Muslims marched on Mecca, ten thousand strong. The Meccans capitulated. Eschewing vengeance and the plunder of conquest, the Prophet instead accepted a settlement, granting amnesty rather than wielding the sword toward his former enemies. For their part, the Meccans converted to Islam, accepted Muhammad's leadership, and were incorporated within the *umma.*

During the next two years, Muhammad established his authority over much of Arabia. The Bedouins who resisted were defeated militarily. At the same time, so many tribes in Arabia sent delegations to come to terms with the successor to the

Quraysh that Muslim history remembers this period as the year of deputations. Alliances were forged. While many converted to Islam, others did not. Representatives were sent from Medina to teach the Quran and the duties and rituals of Islam, and to collect the taxes due Medina. In the spring of 632, Muhammad led the pilgrimage to Mecca, where the sixty-two-year-old leader preached his farewell sermon, exhorting his followers:

> Know ye that every Moslem is a brother unto every other Moslem, and that ye are now one brotherhood. It is not legitimate for any one of you, therefore, to appropriate unto himself anything that belongs to his brother unless it is willingly given him by that brother.[2]

These words summarize both the nature of the Islamic community and the accomplishment of the Prophet Muhammad. When he died three months later in June 632, all Arabia was united under the banner of Islam.

    2. Ibn Hisham, as quoted in Philip K. Hitti, *History of the Arabs,* 9th ed. (New York: St. Martin's Press, 1966), p. 120.

Selections, *The Koran*

A. J. Arberry (translator)

One of the acclaimed translators of the Qur'an was Mohammed Marmaduke Pick-thall, an Englishman who converted to Islam. He entitled his work The Meaning of the Glorious Koran: An Explanatory Translation *(1930) and said flatly in his Fore-word, "The* Koran *cannot be translated. That is the view of the old-fashioned Sheykhs [sheiks] and the view of the present writer."**

Arthur J. Arberry (1905–69), translator of the selections offered here, had similar doubts about his efforts: "Briefly, the rhetoric and rhythm of the Arabic of the Koran *are so characteristic, so powerful, so highly emotive, that any version whatsoever is bound in the nature of things to be but a poor copy of the glittering spendour of the original."***

Dr. Arberry was born in England and educated at Cambridge (Litt. D.). He was head of the Department of Classics in Cairo University and then professor of Persian at the University of London. The last two decades of his life he spent at Cambridge University as Sir Thomas Adams Professor of Arabic and fellow of Pembroke College. He has written a score of books in the field of Islamic studies, including Sufism, Rev-elation and Reason in Islam, The Doctrine of the Sufis, *and* An Introduction to the History of Sufism.

I
The Opening

In the Name of God, the Merciful, the Compassionate

Praise belongs to God, the Lord of all Being,
the All-merciful, the All-compassionate,
the Master of the Day of Doom.

5   Thee only we serve; to Thee alone we pray for succour.
Guide us in the straight path,

*(London: George Allen & Unwin, Ltd., 1930), p. vii.

**Preface, *The Koran Interpreted* (New York: Macmillan, 1973), p. 24.

Reprinted with the permission of the Macmillan Publishing Company from *The Koran Interpreted* by A. J. Arberry, translator. Copyright © George Allen and Unwin Ltd., 1955.

the path of those whom Thou hast blessed,
not of those against whom Thou art wrathful,
nor of those who are astray.

II
The Cow

In the Name of God, the Merciful, the Compassionate

ALIF LAM MIM[1]

That is the book, wherein is no doubt,
a guidance to the godfearing
who believe in the Unseen, and perform the prayer,
and expend of that We have provided them;
who believe in what has been sent down to thee
and what has been sent down before thee,
and have faith in the Hereafter;
those are upon guidance from their Lord,
those are the ones who prosper.

5 As for the unbelievers, alike it is to them
whether thou hast warned them or hast not warned them,
they do not believe.
God has set a seal on their hearts and on their hearing,
and on their eyes is a covering,
and there awaits them a mighty chastisement.

And some men there are who say,
"We believe in God and the Last Day";
but they are not believers.
They would trick God and the believers,
and only themselves they deceive,
and they are not aware.
In their hearts is a sickness,
and God has increased their sickness,
and there awaits them a painful chastisement
for that they have cried lies.
10 When it is said to them, "Do not corruption in the land,"
they say, "We are only ones that put things right."
Truly, they are the workers of corruption

---

1. *Editor's note:* A number of surahs begin with letters of the Arabic alphabet. Their significance is not known.

III
The House of Imran

In the Name of God, the Merciful, the Compassionate

ALIF LAM MIM

God
there is no god but He, the
Living, the Everlasting.

He has sent down upon thee the Book
with the truth, confirming what was before it,
and He sent down the Torah and the Gospel
aforetime, as guidance to the people,
    and He sent down the Salvation.

As for those who disbelieve in God's signs, for
them awaits a terrible chastisement; God is
    All-mighty, Vengeful.

From God nothing whatever is hidden
in heaven and earth. It is He who forms you
in the womb as he will. There is no god but He,
    the All-mighty, the All-wise.

5   It is He who sent down upon thee the Book,
wherein are verses clear that are the Essence
of the Book, and others ambiguous.
As for those in whose hearts is swerving,
they follow the ambiguous part, desiring
dissension, and desiring its interpretation;
and none knows its interpretation, save
only God. And those firmly rooted in
knowledge say, "We believe in it; all
is from our Lord"; yet none remembers, but men
    possessed of minds.

Our Lord, make not our hearts to swerve
after that Thou hast guided us; and give us
    mercy from Thee;
    Thou art the Giver.
Our Lord, it is Thou that shall gather
mankind for a day whereon is no doubt;
    verily God will
    not fail the tryst.
As for the unbelievers, their riches
will not avail them, neither their children,
    but they are not aware.

When it is said to them, "Believe as the people believe",
they say, "Shall we believe, as fools believe?"
     Truly, they are the foolish ones,
       but they do not know.
When they meet those who believe, they say, "We believe";
but when they go privily to their Satans, they say,
   "We are with you; we were only mocking."
   God shall mock them, and shall lead them on
   blindly wandering in their insolence.
   Those are they that have bought error
     at the price of guidance,
   and their commerce has not profited them,
     and they are not right-guided.
The likeness of them is as the likeness of a man
who kindled a fire, and when it lit all about him
God took away their light, and left them in darkness
         unseeing,
      deaf, dumb, blind—
    so they shall not return;
    or as a cloudburst out of heaven
in which is darkness, and thunder, and lightning—
    they put their fingers in their ears
   against the thunderclaps, fearful of death;
    and God encompasses the unbelievers;
the lightning wellnigh snatches away their sight;
whensoever it gives them light, they walk in it,
and when the darkness is over them, they halt;
   had God willed, He would have taken away
    their hearing and their sight.
   Truly, God is powerful over everything.

              · · ·

aught against God; those—they shall be
    fuel for the Fire
like Pharaoh's folk, and the people before them,
who cried lies to Our signs; God seized them
because of their sins; God is terrible
     in retribution.
10   Say to the unbelievers: "You shall be
overthrown, and mustered into Gehenna—
    an evil cradling!"

There has already been a sign for you
in the two companies that encountered,
one company fighting in the way of God
and another unbelieving; they saw them
twice the like of them, as the eye sees,

but God confirms with His help whom He will.
Surely in that is a lesson for men
    possessed of eyes.

Decked out fair to men is the love of lusts—
women, children, heaped-up heaps of gold
and silver, horses of mark, cattle
and tillage. That is the enjoyment of
the present life; but God—with Him is
    the fairest resort.
Say: "Shall I tell you of a better than that?"
For those that are godfearing, with their Lord
are gardens underneath which rivers flow,
therein dwelling forever, and spouses
purified, and God's good pleasure. And God
    sees His servants
who say, "Our Lord, we believe; forgive us
our sins, and guard us against the chastisement
    of the Fire"—
15   men who are patient, truthful, obedient,
expenders in alms, imploring God's pardon
    at the daybreak.

    God bears witness that
      there is no god but He—
and the angels, and men possessed of knowledge—
    upholding justice;
    there is no god but He,
  the All-mighty, the All-wise.

The true religion with God is Islam.

. . .

XXII
The Pilgrimage

In the Name of God, the Merciful, the Compassionate

    O men, fear your Lord!
Surely the earthquake of the Hour is a mighty thing;
on the day when you behold it, every suckling woman shall
neglect the child she has suckled, and every pregnant woman
shall deposit her burden, and thou shalt see mankind drunk,
yet they are not drunk, but God's chastisement is terrible.

    And among men there is such a one
    that disputes concerning God without knowledge
      and follows every rebel Satan,
    against whom it is written down that

whosoever takes him for a friend, him he
leads astray, and he guides him to the
        chastisement of the burning.
                O men,
if you are in doubt as to the Uprising,
    surely We created you of dust
            then of a sperm-drop,
            then of a blood clot,
then of a lump of flesh, formed and unformed
    that We may make clear to you.
    And We establish in the wombs
    what We will, till a stated term,
    then We deliver you as infants,
    then that you may come of age;
        and some of you die,
        and some of you are kept back
unto the vilest state of life, that after
knowing somewhat, they may know nothing.
And thou beholdest the earth blackened,
then, when We send down water upon it,
    it quivers, and swells, and puts forth
        herbs of every joyous kind.
    That is because God—He is the Truth,
    and brings the dead to life, and is powerful
            over everything,
and because the Hour is coming, no doubt of it, and
God shall raise up whosoever is within the tombs.

    And among men there is such a one
    that disputes concerning God without knowledge
    or guidance, or an illuminating Book,
    turning his side to lead astray
    from God's way; for him is degradation
    in this world, and on the Resurrection Day
    We shall let him taste the chastisement
        of the burning:
10   "That is for what thy hands have forwarded
    and for that God is never unjust
            unto His servants."

    And among men there is such a one
    as serves God upon the very edge—
    if good befalls him he is at rest in it,
    but if a trial befalls him he turns
    completely over; he loses this world
    and the world to come; that is indeed
        the manifest loss.
    He calls, apart from God, upon that

which hurts him not, and which neither
profits him anything; that is indeed
       the far error.
He calls upon him who is likelier
to hurt him, rather than to profit him—
an evil protector indeed, he,
       an evil friend!

God shall surely admit those who believe
and do righteous deeds into gardens
underneath which rivers flow; surely God does
       that He desires.

15   Whosoever thinks God will not help him
in the present world and the world to come,
let him stretch up a rope to heaven,
then let him sever it, and behold
whether his guile does away with what
       enrages him.

Even so We have sent it down as signs,
clear signs, and for that God guides
       whom He desires.
Surely they that believe, and those of Jewry,
the Sabaeans, the Christians, the Magians
and the idolaters—God shall distinguish
between them on the Day of Resurrection;
assuredly God is witness
       over everything.
Hast thou not seen how to God bow all who are in the heavens
       and all who are in the earth,
the sun and the moon, the stars and the mountains,
       the trees and the beasts,
and many of mankind? And many merit the chastisement;
       and whom God abases,
there is none to honour him. God does whatsoever He will.

20   These are two disputants who have disputed
concerning their Lord. As for the unbelievers,
for them garments of fire shall be cut,
and there shall be poured over their heads
       boiling water
whereby whatsoever is in their bellies
and their skins shall be melted; for them await
       hooked iron rods;
as often as they desire in their anguish
to come forth from it, they shall be restored
into it, and: "Taste the chastisement
       of the burning!"

God shall surely admit those who believe
and do righteous deeds into gardens
underneath which rivers flow; therein
they shall be adorned with bracelets of gold
and with pearls, and their apparel there
      shall be of silk;
and they shall be guided unto goodly speech,
and they shall be guided unto the path
      of the All-laudable.

25   Those who disbelieve, and bar from God's way
and the Holy Mosque that We have appointed
equal unto men, alike him who cleaves to it
      and the tent-dweller,
and whosoever purposes to violate it
wrongfully, We shall let him taste
      a painful chastisement.

. . .

LVI
The Terror

In the Name of God, the Merciful, the Compassionate

When the Terror descends
(and none denies its descending)
abasing, exalting,
when the earth shall be rocked
5   and the mountains crumbled
and become a dust scattered,
and you shall be three bands—

Companions of the Right (O Companions of the Right!)
Companions of the Left (O Companions of the Left!)
10   and the Outstrippers: the Outstrippers
those are they brought nigh the Throne,
in the Gardens of Delight
(a throng of the ancients
and how few of the later folk)
15   upon close-wrought couches
reclining upon them, set face to face,
immortal youths going round about them
with goblets, and ewers, and a cup from a spring
(no brows throbbing, no intoxication)
20   and such fruits as they shall choose,
and such flesh of fowl as they desire,
and wide-eyed houris
as the likeness of hidden pearls,

a recompense for that they laboured.
Therein they shall hear no idle talk, no cause of sin,
25   only the saying "Peace, Peace!"

The companions of the Right (O Companions of the Right!)
mid thornless lote-trees and serried acacias,
30   and spreading shade and outpoured waters,
and fruits abounding
unfailing, unforbidden,
and upraised couches,
Perfectly We formed them, perfect,
35   and We made them spotless virgins,
chastely amorous, like of age
for the Companions of the Right.
A throng of the ancients
and a throng of the later folk.

40 The Companions of the Left (O Companions of the Left!)
mid burning winds and boiling waters
and the shadow of a smoking blaze
neither cool, neither goodly;
and before that they lived at ease,
45   and persisted in the Great Sin,
ever saying,
"What, when we are dead and become
dust and bones, shall we indeed
be raised up?
What, and our fathers, the ancients?"

Say: "The ancients, and the later folk
shall be gathered to the appointed time
of a known day.
50 Then you erring ones, you that cried lies,
you shall eat of a tree called Zakkoum,
and you shall fill therewith your bellies
and drink on top of that boiling water
55 lapping it down like thirsty camels."
This shall be their hospitality on the
Day of Doom.

. . .

XCVI
The Blood-Clot

In the Name of God, the Merciful, the Compassionate

Recite: In the Name of thy Lord who created,
created Man of a blood-clot.

Recite: And thy Lord is the Most Generous,
who taught by the Pen,
5   taught Man that he knew not

No indeed; surely Man waxes insolent,
for he thinks himself self-sufficient.
Surely unto thy Lord is the Returning.

What thinkest thou? He who forbids
10   a servant when he prays—
What thinkest thou? If he were upon guidance
or bade to godfearing—
What thinkest thou? If he cries lies, and turns away—
Did he not know that God sees?

15   No indeed; surely, if he gives not over,
We shall seize him by the forelock,
a lying, sinful forelock.
So let him call on his concourse!
We shall call on the guards of Hell.

No indeed; do thou not obey him,
and bow thyself, and draw nigh.

CXII
Sincere Religion

In the Name of God, the Merciful, the Compassionate

Say: "He is God, One,
God, the Everlasting Refuge,
who has not begotten, and has not been begotten,
and equal to Him is not any one."

The Qur'ānic Teaching

Fazlur Rahman

Born in 1919 in India (in an area later to become part of Pakistan), Fazlur Rahman was raised in a deeply religious Muslim family. He has said that by the age of ten he could recite the entire Qur'ān by memory. He received his undergraduate education in India, but earned his doctorate from Oxford University. He taught at the University of Durham in England, and then at McGill University in Montreal, Canada. During most of the 1960s he was in Pakistan as head of the Islamic Research Institute, which had been established to advise the government on religious policies. Conservative opposition to him grew dangerous by 1968; he moved to a safer environment in California and a position at UCLA. After a brief tenure there, he was appointed, in 1969, professor of Islamic thought at the University of Chicago, where he remained until his death in 1988.

Rahman's many publications include Health and Medicine in the Islamic Tradition, Major Themes of the Qur'ān, *and* Islam and Modernity.

Rahman has been acclaimed the leading Muslim modernist scholar of his generation.*

What is the Qur'ān?

The Qur'ān is divided into Chapters or Sūras, 114 in number and very unequal in length. The early Meccan Sūras are among the shortest; as time goes on, they become longer. The verses in the early Sūras are charged with an extraordinarily deep and powerful "psychological moment"; they have the character of brief but violent volcanic eruptions. A voice is crying from the very depths of life and impinging forcefully on the Prophet's mind in order to make itself explicit at the level of consciousness. This tone gradually gives way, especially in the Medina period, to a more fluent and easy style as the legal content increases for the detailed organization and direction of the nascent community-state. This is certainly not to say either that the voice had been stilled or even that its intensive quality had changed: a Medinese verse declares "If We had sent down this Qur'ān on a mountain, you would have

*Frederick M. Denny, "The Legacy of Fazlur Rahman," in Yvonne Yazbeck Haddad (ed.), *The Muslims of America* (New York: Oxford University Press, 1991), p. 97.

From Fazlur Rahman, *Islam, Second Edition,* copyright © 1979 by The University of Chicago Press. Reprinted by permission of the publisher.

seen it humbly submit (to the Command) and split asunder out of fear of God" (LIX, 21). But the task itself had changed. From the thud and impulse of purely moral and religious exhortation, the Qur'ān had passed to the construction of an actual social fabric.

For the Qur'ān itself, and consequently for the Muslims, the Qur'ān is the Word of God *(Kalām Allāh)*. Muḥammad, too, was unshakeably convinced that he was the recipient of the Message from God, the totally Other (we shall presently try to discover more precisely the sense of that total otherness), so much so that he rejected, on the strength of this consciousness, some of the most fundamental historical claims of the Judaeo-Christian tradition about Abraham and other Prophets. This "Other" through some channel "dictated" the Qur'ān with an absolute authority. The voice from the depths of life spoke distinctly, unmistakably, and imperiously. Not only does the word *qur'ān,* meaning "recitation," clearly indicate this, but the text of the Qur'ān itself states in several places that the Qur'ān is *verbally revealed and not merely in its "meaning" and ideas. The Qur'ānic term for "Revelation" is waḥy* which is fairly close in its meaning to "inspiration," provided this latter is not supposed to exclude the verbal mode necessarily (by "Word," of course, we do not mean sound). The Qur'ān says, "God speaks to no human (i.e., through sound-words) except through *waḥy* (i.e., through idea-word inspiration) or from behind the veil, or He may send a messenger (an angel) who speaks through *waḥy*. . . . Even thus have We inspired you with a spirit of Our Command . . ." (XLII, 51–52).

When, however, during the second and the third centuries of Islam, acute differences of opinion, controversies partly influenced by Christian doctrines, arose among the Muslims about the nature of Revelation, the emerging Muslim "orthodoxy," which was at the time in the crucial stage of formulating its precise content, emphasized the *externality* of the Prophet's Revelation in order to safeguard its "otherness," objectivity, and verbal character. The Qur'ān itself certainly maintained the "otherness," the "objectivity," and the verbal character of the Revelation, but had equally certainly rejected its externality *vis-à-vis* the Prophet. It declares, "The Trusted Spirit has brought it down upon your heart that you may be a warner" (XXVI, 194), and again, "Say: He who is an enemy of Gabriel (let him be), for it is he who has brought it down upon your heart" (II, 97). But orthodoxy (indeed, all medieval thought) lacked the necessary intellectual tools to combine in its formulation of the dogma the otherness and verbal character of the Revelation on the one hand, and its intimate connection with the work and the religious personality of the Prophet on the other, i.e., it lacked the intellectual capacity to say both that the Qur'ān is entirely the Word of God and, in an ordinary sense, also entirely the word of Muḥammad. The Qur'ān obviously holds both, for if it insists that it has come to the "heart" of the Prophet, how can it be external to him? This, of course, does not necessarily imply that the Prophet did not perceive also a projected figure, as tradition has it, but it is remarkable that the Qur'ān itself makes no mention of any figure in this connection: it is only in connection with certain special experiences (commonly connected with the Prophet's Ascension) that the Qur'ān speaks of the Prophet having seen a figure or a spirit, or some other object "at the farthest end" or "on the horizon," although here also, . . . the experience is described as a spiritual one. But orthodoxy, through the Ḥadīth or the "tradition" from the Prophet, partly suitably interpreted and partly coined, and through the science of theology based largely on the Ḥadīth, made the Revelation of the Prophet entirely through the ear and external to him and regarded the angel or the spirit "that comes to the heart" an entirely external agent. The modern Western picture of the Prophetic Revelation rests largely on this orthodox formulation rather than on the Qur'ān, as does, of course, the belief of the common Muslim.

The present work is not the place to elaborate a theory of the Qur'ānic Revelation in detail. Yet, if we are to deal with facts of Islamic history, the factual statements of the Qur'ān about itself call for some treatment. In the following brief outline an attempt is made to do justice both to historical and Islamic demands. . . . The basic élan of the Qur'ān is moral, whence flows its emphasis on monotheism as well as on social justice. The moral law is immutable: it is God's "Command." Man cannot make or unmake the Moral Law: he must submit himself to it, this submission to it being called *islām* and its implementation in life being called *'ibāda* or "service to God." It is because of the Qur'ān's paramount emphasis on the Moral Law that the Qur'ānic God has seemed to many people to be primarily the God of justice. But the Moral Law and spiritual values, in order to be implemented, must be known. Now, in their power of cognitive perception men obviously differ to an indefinite degree. Further, moral and religious perception is also very different from a *purely* intellectual perception, for an intrinsic quality of the former is that along with perception it brings an extraordinary sense of "gravity" and leaves the subject significantly transformed. Perception, also moral perception, then has degrees. The variation is not only between different individuals, but the inner life of a given individual varies at different times from this point of view. We are not here talking of an intrinsic moral and intellectual development and evolution, where variation is most obvious. But even in a good, mature person whose average intellectual and moral character and calibre are, in a sense, fixed, these variations occur.

Now a Prophet is a person whose average, overall character, the sum total of his actual conduct, is far superior to those of humanity in general. He is a man who is *ab initio* impatient with men and even with most of their ideals, and wishes to re-create history. Muslim orthodoxy, therefore, drew the logically correct conclusion that Prophets must be regarded as immune from serious errors (the doctrine of *'iṣma*). Muḥammad was such a person, in fact the only such person really known to history. That is why his overall behaviour is regarded by the Muslims as Sunna or the "perfect model." But, with all this, there were moments when he, as it were, "transcends himself" and his moral cognitive perception becomes so acute and so keen that his consciousness becomes identical with the moral law itself. "Thus did we inspire you with a Spirit of Our Command: You did not know what the Book was. But We have made it a light" (XLII, 52). But the moral law and religious values are God's Command, and although they are not identical with God entirely, they are part of Him. The Qur'ān is, therefore, purely divine. Further, even with regard to ordinary consciousness, it is a mistaken notion that ideas and feelings float about in it and can be mechanically "clothed" in words. There exists, indeed, an organic relationship between feelings, ideas, and words. In inspiration, even in poetic inspiration, this relationship is so complete that feeling-idea-word is a total complex with a life of its own. When Muḥammad's moral intuitive perception rose to the highest point and became identified with the moral law itself (indeed, in these moments his own conduct at points came under Qur'ānic criticism, . . . as is evident from the pages of the Qur'ān), the Word was given with the inspiration itself. The Qur'ān is thus pure Divine Word, but, of course, it is equally intimately related to the inmost personality of the Prophet Muḥammad whose relationship to it cannot be mechanically conceived like that of a record. The Divine Word flowed through the Prophet's heart.

But if Muḥammad, in his Qur'ānic moments, became one with the moral law, he may not be absolutely identified either with God or even with a part of Him. The Qur'ān categorically forbids this, Muḥammad insistently avoided this and all Muslims worthy of the name have condemned as the gravest error associating *(shirk)* a creature with God. The reason is that no man may say, "I am the Moral Law." Man's duty is carefully to formulate this Law and to submit to it with all his physical, mental, and spiritual faculties. Besides this, Islam knows of no way of assigning any meaning to the sentence, "So-and-so is Divine."

The Qur'ānic Teaching

In the foregoing we have repeatedly emphasized that the basic élan of the Qur'ān is moral and we have pointed to the ideas of social and economic justice that immediately followed from it in the Qur'ān. This is absolutely true so far as man and his destiny are concerned. As the Qur'ān gradually worked out its world-view more fully, the moral order for men comes to assume a central point of divine interest in a full picture of a cosmic order which is not only charged with a high religious sensitivity but exhibits an amazing degree of coherence and consistency. A concept of God, the absolute author of the universe, is developed where the attributes of creativity, order, and mercy are not merely conjoined or added to one another but interpenetrate completely. To Him belong creativity and "ordering" or "commanding" (VII, 54). "My mercy encompasses everything" (VII, 156). Indeed, the "Merciful" (Raḥmān) is the only adjectival name of God that is very frequently used in the Qur'ān as a substantive name of God besides Allāh. It is of course, true, as modern research has revealed, that Raḥmān was used as name for the Deity in South Arabia before Islam, but this fact of historical transportation from the South is obviously irrelevant from our point of view. If we leave out man, for the time being, i.e., his specific spiritual-moral constitution, and consider the rest of the entire created universe, the interpretation of these three ultimate attributes is that God creates everything, and that in the very act of this creation order or "command" is ingrained in things whereby they cohere and fall into a pattern, and rather than "go astray" from the ordained path, evolve into a cosmos; that, finally, all this is nothing but the sheer mercy of God for, after all, existence is not the absolute desert of anything, and in the place of existence there could just as well be pure, empty nothingness.

Indeed, the most intense impression that the Qur'ān as a whole leaves upon a reader is not of a watchful, frowning, and punishing God, as the Christians have generally made it out to be, nor of a chief judge as the Muslim legalists have tended to think, but of a unitary and purposive will creative of order in the universe: the qualities of power or majesty, of watchfulness or justice and of wisdom attributed to God in the Qur'ān with unmistakable emphasis are, in fact, immediate inferences from the creative orderliness of the cosmos. Of all the Qur'ānic terms, perhaps the most basic, comprehensive, and revelatory at once of divine nature of the universe is the term *amr* which we have translated above as order, orderliness, or command. To everything that is created is *ipso facto* communicated its *amr* which is its own law of being but which is also a law whereby it is integrated into a system. This *amr*, i.e., order or command of God, is ceaseless. The term used to indicate the communication of *amr* to all things, including man, is *waḥy*, which we have translated in the previous section as "inspiration." With reference to inorganic things it should be translated as "ingraining." This is because with reference to man, who constitutes a special case, it is not just *amr* that is sent down from high, but a "spirit-from-*amr*" *(rūh min al-amr),* as the Qur'ān repeatedly tells us.

With reference to man (and possibly also to the *jinn,* an invisible order of creation, parallel to man but said to be created of a fiery substance, a kind of duplicate of man which is, in general, more prone to evil, and from whom the devil is also said to have sprung), both the nature and the content of *amr* are transformed, because *amr* really becomes here the moral command: it is not that which actually is an order but that which actually is a disorder wherein an order *is to be* brought about. The actual moral disorder is the result of a deep-seated moral fact to remedy which God and man must collaborate. This fact is that coeval with man is the devil *(shayṭān)* who beguiles him unceasingly.

The Qur'ān portrays the moral dualism in man's character which gives rise to the moral struggle, and the potentialities man and man alone possesses, by two strikingly effective stories. According to one, when God intended to create man as his vicegerent, the angels protested to Him saying that man would be prone to evil, "corrupt the earth and shed blood," while they were utterly obedient to the Divine Will, whereupon God replied, "I have knowledge of that which you do not know" (II, 30). The other story tells us that when God offered "The Trust" to the Heavens and the Earth, the entire Creation refused to accept it, until man came forward and bore it, adding with a sympathetic rebuke, "Man is so ignorant and foolhardy!" (XXXIII, 72). There can be hardly a more penetrating and effective characterization of the human situation and man's frail and faltering nature, yet his innate boldness and the will to transcend the actual towards the ideal constitutes his uniqueness and greatness. This fact of the devil creates an entirely new dimension in the case of man. God "has ingrained in it (i.e., the human soul) a discernment of good and evil" (XCI, 8); but so artful and powerful is the devil's seduction that men normally fail even to decipher properly this eternal inscription of God on the human heart, while some who can decipher it fail to be moved and impelled by it sufficiently strongly. At times of such crisis God finds and selects some human to whom he sends the angel "the spirit of the Command" that is "with Him." The Command that is with Him is so sure, so definite in what it affirms and denies that it is, indeed, the "Invisible Book" written on a "Preserved Tablet," the "Mother of (all) Books"

(LVI, 78; LXXXV, 21–22; XIII, 39). Men charged with these fateful messages to humanity are the Prophets. The Qur'ān "sent" to Muḥammad is the Book that reveals the Command: Muḥammad is the final Prophet and the Qur'ān the last Book that has been so revealed.

With this background, therefore, the Qur'ān emerges as a document that from the first to the last seeks to emphasize all those moral tensions that are necessary for creative human action. Indeed, at bottom the centre of the Qur'ān's interest is man and his betterment. For this it is essential that men operate within the framework of certain tensions which, indeed, have been created by God in him. First and foremost, man may not jump to the suicidal conclusion that he can make and unmake moral law according to his "heart's desire" from the obvious fact that this law is there *for him.* Hence the absolute supremacy and the majesty of God are most strikingly emphasized by the Qur'ān. On the other hand among all creation, man has been given the most immense potentialities and is endowed with the "Trust" which entire creation shrank back in fear from accepting. Again, the idea of justice flows directly from that of the supremacy of the moral law, an idea equally emphasized by the Qur'ān. But with the same insistence the Qur'ān condemns hopelessness and lack of trust in the mercy of God, which it declares to be a cardinal infidelity. The same is true of the whole range of moral tensions, including human power and weakness, knowledge and ignorance, sufferance and retaliation, etc. While the potentialities of man are immense, equally immense, therefore, are the penalties which man must face as a result of his failure.

In pursuance of this picture, belief in one God stands at the apex of the Muslim system of belief derived from the Qur'ān. From this belief is held to follow belief in angels (spirits of the Command) as transmitters of the Divine message to man, in the Prophets, the human repositories of the Divine revelation (the last in the series being Muḥammad), in the genuineness of the messages of the Prophets, the "Book," and in the Day of Reckoning.

Deliverance from Error

Al-Ghazali

Abu Hamid Muhammad al-Ghazali (1058–1111) was born in Tus, Persia. Showing signs of genius from his earliest days, he received a good education and was soon launched into a brilliant academic career. He lectured, published, and enjoyed a growing reputation, but at the same time grew increasingly troubled by spiritual questions until he finally found himself unable to continue. That crisis and his decision to withdraw from all activities—even from his family—is described in the pages that follow. He became a Sufi and, after a decade of study, meditation, and a pilgrimage to Mecca, he returned, at peace with himself, to public life.

"Deliverance from Error" is from al-Ghazali's work by the same title, translated here by W. Montgomery Watt. Professor Watt (1909–) was born in Scotland and educated at the University of Edinburgh and Balliol College, Oxford. His career was spent mainly at the University of Edinburgh as a professor, over the years, of moral philosophy, ancient philosophy, and Arabic and Islamic studies. He is the author of Muslim Intellectual: A Study of al-Ghazali, *as well as other books on Islam* (Muhammad at Mecca, Muhammad at Medina, Islamic Philosophy and Theology, Islamic Revelation in the Modern World, What Is Islam?, *and many more. His books have been translated into eight languages.*

You must know—and may God most high perfect you in the right way and soften your hearts to receive the truth—that the different religious observances and religious communities of the human race and likewise the different theological systems of the religious leaders, with all the multiplicity of sects and variety of practices, constitute ocean depths in which the majority drown and only a minority reach safety. Each separate group thinks that it alone is saved, and "each party is rejoicing in what they have" (Q. 23, 55; 30, 31).[1] This is what was foretold by the prince of the Messengers (God bless him), who is true and trustworthy, when he said, "My community will be split up into seventy-three sects, and but one of them is saved"; and what he foretold has indeed almost come about.

From my early youth, since I attained the age of puberty before I was twenty, until the present time when I am over fifty, I have ever recklessly launched out into

---

1. *Editor's note:* The reference is to the Qur'an, Sura 23, Verse 55; Sura 30, Verse 31.

From W. Montgomery Watt, *The Faith and Practice of Al-Ghazali,* copyright © 1956 George Allen and Unwin Ltd. Reprinted by permission of HarperCollins, Publishers.

the midst of these ocean depths, I have ever bravely embarked on this open sea, throwing aside all craven caution; I have poked into every dark recess, I have made an assault on every problem, I have plunged into every abyss, I have scrutinized the creed of every sect, I have tried to lay bare the inmost doctrines of every community. . . .

To thirst after a comprehension of things as they really are was my habit and custom from a very early age. It was instinctive with me, a part of my God-given nature, a matter of temperament and not of my choice or contriving. Consequently as I drew near the age of adolescence the bonds of mere authority *(taqlīd)* ceased to hold me and inherited beliefs lost their grip upon me, for I saw that Christian youths always grew up to be Christians, Jewish youths to be Jews and Muslim youths to be Muslims. . . .

The Ways of Mysticism

When I had finished with these sciences, I next turned with set purpose to the method of mysticism (or Sufism). I knew that the complete mystic "way" includes both intellectual belief and practical activity; the latter consists in getting rid of the obstacles in the self and in stripping off its base characteristics and vicious morals, so that the heart may attain to freedom from what is not God and to constant recollection of Him.

The intellectual belief was easier to me than the practical activity. . . . It became clear to me, however, that what is most distinctive of mysticism is something which cannot be apprehended by study, but only by immediate experience *(dhawq*—literally "tasting"), by ecstasy and by a moral change. What a difference there is between *knowing* the definition of health and satiety, together with their causes and presuppositions, and *being* healthy and satisfied! What a difference between being acquainted with the definition of drunkenness—namely, that it designates a state arising from the domination of the seat of the intellect by vapours arising from the stomach—and being drunk!

. . .

It had already become clear to me that I had no hope of the bliss of the world to come save through a God-fearing life and the withdrawal of myself from vain desire. It was clear to me too that the key to all this was to sever the attachment of the heart to worldly things by leaving the mansion of deception and returning to that of eternity, and to advance towards God most high with all earnestness. It was also clear that this was only to be achieved by turning away from wealth and position and fleeing from all time-consuming entanglements.

Next I considered the circumstances of my life, and realized that I was caught in a veritable thicket of attachments. I also considered my activities, of which the best was my teaching and lecturing, and realized that in them I was dealing with sciences that were unimportant and contributed nothing to the attainment of eternal life.

After that I examined my motive in my work of teaching, and realized that it was not a pure desire for the things of God, but that the impulse moving me was the desire for an influential position and public recognition. I saw for certain that I was on the brink of a crumbling bank of sand and in imminent danger of hell-fire unless I set about to mend my ways.

I reflected on this continuously for a time, while the choice still remained open to me. One day I would form the resolution to quit Baghdad and get rid of these adverse circumstances; the next day I would abandon my resolution. I put one foot forward and drew the other back. If in the morning I had a genuine longing to seek eternal life, by the evening the attack of a whole host of desires had reduced it to impotence. Worldly desires were striving to keep me by their chains just where I was, while the voice of faith was calling, "To the road! to the road! What is left of life is but little and the journey before you is long. All that keeps you busy, both intellectually and practically, is but hypocrisy and delusion. If you do not prepare *now* for eternal life, when will you prepare? If you do not now sever these attachments, when will you sever them?" On hearing that, the impulse would be stirred and the resolution made to take to flight.

Soon, however, Satan would return. "This is a passing mood," he would say; "do not yield to it, for it will quickly disappear; if you comply with it and leave this influential position, these comfortable and dignified circumstances where you are free from troubles and disturbances, this state of safety and security where you are untouched by the contentions of your adversaries, then you will probably come to yourself again and will not find it easy to return to all this."

For nearly six months beginning with Rajab A.H. 488 (= July A.D. 1095),[2] I was continuously tossed about between the attractions of worldly desires and the impulses towards eternal life. In that month the matter ceased to be one of choice and became one of compulsion. God caused my tongue to dry up so that I was prevented from lecturing. One particular day I would make an effort to lecture in order to gratify the hearts of my following, but my tongue would not utter a single word nor could I accomplish anything at all.

This impediment in my speech produced grief in my heart, and at the same time my power to digest and assimilate food and drink was impaired; I could hardly swallow or digest a single mouthful of food. My powers became so weakened that the doctors gave up all hope of successful treatment. "This trouble arises from the heart," they said, "and from there it has spread through the constitution; the only method of treatment is that the anxiety which has come over the heart should be allayed."

Thereupon, perceiving my impotence and having altogether lost my power of choice, I sought refuge with God most high as one who is driven to Him, because he is without further resources of his own.

. . .

I left Baghdad, then. I distributed what wealth I had, retaining only as much as would suffice myself and provide sustenance for my children. This I could easily

---

2. *Editor's note:* As John L. Esposito mentioned in his essay, the Muslim calendar begins with the first day of Muhammad's Hijrah (or Hegira) from Mecca to Medina. On the Julian/Gregorian calendar, it was July 16, 622. The Muslim calendar is a lunar calendar.

manage, as the wealth of 'Iraq was available for good works, since it constitutes a trust fund for the benefit of the Muslims. Nowhere in the world have I seen better financial arrangements to assist a scholar to provide for his children.

In due course I entered Damascus, and there I remained for nearly two years with no other occupation than the cultivation of retirement and solitude, together with religious and ascetic exercises, as I busied myself purifying my soul, improving my character, and cleansing my heart for the constant recollection of God most high, as I had learnt from my study of mysticism. I used to go into retreat for a period in the mosque of Damascus, going up the minaret of the mosque for the whole day and shutting myself in so as to be alone.

At length I made my way from Damascus to the Holy House (that is, Jerusalem). There I used to enter into the precinct of the Rock every day and shut myself in.

Next there arose in me a prompting to fulfil the duty of the Pilgrimage, gain the blessings of Mecca and Medina, and perform the visitation of the Messenger of God most high (peace be upon him), after first performing the visitation of al-Khalīl, the Friend of God (God bless him).[3] I therefore made the journey to the Hijaz. Before long, however, various concerns, together with the entreaties of my children, drew me back to my home (country); and so I came to it again, though at one time no one had seemed less likely than myself to return to it. Here, too, I sought retirement, still longing for solitude and the purification of the heart for the recollection (of God). The events of the interval, the anxieties about my family, and the necessities of my livelihood altered the aspect of my purpose and impaired the quality of my solitude, for I experienced pure ecstasy only occasionally, although I did not cease to hope for that; obstacles would hold me back, yet I always returned to it.

I continued at this stage for the space of ten years, and during these periods of solitude there were revealed to me things innumerable and unfathomable. This much I shall say about that in order that others may be helped: I learnt with certainty that it is above all the mystics who walk on the road of God; their life is the best life, their method the soundest method, their character the purest character; indeed, were the intellect of the intellectuals and the learning of the learned and the scholarship of the scholars, who are versed in the profundities of revealed truth, brought together in the attempt to improve the life and character of the mystics, they would find no way of doing so; for to the mystics all movement and all rest, whether external or internal, brings illumination from the light of the lamp of prophetic revelation; and behind the light of prophetic revelation there is no other light on the face of the earth from which illumination may be received.

In general, then, how is a mystic "way" *(tarīqah)* described? The purity which is the first condition of it (as bodily purity is the prior condition of formal Worship for Muslims) is the purification of the heart completely from what is other than God most high; the key to it, which corresponds to the opening act of adoration in prayer, is the sinking of the heart completely in the recollection of God; and the end

---

3. That is, Abraham, who is buried in the cave of Machpelah under the mosque at Hebron, which is called "al-Khalīl" in Arabic; similarly the visitation of the Messenger is the formal visit to his tomb at Medina.

of it is complete absorption *(fanā')* in God. At least this is its end relatively to those first steps which almost come within the sphere of choice and personal responsibility; but in reality in the actual mystic "way" it is the first step, what comes before it being, as it were, the antechamber for those who are journeying towards it.

With this first stage of the "way" there begin the revelations and visions. The mystics in their waking state now behold angels and the spirits of the prophets; they hear these speaking to them and are instructed by them. Later, a higher state is reached; instead of beholding forms and figures, they come to stages in the "way" which it is hard to describe in language; if a man attempts to express these, his words inevitably contain what is clearly erroneous.

In general what they manage to achieve is nearness to God. . . .

The True Nature of Prophecy

You must know that the substance of man in his original condition was created in bareness and simplicity without any information about the worlds of God most high. These worlds are many, not to be reckoned save by God most high Himself. As He said, "None knows the hosts of thy Lord save He" (Q. 74, 34). Man's information about the world is by means of perception; and every perception of perceptibles is created so that thereby man may have some acquaintance with a world (or sphere) from among existents. By "worlds (or spheres)" we simply mean "classes of existents."

The first thing created in man was the sense of *touch,* and by it he perceives certain classes of existents, such as heat and cold, moisture and dryness, smoothness and roughness. Touch is completely unable to apprehend colours and noises. These might be non-existent so far as concerns touch.

Next there is created in him the sense of *sight,* and by it he apprehends colours and shapes. This is the most extensive of the worlds of sensibles. Next *hearing* is implanted in him, so that he hears sounds of various kinds. After that *taste* is created in him; and so on until he has completed the world of sensibles.

Next, when he is about seven years old, there is created in him *discernment* (or the power of distinguishing—*tamyīz*). This is a fresh stage in his development. He now apprehends more than the world of sensibles; and none of these additional factors (relations, etc.) exists in the world of sense.

From this he ascends to another stage, and *intellect* (or reason) *('aql)* is created in him. He apprehends things necessary, possible, impossible, things which do not occur in the previous stages.

Beyond intellect there is yet another stage. In this another eye is opened, by which he beholds the unseen, what is to be in the future, and other things which are beyond the ken of intellect in the same way as the objects of intellect are beyond the ken of the faculty of discernment and the objects of discernment are beyond the ken of sense. Moreover, just as the man at the stage of discernment would reject and disregard the objects of intellect were these to be presented to him, so some intellectuals reject and disregard the objects of prophetic revelation. That is sheer ignorance. They have no ground for their view except that this is a stage which they have not reached and which for them does not exist; yet they suppose that it is non-existent in itself. When a man blind from birth, who has not learnt about colours and shapes by listening to people's talk, is told about these things for the first time, he does not understand them nor admit their existence.

.   .   .

Teaching Again

I had persevered thus for nearly ten years in retirement and solitude. I had come of necessity—from reasons which I do not enumerate, partly immediate experience, partly demonstrative knowledge, partly acceptance in faith—to a realization of various truths. I saw that man was constituted of body and heart; by "heart" I mean the real nature of his spirit which is the seat of his knowledge of God, and not the flesh and blood which he shares with the corpse and the brute beast. I saw that just as there is health and disease in the body, respectively causing it to prosper and to perish, so also there is in the heart, on the one hand, health and soundness—and "only he who comes to God with a sound heart" (Q. 26, 89) is saved—and, on the other hand, disease, in which is eternal and other worldly destruction—as God most high says, "in their hearts is disease" (Q. 2, 9). I saw that to be ignorant of God is destructive poison, and to disobey Him by following desire is the thing which produces the disease, while to know God most high is the life-giving antidote and to obey Him by opposing desire is the healing medicine. I saw, too, that the only way to treat the heart, to end its disease and procure its health, is by medicines, just as that is the only way of treating the body.

.   .   .

In general, the prophets are the physicians of the diseases of hearts.

The Originality of Sufism
Martin Lings

Martin Lings (1909–) was born in England and educated at Magdalen College, Oxford, and London University, from which he earned his doctorate. He taught abroad for several years, at the University of Kaunas (Lithuania) and the University of Cairo, and then returned to England with a position as keeper of oriental manuscripts and books, first at the British Museum, later at the British Library in London.

He is the author of several books: A Book of Certainty, A Muslim Saint of the Twentieth Century *(a second edition was entitled* A Sufi Saint of the Twentieth Century), Ancient Beliefs and Modern Superstitions, Shakespeare in the Light of Sacred Art, The Elements and Other Poems, *and* The Heralds and Other Poems. *He has also been a contributor to the* Encyclopedia Britannica *and to the* New Encyclopedia of Islam.

Dr. Lings is a practicing Sufi.

The great Andalusian Sufi, Muhyi 'd-Dīn Ibn 'Arabī, used to pray a prayer which begins: "Enter me, O Lord, into the deep of the Ocean of Thine Infinite Oneness,"[1] and in the treatises of the Sufis this "Ocean" is mentioned again and again, likewise by way of symbolic reference to the End towards which their path is directed. Let us therefore begin by saying, on the basis of this symbol, in answer to the question "What is Sufism?": From time to time a Revelation "flows" like a great tidal wave from the Ocean of Infinitude to the shores of our finite world; and Sufism is the vocation and the discipline and the science of plunging into the ebb of one of these waves and being drawn back with it to its Eternal and Infinite Source.

"From time to time": this is a simplification which calls for a commentary; for since there is no common measure between the origin of such a wave and its destination, its temporality is bound to partake, mysteriously, of the Eternal, just as its finiteness is bound to partake of the Infinite. Being temporal, it must first reach this world at a certain moment in history; but that moment will in a sense escape from time. *Better than a thousand months*[2] is how the Islamic Revelation describes the

1. British Museum Ms. Or. 13453 (3).

2. Qur'ān XCVII: 3.

night of its own advent. There must also be an end which corresponds to the beginning; but that end will be too remote to be humanly foreseeable. Divine institutions are made *for ever*.[3] Another imprint of the Eternal Present upon it will be that it is always flowing and always ebbing in the sense that it has, virtually, both a flow and an ebb for every individual that comes within its scope.

There is only one water, but no two Revelations are outwardly the same. Each wave has its own characteristics according to its destination, that is, the particular needs of time and place towards which and in response to which it has providentially been made to flow. These needs, which include all kinds of ethnic receptivities and aptitudes such as vary from people to people, may be likened to the cavities and hollows which lie in the path of the wave. The vast majority of believers are exclusively concerned with the water which the wave deposits in these receptacles and which constitutes the formal aspect of the religion.

Mystics on the other hand—and Sufism is a kind of mysticism—are by definition concerned above all with "the mysteries of the Kingdom of Heaven"; and it would therefore be true to say, in pursuance of our image, that the mystic is one who is consequently more preoccupied by the ebbing wave than by the water which it has left behind. He has none the less need of this residue like the rest of his community—need, that is, of the outward forms of his religion which concern the human individual as such. For if it be asked what is it in the mystic that can ebb with the ebbing wave, part of the answer will be: not his body and not his soul. The body cannot ebb until the Resurrection, which is the first stage of the reabsorption of the body—and with it the whole material state—into the higher states of being. As to the soul, it has to wait until the death of the body. Until then, though immortal, it is imprisoned in the world of mortality. At the death of Ghazālī, the great eleventh-century Sufi, a poem which he had written in his last illness was found beneath his head. In it are the lines:

> A bird I am: this body was my cage
> But I have flown leaving it as a token.[4]

Other great Sufis also have said what amounts to the same: but they have also made it clear in their writing or speaking or living—and this is, for us, the measure of their greatness—that something in them had already ebbed before death despite the "cage," something incomparably more important than anything that has to wait for death to set it free.

What is drawn back by spiritual realisation towards the Source might be called the centre of consciousness. The Ocean is within as well as without; and the path of the mystics is a gradual awakening as it were "backwards" in the direction of the root of one's being, a remembrance of the Supreme Self which infinitely transcends the human ego and which is none other than the Deep towards which the wave ebbs.

To use a very different image which will help to complete the first, let us liken this world to a garden—or more precisely, to a nursery garden, for there is nothing

---

3. Exodus XII: 14.

4. British Museum Ms. Or. 7561, f. 86. The whole poem is translated in Margaret Smith's *Al-Ghazālī the Mystic* (Luzac, 1944), pp. 36–37.

in it that has not been planted there with a view to its being eventually transplanted elsewhere. The central part of the garden is allotted to trees of a particularly noble kind, though relatively small and growing in earthenware pots; but as we look at them, all our attention is caught by one that is arrestingly finer than any of the others, which it far excels in luxuriance and vigour of growth. The cause is not naked to the eye, but we know at once what has happened, without the need for any investigation: the tree has somehow been able to strike root deep into the earth through the base of its receptacle.

The trees are souls, and that tree of trees is one who, as the Hindus say, has been "liberated in life," one who has realised what the Sufis term "the Supreme Station"; and Sufism is a way and a means of striking a root through the "narrow gate" in the depth of the soul out into the domain of the pure and unimprisonable Spirit which itself opens out on to the Divinity. The full-grown Sufi is thus conscious of being, like other men, a prisoner in the world of forms, but unlike them he is also conscious of being free, with a freedom which immeasurably outweighs his imprisonment. He may therefore be said to have two centres of consciousness, one human and one Divine, and he may speak now from one and now from the other, which accounts for certain apparent contradictions.

To follow the path of the mystics is to acquire as it were an extra dimension, for this path is nothing other than the dimension of depth.[5] Consequently, . . . even those rites which the mystic shares with the rest of his community, and which he too needs for the balance of his soul, are not performed by him exoterically as others perform them, but from the same profound esoteric point of view which characterises all his rites and which he is methodically forbidden to forsake. In other words he must not lose sight of the truth that the water which is left behind by the wave is the same water as that which ebbs. Analogously, he must not forget that his soul, like the water that is "imprisoned" in forms, is not essentially different from the transcendent Spirit, of which it is a prolongation, like a hand that is held out and inserted into a receptacle and then, eventually, withdrawn.

If the reason for the title of this [selection] is not yet apparent, this is partly because the word "original" has become encrusted with meanings which do not touch the essence of originality but which are limited to one of its consequences, namely difference, the quality of being unusual or extraordinary. "Original" is even used as a synonym of "abnormal" which is a monstrous perversion, since true originality is always a norm. Nor can it be achieved by the will of man, whereas the grotesque is doubly easy to achieve, precisely because it is no more than a chaos of borrowings.

The original is that which springs directly from the origin or source, like pure uncontaminated water which has not undergone any "side" influences. Originality is thus related to inspiration, and above all to revelation, for the origins are transcendent, being beyond this world, in the domain of the Spirit. Ultimately the origin is no less than the Absolute, the Infinite, and the Eternal—whence the Divine Name

---

5. Or of height, which is the complementary aspect of the same dimension. The Tree of Life, of which the Saint is a personification, is sometimes depicted as having its roots in Heaven, lest it should be forgotten that depth and height are spiritually identical.

"The Originator," in Arabic *al-Badī'*, which can also be translated "the Marvellous." It is from this Ocean of Infinite Possibility that the great tidal waves of Revelation flow, each "marvellously" different from the others because each bears the imprint of the One-and-Only from which it springs, this imprint being the quality of uniqueness, and each profoundly the same because the essential content of its message is the One-and-Only Truth.

In the light of the image of the wave we see that originality is a guarantee of both authenticity and effectuality. Authenticity, of which orthodoxy is as it were the earthly face, is constituted by the flow of the wave, that is, the direct provenance of the Revelation from its Divine Origin; and in every flow there is the promise of an ebb, wherein lies effectuality, the Grace of the Truth's irresistible power of attraction.

Sufism is nothing other than Islamic mysticism, which means that it is the central and most powerful current of that tidal wave which constitutes the Revelation of Islam; and it will be clear from what has just been said that to affirm this is in no sense a depreciation, as some appear to think. It is on the contrary an affirmation that Sufism is both authentic and effectual.

As to the thousands of men and women in the modern Western world who, while claiming to be "Sufis," maintain that Sufism is independent of any particular religion and that it has always existed, they unwittingly reduce it—if we may use the same elemental image—to a network of artificial inland waterways. They fail to notice that by robbing it of its particularity and therefore of its originality, they also deprive it of all impetus. Needless to say, the waterways exist. For example, ever since Islam established itself in the subcontinent of India, there have been intellectual exchanges between Sufis and Brahmins; and Sufism eventually came to adopt certain terms and notions from Neoplatonism. But the foundations of Sufism were laid and its subsequent course irrevocably fixed long before it would have been possible for extraneous and parallel mystical influences to have introduced non-Islamic elements, and when such influences were finally felt, they touched only the surface.

In other words, by being totally dependent upon one particular Revelation, Sufism is totally independent of everything else. But while being self-sufficient it can, if time and place concur, pluck flowers from gardens other than its own. The Prophet of Islam said: "Seek knowledge even if it be in China."

Moments of the Religious Life

Isma'il R. al-Faruqi

Isma'il Raji al-Faruqi (1921–86) was born in Jaffa, Palestine (now Israel), and immigrated to the United States in 1948, eventually becoming a naturalized citizen. He was a graduate of the American University of Beruit (B.A.), Harvard University (M.A.), and Indiana University (M.A. and Ph.D.); and for four years in Cairo he was engaged in Islamic studies at al-Azhar University. He taught at McGill University, the Central Institute of Islamic Research (Karachi, Pakistan), the University of Chicago, Syracuse University, and for many years at Temple University.

Among his numerous books are Islam and Culture, Islam and the Problem of Israel, Tawhid: Its Implications for Thought and Life, Divine Transcendence and Its Expression, *and* The Hijrah. *There were scores of articles, and he was on the editorial boards of several major journals.**

In "Moments of the Religious Life," al-Faruqi explains in some detail the "Five Pillars" of Islam, the five elementary religious responsibilities of the Muslim. What it means to live as a Muslim begins here.

The Shahadah (The Confession of Faith)

The Muslim confesses that there is no God but God and that Muhammad is the Prophet of God. This confession is the *shahadah,* or "witness." It is not only the Muslim's legal passport into the Muslim community but also the quintessence of the Muslim's faith and an expression of identity. This confession of faith is recited many times a day on many different occasions. . . .

To confess that Muhammad is the Prophet of God is tantamount to declaring that the Qur'an is indeed the holy word of God, complete, verbatim (word for word exactly), and in the order set forth by the Prophet. It also means the confessor believes that the Qur'an's commandments and directives are God's norms and standards of behavior to which Muslims must conform.

· · ·

*John L. Esposito, who was one of his students, has written an extended essay on al-Faruqi's life and accomplishments in "Ismail R. al-Faruqi: Muslim Scholar-Activist," in Yvonne Yazbeck Haddad (ed.), *The Muslims of America* (New York: Oxford University Press, 1991), pp. 65–79.

From Isma'il R. Al Faruqi, *Islam.* Reprinted by permission of the International Institute of Islamic Thought.

The prophethood of Muhammad, restricting itself to the verbatim conveyance of the word of God, presents a capstone of the whole phenomenon of prophecy in Semitic culture. Certainly Moses represented another apex in that history, after which, Muslims believe, prophecy degenerated in Israel to the point of there being many false prophets loose in the marketplaces without any being able to prove his prophethood conclusively.

Islam reinstated prophecy to its place of high honor. The change in times, however, prescribed that prophets no longer justify themselves with miracles which boggle the mind. Hence, Muslims do not claim any miracles for Muhammad. In their view, what proves Muhammad's prophethood is the sublime beauty and greatness of the revelation itself, the Holy Qur'an, not any inexplicable breaches of natural law which confound human reason or pass the human powers of understanding. The Qur'anic revelation is a presentation to one's mind, to reason. It makes its claim critically, not authoritarianly. Instead of commanding blind belief, it invites people to consider the evidence, to compare and contrast the claims and the data, and to judge only in certainty and conviction of the truth.

This is why Islam never had a religious synod or council or church empowered with the right to impose its own views about Islam on the rest of humankind. In Islam, religious truth is a matter of argument and conviction, a cause in which everybody is entitled to contend and everybody is entitled to convince and be convinced. To witness that Muhammad is the Prophet of God means in final analysis that one is convinced that religious truth is critical, arguable, and convincing of itself. This affects the first part of the *shahadah,* namely, "There is no God but God." It tells the Muslim that this is a rational claim, and one can be convinced of its truth without authority or coercion. One has to reason, to consider all the evidence, in seriousness and responsibility.

Salat (Worship)

The word *salat* is better translated as "worship" than as "prayer." Prayer is not necessarily formal. It is not obligatory, has no prescribed style, and can be recited almost anywhere, anytime. Islam knows a form of communion with God which fits the appellation "prayer," and it is called *du'a',* literally "invocation" or "calling." Like "prayer," it varies according to the content, as in prayer of thanksgiving, of praise, of supplication, of forgiveness, and so on.

Unlike *du'a', salat* has a definite and precise form. It must be recited five times a day at given intervals. If the time assigned to it is missed, it can be made up, but with the understanding that one is only making up what has been missed. *Salat* is an absolute commandment of God imposed upon all adult Muslims. To deny it is to leave Islam. To neglect it is to commit a grave sin which must be repented and made up.

Salat is preceded by ablution—that is, the body, or parts of it, is washed. This ablution is both real and symbolic, and both levels of meaning are required in Islam. The Muslim may not approach the divine Presence, as one does in *salat,* with a dirty body or appearance. Just as the place where one prays must be clean (and hence the ubiquitous "prayer" rug throughout the world of Islam), so one's clothing and body must be equally clean. Soiled clothes have to be changed. Hands, mouth and teeth, nose, face, top of head, neck, ears, arms to the elbows, and feet to the ankle—all have to be washed in clean, preferably running, water. The whole operation must be preceded with a silent declaration of intention to oneself that one is entering into it for the sake of God.

Salat can be performed anywhere; for wherever the Muslim stands, there is God present. No ground is holy; the mosque is a place dedicated to worship, but not "consecrated." *Salat* can be performed by the worshipper alone, since there is no sacrament and no priesthood in Islam. Performing it together with one's fellow worshippers is desirable but not obligatory except for the congregational *salat* on Friday *(Jum'ah)* which must be performed with the other members of the congregation. The congregational *salat* is led by an *imam* (leader) whose function is to synchronize the movements of beginning and ending, of genuflection and prostration. Any Muslim may lead the *salat,* provided one's recitation of the Qur'an is correct. On Friday, the *imam* delivers a *khutbah,* or sermon, in addition to these duties. The subject of the sermon should be a living issue in Muslim life, and the *imam* should try to relate the relevant passages of the Qur'an and *hadith* (report of the example of the Prophet's behavior) to the problems or situation at hand.

For the congregational *salat,* the Qur'an advises that beautiful clothes be worn with decorum. Before starting, the *imam* makes sure that the lines of worshippers are full and solid and straight. All face in the direction of the Ka'bah in Makkah. The sight of Muslims in *salat,* whether standing in their straight rows or kneeling and prostrating themselves, is indeed a forcefully expressive and deeply moving sight. The straight line represents the equality of all; the rows represent the fullness and solidity of the community.

The night ends at dawn and the day begins. Islam prescribes that each day begin with *salat.* Between dawn and the noon *salat,* there is usually a period of seven to eight hours which can and should be used to do the day's work. Where the work is of a heavy nature, this period is adequate to satisfy the needs of a progressive, well-organized economy. Where the work is light, it can be resumed after the noon *salat,* which can also constitute a refreshing break. No one need work beyond the midafternoon *salat,* unless it is for an emergency situation or for one's own pleasure and desire. The sunset *salat* terminates the day, and the night *salat* marks the Muslim's retirement.

Salat is a discipline. Its ablution, its form, its movement, the timing and number of genuflections and prostrations—all these constitute exercises in self-attunement to the call of God. The Qur'an says that *salat* is futile unless it leads to moral action and self-exertion in the greater cause, the cause of God. It is supposed to be more than just a reminder of God. For its duration, five times a day, it is to bring people for a time face to face, as it were, with their Lord, Master, and Creator.

Zakat (Wealth Sharing)

Zakat, which literally means "sweetening," justifies or renders legitimate, innocent, and good that which it is supposed to affect. The term can be used with a
human being as object, in which case it means recommendation or acclamation.
When used with wealth as its object—and that is the greater usage—it means making that wealth "sweet" (just, legitimate, innocent, good, and worthy). Obviously,
the worth *zakat* adds to wealth is not utilitarian, but moral.

Islam regards all wealth as belonging to God. One may appropriate as much of
it as one pleases, by all the means which economic life makes possible, as long as
such means do not violate the moral law. Wealth gathering is legitimate activity as
long as it implies no theft, cheating, or coercion. . . .

But even if the moral law has been strictly observed in every step of the process
of acquiring wealth, that wealth still needs justification on another level. This is
what the institution of wealth sharing, or *zakat,* seems to require. If one violates no
moral law in acquiring wealth, why does Islam hold such wealth nonetheless illegitimate until one has justified it by means of *zakat?*

.   .   .

The answer is that while the moral law governs the acquisition of wealth, its
consumption and/or continued possession must also be governed by moral considerations. Were there no purpose to life but existence, and no meaning to that existence except pleasure, comfort, and satisfaction, no demand could be made of the
owner of wealth. But there is more to life than this.

Islam's tenet is that wealth, once acquired, ought to be shared with others in
some proportion. This is equally the requirement of charity, and charity is as old as
humanity. Charity has always been regarded as high moral value. Its proportion—
nay, its very observance—has been left to the personal discretion of the giver. True,
morality has always taught that the greater the portion one shares, the greater the
merit. Jesus moved charity to higher moral grounds when he taught that the purer
the motivation with which the giver gives his wealth, the greater the *moral* worth of
the deed. With all this Islam fully agrees, recognizing this teaching of Jesus as genuine revelation from God. It called the institution of almsgiving *sadaqah,* a derivative from the act of faith itself by which people acknowledge God to be God.

No religion or morality before Islam has made charity itself obligatory in the
sense of institutionalizing it and empowering somebody to levy, collect, and distribute it. It is nice to have charity as a moral ideal. But what would be its worth if
it remained an unobserved ideal? An ideal satisfiable by the millionaire who gives
a few pennies to the poor on the sidewalk? An ideal whose observance is subject
only to one's conscience, or to God in the Hereafter, but to no regulation by one's
peers in this world?

This is the need to which Islam addressed itself by the institution of *zakat:* "You
may give your wealth to your fellow humans as much as you please, when you
please, in the manner you please. That is your *sadaqah,* of which your conscience
and God are the only judges. But you may not escape the requirement of giving
every year two and one-half percent of your total wealth to a corporate institution,

the Islamic state, for distribution to the less fortunate, to those in need." Thus, Islam sought to preserve the moral value of charity, and to add to it the equally moral value of wealth sharing, or *zakat*. . . .

Siyam (Fasting)

Fasting is an old religious custom. It was practiced by lay persons and clergy in ancient religions, as well as by Jews and Christians. Though its purposes differed from religion to religion, there was general agreement that fasting was a self-preparation for communion with divinity.

Islam prescribes a rigorous fast (called *siyam* in Arabic) for all healthy adult Muslims. This fast requires total abstention from food, drink, and sex from dawn to sunset during every day of the month of Ramadan, the ninth month in the Islamic calendar, which is based on the lunar year. The body may not partake of anything in any way or contact another of the opposite sex without breaking the fast. Exempted from this duty are children and persons suffering from sickness or undergoing the tremendously heavy burden of desert travel. In such cases, the exempted person is not to forego the fast but to postpone it to another, healthier or more restful time before recurrence of the following Ramadan.

Long before Islam, the month of Ramadan was regarded by the Arabs as a holy month. Its occasion imposed upon them the prohibition of war and hunting, and brought about an uninterrupted peace during which travel and movement of goods across the desert were safe from attack. The Arabs reckoned Ramadan as the month of spiritual stocktaking. Throughout its duration, they were especially keen to please, to settle old debts and disputes, to do good to their neighbors. The more morally sensitive among them underwent a retreat to a temple, or into their homes, to avoid disturbing their concentration and meditation. Before his commission as Prophet, Muhammad was in the habit of retreating during Ramadan to Hira', a cave outside Makkah, where he would spend several days in meditation. His wife used to send him daily provisions with a servant, knowing that her husband was devoting himself exclusively to worship.

Islam continued the tradition of dedicating the month of Ramadan to religious pursuits. Besides the fast, the Islamic tradition regarded moral and religious action during Ramadan as especially meritorious, and urged Muslims to increase their service to God during the month. It was during Ramadan that Muhammad received his first revelation.

Islam assigned two purposes to fasting: self-discipline and commiseration with the hungry of the earth. . . .

Self-discipline through fasting is a novel religious idea. Hunger and sexual desire are pivotal instincts of life. Their satisfaction is a capital requirement of any social order. But they are precisely two of the most sensitive areas of human life. Prohibition of food and sex constitutes a threat to life, the former to individual life and the latter to group life. Deliberate abstinence from food and sex stirs up the consciousness of imminent death to both the individual and the group, and provides ample opportunity to mobilize consciousness and launch it into combat, in defense of life.

Islam has prescribed total abstinence from food and sex from dawn to sunset precisely for that reason. The threat to individual and group life must be resisted, and the Muslim must be taught and trained in the art of resistance. Patience, forbearance, perseverence, steadfastness in suffering and privation—these are the qualities Islam seeks to cultivate through fasting. Conversely, the areas of food and sex are regarded as two of humanity's weakest spots in regard to morality and righteousness. The Muslim sees them as avenues for vice and immorality to find their way into the world. To learn how to block those avenues of immoral use, fortify the individual against temptation, and make one's moral house impregnable is the purpose of Islamic fasting.

Hajj (Pilgrimage)

Pilgrimage is the last of the five pillars of Islam, the religious duties which constitute the fundamental obligations of Islam. The pilgrimage to Makkah is incumbent only upon the adult Muslims who have earned the wealth needed for the trip, have paid the *zakat* ("sweetening") due on it, have fulfilled all their debts, and have provided adequately for all their dependents during their projected absence.

Once the decision to undertake it is reached, the pilgrimage begins with many celebrations and preparations at home. When the time comes for travel, the whole community goes out to bid the pilgrims farewell and wish them a pilgrimage acceptable to God. Upon arriving near Makkah al Mukarramah (Mecca the blessed), but before actually entering it, the pilgrims shed their clothes and ornaments, take a purifying ablution, and declare to God their *niyyah,* or intention, to perform the pilgrimage. Each pilgrim then puts on two pieces of unsewn white linen or cotton. One piece covers the body from the waist down, the other from the waist up, leaving the head bare. Henceforth pilgrims may not shave, cut their hair, clip their fingernails, or wear anything which might distinguish them from the other pilgrims. They can, of course, change their wraps, called *ihram,* for clean ones whenever they wish.

This clothing requirement is charged with religious meaning. The pilgrim, who comes to Makkah to meet the Creator, is a creature on a par with all other human creatures of God. Wealth, social class, political power, knowledge, wisdom, even previous piety—none of these is allowed to show itself. The distinctions of history are wiped out. All humans are creatures equal before God, and the wearing of *ihram* signifies this equality.

Pilgrims begin their ritual with a visit to the *haram,* an area about eighteen miles long and encompassing Makkah, the plain of Arafat, and other points sacred to Muslims. Immediately upon entering the sanctuary, the pilgrims proceed to the heart of Makkah where the Ka'bah stands. According to tradition, confirmed in the Qur'an, the Ka'bah was the first house of worship built for the worship of God. It was built by Abraham and his son Ishmael, whom the Arabs regard as their ancestors and Muslims regard as the first monotheists in the region. The pilgrims walk around the Ka'bah seven times while reciting a prayer affirming their submission to God's call.

The pilgrims then go on to Safa and Marwah, two little hills a bit less than a mile apart and also within the sanctuary. They cover the distance between the hills seven times at a trotting pace. This ritual, called *al sa'* ("the striving"), is a symbolic reenactment of the experience of Hagar, Abraham's wife and the mother of Ishmael. At God's command, Abraham had left her in that locality with her newborn son. Anxious for the baby's safety and her own, she searched the area for water, running to and fro between the two hills. Hagar did eventually find water when, as tradition reveals, it sprang miraculously from under Ishmael's little feet. The fountain, called Zamzam, still gives its water to the pilgrims, many of whom take bottles of it to their relatives back home.

On the second day, the pilgrims begin their journey to Arafat, a plain a few miles northeast of Makkah where they camp. On the day of Arafat, the pilgrims stand together in prayer from the noon to the sunset *salat,* gathering around the very spot where Muhammad stood to deliver his farewell sermon on his last pilgrimage in the tenth year of the Muslim calendar (632 C.E.).

The pilgrims then proceed to Mina, an oasis eight miles away from Arafat, stopping to throw pebbles at one of three pillars that represents Satan. This is a condemnation of the devil and his ways and symbolically reaffirms the pilgrims' resolution to resist temptation.

At Mina the pilgrims buy a sheep or goat which they then sacrifice, giving the meat to the poor. This sacrifice, called the *'d al Adha* (feast of sacrifice), is a high point of the pilgrimage, marking the pilgrims' willingness to sacrifice for God and to give thanks to Him, while also reminding the pilgrims that they should share with those who are less fortunate.

The most important parts of the pilgrimage are now complete, and at this point the pilgrims may take off the *ihram* and put on their usual clothes. They also clip their nails and hair as a sign of their partial return to everyday life.

But the pilgrimage is not yet ended. The pilgrims now return to Makkah, where they repeat *al sa'y* and once again walk seven times around the Ka'bah as they did at the beginning.

This concludes the pilgrimage itself, but most pilgrims also visit Madinah al Munawwarah (Medina the illuminated city of the Prophet) to pay their respects to the Prophet buried within its mosque. They then prepare to return home where relatives and communities will be waiting for them with a warm welcome and prayers that their pilgrimage has been accepted.

Male and Female in Islamic Perspective

Seyyed Hossein Nasr

Born in Teheran in 1933, Seyyed Hossein Nasr received his early education there, but came to the United States to study physics at the Massachusetts Institute of Technology. He went on to earn a doctorate from Harvard in the History of Science and Learning with special concentration on Islamic science and philosophy. He taught for many years at Teheran University, then Temple University, and now George Washington University, where he is University Professor of Islamic Studies.

One of the most influential of contemporary Muslim scholars, Nasr is equally vigorous as a defender of traditional Islam and as a critic of modern Western values. Among his most recent titles are Traditional Islam in the Modern World *(from which the present reading selection is taken),* Knowledge and the Sacred *(the Gifford Lectures of 1981, published in 1989), and* Man and Nature: The Spiritual Crisis of Modern Man.

O Mankind! Lo! We have created you male and female. The noblest among you, in the sight of Allah, is the best in conduct.   Quran; XLVI; 13

No tradition can pass over in silence the central question of the relationship between man and woman in religious as well as in social life. Islam is no exception to this rule. On the contrary, traditional Islam, basing itself on the explicit teachings of the Quran and the guiding principles of the life of the Prophet, has developed the doctrine of the relationship between the male and the female and formulated the norms according to which the two sexes should live and cooperate in the social order. At a time when innovations of every sort have destroyed for most contemporary people, including many Muslims, the perennial teachings of Islam concerning the male and female relationship, from its metaphysical and spiritual to its most outward aspects, it is particularly necessary to reinstate the traditional Islamic point of view, beginning with the metaphysical principles which govern human nature and the complementary relationship between the male and the female on the highest level.

To speak of creation or manifestation is to speak of the manifold, or multiplicity, whose first stage is that primordial polarization between the two contending and complementary principles that are seen throughout cosmic manifestation and which in human life appear as the male and female sexes. In relation to the Divine Unity, all multiplicity is a veil, and from the perspective of the Divine Substance everything else is an accident embracing all the reverberations of the One in the mirror of the many which we call the world; or in fact the many worlds that at once hide and manifest the One. But from the point of view of the created order, the polarization or duality expressed by the differentiation of the microcosm into man and woman is far from being an accident. It is a most profound feature of what constitutes human nature. That is why in the Quranic verse quoted above, as well as in certain other verses, God refers to His creating mankind in pairs, in two different forms, as both man and woman. God is Himself the creator of both man and woman, and whatever ensues from the distinction between the two sexes must be related to His Wisdom and Providence. The distinction between the sexes is not a later accident or accretion but is essential to the meaning of the human state, without this distinction in any way destroying the significance of the androgynic reality (identified with the Universal or Perfect man—*al-insān al-kāmil*) which both men and women carry within the depths of their being.[1]

Since God has created mankind in pairs, logically and metaphysically there must exist some element of difference which distinguishes one member of the pair from the other, for if two things were the same in every way they would be identical. There is, therefore, of necessity a difference between the two sexes. They are not the same, at least if one takes the totality of being of each sex into consideration, while they may be equal under certain aspects and features. From the Islamic point of view, their equality in fact first and foremost involves the entelechy of the human state as such, in which both men and women participate by virtue of belonging to the human race. Both man and woman were created for immortality and spiritual deliverance. Below that level, however, there are differences between the two sexes whose reality cannot be ignored in the name of any form of egalitarianism.

Furthermore, the difference between the two sexes cannot be only biological and physical because, in the traditional perspective, the corporeal level of existence has its principle in the subtle state, the subtle in the spiritual and the spiritual in the Divine Being Itself. The difference between the sexes cannot be reduced to anatomy and biological function. There are also differences of psychology and temperament, of spiritual types and even principles within the Divine Nature which are the sources *in divinis* of the duality represented on the microcosmic level as male and female. God is both Absolute and Infinite. Absoluteness—and Majesty, which is inseparable from it—are manifested most directly in the masculine state; Infinity and Beauty in the feminine state. The male body itself reflects majesty, power, absoluteness; and the female body reflects beauty, beatitude, and infinity. But these principles are also reflected in all the intermediate realms of existence which, in each

---

1. It is significant to note that the Quranic term for "man" is *insān*, which refers to the human state as such and not to one of the sexes. The Arabic term is closer to the Latin *homo* or the German *mensch* than the English *man*.

type of microcosm, male and female, separate the corporeal state from the Divine Presence.

But since God is one and man, that is, the human being of whichever sex it might be, a theomorphic being who reflects God's Names and Qualities,[2] each human being also reflects the One and seeks to return to the One. Hence there is at once complementarity and rivalry between the sexes. There is union and polarization. The female is at once Mary, who symbolizes the Divine Mercy in the Abrahamic traditions and the beatitude which issues from this Mercy, and Eve, who entices, seduces, and externalizes the soul of man, leading to its dissipation, although in Islam Eve is not the cause of man's loss of the Edenic state. The female is at once the source of concupiscence and the theater for the contemplation of the Divinity in Its uncreated aspect. Likewise, man is at once the symbol of the Lord and Creator and a being who, having lost sight of his ontological dependence upon the Lord, would seek, as a usurper, to play the role of Lord and Creator while he remains a mortal and perishable being. The veil of cosmic manifestation, the *hijāb* of Islamic metaphysics, makes the relation between the sexes an ambivalent one. But the profound metaphysical relationship between the two sexes is such that there is at once the inclination for union with a member of the opposite sex, which means ultimately the need to regain the consciousness of beatific union possessed by the androgynic ancestor of humanity in the paradisal state, and rivalry between the sexes, since each human being is in turn a total image of the primordial *insān*.

While some religions have emphasized the negative aspect of sexuality, Islam bases itself on its positive aspect as a means of perfection of the human state and, on the highest level, a symbol of union with God, sexual relations being of course governed by the injunction of the Divine Law. Addressing itself to man in his primordial nature *(al-fiṭrah)*, to "man as such,"[3] Islam envisages the love of man and woman as being inseparable from the love of God, and leading to God on the highest level.[4] There exists in Islamic spirituality, as a result of this perspective, a hierarchy of love stretching from what is called "metaphorical love" *(al-'ishq al-majāzī)* to "real love" *(al-'ishq al-ḥaqīqī)*, which is the love of God Himself.[5] The well-known but elliptical *ḥadīth* of the Prophet, that of the things of this world he loved above anything else women, perfume, and prayer alludes, spiritually speaking, to

2. On the meaning of man as a theomorphic being, a doctrine which does not at all imply any kind of anthropomorphism, see F. Schuon, *Understanding Islam,* pp. 13ff.

3. Schuon begins his well-known work, *Understanding Islam,* with the phrase, "Islam is the meeting between God as such and man as such: that is to say, man envisaged, not as a fellow being needing a miracle to save him, but as man, a theomorphic being endowed with intelligence capable of conceiving of the Absolute and with a will capable of choosing what leads to the Absolute."

4. "Loving each other, Adam and Eve loved God; they could neither love nor know outside God. After the fall, they loved each other outside God and for themselves, and they knew each other as separate phenomena and not as theophanies; this new kind of love was concupiscence and this new kind of knowing was profanity." Schuon, *Islam and the Perennial Philosophy,* p. 191.

5. This theme is particularly developed among certain Sufis who have been aptly called the *fedeli d'amore* of Islam. See H. Corbin, *En Islam iranien* (Paris, 1972, Vol. III) (sub-titled *Les Fidèles d'amour*), especially pp. 9–146, concerning Rūzbahān Baqlī, the patron saint of Shiraz.

the positive aspect of sexuality in Islam, as well as to the relation of the spiritual nature of womanhood to prayer, which is the most direct means of access to God for human beings, and to the most subtle of sensual experiences having to do with the olfactory faculty.[6] Moreover, the Quran (XXIV; 26) specifically relates the symbolism of perfume to sexual union.

It is because of the positive role accorded to sexuality in the Islamic perspective that the theme of love, as realized gnosis, dominates its spirituality, that God appears as the Beloved and the female as a precious being symbolizing inwardness and the inner paradise which is hidden from man as a result of the loss of "the eye of the heart" and the power to perceive beings *in divinis*.[7] The fall of man into the state of separation and forgetfulness has brought about an exteriorization and inversion in that contemplation of female beauty which can aid man to return to the Center once again, and which brings with it the beatitude in whose quest he spends his efforts, knowingly or unknowingly. This power has ceased to operate for most human beings, except in a potential manner. Yet its echo persists; even the physical joy of sexual union reflects something of its paradisal archetype and is itself proof of the sacred union which is the celestial prototype of all earthly union between the sexes, and which imparts upon the biological act, despite the ontological hiatus between archetype and earthly reflection as well as the element of inversion which is also present between the symbol and the symbolized, something of the experience of the Infinite and the Absolute.

Ibn 'Arabī goes to the point of describing the contemplation of God in woman as the highest form of contemplation possible; he writes:

> When man contemplates God in woman, his contemplation rests on that which is passive; if he contemplates Him in himself, seeing that woman comes from man, he contemplates Him in that which is active; and when he contemplates Him alone, without the presence of any form whatsoever issued from Him, his contemplation corresponds to a state of passivity with regard to God, without intermediary. Consequently his contemplation of God in woman is the most perfect, for it is then God, in so far as He is at once active and passive, that he contemplates, whereas in the pure interior contemplation, he contemplates Him only in a passive way. So the Prophet—Benediction and Peace be upon him—was to love women because of the perfect contemplation of God in them. One would never be able to contemplate God directly in absence of all (sensible or spiritual)

---

6. Ibn 'Arabī devotes many pages of the last chapters of his *Fuṣūṣ al-ḥikam* to an exposition of the metaphysical significance of this *ḥadīth* of the Prophet and why in fact women, perfume, and prayer are mentioned in this order.

7. The beauty of woman is, for spiritual man, an unveiling of the beauty of the paradise that he carries at the center of his being and to which the Quran alludes when it speaks of the *houris* of paradise. Likewise, the goodness of man is for woman a confirmation and support of her inner goodness. According to an Arabic proverb, goodness is outward and beauty inward in man, while in woman beauty is outward and goodness inward. There is not only a complementarity between the sexes but also an inversion of relationships. From a certain point of view, man symbolizes outwardness and woman inwardness. She is the theophany of esotericism and, in certain modes of spirituality, Divine Wisdom (which, as *al-ḥikmah*, is feminine in Arabic) reveals itself to the gnostic as a beautiful woman.

support, for God, in his Absolute Essence, is independent of all worlds. But, as the (Divine) Reality is inaccessible in respect (of the Essence), and there is contemplation *(shahādah)* only in a substance, the contemplation of God in women is the most intense and the most perfect; and the union which is the most intense (in the sensible order, which serves as support for this contemplation) is the conjugal act.[8]

Since religion concerns the final ends of man and his perfection, Islam has legislated and provided spiritual and ethical principles which, in conformity with its perspective, make use of this very important aspect of human nature, namely sexuality, to help perfect human beings and bring them felicity in both this world and the hereafter. This is especially true since Islam is a social order as well as a spiritual path, a *Sharī'ah* as well as a *Ṭarīqah.*[9] Also as already mentioned, Islam envisages the quest after God, which is the ultimate goal of human existence, upon the basis of social and personal equilibrium. Islamic spirituality is always based on the foundation of an equilibrium which is inseparable from the name of *al-islām,* "peace": an equilibrium which is reflected in a blinding fashion in all authentic manifestations of Islam, especially its sacred art.[10]

To make this equilibrium and the spiritual life based upon it possible, Islam has envisaged a human order in which the sexes are seen in their complementary rather than contending aspects. On the social and family levels, it has legislated for a social order in which there should be a maximum amount of stability, the greatest possible degree of attachment of men and women to a family structure, and emphasis upon marriage as a religious duty. Marriage is not seen, however, as a sacrament, since from an "alchemical" and also a metaphysical point of view—which is that of Islam—the sexual act is already a sacred act which must be kept within the bounds of the Sacred Law to govern human passions, but which does not need another sacrament in order to become sacralized. Islamic legislation and the social structure based upon it do not, of course, imply an order in which everyone could be satisfied in every way, for to speak of manifestation and multiplicity is to speak of separation from the unique source of goodness, and hence to be in the realm of imperfection. What the Islamic social order has always sought to achieve is the creation of the maximum amount of equilibrium possible, upon whose basis human beings can lead a life centered around and pointing to man's entelechy and end. Otherwise, there is no doubt that some people have been unhappy in a polygamous family situation, as others have been unhappy in a monogamous one—or even as totally "free" persons living as atomized beings within an atomized society where each entity is, or at least appears to be, free to do and move about at will. The question for Islam has not been how to make everyone happy, because that is something which is not possible in this world. In fact, the world would not be the world *(al-*

8. See Muḥyī al-Dīn Ibn 'Arabī, *The Wisdom of the Prophets,* translated from the Arabic into French with notes by T. Burckhardt; translated from the French by A. Culme-Seymour (Gloucestershire, 1975), p. 120.

9. See S. H. Nasr, *Ideals and Realities of Islam,* chaps. I, IV, and V.

10. T. Burckhardt has dealt with this subject in many of his penetrating studies of Islamic art. See especially his *The Art of Islam.*

dunyā in the language of the Quran) if it were possible. The question has rather been how to create a state in which there would be the maximum amount of harmony and equilibrium, and which would be most conducive to man's living as God's vice-gerent *(khalīfatallāh)* on earth and with awareness of His Will during this fleeting journey called human life.

Since sexuality, far from being just a biological accident, possesses a profound metaphysical significance,[11] it has been possible for Islam to place its perspective on the positive rather than negative aspect of this powerful and profound force within human life.[12] Although both man and woman are *insān,* that is, both are the image of God and carry the androgynic reality within the depth of their beings, they cannot reach this interior and also superior reality through the attainment of a kind of least common denominator between the two sexes. Of course, both sexes contain something of both the male and female principles, the *yin* and *yang* of the Far Eastern traditions, within themselves; only in men, the male principle, and in women, the female principle, are dominant. To attain this state is to move in the other direction. Islamic spirituality tends in fact towards a clarification and complete differentiation of the two human types. Its social patterns and art of dress, among other things help to create masculine types who are very masculine and feminine types who are very feminine. If sexual union symbolizes the androgynic totality which both sexes seek consciously or even unconsciously, this union itself requires the distinction and separation of the two sexes, which can in fact participate in the sacred act precisely because of their very distinctness.

Moreover, each sex symbolizes in a positive manner a Divine aspect. Therefore, not only is sexual deviation and perversion a further step away from spiritual perfection, and a great obstacle to it, but also the loss of masculinity and femininity, and movement both psychologically and emotionally toward a neuter common type and ground implies, from the Islamic perspective, an irreparable loss and further fall from the perfection of the primordial *insān,* who was both male and female. The "neuter" person is in fact a parody of the primordial human being, who was both Adam and Eve. Islamic teachings have emphasized this point very clearly. There are in fact *ḥadīths* of the Prophet which allude to men dressing and acting like women and vice-versa as being signs of the world coming to an end. In Islam, both the male and the female are seen as two creatures of God, each manifesting certain aspects of His Names and Qualities, and in their complementary union

---

11. On the metaphysical principles pertaining to sexuality and its character as found in sources drawn mostly from the Western traditions, see G. Evola, *Metafisica del sesso* (Rome, 1958).

12. Since sexuality is a double-edged sword, the other point of view, which is based on the monastic ideal, has also its metaphysical basis and had to manifest itself in certain religions such as Buddhism and Christianity. Even in Islam the positive attitude of monasticism as separation from the world is realized inwardly, since there is no institution of monasticism in Islam. And despite the emphasis of Islam upon marriage and the positive role accorded to sexuality in Islamic spirituality, there have been many saintly men and women who have practiced sexual abstinence. In fact, it would not be possible to experience the paradisal archetype of sexual union without the primary phase of asceticism which allows the soul to experience phenomena as symbols rather than facts. That is also why the experience of the spiritual aspect of sexuality remains inaccessible outside the cadre of tradition and sacred laws which regulate all human relations, including sexuality.

achieving the equilibrium and perfection that God has ordained for them and made the goal of human existence.

The tenets of Islam based upon sexual purity, separation of the sexes in many aspects of external life, the hiding of the beauty of women from strangers, division of social and family duties, and the like all derive from the principles stated above. Their specific applications have depended on the different cultural and social milieus in which Islam has grown and have been very diverse. For example, the manner in which a Malay woman hides her female beauty is very different from the way of a Syrian, a Pakistani, or a Senegalese; and even within a single country, what is called the veil *(hijāb)* has never been the same among nomads, villagers, and city dwellers. Nor has the complementary role of the two sexes in all walks of life pre-vented Muslim women from participating in nearly all aspects of life, from ruling countries to owning major businesses in bazaars or even running butcher shops. Nor has the Islamic world been without eminent female religious and intellectual figures such as Fāṭimah, the daughter of the Prophet, who was a perfect saint; 'Ā'is-hah, the wife of the Prophet through whom so much of Sunni *ḥadīth* has been trans-mitted; Zaynab, the granddaughter of the Prophet, who gave one of the most elo-quent discourses in Islamic history before Yazīd after the death of her brother Imām Ḥusayn in Karbalā'; Rābi'ah, one of the most celebrated of Muslim saints; or Sayyidah Nafīsah, who was a renowned authority on Islamic Law. The existence of these and many other personalities, from antiquity right down to our own day, demonstrates the undeniable fact that learning as well as the fields of commerce, agriculture, etc., were open to those women who chose to or were allowed to pursue them. But the principle of complementarity, as opposed to uniformity and com-petition, dominated.

This complementarity was rooted in equity rather than equality and sought to base itself on what served best the interests of society as a sacred body and men and women as immortal beings. Although spiritually it saw woman as symbolizing God as Infinity and the aspect of the Divinity above creation to the extent that Jalāl al-Dīn Rūmī refers to woman as "uncreated," on the cosmic and human levels it rec-ognized the role of the male as the immutable pole around which the family was constructed and in whose hand responsibility for the welfare of the women and chil-dren, as well as protection for God's Law and social order, were placed. In the Quran, man is given domination over woman but he is not given this responsibility as a two-legged animal. Rather, he has been entrusted with this task as the *imām* of God and His vice-gerent, whose soul is surrendered to Him. In a sense, man's soul must be the consort of the Spirit in order for him to be able to play his full role as husband for his wife and father for his children. The revolt of the female sex against the male did not precede but followed in the wake of the revolt of the male sex against Heaven.

But even the relative predominance given to the male function, which brings with it not privilege but rather responsibility, has not in any way compromised the view of Islam that both men and women were born for immortality, that the rites of religion are incumbent upon both of them and that its rewards are accessible to men and women alike. The *Sharī'ite* rites of Islam are meant for members of both sexes and the Quran explicitly states:

Lo! Men who surrender unto Allah, and women who surrender, and men who believe and women who believe, and men who obey and women who obey, and men who speak the truth and women who speak the truth, and men who persevere (in righteousness) and women who persevere, and men who are humble and women who are humble, and men who give alms and women who give alms, and men who fast and women who fast, and men who guard their modesty and women who guard (their modesty), and men who remember Allah much and women who remember—Allah hath prepared for them forgiveness and a vast reward.[13]

Even in instances where certain rites are reserved for men, such as the prayer for the dead, this does not imply a particular privilege for though God has not made women responsible for such rites. He still asks them to seek to reach those highest spiritual goals that are the *raison d'être* of such rites. As for the spiritual practices associated with Sufism, they have always been accessible to women and there have always been many women followers in various Sufi orders, some of whom have attained the level of sanctity and become spiritual guides. There is, in fact, a feminine dimension within Sufism which possesses a distinct perfume of its own.[14]

In conclusion we must remember again the Origin which, in its essence, is above the sexes and all other dualities but which yet, in its Majesty and Beauty, contains the roots of what on the plane of cosmic existence appears as the masculine and feminine principles, and on the human level as male and female. Individual human beings are born as men and women, not accidentally but according to their destiny. They can fulfil their function in life, reach the perfection which alone can bestow felicity and even transcend all traces of separative existence and return unto the One, only in accepting their destiny and transcending from above the form into which they have been born, not by rebelling against it. In the Holy Name of God, there is neither male nor female, but no-one can penetrate into the inner sanctum of that Name without having fully integrated into his or her own being the positive elements of the sex into which he or she has been born. The Universal Man is inwardly the androgynic being who possesses the perfection of both sexes, but he or she does not come to that perfection save by remaining faithful to the norms and

13. Quran XXXII; 35, Pickthall translation. On this point see Aisha Lemu, "Women in Islam," in A. Gauhar (ed.), *The Challenge of Islam* (London, 1978), pp. 249–67. The Quran also asserts "Whosoever doeth right, whether male or female, and is a believer, him verily We shall quicken with good life, and We shall pay them a recompense in proportion to the best of what they used to do" (XVI; 97).

On Islamic views concerning women and their rights and responsibilities from a religious as well as sociological and anthropological point of view see Muhammad Abdul-Rauf, *The Islamic View of Women and the Family* (New York, 1977); E. W. Fernea and B. Q. Bezirgan (ed.), *Middle Eastern Women Speak* (Austin, 1977); and D. H. Dwyer, *Images and Self-Images: Male and Female in Morocco* (New York, 1978). There is, needless to say, a vast literature on the subject but most of the works are written from the perspective of current prejudices in the West, as well as from the profane point of view as far as the nature of the human state itself is concerned. There is also very little which, by way of translation, would make accessible authentic writings by Muslim women on religious and spiritual themes.

14. A great master such as Ibn 'arabī had female spiritual guides (*shaykhah* in Arabic) while he was in Andalusia. On the female element in Sufism, see A. M. Schimmel, "The Feminine Element in Sufism," *Mystical Dimensions of Islam* (Chapel Hill, 1975), pp. 426ff.; and L. Bakhtiar, *Sufi Art and Imagination* (London, 1976); see also J. Nurbakhsh, *Sufi Women* (New York, 1983).

conditions his or her sex implies. The revolt of the sexes against that equilibrium which results from their complementarity and union is both the result and a concomitant of the revolt of modern man against Heaven. Man cannot reach that peace and harmony which is the foretaste of the paradise human beings carry at the center of their being, except by bringing to full actualization and realization the possibilities innate in the human state, both male and female. To reject the distinct and distinguishing features of the two sexes and the Sacred Legislation based on this objective cosmic reality is to live below the human level; to be, in fact, only accidentally human. It is to sacrifice and compromise the eternal life of man and woman for an apparent earthly justice based on a uniformity which fails, ultimately even on the purely earthly level, since it does not take into consideration the reality of that which constitutes the human state in both its male and female aspects.

Further Reading

Jane I. Smith, "The Experience of Muslim Women: Considerations of Power and Authority," in Yvonne Y. Haddad et al. (eds.), *The Islamic Impact* (1984). The topics are marriage, divorce, inheritance and ownership of property, veiling and seclusion, education, and employment opportunities.

Frederick M. Denny, *Islam and the Muslim Community* (1987). A sympathetic and concise overview of the religion—its history, practices, and place in today's world.

In *Covering Islam* (1981) Edward Said objects to the "recklessly general and repeatedly deployed cliches" so often used to describe Islam. Worse, much that is written consists of "expressions of unrestrained ethnocentrism, cultural and even racial hatred." Said's *Orientalism* (1978) is similarly a study of the misguided perceptions fostered in the West by the division of the world into Occident and Orient, with the superficial stereotyping of the latter.

Yvonne Yazbeck Haddad (ed.), *The Muslims of America* (1991). A number of papers by leading scholars from a "Muslims of America" conference held in 1989. Haddad notes the "dramatic" growth of the Muslim presence in America: "more than 600 mosques/ Islamic centers, two Islamic colleges." It is estimated that in 1986 there were 4 million Muslims in America.

Cyril Glasse, *The Concise Encyclopedia of Islam* (1989). Some 1200 entries, 472 pages, maps and illustrations, with an introduction by Huston Smith.

Bernard Lewis, Professor of Near Eastern Studies Emeritus at Princeton, puts tensions and events into historical perspective in "The Roots of Muslim Rage," *The Atlantic Monthly,* September 1990.

"To write about Sufism . . . is an almost impossible task. At the first step a wide mountain range appears before the eye—and the longer the seeker pursues the path, the more difficult it seems to reach any goal at all." So writes Annemarie Schimmel, Professor of Indo-Muslim Culture at Harvard, in *Mystical Dimensions of Islam* (1975).

James Kritzeck (ed.), *Anthology of Islamic Literature: From the Rise of Islam to Modern Times* (1964). Over forty selections, from the Qur'an to *The Thousand and One Nights,* with excellent introductory notes by Princeton scholar Kritzeck.

Jalal al-Din Rumi (1207–73) was the greatest of the Persian mystical poets. Among his better translators are William C. Chittick, *The Sufi Path of Love: The Spiritual Teachings of Rumi* (1983); and A. J. Arberry, *Mystical Poems of Rumi* (1968).

X

AFRICAN RELIGIONS
The Dawn of All Things

Great Spirit . . . you are on high with the spirits of the great. You raise the grass-covered hills above the earth and you create the rivers. Gracious one.

Prayer of the Shona

The term "African traditional religions" is now commonly used to denote that continent's indigenous religions, which are generally to be found south of the Sahara. It should be noted that this is an umbrella term and that "religions" is in the plural: there are a great number of traditional religions. Many share certain characteristics, but there are also differences among them. Generalizations are risky.

"Traditional" in this context means native to Africa. Excluded, at least for present purposes, are those religions whose origins are in lands other than Africa, though there are in fact enormous numbers of Christians, Muslims, and others in sub-Saharan Africa. The situation has been described as fluid: "In one household, say in western Nigeria or the southern Sudan, may be found brothers who follow, respectively, traditional beliefs, Islam, and Christianity. In very many cases the parents are still followers of traditional religion while all their children have become Christians or Muslims. Again, men and women move from one set of beliefs and practices to another and back again, as life crises occur which appear to be helped by one faith or another."[1]

The study of religion in Africa has been complicated by several circumstances. The most obvious difficulty is that Africa is a vast continent and its various peoples speak hundreds upon hundreds of different languages. Also a problem, at least to researchers, is that until modern times the remarkable arts of Africa did not include the art of writing, and thus there are no sacred scriptures, no personal accounts of religious experience from earlier centuries, no historical documents. Religious traditions have been transmitted orally, generation to generation. Again, this is a stumbling block for research, not for those practicing the religions:

Religion in African societies is written not on paper but in people's hearts, minds, oral history, rituals, and religious personages like the priests, rainmakers, officiating elders, and even kings. Everybody is a religious carrier.

1. Jocelyn Murray (ed.), *Cultural Atlas of Africa* (New York: Facts on File, 1981), p. 31.

421

. . .

> Where the individual is, there is his religion, for he is a religious being. It
> is this that makes Africans so religious: religion is their whole system of
> being.[2]

And then, too, there is the handicap of the slew of misconceptions about the "dark
continent" and the peoples who inhabit it. Some of us grew up thinking of Africa
in images drawn largely from Hollywood's Tarzan movies, and we were not always
set right by what was written of the history of Africa. Peter Stansky has observed
that the older version of that history was "heavily Eurocentric and concentrated on
tales of exploration and diplomacy. It was written as if those who lived in Africa
were hardly there. The continent was considered vacant, or at best populated by a
colorful group of savages."[3] Still more seriously, scholars have in the past frequently
been guilty of imposing on African belief systems presumptions about what religion
is and is not. Value judgments abound in the very language employed to discuss
Africa and Africans. E. Bolaji Idowu, in the essay that opens this chapter, discusses
the terms "primitive," "savage," and others.[4]

Geoffrey Parrinder, in an essay drawn from his *Belief in Africa,* observes that
faith in a Supreme Being is a basic feature of most African religions, and God's
attributes are those typically ascribed to God in the theistic Western religions. Thus
God is conceived to be all-powerful and all-knowing; God created the world and
sustains it. God is "mysterious and nobody can understand him, he creates and
destroys, he gives and takes away. God is invisible, infinite, and unchangeable."
The good and bad acts of human beings result in rewards and punishments, either
in this life or in the next. Prayers are commonly addressed to God, who hears them
because "his ears are long."

Marcel Griaule's "Ogotemmêli and the Dawn of All Things" is an introduction
to the mythology and religion of the Dogen in the western Sudan. Griaule heard it
from a blind old man, Ogotemmêli, who knew the traditions.

> From the age of fifteen he had been initiated in the mysteries of religion by
> his grandfather. After the latter's death his father had continued the
> instruction. It seemed that the "lessons" had gone on for more than twenty
> years, and that Ogotemmêli's family was not one that took these things
> lightly.

The final essay of the chapter, John S. Mbiti's "Divinities, Spirits, and the Living-Dead," illustrates, among other things, the extent to which the thinking and the
lives of African peoples are steeped in religion. Their spiritual world (that inter-

---

2. John S. Mbiti, *African Religions and Philosophy* (New York: Doubleday, 1979), pp. 4, 5.

3. *The New York Times Book Review,* 8 December 1991, p. 1.

4. Also in circulation and questionable are "preliterate," "nonliterate," "precivilized," and "tribal."
"Primal" has appeared of late, but it sounds very much like "primitive," with which it shares the same
Latin root.

mediate realm between God and man), Mbiti observes, "is very densely populated." Classification of the spirits is difficult, but they generally fall into three groups: (1) *divinities,* who are created as such by God; (2) *"common" spirits,* often believed to have once been men; and (3) the *living-dead,* men who have died not more than five generations ago.

Errors of Terminology

E. Bolaji Idowu

E. Bolaji Idowu is the author of Olódùmarè, God in Yoruba Belief *and* African Traditional Religion, *the latter of which is the source for "Errors of Terminology." The distinguished Nigerian professor of religious studies is here concerned with some of the derogatory terms so often used to describe Africans and their religions. It need hardly be noted that these "errors of terminology" are only a small part of a massive pattern of injustice. Africa, Idowu has written, "has been callously and frequently raped and despoiled by the strong ones of the world who are adepts in the art of benevolent exploitation and civilized savagery."**

Primitive. *The Concise Oxford Dictionary* defines this word as "Early, ancient, old-fashioned, simple, rude; original, primary." It should be obvious that in the light of some of the words in this definition, "primitive" cannot be appropriate in certain contexts in which it is being currently applied. With reference to any people in the world today, "early," "ancient," "original," or "primary" does not apply. Primitive man, in the sense conveyed by the words quoted, disappeared from this world thousands of years ago. The peoples who are being so described today are contemporaries of, and as old or as recent in earthly lineage as, the races of those who are so describing them.[1]

The fashion that perpetuates the incongruous use of the word stems from the notion that anything that does not conform to a certain cultural pattern accepted as the norm by the Western investigator is regarded automatically as primitive; that is, that which belongs to the category of those things which have somehow been left behind in the race of cultural sophistication. "Primitive" in this connection means, categorically, "backward," "rude," or "uncouth."

The anthropological or sociological use of the word "primitive" has been defended on the ground that it only refers to that which is adjudged to be nearer in behaviour or pattern to the original with reference to the human race or culture. It is with this excuse that Western writers still persist in applying the word to Africa, and to African beliefs and practices. This follows also the slothful pattern that where

---

**African Traditional Religion* (London: SCM Press Ltd., 1973), p. 76.

1. See E. S. Waterhouse, *The Dawn of Religion*, (1936), p. 13.

From E. Bolaji Idowu, *African Traditional Religion.* Copyright © 1973 by SCM Press Ltd.

a new, adequate term is not conveniently ready to hand for any situation, an old one, however outmoded or unsuitable, is applied without any apology.

.   .   .

It is especially wrong to speak of the religion of any living people as "primitive" simply on the ground of racial or ethnic prejudice. "Primitive" in most Western writings is a derogatory term and therefore obnoxious. Therefore, it is not only inappropriate but also offensive to describe African traditional religion unreservedly as "primitive."

Savage. Here, in the use of the word "savage," we meet again the inveterate streak in race-proud man.

.   .   .

"Savage" stands at the opposite end of the pole from "civilized." The terms are antithetic to each other. Too often, peoples or cultures and religious practices are described as savage through sheer prejudice, lack of sympathy, or understanding.

.   .   .

A few comparative illustrations will illuminate the subject for us. First, capital has been made out of the fact of human sacrifice in Africa. Human sacrifice, we trust, has become or is fast becoming a thing of the past throughout Africa. I have discussed the subject at some length in *Olódùmarè*.[2] The fundamental principle behind it is that "it is expedient . . . that one man should die for the people, and that the whole nation should not perish." This substitutionary principle has been put into practice from time immemorial, though, more often than not, its expression has been the perversion which has acquired the name of human sacrifice. What is both interesting and disappointing is that the Western world is putting on blinkers with regard to the perversion of this principle which is daily occurring in its midst. Political murders, euphemistically glorified as "assassinations," negro lynching resulting in the death of countless numbers of people of African descent in America, the extermination of the aboriginal peoples in America, Australia, and New Zealand in order that those who came to acquire their lands forcibly might possess the lands for themselves and for their posterity, the German gas-chambers which, like Moloch, devoured countless numbers of Jews, the wanton and wholesale murders of apartheid South Africa and Rhodesia: these perversions, in each case, are of the same character as ritual human sacrifice, although in these euphemistic instances, the case for it is very much weaker.

Secondly, I have never watched on the television the films on "Wrestling from Canada" and "Wrestling from Britain" without being filled with horror at what to me as an African is the sheer "savagery" of the whole performance. In Yorubaland for instance, wrestling is an art implying artistic movements and beauty of strategy; and when once any part of a contestant's body (apart from the feet) has touched the ground, be it no more than the tip of a finger, that contestant has been defeated and

---

2. E. B. Idowu, *Olódùmarè: God in Yoruba Belief* (1962), pp. 120f.

the contest is over. There is nothing of the callous, cruel assault on the contestant, twistings of, or attempts to damage, any organs of the body, or sitting upon a person and buffeting him when he is down.

Thirdly, there are undoubtedly several parts of Africa where feuds are settled with hatchets and spears, dane guns or arson. The difference between this and such undertakings in the Western world is that weapons have been scientifically perfected—pistols, revolvers, bombs, and nuclear appliances are civilized Western counterparts.

. . .

No people should be called savages simply because they are technologically backward or because their own ways of reverting to the raw "natural" state have not yet acquired scientific justification and technological polish.

Native. My wife and I were on a week's holiday, residing at a Quaker Guest House called "The Blue Idol" somewhere in Sussex. There were other guests staying at the same time in the house. One evening, after supper, several of us sat round a table, playing a game of cards. It was my turn to shuffle the cards and I did it in a way which a British woman considered admirable: for she burst out, "Oh, how wonderfully you do it! Do all natives do it the same way?" "*Natives* of where—England, Scotland, or Ireland?" I asked her. By the way she was taken aback and by the expression on the faces of the other Europeans in that room, it was patent that they were probably realizing for the first time that they themselves must have been *born* somewhere! The fact is that to her and, by and large, to the peoples of the Western world, the word "native" has acquired a derogatory nuance and has become one that is reserved for the "unfortunate," "backward," non-Western peoples of the world. This is so, thanks to the anthropologists and missionaries, and the stay-at-home investigators who must always find terms of unmistakable distinction between themselves and "those others." "Prayers for native Christians" are still being offered in churches of Europe and America; "native Christians" being not Christians who are born and are living in Europe and America, but Christians of Africa and Asia and those other "benighted climes." This defines the Western mind on the issue beyond doubt:

> It was about this time that Damu, quite unknown to himself, developed two minds, or rather his own mind split in two parts. One part was his civilized or white mind, the other his native mind which, gradually submerged by his life in England, had been reawakened by contact with his present surrounding. It was his native mind that trifled with the idea of rising against the people he hated, while his white mind laughed at the fantastic notions. Conversely, it was his white mind that made him curious about the Leopard cult, for a native would have been terror-stricken at the very notion of probing into such mysteries.[3]

3. Webster, *Son of Abdan,* pp. 85f.

So also is this:

> Oh yes. Abu bin Zaka is a pure European. Not a drop of native blood in him.[4]

. . .

Paganism. This is probably the oldest of the names adopted to describe the religion of the so-called primitive or "uncivilized" peoples of the world. This word has a Latin origin—*paganus*—and means originally a village-dweller or a countryman, a person who lives away from the civilized community. Thus, originally, the word was a sociological term, a mark of distinction between the enlightened, the civilized, and the sophisticated, on the one hand and the rustic, the unpolished, and the unsophisticated on the other.

The word must have travelled some curious distance in order to become a term with an exclusively religious connotation. In the world to which it originally belonged, what came under the term now was all the religion that there was. And yet, the *Pocket Oxford Dictionary* appears to be unaware of this when it defines "pagan" as "acknowledging neither Jehovah, Christ, nor Allah; non-Christian." The *Encyclopaedia of Religion and Ethics* in a passing reference links the term with "primitive peoples."[5]

. . .

Heathenism. . . . [This] is a word of Germanic root. The suffix -en has the same meaning as the -en in wood*en;* and the heath, originally, was the waste land removed from the outskirts of the town, where outlaws, vagabonds, and brigands had their abode; "heathen" means a dweller on the heath. Thus, the "heathen" is, primarily, one who belongs to, or has the habit of, or has the forbidding quality or characteristics of, heath-dwellers. "Heathenism" means the habit or the characteristics, or the disposition, of heath-dwellers.

The Concise Oxford Dictionary, however, defines "heathen" as (one who is) "neither Christian, Jewish, nor Mohammedan; unenlightened persons." Like the *Pocket Oxford Dictionary,* it makes "pagan" and "heathen" synonymous. . . .

It is needless to say, after all that has been discussed so far, that with regard to African traditional religion, the name *heathenism* is most unsuitable and is, in fact, a very obnoxious misnomer. It has nothing to do with religion, basically. It is of all opprobrious labels the most opprobrious, and is culpably inexcusable.

---

4. P. C. Wren, *Sinbad the Soldier* (John Murray, 1958), p. 148.
5. On "Abyssinia," *Encyclopaedia of Religion and Ethics* 1, pp. 55ff.

God in African Belief

E. Geoffrey Parrinder

Born in London in 1910, E. Geoffrey Parrinder has had the proverbial long and distinguished career. He received doctorates of philosophy and divinity from the University of London and went to Africa in 1933, where he taught for twenty-five years. The religions of that continent have been the subject of his Religion in Africa, African Traditional Religion, African Mythology, Religion in an African City, West African Religion, Witchcraft, Africa's Three Religions, *and other of his books. In 1958 he became reader and then professor of the comparative study of religions at King's College, the University of London, retiring in 1977. He has been Wilde Lecturer in Natural and Comparative Religion at Oxford University; Teape Lecturer at the University of Delhi; and a visiting professor at the University of Tokyo. In addition to his books about Africa are many that concern other religions, including* Avatar and Incarnation, The Indestructible Soul, The Faiths of Mankind, Worship in the World's Religions, *and* Encountering World Religions.

From the earlier view that African religion was crudely fetishistic, with an idea of God where it existed being an importation, informed opinion has now swung round to the conviction that most, if not all African peoples have had a belief in a Supreme Being as an integral part of their world view and practised religion. The symposium *African Ideas of God*[1] did much to establish this finally, but it has been supported by countless books and articles. Missionaries have found, often to their surprise, that they did not need to argue for the existence of God, or faith in a life after death, for both these fundamentals of world religion are deeply rooted in Africa.

Some writers refer to "the High God," but this term sounds derogatory to educated African ears, suggesting that God is merely distant or transcendent. Here we shall speak of the Supreme Being, or God, as in normal English usage. . . . African myths express many beliefs about God in graphic form. It is not necessary to accept the myths as true in detail; but they express a conviction in the spiritual direction of the universe. Modern science may express its theories in different ways, and in new symbols, but it is also making a religious search for truth and purpose in the universe. Myths speak about God in picture language, and other sources for an

1. E. W. Smith (ed.), (1950).

understanding of his character in African traditional religion are found in prayers, songs, proverbs, riddles, and some rituals.

The nature of God in African belief can be gathered from the qualities attributed to him. These correspond generally to many of the divine attributes postulated in other religions. That God is almighty is one of the most obvious assertions, since supremacy implies it. All-powerful is a common name for him and he receives many similar titles: creator, allotter, giver of rain and sunshine, the one who began the forest, the one "who gives and rots," maker of souls, father of the placenta, the one who exists by himself. The omnipresence of God, less commonly expressed, is found in sayings such as "the one who is met everywhere," and "the great ocean whose head-dress is the horizon." More clearly God is omniscient: the wise one, the all-seeing, the "one who brings round the seasons."[2]

These attributes imply the transcendence of God, and to some extent his immanence. God is always creator and ruler, the one beyond all thanks, the ancient of days who is from the first, the everlasting who has no limits, and he who alone is full of abundance. The Zulu particularly delighted in such titles: "he who bends down even majesties," the irresistible, and "he who roars so that all nations are struck with terror." Then the nearness of God comes in such titles as "the one you meet everywhere," "the great pool contemporary of everything," and "the one who fills everything." In his immanence God may be conceived more physically or naturally. He may be found in big trees or thickets, on mountains or rocky places, and especially in rivers and streams. He may be spoken of as one but many, invisible at ordinary times but seen by a man about to die, and his voice may be heard when the bush is burnt or when a whirlwind blows.

It is clear that God exists by himself; he is not the creature of any other being but is the cause of everything else. His pre-eminence and his greatness go together. But since he is greater than any other spirit or man, God is mysterious and nobody can understand him, he creates and destroys, he gives and takes away. God is invisible, infinite, and unchangeable. Although his wife or wives and children appear in myths, yet in himself God is one, and only rarely is the notion found of a twin deity. Heaven and earth, sun and moon, day and night, man and woman, are dual but God is the unity beyond all this. The duality is not discussed as it is in Hindu speculation, but the unity of God follows from his pre-eminence and sole creation. It has been said that God might have been banished from Greek thought without damaging its logical architecture, but this cannot be said of African thought, as God is both the creator and the principle of unity that holds everything together. He is the source and essence of force, Ntu, which inspires the whole vital organism.

The character of God appears not just in abstract attributes, but in more humane and moral qualities. Although he is supremely great, mysterious and irresistible, yet he is also kindly disposed towards men and his providence is mentioned not infrequently. He is the God of destinies but also of comfort, the kindly-disposed and "the providence which watches over all like the sun"; he can be angry but is also "full of pity," the father of babies and the great friend. In the enigmatic Akan title he is "the one on whom men lean and do not fall."

2. See the Index of God-names in *African Ideas of God,* p. 305 f.

The natural attributes of God come from his primary function as creator. Not only did he make the world, but he established the laws of society and the existence of justice depends upon obedience to him. Creation is not only in the past; the divine work is continued in sustaining the universe, and men turn to God if things go wrong today, complaining if they have been treated unjustly. God is the giver of destinies, and may appear harsh or inscrutable, but that does not make people fatalistic or console them if justice is perverted.

A well known Ila story tells of an old woman who came from a large family and had many troubles. God, Leza, "the one who besets," smote all the family in turn. Her parents died and then other relatives. Although she married and had children, her husband died and then the children. Some had borne her grand-children but these also passed away. The crone was left and hoped to die, but strangely she grew young again (some would have said that she had eaten the soul-stuff of her relatives), and she decided to use her new powers to find out God and get an explanation of her troubles. First she tried to make a ladder to heaven out of forest trees, but as this Tower of Babel neared the sky the whole structure collapsed. So the woman resolved to travel to every country till she found the place where heaven touches earth and provides the road to God. In every land that she visited people asked why she was travelling and she replied that she had suffered so much at the hands of God that she was seeking him out. But her hearers said this was not strange, for such troubles come to all people and nobody can ever get free of them.

Although the ways of God are beyond man and can never be fully known, yet numerous titles speak of his sustaining and cherishing work. He gives rain and sun, health and fertility. He is also the deliverer and Saviour, moulder and providence. Disease and poverty, drought and famine, locusts and death come to plague man, but they are part of the mystery of nature. Although life is viewed, inevitably, from the human standpoint, yet man is not the centre of the universe in African thought, any more than in Christian theology. It is God who is supreme and the central moving force, and man submits to him as the great chief.

How far God is regarded in anthropomorphic fashion, as a big man projected into the heavens, or a glorified ancestor, has been debated. Human titles have been given to him: ruler, father, mother, and even more grandfather, the originator of the people. J. B. Danquah asserted that for the Akan God is the Great Ancestor, but other writers disagree. It seems rare for God to be thought of as linked to man in a family relationship. Rather man is his creation and God is the inscrutable maker. Other gods are spoken of but it is not normal to find the same generic term for "a god" applied to the Supreme Being, who is in a class apart. And it has been noted that there are few, if any, sculptures of the great God.

Occasionally God may be spoken about in terms of either sex. Mawu-Lisa of the Fon is the supreme female-male, and Dr. Aggrey, the Ghanaian educationalist, spoke of "Father-mother God." The southern Nuba, who have a system of matrilineal descent, refer to God as "the Great Mother" and when praying beside a dying person they say, "Our God, who has brought us into this world, may she take you."[3] This is very unusual, and though most African languages have no sex in the pro-

3. *African Ideas of God*, p. 215 f.

noun, God is generally clearly personified as a great male ruler. In mythology God may have a wife and children, servants and messengers, and other gods act as his partners or agents in creation. God may be described with a body, head, eyes, ears, mouth, arms, and legs. But both the Bible and the Koran speak of the divine body in this way, though theologians take such language as symbolical or, in a common Muslim phrase, assert the paradox that God has two eyes "but without asking how." Men have to use language, with its solid imagery, even when speaking of the invisible and indescribable God, and anything more than negatives is bound to involve metaphor.

Similarly God is related to heavenly objects, and at times apparently identified with them. His virtual identification with the sky, in myths of divine withdrawal, has been noted. In other stories God is closely linked with the sun, though this is not common. Some peoples may seem almost to identify God with the sun, but this appears to be metaphorical and due to the similarity of words used about God and the sun. The sun is sometimes personified in myths, or is regarded as a manifestation of God, but there are few clear indications that the sun is God or God is the sun. There is little ritual in connexion with the sun, such as that which was performed in ancient Europe or Japan to make the sun return from its winter journey to the south. In the tropics the sun is always overhead, and needs no encouragement to shine. However, as it is supreme in the heavens the sun may be an apt symbol for God, and stories are told of men visiting the sky and reaching the sun or God.

The Bakuta of the Congo speak of two supreme Gods: Nzambi above and Nzambi below. Often regarded as twins they act heroic roles in many stories, and have villages and families in heaven and earth. But in myths of creation it is Nzambi above who is supreme and his twin disappears, so that the function of Nzambi is creation. His first children were twins, the sun and moon, and death is attributed to his faulty messenger, here the goat. As in other myths it is said that Nzambi retired from the earth after a human offence and he has no regular worship. But he still has a concern for men and death is under his control. His name occurs in proverbs and exclamations: "God sees him" is said about a man who escapes punishment from earthly courts, "we have the grace of Nzambi" is uttered when people are spared by flashes of lightning, and "Nzambi is with me" is said by a woman after childbirth. Some writers have identified this celestial Nzambi with the sun, but men prayed to him also at night, looking up to the sky, and when a thunderbolt falls at night it is his axe.

Any of the celestial bodies may be connected with God. The Akan of Ghana also say that thunderbolts are God's axes, though some other peoples have storm gods, inferior to the Supreme Being, who control the thunder. The rainbow is God's bow, and lightning is his weapon against evildoers. Different reasons are given for eclipses; they are due to the quarrel of sun and moon, or to clouds or storms devouring the moon, but ultimately God is responsible. An eclipse is viewed with alarm, since all nature goes quiet at this time, and drums are beaten to ensure the victory of good, but wise men know that the darkness never lasts long.

Earthly objects, and especially high mountains like Mount Kenya, are apt symbols for the dwelling or place of manifestation of a transcendent God, as in the Bible. They provide places where prayers and sacrifices can be made in time of need.

Groves of trees are sacred, and the Gikuyu on important occasions pray to the Supreme Being there in the open. There are spirits of the earth, but unusual phenomena like earthquakes or floods may be ascribed to the direct action of God, and desolate places may be thought of as his special abodes, and precious metals in the ground as his gift. The regularity of nature is also ascribed to him, the succession of day and night, heat and cold, dry and rainy seasons. Although nature gods and ancestors are both objects of prayers for good harvests and plentiful rain, yet ultimately they are the concern of the supreme God.

Worship of God

The relationship of men with God is complex. Man is always the creature of the Most High, as mythology shows. The first man and woman are often called children of God, even though some stories say that they came from the earth instead of from heaven. Traffic between heaven and earth was easy in the olden days, according to the stories, but the separation came about by human fault, usually that of a woman. One result of the misunderstanding between God and man is that death has come, though a further reason is often given for this, and generally an animal is blamed.

Human life should be conducted according to principles which God gave to the founding fathers of the clan. Every clan has traditional history, some of it fact, some legend, but always important for revealing ideals and attitudes. The ancient heroes are often described as coming from God, or entrusted by him with ordering their lives and settling on their land. Morality is traditional, but it depends on the ultimate creation and the purpose of the world to maintain harmony and prosperity. Rewards and punishments for good or bad acts may be applied in this present life. Even notorious evildoers who manage to flourish like the green bay tree and avoid justice for a long time are believed, rather optimistically, to be due for punishment before death. Only rarely, it seems, is a judgement predicted for good and evil men after death. But the Yoruba say that all that is done on earth will be accounted for in heaven, and men will have to state their case kneeling before God. Then the final lot of the righteous will be a heaven of cool breezes, and for the wicked a heaven of potsherds, a sort of celestial rubbish-heap like the midden of every village where refuse and broken pots are thrown.

The above statements suggest that God is close to most African peoples and that he receives regular worship, as in Christianity or Islam. Therefore it is surprising to find that there is little ordered worship of God and few places where rituals are performed for him. That a Supreme Being is widely believed in, that he is the background of life, and is thought to be near to many people, is true, though there are exceptions. But regular worship is not usual.

The Dogon have group altars for Amma, at which the village chief usually officiates. Additional altars are made if some special object is found which is imbued with the divine presence, and there are special priests and priestesses who sacrifice here and at annual communal rites. Rattray provided invaluable photographs of temples of Nyame in Ashanti, with their priests, and of the small "God's altars," forked sticks holding bowls for offerings which stood in front of houses. But the temples were relatively few even in the 1920s, and many of the forked altars have disappeared today, though the worship of God has increased through the Christian churches. The Gikuyu and Shona also worship God on occasion or at special and communal ceremonies, but few other African peoples have organized cults for him.

Generally there are no temples or priests for God, though there may be many temples for the nature gods, and there are always sacrifices and prayers made to the ancestors. Yet occasional worship of God, by libation or simple invocation, is quite common. Prayer is worship, and it can be made by any layman or woman, at any place or time. When the gods and ancestors fail, or when appeal is needed to the highest authority, then despite his greatness God can be appealed to directly, without any special formula or intermediary priest.

The lesser spirits are also important in this connexion. Although they may appear to receive most attention in sacrifices, it is often said that they receive the externals of the offering but the essence of it is taken by them to God. The gods are subordinates and may pray to God for men, and in prayers to them the Supreme Being is often mentioned first, in a recital of the spiritual powers that are being invoked. Even when God is thought to be far away and fearsome, he can be called upon in time of distress because "his ears are long."

The study of the idea of God in Africa has been weakened by theorists, some of whom think that there has been an inevitable evolution from fetishism, to animism, to polytheism, and finally to monotheism. Others consider that there was an original monotheism from which all Africans fell, in a kind of Fall of Adam. Looking at things as they are today there is a picture of a mixed religion, which is not mere animism, nor a democratic polytheism, nor a pure monotheism. E. B. Idowu calls it "diffused monotheism."[4]

Evans-Pritchard, in one of his thoughtful conclusions, says that "a theistic religion need not be either monotheistic or polytheistic. It may be both. It is a question of the level, or situation, of thought rather than of exclusive types of thought. On one level Nuer religion may be regarded as monotheistic, at another level as polytheistic; and it can also be regarded at other levels as totemistic or fetishistic. These conceptions of spiritual activity are not incompatible. They are rather different ways of thinking of the numinous at different levels of experience. . . . At no level of thought and experience is Spirit thought of as something altogether different from God."[5]

---

4. *Editor's note:* He calls it a diffused monotheism "because here we have a monotheism in which there exist other powers which derive from Deity such being and authority that they can be treated, for practical purposes, almost as ends in themselves." *African Traditional Religion* (London: SCM Press Ltd., 1973), p. 135.

5. *Nuer Religion* (1956), p. 316.

Ogotemmêli and the Dawn of All Things
Marcel Griaule

Marcel Griaule (1898–1956), a French ethnologist, engaged in field studies in Africa for over a quarter of a century. During those years the Dogen, a Sudanese people, came to hold Griaule in especially high regard, and in 1946 the elders and priests of the Dogen decided to reveal more than just the "simple" teachings they customarily dispensed to outsiders. Assigned to this task was Ogotemmêli.

Until he lost his sight [in a hunting accident], he was a mighty hunter who, though one-eyed from childhood as a result of smallpox, would always come back from the chase with a full bag, while the others were still toiling in the gorges. His skill as a hunter was the fruit of his profound knowledge of nature, of animals, of men, and of gods. After his accident he learnt still more. Thrown back on his own resources, on his altars and on whatever he was able to hear, he had become one of the most powerful minds on the cliffs.

Indeed his name and his character were famous throughout the plateau and the hills, known (as the saying was) to the youngest boy. People came to his door for advice every day and even by night.

Arrangements were made, and Griaule met Ogotemmêli:

Then a head bent beneath the lintel of the door, and the man stood up to his full height, turning towards the stranger a face that no words can describe.

"Greetings!" he said, "Greetings to those who are athirst!"

The thick lips spoke the purest Sanga language. So alive were they that one saw nothing else. All the other features seemed to be folded away, particularly as, after the first words, the head had been bent. The cheeks, the cheek-bones, the forehead, and the eyelids seemed all to have suffered the same ravages; they were creased by a hundred wrinkles which had caused a painful contortion as of a face exposed to too strong a light or battered by a hail of stones. The eyes were dead.

Following that initial meeting were thirty-two consecutive days of instruction, the first of which is described here.

Ogotemmêli, seating himself on his threshold, scraped his stiff leather snuff-box, and put a pinch of yellow powder on his tongue.

From Marcel Griaule, *Conversations with Ogotemmeli.* Published by Oxford University Press for the International African Institute. Reprinted by permission of the International African Institute.

"Tobacco," he said, "makes for right thinking."

So saying, he set to work to analyse the world system, for it was essential to begin with the dawn of all things. He rejected as a detail of no interest, the popular account of how the fourteen solar systems were formed from flat circular slabs of earth one on top of the other. He was only prepared to speak of the serviceable solar system; he agreed to consider the stars, though they only played a secondary part.

"It is quite true," he said, "that in course of time women took down the stars to give them to their children. The children put spindles through them and made them spin like fiery tops to show themselves how the world turned. But that was only a game."

The stars came from pellets of earth flung out into space by the God Amma, the one God. He had created the sun and the moon by a more complicated process, which was not the first known to man but is the first attested invention of God: the art of pottery. The sun is, in a sense, a pot raised once for all to white heat and surrounded by a spiral of red copper with eight turns. The moon is the same shape, but its copper is white. It was heated only one quarter at a time. Ogotemmêli said he would explain later the movements of these bodies. For the moment he was concerned only to indicate the main lines of the design, and from that to pass to its actors.

He was anxious, however, to give an idea of the size of the sun.

"Some," he said, "think it is as large as this encampment, which would mean thirty cubits. But it is really bigger. Its surface area is bigger than the whole of Sanga Canton."

And after some hesitation he added:

"It is perhaps even bigger than that."

He refused to linger over the dimensions of the moon, nor did he ever say anything about them. The moon's function was not important, and he would speak of it later. He said however that, while Africans were creatures of light emanating from the fullness of the sun, Europeans were creatures of the moonlight: hence their immature appearance.

He spat out his tobacco as he spoke. Ogotemmêli had nothing against Europeans. He was not even sorry for them. He left them to their destiny in the lands of the north.

The God Amma, it appeared, took a lump of clay, squeezed it in his hand and flung it from him, as he had done with the stars. The clay spread and fell on the north, which is the top, and from there stretched out to the south, which is the bottom, of the world, although the whole movement was horizontal. The earth lies flat, but the north is at the top. It extends east and west with separate members like a foetus in the womb. It is a body, that is to say, a thing with members branching out from a central mass. This body, lying flat, face upwards, in a line from north to south, is feminine. Its sexual organ is an anthill, and its clitoris a termite hill. Amma, being lonely and desirous of intercourse with this creature, approached it. That was the occasion of the first breach of the order of the universe.

Ogotemmêli ceased speaking. His hands crossed above his head, he sought to distinguish the different sounds coming from the courtyards and roofs. He had reached the point of the origin of troubles and of the primordial blunder of God.

"If they overheard me, I should be fined an ox!"

At God's approach the termite hill rose up, barring the passage and displaying its masculinity. It was as strong as the organ of the stranger, and intercourse could not take place. But God is all-powerful. He cut down the termite hill, and had intercourse with the excised earth. But the original incident was destined to affect the course of things for ever; from this defective union there was born, instead of the intended twins, a single being, the *Thos aureus* or jackal, symbol of the difficulties of God. Ogotemmêli's voice sank lower and lower. It was no longer a question of women's ears listening to what he was saying; other, non-material, ear-drums might vibrate to his important discourse. The European and his African assistant, Sergeant Koguem, were leaning towards the old man as if hatching plots of the most alarming nature.

But, when he came to the beneficent acts of God, Ogotemmêli's voice again assumed its normal tone.

God had further intercourse with his earth-wife, and this time without mishaps of any kind, the excision of the offending member having removed the cause of the former disorder. Water, which is the divine seed, was thus able to enter the womb of the earth and the normal reproductive cycle resulted in the birth of twins. Two beings were thus formed. God created them like water. They were green in colour, half human beings and half serpents. From the head to the loins they were human: below that they were serpents. Their red eyes were wide open like human eyes, and their tongues were forked like the tongues of reptiles. Their arms were flexible and without joints. Their bodies were green and sleek all over, shining like the surface of water, and covered with short green hairs, a presage of vegetation and germination.

These spirits, called Nummo, were thus two homogeneous products of God, of divine essence like himself, conceived without untoward incidents and developed normally in the womb of the earth. Their destiny took them to Heaven, where they received the instructions of their father. Not that God had to teach them speech, that indispensable necessity of all beings, as it is of the world-system; the Pair were born perfect and complete; they had eight members, and their number was eight, which is the symbol of speech.

They were also of the essence of God, since they were made of his seed, which is at once the ground, the form, and the substance of the life-force of the world, from which derives the motion and the persistence of created being. This force is water, and the Pair are present in all water: they *are* water, the water of the seas, of coasts, of torrents, of storms, and of the spoonfuls we drink.

Ogotemmêli used the terms "Water" and "Nummo" indiscriminately.

"Without Nummo," he said, "it was not even possible to create the earth, for the earth was moulded clay and it is from water (that is, from Nummo) that its life is derived."

"What life is there in the earth?" asked the European.

"The life-force of the earth is water. God moulded the earth with water. Blood too he made out of water. Even in a stone there is this force, for there is moisture in everything.

"But if Nummo is water, it also produces copper. When the sky is overcast, the sun's rays may be seen materializing on the misty horizon. These rays, excreted by the spirits, are of copper and are light. They are water too, because they uphold the earth's moisture as it rises. The Pair excrete light, because they are also light."

While he was speaking, Ogotemmêli had been searching for something in the dust. He finally collected a number of small stones. With a rapid movement he flung them into the courtyard over the heads of his two interlocutors, who had no time to bend down. The stones fell just where the Hogon's cock had been crowing a few seconds before.

"That cock is a squalling nuisance. He makes all conversation impossible."

The bird began to crow again on the other side of the wall, so Ogotemmêli sent Koguem to throw a bit of wood at him. When Koguem came back, he asked whether the cock was now outside the limits of the Tabda quarter.

"He is in the Hogon's field," said Koguem. "I have set four children to watch him."

"Good!" said Ogotemmêli with a little laugh. "Let him make the most of what remains to him of life! They tell me he is to be eaten at the next Feast of Twins."

He returned to the subject of the Nummo spirits, or (as he more usually put it, in the singular) of Nummo, for this pair of twins, he explained, represented the perfect, the ideal unit.

The Nummo, looking down from Heaven, saw their mother, the earth, naked and speechless, as a consequence no doubt of the original incident in her relations with the God Amma. It was necessary to put an end to this state of disorder. The Nummo accordingly came down to earth, bringing with them fibres pulled from plants already created in the heavenly regions. They took ten bunches of these fibres, corresponding to the number of their ten fingers, and made two strands of them, one for the front and one for behind. To this day masked men still wear these appendages hanging down to their feet in thick tendrils.

But the purpose of this garment was not merely modesty. It manifested on earth the first act in the ordering of the universe and the revelation of the helicoid sign in the form of an undulating broken line.

For the fibres fell in coils, symbol of tornadoes, of the windings of torrents, of eddies and whirlwinds, of the undulating movement of reptiles. They recall also the eight-fold spirals of the sun, which sucks up moisture. They were themselves a channel of moisture, impregnated as they were with the freshness of the celestial plants. They were full of the essence of Nummo: they *were* Nummo in motion, as shown in the undulating line, which can be prolonged to infinity.

When Nummo speaks, what comes from his mouth is a warm vapour which conveys, and itself constitutes, speech. This vapour, like all water, has sound, dies away in a helicoid line. The coiled fringes of the skirt were therefore the chosen vehicle for the words which the Spirit desired to reveal to the earth. He endued his hands with magic power by raising them to his lips while he plaited the skirt, so that the moisture of his words was imparted to the damp plaits, and the spiritual revelation was embodied in the technical instruction.

In these fibres full of water and words, placed over his mother's genitalia, Nummo is thus always present.

Thus clothed, the earth had a language, the first language of this world and the most primitive of all time. Its syntax was elementary, its verbs few, and its vocabulary without elegance. The words were breathed sounds scarcely differentiated from one another, but nevertheless vehicles. Such as it was, this ill-defined speech sufficed for the great works of the beginning of all things.

In the middle of a word Ogotemmêli gave a loud cry in answer to the hunter's halloo which the discreet Akundyo, priest of women dying in childbirth and of stillborn children, had called through the gap in the wall.

Akundyo first spat to one side, his eye riveted on the group of men. He was wearing a red Phrygian cap which covered his ears, with a raised point like a uraeus on the bridge of the nose in the fashion known as "the wind blows." His cheekbones were prominent, and his teeth shone. He uttered a formal salutation to which the old man at once replied and the exchange of courtesies became more and more fulsome.

"God's curse," exclaimed Ogotemmêli, "on any in Lower Ogol who love you not!"

With growing emotion Akundyo made shift to out-do the vigour of the imprecation.

"May God's curse rest on me," said the blind man at last, "if I love you not!"

The four men breathed again. They exchanged humorous comments on the meagreness of the game in the I valley. Eventually Akundyo took his leave of them, asserting in the slangy French of a native soldier that he was going to "look for porcupine," an animal much esteemed by these people.

The conversation reverted to the subject of speech. Its function was organization, and therefore it was good; nevertheless from the start it let loose disorder.

This was because the jackal, the deluded and deceitful son of God, desired to possess speech, and laid hands on the fibres in which language was embodied, that is to say, on his mother's skirt. His mother, the earth, resisted this incestuous action. She buried herself in her own womb, that is to say, in the anthill, disguised as an ant. But the jackal followed her. There was, it should be explained, no other woman in the world whom he could desire. The hole which the earth made in the anthill was never deep enough, and in the end she had to admit defeat. This prefigured the even-handed struggles between men and women, which, however, always end in the victory of the male.

The incestuous act was of great consequence. In the first place it endowed the jackal with the gift of speech so that ever afterwards he was able to reveal to diviners the designs of God.

It was also the cause of the flow of menstrual blood, which stained the fibres. The resulting defilement of the earth was incompatible with the reign of God. God rejected that spouse, and decided to create living beings directly. Modelling a womb in damp clay, he placed it on the earth and covered it with a pellet flung out into space from heaven. He made a male organ in the same way and having put it on the ground, he flung out a sphere which stuck to it.

The two lumps forthwith took organic shape; their life began to develop. Members separated from the central core, bodies appeared, and a human pair arose out of the lumps of earth.

At this point the Nummo Pair appeared on the scene for the purpose of further action. The Nummo foresaw that the original rule of twin births was bound to disappear, and that errors might result comparable to those of the jackal, whose birth was single. For it was because of his solitary state that the first son of God acted as he did.

"The jackal was alone from birth," said Ogotemmêli, "and because of this he did more things than can be told."

The Spirit drew two outlines on the ground, one on top of the other, one male and the other female. The man stretched himself out on these two shadows of himself, and took both of them for his own. The same thing was done for the woman. Thus it came about that each human being from the first was endowed with two souls of different sex, or rather with two principles corresponding to two distinct persons. In the man the female soul was located in the prepuce; in the woman the male soul was in the clitoris.

But the foreknowledge of the Nummo no doubt revealed to him the disadvantages of this makeshift. Man's life was not capable of supporting both beings: each person would have to merge himself in the sex for which he appeared to be best fitted.

The Nummo accordingly circumcised the man, thus removing from him all the femininity of his prepuce. The prepuce, however, changed itself into an animal which is "neither a serpent nor an insect, but is classed with serpents." This animal is called a *nay*. It is said to be a sort of lizard, black and white like the pall which covers the dead. Its name also means "four," the female number, and "Sun," which is a female being. The *nay* symbolized the pain of circumcision and the need for the man to suffer in his sex as the woman does.

The man then had intercourse with the woman, who later bore the first two children of a series of eight, who were to become the ancestors of the Dogon people. In the moment of birth the pain of parturition was concentrated in the woman's clitoris, which was excised by an invisible hand, detached itself and left her, and was changed into the form of a scorpion. The pouch and the sting symbolized the organ: the venom was the water and the blood of the pain.

The European, returning through the millet field, found himself wondering about the significance of all these actions and counteractions, all these sudden jerks in the thought of the myth.

Here, he reflected, is a Creator God spoiling his first creation; restoration is effected by the excision of the earth, and then by the birth of a pair of spirits, inventive beings who construct the world and bring to it the first spoken words; an incestuous act destroys the created order, and jeopardizes the principle of twin-births. Order is restored by the creation of a pair of human beings, and twin-births are replaced by dual souls. (But why, he asked himself, twin-births at all?)

The dual soul is a danger; a man should be male, and a woman female. Circumcision and excision are once again the remedy. (But why the *nay*? Why the scorpion?)

The answers to these questions were to come later, and to take their place in the massive structure of doctrine, which the blind old man was causing to emerge bit by bit from the mists of time.

Over the heads of the European and Koguem the dark millet clusters stood out against the leaden sky. They were passing through a field of heavy ears, stiffly erect and motionless in the breeze. When the crop is backward and thin, the ears are light and move with the slightest breath of wind. Thin crops are therefore full of sound. An abundant crop, on the other hand, is weighed down by the wind and bows itself in silence.

Postscript

What was revealed to Professor Griaule was an incredibly complex, detailed, and systematic mythology. In the years that followed, however, Griaule continued his research and discovered that there was an even deeper strata of myth and thought—and it was significantly different from the one revealed by Ogotemmêli. Then still later another level was plummeted. Evan M. Zuesse speculates that "Griaule and his students were being led slowly along the path that Dogen candidates themselves had to traverse."*

Ogotemmêli died in 1947. When Griaule died in 1956 he was buried in Paris, but in the Sudan the Dogen performed for him the elaborate rituals usually reserved for the death of a revered leader.**

**Ritual Cosmos: The Sanctification of Life in African Religions* (Athens, Ohio: Ohio University Press, 1979), pp. 156ff.

***Life,* 3 December 1956, pp. 111 ff.

Divinities, Spirits, and the Living-Dead

John S. Mbiti

John S. Mbiti was born in 1931 in Kitui, Kenya. He received undergraduate degrees from Makerere University, Uganda, and Barrington College, Rhode Island; his doctorate is from Cambridge University. He has been a professor of theology and comparative religion at Makerere University, a visiting lecturer at the University of Hamburg, and he has taught at Union Theological Seminary. Among his books are Akamba Stories *(a collection of folktales),* Concepts of God in Africa, African Religions and Philosophy, *and* The Prayers of African Religion. *He speaks Kikamba, Swahili, Gikuyu, English, French, and German; he reads New Testament Greek and some Old Testament Hebrew.*

Stressing the degree to which Africans are immersed in their religions, Mbiti has written that the

> names of people have religious meanings in them; rocks and boulders are not just empty objects, but religious objects; the sound of the drum speaks a religious language; the eclipse of the sun or moon is not simply a silent phenomenon of nature, but one which speaks to the community that observes it. . . . For Africans, the whole of existence is a religious phenomenon; man is a deeply religious being living in a religious universe.*

The spiritual world of African peoples is very densely populated with spiritual beings, spirits and the living-dead. Their insight of spiritual realities, whether absolute or apparent, is extremely sharp. To understand their religious ethos and philosophical perception it is essential to consider their concepts of the spiritual world in addition to concepts of God. We have repeatedly emphasized that the spiritual universe is a unit with the physical, and that these two intermingle and dovetail into each other so much that it is not easy, or even necessary, at times to draw the distinction or separate them. . . .

The spirits in general belong to the ontological mode of existence between God and man. Broadly speaking, we can recognize two categories of spiritual beings:

African Religions and Philosophy (New York: Doubleday, 1970), p. 19.

From *African Religions and Philosophy* by J. S. Mbiti. Copyright © 1969 by John S. Mbiti. Reprinted by permission of the publisher, Heinemann International.

those which were created as such, and those which were once human beings. These can also be subdivided into divinities, associates of God, ordinary spirits and the living-dead. Our time analysis[1] is here very useful in helping us to place the spiritual beings in their proper category, and to grasp the logic behind their recognition by African peoples. We can now take a closer look at these beings that populate the spiritual realm.

Divinities and God's Associates

I am using the word "divinity" to cover personifications of God's activities and manifestations, of natural phenomena and objects, the so-called "nature spirits," deidied heroes, and mythological figures. Sometimes it is difficult to know where to draw the line, especially since different writers loosely speak of "gods," "demigods," "divinities," "nature spirits," "ancestral spirits," and the like.

Divinities are on the whole thought to have been created by God, in the onto-logical category of the spirits. They are associated with Him, and often stand for His activities or manifestations either as personifications or as the spiritual beings in charge of these major objects or phenomena of nature. Some of them are national heroes who have been elevated and deified, but this is rare, and when it does happen the heroes become associated with some function or form of nature. Concrete examples will make these points clearer.

It is reported that the Ashanti have a pantheon of divinities through whom God manifests Himself. They are known as *abosom;* are said to "come from Him" and to act as His servants and intermediaries between Him and other creatures. They are increasing numerically; and people hold festivals for major tribal divinities. Minor divinities protect individual human beings; and it is believed that God pur-posely created the *abosom* to guard men.[2] Banyoro divinities are departmentalized according to people's activities, experiences and social-political structure. They include the divinities of war, of smallpox, of harvest, of health and healing, of the weather, of the lake, of cattle, and minor ones of different clans. The same pattern of divinities is reported among Basoga, Edo, and others.

The Yoruba have one thousand and seven hundred divinities *(orisa),* this being obviously the largest collection of divinities in a single African people. These divin-ities are associated with natural phenomena and objects, as well as with human activities and experiences. They are said to render to God "annual tributes of their substance in acknowledgment of His Lordship." Parallel to the Yoruba social-polit-ical structure, these divinities form a hierarchy. *Orisa-nla* is "the supreme divinity" in the country, and acts as God's earthly deputy in creative and executive functions. *Orunmila* is reputed to be an omnilinguist divinity who understands "every lan-

1. EDITOR'S NOTE: In contrast to the Western linear concept of time, with its past, present, and future, the African concept of time is two-dimensional: there is a past (the Zamani period), a present (the Sasa period), but virtually no future. "Time has to be experienced in order . . . to become real." John S. Mbiti, *African Religions and Philosophy* (New York: Doubleday, 1970), pp. 19–36.]

2. K. A. Busia in D. Forde (ed.), *African Worlds* (Oxford, 1954), p. 191 f.; R. A. Lystad, *The Ashanti* (New Brunswick, 1958), p. 163 f.

guage spoken on earth," and who represents God's omniscience and knowledge. This divinity shows itself among men through the oracle of divination, and has the fame of being a great doctor. *Ogun* is the owner of all iron and steel, being originally a hunter who paved the way for other divinities to come to earth, for which reason they crowned him as "Chief among the divinities." He is ubiquitous, and is the divinity of war, hunting, and activities or objects connected with iron. *Sango* represents the manifestation of God's wrath, though legend makes him a historical figure in the region of Oyo near Ibadan. He is the divinity of thunder and lightning, and there is a cult for him. These are but a few of the Yoruba divinities, an interesting study of which can be found in Idowu's book.[3]

There are many societies which have only one or two divinities of any major status. The Bambuti recognize *Tore* as the divinity in charge of death, to whom they refer as "the Gate of the Abyss" and "the Spirit of the dead."[4] Although the Dinka have several, three are most prominent. These are *Macardit* who is the final explanation of sufferings and misfortunes; *Garang* who is associated with men, and falling from heaven enters their bodies; and *Abuk* who is in charge of women's occupations.[5] The Vugusu blame their experiences of evil and suffering upon an evil divinity *(Wele gumali)* who is said to have servants.[6] The Walamo have one divinity connected with rain, said to dwell on a mountain where people take gifts in time of drought.

.   .   .

Spirits

Myriads of spirits are reported from every African people, but they defy description almost as much as they defy the scientist's test tubes in the laboratory. Written sources are equally confusing. We have tried to include under the term "divinity," those spiritual beings of a relatively high status. If we pursue the hierarchical consideration, we can say that the spirits are the "common" spiritual beings beneath the status of divinities, and above the status of men. They are the "common populace" of spiritual beings.

As for the origin of spirits, there is no clear information what African peoples say or think about it. Some spirits are considered to have been created as a "race" by themselves. These, like other living creatures, have continued to reproduce themselves and add to their numbers. Most peoples, however, seem to believe that the spirits are what remains of human beings when they die physically. This then becomes the ultimate status of men, the point of change or development beyond which men cannot go apart from a few national heroes who might become deified. Spirits are the destiny of man, and beyond them is God. Societies that recognize divinities regard them as a further group in the ontological hierarchy between spirits

3. E. B. Idowu, *Olódùmarè: God in Yoruba Belief* (London/New York, 1962), pp. 55–106.

4. P. Schebesta, *Revisiting My Pygmy Hosts* (E. T. London, 1936), p. 174 f.

5. G. Lienhardt, *Divinity and Experience: The Religion of the Dinka* (Oxford, 1961), p. 81 f.

6. G. Wagner, *The Bantu of North Kavirondo* (Oxford, 1949), Vol. I, p. 175 f.

and God. Man does not, and need not, hope to become a spirit: he is inevitably to become one, just as a child will automatically grow to become an adult, under normal circumstances. A few societies have an additional source of the spirits, believing that animals also have spirits which continue to live in the spirit world together with human and other spirits.

Spirits are invisible, but may make themselves visible to human beings. In reality, however, they have sunk beyond the horizon of the Zamani period, so that human beings do not see them either physically or mentally. Memory of them has slipped off. They are "seen" in the corporate belief in their existence. Yet, people experience their activities, and many folk stories tell of spirits described in human form, activities, and personalities, even if an element of exaggeration is an essential part of that description. Because they are invisible, they are thought to be ubiquitous, so that a person is never sure where they are or are not.

Since the spirits have sunk into the horizon of the Zamani, they are within the state of collective immortality, relative to man's position. They have no family or personal ties with human beings, and are no longer the living-dead. As such, people fear them, although intrinsically the spirits are neither evil nor good. They have lost their human names, as far as men are concerned—i.e., those that once were human beings. To men, therefore, the spirits are strangers, foreigners, outsiders, and in the category of "things." They are often referred to as *"its."* Viewed anthropocentrically, the ontological mode of the spirits is a depersonalization and not a completion or maturation of the individual. Therefore, death is a loss, and the spirit mode of existence means the withering of the individual, so that his personality evaporates, his name disappears, and he becomes less and not more of a person: a thing, a spirit, and not a man any more.

Spirits as a group have more power than men, just as in a physical sense the lions do. Yet, in some ways men are better off, and the right human specialists can manipulate or control the spirits as they wish. Men paradoxically may fear, or dread, the spirits and yet they can drive the same spirits away or use them to human advantage. In some societies only the major spirits (presumably in the category of divinities) are recognized, and often these are associated with natural phenomena or objects.

Although the spirits are ubiquitous, men designate different regions as their places of abode. Among some societies like the Abaluyia, Banyarwanda, and Igbo, it is thought that the spirits dwell in the underground, netherworld, or the subterranean regions. The Banyarwanda say, for example, that this region is ruled by "the one with whom one is forgotten"; and the Igbo consider it to be ruled by a queen. The idea of the subterranean regions is suggested, obviously, by the fact that the bodies of the dead are buried and the ground points to, or symbolizes, the new homeland of the departed. A few societies like some Ewe, some Bushmen, and the Mamvu-Mangutu, situate the land of the spirits above the earth, in the air, the sun, moon, or stars.

The majority of peoples hold that the spirits dwell in the woods, bush, forest, rivers, mountains, or just around the villages. Thus, the spirits are in the same geographical region as men. This is partly the result of human self-protection and partly because man may not want to imagine himself in an entirely strange environment when he becomes a spirit. There is a sense in which man is too anthropocentric to get away from himself and his natural, social, political, and economic surroundings. This then makes the spirits men's contemporaries: they are ever with men, and man would feel uncomfortable if the ontological mode of the spirits were too distant from his own. This would mean upsetting the balance of existence, and if that balance is upset, then men make sacrifices, offerings, and prayers, to try and restore it. In effect, men visualize their next ontological stage, in form of spirits, but geographically it is not another stage. The world of the spirits, wherever it might be situated, is very much like the carbon copy of the countries where they lived in this life. It has rivers, valleys, mountains, forests, and deserts. Their activities of the spirits are similar to those of human life here, in addition to whatever other activities of which men may not know anything.

Yet, in certain aspects, the spirit world differs radically from the human world. It is invisible to the eyes of men: people only know or believe that it is there, but do not actually "see" it with their physical eyes. But more important, even if the spirits may be the depersonalized residue of individual human beings, they are ontologically "nearer" to God: not ethically, but in terms of communication with Him. It is believed that whereas men use or require intermediaries, the spirits do not, since they can communicate directly with God. . . . In many African societies the spirits and the living-dead act as intermediaries who convey human sacrifices or prayers to God, and may relay His reply to men. . . . [Also] in some societies it is believed that God has servants or agents whom He employs to carry out His intentions in the universe. The spirits fill up the ontological region of the Zamani between God and man's Sasa. The ontological transcendence of God is bridged by the spirit mode of existence. Man is forever a creature, but he does not remain forever man, and these are his two polarities of existence. Individual spirits may or may not remain for ever, but the class of the spirits is an essential and integral part of African ontology.

Becoming spirits is, in a sense, a social elevation. For this reason, African peoples show respect and high regard for their living-dead and for some of the important spirits. Spirits are "older" than men, when viewed against the Sasa and Zamani periods—they have moved completely into the Zamani period. Their age which is greater than that of human beings compels the latter to give them respect along the same pattern that younger people give respect to older men and women, whether or not they are immediately members of the same family. In relation to the spirits, men are the younger generation, and social etiquette requires that they respect those who have fully entered and settled in the Zamani period.

Spirits do not appear to human beings as often as do the living-dead, and where mention of their appearances is made it is generally in folk stories. They act in malicious ways, as well as in a benevolent manner. People fear them more because of their being "strangers" than because of what they actually are or do. They are said to have a shadowy form of body, though they may assume different shapes like human, animal, plant forms or inanimate objects. People report that they see the spirits in ponds, caves, groves, mountains, or outside their villages, dancing, singing, herding cattle, working in their fields, or nursing their children. Some spirits appear in people's dreams, especially to diviners, priests, medicine-men, and rainmakers to impart some information. These personages may also consult the spirits as part of their normal training and practice. In many societies it is said and believed that spirits call people by name, but on turning round to see who called them there would be nobody. This sounds like a naughty game on the part of the spirits who probably derive a lot of fun from it. In folk stories it is told that the spirits sleep in the daytime and remain awake at night.

As the spirits are invisible, ubiquitous, and unpredictable, the safest thing is to keep away from them. If they, or the living-dead, appear too frequently to human beings people feel disturbed. Then the spirits possess men, and are blamed for forms of illness like madness and epilepsy. Spirit possession occurs in one form or another in practically every African society. Yet, spirit possession is not always to be feared, and there are times when it is not only desirable but people induce it through special dancing and drumming until the person concerned experiences spirit possession during which he may even collapse. When the person is thus possessed, the spirit may speak through him, so that he now plays the role of a medium, and the messages he relays are received with expectation by those to whom they are addressed. But on the whole, spirit possessions, especially unsolicited ones, result in bad effects. They may cause severe torment in the possessed person; the spirit may drive him away from his home so that he lives in the forests; it may cause him to jump into the fire and get himself burnt, to torture his body with sharp instruments, or even to do harm to other people. During the height of spirit possession, the individual in effect loses his own personality and acts in the context of the "personality" of the spirit possessing him. The possessed person becomes restless, may fail to sleep properly, and if the possession lasts a long period it results in damage to health. Women are more prone to spirit possession than men. Exorcism is one of the major functions of the traditional doctors and diviners; and when spirits "endanger" a village, there are usually formal ceremonies to drive away the notorious spirits. In some societies family spirits have to be moved ceremoniously when the villagers move from one place to another. This insures that the family spirits and especially the living-dead, move with members of their human relatives and are not forsaken where there is nobody to "remember" them in their personal immortality.

Human relationships with the spirits vary from society to society. It is, however, a real, active, and powerful relationship, especially with the spirits of those who have recently died—whom we have called the living-dead. Various rites are performed to keep this contact, involving the placing of food and other articles, or the pouring of libation of beer, milk, water, and even tea or coffee (for the spirits who have been "modernized"). In some societies this is done daily, but most African peoples do it less often. Such offerings are given to the oldest member of the departed—who may still be a living-dead, or may be remembered only in genealogies. This is done with the understanding that he will share the food or beverage with the other spirits of the family group. Words may or may not accompany such offerings, in form of prayers, invocations, or instructions to the departed. These words are the bridge of communion, the people's witness that they recognize the departed to be still alive. Failure to observe these acts means in effect that human beings have completely broken off their links with the departed, and have therefore forgotten the spirits. This is regarded as extremely dangerous and disturbing to the social and individual conscience. People are then likely to feel that any misfortune that befalls them is the logical result of their neglect of the spirits, if not caused by magic and witchcraft.

For spirits which are not associated with a particular family, offerings may be placed in spirit shrines where these exist. Such shrines belong to the community, and may be cared for by priests. Some of the spirits who are accorded this honour are venerated according to their functions, for example the spirits of the water may receive offerings when people want to fish or sail in the water; and the spirits of the forests may be consulted when people want to cut down the forest and make new fields. Here we merge with the category of the divinities, which we have already described above.

The Living-Dead

The departed of up to five generations are in a different category from that of ordinary spirits which we have been considering. They are still within the Sasa period, they are in the state of personal immortality, and their process of dying is not yet complete. We have called them the living-dead. They are the closest links that men have with the spirit world. Some of the things said about the spirits apply also to the living-dead. But the living-dead are bilingual: they speak the language of men, with whom they lived until "recently"; and they speak the language of the spirits and of God, to Whom they are drawing nearer ontologically. These are the "spirits" with which African peoples are most concerned: it is through the living-dead that the spirit world becomes personal to men. They are still part of their human families, and people have personal memories of them. The two groups are bound together by their common Sasa which for the living-dead is, however, fast disappearing into the Zamani. The living-dead are still "people," and have not yet become "things," "spirits," or "its." They return to their human families from time to time, and share meals with them, however symbolically. They know and have interest in what is going on in the family. When they appear, which is generally to the oldest members of the household, they are recognized by name as "so and so"; they enquire about family affairs, and may even warn of impending danger or rebuke those who have failed to follow their special instructions. They are the guardians of family affairs, traditions, ethics, and activities. Offence in these matters is ultimately an offence against the forefathers who, in that capacity, act as the invisible police of the families and communities. Because they are still "people," the living-dead are therefore the best group of intermediaries between men and God: they know the needs of men, they have "recently" been here with men, and at the same time they have full access to the channels of communicating with God directly or, according to some societies, indirectly through their own forefathers. Therefore men approach them more often for minor needs of life than they approach God. Even if the living-dead may not do miracles or extraordinary things to remedy the need, men experience a sense of psychological relief when they pour out their hearts' troubles before their seniors who have a foot in both worlds.

All this does not mean that the relationship between men and the living-dead is exclusively paradisal. People know only too well that following physical death, a barrier has been erected between them and the living-dead. When the living-dead return and appear to their relatives, this experience is not received with great enthusiasm by men; and if it becomes too frequent, people resent it. Men do not say to the living-dead: "Please sit down and wait for food to be prepared!"; nor would they bid farewell with the words: "Great so-and-so in the spirit world!" And yet these are two extremely important aspects of social friendliness and hospitality among men in African communities. The food and libation given to the living-dead are paradoxically acts of hospitality and welcome, and yet of informing the living-dead to move away. The living-dead are wanted and yet not wanted. If they have been improperly buried or were offended before they died, it is feared by the relatives or the offenders that the living-dead would take revenge. This would be in the form of misfortune, especially illness, or disturbing frequent appearances of the living-dead. If people neglect to give food and libation where this is otherwise the normal practice, or if they fail to observe instructions that the living-dead may have given before dying, then misfortunes and sufferings would be interpreted as resulting from the anger of the living-dead. People are, therefore, careful to follow the proper practices and customs regarding the burial or other means of disposal of dead bodies, and make libation and food offerings as the case might be. In some societies, special care of the graves is taken, since the living-dead may be considered to dwell in the area of the graves, some of which are in the former houses of the departed. Attention is paid to the living-dead of up to four or five generations, by which time only a few, if any, immediate members of their families would still be alive. When the last person who knew a particular living-dead also dies, then in effect the process of death is now complete as far as that particular living-dead is concerned. He is now no longer remembered by name, no longer a "human being," but a spirit, a thing, an *it*. He has now sunk beyond the visible horizon of the Zamani. It is no more necessary to pay close attention to him in the family obligation of making food offerings and libation, except, in some societies, within the context of genealogical remembrances or in the chain of the intermediaries. By that time also, additional living-dead have come into the picture and deserve or require more attention from the living. Those who have "moved on" to the stage of full spirits, merge into the company of spirits, and people lose both contact with and interest in them. They are no longer in the human period of the Sasa, even if they may continue to be men's contemporaries. Their plane of existence is other than that of men, they are ontologically spirits and spirits only. In some societies it is believed that some living-dead are "reborn." This is, however, only partial reincarnation since not the entire person is reborn as such, but only certain of his characteristics or physical distinctions.

Further Reading

Two internationally acclaimed authors must head the listings here.

The Nigerian Chinua Achebe provides a vivid portrait of African life and belief in his novels. *Things Fall Apart* (1959) was his first; *Anthills of the Savannah* (1988) his most recent. "The moment I realized," he has written, "in reading [Conrad's] *Heart of Darkness,* that I was not supposed to be part of Marlowe's crew, sailing down the Congo, but I was one of those on the shore jumping up, clapping, and making faces—the moment I realized that, then I realized that that was not me, and that story had to be told again."

Wole Soyinka, also a Nigerian, is a playwright, poet, novelist, editor, and essayist; he was awarded the Noble Prize for literature in 1986. A good way to meet Soyinka would be in his autobiography, one part of which has been published as *Ake: The Years of Childhood* (1981).

Jerome Rothenberg (ed.), *Technicians of the Sacred: A Range of Poetries from African, America, and Oceania* (2d ed., 1985). A remarkable collection of prayers, hymns, songs, incantations—with notes and commentaries.

Religions of Africa: Traditions in Transformation (1985) by E. Thomas Lawson is a very brief textbook that focuses on Zulu and Yoruba religious systems.

Ritual Cosmos: The Sanctification of Life in African Religions (1979) by Evan M. Zuesse is "an attempt to bring together the two disciplines that are most concerned with the investigation of African religions: anthropology and religious studies. There has been a tendency," the author writes, "on the part of each discipline to go its own way. . . . Many of the basic theoretical approaches in religious studies are still determined by Christian theology, and are essentially irrelevant for a study of African religions."

In *The Religion, Spirituality, and Thought of Traditional Africa* (1970), Dominique Zahan observes that the word "religion" suggests to us a "corpus of doctrines and practices expressing the relationship between man and the Invisible, and by giving the word this meaning we immediately establish a fundamental distinction between man and the divine powers. But in actuality," he asks, "how do Africans themselves conceive of this aspect of culture?"

John S. Mbiti, *Concepts of God in Africa* (1970). Topics include the nature and attributes of God, the problem of evil, anthropomorphism, the creation of man, worship, ethics, and death.

XI

RELIGION IN AMERICA
A Sampler

It is not enough to be busy. . . . The question is: what are we busy about?

Henry David Thoreau

Alexis de Tocqueville, still only twenty-five years of age, began his travels in the United States in 1831. Later, in his classic *Democracy in America,* he wrote that "the religious aspect of the country was the first thing that struck my attention." Though his visit here was brief—barely over nine months—the young Frenchman was often uncannily perceptive. ("I think that in no country in the civilized world is less attention paid to philosophy than in the United States." He noted the "restless ambition" of Americans, and said with alarm, "This race is entirely commercial.") He was pleased that "every man is allowed freely to take that road which he thinks will lead him to heaven." The consequences of that freedom were also apparent: "Christian sects are infinitely diversified and perpetually modified." But then, in a somewhat less complimentary vein: "Religious insanity is very common in the United States." He did not name names.

In view of the number of religions (and denominations and sects) that have prospered in this land, there is no denying that there has been religious freedom—but it was never easy and is not today. The Puritans wanted freedom, really, for no one but themselves, and that was the beginning of a long, sorry story. "The mind of the bigot is like the pupil of the eye," said Oliver Wendell Holmes, Jr., "the more light you pour upon it, the more it will contract."

Peter Cartwright, the Davy Crockett of Methodism,[1] appears first in the pages that follow. Converted to Methodism at the age of sixteen (in 1801), Cartwright became a frontier preacher who tirelessly "exhorted" others to come to Christ. Self-confident, zealous, physically powerful, he was a force to be reckoned with. He himself testified that he never doubted for a moment that his church (he frequently calls it the "Methodist Episcopal") was anything but the one true faith. Accordingly, he roundly denounced Deists, "diabolical Mormons," Universalists, Unitarians, Predestinarians, Baptists, and Presbyterians. Those in the "muddy pool of Shakerism"

---

1. So aptly termed by Edwin Scott Gaustad, *Historical Atlas of Religion in America* (New York: Harper & Row, 1962), p. 78.

were "blasphemous"; Shakerism was a "dreadful delusion." Cartwright was nothing if not forthright.

In 1820 Joseph Smith was fifteen years old and lived with his family in the village of Manchester in New York. Confused by the "great clash in religious sentiment" of different churches, he went one day to a grove and fervently prayed. Abruptly there came a vision of "two glorious personages . . . surrounded with a brilliant light which eclipsed the sun at noon day. They told me that all religious denominations were believing in incorrect doctrines." Thus were begun the revelations to a new prophet and what he and his followers have termed a "restoration" of the Gospel of Jesus Christ. The revelations continued after Joseph Smith's death: each succeeding president of the Church is also a prophet of God.

Christian Science is represented here by two brief selections. The first is "Christian Science in Tremont Temple," an address by founder Mary Baker Eddy that marked a turning point in the early history of that Church. As the number of her followers had grown, other churches had been forced to take notice of Mrs. Eddy, and some did so by attacking her, charging blasphemy and leveling ridicule. She responded by challenging one of her most eminent critics to allow her to answer his criticisms at Tremont Temple in Boston, the proverbial bastion of respectability and orthodoxy. She was given only ten minutes, but the occasion signaled the arrival of Christian Science.[2] The second reading selection is a chapter from *Science and Health with Key to the Scriptures,* the volume by Mrs. Eddy that members of her Church believe reveals the true spiritual meaning of the Bible.

The Souls of Black Folk (1903), from which the reading selection by W. E. B. DuBois is taken, was the result of a great shift in the work of its author. DuBois had previously written sociological studies of the African-American experience in America: his hope had been that the presentation of "scientific facts" would call attention to problems and lead to reforms. Disappointed in those hopes, he wrote *The Souls of Black Folk,* the very title of which indicates that DuBois was not writing sociology or science, but much more.

It is ironic that the much maligned Native Americans—the "savages" of this continent and of popular entertainment since the days of ten-cent novels—are now so widely admired for their values. As Joseph Epes Brown has explained elsewhere, the Native American of the plains (for example) felt "the world of nature itself was his temple, and within this sanctuary he showed great respect to every form, function, and power." This reverence for nature and for life was central to Native American religion: the human being was linked to the heavens and the earth, and had the responsibility of "guardianship over the world of nature." The Great Spirit was both immanent and transcendent, and thus was the world of the Native American pervaded and encompassed by a sense of the sacred. All of this, finally, was manifested in a life rich with religious ritual and symbol. The circular shape of the *tipi* had cosmic meaning, and the rite of smoking the sacred pipe was compared by Brown to the Christian rite of Holy Communion.[3]

---

2. For a full account of this occasion and, for that matter, of Christian Science in general, see Stephan Gottschalk, *The Emergence of Christian Science in American Religious Life* (Berkeley: University of California Press, 1973), which is also the source of my notes here about the Tremont Temple address.

3. Joseph Epes Brown, *The Spiritual Legacy of the American Indian* (Wallingford, Penn.: Pendle Hill Publications, 1964).

Frontier Preacher

Peter Cartwright

In his Autobiography, *Peter Cartwright (1785–1872) recalled his family's move from Virginia, where he was born, to the wilds of Kentucky: "After we struck the wilderness we rarely traveled a day but we passed some white persons, murdered and scalped by the Indians." Cartwright survived not only Indians but outlaws and the other rigors of frontier life, in most frays giving much more than he took. For years he was a "circuit rider," that is, a preacher who traveled by foot or horseback a given route to meet with the faithful at appointed times and places to preach and "exhort." "Many nights, in early times, the itinerant [preacher] had to camp out, without fire or food for man or beast." He preached, he said, fourteen thousand sermons and baptized twelve thousand persons. His circuits, over the years, took him also to Tennessee, Indiana, Ohio, and Illinois.*

The Autobiography, *from which the following excerpts are taken, was published in 1856, when he said he was "old and well stricken in years." But he lived another sixteen years, and he was robust until his last days. At his death at the age of eighty-seven, his family numbered nine children, fifty grandchildren, thirty-seven great-grandchildren, and seven great-great-grandchildren.*

When my father settled in Logan County, there was not a newspaper printed south of Green River, no mill short of forty miles, and no schools worth the name. Sunday was a day set apart for hunting, fishing, horseracing, card-playing, balls, dances, and all kinds of jollity and mirth. We killed our meat out of the woods, wild; and beat our meal and hominy with a pestle and mortar. We stretched a deer skin over a hoop, burned holes in it with the prongs of a fork, sifted our meal, baked our bread, eat it, and it was first-rate eating too. We raised, or gathered out of the woods, our own tea. We had sage, bohea, cross-vine, spice, and sassafras teas, in abundance. As for coffee, I am not sure that I ever smelled it for ten years. We made our sugar out of the water of the maple-tree, and our molasses too. These were great luxuries in those days.

We raised our own cotton and flax. We water-rotted our flax, broke it by hand, scutched it; picked the seed out of the cotton with our fingers; our mothers and sisters carded, spun, and wove it into cloth, and they cut and made our garments

From *The Autobiography of Peter Cartwright,* with an Introduction, Bibliography, and Index by Charles L. Wallis. Reprinted by permission of Abingdon Press.

and bed-clothes, &c. And when we got on a new suit thus manufactured, and sallied out into company, we thought ourselves *"so big as anybody."*

. . .

I was naturally a wild, wicked boy, and delighted in horse-racing, card-playing, and dancing. My father restrained me but little, though my mother often talked to me, wept over me, and prayed for me, and often drew tears from my eyes; and though I often wept under preaching, and resolved to do better and seek religion, yet I broke my vows, went into young company, rode races, played cards, and danced.

At length my father gave me a young race-horse, which well-nigh proved my everlasting ruin; and he bought me a pack of cards, and I was a very successful young gambler; and though I was not initiated into the tricks of regular gamblers, yet I was very successful in winning money. This practice was very fascinating, and became a special besetting sin to me, so that, for a boy, I was very much captivated by it. My mother remonstrated almost daily with me, and I had to keep my cards hid from her; for if she could have found them, she would have burned them, or destroyed them in some way. O, the sad delusions of gambling! How fascinating, and how hard to reclaim a practiced gambler! Nothing but the power of Divine grace saved me from this wretched sin.

My father sent me to school, boarding me at Dr. Beverly Allen's; but my teacher was not well-qualified to teach correctly, and I made but small progress. I, however, learned to read, write, and cipher a little, but very imperfectly.

. . .

Conversion

In 1801, when I was in my sixteenth year, my father, my eldest half brother, and myself, attended a wedding about five miles from home, where there was a great deal of drinking and dancing, which was very common at marriages in those days. I drank little or nothing; my delight was in dancing. After a late hour in the night, we mounted our horses and started for home. I was riding my race-horse.

A few minutes after we had put up the horses, and were sitting by the fire, I began to reflect on the manner in which I had spent the day and evening. I felt guilty and condemned. I rose and walked the floor. My mother was in bed. It seemed to me, all of a sudden, my blood rushed to my head, my heart palpitated, in a few minutes I turned blind; an awful impression rested on my mind that death had come and I was unprepared to die. I fell on my knees and began to ask God to have mercy on me.

My mother sprang from her bed, and was soon on her knees by my side, praying for me, and exhorting me to look to Christ for mercy, and then and there I promised the Lord that if he would spare me, I would seek and serve him; and I never fully broke that promise. My mother prayed for me a long time. At length we lay down, but there was little sleep for me. Next morning I rose, feeling wretched beyond expression. I tried to read in the Testament, and retired many times to secret prayer through the day, but found no relief. I gave up my race-horse to my father, and requested him to sell him. I went and brought my pack of cards, and gave them to mother, who threw them into the fire, and they were consumed. I fasted, watched, and prayed, and engaged in regular reading of the Testament. I was so distressed and miserable, that I was incapable of any regular business.

.   .   .

At length one day I retired to the horse-lot, and was walking and wringing my hands in great anguish, trying to pray, on the borders of utter despair. It appeared to me that I heard a voice from heaven, saying, "Peter, look at me." A feeling of relief flashed over me as quick as an electric shock. It gave me hopeful feelings, and some encouragement to seek mercy, but still my load of guilt remained. I repaired to the house, and told my mother what had happened to me in the horse-lot. Instantly she seemed to understand it, and told me the Lord had done this to encourage me to hope for mercy, and exhorted me to take encouragement, and seek on, and God would bless me with the pardon of my sins at another time.

Some days after this, I retired to a cave on my father's farm to pray in secret. My soul was in an agony; I wept, I prayed, and said, "Now, Lord, if there is mercy for me, let me find it," and it really seemed to me that I could almost lay hold of the Saviour, and realize a reconciled God. All of a sudden, such a fear of the devil fell upon me that it really appeared to me that he was surely personally there, to seize and drag me down to hell, soul and body, and such a horror fell on me that I sprang to my feet and ran to my mother at the house. My mother told me this was a device of Satan to prevent me from finding the blessing then. Three months rolled away, and still I did not find the blessing of the pardon of my sins.

.   .   .

There were no camp-meetings in regular form at this time, but as there was a great waking up among the Churches, from the revival that had broken out at Cane Ridge, . . . many flocked to those sacramental meetings. The church would not hold the tenth part of the congregation. Accordingly, the officers of the Church erected a stand in a contiguous shady grove, and prepared seats for a large congregation.

The people crowded to this meeting from far and near. They came in their large wagons, with victuals mostly prepared. The women slept in the wagons, and the men under them. Many stayed on the ground night and day for a number of nights and days together. Others were provided for among the neighbors around. The power of God was wonderfully displayed; scores of sinners fell under the preaching, like men slain in mighty battle; Christians shouted aloud for joy.

To this meeting I repaired, a guilty, wretched sinner. On the Saturday evening of said meeting, I went, with weeping multitudes, and bowed before the stand, and earnestly prayed for mercy. In the midst of a solemn struggle of soul, an impression was made on my mind, as though a voice said to me, "Thy sins are all forgiven thee." Divine light flashed all round me, unspeakable joy sprung up in my soul. I rose to my feet, opened my eyes, and it really seemed as if I was in heaven; the trees, the leaves on them, and everything seemed, and I really thought were, praising God. My mother raised the shout, my Christian friends crowded around me and joined me in praising God; and though I have been since then, in many instances, unfaithful, yet I have never, for one moment, doubted that the Lord did, then and there, forgive my sins and give me religion.

Our meeting lasted without intermission all night, and it was believed by those who had a very good right to know, that over eighty souls were converted to God during its continuance. I went on my way rejoicing for many days. This meeting was in the month of May. In June our preacher, John Page, attended at our little church, *Ebenezer,* and there in June, 1801, I joined the Methodist Episcopal Church, which I have never for one moment regretted. I have never for a moment been tempted to leave the Methodist Episcopal Church, and if they were to turn me out, I would knock at the door till taken in again.

.   .   .

Cane Ridge Camp-Meeting

Somewhere between 1800 and 1801, in the upper part of Kentucky, at a memorable place called "Cane Ridge," there was appointed a sacramental meeting by some of the Presbyterian ministers, at which meeting, seemingly unexpected by ministers or people, the mighty power of God was displayed in a very extraordinary manner; many were moved to tears, and bitter and loud crying for mercy. The meeting was protracted for weeks. Ministers of almost all denominations flocked in from far and near. The meeting was kept up by night and day. Thousands heard of the mighty work, and came on foot, on horseback, in carriages and wagons. It was supposed that there were in attendance at times during the meeting from twelve to twenty-five thousand people. Hundreds fell prostrate under the mighty power of God, as men slain in battle. Stands were erected in the woods from which preachers of different Churches proclaimed repentance toward God and faith in our Lord Jesus Christ, and it was supposed, by eye and ear witnesses, that between one and two thousand souls were happily and powerfully converted to God during the meeting. It was not unusual for one, two, three, and four to seven preachers to be addressing the listening thousands at the same time from the different stands erected for the purpose. The heavenly fire spread in almost every direction. It was said, by truthful witnesses, that at times more than one thousand persons broke out into loud shouting all at once, and that the shouts could be heard for miles around.

From this camp-meeting, for so it ought to be called, the news spread through all the Churches, and through all the land, and it excited great wonder and surprise; but it kindled a religious flame that spread all over Kentucky and through many other states. And I may here be permitted to say, that this was the first camp-meeting ever held in the United States, and here our camp-meetings took their rise.

As Presbyterian, Methodist, and Baptist ministers all united in the blessed work at this meeting, when they returned home to their different congregations, and carried the news of this mighty work, the revival spread rapidly throughout the land; but many of the ministers and members of the synod of Kentucky thought it all disorder, and tried to stop the work. They called their preachers who were engaged in the revival to account, and censured and silenced them. These ministers then rose up and unitedly renounced the jurisdiction of the Presbyterian Church, organized a Church of their own, and dubbed it with the name *Christian*. Here was the origin of what was called the *New Lights*. They renounced the Westminster Confession of Faith, and all Church discipline, and professed to take the New Testament for their Church discipline. They established no standard of doctrine; every one was to take the New Testament, read it, and abide his own construction of it. Marshall, M'Namar, Dunlevy, Stone, Huston, and others, were the chief leaders in this *trash trap*. Soon a diversity of opinion sprang up, and they got into a Babel confusion. Some preached Arian, some Socinian, and some Universalist doctrines; so that in a few years you could not tell what was *harped* or what was *danced*. They adopted the mode of immersion, the water-god of all exclusive errorists; and directly there was a mighty controversy about the way to heaven, whether it was by water or by dry land.

. . .

The Great Revival

I have seen and heard more than five hundred Christians all shouting aloud the high praises of God at once; and I will venture to assert that many happy thousands were awakened and converted to God at these camp-meetings. Some sinners mocked, some of the old dry professors opposed, some of the old starched Presbyterian preachers preached against these exercises, but still the work went on and spread almost in every direction, gathering additional force, until our country seemed all coming home to God.

In this great revival the Methodists kept moderately balanced; for we had excellent preachers to steer the ship or guide the flock. But some of our members ran wild, and indulged in some extravagancies that were hard to control.

The Presbyterian preachers and members, not being accustomed to much noise or shouting, when they yielded to it went into great extremes and downright wilderness, to the great injury of the cause of God.

. . .

Just in the midst of our controversies on the subject of the powerful exercises among the people under preaching, a new exercise broke out among us, called the *jerks*, which was overwhelming in its effects upon the bodies and minds of the people. No matter whether they were saints or sinners, they would be taken under a warm song or sermon, and seized with a convulsive jerking all over, which they could not by any possibility avoid, and the more they resisted the more they jerked. If they would not strive against it and pray in good earnest, the jerking would usually abate. I have seen more than five hundred persons jerking at one time in my large congregations. Most usually persons taken with the jerks, to obtain relief, as they said, would rise up and dance. Some would run, but could not get away. Some would resist; on such the jerks were generally very severe.

To see those proud young gentlemen and young ladies, dressed in their silks, jewelry, and prunella, from top to toe, take the *jerks,* would often excite my risibilities. The first jerk or so, you would see their fine bonnets, caps, and combs fly; and so sudden would be the jerking of the head that their long loose hair would crack almost as loud as a wagoner's whip.

At one of my appointments in 1804 there was a very large congregation turned out to hear the Kentucky boy, as they called me. Among the rest there were two very finely-dressed, fashionable young ladies, attended by two brothers with loaded horsewhips. Although the house was large; it was crowded. The two young ladies, coming in late, took their seats near where I stood, and their two brothers stood in the door. I was a little unwell, and I had a phial of peppermint in my pocket. Before I commenced preaching I took out my phial and swallowed a little of the peppermint. While I was preaching, the congregation was melted into tears. The two young gentlemen moved off to the yard fence, and both the young ladies took the jerks, and they were greatly mortified about it. There was a great stir in the congregation. Some wept, some shouted, and before our meeting closed several were converted.

As I dismissed the assembly a man stepped up to me, and warned me to be on my guard, for he had heard the two brothers swear they would horsewhip me when meeting was out, for giving their sisters the jerks. "Well," said I, "I'll see to that."

I went out and said to the young men that I understood they intended to horsewhip me for giving their sisters the jerks. One replied that he did. I undertook to expostulate with him on the absurdity of the charge against me, but he swore I need not deny it; for he had seen me take out a phial, in which I carried some truck that gave his sisters the jerks. As quick as thought it came into my mind how I would get clear of my whipping, and, jerking out the peppermint phial, said I, "Yes; if I give your sisters the jerks I'll give them to you." In a moment I saw he was scared. I moved toward him, he backed, I advanced, and he wheeled and ran, warning me not to come near him, or he would kill me. It raised the laugh on him, and I escaped my whipping. I had the pleasure, before the year was out, of seeing all four soundly converted to God, and I took them into the Church.

While I am on this subject I will relate a very serious circumstance which I knew to take place with a man who had the jerks at a camp-meeting, on what was called the Ridge, in William Magee's congregation. There was a great work of religion in the encampment. The jerks were very prevalent. There was a company of drunken rowdies who came to interrupt the meeting. These rowdies were headed by a very large drinking man. They came with their bottles of whiskey in their pockets. This large man cursed the jerks, and all religion. Shortly afterward he took the jerks, and he started to run, but he jerked so powerfully he could not get away. He halted among some saplings, and, although he was violently agitated, he took out his bottle of whiskey, and swore he would drink the damned jerks to death; but he jerked at such a rate he could not get the bottle to his mouth, though he tried hard. At length he fetched a sudden jerk, and the bottle struck a sapling and was broken to pieces, and spilled his whiskey on the ground. There was a great crowd gathered round him, and when he lost his whiskey he became very much enraged, and cursed and swore very profanely, his jerks still increasing. At length he fetched a very violent jerk, snapped his neck, fell, and soon expired, with his mouth full of cursing and bitterness.

I always looked upon the jerks as a judgment sent from God, first, to bring sinners to repentance; and, secondly, to show professors that God could work with or without means, and that he could work over and above means, and do whatsoever seemeth him good, to the glory of his grace and the salvation of the world.

There is no doubt in my mind that, with weak-minded, ignorant, and superstitious persons, there was a great deal of sympathetic feeling with many that claimed to be under the influence of this jerking exercise; and yet, with many, it was perfectly involuntary. It was, on all occasions, my practice to recommend fervent prayer as a remedy, and it almost universally proved an effectual antidote.

There were many other strange and wild exercises into which the subjects of this revival fell; such, for instance, as what was called the running, jumping, barking exercise. The Methodist preachers generally preached against this extravagant wildness. I did it uniformly in my little ministrations, and sometimes gave great offense; but I feared no consequences when I felt my awful responsibilities to God. From these wild exercises, another great evil arose from the heated and wild imaginations of some. They professed to fall into trances and see visions; they would fall at meetings and sometimes at home, and lay apparently powerless and motionless for days, sometimes for a week at a time, without food or drink; and when they came to, they professed to have seen heaven and hell, to have seen God, angels, the devil, and the damned; they would prophesy, and, under the pretense of Divine inspiration, predict the time of the end of the world, and the ushering in of the great millennium.

This was the most troublesome delusion of all; it made such an appeal to the ignorance, superstition, and credulity of the people, even saint as well as sinner. I watched this matter with a vigilant eye. If I opposed it, I would have to meet the clamor of the multitude; and if any one opposed it, these very visionists would single him out, and denounce the dreadful judgments of God against him. They would even set the very day that God was to burn the world, like the self-deceived modern Millerites. They would prophesy, that if any one did oppose them, God would send fire down from heaven and consume him, like the blasphemous Shakers. They would proclaim that they could heal all manner of diseases, and raise the dead, just like the diabolical Mormons. They professed to have converse with spirits of the dead in heaven and hell, like the modern spirit rappers. Such a state of things I never saw before, and I hope in God I shall never see again.

I pondered well the whole matter in view of my responsibilities, searched the Bible for the true fulfillment of promise and prophecy, prayed to God for light and Divine aid, and proclaimed open war against these delusions. In the midst of them along came the Shakers, and Mr. Rankin, one of the Presbyterian revival preachers, joined them; Mr. G. Wall, a visionary local preacher among the Methodists, joined them; all the country was in commotion.

I made public appointments and drew multitudes together, and openly showed from the Scriptures that these delusions were false. Some of these visionary men and women prophesied that God would kill me. The Shakers soon pretended to seal my damnation. But nothing daunted, for I knew Him in whom I had believed, I threw my appointments in the midst of them, and proclaimed to listening thousands the more sure word of prophecy. This mode of attack threw a damper on these visionary, self-deluded, false prophets, sobered some, reclaimed others, and stayed the fearful tide of delusion that was sweeping over the country.

. . .

Primitive Methodism

At [a] conference, in October, 1804, I was sent as the junior preacher to Salt River and Shelbyville Circuits, which were joined together, Benjamin Lakin in charge, and William M'Kendree presiding elder.

The circuit was in Kentucky District. It was a large six weeks' circuit, and extended from the rolling fork of Green River south, to the Ohio River north, and even crossed the Ohio into what was then called Clark's or the Illinois Grant, now in the eastern portion of Indiana State. We had a little Book Concern then in its infancy, struggling hard for existence. We had no Missionary Society; no Sunday-school Society; no Church papers; no Bible or Tract Societies; no colleges, seminaries, academies, or universities; all the efforts to get up colleges under the patronage of the Methodist Episcopal Church in these United States and Territories, were signal failures. We had no pewed churches, no choirs, no organs; in a word, we had no instrumental music in our churches anywhere. The Methodists in that early day dressed plain; attended their meetings faithfully, especially preaching, prayer, and class meetings; they wore no jewelry, no ruffles; they would frequently walk three or four miles to class-meetings and home again, on Sunday; they would go thirty or forty miles to their quarterly meetings, and think it a glorious privilege to meet their presiding elder, and the rest of the preachers. They could, nearly every soul of them, sing our hymns and spiritual songs. They religiously kept the Sabbath day: many of them abstained from dram-drinking, not because the temperance reformation was ever heard of in that day, but because it was interdicted in the General Rules of our Discipline. The Methodists of that day stood up and faced their preacher when they sung; they kneeled down in the public congregation as well as elsewhere, when the preacher said, "Let us pray." There was no standing among the members in time of prayer, especially the abominable practice of sitting down during that exercise was unknown among early Methodists. Parents did not allow their children to go to balls or plays; they did not send them to dancing-schools; they generally fasted once a week, and almost universally on the Friday before each quarterly meeting. If the Methodists had dressed in the same "superfluity of naughtiness" then as they do now, there were very few even out of the Church that would have any confidence in their religion. But O, how have things changed for the worse in this educational age of the world!

. . .

I traveled in the State of Ohio in 1806, and at a largely attended camp-meeting near New Lancaster, there was a great work of God going on; many were pleading for mercy; many were getting religion; and the wicked looked solemn and awful. The pulpit in the woods was a large stand; it would hold a dozen people, and I would not let the lookers-on crowd into it, but kept it clear that at any time I might occupy it for the purpose of giving directions to the congregation.

There were two young ladies, sisters, lately from Baltimore, or somewhere down east. They had been provided for on the ground in the tent of a very religious sister of theirs. They were very fashionably dressed; I think they must have had, in rings, earrings, bracelets, gold chains, lockets, etc., at least one or two hundred dollars' worth of jewelry about their persons. The altar was crowded to overflowing with mourners; and these young ladies were very solemn. They met me at the stand, and asked permission to sit down inside it. I told them that if they would promise me to pray to God for religion, they might take a seat there. They were too deeply affected to be idle lookers-on; and when I got them seated in the stand, I called them, and urged them to pray; and I called others to my aid. They became deeply engaged; and about midnight they were both powerfully converted. They rose to their feet, and gave some very triumphant shouts; and then very deliberately took off their gold chains, ear-rings, lockets, etc., and handed them to me, saying, "We have no more use for these idols. If religion is the glorious, good thing you have represented it to be, it throws these idols into eternal shade."

.   .   .

A Methodist preacher in those days, when he felt that God had called him to preach, instead of hunting up a college or Biblical institute, hunted up a hardy pony of a horse, and some traveling apparatus, and with his library always at hand, namely, Bible, Hymn Book, and Discipline, he started, and with a text that never wore out nor grew stale, he cried, "Behold the Lamb of God, that taketh away the sin of the world." In this way he went through storms of wind, hail, snow, and rain; climbed hills and mountains, traversed valleys, plunged through swamps, swam swollen streams, lay out all night, wet, weary, and hungry, held his horse by the bridle all night, or tied him to a limb, slept with his saddle blanket for a bed, his saddle or saddle-bags for his pillow, and his old big coat or blanket, if he had any, for a covering. Often he slept in dirty cabins, on earthen floors, before the fire; ate roastingears for bread, drank butter-milk for coffee, or sage tea for imperial; took, with a hearty zest, deer or bear meat, or wild turkey, for breakfast, dinner, and supper, if he could get it. His text was always ready, "Behold the Lamb of God," &c. This was old-fashioned Methodist preacher fare and fortune. Under such circumstances, who among us would now say, "Here am I, Lord, send me?"

The Faith of the Latter-Day Saints
Joseph Smith

The document that follows is known as "The Wentworth Letter," and it is greatly esteemed by members of the Church of Jesus Christ of Latter-day Saints—the Mormons, as they are popularly known. Its author is Joseph Smith (1805–44), the prophet-founder of the church, and it contains both his own story of his life and an account of the early history of the church. The letter concludes, moreover, with a summary listing of beliefs, which have since been entitled "The Articles of Faith."

The persecution mentioned in the letter was to continue: only two years after it was written, Joseph Smith and his brother Hyrum were murdered by a mob in Carthage, Illinois. The leadership of the church passed to Brigham Young,* and it was he who led the final migration to the valley of the great Salt Lake.

March 1, 1842—At the request of Mr. John Wentworth, Editor and Proprietor of the Chicago *Democrat,* I have written the following sketch of the rise, progress, persecution, and faith of the Latter-day Saints, of which I have the honor, under God, of being the founder. Mr. Wentworth says that he wishes to furnish Mr. Bastow, a friend of his, who is writing the history of New Hampshire, with this document. As Mr. Bastow has taken the proper steps to obtain correct information, all that I shall ask at his hands, is, that he publish the account entire, ungarnished, and without misrepresentation.

I was born in the town of Sharon, Windsor County, Vermont, on the 23rd of December, A.D. 1805. When ten years old, my parents removed to Palmyra, New York, where we resided about four years, and from thence we removed to the town of Manchester. My father was a farmer and taught me the art of husbandry. When about fourteen years of age, I began to reflect upon the importance of being prepared for a future state, and upon inquiring [about] the plan of salvation, I found that there was a great clash in religious sentiment; if I went to one society they referred me to one plan, and another to another; each one pointing to his own particular creed as the *summum bonum* of perfection. Considering that all could not be right, and that God could not be the author of so much confusion, I determined

---

*The Reorganized Church of Jesus Christ of Latter-day Saints, with headquarters in Independence, Missouri, grew from a group that disputed Young's leadership. And there are still other independent Mormon churches.

Joseph Smith, "The Wentworth Letter," 1842.

to investigate the subject more fully, believing that if God had a Church it would not be split up into factions, and that if he taught one society to worship one way, and administer in one set of ordinances, he would not teach another, principles which were diametrically opposed.

Believing the word of God, I had confidence in the declaration of James—"If any of you lack wisdom, let him ask of God, that giveth to all men liberally, and upbraideth not; and it shall be given him." I retired to a secret place in a grove, and began to call upon the Lord; while fervently engaged in supplication, my mind was taken away from the heavenly vision, and saw two glorious personages, who exactly resembled each other in features and likeness, surrounded with a brilliant light which eclipsed the sun at noon day. They told me that all religious denominations were believing in incorrect doctrines, and that none of them was acknowledged of God as his Church and kingdom: and I was expressly commanded "to go not after them," at the same time receiving a promise that the fulness of the Gospel should at some future time be made known unto me.

On the evening of the 21st of September, A.D. 1823, while I was praying unto God, and endeavoring to exercise faith in the precious promises of scripture, on a sudden a light like that of day, only of a far purer and more glorious appearance and brightness, burst into the room, indeed the first sight as though the house was filled with consuming fire; the appearance produced a shock that affected the whole body; in a moment a personage stood before me surrounded with a glory yet greater than that with which I was already surrounded. This messenger proclaimed himself to be an angel of God, sent to bring the joyful tidings that the covenant which God made with ancient Israel was at hand to be fulfilled, that the preparatory work for the second coming of the Messiah was speedily to commence; that the time was at hand for the Gospel in all its fulness to be preached in power, unto all nations that a people might be prepared for the millennial reign. I was informed that I was chosen to be an instrument in the hands of God to bring about some of his purposes in this glorious dispensation.

I was also informed concerning the aboriginal inhabitants of this country and shown who they were, and from whence they came; a brief sketch of their origin, progress, civilization, laws, governments, of their righteousness and iniquity, and the blessings of God being finally withdrawn from them as a people, was made known unto me; I was also told where were deposited some plates on which were engraven an abridgment of the records of the ancient Prophets that had existed on this continent. The angel appeared to me three times the same night and unfolded the same things. After having received many visits from the angels of God unfolding the majesty and glory of the events that should transpire in the last days, on the morning of the 22nd of September, A.D. 1827, the angel of the Lord delivered the records into my hands.

These records were engraven on plates which had the appearance of gold, each plate was six inches wide and eight inches long, and not quite so thick as common tin. They were filled with engravings, in Egyptian characters, and bound together in a volume as the leaves of a book, with three rings running through the whole. The volume was something near six inches in thickness, a part of which was sealed. The characters on the unsealed part were small, and beautifully engraved. The whole book exhibited many marks of antiquity in its construction, and much skill in the art of engraving. With the records was found a curious instrument, which the ancients called "Urim and Thummim," which consisted of two transparent stones set in the rim of a bow fastened to a breast plate. Through the medium of the Urim and Thummim I translated the record by the gift and power of God.

In this important and interesting book the history of ancient America is unfolded, from its first settlement by a colony that came from the Tower of Babel, at the confusion of languages to the beginning of the fifth century of the Christian Era. We are informed by these records that America in ancient times has been inhabited by two distinct races of people. The first were called Jaredites, and came directly from the Tower of Babel. The second race came directly from the city of Jerusalem, about six hundred years before Christ. They were principally Israelities, of the descendants of Joseph. The Jaredites were destroyed about the time that the Israelites came from Jerusalem, who succeeded them in the inheritance of the country. The principal nation of the second race fell in battle towards the close of the fourth century. The remnants are the Indians that now inhabit this country. This book also tells us that our Savior made his appearance upon this continent after his resurrection; that he planted the Gospel here in all its fullness, and richness, and power, and blessing; that they had Apostles, Prophets, Pastors, Teachers, and Evangelists; the same order, the same priesthood, the same ordinances, gifts, powers, and blessing, as were enjoyed on the eastern continent, that the people were cut off in consequence of their transgressions, that the last of their prophets who existed among them was commanded to write an abridgment of their prophecies, history, etc., and to hide it up in the earth, and that it should come forth and be united with the Bible for the accomplishment of the purposes of God in the last days. For a more particular account I would refer to the Book of Mormon, which can be purchased at Nauvoo, or from any of our Traveling Elders.

As soon as the news of this discovery was made known, false reports, misrepresentation, and slander flew, as on the wings of the wind, in every direction; the house was frequently beset by mobs and evil designing persons. Several times I was shot at, and very narrowly escaped, and every device was made use of to get the plates away from me; but the power and blessing of God attended me, and several began to believe my testimony.

On the 6th of April, 1830, the "Church of Jesus Christ of Latter-day Saints" was first organized in the town of Fayette, Seneca county, state of New York. Some few were called and ordained by the Spirit of revelation and prophecy, and began to preach as the Spirit gave them utterance, and though weak, yet were they strengthened by the power of God, and many were brought to repentance, were immersed in the water, and were filled with the Holy Ghost by the laying on of hands. They saw visions and prophesied, devils were cast out, and the sick healed by the laying on of hands. From that time the work rolled forth with astonishing rapidity, and churches were soon formed in the states of New York, Pennsylvania, Ohio, Indiana, Illinois, and Missouri; in the last named state a considerable settlement was formed in Jackson county: numbers joined the Church and we were increasing rapidly; we made large purchases of land, our farms teemed with plenty, and peace and happiness were enjoyed in our domestic circle, and throughout our neighborhood; but as we could not associate with our neighbors (who were, many of them, of the basest of men, and had fled from the face of civilized society, to the frontier country to escape the hand of justice,) in their midnight revels, their Sabbath breaking, horse racing and gambling; they commenced at first to ridicule, then to persecute, and finally an organized mob assembled and burned our houses, tarred and feathered and whipped many of our brethren, and finally, contrary to law, justice and humanity, drove them from their habitations; who, houseless and homeless, had to wander on the bleak prairies till the children left the tracks of their blood on the prairie. This took place in the month of November, and they had no other covering but the canopy of heaven, in this inclement season of the year; this proceeding was winked at by the government, and although we had warrantee deeds for our land, and had violated no law, we could obtain no redress.

There were many sick, who were thus inhumanly driven from their houses, and had to endure all this abuse and to seek homes where they could be found. The result was, that a great many of them being deprived of the comforts of life, and the necessary attendances, died; many children were left orphans, wives, widows, and husbands, widowers; our farms were taken possession of by the mob, many thousands of cattle, sheep, horses, and hogs were taken, and our household goods, store goods, and printing press and type were broken, taken, or otherwise destroyed.

Many of our brethren removed to Clay county, where they continued until 1836, three years; there was no violence offered, but there were threatenings of violence. But in the summer of 1836 these threatenings began to assume a more serious form, from threats, public meetings were called, resolutions were passed, vengeance and destruction were threatened, and affairs again assumed a fearful attitude, Jackson county was a sufficient precedent, and as the authorities in that county did not interfere they boasted that they would not in this; which on application to the authorities we found to be true, and after much privation and loss of property, we were again driven from our homes.

We next settled in Caldwell and Daviess counties, where we made large and extensive settlements, thinking to free ourselves from the power of oppression, by settling in new counties, with very few inhabitants in them; but here we were not allowed to live in peace, but in 1838 we were again attacked by mobs, an exterminating order was issued by Governor Boggs, and under the sanction of law, an organized banditti ranged through the country, robbed us of our cattle, sheep, hogs, etc., many of our people were murdered in cold blood, the chastity of our women was violated, and we were forced to sign away our property at the point of the sword; and after enduring every indignity that could be heaped upon us by an inhuman, ungodly band of marauders, from twelve to fifteen thousand souls, men, women, and children were driven from their own firesides, and from lands to which they had warantee deeds, houseless, friendless, and homeless (in the depths of winter) to wander as exiles on the earth or to seek asylum in more genial clime, and among a less barbarous people. Many sickened and died in consequence of the cold and hardships they had to endure; many wives were left widows, and children, orphans, and destitute. It would take more time than is allotted me here to describe the injustice, the wrongs, the murders, the bloodshed, the theft, misery and woe that have been caused by the barbarous, inhuman, and lawless proceedings of the state of Missouri.

In the situation before alluded to, we arrived in the state of Illinois in 1839, where we found a hospitable people and a friendly home: a people who were willing to be governed by the principles of law and humanity. We have commenced to build a city called "Nauvoo," in Hancock county. We number from six to eight thousand here, besides vast numbers in the county around, and in almost every county of the state. We have a city charter granted us, and charter for a Legion, the troops of which now number 1,500. We have also a charter for a University, for an Agricultural and Manufacturing Society, have our own laws and administrators, and possess all the privileges that other free and enlightened citizens enjoy.

Persecution has not stopped the progress of truth, but has only added fuel to the flame, it has spread with increasing rapidity. Proud of the cause which they have espoused, and conscious of our innocence, and of the truth of their system, amidst calumny and reproach, have (the Elders of this Church) gone forth, and planted the Gospel in almost every state of the Union; it has penetrated our cities, it has spread over our villages, and has caused thousands of our intelligent, noble, and patriotic citizens to obey its divine mandates, and be governed by its sacred truths. It has also spread into England, Ireland, Scotland, and Wales, where, in the year 1840, a few of our missionaries were sent, and over five thousand joined the Standard of Truth; there are numbers now joining in every land.

Our missionaries are going forth to different nations, and in Germany, Palestine, New Holland, Australia, the East Indies, and other places the Standard of Truth has been erected; no unhallowed hand can stop the work from progressing; persecutions may rage, mobs may combine, armies may assemble, calumny may defame, but the truth of God will go forth boldly, nobly, and independently till it has penetrated every continent, visited every clime, swept every country, and sounded in every ear, till the purposes of God shall be accomplished, and the Great Jehovah shall say the work is done.

We believe in God the eternal Father, and in his Son Jesus Christ, and in the Holy Ghost.

We believe that men will be punished for their own sins, and not for Adam's transgression.

We believe that through the atonement of Christ all mankind may be saved by obedience to the laws and ordinances of the Gospel.

We believe that the first principles and ordinances of the Gospel are: (1) Faith in the Lord Jesus Christ; (2) Repentance; (3) Baptism by immersion for the remission of sins; (4) Laying on of hands for the gift of the Holy Ghost.

We believe that a man must be called of God by prophecy and by the laying on of hands, by those who are in authority, to preach the Gospel and administer in the ordinances thereof.

We believe in the same organization that existed in the primitive Church, viz: apostles, prophets, pastors, teachers, evangelists, etc.

We believe in the gift of tongues, prophecy, revelation, visions, healing, interpretation of tongues, etc.

We believe the Bible to be the word of God, as far as it is translated correctly; we also believe the Book of Mormon to be the word of God.

We believe all that God has revealed, all that he does now reveal, and we believe that he will yet reveal many great and important things pertaining to the kingdom of God.

We believe in the literal gathering of Israel and in the restoration of the Ten Tribes: that Zion will be built upon this [the American continent;] that Christ will reign personally upon the earth; and that the earth will be renewed and receive its paradisiacal glory.

We claim the privilege of worshiping almighty God according to the dictates of our own conscience, and allow all men the same privilege, let them worship how, where, or what they may.

We believe in being subject to kings, presidents, rulers, and magistrates, in obeying honoring and sustaining the law.

We believe in being honest, true, chaste, benevolent, virtuous, and in doing good to all men; indeed we may say that we follow the admonition of Paul, We believe all things, we hope all things, we have endured many things, and hope to be able to endure all things. If there is anything virtuous, lovely, or of good report or praiseworthy, we seek after these things.

Christian Science
Mary Baker Eddy

Born on a farm in New Hampshire in 1821, Mary Baker was unwell through much of her life. The nature and causes of her ailments, early and late, are disputed, as is everything else about her and the church she founded, Christian Science. She married in 1843, was widowed six months later, and gave birth to her only child shortly thereafter. Difficult years followed: unable to support herself, she was forced to live with relatives and was often ill. A second marriage in 1853 was an unhappy one; she and her husband were first separated and later divorced.

Coming under the care of Phineas Parkhurst Quimby, a doctor in Maine who practiced mental healing, her condition improved dramatically. She became for a time an enthusiastic admirer and student of Dr. Quimby, but the extent of his influence on her is another matter of controversy.

Mrs. Eddy dates Christian Science specifically from an incident in 1866: injured in a fall, she lay in bed studying the New Testament—especially about Jesus's healing powers—when she experienced a sudden healing. In the ensuing years she studied and wrote; in 1875 she published Science and Health with Key to the Scriptures, *the basic text of the church. She revised the work many times over a period of thirty years; the edition of 1906 was pronounced the final and official one.*

In 1877 she married Asa Gilbert Eddy; five years later she was again widowed when he died of heart failure. In the meanwhile, the number of her followers grew under her vigorous and firm leadership; the Church of Christ, Scientist, was established in 1879; the First Church of Christ, Scientist—the Mother Church—was organized in 1892. All other Christian Science churches are branches.

Mrs. Eddy passed on, as Christian Scientists prefer to word it, in 1910, at the age of 89.

Christian Science in Tremont Temple

From the platform of the Monday lectureship in Tremont Temple, on Monday, March 16, 1885, as will be seen by what follows, Reverend Mary Baker G. Eddy was presented to Mr. Cook's audience, and allowed ten minutes in which to reply

Mary Baker Eddy, "Christian Science in Tremont Temple," from *Miscellaneous Writings, 1883–1896;* and Chapter VI, "Science, Theology, Medicine," from *Science and Health with Key to the Scriptures* (1906).

to his public letter condemning her doctrines; which reply was taken in full by a shorthand reporter who was present, and is transcribed below.

Mrs. Eddy responding, said:—

As the time so kindly allotted me is insufficient for even a synopsis of Christian Science, I shall confine myself to questions and answers.

Am I a spiritualist?

I am not, and never was. I understand the impossibility of intercommunion between the so-called dead and living. There have always attended my life phenomena of an uncommon order, which spiritualists have miscalled mediumship; but I clearly understand that no human agencies were employed,—that the divine Mind reveals itself to humanity through spiritual law. And to such as are "waiting for the adoption, to wit, the redemption of our body," Christian Science reveals the infinitude of divinity and the way of man's salvation from sickness and death, as wrought out by Jesus, who robbed the grave of victory and death of its sting. I understand that God is an ever-present help in all times of trouble,—have found Him so; and would have no other gods, no remedies in drugs, no material medicine.

Do I believe in a personal God?

I believe in God as the Supreme Being. I know not what the person of omnipotence and omnipresence is, or what the infinite includes; therefore, I worship that of which I can conceive, first, as a loving Father and Mother; then, as thought ascends the scale of being to diviner consciousness, God becomes to me, as to the apostle who declared it, "God is Love,"—divine Principle,—which I worship; and "after the manner of my fathers, so worship I God."

Do I believe in the atonement of Christ?

I do; and this atonement becomes more to me since it includes man's redemption from sickness as well as from sin. I reverence and adore Christ as never before.

It brings to my sense, and to the sense of all who entertain this understanding of the Science of God, a *whole* salvation.

How is the healing done in Christian Science?

This answer includes too much to give you any conclusive idea in a brief explanation. I can name some means by which it is not done.

It is not one mind acting upon another mind; it is not the transference of human images of thought to other minds; it is not supported by the evidence before the personal senses,—Science contradicts this evidence; it is not of the flesh, but of the Spirit. It is Christ come to destroy the power of the flesh; it is Truth over error; that understood, gives man ability to rise above the evidence of the senses, take hold of the eternal energies of Truth, and destroy mortal discord with immortal harmony,—the grand verities of being. It is not one mortal thought transmitted to another's thought from the human mind that holds within itself all evil.

Our Master said of one of his students, "He is a devil," and repudiated the idea of casting out devils through Beelzebub. Erring human mind is by no means a desirable or efficacious healer. Such suppositional healing I deprecate. It is in no way allied to divine power. All human control is animal magnetism, more despicable than all other methods of treating disease.

Christian Science is not a remedy of faith alone, but combines faith with understanding, through which we may touch the hem of His garment; and know that omnipotence has all power. "I am the Lord, and there is none else, there is no God beside me."

Is there a personal man?

The Scriptures inform us that man was made in the image and likeness of God. I commend the Icelandic translation: "He created man in the image and likeness of Mind, in the image and likeness of Mind created He him." To my sense, we have not seen all of man; he is more than personal sense can cognize, who is the image and likeness of the infinite. I have not seen a perfect man in mind or body,—and such must be the personality of him who is the true likeness: the lost image is not this personality, and corporeal man is this lost image; hence, it doth not appear what is the real personality of man. The only cause for making this question of personality a point, or of any importance, is that man's perfect model should be held in mind, whereby to improve his present condition; that his contemplation regarding himself should turn away from in harmony, sickness, and sin, to that which is the image of his Maker.

Science and Health

In the year 1866, I discovered the Christ Science or divine laws of Life, Truth, and Love, and named my discovery Christian Science. God had been graciously preparing me during many years for the reception of this final revelation of the absolute divine Principle of scientific mental healing.

This apodictical Principle points to the revelation of Immanuel, "God with us,"—the sovereign ever-presence, delivering the children of men from every ill "that flesh is heir to." Through Christian Science, religion and medicine are inspired with a diviner nature and essence; fresh pinions are given to faith and understanding, and thoughts acquaint themselves intelligently with God.

Feeling so perpetually the false consciousness that life inheres in the body, yet remembering that in reality God is our Life, we may well tremble in the prospect of those days in which we must say, "I have no pleasure in them."

Whence came to me this heavenly conviction,—a conviction antagonistic to the testimony of the physical senses? According to St. Paul, it was "the gift of the grace of God given unto me by the effectual working of His power." It was the divine law of Life and Love, unfolding to me the demonstrable fact that matter possesses neither sensation nor life; that human experiences show the falsity of all material things; and that immortal cravings, "the price of learning love," establish the truism that the only sufferer is mortal mind, for the divine Mind cannot suffer.

My conclusions were reached by allowing the evidence of this revelation to multiply with mathematical certainty and the lesser demonstration to prove the greater, as the product of three multiplied by three, equalling nine, proves conclusively that three times three duodecillions must be nine duodecillions,—not a fraction more, not a unit less.

When apparently near the confines of mortal existence, standing already within the shadow of the death-valley, I learned these truths in divine Science: that all real being is in God, the divine Mind, and that Life, Truth, and Love are all-powerful and ever-present; that the opposite of Truth,—called error, sin, sickness, disease, death,—is the false testimony of false material sense, of mind in matter; that this false sense evolves, in belief, a subjective state of mortal mind which this same so-called mind names *matter,* thereby shutting out the true sense of Spirit. My discovery, that erring, mortal, misnamed *mind* produces all the organism and action of the mortal body, set my thoughts to work in new channels, and led up to my demonstration of the proposition that Mind is All and matter is naught as the leading factor in Mind-science.

Christian Science reveals incontrovertibly that Mind is All-in-all, that the only realities are the divine Mind and idea. This great fact is not, however, seen to be supported by sensible evidence, until its divine Principle is demonstrated by healing the sick and thus proved absolute and divine. This proof once seen, no other conclusion can be reached.

For three years after my discovery, I sought the solution of this problem of Mind-healing, searched the Scriptures and read little else, kept aloof from society, and devoted time and energies to discovering a positive rule. The search was sweet, calm, and buoyant with hope, not selfish nor depressing. I knew the Principle of all harmonious Mind-action to be God, and that cures were produced in primitive Christian healing by holy, uplifting faith; but I must know the Science of this healing, and I won my way to absolute conclusions through divine revelation, reason, and demonstration. The revelation of Truth in the understanding came to me gradually and apparently through divine power. When a new spiritual idea is borne to earth, the prophetic Scripture of Isaiah is renewedly fulfilled: "Unto us a child is born, . . . and his name shall be called Wonderful."

Jesus once said of his lessons: "My doctrine is not mine, but His that sent me. If any man will do His will, he shall know of the doctrine, whether it be of God, or whether I speak of myself" (John vii. 16, 17).

The three great verities of Spirit, omnipotence, omnipresence, omniscience,— Spirit possessing all power, filling all space, constituting all Science,—contradict forever the belief that matter can be actual. These eternal verities reveal primeval existence as the radiant reality of God's creation, in which all that He has made is pronounced by His wisdom good.

Thus it was that I beheld, as never before, the awful unreality called evil. The equipollence of God brought to light another glorious proposition,—man's perfectibility and the establishment of the kingdom of heaven on earth.

In following these leadings of scientific revelation, the Bible was my only textbook. The Scriptures were illumined; reason and revelation were reconciled, and afterwards the truth of Christian Science was demonstrated. No human pen nor tongue taught me the Science contained in this book, *Science and Health;* and neither tongue nor pen can overthrow it. This book may be distorted by shallow criticism or by careless or malicious students, and its ideas may be temporarily abused and misrepresented; but the Science and truth therein will forever remain to be discerned and demonstrated.

Jesus demonstrated the power of Christian Science to heal mortal minds and bodies. But this power was lost sight of, and must again be spiritually discerned, taught, and demonstrated according to Christ's command, with "signs following."

Its Science must be apprehended by as many as believe on Christ and spiritually understand Truth.

No analogy exists between the vague hypotheses of agnosticism, pantheism, theosophy, spiritualism, or millenarianism and the demonstrable truths of Christian Science; and I find the will, or sensuous reason of the human mind, to be opposed to the divine Mind as expressed through divine Science.

Christian Science is natural, but not physical. The Science of God and man is no more supernatural than is the science of numbers, though departing from the realm of the physical, as the Science of God, Spirit, must, some may deny its right to the name of Science. The Principle of divine metaphysics is God; the practice of divine metaphysics is the utilization of the power of Truth over error; its rules demonstrate its Science. Divine metaphysics reverses perverted and physical hypotheses as to Deity, even as the explanation of optics rejects the incidental or inverted image and shows what this inverted image is meant to represent.

A prize of one hundred pounds, offered in Oxford University, England, for the best essay on Natural Science,—an essay calculated to offset the tendency of the age to attribute physical effects to physical causes rather than to a final spiritual cause,—is one of many incidents which show that Christian Science meets a yearning of the human race for spirituality.

After a lengthy examination of my discovery and its demonstration in healing the sick, this fact became evident to me,—that Mind governs the body, not partially but wholly. I submitted my metaphysical system of treating disease to the broadest practical tests. Since then this system has gradually gained ground, and has proved itself, whenever scientifically employed, to be the most effective curative agent in medical practice.

Is there more than one school of Christian Science? Christian Science is demonstrable. There can, therefore, be but one method in its teaching. Those who depart from this method forfeit their claims to belong to its school, and they become adherents of the Socratic, the Platonic, the Spencerian, or some other school. By this is meant that they adopt and adhere to some particular system of human opinions. Although these opinions may have occasional gleams of divinity, borrowed from that truly divine Science which eschews man-made systems, they nevertheless remain wholly human in their origin and tendency and are not scientifically Christian.

From the infinite One in Christian Science comes one Principle and its infinite idea, and with this infinitude come spiritual rules, laws, and their demonstration, which, like the great Giver, are "the same yesterday, and to-day, and forever;" for thus are the divine Principle of healing and the Christ-idea characterized in the epistle to the Hebrews.

Any theory of Christian Science, which departs from what has already been stated and proved to be true, affords no foundation upon which to establish a genuine school of this Science. Also, if any so-called new school claims to be Christian Science, and yet uses another author's discoveries without giving that author proper credit, such a school is erroneous, for it inculcates a breach of that divine commandment in the Hebrew Decalogue, "Thou shalt not steal."

God is the Principle of divine metaphysics. As there is but one God, there can be but one divine Principle of all Science; and there must be fixed rules for the demonstration of this divine Principle. The letter of Science plentifully reaches humanity to-day, but its spirit comes only in small degrees. The vital part, the heart and soul of Christian Science, is Love. Without this, the letter is but the dead body of Science,—pulseless, cold, inanimate.

The fundamental propositions of divine metaphysics are summarized in the four following, to me, *self-evident* propositions. Even if reversed, these propositions will be found to agree in statement and proof, showing mathematically their exact relation to Truth. De Quincey says mathematics has not a foot to stand upon which is not purely metaphysical.

1. God is All-in-all.
2. God is good. Good is Mind.
3. God, Spirit, being all, nothing is matter.
4. Life, God, omnipotent good, deny death, evil, sin, disease.—Disease, sin, evil, death, deny good, omnipotent God, Life.

Which of the denials in proposition four is true? Both are not, cannot be, true. Accordig to the Scripture, I find that God is true, "but every [mortal] man a liar."

The divine metaphysics of Christian Science, like the method in mathematics, proves the rule by inversion. For example: There is no pain in Truth, and no truth in pain; no nerve in Mind, and no mind in nerve; no matter in Mind, and no mind in matter; no matter in Life, and no life in matter; no matter in good, and no good in matter.

The Souls of Black Folk

W.E.B. DuBois

A man of remarkable commitment and ability, William Edward Burghardt DuBois (1868–1963) was a professor, civil rights leader, and author. Born in Massachusetts, he earned his bachelor, masters, and doctoral degrees at Harvard and was a professor of history and economics at Atlanta University from 1897 to 1910, and again from 1932 to 1944. In 1909 he was a cofounder of the National Negro Committee, which shortly thereafter became the National Association for the Advancement of Colored People, and in the years between his two tenures as a professor he was the editor of the NAACP magazine, Crisis. *He participated in Pan African Congresses and lived in Ghana for the last two years of his life. Along the way, he wrote books, most notably* The Souls of Black Folk *(1903), but also* The Philadelphia Negro: A Social Study *(1899),* John Brown *(1909),* Black Reconstruction *(1935),* The World and Africa *(1947), and* The Black Flame *(1957–61). His* Autobiography *(1968) appeared posthumously. He has been honored recently by inclusion in the distinguished series,* The Library of America.

It was out in the country, far from home, far from my foster home, on a dark Sunday night. The road wandered from our rambling log-house up the stony bed of a creek, past wheat and corn, until we could hear dimly across the fields a rhythmic cadence of song,—soft, thrilling, powerful, that swelled and died sorrowfully in our ears. I was a country school-teacher then, fresh from the East, and had never seen a Southern Negro revival. To be sure, we in Berkshire were not perhaps as stiff and formal as they in Suffolk of olden time; yet we were very quiet and subdued, and I know not what would have happened those clear Sabbath mornings had some one punctuated the sermon with a wild scream, or interrupted the long prayer with a loud Amen! And so most striking to me, as I approached the village and the little plain church perched aloft, was the air of intense excitement that possessed that mass of black folk. A sort of suppressed terror hung in the air and seemed to seize us,—a pythian madness, a demoniac possession, that lent terrible reality to song and word. The black and massive form of the preacher swayed and quivered as the words crowded to his lips and flew at us in singular eloquence. The people moaned and fluttered, and then the gaunt-cheeked brown woman beside me suddenly leaped straight into the air and shrieked like a lost soul, while round about came

From W.E.B. DuBois, *The Souls of Black Folk,* 1903.

wail and groan and outcry, and a scene of human passion such as I had never conceived before.

Those who have not thus witnessed the frenzy of a Negro revival in the untouched backwoods of the South can but dimly realize the religious feeling of the slave; as described, such scenes appear grotesque and funny, but as seen they are awful. Three things characterized this religion of the slave,—the Preacher, the Music, and the Frenzy. The Preacher is the most unique personality developed by the Negro on American soil. A leader, a politician, an orator, a "boss," an intriguer, an idealist,—all these he is, and ever, too, the centre of a group of men, now twenty, now a thousand in number. The combination of a certain adroitness with deep-seated earnestness, of tact with consummate ability, gave him his preëminence, and helps him maintain it. The type, of course, varies according to time and place, from the West Indies in the sixteenth century to New England in the nineteenth, and from the Mississippi bottoms to cities like New Orleans or New York.

The Music of Negro religion is that plaintive rhythmic melody, with its touching minor cadences, which, despite caricature and defilement, still remains the most original and beautiful expression of human life and longing yet born on American soil. Sprung from the African forests, where its counterpart can still be heard, it was adapted, changed, and intensified by the tragic soul-life of the slave, until, under the stress of law and whip, it became the one true expression of a people's sorrow, despair, and hope.

Finally the Frenzy or "Shouting," when the Spirit of the Lord passed by, and, seizing the devotee, made him mad with supernatural joy, was the last essential of Negro religion and the one more devoutly believed in than all the rest. It varied in expression from the silent rapt countenance or the low murmur and moan to the mad abandon of physical fervor,—the stamping, shrieking, and shouting, the rushing to and fro and wild waving of arms, the weeping and laughing, the vision and the trance. All this is nothing new in the world, but old as religion, a Delphi and Endor. And so firm a hold did it have on the Negro, that many generations firmly believed that without this visible manifestation of the God there could be no true communion with the Invisible.

These were the characteristics of Negro religious life as developed up to the time of Emancipation. Since under the peculiar circumstances of the black man's environment they were the one expression of his higher life, they are of deep interest to the student of his development, both socially and psychologically. Numerous are the attractive lines of inquiry that here group themselves. What did slavery mean to the African savage? What was his attitude toward the World and Life? What seemed to him good and evil,—God and Devil? Whither went his longings and strivings, and wherefore were his heart-burnings and disappointments? Answers to such questions can come only from a study of Negro religion as a development, through its gradual changes from the heathenism of the Gold Coast to the institutional Negro church of Chicago.

Moreover, the religious growth of millions of men, even though they be slaves, cannot be without potent influence upon their contemporaries. The Methodists and Baptists of America owe much of their condition to the silent but potent influence of their millions of Negro converts. Especially is this noticeable in the South,

where theology and religious philosophy are on this account a long way behind the
North, and where the religion of the poor whites is a plain copy of Negro thought
and methods. The mass of "gospel" hymns which has swept through American
churches and well-nigh ruined our sense of song consists largely of debased imita-
tions of Negro melodies made by ears that caught the jingle but not the music, the
body but not the soul, of the Jubilee songs. It is thus clear that the study of Negro
religion is not only a vital part of the history of the Negro in America, but an interesting part of American history.

The Negro church of to-day is the social centre of Negro life in the United States,
and the most characteristic expression of African character. Take a typical church
in a small Virginia town: it is the "First Baptist"—a roomy brick edifice seating five
hundred or more persons, tastefully finished in Georgia pine, with a carpet, a small
organ, and stained-glass windows. Underneath is a large assembly room with
benches. This building is the central club-house of a community of a thousand or
more Negroes. Various organizations meet here,—the church proper, the Sunday-
school, two or three insurance societies, women's societies, secret societies, and
mass meetings of various kinds. Entertainments, suppers, and lectures are held
beside the five or six regular weekly religious services. Considerable sums of money
are collected and expended here, employment is found for the idle, strangers are
introduced, news is disseminated and charity distributed. At the same time this
social, intellectual, and economic centre is a religious centre of great power.
Depravity, Sin, Redemption, Heaven, Hell, and Damnation are preached twice a
Sunday with much fervor, and revivals take place every year after the crops are laid
by; and few indeed of the community have the hardihood to withstand conversion.
Back of this more formal religion, the Church often stands as a real conserver of
morals, a strengthener of family life, and the final authority on what is Good and
Right.

Thus one can see in the Negro church to-day, reproduced in microcosm, all that
great world from which the Negro is cut off by color-prejudice and social condition.
In the great city churches the same tendency is noticeable and in many respects
emphasized. A great church like the Bethel of Philadelphia has over eleven hundred
members, an edifice seating fifteen hundred persons and valued at one hundred
thousand dollars, an annual budget of five thousand dollars, and a government consisting of a pastor with several assisting local preachers, an executive and legislative
board, financial boards and tax collectors; general church meetings for making
laws; subdivided groups led by class leaders, a company of militia, and twenty-four
auxiliary societies. The activity of a church like this is immense and far-reaching,
and the bishops who preside over these organizations throughout the land are
among the most powerful Negro rulers in the world.

Such churches are really governments of men, and consequently a little investigation reveals the curious fact that, in the South, at least, practically every American Negro is a church member. Some, to be sure, are not regularly enrolled, and a
few do not habitually attend services; but, practically, a proscribed people must
have a social centre, and that centre for this people is the Negro church. The census
of 1890 showed nearly twenty-four thousand Negro churches in the country, with
a total enrolled membership of over two and a half millions, or ten actual church

members to every twenty-eight persons, and in some Southern States one in every two persons. Besides these there is the large number who, while not enrolled as members, attend and take part in many of the activities of the church. There is an organized Negro church for every sixty black families in the nation, and in some States for every forty families, owning, on an average, a thousand dollars' worth of property each, or nearly twenty-six million dollars in all.

Such, then, is the large development of the Negro church since Emancipation. The question now is, What have been the successive steps of this social history and what are the present tendencies? First, we must realize that no such institution as the Negro church could rear itself without definite historical foundations. These foundations we can find if we remember that the social history of the Negro did not start in America. He was brought from a definite social environment,—the polygamous clan life under the headship of the chief and the potent influence of the priest. His religion was nature-worship, with profound belief in invisible surrounding influences, good and bad, and his worship was through incantation and sacrifice. The first rude change in this life was the slave ship and the West Indian sugarfields. The plantation organization replaced the clan and tribe, and the white master replaced the chief with far greater and more despotic powers. Forced and long-continued toil became the rule of life, the old ties of blood relationship and kinship disappeared, and instead of the family appeared a new polygamy and polyandry, which, in some cases, almost reached promiscuity. It was a terrific social revolution, and yet some traces were retained of the former group life, and the chief remaining institution was the Priest or Medicine-man. He early appeared on the plantation and found his function as the healer of the sick, the interpreter of the Unknown, the comforter of the sorrowing, the supernatural avenger of wrong, and the one who rudely but picturesquely expressed the longing, disappointment, and resentment of a stolen and oppressed people. Thus, as bard, physician, judge, and priest, within the narrow limits allowed by the slave system, rose the Negro preacher, and under him the first Afro-American institution, the Negro church. This church was not at first by any means Christian nor definitely organized; rather it was an adaptation and mingling of heathen rites among the members of each plantation, and roughly designated as Voodooism. Association with the masters, missionary effort and motives of expediency gave these rites an early veneer of Christianity, and after the lapse of many generations the Negro church became Christian.

Two characteristic things must be noticed in regard to this church. First, it became almost entirely Baptist and Methodist in faith; secondly, as a social institution it antedated by many decades the monogamic Negro home. From the very circumstances of its beginning, the church was confined to the plantation, and consisted primarily of a series of disconnected units; although, later on, some freedom of movement was allowed, still this geographical limitation was always important and was one cause of the spread of the decentralized and democratic Baptist faith among the slaves. At the same time, the visible rite of baptism appealed strongly to their mystic temperament. To-day the Baptist Church is still largest in membership among Negroes, and has a million and a half communicants. Next in popularity came the churches organized in connection with the white neighboring churches, chiefly Baptist and Methodist, with a few Episcopalian and others. The Methodists still form the second greatest denomination, with nearly a million members. The faith of these two leading denominations was more suited to the slave church from the prominence they gave to religious feeling and fervor. The Negro membership in other denominations has always been small and relatively unimportant, although the Episcopalians and Presbyterians are gaining among the more intelligent classes to-day, and the Catholic Church is making headway in certain sections. After Emancipation, and still earlier in the North, the Negro churches largely severed such affiliations as they had had with the white churches, either by choice or by compulsion. The Baptist churches became independent, but the Methodists were compelled early to unite for purposes of episcopal government. This gave rise to the great African Methodist Church, the greatest Negro organization in the world, to the Zion Church and the Colored Methodist, and to the black conferences and churches in this and other denominations.

The second fact noted, namely, that the Negro church antedates the Negro home, leads to an explanation of much that is paradoxical in this communistic institution and in the morals of its members. But especially it leads us to regard this institution as peculiarly the expression of the inner ethical life of a people in a sense seldom true elsewhere. Let us turn, then, from the outer physical development of the church to the more important inner ethical life of the people who compose it. The Negro has already been pointed out many times as a religious animal,—a being of that deep emotional nature which turns instinctively toward the supernatural. Endowed with a rich tropical imagination and a keen, delicate appreciation of Nature, the transplanted African lived in a world animate with gods and devils, elves and witches; full of strange influences,—of Good to be implored, of Evil to be propitiated. Slavery, then, was to him the dark triumph of Evil over him. All the hateful powers of the Underworld were striving against him, and a spirit of revolt and revenge filled his heart. He called up all the resources of heathenism to aid,— exorcism and witchcraft, the mysterious Obi worship with its barbarous rites, spells, and blood-sacrifice even, now and then, of human victims. Weird midnight orgies and mystic conjurations were invoked, the witch-woman and the voodoo-priest became the centre of Negro group life, and that vein of vague superstition which characterizes the unlettered Negro even to-day was deepened and strengthened.

In spite, however, of such success as that of the fierce Maroons, the Danish blacks, and others, the spirit of revolt gradually died away under the untiring energy and superior strength of the slave masters. By the middle of the eighteenth century the black slave had sunk, with hushed murmurs, to his place at the bottom of a new economic system, and was unconsciously ripe for a new philosophy of life. Nothing suited his condition then better than the doctrines of passive submission embodied in the newly learned Christianity. Slave masters early realized this, and cheerfully aided religious propaganda within certain bounds. The long system of repression and degradation of the Negro tended to emphasize the elements in his character which made him a valuable chattel: courtesy became humility, moral strength degenerated into submission, and the exquisite native appreciation of the beautiful became an infinite capacity for dumb suffering. The Negro, losing the joy of this world, eagerly seized upon the offered conceptions of the next; the avenging Spirit of the Lord enjoining patience in this world, under sorrow and tribulation until the

Great Day when He should lead His dark children home,—this became his comforting dream. His preacher repeated the prophecy, and his bards sang,—

> "Children, we all shall be free
> When the Lord shall appear!"

This deep religious fatalism, painted so beautifully in "Uncle Tom," came soon to breed, as all fatalistic faiths will, the sensualist side by side with the martyr. Under the lax moral life of the plantation, where marriage was a farce, laziness a virtue, and property a theft, a religion of resignation and submission degenerated easily, in less strenuous minds, into a philosophy of indulgence and crime. Many of the worst characteristics of the Negro masses of to-day had their seed in this period of the slave's ethical growth. Here it was that the Home was ruined under the very shadow of the Church, white and black; here habits of shiftlessness took root, and sullen hopelessness replaced hopeful strife.

With the beginning of the abolition movement and the gradual growth of a class of free Negroes came a change. We often neglect the influence of the freedman before the war, because of the paucity of his numbers and the small weight he had in the history of the nation. But we must not forget that his chief influence was internal,—was exerted on the black world; and that there he was the ethical and social leader. Huddled as he was in a few centres like Philadelphia, New York, and New Orleans, the masses of the freedmen sank into poverty and listlessness; but not all of them. The free Negro leader early arose and his chief characteristic was intense earnestness and deep feeling on the slavery question. Freedom became to him a real thing and not a dream. His religion became darker and more intense, and into his ethics crept a note of revenge, into his songs a day of reckoning close at hand. The "Coming of the Lord" swept this side of Death, and came to be a thing to be hoped for in this day. Through fugitive slaves and irrepressible discussion this desire for freedom seized the black millions still in bondage, and became their one ideal of life. The black bards caught new notes, and sometimes even dared to sing.—

> "O Freedom, O Freedom, O Freedom over me!
> Before I'll be a slave
> I'll be buried in my grave,
> And go home to my Lord
> And be free."

For fifty years Negro religion thus transformed itself and identified itself with the dream of Abolition, until that which was a radical fad in the white North and an anarchistic plot in the white South had become a religion to the black world. Thus, when Emancipation finally came, it seemed to the freedman a literal Coming of the Lord. His fervid imagination was stirred as never before, by the tramp of armies, the blood and dust of battle, and the wail and whirl of social upheaval. He stood dumb and motionless before the whirlwind: what had he to do with it? Was it not the Lord's doing, and marvellous in his eyes? Joyed and bewildered with what came, he stood awaiting new wonders till the inevitable Age of Reaction swept over the nation and brought the crisis of to-day.

It is difficult to explain clearly the present critical stage of Negro religion. First, we must remember that living as the blacks do in close contact with a great modern nation, and sharing, although imperfectly, the soul-life of that nation, they must necessarily be affected more or less directly by all the religious and ethical forces that are to-day moving the United States. These questions and movements are, however, overshadowed and dwarfed by the (to them) all-important question of their civil, political, and economic status. They must perpetually discuss the "Negro Problem,"—must live, move, and have their being in it, and interpret all else in its light or darkness. With this come, too, peculiar problems of their inner life,—of the status of women, the maintenance of Home, the training of children, the accumulation of wealth, and the prevention of crime. All this must mean a time of intense ethical ferment, of religious heart-searching and intellectual unrest. From the double life every American Negro must live, as a Negro and as an American, as swept on by the current of the nineteenth while yet struggling in the eddies of the fifteenth century,—from this must arise a painful self-consciousness, an almost morbid sense of personality and a moral hesitancy which is fatal to self-confidence. The worlds within and without the Veil of Color are changing, and changing rapidly, but not at the same rate, not in the same way; and this must produce a peculiar wrenching of the soul, a peculiar sense of doubt and bewilderment. Such a double life, with double thoughts, double duties, and double social classes, must give rise to double words and double ideals, and tempt the mind to pretence or revolt, to hypocrisy or radicalism.

In some such doubtful words and phrases can one perhaps most clearly picture the peculiar ethical paradox that faces the Negro of to-day and is tingeing and changing his religious life. Feeling that his rights and his dearest ideals are being trampled upon, that the public conscience is ever more deaf to his righteous appeal, and that all the reactionary forces of prejudice, greed, and revenge are daily gaining new strength and fresh allies, the Negro faces no enviable dilemma. Conscious of his impotence, and pessimistic; he often becomes bitter and vindictive; and his religion, instead of a worship, is a complaint and a curse, a wail rather than a hope, a sneer rather than a faith. On the other hand, another type of mind, shrewder and keener and more tortuous too, sees in the very strength of the anti-Negro movement its patent weaknesses, and with Jesuitic casuistry is deterred by no ethical considerations in the endeavor to turn this weakness to the black man's strength. Thus we have two great and hardly reconcilable streams of thought and ethical strivings; the danger of the one lies in anarchy, that of the other in hypocrisy. The one type of Negro stands almost ready to curse God and die, and the other is too often found a traitor to right and a coward before force; the one is wedded to ideals remote, whimsical, perhaps impossible of realization; the other forgets that life is more than meat and the body more than raiment. But, after all, is not this simply the writhing of the age translated into black,—the triumph of the Lie which to-day, with its false culture, faces the hideousness of the anarchist assassin?

To-day the two groups of Negroes, the one in the North, the other in the South, represent these divergent ethical tendencies, the first tending toward radicalism, the other toward hypocritical compromise. It is no idle regret with which the white South mourns the loss of the old-time Negro,—the frank, honest, simple old servant who stood for the earlier religious age of submission and humility. With all his laziness and lack of many elements of true manhood, he was at least open-hearted, faithful, and sincere. To-day he is gone, but who is to blame for his going? Is it not those very persons who mourn for him? Is it not the tendency, born of Reconstruction and Reaction, to found a society on lawlessness and deception, to tamper with the moral fibre of a naturally honest and straight-forward people until the whites threaten to become ungovernable tyrants and the blacks criminal and hypocrites? Deception is the natural defence of the weak against the strong, and the South used it for many years against its conquerors; to-day it must be prepared to see its black proletariat turn that same two-edged weapon against itself. And how natural this is! The death of Denmark Vesey and Nat Turner proved long since to the Negro the present hopelessness of physical defence. Political defence is becoming less and less available, and economic defence is still only partially effective. But there is a patent defence at hand,—the defence of deception and flattery, of cajoling and lying. It is the same defence which peasants of the Middle Age used and which left its stamp on their character for centuries. To-day the young Negro of the South who would succeed cannot be frank and outspoken, honest and self-assertive, but rather he is daily tempted to be silence and wary, politic and sly; he must flatter and be pleasant, endure petty insults with a smile, shut his eyes to wrong; in too many cases he sees positive personal advantage in deception and lying. His real thoughts, his real aspirations, must be guarded in whispers; he must not criticise, he must not complain. Patience, humility, and adroitness must, in these growing black youth, replace impulse, manliness, and courage. With this sacrifice there is an economic opening, and perhaps peace and some prosperity. Without this there is riot, migration, or crime. Nor is this situation peculiar to the Southern United States, is it not rather the only method by which undeveloped races have gained the right to share modern culture? The price of culture is a Lie.

On the other hand, in the North the tendency is to emphasize the radicalism of the Negro. Driven from his birthright in the South by a situation at which every fibre of his more outspoken and assertive nature revolts, he finds himself in a land where he can scarcely earn a decent living amid the harsh competition and the color discrimination. At the same time, through schools and periodicals, discussions and lectures, he is intellectually quickened and awakened. The soul, long pent up and dwarfed, suddenly expands in new-found freedom. What wonder that every tendency is to excess,—radical complaint, radical remedies, bitter denunciation or angry silence. Some sink, some rise. The criminal and the sensualist leave the church for the gambling-hell and the brothel, and fill the slums of Chicago and Baltimore; the better classes segregate themselves from the group-life of both white and black, and form an aristocracy, cultured but pessimistic, whose bitter criticism stings while it points out no way of escape. They despise the submission and subserviency of the Southern Negroes, but offer no other means by which a poor and oppressed minority can exist side by side with its masters. Feeling deeply and keenly the tendencies and opportunities of the age in which they live, their souls are bitter at the fate which drops the Veil between; and the very fact that this bitterness is natural and justifiable only serves to intensify it and make it more maddening.

Between the two extreme types of ethical attitude which I have thus sought to make clear wavers the mass of the millions of Negroes, North and South; and their religious life and activity partake of this social conflict within their ranks. Their churches are differentiating,—now into groups of cold, fashionable devotees, in no way distinguishable from similar white groups save in color of skin; now into large social and business institutions catering to the desire for information and amusement of their members, warily avoiding unpleasant questions both within and without the black world, and preaching in effect if not in word: *Dum vivimus, vivamus.*

But back of this still broods silently the deep religious feeling of the real Negro heart, the stirring, unguided might of powerful human souls who have lost the guiding star of the past and seek in the great night a new religious, ideal. Some day the Awakening will come, when the pentup vigor of ten million souls shall sweep irresistibly toward the Goal, out of the Valley of the Shadow of Death, where all that makes life worth living—Liberty, Justice, and Right—is marked "For White People Only."

The Spiritual Values of Native Americans
Joseph Epes Brown

After graduating from Haverford College in Pennsylvania, Joseph Epes Brown spent a number of years living and traveling with several of the Indian nations, particularly those of the prairies. He observed in Native Americans "degrees of spirituality rarely found in the world today," and "in the rhythm of their society, and in the beauty of the forms of their ancient culture, those great qualities for want of which the modern world is becoming impoverished, in spite of its material wealth."* The Sacred Pipe: Black Elk's Account of the Seven Rites of the Oglala Sioux, which Brown recorded and edited, was the product of his having lived with Black Elk for eight months. Brown has also written The Spiritual Legacy of the American Indian *(1982) and* Animals of the Soul: A Native American Bestiary *(1991). He has served as a consulting editor for* Parabola, *taught at the Valley Verde School in Arizona, and is now in the Department of Religious Studies at the University of Montana.*

Although greatly oversimplified and generalized, let me give at least a brief sampling of what I think are some of the core Native American values and perspectives, through which we can perhaps come to relearn a little bit about ourselves and about our own proper spiritual heritage, the hope being that what has been lost can still be rediscovered. Certainly the Native American people themselves, especially the younger ones today, are trying to regain and revitalize their own traditions which may have been lost, or taken from them through a variety of pressures and prejudices. We have, I suggest, in this struggle a model for our own proper quest. What are some of its contours?

Tribal cultures, it seems to me, present a model of what a religious tradition *is;* and this is a basic reality which we have lost sight of. That is, what really is a true religious tradition? What does it encompass, what are its dimensions? These cultures demonstrate how all components of a culture can be interconnected: how the presence of the sacred can permeate all lifeways to such a degree that what we call

---

* *The Sacred Pipe* (Norman: University of Oklahoma Press, 1953), p. x.

From Joseph Epes Brown, "Becoming Part of It," reprinted from D. M. Dooling and Paul Jordan-Smith, eds., *I Become Part Of It* (New York: PARABOLA Books, 1989). Reprinted by permission of PARABOLA Books and the author.

religion is here integrated into the totality of life and into all of life's activities. Religion here is so pervasive in life that there is probably no Native American language in which there is a term which could be translated as "religion" in the way we understand it. As Peter Nabokov tells us in his book, *Indian Running,* when you track down a seemingly isolated or minimal feature of Indian life, such as running, the whole system opens before your eyes; and this is true because of the interrelatedness of all the components of a genuine tradition. Obviously in such a system life cannot be fragmented, due to that binding and interconnecting thread of the presence of the sacred.

In terms of interconnections, a dominant theme in all Native American cultures is that of relationship, or a series of relationships that are always reaching further and further out; relationships within the immediate family reaching out to the extended family, to the band, outward again to the clan, to the tribal group; and relationships do not stop there but extend out to embrace and relate to the environment; to the land, to the animals, to the plants, and to the clouds, the elements, the heavens, the stars; and ultimately those relationships that people express and live, extend to embrace the entire universe.

In the Plains area, to give an example, one of the most profound rites is that of the smoking of the pipe. In this ritual smoking of the pipe, all who participate are joined in a communal ritual, and when it is finished, everybody who has shared in the smoking of the pipe recites the phrase, in Lakota in this case, "*mitakuye oyasin*"—"we are all relatives." We *are* all related, because in this rite we have all become one within a mystery that is greater than any of its parts. I shall talk more about the general importance of rituals and ceremonies later.

Associated with relationship there should be mentioned the theme of reciprocity which permeates so many aspects of North American cultures. Put very simply, reciprocity here refers again to that process wherein if you receive or take away you must also give back. This is a living statement of the importance of the cycle permeating all of life. Everything in their world of experience is conceived in terms of such cycles or of the circle; everything comes back upon itself. Black Elk so often said that all the forces of the world work in cycles or circles; the birds build their nests in circular form, the foxes have their dens in circles, the wind in its greatest power moves in a circle, and life is as a circle. I recall once how this reality was beautifully expressed in a living manner, when I noticed how this dignified old man would relate to little children. He would get down on his hands and knees and pretend he was a horse, and the children would squeal with joy on the old man's back. Here there obviously was no generation gap; he was one with the child. I once asked him how it was that he could so relate to the child, and he replied: "I who am an old man am about to return *to* the Great Mysterious" (*Wakan Tanka,* Lakota) "and a young child is a being who has just come *from* the Great Mysterious; so it is that we are very close together." Because of such cyclical understanding, both are very nearly at the same point.

Such attitudes could be spelled out in terms of any number of cultural expressions, but the point I want to draw from this is that we have here an example which contrasts with our own dominant concept of process which is in terms of linearity— the straight line which moves from here to there and onward indefinitely. Indeed, this theme of linearity permeates all aspects of our life. The way we read, for instance, is in lines; we have sayings in our vocabulary that tell us to "Line up!" "Let's get this straight!" Or if we refer to somebody who is a little bit crazy, we make a circular motion alongside our head, by which we indicate the reason is going in circles. There is something here from which we can learn, something about ourselves and our concept of progress, with all the loaded meanings which this term bears.

One must mention also the special nature of Native American languages, which contrasts with our understanding of language and our use of words. In Native languages the understanding is that the meaning *is* in the sound, it *is* in the word; the word is not a symbol for a meaning which has been abstracted out, word and meaning are together in one experience. Thus, to name a being, for example an animal, is actually to conjure up the powers latent in that animal. Added to this is the fact that when we create words we use our breath, and for these people and these traditions breath is associated with the principle of life; breath is life itself. And so if a word is born from this sacred principle of breath, this lends an added sacred dimension to the spoken word. It is because of this special feeling about words that people avoid using sacred personal names, because they contain the power of the beings named, and if you use them too much the power becomes dissipated. So usually one has to refer to a person in a very circuitous manner, or use a term which expresses relationship.

In this context one must also emphasize the positive values that could be attached to non-literacy. I use that term rather than illiteracy, which connotes the *inability* to read and write, which is negative and derogatory. Too often we have branded people as being backward and uncivilized if they are *illiterate,* whereas one can make a strong case for the advantages of growing up and living in a society which is *non-literate.* For in such a society all the lore which is central and sacred to the culture is borne *within* the individual in a living manner; you do not have to go outside of yourself, for all that is essential to life is carried with you, is ever-present. It seems that where you have people who are non-literate in this positive sense, you tend to have a special quality of person, a quality of being that cannot be described—a very different quality from that of the literate person. It has been my experience when among primal peoples in many parts of the world that there is something here that is very special.

Paralleling this primal concept of language, and of the word not as "symbol" but as an immediate event, is the quality of experiencing the visual arts and crafts. I should stress first of all that for primal peoples generally there is no dichotomy between the arts and crafts, in the manner that our art historians insist on, where art is one kind of thing that can be placed on a mantelpiece or hung on the wall, and the craft item is inferior because it is made for utilitarian ends. This seems to me a most artificial distinction and I think it is time that we outgrew it; indeed there is today evidence that we *are* re-evaluating such prejudiced dichotomies. For why cannot a utilitarian object also be beautiful? All necessary implements, utensils, and tools in Native American life-ways are of technical excellence and are also beautiful. They must be made in special sacred ways, and the materials of the tools and objects made have to be gathered with prayer and offerings. Beauty and truth are here one! When a Pomo basketmaker, for example, goes out to collect the grasses for her basket, she prays to the grasses, she enters into a relationship with them as she gathers, and makes offerings in return for having taken their life. When a woman weaves a basket she will pass the grass between her lips to moisten it, but also to breathe upon it, to give her life breath into the grass and thus give to the basket a special sacred quality that is always present in its use and tangible presence.

Through these few selected examples which have been given, I am suggesting that, where such traditions are still alive and spiritually viable, there tend to be present, within all of life's necessary activities, dimensions and expressions of the sacred. Actions of such quality could therefore be considered to manifest a ritual element in the sense that they tend to *order* life around and toward a Center. In this context, however, one must also speak of those special great rites and ceremonies, many often related to the seasonal cycles, which serve not just to support continuing orientations toward the sacred in everyday activities, but work for the *intensification* of such Presence and experience; such rites may also be the source and origin of new rites, ceremonies, and other sacred expressions through the visual arts, songs, or special dance forms.

One example of a ritual complex which is central to the lives of Plains people is the well known "vision" or "guardian spirit quest." This ritualized retreat is for the benefit of the individual man and woman, and yet means are present for the eventual sharing of received vision powers or messages with the larger community. After rigorous preparations, which always include the rites of the purifying sweat lodge and instructions by a qualified elder, the candidate goes to a high and remote place with the resolve to fast and pray continually and to suffer through acts of sacrifice and exposure to the elements for a specified number of days. The ordeal is highly ritualized and may involve the establishing of an altar, or the setting out of poles at the center and to the four directions of space. The person may also be instructed to remain within this established space and not to move about casually but to walk only out from the center to each of the poles in turn, always returning to the center. Prayers may be addressed to the powers of the four directions, and one may also use repetitive prayers such as the one the Lakota Black Elk has given us: "Grandfather, Great Mysterious, have pity on me." One may also remain silent, for it has been said that "silence *is* the voice of *Wakan Tanka,* the *Great Mysterious.*" If tired, one may sleep, for dreams of power may come to the candidate in this manner; yet it is understood that the true vision is of greater power than the dream. Often the sacred experience comes in the mysterious appearance of an animal or a winged being, or perhaps in one of the powers of nature. A special message is often communicated to the seeker, and this will serve as a guide and reminder throughout the person's life. After three or four days one returns to camp where a sweat lodge has again been prepared; within this lodge the candidate will explain the vision or dream which will be interpreted by the guiding elder, who will then give instructions as to what should now be accomplished in order to insure the continuity of the participation of the spiritual throughout the person's life. From such experiences have come the "medicine bundles" with rich and complex rites specific to each bundle and their ceremonial opening on special occasions. They have also been the origin of sacred types of art forms, such as the painted shields, or special songs of power, or even the great ritual dances, such as the horse dance, involving four groups of eight horses not representing, but *being* the powers of the four directions of space. It is in this manner that something of the sacred experience which had come to a particular individual is shared by all members of the larger community.

What is remarkable about the rites of the vision quest among the Plains peoples is that it is accomplished not just by special people as is the case in the Arctic, but that every man or woman after the age of puberty is expected to participate either once or even repeatedly throughout his or her life.

What concerns us in this example is not just the detailed pattern of the ritual elements of the quest as such, which can encompass a multitude of very diverse possibilities, but that here we have one sample as a model of traditional ritual structures and acts which must involve initial purification, choice of appropriate site, the defining and delimiting of a special sacred place, and the fixing of a center. Further, ritualized *actions* are prescribed for the participant, which means that participation is not just with the mind, or a part of one's being, but with the totality of who one is. Also provided are means for continuity and development of the sacred experiences received, and the eventual responsibility for sharing something of them with the larger community.

As complement to the individually oriented "vision quest," one could mention the great communal "Sun Dance," referred to in different terms across the Plains groups. For this great complex of solemn rites, ceremonies, fasting, sacred song and dance fulfills not just the particular spiritual needs of the actively participating individuals, but also those of the entire tribal group gathered in circular camp for the occasion. The event is indeed for the welfare of the entire world. These are ceremonies, interspersed with special sacred rites, which celebrate world and life renewal at the time of spring. The ritualized dance forms again involve orientation around and towards a center which is either the sun itself or the cottonwood tree as axis of the world, standing at the center of a circular frame lodge carefully constructed in imitation of the cosmos. The ritual and ceremonial language of the total celebration speaks to and encompasses a plurality of spiritual possibilities at the levels of microcosm, macrocosm, and metacosm. It is believed by many that should the sacrificial rites of this "thirst lodge" be neglected or forgotten, the energy of the world will run out and the cycle in which we are living will close. It is an example to the world that these rites and ceremonies are far from being neglected, for today in ever increasing numbers the people are participating and are finding renewed strength and spiritual resolve.

All spiritually effective rites must accomplish three cumulative possibilities which may be termed purification, expansion—in wholeness or virtue—and identity. A ritual means which embodies these possibilities may be found in the sacred nature and use of the Plains Indian tobacco pipe, the smoking of which constitutes a communion. The shape of the pipe with its stem, bowl or "heart," and foot, is identified with the human person. In purifying the pipe before a ritual smoking there is an analogy to man's own purification; for in concentrating on the hollow of the straight stem leading to the bowl comes the understanding that one's mind should be this straight and pure. In filling the bowl of the pipe a prayer is said for each grain of tobacco in such a manner that everything in the world is mentioned

The filled bowl or the heart of man, in thus containing all possibilities, is then the universe. Finally, the fire which is put to the tobacco is the Presence of the ultimate all-inclusive Principle, *Wakan Tanka,* the "Great Mysterious." In smoking the pipe, through the aid of breath the totality of all creation is absorbed within this ultimate Principle. And since in the pipe there is a grain of tobacco identified with the one who smokes, there is here enacted a sacrificial communion of identity. With this understanding, the phrase "we are all related," recited by the individual or group after the smoking, takes on the deepest possible meaning.

I will sum up by simply saying that in all that I have tried to speak of in such brief fashion, we have expressions through different means of a special quality among traditional peoples that could be called oneness of experience: a lack of dichotomizing or fragmenting, a unity in the word and in visual image. In the painted image, for example, the understanding is that in the being that is represented, or even in a depicted part of that being—the paw of a bear, let us say—all the power of the animal is present. One can draw from all Native American cultures examples to reinforce such interpretation. One final example I will use is that of the Navajo dry painting or "sand painting" as it is sometimes called. These are made in a rich ceremonial context for the curing of individuals who have gotten out of balance with their world. They are long ceremonies which can go on for four or five or up to ten days, during which time sacred chants are used with all the meaning of the *word* as I have tried to explain it. At a certain moment during the ceremony the ill person is placed at the center of one of the dry paintings; the understanding is that the person thus becomes identified with the power that is in the image painted on the earth with colored sand and pollen. And the singer takes some of the painted image and presses it to the body of the ill person, again to emphasize this element of identity: the painting is not a symbol of some meaning or power, the power *is* there present in it, and as the person identifies with it the appropriate cure is accomplished.

I conclude with this portion of a Navajo chant:

> The mountains, I become part of it . . .
> The herbs, the fir tree, I become part of it.
> The morning mists, the clouds, the gathering waters,
> I become part of it.
> The wilderness, the dew drops, the pollen . . .
> I become part of it.

And in the context of other chants, there is always the conclusion that indeed, I *am* the universe. We are not separate, but are one.